Please remember that this is a library book,
and that it belongs only temporarily to each
person who uses it. Be considerate. Do
not write in this, or any, library book.

THE CAMBRIDGE HISTORY OF
ENGLISH LITERATURE

VOLUME XIII

THE NINETEENTH CENTURY

II

LONDON
Cambridge University Press
FETTER LANE

NEW YORK · TORONTO
BOMBAY · CALCUTTA · MADRAS
Macmillan

TOKYO
Maruzen Company Ltd

Copyrighted in the United States of
America by the Macmillan Company

THE
CAMBRIDGE HISTORY OF
ENGLISH LITERATURE

EDITED

BY

SIR A. W. WARD

AND

A. R. WALLER

VOLUME XIII

THE NINETEENTH CENTURY

II

CAMBRIDGE

AT THE UNIVERSITY PRESS

1932

First edition   **1916**
New impression   **1922**
Cheap edition (text only)   **1932**

PRINTED IN GREAT BRITAIN

PREFATORY NOTE

The Cambridge History of English Literature was first published between the years 1907 and 1916. The General Index Volume was issued in 1927.

In the preface to Volume I the general editors explained their intentions. They proposed to give a connected account of the successive movements of English literature, to describe the work of writers both of primary and of secondary importance, and to discuss the interaction between English and foreign literatures. They included certain allied subjects such as oratory, scholarship, journalism and typography, and they did not neglect the literature of America and the British Dominions. The History was to unfold itself, "unfettered by any preconceived notions of artificial eras or controlling dates," and its judgments were not to be regarded as final.

This reprint of the text and general index of the *History* is issued in the hope that its low price may make it easily available to a wider circle of students and other readers who wish to have on their shelves the full story of English literature.

CAMBRIDGE
1932

CONTENTS

Chap. I. Carlyle . . . . *page* 1
By J. G. ROBERTSON

II. The Tennysons 23
By H. J. C. GRIERSON

III. Robert Browning and Elizabeth Barrett
Browning 49
By SIR HENRY JONES

IV. Matthew Arnold, Arthur Hugh Clough,
James Thomson 85
By W. LEWIS JONES

V. The Rossettis, William Morris, Swinburne
and others 110
By A. HAMILTON THOMPSON

VI. Lesser Poets of the Middle and Later Nineteenth Century 147
By GEORGE SAINTSBURY

VII. The Prosody of the Nineteenth Century 225
By GEORGE SAINTSBURY

VIII. Nineteenth-century Drama 225
By HAROLD CHILD

IX. Thackeray 275
By A. HAMILTON THOMPSON

X. Dickens 303
By GEORGE SAINTSBURY

XI. The Political and Social Novel. Disraeli,
Charles Kingsley, Mrs Gaskell, 'George
Eliot' 340
By SIR A. W. WARD

Chap. XII. The Brontës . . . . . *page* 403
By A. A. JACK

XIII. Lesser Novelists 417
By W. T. YOUNG

XIV. George Meredith, Samuel Butler, George
Gissing 440
By W. T. YOUNG

CHAPTER I

CARLYLE

WHEN Goethe, in 1827, declared Carlyle—the Carlyle of the *Life of Schiller*—to be 'a moral force of great significance,' he showed, as often in his judgments of men, an insight which, at the same time, was prophetic; for Carlyle, unquestionably, was the strongest moral force in the English literature of the nineteenth century. In an age which dealt pre-eminently in ethical and religious ideas; an age in which the intellectual currency was expressed in terms of faith and morality, rather than of abstract metaphysics; when the rapid widening of knowledge was viewed in many quarters with suspicion and apprehension; and, especially, when the new-born science of biology appeared as a sinister force threatening the very foundations of belief—in such an age, Carlyle was a veritable leader to those who walked in uncertainty and darkness. He laughed to scorn the pretensions of scientific materialism to undermine man's faith in the unseen; he heaped obloquy on the much vaunted science of political economy; he championed the spiritual against the material, demanded respect for justice and for the moral law and insisted on the supreme need of reverence—reverence, as Goethe had taught him, not merely for what is above us, but, also, for what is on the earth, beside us and beneath us. Nowadays, when the interest in many of these questions has ceased to be a burning one, when a tolerance, not far removed from indifference, has invaded all fields of mental and moral speculation, and when a calmer historical contemplation of human evolution has taken the place of the embittered controversy of Victorian days, Carlyle's power over men's minds is, necessarily, no longer what it was. But it is, perhaps, just on this account the easier to take a dispassionate view of his life and work, to sum up, as it were, and define his place in the national literature. Such is the chief problem which we propose to deal with in the present chapter.

Born in the little Dumfriesshire village of Ecclefechan on
4 December 1795, when the lurid light of the French revolution
still lit up the European sky, Thomas Carlyle came of a typical
lowland Scottish peasant stock, and, to the last, he remained
himself a peasant, bound by a thousand clannish bonds to his
provincial home. The narrow ties of blood and family always
meant more to him than that citizenship of the world which is
demanded of a man of genius; and, in spite of his forty years'
life in the metropolis, he never succeeded in shaking off the
unpliant instincts of the south of Scotland peasant. His prickly
originality and sturdy independence had something Celtic about
them, and these characteristics clung to him all his life, even
although he had early found an affinity in the Germanic mind.
In the *Dichtung und Wahrheit* of *Sartor Resartus* and the
preternaturally vivid pictures of *Reminiscences*, a kindly light
of retrospect is thrown over Carlyle's childhood and early life;
but, none the less, the reader is conscious of the atmosphere
of oppressive frugality, through which, as a child and youth,
he fought his way to the light. At the grammar school of
Annan, to which, after sparse educational beginnings in his native
village, he was sent in 1805, he was too sensitive a child to
distinguish himself other than as the tearful victim of his rougher
schoolmates; and, at the early age of fourteen, he passed to the
university of Edinburgh, where he attended lectures through five
sessions. The Scottish universities, still medieval in character and
curriculum, were then veritable bear-gardens, where the youth of
the land, drawn from every rank of the population, were let loose
to browse as they listed; the formalities and entrance-examina-
tions which now guard these institutions, and have destroyed
their old democratic character, were, as yet, undreamt of: but
the Scottish students of the early nineteenth century enjoyed a
Lernfreiheit as complete as, if, in its opportunities, more restricted
than, that of German students of our own time; and Carlyle, while
following, nominally, the usual courses, availed himself of this
freedom to the full. Ever intolerant of teachers and of the
systematic acquisition of knowledge, he benefited little from his
classes in Edinburgh. Like many of our men of genius, he—one
of the least academically minded of them all—always stood outside
the academic pale. He had no high opinion of centres of learning,
from this, his first experience—which, doubtless, provoked the
outburst in *Sartor*, 'that out of England and Spain, ours was the
worst of all hitherto discovered universities'—to the day when he

recalled to students of Edinburgh university, more than fifty years later, his dictum from *Lectures on Heroes*, that 'the true university of our days is a collection of books.'

Edinburgh had thus little share in Carlyle's development; at most, he succeeded, like his own Teufelsdröckh, 'in fishing up from the chaos of the library more books perhaps than had been known to the very keepers thereof.' He had begun his studies with certain vague and half-hearted aspirations towards the ministry; but these were soon discarded. His only tie with academic learning was mathematics, for which he had a peculiar aptitude, and in which he even won the praise of his professor. He left the university in 1814 without taking a degree. On his return to Dumfriesshire, he was appointed a teacher of mathematics in Annan, in which post he succeeded a friend who was also to make some mark in the world, Edward Irving. From Annan, Carlyle, now in his twenty-first year, passed, with the help of a recommendation from his Edinburgh professor, to Kirkcaldy, whither Irving had preceded him—still as mathematical master, still without any kind of clearness as to what kind of work he was ultimately to do in the world. In Fifeshire, however, he appears to have had his first experience of romance, which presented itself to him in the shape of a pupil of higher social station than his own; Margaret Gordon, Carlyle's first love, may, possibly, have hovered before him as a kind of model for the 'Blumine' of *Sartor*; although it seems hardly necessary to seek any specific model for so purely 'literary' a figure. No doubt, this love-affair, which, through the timely interposition of a relative of Miss Gordon, came to an abrupt end, upset many of the presuppositions with which Carlyle set out in life. Another significant event was the chance reading, in September 1817, of Madame de Staël's *De l'Allemagne*, then quite new, which did more than all the treasures of the university library in Edinburgh to bring order and direction into Carlyle's intellectual world. Considerable emphasis must be laid on this, the accident of his first introduction to the literature that was to mean much to him. Madame de Staël's work, which opened up the wonderland of German thought and poetry, not only to Carlyle, but, also, to all Europe outside Germany, was a product of German romanticism, having been written, in great measure, under the guidance of August Wilhelm Schlegel, the chief critic of that movement; it was responsible for the fact that the impress which the new literature of Germany made on the European mind was, in the main, romantic. Even

Goethe and Schiller are here seen essentially as Schlegel saw them; and Carlyle, all his life long, viewed the German writers whom he loved and looked up to as his masters from the romantic angle.

Heartily weary of school-teaching, Carlyle, once more, made an effort towards a profession; he returned with his friend Irving to Edinburgh, and, in September 1818, took up the study of law. But he soon found that law had even less grip on him than had his previous studies for the church; and, gradually, he drifted into the undefined, and, for a man of Carlyle's temperament infinitely disheartening and uphill, profession of the 'writer of books.' His task was the harder, as he had already begun to be tortured by dyspepsia, and by the melancholy and depression which that disease brought in its train. Nevertheless, he made a beginning towards a literary activity with a number of articles contributed to Sir David Brewster's *Edinburgh Encyclopaedia*; this was the merest hackwork, but, at least, it was hackwork honestly performed. Meanwhile, in the summer of 1820, when at home in Dumfriesshire, he entered on a systematic study of the German language, and threw himself with passionate ardour into the works of the new writers, from whom Madame de Staël's book had led him to hope that he would find guidance. And, in his early efforts to make money by his pen, it was only natural that he should have turned his German studies to account; while translating—again for Brewster—Legendre's *Elements of Geometry and Trigonometry*, he found time to write an essay on Goethe's *Faust*, which appeared in *The New Edinburgh Review* in April 1822. But his first serious task as an interpreter of German literature was a *Life of Schiller*, the German writer to whom, as was to be expected, he had been first attracted. This is an excellent piece of work, if it be remembered how meagre were the materials at his disposal; and it is hardly surprising that Schiller's personality—in which Carlyle saw mirrored his own early struggles—and Schiller's work as a historian, are more adequately treated than are his dramatic poetry and aesthetic studies. Carlyle's *Life of Schiller* came out serially in *The London Magazine* in 1823 and 1824, and appeared in book form in 1825. Meanwhile, he had turned to Goethe, and translated, not without occasional secret misgivings, *Wilhelm Meister's Apprenticeship*, which was published in 1824. This was followed by four volumes entitled *German Romance*, which included stories by Musäus— something of an intruder in this circle of romanticists—Fouqué, Tieck, Hoffmann, Richter, as well as the continuation of Goethe's novel, *Wilhelm Meister's Travels*, the translation of which was, naturally, more to his mind than that of the *Apprenticeship* had been. *German Romance* appeared in 1827, and found little favour with the reading public; but in that same year Carlyle had begun to write the remarkable series of essays on German literature, contributed to *The Edinburgh Review, Foreign Review* and *Foreign Quarterly Review*, which now form a considerable part of *Critical and Miscellaneous Essays*.

The beginnings of Carlyle's career as man of letters, all things considered, had been auspicious: perhaps, indeed, more auspicious than was justified by subsequent developments. But, at least, all thought of the bar as a profession was given up. Through Edward Irving, who, in the meantime, had settled in London, Carlyle became tutor to Charles Buller in 1822, and had the opportunity of getting to know something of a social world much above his own and of seeing London and even Paris. Before this, however, a new chapter in his life had begun with his introduction, in the early summer of 1821, to Jane Welsh of Haddington. Again, it was Irving whom he had to thank for this introduction, which formed a momentous turning-point in his life. Irving had himself been attracted by Miss Welsh, and she by him; but he was under other obligations; and the friendship between her and Carlyle was free to drift, in spite of many points of friction, into love. In 1826, the many difficulties and scruples which had arisen were successfully overcome, and she became Carlyle's wife. After a short spell in Edinburgh, the young couple took up their abode amid the solitudes of the Dumfriesshire moors, at Craigen-puttock, 'the dreariest spot in all the British dominions,' where Mrs Carlyle, born, if ever woman was, to grace a *salon*, spent six of her best years in oppressive solitude added to household work. With these years, which produced the essays on German literature, as well as *Sartor Resartus*, Carlyle's apprenticeship to literature may be said to have come to a close.

It will be convenient, at this stage, to consider what these literary beginnings under German influence meant for Carlyle. He was by no means, as has been often asserted, a pioneer of German studies in this country; he rather took advantage of an already existing interest in, and curiosity about, things German, to which many translations and magazine articles—*Blackwood's Magazine*, for instance, had, since its inception in 1817, manifested a strong interest in German poetry—bear witness. Carlyle, however, had an advantage over other writers and translators of his day, in so far as his work is free from the taint of dilettantism, the besetting sin of all who, in those days, wrote on German literature in English magazines; he spoke with the authority of one who knew, whose study had been deep and fundamental, even although his practical knowledge of German at no time reached a very high degree of proficiency.

Carlyle was never weary, all his life long, of proclaiming his personal debt to his German masters, above all, to Goethe; and, no doubt, the debt, especially to the latter, was a very real one. It was Goethe who helped him out of the Slough of Despond in the early twenties, when he was searching for a solution to the problem: 'What canst thou work at?'—Goethe who showed him how to work his way through blank despair to the 'Everlasting Yea.'

'If I have been delivered from darkness into any measure of light,' he himself wrote to the German poet, 'if I know aught of myself and my duties and destination, it is to the study of your writings more than to any other circumstance that I owe this; it is you more than any other man that I should always thank and reverence with the feeling of a Disciple to his Master, nay of a Son to his spiritual Father.'

Carlyle has himself said that the famous incident in *Sartor Resartus*, where the light breaks on Teufelsdröckh in the rue Saint Thomas de l'Enfer, really took place in his own life one June afternoon in 1821, as he went down Leith walk to bathe in the firth of Forth. He, too, like his hero, had dwelt with the 'Everlasting No'; difficulties of all kinds had beset him, religious difficulties, moral difficulties, above all, the racking problem of the end of life—happiness *versus* renunciation. He had, perhaps, also to face problems of a more practical kind than those which assailed his Teufelsdröckh; for it was only a few weeks before the crisis that he had met Miss Welsh; and, doubtless, in a dim way, he felt that the problem of life was now, or would become for him, not merely what canst thou work at, but what canst thou work at with sufficient worldly success to allow of sharing thy life with another. Moreover, the spiritual crisis, when it did break over Carlyle, assuredly did not come and go with the dramatic vividness of the chapters in *Sartor*; Carlyle's struggles with the powers of darkness extended over years, and it may be questioned if he ever found complete deliverance, ever succeeded in setting the 'Everlasting No' completely and finally at defiance.

When, however, we scrutinise Carlyle's relation to Goethe more closely, we see how strangely few points actually existed between the two men. Carlyle's Goethe was by no means the whole Goethe, not even the real Goethe. Carlyle's hero and saviour was a fantastic, romantic Goethe, on whom was grafted a modern individualism that was assuredly not Goethe's. Carlyle attributed to Goethe a disharmony between the emotional and the intellectual life, which the German poet had never really known; for Goethe's 'storm and stress' crisis, which had been lived through, once and for all, years before Carlyle was born, was of quite another kind. The 'Everlasting Yea' of *Sartor*, tinged, as it was, by puritanic abnegations, had not been Goethe's solution to the inner dissonance of his early years; and *Entsagen*, to 'the Great Heathen,' was a very different thing from the drab and austere interpretation which Carlyle put on the English word 'renunciation.' In truth, Carlyle was no true Goethean, but a romanticist to the core; not in the vague English sense of that word, but as it is used in Germany, where it connotes a particular school of thought at the beginning of the nineteenth century. He drew his spiritual transcendentalism from Novalis, who is the theme of one of the most beautiful of his German essays; he sought his philosophic and political inspiration in Fichte; he regarded Richter's Sterne-like genius, his fantastic and often incongruous mingling of crude melodrama, eccentric humour and soaring imaginative flight, as something divinely inspired; and Goethe, to him, was no calm Olympian, but a hero of self-abnegation, who had emerged, scarified and broken, from a 'sanctuary of sorrows.' And yet, in a kind of dim way, even if much of Goethe's life and thinking was a closed book to him, Carlyle realised that the German poet had solved the riddle of the spiritual life which tortured himself, and had arrived at a peace and serenity to which it was never his own lot to attain. Carlyle's interest in German literature virtually came to a close with Goethe's death and the end of romantic ascendancy in Germany. For the later men and movements of that literature he had no sympathy or understanding; and the chief German friend of his later life, Varnhagen von Ense, was, pre-eminently, an upholder of the traditions of the past. Thus, it is to Carlyle, rather than to Byron, or to Coleridge and Wordsworth, that we must look to find the analogue in English literature of continental romanticism, that movement which, built up on a faith in the spiritual and the unseen, had risen superior to the 'enlightenment,' as well as to the *Weltschmerz*, of the previous century. This was what Carlyle's English contemporaries endeavoured to express when they said that he belonged to the 'mystic' school. At the same time, he by

no means represents romanticism in all its variety and extent;
he stands rather for its ethical and religious side only; while, to
find an English equivalent for the no less fruitful aesthetic side of
the romantic movement—with which Carlyle had no sympathy—
we have to turn to the later pre-Raphaelites and to Carlyle's
disciple Ruskin.

The romantic stamp on Carlyle's work is nowhere more clearly
apparent than in his critical writings. His method as a literary
critic is summed up in the title of one of his essays, *Characteristics*,
a title which had been used for a volume of criticism by the two
leaders of German romanticism, the brothers Schlegel. The older
ideals of criticism, which had held uninterrupted sway in Europe
from the renascence to the end of the eighteenth century, had
been established on the assumption that the critic was a man of
superior knowledge and juster instincts; the critic, according to
this view, sat in judgment, and looked down on the criticised from
his higher standpoint; or, as Carlyle himself put it: 'perched himself resolutely, as it were, on the shoulders of his author, and
therefrom showed as if he commanded and looked down upon
him by a natural superiority of stature.' This type of critic
persisted in England in the school of Jeffrey and *The Edinburgh
Review*; its most brilliant representative among Carlyle's contemporaries was Macaulay. It was Carlyle's mission, as a literary
critic, to complete the revolution already tentatively foreshadowed
by Coleridge, and to establish the new standpoint which had been
ably maintained by the Schlegels. According to these writers,
the first function of the critic is not to pass superior judgments, but
to 'characterise'; to interpret, in humble respect for the higher
rights and claims of creative genius; to approach poetry through
the personality of the poet. This is the attitude which Carlyle
consistently maintains in all his essays. He insists that it is the
critic's chief task to get into sympathy with his author, to understand and appreciate his aims and intentions, not to impose on
him purposes which may have lain entirely outside his plan. It was
this ideal, Carlyle's adaptation of the interpretative method of the
Schlegels to English needs, that makes his critical essays a land-
mark of the first importance in the history of English criticism.

In practice, criticism of this kind is, obviously, at the mercy of the
personal attitude of the critic to literature; it allows freer play to
subjective likes and dislikes than is permitted to the critic who proceeds by rule of thumb. One might say that it postulates an original
sympathy between critic and criticised; at least, it is to be seen

at its best where such sympathy is strong, as, for instance, in Carlyle's essays on his German masters, Goethe, Jean Paul Friedrich Richter, Novalis, and in his masterly essay on Burns. But, where such sympathy does not exist, the method may be responsible for an even greater unfairness than is to be laid at the door of the older, objective criticism. This disadvantage, to some extent, is apparent in Carlyle's essay on Scott; it comes out with disagreeable emphasis in his personal utterances on men like Heine, on the leaders of the French romantic school and on many of his English contemporaries, such as Coleridge, Wordsworth and Lamb. On the other hand, one must not overlook the eminent fairness with which Carlyle has written of the eighteenth century—a century which appeared to him only as an age of paralysing scepticism and un- belief—and on writers so far away from his own way of thinking as Diderot and Voltaire.

Apart from his essays, the work by which Carlyle takes his place as the English representative of German romanticism is *Sartor Resartus*, an immediate product of his affectionate study of Jean Paul. The ideas, form, the very style, of this work, which repelled many when it first appeared and had made the search for a publisher dishearteningly difficult, have all the stamp of Jean Paul on them. But, into the German fabric, which has more consistency of plan, and a more original imagi- native basis than it is usually credited with, Carlyle wove his own spiritual adventures, which had already found expression in a cruder and more verbose form in an unfinished autobiographical novel, *Wotton Reinfred*. *Sartor Resartus* falls into two parts, a disquisition on 'the philosophy of clothes'—which, doubtless, formed the original nucleus of the book—and an autobiographic romance, modelled, to a large extent, on the writings of Jean Paul. The philosophy of clothes left most of Carlyle's contemporaries cold; and, indeed, to his early critics, it seemed lacking in origi- nality, as a mere adaptation of an idea from Swift's *Tale of a Tub*; in their eyes, it was overshadowed by the subjective romance, as it seems to have been in the case of Carlyle himself as he proceeded with it. The German village of Entepfuhl took on the colouring of Ecclefechan; the German university, the name of which Teufels- dröckh forbears to disclose, was suggested by what Carlyle had experienced in Edinburgh; the clothes-philosophy made way, more and more, for a vivid depiction of the spiritual and moral crisis in the author's own life. The three chapters, 'The Ever- lasting No,' 'Centre of Indifference' and 'The Everlasting Yea, were, as we have seen, an epitome of what Carlyle had himself come through acutely in 1821. Here, moreover, and not in its metaphysics, lay the significance of *Sartor Resartus* for more than one generation of young Englishmen; in Carlyle's cry of defiance—for defiance it was, rather than meek resignation—in his 'Close thy Byron, open thy Goethe!' 'Love not Pleasure; love God. This is the Everlasting Yea, wherein all contradiction is solved; wherein whoso walks and works, it is well with him,' they found a veritable finger-post pointing to the higher moral and spiritual life. Here was a basis for that new spiritual idealism, based on suffering and resignation, but 'strong in will to strive, to seek, to find, and not to yield,' which, later, was to pass into the poetry of *In Memoriam*, and into the more assured optimism of Browning.

In 1833, the Carlyles' six years' exile in their Dumfriesshire Patmos came to an end; after a few months' trial of Edinburgh, which proved unsatisfactory, they migrated—with no more than two hundred pounds to their credit—to London, 'the best place,' as he realised, 'for writing books, after all the one use of living.' In May 1834, they took up their abode at 5 Cheyne row, Chelsea, which remained their home for the rest of their lives. Although London meant an accession of new friends, and the stimulus of congenial intercourse, Carlyle's life had by no means yet passed into smoother waters. For the first time, in fact, financial difficulties began seriously to press on him. *Sartor* had begun to appear in *Fraser's Magazine* before the move was made; but, owing to what the editor regarded as its dubious quality, it was not paid for at the full rate, and the result went far towards justifying the editorial attitude. The publication met, indeed, with a storm of disapprobation, one critic even dismissing it as 'a heap of clotted nonsense.' There seemed little hope that it would ever attain to book-form at all; and it might have taken much longer to do so had not Emerson taken the initiative in America; *Sartor Resartus* appeared as a book in New York in 1836, in London in 1838. Meanwhile, however, Carlyle, having more or less turned his back on German literature and German thought, was deep in a historical work, the subject of which was the French revolution.

The labour on this new book meant even more self-abnegation than that on *Sartor* had implied. On the lonely Scottish moors at Craigenputtock there had been little or nothing to tempt Carlyle to deviate from his singleness of purpose; but London opened up alluring avenues to a literary life which might have led to freedom from material cares, to comfort, perhaps even to affluence. Had Carlyle stooped to journalism and adapted himself to the everyday routine of the professional man of letters—*The Times*, for instance, was thrown open to him—he might rapidly have won an assured position for himself. Instead, he buried himself in French history, laboured unremittingly at his *French Revolution*, while months passed when not a penny came into the domestic exchequer. And, as if the struggles to produce the book were not enough, the work of many weeks, the manuscript of the first volume, was accidentally destroyed in the early part of 1835, when in the hands of John Stuart Mill. Rarely has the virtue of 'the hero as man of letters' shone in fairer light than in the manner in which Carlyle received the terrible news, and grimly determined to sit down and rewrite the volume. At last, in January 1837, the *History of the French Revolution* was finished. The English reading world did not, at first, know what to make of this strange history, any more than it had known what to make of *Sartor*; but it was, at least, quicker to feel the power of the book; and enthusiastic recognition soon began to pour in from the most unexpected quarters. Fame came at last, the right kind of fame, a fame, too, that, in course of time, brought reasonable remuneration in its train.

Carlyle's *French Revolution* is, again in the continental sense of the word, a 'romantic' work; once more, as in his literary criticism, he stands out in sharp antagonism to Macaulay, the heir of rationalism, whose *History of England* began to appear some ten years later. *The French Revolution* is individualistic history, interpretative history on a subjective basis; it is as far removed from the sober ideals of a scientific age of faithful chronicling of 'things as they were,' as it is from the 'enlightened' history-writing of the eighteenth century. Carlyle's work is, essentially, a personal 'confession.' 'You have not,' he declared to the world, 'had for two hundred years any book that came more truly from a man's very heart.' The French revolution, as Carlyle sees it, becomes a vindication of the ways of God to man; a sermon on the text: 'Whatsoever a man soweth, that shall he also reap,' on the nemesis that follows the abuse of power or the neglect of the duties and responsibilities of those in whom power has been placed by Providence. And Carlyle ranges himself unmistakably on the side of that nemesis; he makes no attempt, so to speak, to write 'fair' history, to hold the balance between the two great antagonistic forces that clashed in the revolution. *The French Revolution*, rightly read, is a declaration of its author's convictions on problems of his own time; a solemn warning to the England of his own day to avoid a catastrophe which Carlyle believed, and never ceased to believe all his life long, was imminent. But this work is, also, something more precious than a subjective history combined with a tract for the times; it is a prose epic, a work of creative genius, in which the facts of history are illumined by the imagination of a poet. Light and shadow, colour and darkness, are distributed over the picture with the eye and the instinctive judgment of an artist. Carlyle does not dilate on motives or on theories of government; he does not even, in a straightforward way, narrate facts; he paints pictures; he brings before us only what, as it were, he has first seen with his own eyes. Setting out from the conviction that biographies are the most precious of all records of the past—or, as he put it in lectures *On Heroes*, 'the History of the World is the Biography of Great Men'—he writes a history which is a collection of marvellously clear-cut portraits; more than this, he deals with the history of a nation itself as if it were a human biography; distils, so to speak, the life of the whole from innumerable lives of individuals. Thus, the events he has to narrate are overshadowed and dominated by the men that were responsible for them; Danton, Mirabeau, the 'sea-green incorruptible' Robespierre, are masterpieces of historical portraiture; and the imaginative literature of Carlyle's age knew nothing more graphic and unforgettable than the description of the royal flight to Varennes.

Meanwhile, until the material harvest of the labour on *The French Revolution* came in, Carlyle was induced, in order to keep the wolf from the door, to give several series of popular lectures in London. For the first of these, delivered in May 1837, he utilised the materials he had gathered for a history of German literature; the second course, in the following year, was also on literature, but took a wider sweep of literary history, beginning with classical times and coming down to the eighteenth century. A third series dealt with the revolutions of modern Europe, while the fourth and last, delivered in the early summer of 1840, and published in the following year under the title *On Heroes, Hero-Worship, and the Heroic in History*, was most successful of all. This has always been one of Carlyle's most attractive and popular works. It elucidates, with the help of picturesque and contrasting portraits, the cardinal doctrines of his own romantic creed of individualism, a creed which went back in its essentials to the philosophy of Fichte, namely, that personality alone matters in the world; that history is the record of the thoughts and actions of great men; and that greatness lies in the exercise of the 'heroic' virtues, that is to say, in the power to renounce, coupled with the will to achieve. On the basic assumption that the quality of heroism, which makes a man a leader of men, is capable of realisation in any sphere of human activity in which the hero happens to be placed, Carlyle applied his doctrine to the most varied forms of leadership. Odin, chosen to illustrate the hero as god, gave Carlyle his first opportunity to proclaim his sympathy with the virile religion of our Germanic ancestors, a sympathy that grew with the years and found expression again in his very last work. Mahomet, the hero as prophet, led him to seek a solid foundation of sincerity for the faith of Islam. Dante and Shakespeare, again in contrasting spheres, served to illustrate the hero as *vates* or poet; while, for examples of the less soaring activity of the 'man of letters,' Carlyle turned to the century he found it hardest to understand, and singled out as sympathetic figures against an unsympathetic background, Samuel Johnson, Rousseau and Burns. For the hero as priest, he chose Luther and John Knox; for the hero as king, Cromwell and Napoleon; but the last two lectures show some falling off in comparison with the earlier ones.

The interest in *Heroes* was, in the main, literary rather than historical, although, with *The French Revolution*, Carlyle had appeared to turn his back definitely on literary criticism; but readers, not merely of the latter work, but, also, of *Heroes*, began to discern a trend in his mind which was neither literary nor historical, a trend towards actuality and the present. Literature was never, indeed, for Carlyle, merely literature; its value as an aesthetic expression had always been subordinate to its potentiality as an intellectual and moral factor. Great poetry, for him, was not the embodiment of the highest beauty, but the poetry that contained the deepest lessons for mankind. So, too, had it been with history; history was not merely a record of how things had been, but, also, a writing on the wall for the benefit of the historian's contemporaries. Carlyle's mission in life, as he interpreted it, was, in fact, neither to be a critic of literature nor a chronicler of history; but to be a teacher and a prophet to his own time. With every new book his writing was becoming more 'actual' in its aims; the past was becoming more and more a medium through which he spoke to the present.

Before the lectures *On Heroes* were published, Carlyle threw off all historical disguise and entered the arena of practical, contemporary politics. This was with the little book, originally planned as a review article, entitled *Chartism* (end of 1839). Carlyle had begun life as a radical of the radicals; the disturbances of the Peterloo time had made a deep impression on him in his student years, and the Corn law agitation had stirred up his sympathies with the oppressed classes. In his early London days, he was heart and soul with the reform agitation. But, by the time he came to write on chartism, his radicalism had undergone a change. He was still convinced that a root-and-branch reform was urgent; but his faith in the nostrums of political radicalism was rapidly waning. In his antagonism to what he stigmatised as the 'quackery' of the radicalism of his day, he appeared almost conservative; it only meant that his radicalism had become more radical than before. 'I am not a Tory,' he said in *Chartism*, 'no, but one of the deepest though perhaps the quietest of radicals.' The only radicalism, as it now seemed to him, which would avail against the ills and cankers of the day was the hand of the just, strong man. The salvation of the working-classes was not to be attained by political enfranchisement and the dicta of political economists, but by reverting to the conditions of the middle ages, when the labourer was still a serf. The freedom of the working-man was a delusion; it meant only freedom to be sucked out in the labour market, freedom to be a greater slave than he had ever been before. Carlyle's warfare against political economy was part and parcel of his crusade against the scientific materialism of his time. The 'dismal science' eliminated the factors of religion and morality from the relation of man to man, and established that relation on a scientific 'profit and loss' basis; it preached that the business of each man was to get as large a share of the world's goods as he could, at the expense—strictly regulated by laws of contract—of his fellow-man. Carlyle believed that the path marked out by such a science was the way to perdition and national ruin.

These doctrines were repeated in a more picturesque form in Carlyle's next contribution to political literature, *Past and Present*. In the beginning and end of this little work, which, perhaps, is his most inspired, as it was his most spontaneous, production—it was written within the space of two months early in 1843—he unrolls once again 'The condition of England question,' in its familiar form; he reiterates the old demands for duty and responsibility, for earnestness and just dealing on the part of England's rulers; and he sets up the strong man as the only remedy for political rottenness. The arguments are the same as before; but they are put even more trenchantly and vividly; the scornful contempt which he heaps on the democratic remedies of his radical friends is more scathing. Encased within these two sections of the book lies the contrasting picture of the past; he takes the chronicle of Jocelyn of Brakelond, which, not long before, had been unearthed by the Camden society, and, with a clearness of delineation and dramatic actuality hardly surpassed by Scott himself, he puts life into the records of the abbot Samson and his monks of St Edmund's and transmutes these dry records into a veritable prose idyll. Here, Carlyle stands out emphatically as the poet and the artist, rather than as the politician or economist.

Seven years later, in 1850, Carlyle again essayed the *rôle* of political critic and prophet, namely in his *Latter-Day Pamphlets*. In these papers, he brought his doctrines to a still sharper focus on the actual problems of the day, and expressed them with a virulence and passionate exaggeration which left his earliest utterances far behind. The consequence was that many of his old friends—friends of many years' standing like Mazzini and Mill—were estranged. Carlyle's wholehearted denunciation of philanthropy, in particular, appeared to that eminently philanthropic age as the utterances of a misanthrope and a barbarian. Possibly, he overshot the mark, although the *Pamphlets* contain little that he had not already said—in point of fact, Carlyle's political creed turns round a very few cardinal ideas which are repeated again and again in different keys throughout his writings. So long as he had been content to enunciate these political theories as abstractions, they were accepted—no doubt with some demur, but still accepted—as the curious views of an interesting personality; it was when he brought them to bear on the concrete questions of the day that he caused real offence. Looking back on the storm that *Latter-Day Pamphlets* called forth, one cannot help thinking that this book was, in some way, a reflex of the great political upheaval of 1848, from which England had emerged much less scathed than the nations of the continent. Doubtless, Carlyle saw in the March revolution and its dire consequences in other lands a realisation of his forebodings. 'It is long years,' he wrote to Emerson of that revolution, 'since I felt any such deep-seated satisfaction at a public event, showing once again that the righteous Gods do yet live and reign.' He felt the surer that England would not escape the nemesis, that nemesis, indeed, might be all the more terrible in consequence of the delay of its coming.

As a political preacher and prophet, Carlyle was as one crying in the wilderness; his hand was against every man's; he was disowned by all parties, and, apart from a certain confidence which, in earlier days, he had felt in Peel, he was notoriously out of sympathy with the leaders of the two great political parties. He trampled ruthlessly on the toes of Victorian liberals, and flouted their most cherished ideas. Deep down in his heart, he remained the democratic Scottish peasant, who demanded, with Burns-like radicalism, that the innate nobility of manhood, whether in king or peasant, must be recognised; he claimed the right of nobly born souls to rise to be rulers of men. His own cure for all political ills was government by the ablest and the best: but he denied vehemently the possibility of the ablest and best being discoverable by the vote of a majority; for such a purpose, reform bills and secret ballots were wholly unsuitable. No nation could be guided aright—any more than a ship could double cape Horn—by the votes of a majority. Exactly in what manner the best man, the hero, is to be discovered and endowed with power, is a problem Carlyle never reduces to practical terms or intelligible language; and methods similar to those whereby abbot Samson became the head of his monastery, if applied to the conditions of modern life, would—he must himself have admitted it—lead to anarchy, not stable government. Carlyle had rather a kind of mystic belief in the able man entering into his inheritance by virtue of a supernatural right; that the choice of the man who should rule over men lay not so much with the ruled themselves as with a higher Power; and that the right to govern was enforced by a divinely endowed might to compel the obedience of one's fellow-men.

But the world, as Carlyle clearly saw, was not planned on so orderly a scheme as his faith implied. 'Might' showed itself by no means always to be the same thing as 'right'; and, in spite of his belief in the virtue of strength, none could be more denunciatory than Carlyle of the victorious usurper, if the usurper's ends were not in accordance with Carlyle's own interpretation of God's purpose. Behind all his political writings, and his asseveration of the right of might, there thus lay a serious and irreconcilable schism. 'The strong thing is the just thing,' he proclaimed with increasing

vehemence; but he was forced to add that it might need centuries
to show the identity of strength and justice. In truth, with all his
belief in the strong man, Carlyle never came entirely out into the
open; never expressed himself with the ruthless logical consistency
of the individualistic thinkers of our own time; the doctrine of the
Übermensch was not yet ripe. On the other hand, in the modern
democratic ideal of a state built up on mutually helpful citizenship, Carlyle had little faith.

Amid all these incursions into the politics of the moment, however, he still felt on surer ground as a historian; the lesson he
had to teach, he felt, could be more effectually set forth from the
platform of history, than by descending into the dusty and noisy
arena of political controversy. His wish to serve the present
by reviving the past is indicated by the masterly portrait he
put together from the letters and utterances of Oliver Cromwell.
The work had been long in preparation; indeed, none of Carlyle's
writings, not even his *Frederick the Great*, was heralded by so
many groans and despairs as this; in the case of none did he find
it so difficult to discover the form best suited to the matter.
At first, he had some idea of writing a history of the civil wars,
or a history of the commonwealth; but the ultimate result was
very different from that originally contemplated; in fact, he
arrived at that result unawares. The publication of the letters
and speeches was to have been a mere by-product, but, this
done, he saw that there was nothing more left for him to do.
The Letters and Speeches of Oliver Cromwell (1845) has been
described by Froude as 'the most important contribution to
English history which has been made in the nineteenth century.'
This opinion may be debatable; but it might, at least, be said
that the task of rehabilitating the protector, of destroying false
legends which had gathered round him, was peculiarly made for
Carlyle's hand. Cromwell lives again here in all his rugged
strength; and lives precisely because his was one of those natures
into which Carlyle could, so to speak, project something of his
own. Again, Carlyle is the artist here: not the artist in form;
nor the Protean artist of many parts, as in *The French Revolution* or *Frederick the Great*, where the stage is crowded with
varied figures; but the artist who has concentrated all his creative
power on one great figure.

Standing apart from the turmoil of political controversy as well
as the more serious historical studies in these years, is a work
which cannot be overlooked in an estimate of Carlyle's activity as

a man of letters, the biography of his friend *John Sterling*, which appeared in 1851. Sterling himself, whose life of brilliant promise had been darkened and prematurely eclipsed by consumption, was hardly a significant enough figure to warrant the monument which Carlyle has erected to him; but Carlyle felt that a duty was imposed upon him to remove the stigma which Sterling's first biographer, Christopher Hare, had placed on his memory, in presenting him too exclusively as a renegade from church of England orthodoxy. Carlyle's book has been declared by more than one critic to be his best from the point of view of pure literature; but it is unduly long, and suffers by excessive and unnecessary detail. It contains, however, some of Carlyle's most trenchant writing, notably the often quoted pen-portrait of Coleridge. Its chief value, perhaps, is the light it throws on Carlyle himself. We obtain from it an instructive glimpse of the writer's own religion, that religion which was an almost ludicrous combination of the 'dourest' Scottish Calvinism and the Spinozistic pantheism of Goethe; we get a pleasanter, less atrabilious picture in it, too, of the Carlyle of the early London days, than is to be obtained from Froude's biography; and, most valuable of all, we are able to gather from it, not merely what he felt towards one disciple, but towards all the young aspiring souls of the time who, setting out in life, looked to him for spiritual guidance.

The most ambitious of Carlyle's work had still to come, *The History of Friedrich II of Prussia, called Frederick the Great*. The first volume appeared in 1858, the sixth and last in March 1865. There has been much difference of opinion concerning Carlyle's *Frederick*, much questioning of the wisdom which led him to spend many years of racking labour, torments and misery over the production of this work. It was asserted quite openly in the sixties and seventies, and it is a very generally held opinion today, that the result of those labours was in no fair proportion to what they meant to the author. It cannot be said that Carlyle has uttered any very final word about his hero; it is doubtful if any of the acknowledged standard writings on Frederick in our day would have been essentially different had Carlyle never laboured. At most, he has been commended by German historians for his vivid and accurate accounts of Frederick's decisive battles. In point of fact, Carlyle had once more set out, in his imperturbable romantic way, to do something more than make known to the world 'what had happened.' Not but what he was, in respect of the truth of history, just as conscientious in his way as historians of the scientific school are. This is to be seen in the unwearying labour with which he collected his materials, poring over libraries of 'dull books'; and in his efforts, notwithstanding that travel was to him a torture, to see with his own eyes the backgrounds against which Frederick's life was played, the battlefields on which he fought. But there was another purpose which, in the first instance, moved him to undertake the work; he set out with the object of demonstrating the heroic in Frederick, of illustrating his thesis of 'the hero as king.' He had written his previous histories—*The French Revolution* and *Cromwell*—with similar preconceived ends; but there was an essential difference in these cases, in so far as hypotheses and fact are dovetailed into one another. The French revolution, in reality, was an illustration of the nemesis of misrule; and Cromwell was well adapted to the *rôle* of Carlylean strong man; whereas, it is very much open to question if the friend and patron of the French encyclopedists, the extremely practical and hardheaded ruler who built up the modern Prussian state, could be adjudged a hero in Carlyle's sense at all. Thus, the history suffers from a too apparent dissonance; it suffers, also, from a certain futility in its author's efforts to make it throw a shadow across the world of his own day. For, just as *The French Revolution* was intended to be an overwhelming object-lesson to an England which Carlyle believed to be rushing blindly into the whirlpool of chartism, so, his *Frederick the Great* was intended to clinch his gospel of might as right, to be an embodiment, in its highest form, of the ideal of romantic individualism. Of all men of the past, none, it seems to us, was less suited to such an interpretation than Frederick the great. There are, however, many pages in this history which bear witness to the cunning of the artist; the gallery of living portraits is even wider than that in the first history, the battle scenes are on a grander scale.

In 1865, an event happened which brought peculiar gratification to Carlyle: he was invited by the students of his own university of Edinburgh to become their lord rector. At last, the prophet was to find honour in his own country. In many ways —bound as he was by every fibre of his nature to his native land —he regarded 2 April 1866, when he delivered his inaugural address *On the Choice of Books*, in Edinburgh, as a kind of coping-stone to his career. The address, although it makes but ineffective reading, was a triumph in delivery. Very shortly afterwards, however, a blow fell on him of the direst kind. Before he got back to London, the news reached him that his wife had been found dead in her carriage when driving in Hyde park. 'She died at London 21 April 1866, suddenly snatched from him, and the light of his life as if gone out.' The light of his life was very literally gone out; the remaining fifteen years he had still to live were years of gradual decadence. Still one other book it was given to him to publish, entitled *The Early Kings of Norway* (1875), but it has little of the old fire and strength; and his name appeared frequently attached to letters in the press. Notable among such letters was his vigorous appeal in *The Times* in behalf of Germany in her war with France, an appeal which, no doubt, had weight with Bismarck when, later, he conferred on him the much prized Prussian order of merit. Disraeli made an effort to get Carlyle to accept an honour from the British government, but he declined. Years before the end, his right hand failed him and made literary work impossible, even although his intellectual power and energy remained unimpaired. His death took place on 4 February 1881. He lies buried, not as his friends would have wished, in Westminster abbey, but with his own kinsfolk in Ecclefechan.

Carlyle is not to be regarded as a mere apostle or transmitter of German ideas and German ideals; he built up, under the stimulus, and with the help, of these ideas, a spiritual and moral world of his own. He saw human life and earthly happenings against a vast background of mystic spiritualism, of eternities and immensities; he was an individualist, to whom the development of the race depends on great personal virtues, on heroic abnegation and self-sacrificing activity. His rugged independence made it difficult for his contemporaries to 'place' him; he resolutely refused to be labelled, or to be identified with any specific intellectual, literary or political creed. He would admit allegiance to no one; he treated his peers and contemporaries with crying injustice, often with quite indefensible contumely; he scorned every link with the world around him. He went through life fighting for high causes, scattering the forces of cant and unbelief, grappling, like a modern Luther, with the very devil himself. No man was ever more terribly in earnest about his 'God-given hest,' than Carlyle; and yet, perhaps, none was less conscious of his own precise place and *rôle* in the world-history. Carlyle's own personal convictions were full of irreconcilable contradictions. At one time, for instance, the making of books, his own craft, is endowed, in his eyes, with priesthood; at another, it is the paltriest and meanest of trades; at one time, his utterances are radical of the radical; at another, his radical friends are appalled and struck dumb by his apparent apostasy. A preacher of the virtue of silence, he himself has left us well-nigh forty volumes of printed speech; a scorner of philanthropy, he was the most generous and open-handed disburser of charity. Possibly, his own love of startling paradox and contrast led him to accentuate such antitheses in his own nature; but, perhaps, they only meant that he saw deeper into the essence of things and relationships than other men; that the irreconcilability was a mere mirage of the surface. One might fittingly apply to Carlyle the phrase with which George Brandes characterised Nietzsche; he is 'an aristocratic radical'; or, as MacCunn has called him, 'an anti-democratic radical.' Equally distraught was his own personal life; it was built up on dissonances. The agonies and despairs which made the life at Cheyne row often a veritable purgatory for his faithful helpmate were not all the emanation of dyspepsia and insomnia; he was the irritable man of genius, who, as his mother had discovered long before, was 'gey ill to live wi'.' Below all his reflections on human things and fates, there lay a deep and ineradicable discord. Outwardly, he would fain have appeared as a convinced optimist, to whom God was 'in his heaven,' and all was 'right with the world'; inwardly, he was often haunted with pessimistic doubts as to the right governance of the world. He proclaimed, incessantly and fervently, that 'the world is God's,' but the converse thought of the 'absentee-God sitting outside the Universe and seeing it go' often tempted and assailed him. Thus, Carlyle's 'Everlasting Yea' is an 'Everlasting Yea' against a background of 'the Everlasting No.' He may well have cried 'Love not Pleasure; love God!' but these words were originally wrung from him by bitter, enforced resignation. He had spurned mere 'happiness' all his life; but it is not given to everyone who thus places himself above the common lot of men to find what he himself calls 'blessedness.' And we sometimes doubt whether Carlyle ever found it. Such a struggle as is reflected in his life is, too often, the consequence when a man sees his own life-happiness slip through his fingers in the pursuit of other ideals, and when all that is left to him is to make of the stern *Entbehren sollst du, sollst entbehren!* such virtue as he can. Certainly, the higher, harmonious life, to which Goethe attained, Carlyle only saw afar off as an ideal beyond his reach. Rather, we have to think of him, even in his maturity, as he appears in early days, when he chose as a symbol of his life the burning candle with the motto: *terar dum prosim.*

But it is just this discord, this *Misston auf der grossen Laute* of which Schiller sang, that gave the enormous impetus to Carlyle's influence; it was this optimism, tossed fitfully on a vast ocean of pessimism, that acted as a tonic on the national life of the Victorian age. Carlyle's idealism, whether in literature or in morals, was an impracticable creed, but idealisms, after all, are not there to be practicable, but, rather, to leaven the practice of life. It was this leaven that Carlyle brought to many who, in youth, fell under the spell of his teaching. We have already claimed Carlyle as the greatest moral force in the England of his day, and it is difficult to say more. His influence penetrated deep into English intellectual life, at no time overprone to impracticable idealisms; and it acted as a deterrent and antidote to the allurements held out by Benthamism, Saint-Simonism, Comtism; it helped to counteract the secondary effects of the re-birth and advance of science—a re-birth which made appalling havoc on intellectual idealism in Germany itself. To Carlyle, the first of all practical problems was for a man to discover his appointed activity, the activity which alone is capable of destroying the canker of doubt. The life of the individual man passes, but his work remains.

The only happiness a brave man ever troubled himself with asking much about was happiness enough to get his work done. Not 'I can't eat!' but 'I can't work!' that was the burden of all wise complaining among men. It is, after all, the one unhappiness of a man, that he cannot work; that he cannot get his destiny as a man fulfilled. Behold the day is passing swiftly over, our life is passing swiftly over; and the night cometh when no man can work. The night once come, our happiness, our unhappiness—it is all abolished; vanished; clean gone; a thing that has been.... But our work—behold, that is not abolished, that has not vanished; our work, behold it remains, or the want of it remains; for endless Times and Eternities remains; and that is now the sole question for us for evermore!

This was Carlyle's firm positive faith, his panacea for the temptations and despairs that assail human life; it stands out now as his greatest message to his generation.

CHAPTER II

THE TENNYSONS

ALFRED TENNYSON, the most representative, and by far the most popular, poet of Victorian England, born in 1809, was the fourth son of the rector of Somersby in Lincolnshire. His two elder brothers, Frederick and Charles, were also poets and must receive some mention later. They were all, not least the greatest of them, men of singular physical beauty and strength, dark and stalwart, and through most of them ran a vein of almost morbid hyper-sensitiveness and melancholy, to which, in Alfred, we may trace the rare delicacy and intensity of his sensuous and emotional renderings of nature and mood and dream, as well as the hysterical extravagances of some of the poems in which he touched on subjects, political and religious, that moved him deeply.

Educated at Louth grammar school (of which his only pleasant memory was the music of the Latin words *sonus desilientis aquae*) and by his father at home, Tennyson's genius struck its roots deep into that soil of family affection and love of country the alienation from which, in varying degree, of most of the earlier romantic poets—Wordsworth, Coleridge, Byron, Shelley—contributed to the independent, revolutionary tone of their poetry, and the slowness with which some of them gained the ear of English readers. When Tennyson went up to Cambridge, Shelley's was still a name of doubtful omen. Tennyson was always to be—not entirely for the benefit of his poetry—in closer sympathy with the sentiments of the English middle-classes, domestic, distrustful of passion or, at least, of the frank expression and portrayal of passion, patriotic, utilitarian.

And the influence of these classes, politically and morally, was becoming dominant. Tennyson went to Cambridge a few months before Gladstone, the representative statesman of the coming era, went to Oxford. The group of friends who gathered round Tennyson included Arthur Henry Hallam, Gladstone's most intimate

friend at Eton. They were all of them young men of the high
and strenuous seriousness which breathes from the letters of
Sterling and Hallam—James Spedding, Richard Trench, Henry
Alford, Edmund Law Lushington. The life they led was a very
different one from that which Byron describes in his letters of
twenty years earlier. These have the hard, reckless ring of the
age of Fox and his dissipated, aristocratic friends. The young
band of 'Apostles' who debated

> on mind and art,
> And labour, and the changing mart,
> And all the framework of the land

were imbued with the serious, practical temper of the great
merchant class which was to reshape England during the next
fifty years. They were strangers alike to the revolutionary hopes
that intoxicated the youthful Wordsworth, and the reactionary
spirit of 'blood and iron' against which Byron fought and over
which Shelley lamented in strains of ineffable music:

> Oh, cease! must hate and death return?
> Cease! must men kill and die?

The era of conservative reform, of Canning and Peel, of attachment to English institutions combined with a philanthropic ardour
for social betterment, had begun. The repeal of the Test act,
Catholic emancipation, the first great Reform bill were all carried
between the date at which Gladstone and Tennyson went up to
college and a year after they had gone down. Of this movement,
Tennyson was to make conscientious efforts to approve himself
the poet; but, as experience was to show, the conservative instincts
of the would-be liberal poet were deeper and more indestructible
than those of the young statesman who, in these years, was still
'the rising hope of stern and unbending Tories[1].'

The same *via media* was the path followed by Tennyson and
his friends in the region of theology and philosophy. Disciples,
some of them, of Coleridge, they were all more or less broad
churchmen, Christian in sentiment but with little of Gladstone's
reverence for dogma, and sensitive, as Gladstone never was, to
movements of contemporary thought and science. 'Christianity
is always rugging at my heart,' Tennyson said, and his heart and
mind were too often divided against one another to allow of his
attaining to the heights of inspired and inspiring religious
song. But in no mind of his day did the conflict of feeling and

---

[1] Macaulay, *Essays: Gladstone on Church and State*, 1839.

thought produce more sensitive reactions. In the widened and altered vision of the universe which natural science was slowly unfolding, Tennyson was to find, at moments, a fresh justification of the deepest hopes and instincts of his heart, at moments, their utter negation. To the conflict between his sensitive and conservative temperament and that Lucretian vision of the universe which physical science seemed more and more to unroll, we owe some of the most haunting notes of Tennyson's poetry.

But these notes were not sounded at once. Tennyson's first concern was with poetry alone, the object of his assiduous and patient quest being to discover and to master the style and measures in which he could best express the poetry with which his mind was charged to overflowing. *Poems, by Two Brothers* (1827) is negligible. In these early verses, he threw off, as in a kind of mental measles, the infection of the more popular poets of the day—Byron and Moore and Scott. At Cambridge, Wordsworth and Coleridge and Shelley and Keats displaced their more popular rivals, and Tennyson's genius entered upon a period of experiment, of growing clearness and sureness of judgment, of increasing richness and felicity of diction and rhythm, the record of which has been preserved with unusual fulness in the successive *Poems, Chiefly Lyrical* (1830), *Poems* (1833) and *Poems. By Alfred Tennyson,* 2 vols. (1842).

The relation in which these stand to one another is not unlike that of the different 'states' of an etching, the successive 'pulls' in which the artist studies the progress he has made towards the complex perfection of the final plate. Some poems were rejected altogether; others dropped only to reappear; a few suffered little or no alteration between the first edition and the last; yet others (and these are the most interesting and the most important) underwent an elaborate process of rearrangement of the component features, of rehandling that included every kind of erasing, deepening and enriching—processes of which the final outcome was the pomp and magnificence of the 1842 volumes, the beauty and glow presented in their final form by such studies as *The Lady of Shalott, The Miller's Daughter, Œnone, The Palace of Art* (considering the poem only on the side of its music and pictures), *A Dream of Fair Women* and *The Lotos Eaters.*

Tennyson's aim in all this elaboration is clear enough now, though it was not to such early critics as Christopher North and Lockhart—who were justifiably witty at the expense of the poet's lapses, if Lockhart was less justifiably blind to the final result to which the experiments tended. It was no deepening insight into his subjects which guided Tennyson's efforts, for they were to him subjects and no more. They were the common topics of his romantic predecessors, nature, English pastorals, ballad themes, medieval romance, classical legend, love and death. But Tennyson was burdened with no message, no new interpretation of nature or the peasant, no fresh insight into the significance of things medieval or things Hellenic. Each and all were subjects that quickened his poetic imagination, and his concern was to attain to the perfect rendering in melody and picturesque suggestion of the mood which each begat in his brooding temperament. Much has been said of Tennyson's relation to Keats and Wordsworth; but a closer tie unites him to Coleridge, the poet. Like Coleridge, Tennyson is a poet not so much of passion and passionate thinking as of moods—moods subtle and luxurious and sombre, moods in which it is not always easy to discern the line that separates waking from dreaming.

And, like Coleridge, Tennyson, from the outset, was a metrist, bold in experiment and felicitous in achievement. Almost every poem in these volumes was a distinct, conscious experiment in the metrical expression of a single, definite mood. There were some failures, not from inadequate control of the poet's medium of verse (as Coleridge was inclined to think) but because, as Christopher North pointed out, Tennyson occasionally mistook for a poetic mood what was merely a fleeting fancy and recorded it in lines that were, at times, even silly. Of the poems which survived the purgation to which Tennyson subjected his work, some are less happy than others, again not because the poet has failed to make the verse the echo of the mood, but because the mood itself was not one that was altogether congenial to his mind. In lighter and simpler strains, Tennyson is never quite spontaneous. But, when the mood was one of the poet's very soul, luxurious or sombre or a complex blend of both, the metrical expression was, from the first, a triumphant success. *Claribel, Mariana,* 'A spirit haunts the year's last hours,' *Recollections of the Arabian Nights, The Dying Swan, The Lady of Shalott,* the blank verse of *Œnone, A Dream of Fair Women, The Palace of Art, The Vision of Sin, The Lotos Eaters*—all reveal (think what one may of the philosophy of some or of the faults of phrase and figure which marred the first transcripts) a poet with a command of new and surprising and delightful metrical effects as unmistakably as did the early poems of Milton, the masterpieces of

Coleridge, Shelley's songs or Swinburne's *Poems and Ballads*.
The true character of the English verse foot which the romantic
poets had rediscovered without all of them quite knowing what
they had done, the possibilities of what Saintsbury calls 'substitution,' the fact that, in verse whose indicator is a recurring stress,
the foot may be iambic, trochaic, spondaic or monosyllabic without
altering the time-lengths of the rhythmical interval, Tennyson
understood perfectly and he experimented on it with a conscious
and felicitous art, combining with this subtle management of
the foot a careful attention to the musical value of vowel
and consonant combinations in which his precursors are Gray and
Pope and Milton. And, for Tennyson, the guiding principle in
every experiment, from *Claribel* to *The Vision of Sin*, is the
dramatic appropriateness of verse to mood.

Many of the poems, as has been said, underwent drastic
revision; but this revision seldom affected the metre, though the
concluding stanza of *The Lotos Eaters* is a striking exception.
It was the phrasing and imagery, the richly decorative and
picturesque diction, that was revised before the eyes of the reader
with wonderful results. The motive which dictated this labour
was the same as that which controlled the varied cadences of the
poet's verse, the desire to secure the full and exact expression
for the single mood which dominates the poem throughout. For
each of Tennyson's shorter poems, at any rate—hence, perhaps,
his preference of the idyll to the epic—is the expression of a
single mood of feeling. It is seldom that one of his songs or odes
or idylls carries the imagination of the reader from one mood of
feeling to another, as does an ode by Keats or Wordsworth,
while the stream of impassioned thought flows through the mind.
In his longer poems, *In Memoriam* and *Idylls of the King*, as
will be seen later, the plan of construction finally adopted is a
concession to this quality of the poet's genius. A brooding
imagination, a fine ear and a vivid and curious eye, the eye of
an artist who, also, was something of a naturalist—these are the
distinctive qualities of Tennyson's poetic temperament. He
divined, as Keats had before him (but Keats's eye was not, to
a like extent, the dominant factor in his sensibility), that a picture
presented with extraordinary precision of detail may, if every
detail be relevant, contribute potently to the communication of
a mood of feeling—the whole secret of pre-Raphaelitism. But
he was also aware that mere description is no business of the
poet who describes only to communicate feeling. Accordingly,

the alterations which Tennyson introduced into his work, in so far as they were not dictated by the ear, by the desire to secure a purer more flute-like melody of vowel and consonant, had one of two purposes in view, either to present a picture with greater clearness of arrangement and vividness or wealth of detail, or, even more often, to diminish merely descriptive effects, to substitute one or two significant, suggestive details for a fully drawn picture, in every way to intensify the emotional, dramatic effect as by passing the stanza once more through the dyeing vat of the poet's own passionate mood. Of passages in which the first aim predominates, a classical example is the opening landscape in *Œnone*, but a shorter may be cited from *The Palace of Art*:

> One seemed a foreground black with stones and slags,
>   Below sunsmitten icy spires
> Rose striped with long white cloud the scornful crags
>   Deeptrenched with thunderfires,

compared with

> And one a foreground black with stones and slags,
>   Beyond, a line of heights, and higher
> All barr'd with long white cloud the scornful crags,
>   And highest, snow and fire.

Of the other process, the subtle heightening of the emotional thrill, examples will be found in all the poems mentioned; but two short passages may be cited by way of illustration:

> No time hath she to sport and play,
> A charmed web she weaves alway,
> A curse is on her if she stay
> Her weaving either night or day,
>   To look down to Camelot,

compared with

> There she weaves by night and day
> A magic web with colours gay.
> *She has heard a whisper say,*
> A curse is on her if she stay
>   To look down to Camelot,

or,

> She moved her lips, she prayed alone,
> She praying disarrayed and warm
> From slumber, deep her wavy form
> In the darklustrous mirror shone.
> "Madonna," in a low, clear tone
>   Said Mariana, night and morn,
>   Low she mourned, "I am all alone,
> Love-forgotten, and love-forlorn,"

compared with

> Complaining, 'Mother, give me grace
> To help me of my weary load.'
> *And on the liquid mirror glow'd*
> *The clear perfection of her face.*

'*Is this the form,*' she made her moan,
'*That won his praises night and morn?*'
And '*Ah,*' she said, '*but I wake alone,
I sleep forgotten, I wake forlorn.*'

The heightened glow of the picture in the lines italicised is not more striking than the dramatic significance of '*Is this the form,*' etc. But, perhaps, the supreme examples of the poet's power to enrich his verses by passing them once again through the mood in which the whole poem was conceived are the closing stanzas of *The Lady of Shalott* and of *The Lotos Eaters.*

The outcome of the severe course of training to which Tennyson submitted his art—a process that never quite came to an end, for later poems were, also, carefully revised after publication—was a style, the ground and texture of which is a pure, idiomatic English, mannered as, in a different way, the style of Milton is mannered, decorative as, in a different way, the style of Milton is decorative[1], and a verse of wonderful variety, a felicitous adaptability to the mood of the poem, and a curiously elaborated melody of vowel and consonant. With the exception of Gray—for Pope's 'correctness' is not entirely a poetical excellence—English poetry had produced nothing since Milton that is so obviously the result of a strenuous and unwearied pursuit of perfection of form.

Tennyson's range of topics is, also, fully represented in the 1842 volumes—studies of mood and character ranging from the first slight sketches of Adelines and Marianas to the complexities of Simeon Stylites, St Agnes and Sir Galahad, and the nobility of Ulysses; studies of English rural life like *Dora,* among the least successful of Tennyson's poems, not because (as a critic has complained) they have too much of Wordsworth's 'silly sooth,' but because they lack the intense conviction which keeps Wordsworth from ever being 'silly,' though he may at times be absurd, and exalts his 'sooth' into imaginative truth; medieval studies in which was now included *Morte d'Arthur,* starting point of the later *Idylls of the King*; classical legend represented by the early *Œnone* recast and *Ulysses,* for *Tithonus* though written was not yet published; and, lastly, poems in which Tennyson touches on the mysteries of life and death and immortality, themes round

---

[1] The ground-work of Milton's style is English Latinised in syntax, idiom and vocabulary. Of Tennyson's *Idylls of the King,* a contemporary critic says: 'In the history of the English language these poems will occupy a remarkable place as examples of vigorous, unaffected, and almost unmixed Saxon written at a time in which all the ordinary walks of literature are becoming rapidly vulgarised with bastard Latinity,' *The Edinburgh Review,* 1859. Dyboski's *Tennyson's Sprache und Stil* collects Tennyson's usages and throws an instructive light on his mannerisms.

which his brooding imagination was to circle all his life with a sincerer passionate and pathetic interest than he felt for any other subject that engaged his art—seeking, finding, but never long sure that he really had found, like some lone, ghostly sea-bird wheeling round the luring, dazzling, baffling beams of a lighthouse on some stormy headland. For all his questing, Tennyson was never to get much further than the vague hope of the closing section of *The Vision of Sin*:

> At last I heard a voice upon the slope
> Cry to the summit, 'Is there any hope?'
> To which an answer peal'd from that high land,
> But in a tongue no man could understand;
> And on the glimmering limit far withdrawn
> God made Himself an awful rose of dawn.

The sombre note of the scene and the song which precede this close was to be heard more than once again in the verse of the poet who had already written *The Two Voices* and was yet to write *Vastness*. Of political pieces, the volumes included the very characteristic poems 'You ask me, why,' 'Love thou thy land,' 'Of old sat Freedom' and the very popular, if now somewhat faded, trochaics of *Locksley Hall*.

These latter poems, and such additions to his earlier work as *Morte d'Arthur*, *Ulysses* and *Love and Duty*, were proof that not only had Tennyson completely mastered his decorative, musical style but that his poetry had gained in thought, in dramatic insight, in depth and poignancy of feeling; and the question for a lover of Tennyson's poetry in 1842 must have been, was this advance to be continuous, such an increasing dramatic understanding of the passionate heart of man as carried Shakespeare from *A Midsummer Night's Dream* to *Macbeth* and *Othello*, with all the change in style and verse which that process brought with it, or such an absorption in a great theme, the burden of a message, as produced *La Divina Commedia* or *Paradise Lost*. For there were dangers besetting Tennyson's laborious cultivation of a new and rich poetic diction, dangers which betrayed themselves very evidently in the first considerable poem that followed the 1842 volumes, the longest poem Tennyson had yet attempted, and the first in which he set himself conscientiously (in the mood in which he had conceived *The Palace of Art*) to give to his poetry a didactic intention. *The Princess*, first published in 1847 but revised and re-revised in 1851 and 1853, if it exhibits all the characteristic excellences of Tennyson's style, his mellifluous blank verse and polished, jewelled phrasing, reveals with equal clearness its limitations and faults.   The blend of humour and sentiment and serious purpose is not altogether a success—'Alfred, whatever he may think,' said FitzGerald, 'cannot trifle.   His smile is rather a grim one'—and of dramatic interest there is the merest suggestion in the grandiloquent princess, the silly prince and their slightly outlined companions.   Moreover, the style, with all its beauties, reveals, as some of the later *Idylls of the King* were to do, the radical want of simplicity, which is not really disguised by the purity, of Tennyson's style, a tendency to conceit and decoration which seeks to make poetry of a plain statement by periphrasis and irrelevant, even if beautiful, figure.   Gladstone admired the skill with which Tennyson could make poetical the description of a game-pie :

> Where quail and pigeon, lark and leveret lay
> Like fossils of the rock, with golden yolks
> Imbedded and injellied,

and describe mathematics as

> The hard-grain'd Muses of the cube and square.

The Princess abounds in refinements of this kind, as when the prince

> sat down and wrote,
> In such a hand as when a field of corn
> Bows all its ears before the roaring East,

or the remark that Cyril's wilder frolics are not the surest index to his character is thus adorned :

> He has a solid base of temperament:
> But as the waterlily starts and slides
> Upon the level in little puffs of wind,
> Tho' anchor'd to the bottom, such is he.

Even when the poem rises to a higher level of seriousness in the closing sections, the style is still elaborated and brocaded out of all proportion to the theme.   Yet of such art the final perfection is found in an appearance of simplicity, and that, too, Tennyson achieved in the lyrics which were added to the third edition—the subtle 'silly sooth' of 'We fell out' and 'Sweet and low,' the pealing music of 'The splendour falls,' the sophisticated, coloured art of 'Now sleeps the crimson petal,' and, lastly, the melody, the vision and the passionate wail of 'Tears, idle tears' the most moving and finely wrought lyric Tennyson ever wrote.

The quality which such art, with all its wonderful elaboration, lacks is that last secret of a great style which Dante indicates when he defines the *dolce stil nuovo*—for what is true of love is true of any other adequate theme—

> *Ed io a lui: ' Io mi son un che, quando*
> *Amor mi spira, noto, ed a quel modo*
> *Che ditta dentro, vo significando*[1].'

He had not yet written as when a great subject appears to take the pen and write itself. But, in 1850, Tennyson seemed to his readers to have found such an inspiring theme, when the poem on which he had been at work ever since the death in 1833 of his friend Arthur Henry Hallam was published under the simple title *In Memoriam*, for the theme, death and immortality, was that on which Tennyson ever felt most deeply, was most constantly haunted and agitated by conflicting hopes and fears. In no poems had he written with more evident sincerity, more directness, a finer balance of thought and style, than in those poems which, like *Ulysses* and *The Vision of Sin*, were precursors of this longer poem on life and death and immortality, sorrow and sin and the justification of God's ways to men.

In Memoriam is not altogether free from the faults of Tennysonian diction, phrasing such as ' eaves of weary eyes ' or

> And where the kneeling hamlet drains
> The chalice of the grapes of God,

but, with few exceptions, the style is pure, direct and masculine, and to this not only the theme but the verse contributed, a verse which Ben Jonson and lord Herbert of Cherbury had used before him, but which Tennyson made his own by the new weight and melody which he gave to it. In Tennyson's hands, the verse acquired something of the weight and something of the fittingness for a long meditative poem of the *terza rima* as used by Dante, the same perfection of internal movement combined with the same invitation to continue, an eddying yet forward movement[2].

The construction of the poem in separate sections, some of which are linked together in groups by continuity of theme, was that which gave freest scope to Tennyson's genius, allowing him to make of each section the expression of a single, intense mood. But the claim for *In Memoriam*, that it is not merely a collection of poems of varying degrees of beauty but a great poem, rests on

---

[1] *Purgatorio*, xxiv, 52—4.

[2] See Saintsbury, *History of English Prosody*, vol. iii, p. 205, and, on the *terza rima*, as used by Dante and by English poets, *ibid.* pp. 361—5.

the degree of success with which Tennyson has woven these together into a poem portraying the progress of the human spirit from sorrow to joy, not by the loss of love or the mere dulling of grief, but by the merging of the passion for the individual friend, removed but still living, into the larger love of God and of his fellow-men[1]. If the present generation does not estimate *In Memoriam* quite so highly as its first readers, it is because time, which has a way of making clear the interval between a poet's intention and his achievement, the expressed purpose of a *Paradise Lost* and its final effect, has shown that Tennyson failed to make this central experience, this great transition, imaginatively convincing and impressive. It is not in the vague philosophy, with a dash of semi-mystical experience, in which is veiled the simple process by which the heart grows reconciled to loss and life renews her spell, nor in the finished and illuminated style in which all this is clothed—it is not here that the reader of today finds the true Tennyson, the poet with his own unique and splendid gifts, but in the sombre moods and the lovely landscapes of individual sections. 'Old Yew, which graspest at the stones,' 'Dark house, by which once more I stand,' 'Calm is the morn without a sound,' 'To-night the winds begin to rise,' 'With trembling fingers did we weave'—sections such as these, or the passionate sequence beginning 'Oh yet we trust that somehow good,' and later, lovelier flights as 'When on my bed the moonlight falls,' 'I cannot see the features right,' 'Witch-elms that counterchange the floor,' 'By night we linger'd on the lawn,' 'Unwatch'd, the garden bough shall sway,' 'Sad Hesper o'er the buried sun'—these are likely to be dear to lovers of English poetry by their expression of mood in picture and music, long after the philosophy of *In Memoriam* has been forgotten. It is not the mystical experience of the ninety-fifth section which haunts the memory, but the beauty of the sun-rise that follows when

> the doubtful dusk reveal'd
> The knolls once more where, couch'd at ease,
> The white kine glimmer'd, and the trees
> Laid their dark arms about the field:
>
> And suck'd from out the distant gloom
> A breeze began to tremble o'er
> The large leaves of the sycamore,
> And fluctuate all the still perfume,

---

[1] See A. C. Bradley, *A Commentary on Tennyson's 'In Memoriam,'* in which the development of this thought is traced.

And gathering freshlier overhead,
Rock'd the full foliaged elms, and swung
The heavy-folded rose, and flung
The lilies to and fro, and said

'The dawn, the dawn,' and died away;
And East and West, without a breath,
Mixt their dim lights, like life and death,
To broaden into boundless day.

To the theme of the most agitated sections of the poem, those whose theme is not the removal of the friend by death from the sight and touch of those that loved him, but the more terrible doubt as to a life after death, the poet was to recur again, to fight more than one 'weird battle of the west,' before he faced the final issue with courage and resignation and hope.

In the year of *In Memoriam*, Tennyson succeeded Wordsworth in the post of poet laureate, and his first official poem was the fine *Ode on the Death of the Duke of Wellington* (1852), a bold metrical experiment, the *motif* for which is given by the funeral march and the pomp of the obsequies in St Paul's. In the dramatic use of varying metres no poet was ever a more constant and generally felicitous experimenter than Tennyson, and in his next considerable poem *Maud*, issued in *Maud, and Other Poems* (1855), he employed the device of sections, not, as in *In Memoriam*, of like metrical structure, but varying in the boldest fashion from long six-foot to short three-foot lines, to tell in monodrama a story of tragic passion. The hero and narrator is dramatically conceived, and Tennyson was very anxious not to be identified with the Hamlet of his story. But the political opinions which he put into his mouth were his own, in the main, and the morbid, hysterical temperament was his own, too, dramatically intensified and elaborated. The result was a poem which greatly disconcerted his admirers —alike those who would have had him content to remain the Theocritus of idylls like *The Gardener's Daughter* and *The Brook* (which was published in the same volume as *Maud*), and those who were calling on him for a great poem, and were prepared to acclaim him—mainly on the strength of *Locksley Hall*—as the laureate of an age of 'unexampled progress.' The latter were profoundly shocked at the poet's fierce exultation over war for a cause, his clear perception of the seamy side of commercial prosperity and his contempt for what he thought a mean conception of the blessing of peace. A great poem *Maud* is not. The heroine is too shadowy, the hero a Hamlet only in the hysterical instability of his temperament, with none of Hamlet's range of thought, or

that ultimate strength of soul which held madness and suicide at
arm's length ; but 'I have led her home,' 'Come into the garden,
Maud,' and 'O that 'twere possible' are among the most perfect of
Tennyson's dramatic love-lyrics.

The great poem, the *magnum opus*, to which Tennyson's critics
summoned him insistently[1] and on which his mind dwelt with
almost too conscientious a desire to fulfil what was expected of
him, began to take shape finally, in the only form in which his
genius could work at ease (the concentration, in a poem of not too
great length, on a single mood of feeling), with the composition of
Idylls of the King. Malory's *Morte d'Arthur* had early arrested
his attention.

I could not read *Palmerin of England* nor *Amadis*, nor any other of
those Romances through. The *Morte d'Arthur* is much the best: there are
very fine things in it; but all strung together without Art.

So he told FitzGerald, and his first experiment in the retelling of
the old legends, *Morte d'Arthur*, had appeared in 1842 as a
fragment of Homeric epic. Nothing more was added till 1857,
when *Enid and Nimuë* was issued in an edition of some six
copies. This issue was followed, in 1859, by *The True and the
False, Four Idylls of the King,* containing *Enid, Nimuë (Vivien),
Elaine* and *Guinevere.* In the same year, the four idylls were
issued as *Idylls of the King.* In 1869 were added *The Coming
of Arthur, The Holy Grail, Pelleas and Ettarre* and *The
Passing of Arthur. The Last Tournament* (1871), *Gareth and
Lynette* (1872), *Balin and Balan* (1885) came later, and, in the
final arrangement, *Geraint and Enid* was divided into two
parts.

In the later poems, the epic, Homeric flavour of the first *Morte*
is abandoned for a more purely idyllic tone, a chiselled, polished,
jewelled exquisiteness of Alexandrian art. Of blank verse,
Tennyson was an exacting critic and a master in a manner as
definitely his own as Thomson's, but with a greater claim to be
compared with the finest of English non-dramatic blank verse,
that is Milton's. And when the theme is reflective, oratorical or
dramatic—at least in monologue—Tennyson's blank verse is
melodious and sonorous, variously paused and felicitously drawn
out into effective paragraphs. A continuous study reveals a
greater monotony of effect than in Milton's ever varied harmonies,

---

[1] 'We once more call upon him to do the duty which England has long expected
of him, and to give us a great poem on a great subject,' *The Edinburgh Review*,
1855.

and there is never the grand undertone of passion, of the storm
that has raised the ground swell. It is in narrative that the faults
of Tennyson's blank verse become apparent—its too flagrant
artificiality. The pauses and cadences are too carefully chosen,
the diction too precious, the movement too mincing, the whole
' too picked, too spruce, too affected ' :

> So coming to the fountain-side beheld
> Balin and Balan sitting statuelike,
> Brethren, to right and left the spring, that down,
> From underneath a plume of lady-fern
> Sang, and the sand danced at the bottom of it.

One could multiply such instances—taken quite at random—from
the *Idylls*, especially from the descriptions of tournament or
combat. In his parody of *The Brook*, Calverley has caught to
perfection the mincing gait and affected phrasing of this
Tennysonian fine-writing :

> Thus on he prattled like a babbling brook,
> Then I, " The sun hath slipt behind the hill,
> And my Aunt Vivian dines at half-past six."
> So in all love we parted; I to the Hall,
> They to the village. It was noised next noon
> That chickens had been miss'd at Syllabub Farm.

The over-exquisite elaboration of form is in keeping with
Tennyson's whole treatment of the old legends, rich in a colour
and atmosphere of their own. With the spirit of the Arthurian
stories, in which elements of a Celtic, primitive world are blended
in a complex, now hardly to be disentangled, fashion with medieval
chivalry and catholic, sacramental symbolism, the Victorian poet
was out of sympathy. Neither the aimless fighting in which they
abound, nor the cult of love as a passion so inspiring and ennobling
that it glorified even sin, nor the mystical adoration of the Host
and the ascetic quest of a spotless purity in the love and service
of God, appealed deeply to Tennyson, who wished to give to the
fighting a philanthropic purpose, to combine love with purity in
marriage and to find the mystic revelation of God in the world
in which we move and serve.

It is not easy to pour new wine into old bottles, to charge old
stories with a new spirit. If Milton's classical treatment of Biblical
themes is a wonderful *tour de force*—and it is not a complete
success—it is because the spirit of the poet and the poem is, after
all, rather Hebraic than Hellenic. There is as much of the Hebrew
prophets in his work as of the Greek poets. It is still harder to
give a new soul to old legends if one is not quite sure what that

soul is to be. The allegory which was to connect the whole, 'the conflict continually maintained between the spirit and the flesh,' is, at once, too obvious and too vague, too vague as an interpretation of the story as a whole, too obvious when it appears as an occasional intrusion of a double meaning—in *Gareth and Lynette* or *The Holy Grail*. It was, indeed, a misfortune that Tennyson was determined to tie the tin kettle of a didactic intention to the tail of all poems of this period. The general moral significance of the old story was clear enough—'do after the good and leave the evil and it shall bring you to good fame and renommee'—and needed no philosophic pointer. The sole justification for rehandling the legends was the possibility of giving them a new and heightened poetic beauty and dramatic significance.

In the latter, the poet has certainly not wholly failed, and it is this dramatic significance, rather than the vague allegory, which connects the stories and gives to the series a power over and above the charm of the separate tales. As in *In Memoriam*, so in *Idylls of the King*, the connecting link between the parts is a gradually induced change of mood. Each *Idyll* has its dominant mood reflected in the story, the characters and the scenery in which these are set, from the bright youth and glad spring-tide of *Gareth and Lynette* to the disillusionment and flying yellow leaves of *The Last Tournament*, the mists and winter-cold of the parting with Guinevere and 'that last, dim, weird battle of the west.' The dramatic background to this change of mood is the story of Lancelot and Guinevere, and the final test of Tennyson's success or failure in his most ambitious work is his handling of this story ; the most interesting group of characters are the four that contemplate each other with mournful and troubled eyes as in some novel of modern life, Arthur, Lancelot, Guinevere and Elaine. In part, Tennyson has succeeded, almost greatly ; in part, he has inevitably failed. Elaine is perfect, a wonderful humanising of the earlier, half mystical Lady of Shalott. Lancelot, too, is surely a great study of the flower of knighthood caught in the trammels of an overpowering, ruining passion, a modern picture drawn on the lines of the old ; and Guinevere, too, slightly, yet distinctly, drawn

in her splendid beauty—wilful, impetuous, self-indulgent—yet full of courtesy and grace and, when she pleases, of self-control also; not without a sense in her of the greatness of the work which she is marring; not without a bitter consciousness of her secret humiliation and the place she has lost; but yet too proud, too passionate, too resolute to yield even to her own compunctions[1].

The failure is Arthur, and it could hardly be otherwise. A shadowy figure in the old legends, Tennyson has made him not more but less real, a 'conception of man as he might be,' Gladstone declared, and, in consequence, of man as he ought not to be in such a dramatic setting. Like the Lady in *Comus*, Arthur has become a symbol, not a human being. As the former, when she speaks, is not a young English girl, but the personification of chastity, so Arthur is, as in Spenser's poem, the embodiment of complete virtue conceived in a Victorian fashion, with a little too much in him of the 'endless clergyman,' which Tennyson said was the Englishman's idea of God. And the last speech he delivers over the fallen Guinevere is, in consequence, at once magnificent and intolerable. The most popular of his works when they appeared, *Idylls of the King*, is, today, probably the chief stumbling-block to a young student of Tennyson. Its Parnassian beauties, its vaguely religious and somewhat timid morality reflect too vividly the spirit of their own day. Yet, even English poetry would need to be richer than it is before we could afford to forget or ignore such a wealth of splendid colour and music as these poems present.

The same excess of sentiment, which, in a great poem, should have given place to thought and passion, and the same over-elaborate art, are apparent in the rustic idyll which gives its name to the volume published in 1864, *Enoch Arden, etc.*, a tragedy of village life founded on a story given to Tennyson by the sculptor Woolner, recalling, in many of its details, Crabbe's *The Parting Hour*. Fundamentally, there is more of Crabbe than of Wordsworth in Tennyson's tales of English country-life, for, though Tennyson is more sentimental than Crabbe and his treatment far more decorative, he does not idealise in the mystical manner of Wordsworth. But, in style and verse, there could not well be a greater difference than that between the vivid pictures, the tropical colouring, the sophisticate simplicity of *Enoch Arden* and the limited, conventional phraseology, the monotonous verse in which Crabbe tells his story with so much more of sheer dramatic truth. But it was in the direction of sheer dramatic truth, mastering and, to some extent, simplifying the style, that Tennyson's genius was advancing most fruitfully, and the earnest of this is two poems which accompany *Enoch Arden*, the dialect

---

[1] From a review of *Idylls of the King* in *The Edinburgh Review*, April 1870.

ballads in six-foot anapaests, *The Grandmother* and *The Northern Farmer—Old Style*, the first of which owes its poignancy to the sorrow with which Tennyson gazed on his own first child born dead, while the latter is the earliest altogether felicitous expression of the vein of dramatic humour which ran through his naturally sombre temperament. Tennyson could not trifle, but he had a gift of caustic satire to which he might have given freer play with advantage to his permanent, if not his immediate, popularity. The two farmer poems and *The Village Wife* are worth several such poems as *Dora* and *Enoch Arden*.

'He bestowed infinite trouble on his dramas,' his son says, and they bear every mark of a careful study of the sources, thoughtful delineation of character, finished expression and versification. What they want is dramatic life and force. The historical plays are the product of his patriotism and his dislike of catholicism; but the political interest is not, as in Shakespeare's plays, quickly superseded by the dramatic. The characters do not become alive and take the conduct of the play into their own hands, as Falstaff and the humorous characters in Shakespeare's English plays tend to do. In *Queen Mary*, no single character arrests and dominates our interest, and the hero of *Harold*, as of many modern plays, is of the Hamlet type of character, without quite being a Hamlet, more interested in the conflict of his own impulses and inhibitions than the driving force of a play full of action and incident. The most single in interest and the most impressive is *Becket*. Thoughtful and accomplished as they are, none of Tennyson's dramas is the product of the imagination which begat the greatest and most characteristic of his poems.

It is in the poems beginning with the above mentioned dialect poems and continued in *Lucretius* (1868), *The Revenge: A Ballad of the Fleet* (1878), the startling *Ballads and Other Poems* of 1880 and the subsequent similar studies, published, some of them, separately and then collected in the successive volumes —*Tiresias, and Other Poems* (1885), *Locksley Hall Sixty Years After* (1886), *Demeter and Other Poems* (1889), *The Death of Œnone, Akbar's Dream, and Other Poems* (1892)—that the later Tennyson appears in poems revealing the same careful structure and metrical cunning as the romantic studies that filled the two volumes of 1842. But the romantic colour and magic are gone; gone, too, is the suggestion of an optimistic philosophy which has tempted some critics to apply the strange epithet 'complacent' to the troubled, sensitive soul of Tennyson. What has taken the place of these is a more poignant dramatic note, a more troubled outlook upon life and the world around him, a severer but, in its severity, a no less felicitous style, rarely a less dramatic adjustment of rhythm to feeling.

Tennyson's sensitive imagination was ever responsive to the moral atmosphere around him. It was the high seriousness of Hallam and his Cambridge friends, their sympathy with moral and political progress, which had encouraged him to endeavour, even too strenuously, to charge his work with didactic intention, which had made him strive, often against his deepest instincts and prejudices, to sympathise with the claims of advancing democracy and which had instilled into his mind the one article of his vague and more emotional than dogmatic Christianity, the belief in the 'far future,' the ultimate triumph of love. And now it seemed as though these high thoughts and hopes were illusions, and the morbid vein in which he had already written *The Two Voices* becomes dominant, strengthened by his consciousness of the times being 'out of joint.' Coleridgean Christianity had given place to modern science and the religion of Lucretius. Romance was yielding ground to a realism as sombre as Crabbe's, but more pathological and irreverent. Democracy had not brought all the blessings that were promised, and it seemed to Tennyson to be relaxing the national spirit, the patriotism and heroism which had made England great. The feelings with which all these changes affected Tennyson are vividly reflected in all his later poems. The patriotic poems breathe a more fervent, a fiercer patriotism. *The Revenge, The Defence of Lucknow, The Charge of the Heavy Brigade* are instinct with a patriotism which allows of scant sympathy with Indian rebels, 'Russian hordes,' or 'the Inquisition dogs and the devildoms of Spain.' The ballads of peasant humours, as *The Spinster's Sweet-Arts* and *The Village Wife; or, The Entail*, and of peasant sorrows and tragedies, like *The Grandmother* and *Rizpah* are as realistic, sombre and humorous as some of the contemporary novels of country life—poems at the opposite pole from *The Gardener's Daughter* and *The Miller's Daughter*. In stories of modern life, as already in the earlier *Aylmer's Field*, there is the note of hysterical feeling which betrays the jarring of the poet's nerves as he contemplated certain aspects of modern life in *Locksley Hall Sixty Years After, Despair, In the Childrens' Hospital*. In the meditative poems in blank verse, classical idylls from *Lucretius* to *Tiresias*, idylls from history as *Sir John Oldcastle, Columbus, St Telemachus*, or more lyrical meditations like *Vastness*, his mind circles ever round one theme in various aspects, the pathos of man's destiny wandering between faiths which are rooted in fear and a widening knowledge that dispels the superstitious fears but leaves him no hope, the tragic grandeur of man's sensitive soul terribly environed, the cost and pain with which he has struggled forwards to

> The worship which is Love, [to] see no more
> The Stone, the Wheel, the dimly-glimmering lawns
> Of that Elysium, all the hateful fires
> Of torment, and the shadowy warrior glide
> Along the silent field of Asphodel,

and the haunting fear that, after all, the purer faith may be a dream, melting in the cold light of physical science :

> What is it all, if we all of us end but in being our own corpse-coffins at last,
> Swallow'd in Vastness, lost in Silence, drown'd in the deeps of a meaningless Past?

Tennyson was not able to expel, though he could subdue, the ghosts which haunted him. He never thought his way through any of the problems, political, moral or metaphysical, which the age presented, and, to the reader of today, it is not the thought of these poems which matters, but the reaction of this thought on their dramatic and poetic quality, the piercing note which it gave to poems that have lost the wonderful fragrance and colour —the rich bouquet if one might change the figure—of the 1842 poems, but in whose autumnal tints and severer outlines there is a charm more deeply felt than in the overwrought perfection, the deliberate intention of the middle period poems.

In one respect, these poems show little, if any, abatement of force, that is in the dramatic adjustment of metre to mood. The blank verse of the later pieces is simpler and less mannered than in *Idylls of the King*, while retaining the variety and dignity of movement which Tennyson's blank verse always has when used for meditative, and not narrative, poetry. *Tithonus* has all, and more than all, the magic of the earlier *Œnone* in the rendering of a passionate mood in a setting of exquisite natural description, and *Lucretius* all, and more than all, the dramatic and psychological subtlety and force of such an earlier study of mental disturbance as *St Simeon Stylites*; and, to the last, in *Tiresias* and *Demeter* and *St Telemachus*, the stately movement, the vowelled melody, hardly flags.

But the metre in which Tennyson experimented most repeatedly in the last poems is the anapaestic, generally in a six-foot line. All the dialect pieces are in this metre and the verse is admirably adapted to the drawling speech of the English rustic. In *The Revenge*, where the anapaest interchanges freely with shorter, more massive, rhythms, the poet has achieved one of his masterpieces in dramatic, picturesque, glowing narrative, following closely, at times adopting the words of, Ralegh's story[1]. It is, perhaps, the greatest war-poem in the language; and, metrically, *The Charge of the Heavy Brigade* is not less felicitous though the story is not so romantic and picturesque. In *The Voyage of Maeldune*, Tennyson opened at the end of his life another storehouse of Celtic legend than the Arthurian, and the metre, again, is perfectly adapted to the monotony of marvel and magic which is the note of Irish story. It is, however, more doubtful whether the six-foot anapaest was so well suited to the tales of modern life, *Despair*, *The Flight*, *The Wreck*, etc., of which Tennyson wrote, perhaps, more than enough in his last years. Certainly, the blank verse poem *The Sisters* is a happier effort. The ballad movement is not well adaptable to such themes, and the verse, quite in keeping with the style of rustic narrative, seems, by its monotony, to heighten the tone of hysterical sensibility, the 'spasmodic' character, of these not very pleasing poems.

Blank verse and anapaests by no means exhaust the metres of these last volumes, though some of these are professedly experiments. In *The Daisy*, published in the *Maud* volume, Tennyson was justly proud of having caught 'a far-off echo of the Horatian Alcaic'; and his trochaics are not less felicitous than his anapaests. The last volumes contain, as well as the second *Locksley Hall*, the lovely echo of Catullus's lament,

> Row us out from Desenzano, to your Sirmione row!

and the clangour of the great lines *To Virgil*,

> Landscape-lover, lord of language,

the worthiest tribute which has been paid to the Roman poet since Dante. To the last, Tennyson was capable of springing such surprises on those who were babbling of his decadence; to the last, he was able to delight by the musical and picturesque interpretation of mood and dream. The author of *Tears, idle tears* could write at the age of eighty:

---

[1] *A report of the truth of the fight about the Iles of Açores.* 1591.

> But such a tide as moving seems asleep,
>   Too full for sound and foam,
> When that which drew from out the boundless deep
>   Turns again home.

The very fullness of Tennyson's popularity, unlike anything since Pope, provoked the inevitable reaction.   To do justice to the great body of varied and splendid poetry he lived to complete without any such subsidence of original inspiration as is evident in all the later work of Wordsworth, relieved though that is by fitful recurrences of the old magic, time was needed, time which separates unerringly the most accomplished writing and interesting thought from poetry, the expression of an imaginative, musical soul.   It was on the thinker, the seer, that the greatest admirers of the old poet, Frederick Myers and others, were tempted to lay stress, the prophet of immortality in an age of positivism.   But Tennyson was no seer like Blake or Wordsworth, no agile dialectician like Browning.   He was a great sensitive soul, full of British prejudices but also with a British conscience, anxious to render a good account of the talent entrusted to him, to make art the handmaid of duty and faith, but troubled by the course of events and unable to find any solution save a faith in the 'far future,' in a process that runs through all things, the

> one far-off divine event,
> To which the whole creation moves

Since Shakespeare, there has been no poet so English in his prejudices and in his love of the soil and scenery of England, her peasants and her great sailors and soldiers.   To speak of him as a representative Victorian is a mistake if it suggests that there was in him anything of Macaulay's complacent pride in the 'progress' of the age, economic and scientific.   He was interested in, and his thought deeply coloured by, these; but, temperamentally, he belonged to the aristocratic, martial England of the period that closed in 1832, and the conflict of his temperament and his conscientious effort to understand and sympathise with his own age gave a complex *timbre* to many of his poems.   At heart, he was an aristocratic Englishman, distrustful of democracy, and disdainful of foreigners and foreign politics, passionately patriotic and troubled, above all, by a fear that democratic England was less jealous of her honour than the old, more intent on material welfare and peace at any price.   At heart, he was a Christian in a quite undogmatic English fashion, a Christian of the old English rectory and village-church type, rich in the charities and the simpler pieties, with no touch of Browning's nonconformist fervour, distrustful of Romanising dogmas and ritual, at once interested in, and profoundly troubled by, the drift of contemporary science and positivism. The beauties of English rural scenery and English gardens and villages are woven through and through the richly coloured tapestry of his poetry. Of his one journey to Italy he remembered only the discomfort of the rain and the daisy which spoke to him of England. Even for the dead it is better to lie in English soil:

> we may stand
> Where he in English earth is laid,
> And from his ashes may be made
> The violet of his native land.

And there are no such achievements by sea or land as those of English sailors and soldiers.

It is not as a thinker or seer that Tennyson will live but as one of the most gifted and, with Milton and Gray, one of the few conscientious workmen among English poets. From *Claribel* to *Crossing the Bar*, the claim of his poetry is always the same, the wonderful felicity with which it renders in vivid picture, in varied but always dramatically appropriate metre, in language of the most carefully wrought euphony—no poet since Milton studied as Tennyson did the finer effects of well adjusted vowels and consonants—the single intense mood in which the poem has been conceived. He was not a great dramatist, he was not a great narrative poet. There is a more passionate, winged movement in the songs of other poets than his, songs that sing themselves more inevitably. His great achievement is in that class of meditative, musical, decorative poetry to which belong Milton's *L'Allegro* and *Il Penseroso*, Gray's *Elegy*, Keats's odes. This is the type towards which all his poems tend even when they take different forms and are lyrical or include an element of narrative. And, if Tennyson has written nothing so fine as Milton's or Keats's poems just named, he has given new qualities to the kind, and he has extended its range by his dramatic use of the idyll, the picture of a mood. Compared with Tennyson, Wordsworth, Shelley and Keats are poets of a single note, nature mystically interpreted, the sensuous delight of beauty, the 'desire of the moth for the star.' The moods to which Tennyson has given poetic expression are as varied as his metres, and include a rare feeling for the beauty of English scenery, the mind of the peasant in many of its phases, humorous and tragic, the interpretation of classical legend, the reproduction of the very soul of some Greek and Roman poets, as Theocritus and Vergil, Lucretius and Catullus, the colour and beauty, if not all the peculiar ethical and religious tone, of medieval romance, complexities of mind and even pathological subtleties of emotion, the brooding of a sensitive spirit over the riddles of life and death and good and evil. Browning has a wider range, is less insular, more curious about exotic types and more subtle in tracing the dialectics of mood and situation. But he does not enter more intensely into the purely emotional aspect of the mood, and he does not steep the whole in such a wealth of colour and melody.

Coming after the great romantics, Tennyson inherited their achievement in the rediscovery of poetic themes, the purification and enrichment of English poetic diction, the liberation and enrichment of English verse, and he uses them all as a conscious, careful artist. His poetry stands to theirs much as a garden to a natural landscape. The free air of passionate inspiration does not blow through it so potently; it lacks the sublimity of sea and moor and the open heavens. But there are compensations. The beauty of nature is enhanced by art, the massing of blooms, the varying of effects, the background of velvet lawn and grassy bank and ordered hedge-row ; above all, by the enrichment of the soil which adds a deeper crimson to the rose, and blends with simpler blooms the splendours of the exotic. An imagination rich in colour, a delicate and highly trained ear, a thought which if not profound was nourished on the literature and philosophy of Greece and Rome—these were among Tennyson's gifts to English poetry, and they go a long way to counterbalance such limitations as are to be found in his thought and feeling. The peerage conferred on him in 1884 was the recognition of the greatness of his reputation and the intensely national spirit of his work.

The name Tennyson may have overshadowed for a time, in the long run it has given an adventitious interest to, the work of the poet laureate's brothers, Frederick and Charles. Frederick went from Louth grammar school to Eton, and from Eton to Cambridge, where, after a year at St John's college, he migrated to Trinity where he was joined by his brothers. He distinguished himself by gaining the Browne medal with a Greek ode on Egypt. The cadence of the closing lines lingered in the ears of Sir Francis Doyle all his life: ὀλλυμένων γὰρ, ἁ χθὼν ἐξαπολεῖται! But he did not make so strong an impression on his contemporaries as the younger brothers. The greater part of his subsequent life was spent in Italy, and the last thirty-five years in Jersey. At Florence, he came under the influence of the spiritualistic influences which attracted Mrs Browning and gave the world *Mr Sludge, 'The Medium'*; and in his later life he became an ardent Freemason and Swedenborgian. He was a great reader, a student of art and a passionate lover of music. His first volume of poems *Days and Hours* was published in 1854. Thereafter, he published nothing until 1890, when he issued a long volume of blank verse idylls called *The Isles of Greece*, followed, in 1891, by a volume of classical stories, *Daphne and other Poems*, and, in 1895, under the title of *Poems of the Day and Year*, a selection from the earlier printed poems with some additions.

Charles Tennyson graduated at Cambridge in 1832 and was ordained in 1835. On succeeding to a small estate by the will of a grand-uncle he took the name of Turner. The greater part of his life was spent as vicar at Grasby in Lincolnshire, where he cultivated his delicate, meditative verse, writing sonnets on incidents in his daily life, public events, theological topics and other subjects. He died at Cheltenham in 1879.

Charles Tennyson's poems, with few exceptions, were sonnets, in the Italian form, but with a fresh set of rimes in the second quartet of the octave. Fifty were published in 1830 and were added to, as occasion suggested, till *Sonnets, Old and New*, published in 1880, numbered more than three hundred. Not many of this number reveal the intensity of feeling and perfection of form which are essential to the sonnet. Coleridge was attracted by the young Tennyson's sonnets, as, at an earlier age, he had been by the not very dissimilar sonnets of Bowles with their pensive sentiment and occasionally felicitous description. But, when at his best, Tennyson-Turner is a finer artist than Bowles. Some of the earlier, indeed, show an uncertain grasp of the form, the last lines betraying an heroic effort to complete the fourteen and finish. He wrote too many on occasional themes and theological polemics. But the best of those inspired by aspects of natural scenery and simple incidents have the charm of felicitous workmanship and delicate feeling. *The Lattice at Sunrise, The Buoy-Bell, The Ocean* and some others suggest Wordsworth in a minor key, and *Letty's Globe*, like the grander sonnet of Blanco White, is a poem in which art and chance seem to have combined to produce a poem surprisingly felicitous alike in conceit and execution.

If Charles Tennyson is a pleasing lesser poet, Frederick strikes one as a poet in whom the possibility of greater things was never realised. His character and occasional lines in his work impressed FitzGerald, who, after 1842, was never a whole-hearted admirer of the poet laureate's work. 'You are now the only man I expect verse from,' he wrote to Frederick in 1850, 'such gloomy, grand stuff as you write ... we want some bits of strong, genuine imagination'; and Browning spoke of him as possessing all the qualities of his brother Alfred, but in solution. 'One always expected them to crystallise—but they never did.'

There is certainly more of the large manner about him than Charles. His imagery, especially his personifications, is more imaginative ; his verse has more of sweep and flow. But he never took to heart, as Alfred did, the lesson of brevity : 'I felt certain of one thing then, if I meant to make any mark at all it must be by shortness, for the men before me had been so diffuse.' Frederick's classical idylls and narratives are excessively diffuse. They contain some of his best work, charming description, tenderness of feeling—passion they lack as, in some degree, does the work of all the Tennysons. There is none that would not have gained by concentration of treatment.

The other notable quality of Frederick Tennyson's poems, longer and shorter, is a certain abstractness. His love of travel and a life apart were the index to a certain aloofness and solitariness of soul, not incompatible with a desire for sympathy and self-expression. Some stanzas called *River of Life* close with a confession of this aloofness :

> River of Life, lo! I have furl'd my sail
> Under the twilight of these ancient trees,
> I listen to the water's sleepless wail,
> I fill mine ears with sighs that never cease,
> If armed hearts come stronger out of ill,
> The dust of conflict fills their eyes and ears;
> Mine unaccustom'd heart will tremble still
> With the old mirth and with the early tears.

He was deeply interested in metaphysical problems. He retells old myths with the purpose of making them messengers of his own thought on immortality and the unseen world. But the message is a little indistinct. Occasionally, as in *Psyche*, he loses himself in a Swedenborgian quagmire. There was something of a mystic in Frederick Tennyson; and his strange, unequal poems are the expression of a solitary soul with a certain distinction of its own. Nature and love and death and immortality are the foci round which his thought, as that of his greater brother, moved, and on each he has written occasional haunting lines:

> Oh! thou must weep, and, in the rain
> Of tears, raise up the prime
> And beauty of thy heart again,
> And toil, and fall with time;
> And look on Fate, and bear to see
> The shadow of Death familiarly.
>
> Thy noblest act is but a sorrow,
> To live—though ill befall;
> Thy great reward—to die to-morrow,
> If God and Nature call;
> In faith to reach what ear and eye
> Dream not, nor all thy phantasy!

CHAPTER III

ROBERT BROWNING

AND

ELIZABETH BARRETT BROWNING

THE best explanation of a poet is to be sought in the best poem he has written, or in that theme which, at his touch, breaks out into the amplest music. There, his very self, the personality which he verily is and which, in a greater or lesser degree, subtly suffuses all that he does, finds fittest and fullest utterance; and the utterance itself, whether in phrase or figure, being faithful to fact, bears that stamp of inevitability which implies perfection.

There is little doubt as to the theme which called forth the fullness of the powers of Elizabeth Barrett and Robert Browning. It was love. It was love in the same cosmic sense as Wordsworth's duty, which 'preserved the stars from wrong,' an omnipresent passion for the best in all nature and in all mankind. To Elizabeth Browning, there was no truth nor substance, save love. It was the essence and wholeness of her being, and it expressed itself with unrestrained prodigality in *Sonnets from the Portuguese.* Everything in her life that went before—the beauty of her early home among the Malverns, the whole practice of her literary industry, the long lone years of illness and weakness, the heavy sorrow of the death-stricken home—is taken up, sanctified and dedicated in these poems; and everything that was to follow was but harvest-gleaning and aftermath. These sonnets, and, one is tempted to say, these sonnets only, of all that Elizabeth Browning wrote, the world will in no wise let go. They are equalled only by her life—in Milton's sense[1], they *are* her life.

Robert Browning cannot be so easily summed and surveyed. His skill was multifarious far beyond the wont even of great poets. There was hardly an instrument in the orchestra which he could not play, his touch was always unique and recognisable; and, within the domain of human character, there was hardly a

[1] *Areopagitica.*

bent or trait, a passion or propensity, which he did not celebrate. Nevertheless, when, like his Arion, he 'gathers his greatness round him,' and 'stands in state,' and 'harp and voice rend air' with his full 'magnificence of song[1],' the theme is almost certain to be some phase of love.   And love had the same cosmic, constitutive character to him, the same, or even greater, moral worth and spiritual splendour.   Speaking of *Sonnets from the Portuguese*, a critic has observed with truth that

as pieces of poetry they are not equal to the sonnets of Wordsworth or of Milton, yet it is not so unreasonable to question whether their removal would not leave a more irreparable gap in literature[2].

The removal of love from among Browning's themes would be, original as he was in everything, the removal of his most original, as well as his most massively valuable, contribution to our literature. It would have left the poet himself a man without a purpose in a universe without meaning.   Love, in the last resort, was the only article in his creed.   For these reasons, the convergence of these two lives into unity and their most intimate commingling ever after, have an artistic meaning no less than an ethical interest, and they concern the literary critic not less than the biographer.   Not that either of the two poets, when their 'prentice days were over, was content to be imitative, or could possibly be conceived as moving in the other's manner.   There was no sacrifice of independence—there never is when the union is spiritual in character and complete.   They even took precautions against influencing one another when a poem was in the making.   Nevertheless, what they meant for one another was more subtle and penetrating and pervasive than any direct and explicit borrowing, over which the critic could cry 'Lo here,' or 'Lo there.'   It is more easy to suggest and to instance than to describe their influence on each other: but a crowning example, I believe, is to be found in Browning's Pompilia.   There are charms, and, above all, there are intensities, scattered abroad in *The Ring and the Book* which would not have been possible, even for him, had it not been for his 'lyric Love.' No one was more eager to be dramatical than Browning, or less willing to expose to a gaping world the pageant of his inner life. But, after all, a poet dips his pen in his own blood when he writes what the world *must* read ; if he be robbed of experience as a man, he stands more bare as a poet; and, in the experience of both Robert and Elizabeth Browning, there was one event paramount,

---

[1] *Fifine at the Fair.*

[2] Hugh Walker, *The Literature of the Victorian Era.*

one sovereign fact that lent meaning to all that followed. This was their discovery of one another and the unique perfection of their wedded life. Criticism of the Brownings and of their meaning to literature dare not disregard or discount a mutual penetration of personalities so intense as theirs, but must, in dealing with the one, be aware that it is dealing with the other as well. In this respect, what went before in their life and work was but preliminary, and what came after mere consequent.

Robert Browning was younger than Elizabeth Barrett by some six years. He was born in Southampton street, Camberwell, on 7 May 1812. His father was a clerk in the bank of England, of literary and artistic tastes, and his mother the daughter of a Dundee shipowner of German extraction.

It is more easy to read the acorn in terms of the oak than the oak in terms of the acorn; and the great man reveals and explains, rather than is revealed and explained by, the capacities that slumbered in his forefathers. While none can deny the heredity of the features of the soul, any more than those of the body, it is idle to pretend that the lineaments of a great man's spirit can be traced back with any degree of accuracy to his ancestors. Every man, even the most meagre in endowment, has so many ancestors! But the psychical structure and propensities of his *immediate* parents have a significance all their own: for these define and determine the environment within which the child's mind lives and moves and has its being. The home, during the years when, most of all, the soul is being made, stands to the child for solid earth and starry firmament, and the influences operative therein are the air and the food and the drink, and, therefore, the very substance embodied in his personality. From this point of view, the simple piety of Browning's mother, her membership of an 'Independent Church' in Walworth, her life-long class in the Sunday school, her box for contributions to the London Missionary society lose their insignificance. In these and other habits, the child saw the spirit of religion made real and ratified by his mother, and it remained with him, much modified it is true, but, owing to his mother's memory, permanently holy and always dominant.

Again, it must not be said that Browning's 'genius was derived from his father.' Genius is not derived. It is always a miracle and has no history. But the father's genius, that of a lover of art and of literature, made the son a lover of books and a collector of them. It led him to write verse—which he did fluently and after the manner of Pope; and he had a great delight in grotesque rimes. Moreover, he was so skilful in the use of his pencil that Rossetti pronounced him to possess 'a real genius for drawing.' Now, 'the handsome, vigorous, fearless child,' unrestingly active, fiery of temper, crowded with energy of mind, observant and most swift to learn, naturally saw all these things and, not less naturally, imitated the ways of his parents and sought to acquire what they valued.

In Browning's case, no educational influence counts at all, in comparison with that of his father's tastes and habits and collection of books. That influence can be traced in the poet's choice of themes, all the way from *Pauline* and *Sordello* to *Parleyings* and *Asolando*, and it even marks his manner of dealing with many of them. He read voraciously in his father's library, apparently without let or guidance, and his acquaintance was very early with the works of Voltaire, the letters of Junius and of Horace Walpole, the *Emblems* of Quarles and Croxall's *Fables*. The first book he ever bought with his own money was Macpherson's *Ossian*.

Side by side with this precocious literary omnivorousness went, from early childhood, careful training in music. 'I was studying the Grammar of Music,' he said, according to Mrs Ireland, 'when most children are learning the Multiplication Table.' Moreover, he was given permission, at an age lower than the rules allowed, to visit the Dulwich gallery, which was hard by his father's home. It became 'a beloved haunt of his childhood.' He was grateful all his life for the privilege and used to recall, in later years, 'the triumphant Murillo pictures,' 'such a Watteau' and 'all the Poussins' he had seen there.

The contribution made by school and college to the education of Browning was even less significant than it has been in the case of most great poets. His *real* masters, besides his father and his father's library in general, were the poets, and especially Byron and Shelley. 'The first composition I was ever guilty of,' he wrote to Elizabeth Barrett in 1846, 'was something in imitation of Ossian.' But he never could 'recollect not writing rhymes,' though he 'knew they were nonsense even then.' 'It is not surprising,' says Herford, 'that a boy of these proclivities was captivated by the stormy swing and sweep of Byron,' and that, as the poet told Elizabeth Barrett, he 'would have gone to Finchley to see a curl of his hair or one of his gloves'; whereas he 'could not get up enthusiasm enough to cross the room if at the other end of it all Wordsworth, Coleridge and Southey were condensed into the little China bottle yonder[1].'

[1] To E. B., 22 August 1846.

When he was twelve years of age, a collection under the title *Incondita* was made of his 'Byronic poems,' and the father would have liked to publish it. No publisher was found willing, and the young author destroyed the manuscript. But the poems had been seen by Eliza Flower (sister of the authoress of the hymn *Nearer, my God, to Thee*), who made a copy of them and showed it to W. J. Fox, editor of *The Monthly Repository*. According to Browning's statement to Gosse, the editor found in them 'too great splendour of language and too little wealth of thought,' but, also, a 'mellifluous smoothness'; and Fox did not forget the boy-poet.

Browning next passed under an influence which was still more inspiring and intimate. He chanced upon Shelley's *Queen Mab* on a bookstall, and became, in consequence of assimilating it, 'a professing atheist and a practising vegetarian.' With some difficulty, his mother secured for him others of 'Mr Shelley's atheistical poems'; and, apparently, through *Adonais*, he was led to Keats. In the winter of 1829—30, he attended classes in Greek and Latin, and, for a very short time, in German, at University college, London; and, afterwards, Blundell's lectures in medicine, at Guy's hospital. Meantime, he carried on his studies in music, and sang, danced, boxed and rode.

This, if any, was his period of *Sturm und Drang*—during which, by the way, he lived on potatoes and bread! He chafed a little at the social limitations of the home he loved well, and he gave his devoted parents a little entirely needless anxiety: his temperament was buoyant, his soul like a ship crowded with sails, and he was a venturesome mariner. But his wanderings were of the imagination, and his 'excesses' were literary both in origin and in outcome. In truth, all the time, he was living within the bounds, nay, drawing his strength and his inspiration from those convictions of the stable things of the world of spirit in the power of which he went forth, in later days, to challenge, in every form of joust and tournament and in many an adventure, the forces of doubt and falsehood and denial and crime. He had not to suffer in his later life from any treacherous aches of half-forgotten wounds to character, but faced life sound in every limb and (one is tempted to add) arrogantly healthy.

The wholesome and wealthy confusion of this seething period of the young poet's life is faithfully rendered or, rather, betrayed, in the brilliant and incoherent *Pauline*—Browning's earliest published poem. Pauline herself, except for the first half-dozen lines and a footnote, is the shadow of a shade—the passive recipient of the psychological confessions of a young poet : a young poet, who, not at all unaware of his curls and lace and ruffles, has been turning himself round and round before the mirror, and has found that he is too noble a being, too bold, reckless, unrestrained, sceptical, brilliant, intense, wide-souled, hungry for knowledge and love for this work-a-day world. The self-consciousness is not 'intense,' as J. S. Mill thought. It is picturesque. It is not 'morbid' or unwholesome, as other critics have averred. It is only the frippery, the most serious mock-believe tragical outpourings of an extraordinarily handsome and innocent youth, who, in truth, had never known disappointment nor looked in the face of sorrow. Browning's dislike of the poem in later years was entirely natural. He resented all prying into private life, and was, of all men, least willing to 'sonnet-sing about himself.' So, the drapery in which he had clothed himself in this early poem seemed to him to be almost transparent, and he felt as if he had been going about nude.

Pauline was published in January 1833, anonymously, when its author was twenty years old. But that fine critic W. J. Fox discerned its merit and dealt with it in generous praise in *The Monthly Repository* for April in the same year. Allan Cunningham, also, praised it in *The Athenaeum*. Some years later (probably in 1850), Rossetti found and transcribed it in the reading room of the British Museum, and he wrote to Browning, who was in Florence, to ask him 'whether he was the author of a poem called *Pauline.*' Beyond this, the poem attracted no attention. Why, it is difficult to say. That it is mastered by its material, flooded by its own wealth, is true. Of all Browning's poems, it is the only one which owes its difficulty to confusion; and it is, in fact, to use the poet's own phrase, a 'boyish work.' But what work for a boy! There are passages in it, not a few, of a beauty that exceeds so much as to belong to a sphere of being into which mediocrity never for a moment gains entry. So long as he has this theatrically earnest boy at his side, the reader is never safe from the surprise of some sudden splash of splendour :

> the boy
> With his white breast and brow and clustering curls
> Streaked with his mother's blood, but striving hard
> To tell his story ere his reason goes.

He is 'exploring passion and mind,' he says, 'for the first time,' 'dreaming not of restraint but gazing on all things.' He is 'borne away, as Arab birds float sleeping in the wind, o'er deserts, towers,

and forests.' He 'nourishes music more than life, and old lore,' and
'knows the words shall move men, like a swift wind.' In every way,
Pauline must remain a supremely interesting poem to Browning's
readers: it holds in bud many of Browning's qualities, powers
and even convictions.

After the publication of *Pauline*, in 1833, Browning visited
Petrograd with Benkhausen, the Russian consul general; and it was
probably this contact with official life which led him, shortly after
his return to England, to apply—in vain—for a post on a Persian
mission. During this period, there is ample evidence of physical
and mental exuberance, but little of poetic activity. It was many
years later that the Russian visit yielded the forest-scene of the
thrilling tale of Ivàn Ivànovitch, and his toying with the Persian
mission (possibly) suggested *Ferishtah*. But his interest in the
complicated subtleties of diplomacy appeared in *Sordello* and
Strafford as well as in *Prince Hohenstiel-Schwangau*—not to
mention *Bishop Blougram* and *Caliban upon Setebos*. In 1834,
however, there appeared in *The Monthly Repository* a series of
five poetic contributions of which the most noteworthy were
Porphyria, afterwards entitled *Porphyria's Lover*, and the six
stanzas beginning 'Still ailing, Wind? Wilt be appeased or no,'
which were republished in *James Lee's Wife*. Then, with a
preface dated 15 March 1835, when its author still lacked two
months of completing his twenty-third year, there appeared one of
the most marvellous productions of youthful poetic genius in the
history of any literature.

Browning is said to have written *Paracelsus* in six months,
meditating not a few of its passages during midnight walks, within
sight of the glare of London lights, and the muffled hearing of its
quieting tumult. This poem belongs to an altogether different
altitude from that of *Pauline*. Instead of a confused rendering
of vague dreams and seething sentiments and passions, we have, in
Paracelsus, the story of the lithe and sinewy strength of early
manhood, the manifold powers of a most gifted spirit braced
together and passionately dedicated to the service of an iron-hard
intellectual ambition. Here is the 'intensest life' resolute upon
acquiring, at any cost, the intellectual mastery of mankind.

The subject was suggested to Browning by a French royalist
and refugee, count Amédée de Ripert-Monclar, and the poem is
dedicated to him. Browning was already acquainted with the
career and character of Paracelsus—his works were in his father's
library. Moreover, it is beyond doubt that, at this stage of his

life, in particular, the poet was driven by a like hunger for knowledge and ambition for intellectual sovereignty. His reading of
his subject implies affinity of mind and is altogether sympathetic.
The eccentricities of behaviour, the charlatanism, the boundless
conceit, the miracles and absurdities with which Paracelsus was
accredited by popular belief, either disappear or are sublimated
into elements of a dramatic romance which has something of the
greatness and seriousness of tragedy. To assume that Browning,
in this poem, was depicting 'the fall of a logician,' or of set design
'destroying the intellectualist fallacy,' is to misunderstand the
spirit in which the poem was written. The adventurous alchemist
was himself too much a poet to serve such an unpoetic purpose,
even if Browning had been so little a poet as to form it.
Paracelsus does not 'fall': he 'attains.'

Far from convicting him of intellectual futility, Browning actually made
him divine the secret he sought, and, in one of the most splendid passages of
modern poetry, declare with his dying lips a faith which is no less Browning's
than his own[1].

True ! knowledge without love is not even power ; but neither is
love without knowledge ; and the consummation of the achievement of Paracelsus is that love becomes the means of knowledge
and intelligence the instrument of love. 'The simultaneous perception of Love and Power in the Absolute' was, in Browning's
view, 'the noblest and predominant characteristic of Shelley'; and,
for Browning, even in his most 'metaphysical' days, when knowledge was always said to have 'failed,' it was still a power.

Paracelsus is the most miraculous and inexplicable of all the
exhibitions of Browning's genius. The promise it contained, with
all the poet's lasting greatness, was not fulfilled. Its form and
artistic manner, the lineaments and the movements of the mind
which works within it, the noble passions which moved the poet
and the faith which inspired and controlled him—these are pre-
eminently illuminating to the student of Browning and by far the
best introduction to all he strove to do. *Paracelsus* is interesting,
also, as touching the new times which were dawning around the
young poet. In its closing pages, something of the spirit of modern
science comes forth, for the moment, at least, wearing the garb of
poetry. Never was the conception of the evolutionary continuity
of nature more marvellously rendered,

> as successive zones
> Of several wonder open on some spirit
> Flying secure and glad from heaven to heaven.

[1] Herford.

The young poet had even grasped, what took the world another
half-century to perceive, that the idea of evolution levelled upwards and not downwards, spiritualised nature rather than
naturalised spirit.

The minor characters of *Paracelsus* need not detain us. Festus
is the commonsense foil of the hero, and the gentle domestic
Michal, maiden and sorrowing mother, is only less of a shadow
than Pauline. Aprile is an unsubstantial moonstruck 'wraith of
a poet,' who 'would love infinitely and be loved'; but his *rôle* is
most significantly derived and borrowed and accidental.

> I saw Aprile—my Aprile there!
> And as the poor melodious wretch disburthened
> His heart, and moaned his weakness in my ear,
> I learned my own deep error.

Paracelsus learnt from him 'the worth of love in man's estate and
what proportion love should hold with power.' It was this new
knowledge which made him wise to know mankind,

> be proud
> Of their half-reasons, faint aspirings, dim
> Struggles for truth, their poorest fallacies,

'all with a touch of nobleness... upward tending,'

> Like plants in mines which never saw the sun,
> But dream of him, and guess where he may be,
> And do their best to climb and get to him.

With this knowledge, this 'splendour of God's lamp' on his dying
brow, he is as secure of 'emerging one day,' as he was when he first
set forth 'to prove his soul.'

Paracelsus, on its publication, was hailed by the ever faithful
and watchful Fox; but the most striking notice it received was
from John Forster. He predicted for the author a brilliant career,
and, in a second article on the poem, said, with unusual daring as
well as insight, 'Without the slightest hesitation we name Mr Robert
Browning at once with Shelley, Coleridge, Wordsworth.' But, by
most journals, *Paracelsus* was simply neglected. In his letters
to Elizabeth Barrett, Browning refers to the contemptuous treatment it received. It brought him neither money nor fame.

But it brought him, first, the acquaintance, and, then, the friendship, of the most distinguished men of the day—among them were
Wordsworth, Dickens, Landor and Carlyle; and in nothing was the
manly munificence of Browning's nature more evident than in his
friendships. His affection for Landor, touched with sympathy as
well as admiration, showed itself, in later years, in a care for him

which was 'one of the most beautiful incidents in a beautiful life.'
The friendship with Carlyle was, on both sides, peculiarly warm
and trustful. 'I have just seen dear Carlyle,' says Browning,
'catch me calling people "dear," in a hurry'; and that Carlyle
should cross over to Paris just to see and dine with Browning is,
assuredly, eloquent of his regard and affection for the young poet.
'Commanded of me by my venerated friend Thomas Carlyle,' says
Browning of his translation of *Agamemnon,* 'and rewarded will it
indeed become if I am permitted to dignify it by the prefatory
insertion of his dear and noble name.' John Forster and William
Macready were also added at this time to the group of Browning's
friends, and his acquaintance with the latter had, for a time, an
important bearing upon his work.

In *Pauline* and *Paracelsus,* it has been well said, Browning
had 'analysed rather than exhibited' character. The soul, 'the
one thing' which he thought 'worth knowing,' was the psycho-
logist's abstract entity, little more than a stage occupied successively
by moods and passions: it was not the concrete, complex self,
veined and blood-tinctured. Moreover (which signifies much),
all its history fell within itself, and external circumstance, instead
of furnishing it with the material out of which character is hewn,
was but 'decoration,' to use Browning's own phrase, and was
purposely put into the background. These two poems were thus
justly called 'confessional': they were subjective and self-conscious.

No sooner was *Paracelsus* finished than Browning contemplated
another 'soul-history.' In it, once more, a greatly aspiring soul
was to recognise, only at the last moment and after much 'apparent
failure,' the mission which could save, fitting to the finite his infinity.
The story that he wished to tell was *Sordello.*

But the material was stubborn as well as rich, and it resisted
easy and early mastery. Possibly, also, the 'confessional' mood
was passing. In any case, Browning, who was always and almost
solely interested in human character, was thinking of depicting
character in action. He was eager, as he said in his preface to
Strafford, 'to freshen a jaded mind by diverting it to the healthy
natures of a grand epoch.' Browning's mind, no doubt, was
turned to Strafford by Forster, who, with some help from Browning,
had written the great statesman's life. But it was at a supper
given by Talfourd to celebrate the first performance of *Ion*
that Macready, to whom Browning had already spoken of his
intention of writing a tragedy, said 'Write a play, Browning, and
keep me from going to America.' *Strafford,* which was the result

of the request, was acted at Covent garden theatre on 1 May 1837
—Macready appearing as Strafford and Helen Faucit as lady
Carlisle. Its stage history was brief. It was not 'damned' on
the first night, but just escaped; it was applauded on the second;
and it died an unnatural death after the fifth. It was betrayed:
the player who acted Pym refusing 'to save England even once
more,' and Browning vowing that 'never again would he write
a play!'

The tragical element in the play is the collision of the two
loyalties—that of Strafford to the king and that of Pym to England: and the tragedy borrows its intensity from the fact that the
king whom Strafford loves will not save him, and that Pym, who
loves Strafford, sends him to his death. Pym 'was used to stroll
with him, arm locked in arm,' and, in early days, had even read the
same needs in England's face, while

> Eliot's brow grew broad with noble thoughts.

The atmosphere of the play is that of 'a thorough self-devotement,
self-forgetting.' The characters are all simple, and apt to be always
in one condition of mind. They have a generous magnitude and
strength and vigour; but they are too consistently in a state of
exaltation, inclined to be declamatory and self-conscious and to be
always expounding the movements of their own minds. Indeed,
not one of Browning's characters in any of his plays fairly comes
out into the open air and on the high road, except, perhaps,
Pippa.

In the preface to *Strafford*, Browning says that 'he had for
some time been engaged on a Poem of a very different nature,
when induced to make the present attempt.' This poem, as already
hinted, was *Sordello*, Browning's second study of a poetic soul,
but a soul, this time, caught in the context of large and imperious
circumstance and quite unlike Aprile.

Many have explained *Sordello*, and some have comprehended
it. It is uncompromisingly and irretrievably difficult reading.
No historical account of the conflicts of Ghibelline and Guelph,
no expository annotation of any kind, not even its own wealth of
luminous ideas or splendour of Italian city scenes and solitudes,
can justify it entirely as a work of art. We may render its main
plot in simple terms: how Sordello, endowed with powers that
might have made him the Apollo of his people and victorious in
a contest of song over Eglamor, his poetic foil, finds, unexpectedly,
eminent station and political power within his grasp, but gains a

victory of another kind, rising superior to the temptation doubly urged by the Ghibelline captain and the beauty of Parma; how the double victory has still left him a dabbler and loiterer, a Hamlet in both poetry and politics; how, clinging to his ideal, the cause of humanity, but failing to make it dominant over his 'finite' world, he 'dies under the strain of choice.' But no simplification of the story suffices. It is dark from the very intensity and multiplicity of the playing cross-lights; for the main ideas are reflected innumerably from the countless facets of the facts which the poet displays in confusingly rapid succession. Brilliancy, swiftness of movement, the sudden exclamation made to convey a complex thought, the crowded intrusion of parenthetical antecedents, the elision of connecting relatives—such are the characteristics which make it difficult to decipher.

It is no wonder that the appearance of *Sordello,* in 1840, destroyed the somewhat timid promise of public favour which *Paracelsus* had brought to the poet. We are told that the 'gentle literary public' of those days had found *Sartor Resartus* unintelligible, and frankly turned away from Browning. But the suggested comparison is misleading and the criticism is unfair. The difficulties of *Sartor* have disappeared with the new times which Carlyle introduced; those of *Sordello* will stay so long as the mental structure of men remains the same.

'I blame no one,' said Browning, 'least of all myself, who did my best then and since.' It was in no perverse mood of intellectual pride or of scorn for the public mind that he wrote *Sordello.* His error was, rather, the opposite. 'Freighted full of music,' crowded with the wealth of his detailed knowledge, rapt with the splendour of his poetic visions, he, in the simplicity of his heart, forgot his public so completely as to assume, as a matter of course, that his readers were able to wing their flight at his side.

There are evidences that the experience was painful and that its effects lasted. In *The Ring and the Book,* and elsewhere, there is, in the resolute simplification of the narrative and the painful iteration, a clue to the effect of the failure of *Sordello* upon his workmanship. Both as he entered upon and as he closed that greatest of all his poetic adventures, there is a hint of a challenge and a touch of reproof, and even scorn, of the 'British Public,'

> ye who like me not,
> (God love you!)—whom I yet have laboured for,
> Perchance more careful whoso runs may read
> Than erst when all, it seemed, could read who ran.

But it is time to turn to the outward events of this period of Browning's life. These were his journey to Italy and the removal of the family to Hatcham. He started for Italy on Good Friday 1838, travelling as sole passenger on a merchantman. On the voyage, he wrote the glorious story of the ride from Ghent to Aix, and *Home Thoughts from the Sea.* One of his objects was to gather materials for *Sordello* ; but he harvested much more from his visit. It was, for him, 'a time of enchantment.' He saw Asolo and Venice and Padua ; he visited mountain solitudes, and he brought home a passionate and enduring love for Italy. Italian themes were, henceforth, to be favourites of his imagination, and his life in that country was, for many years to come, to saturate his experience.

At the time when Browning was 'going to begin the finishing of Sordello,' as he wrote to Miss Haworth, he was also beginning 'thinking a Tragedy.' He had still another tragedy in prospect, he tells us, and 'wrote best so provided.' The two tragedies were *King Victor and King Charles* and *The Return of the Druses.* He was also occupied with what was not strictly a play, but a new poetic form—a series of scenes connected together like pearls on a silken thread by the magic influence of the little silk-winder of Asolo—the exquisitely beautiful and simple *Pippa Passes.* The plays were written with the view of being acted ; but Macready's refusal kept them back, for a time, and they were published. They appeared in a series of what may be called poetical pamphlets, issued between 1841 and 1846, which undoubtedly constituted as remarkable literary merchandise as was ever offered to any public. This plan of publication was suggested by Moxon, and was intended to popularise the poet's works by selling them cheaply. They were at first sold at sixpence. But (among other hindrances) they were called *Bells and Pomegranates,* and it was only at the close of the series and on the instigation of Elizabeth Barrett that Browning explained to the puzzled readers how it was intended by this reference to 'the hem of the robe of the high priest' to indicate 'the mixture of music with discoursing, sound with sense, poetry with thought,' which the pamphlets were. Moreover, literary critics had not forgotten or forgiven *Sordello,* and literary prejudice is stubborn stuff. Even *Pippa Passes,* the first of the series, had a reluctant and frigid reception. A generously appreciative article, in *The Eclectic Review,* in 1849, mentions it along with *Sordello* as one of the poems against which 'the loudest complaints of obscurity have been raised.'

Nothing that Browning ever wrote was better fitted than *Pippa Passes* to arrest the public attention. It was as novel in charm as it was in form. Pippa herself, it has been suggested[1], is Browning's Ariel—a magic influence in the magic isle of man's world. The little silk-winder, walking along the streets of Asolo on her 'one day in the year' and fancying herself to be, in turn, each of its 'Four Happiest Ones,' pours forth her lyric soul in song. The songs striking into the world of passions, plots and crimes, in which the 'Four Happiest Ones' were involved, arrest, cleanse and transform. She is as charming as the lyrics she carols. Elizabeth Barrett 'could find in her heart to envy the Author,' and *Pippa* was Browning's own favourite among the creations of his early manhood. She has 'crept into the study of imagination' of all his readers ever since.

Pippa Passes was followed, in 1842, by *King Victor and King Charles,* and that tragedy, in turn, by a collection of some sixteen short pieces, which were called *Dramatic Lyrics.* Then, in 1843, appeared *The Return of the Druses,* written some years earlier, and two other plays—*A Blot in the 'Scutcheon* and *Colombe's Birthday* (published in 1844). These were followed by another collection of short poems, on the greatest variety of subjects, entitled *Dramatic Romances and Lyrics.* In 1846, the series entitled *Bells and Pomegranates* was brought to an end, and Browning's period of playwriting closed with *Luria* and the dramatic sketch *A Soul's Tragedy.*

At this time, also, the first period of Browning's amazing productiveness came to a close. The poems that appeared cannot even be classified except in the roughest way, and any classification must mislead. The familiar distinctions which criticism sets up fade and become false. There are lyrical effects in most of the dramas, dramatic touches in almost every lyric and romance, and his muse will not be demure and prim. On the other hand, the variety of the subjects, forms, moods, scenes and passions, and of the workings of each of them, baffles classification. And each is so 'clear proclaimed'—whether 'Hope rose a-tiptoe,' or 'Rapture drooped the eyes,' or 'Confidence lit swift the forehead up'—that the distinctions, if they are to be faithful, must be as numerous as the poems themselves. In truth, it is not art but science, not love but knowledge, which classifies. So far as poems are true works of art, each one is, and must be, unique—a carved golden cup filled with its own wine. For the artist, every song in turn is

[1] By Herford.

the one song, and, for the lover, every tress of hair, in turn, 'is the fairest tress of all.'

Browning himself, however, suggests two points of view from which the poems may be observed. He characterises them all as 'dramatic.' How far is this qualification accurate? Was Browning's genius verily dramatic in character? The question is not easily answered, even although it can be profitably asked. In comparison with Wordsworth, who was both the most self-contained and the most impersonal of all our poets, we must answer the question with a clear affirmative. But, compared with Shakespeare, or with Sir Walter Scott (as novelist), the difference is so great as to make the epithet 'dramatic' positively misleading. Of not one of Shakespeare's creations can we say 'Here is the author himself'; of scarcely one of Browning's can we say 'Here the author is not.' Browning, in writing to Elizabeth Barrett, called the poems 'Mere escapes of my inner power, like the light of a revolving lighthouse leaping out at intervals from a narrow chink.' The analogy is true in more than one sense. The poems carry suggestions of the abundance of riches within the poet's own living, alert, enterprising, sense-fraught, passion-fused soul; the motley throng of his *Dramatic Lyrics, Dramatic Romances* and *Dramatis Personae* also stand in the brilliant glare of his personality—not in the unobtrusive, quiet light of common day. There is hardly a stratum of society, an age of history, a corner of the world of man, which is altogether absent from these poems; nevertheless, we never escape the sense of the author's powerful presence. In all the diversities of type, race and character, there are persistent qualities, and they are the poet's own.

There is no quality of Shakespeare's mind which can be found in all his plays, except, perhaps, his gentleness; even as only the one epithet 'gentle' satisfies when we speak of Shakespeare himself. But 'gentleness' is just tolerance suffused with kindliness; and, where tolerance is perfect, preferences disappear, and the poet himself remains always revealing and never revealed.

To deny tolerance to Browning is impossible, and would utterly destroy his claim to be dramatic. There is a real sense in which he stands aloof from his creations, neither approving nor disapproving but letting them go. Bishop Blougram and Mr Sludge; Caliban and the bishop of St Praxed's; the lady of *The Laboratory* and of *The Confessional*; the lion of *The Glove* with 'those eyes wide and steady,'

> leagues in the desert already,
> Driving the flocks up the mountain,

and the live creatures in *Sibrandus Schafnaburgensis*—'worm, slug, eft, with serious features,' tickling and tousing and browsing him all over—all these are given a place in the sun, no less than his Valence or Caponsacchi, Colombe or Constance. It were unpardonable in a critic not to recognise that, for Browning, there was no form which the human soul could take that was too strange, complex, monstrous, magnificent, commonplace and drab, in its hate or love or in any other passion, to be interesting in the artistic and purely impersonal sense. All the same, his tolerant universality is not like Shakespeare's in quality. There are, in Browning, no characters whom we must condemn and, also, must approve; whom we cannot justify and would not miss, but like beyond all speech or sense. There is no Jack Falstaff, nor even a Dogberry, or Bottom, or Launce, far less a Touchstone. There is no Bob Acres, even, or Sir Anthony Absolute.

Browning *will* persist in appealing to our reason. It is always a question of what accepts or refuses to accept its control. Morality, at rare moments, is allowed to see to itself, and the beautiful and ugly stand justified or condemned in their own right. But truth always matters to him, and his intellectualising propensities never rest. The play of fancy is rarely quite irresponsible, and of humour more rarely still. There is no touch in Browning of the singing rogue Autolycus. Some of his lyrics, no doubt, are as light as they are lovely; and *The Pied Piper* is by no means the only first-rate example of joyous story-telling. Nevertheless, Browning, many as are the parts he plays, is not like Bottom—he cannot aggravate his voice and roar us gently. He is never splendidly absurd, nor free of every purpose. Even at this period, he is plagued with problems, crammed with knowledge, crowded with mental energy, a revolving lighthouse bursting with light. In a word, he is intense and purposive, and his purposiveness and intensity had many consequences, not all of them favourable to his dramatic work. A brief study of these is illuminative of his whole work as a poet.

'Hold on, hope hard in the subtle thing that's spirit,' he said, in *Pacchiarotto*. He laid stress 'on the incidents in the development of a soul,' he tells us, in his preface to *Sordello*, 'little else is worth study.' This was more than a fundamental idea to Browning, it was a constitutional propensity; and it drove him to the drama. But the confession of it implies the consciousness of a mission, and the artist, at his best, knows no mission of that kind. He is in the service of no conception that the intellect can shape or express, or of no purpose that the will can frame and fix. His rapture is as fine and careless as that of the thrush, and he is snatched up and away by themes that define themselves only in the process of creation and, in the end, escape all definition and stand forth as miracles. But this absence of purpose we do not often find in Browning. His dramatic pieces are not at leisure; the poet himself never strolls, but is always set upon some business, even among his *Garden Fancies*.

For the same reason, there are no genuine little incidents in Browning's plays. Little things are apt to be symbolic—pin-point rays of intense light coming from afar are imprisoned in them: they suggest grave meanings: possibly, for instance, the failure of the whole life, through making love, at some moment, a merely second-best.

> Why did not you pinch a flower
> In a pellet of clay and fling it?
> Why did not I put a power
> Of thanks in a look, or sing it?[1]

The whole atmosphere of the plays is heavily charged with significance; and many characters, in consequence, are, from beginning to end, in some highly-strung mood. There is tragic tension in the very first words that Mildred speaks: 'Sit, Henry— do not take my hand.' The moral strain deepens with the next question, and it is never relaxed. No breath of fresh air from the unheeding outer world comes to break the spell, and, at the same time, to deepen, by contrast, the pathos and tragedy of Mildred's overmastering consciousness that she does not deserve, and will never hold in her arms, the happiness that seemed to stand close by.

It is, probably, this preliminary, purposive surcharging of the characters and incidents that led Dowden to say that

the dramatic genius of Browning was in the main of the static kind; it studies with extraordinary skill and subtlety character in position; it attains only an imperfect or laboured success with character in movement.

As it stands, this dictum is unsound. Restless energy is always straining against the poet's control. His genius is dramatic, precisely in virtue of the sense of movement which it conveys, and the feeling that life is process and nothing else, a continuous new creation of itself carried on by itself. Even in *The Ring and the Book*, where the poet not only knows but tells the end at the beginning, the dramatic quality of movement is present. The story expands at each telling, like circles in water. The facts are

---

[1] *Youth and Art.*

transformed with each successive telling of them, by one and the other Half-Rome, Guido, Caponsacchi, Pompilia, The Pope and the lawyers. Not for a moment does the story stand still, nor does the reader feel that he is being told of past events, as in listening to an essentially epic poet, like Milton. Browning's poems are never stagnant: tragedy never hangs overhead, as in *Hamlet*, a black, motionless, delayed thunder-cloud ; but the lightning is always ablaze. There are crowded happenings, and the heat and hurry of situations crashing into their consequences. Browning's genius is essentially dynamic, and there is abundant movement.

What Browning's characters lack is objectivity—if we may borrow a term from the philosophers. Such is the intensity of his interest in 'the incidents in the development of a soul' that it transfuses not only the *dramatis personae* but the world in which they live. The outer world is not genuinely outer. It does not exist for its own sake, carrying on its own processes, 'going on just the same,' whether men and women laugh or weep, live or die, utterly indifferent to every fate, distinguishing not in the least between great things and small, evil things and good, allowing 'both the proudly riding and the foundering bark.' It is not a world aloof from man, non-moral and, on surface reading, non-rational, the sphere of sheer caprice and the playground of accident. The world is the stage and background for Browning's characters and supplies the scenery they need.

What is done by his personages, therefore, is not the result of intercourse between human character and what, in itself, is an entirely natural world. And, consequently, what takes place lacks that appearance of contingency in collusion with necessity of which the true dramatist makes tragic use. When he is most completely under the spell of his muse, the true dramatist cannot tell beforehand what will happen to his men and women, or how they will behave. He is at the mercy of two unknowns: the inexhaustible possibilities of man's nature, and of the response which it will make to the never-ending contingencies of an indifferent outer world. He has no preconceived theory, no scheme of life, no uniformities or necessities which can be labelled: the unity of his work, as a work of art, has some more mystic source than any of these things. But we cannot quite say this of Browning. His men and women cannot be called embodiments of *à priori* conceptions, meant to illustrate a doctrine or point a moral; and, yet, their intercourse with their fellows and interaction with the world have no genuinely fashioning potency. Nothing quite new or quite unexpected ever happens to them. They are not in a world where unexpected things are permitted to happen. Had not Macbeth *happened* to meet the witches on the moor, with the excitement of the battle not yet subsided in his blood, he might have lived and died a loyal and victorious general. And what side-winds of mere accidents there are in *Othello* and *Hamlet*! These dramas are like life, because the fate which is irresistible comes clothed in accident and with its chaplet all awry and as careless as that of a Bacchic dancer. The accidents seem trivial, too, and might easily not have taken place or have been turned aside, until they *have* taken place. Then, and not till then, do we feel that they were meant, and that they were as inevitable as destiny.

But Browning's plays can be seen from afar to march straight-forward to their consummation; and the world in which they take place is all too obtrusively 'a moral order.' The personages are, from the first, inwardly charged with some dominant passion or propensity. They are dedicated, even when they are complex, to some one form of good or of evil; and some one misdeed stains the whole of life like ink in water. They are enveloped in their own atmosphere, and outer incidents cannot affect their career; carried along by the powers within as if by a driving storm; freighted full from the first with their destiny: Pym with his love of England; Mildred with the guilt of her innocence; Luria with his 'own East'; Tresham with the pride of family and the 'scutcheon without a blot; Valence with his stormy rectitude and great heart.

This is the only sense in which Browning's dramas lack move-ment, and his method may be called static. His characters are impervious to outward influence, except in so far as it serves to discharge what is already within. Within the inner realm of passions, emotions, volitions, ambitions, and the world which these catch up in their career, there is no lack of movement. A plenitude of powers all active are revealed by him: they co-operate, sever, mingle, collide, combine, and are all astrain—but they are all psychical. Browning places us in the parliament of the mind. It is the powers of mind to which we listen in high debate. And we are reminded by them of the fugues of Master Hugues of Saxe-Gotha:

> One dissertates, he is candid;
> Two must discept—has distinguished;
> Three helps the couple, if ever yet man did;
>   Four protests; Five makes a dart at the thing wished:
> Back to One, goes the case bandied.

And they require scope to declare themselves, as they reveal the wonder-world of the human soul.

Now, we have stated these points somewhat fully because they seem to throw light upon the whole of Browning's work as a poet. The tendency towards dwelling upon ideal issues rather than upon outer deeds, on the significance of facts for souls, and the insignificance of all things save in the soul's context, was always present in Browning; so, also, was the tendency towards monologue, with its deliberate, ordered persistency. And both of these tendencies grew. External circumstance became, more and more, the mere garb of the inner mood; deeds, more and more, the creatures of thoughts; and all real values were, more and more, undisguisedly ideal ministrants to man's need of beauty, or goodness, or love and happiness.

But to say this is to admit not only that the dramatic element in his poetry was on the wane, but that his poetry was itself becoming more deliberately reflective. And the spirit of reflection which rejects first appearances, sublimates sense and its experience into meanings, is, to say the least, as characteristic of philosophy as it is of art. It is philosophy rather than art which concentrates upon principles, and which allows facts and events to dwindle into instances of general laws. Art must value a thing for what it is in itself, not for the truth which it exemplifies. The reference of the beautiful object beyond itself to a beauty that is eternal must be, for art, as undesigned as the music of a harp swung in the wind. And, when a poet takes to illustrating themes, or the unity of his poems, instead of being a mystic harmony of elements mingling of themselves, comes of a set purpose which can be stated in words, then, indeed, is the glory of art passing into the grey. The poet outlived the dramatist in Browning, and, if the poet did not succumb to the philosopher, it was because of the strength of the purely lyrical element in his soul and the marvellous wealth of his sensuous and emotional endowments. His humanity was too richly veined for him to become an abstract thinker; and certain apparent accidents of his outer life conspired with the tendencies of his poetic genius to lead them away from the regular drama.

One of these was his quarrel over *A Blot in the 'Scutcheon* with Macready, for whom and at whose request this play was written. But Macready's affairs were entangled; he would withdraw from his arrangement with Browning, was not frank with him, but shuffled: and Browning was angered, imperious and explosive. The play was produced but 'damned,' apparently not by the audience but by Macready's own stage and press arrangements. *The Times* pronounced it 'one of the most faulty dramas we ever beheld,' and *The Athenaeum* called it 'a puzzling and unpleasant business,' and the characters inscrutable and abhorrent. This was in 1843.

The quarrel with Macready was not the poet's only unpleasant experience of the stage. Soon after this incident, Charles Kean negotiated with Browning for a suitable play, and, in March 1844, *Colombe's Birthday* was read to him and approved. But Kean asked that it should be left with him, unpublished, till the Easter of the following year. Browning, however, thought the long delay unreasonable, was, possibly, doubtful of the actor's good faith and resolved to publish the play at once. It was not acted till 1853, when it was produced by Phelps with Helen Faucit as heroine and ran for a fortnight. But it was reviewed on publication by Forster—who said that he abominated the tastes of Browning as much as he respected his genius. Forster repented, called on Browning and was 'very profuse of graciocities'; but their friendship had received a fatal injury. Browning concluded that there was too much 'spangle' and 'smutch' in connection with actors, and wrote no more for the stage.

During the years 1844—5, Browning made a series of contributions to *Hood's Magazine*. The series included *The Flight of the Duchess* and *The Bishop orders his Tomb at Saint Praxed's Church*. The poet, having gone to Italy in 1844, and having visited the grave of Shelley, had turned into the little church of Saint Prassede near Santa Maria Maggiore.

Returning to England before the end of the year, he read Elizabeth Barrett's newly published *Poems*. They contained *Lady Geraldine's Courtship*, in which he found his work mentioned with that of Tennyson and of Wordsworth, and a reference to his own 'heart blood-tinctured, of a veined humanity.' Elizabeth Barrett had previously, in a series of articles on English poets in *The Athenaeum*, placed Browning among 'high and gifted spirits'; and he had approved of her first series of articles on the early Greek Christian poets. Moreover, each knew of the other through Kenyon, Elizabeth Barrett's second cousin, schoolfellow of Browning's father and the special providence of both Robert Browning and his wife. Kenyon encouraged Browning to express to Elizabeth Barrett his admiration of her poems. The poet wrote to her with the unrestrained freedom of his most magnanimous character, telling her that he 'loved her verses with all his heart'; and his letter the letter 'of the author of *Paracelsus* and king of the mystics,' 'threw her into ecstasies.' They became intimate through a correspondence which was at first dictated by mood and opportunity, and, afterwards, in accordance with formal 'contract.' On 20 May 1845, after the lapse of a winter and a spring, Browning came and saw her for the first time, a 'little figure, which did not rise from the sofa, pale ringleted face, great, eager, wistful eyes,' and, as Elizabeth Barrett said, 'he never went away again.' His declaration of love followed, prompt and decisive as a thunder-clap. It was countered with a refusal that was absolute, but all for his sake, and followed by 'the triumph of a masterful passion and will which could not be put aside.'

The circumstances are too remarkable, and meant too much for both the poets not to require a brief recounting.

Elizabeth Barrett was born at Coxhoe hall, Durham, on 6 March 1806, the eldest of the eleven children of Edward Moulton Barrett, a West Indian planter. When she was still an infant, the family moved to Hope End, Herefordshire, the place with which the early memories recorded in *Aurora Leigh, The Lost Bower* and other poems are associated. Until she was about fifteen years of age, she was healthy and vigorous, although 'slight and sensitive'; and she was a good horsewoman. But, either in endeavouring to saddle her pony for herself, or in riding, she injured her spine ; and the hurt was the occasion, if not the cause, of her being treated as an incurable invalid by her father—so long as she was under his roof.

From Hope End, the family removed first to Sidmouth, afterwards to 74 Gloucester place, and, finally, to Wimpole street, London, where Browning first came to see her. The marriage took place on 12 September 1846; and, a week later, they were on the way to Italy, where they made their permanent home in Casa Guidi, Florence.

The Battle of Marathon, Elizabeth Barrett's juvenile poem, was followed, in 1826, by *An Essay on Mind and other Poems*, a volume which bears in the very title the stamp of Pope, though its authoress, then and always, was quite unqualified to imitate his terse neatness. Then, in 1833, came *Prometheus Bound*, a translation from Aeschylus, with which the translator herself came to be so thoroughly dissatisfied that she suppressed it, so far as she was able, and substituted for it a second translation, which was published in 1850, in the same volume as *Sonnets from the Portuguese. The Seraphim and other Poems* was published in

1838, and, finally, in 1844, the two volumes of *Poems*. No poet ever had less of the Greek spirit of measure and proportion, though she was widely read in Greek literature and delighted in its fair forms. Nor was anyone more unlike Pope. Her work, in fact, was as chaotic and confused as it was luxurious and improvident. Her *Seraphim* is overstrained and misty; her *Drama of Exile* is an uninteresting allegory; nearly all her shorter poems are too long, for she did not know how to omit, or when to stop. Few, if any, poets have sinned more grievously or frequently against the laws of metre and rime.

It was natural and inevitable that the influence of her love for Browning should transfigure her poetry as well as transform her life. In consequence of it, there is one work (and possibly one only) whose quality is unique, and whose worth is permanent, and not easily computed. This is her *Sonnets from the Portuguese*. They had been composed by her during the period of the courtship. Browning knew of them for the first time when, ' one morning, early in 1847, Mrs Browning stole quietly after breakfast into the room where her husband worked, thrust some manuscript into his pocket, and then hastily withdrew[1].' An amazing revelation even to him they must have been of the seraphic intensity of her love.

The form of the sonnet had helped Elizabeth Barrett (as it helped Wordsworth at times) to avoid her besetting sins. Extravagance and diffuseness are not so possible under its rigid rules. On the other hand, the intoxication of her passion helped to secure her against the flatness of the commonplace. They were first privately printed as *Sonnets by E.B.B.*, and, three years later, published under their present title. These forty-four sonnets, unequal as they are, make Elizabeth Browning's title to fame secure and go some way towards explaining, if not also justifying, the esteem of her contemporaries for her poetry. She was deemed the greatest of English poetesses, perhaps rightly; her name was also suggested (with Tennyson's but without her husband's) for the poet laureate-ship on the death of Wordsworth. In March 1849, the Brownings' only child, Robert Wiedemann Barrett, was born, and, shortly afterwards, Robert Browning's mother died, leaving him long depressed. The summers of 1851 and 1852 were spent in England. In the former year, on their return journey to Italy, they travelled as far as Paris with Carlyle. There, among other celebrities, they met George Sand, and, also, Joseph Milsand, who had recently written of Browning in *La Revue des Deux Mondes*. Milsand's

---

[1] *The Life of Robert Browning* by Griffin and Minchin.

friendship was one of the most precious in Browning's life. *Quel homme extraordinaire !* he is reported to have said of the poet, *son centre n'est pas au milieu.* The winter of 1853—4 was spent, by way of variety, at Rome. Of the numerous journeyings from Florence during the remaining years, it is only necessary to record that, in the summer of 1855, the two poets carried to England the MS of *Men and Women* and great part of that of *Aurora Leigh.* Browning completed his volume by the addition of *One Word More,* which is dated London, September 1855. During this visit, Tennyson, in the house of Browning, read aloud his *Maud* and Browning read *Fra Lippo Lippi,* while Dante Rossetti listened and sketched him—Tennyson, according to W. M. Rossetti, 'mouthing out his hollow *o*'s and *a*'s,' while Browning's voice laid stress on all the light and shade of character, its conversational points, its dramatic give and take. They joined Kenyon at West Cowes, and Elizabeth Browning wrote the last pages of *Aurora Leigh* under his roof and dedicated the poem to him.

On their return to Florence, they received news of the immediate and very great success of the poem; and Browning, whose *Men and Women* failed either to attract the public or to please the critics, rejoiced with a great joy in her triumph.

While the Brownings were in England, Daniel D. Home, the most notorious of American exponents of spiritualism, held a *séance* at which they were present. A wreath that 'happened' to be on the table was raised by 'spirit' hands and placed on Elizabeth Browning's brow—the medium's own feet operating also, Browning maintained. Home subsequently visited Florence; and spiritualistic manifestations became for Elizabeth Browning and some of her friends a matter of profoundly serious interest, and for Browning himself an intolerable irritant. Nothing that Browning wrote surpasses *Mr Sludge, 'The Medium'* in dramatic power. It exposes more powerfully even than Blougram and Juan and Hohenstiel-Schwangau that corruption of the soul by a lying and selfish life which infects its whole world, making of it a twilight region in which truth and error, right and wrong are inextricably confused, and nothing said is either sincere or insincere. Sludge, at least in some respects, is the greatest of Browning's magnificent casuists, who themselves are new figures in poetic literature: and, no doubt, it owes something of its vigour to his distasteful experience of Home. But Home was not the subject of the poem. Sludge the medium is as universal and impersonal a creation as Falstaff; and, though Browning 'stamped on the floor in a frenzy of rage at the way some believers and mediums deceived Mrs Browning,' he allows Sludge to be himself and to have his own say in so impartial a way as to make the poem a striking revelation of the strength of the poet's dramatic genius.

In 1859, Elizabeth Browning fell alarmingly ill : political events—the war, the armistice and conference at Villafranca and Napoleon's bargain excited her too much. Browning nursed her, and took charge, also, of his son's lessons. To these, he added the charge of the affairs of Landor, and of Landor himself —a most difficult and delicate task. Landor had quarrelled in his volcanic way with his family, with whom he lived at Fiesole, and appeared homeless, penniless and with nothing but the clothes he stood in at Casa Guidi. Browning took him into his house, arranged and managed his affairs for him, and was loving and tolerant with that wide generosity of spirit which made friends of men of the most untoward temperament. Landor loved Browning, and was tame under his hand, while Browning amused Elizabeth by talking of Landor's 'gentleness and sweetness.'

Notwithstanding the 'transformation' which her marriage was said to have wrought, Elizabeth Browning's health was never completely restored, or secure—'I have never seen a human frame so nearly a transparent veil for a celestial and immortal spirit,' said Hillard of her, when he saw her in Florence. During these years, her strength gradually waned, and on 29 June 1861, suddenly, without any presentiment on her part or fear on his, she passed away. Her death, it is supposed, was hastened by that of Cavour on the sixth of the same month. She had said of him, 'if tears or blood could have saved him to us, he should have had mine.' She was buried in Florence, and a tablet on the walls of Casa Guidi expresses the gratitude of the city for her advocacy of Italian freedom. Browning's sorrow was as deep as his life ; but it was borne in his manly fashion. In order 'to live and work and write,' he had 'to break up everything and go to England.' He never returned to Florence, nor did he visit Italy again until 1878.

Although they lived at first in happy seclusion, 'soundless and stirless hermits,' as Elizabeth Browning said, still, no one followed with fuller sympathy the changing fortunes of Italy. But Browning sang neither its hopes nor its sorrows—'Nationality was not an effectual motive with him'—nor did its contemporary politics mean

so much for him as a poet as its medieval art. But it was otherwise with his wife. She responded to what was present. Even the
art of which we hear in her letters is not the art of the Vatican or
the Capitol, but Story's, or Gibson's, or Page's. She was profoundly
moved by the agitation for freedom. Italy was the land where she
herself first knew freedom, and her emotions swept her into song.
Of the four publications of her later life, two are entirely Italian in
theme—*Casa Guidi Windows* (1851) and *Poems before Congress*
(1860). And both are political.

It was a time of revolution when the Brownings settled in
Italy, and the ferment continued throughout the whole period of
their married life. *Casa Guidi Windows* dealt with the earlier
phases of the movement for liberation. In its later stages, the
part taken in it by Napoleon III and the equivocal character
of his motives and actions were matter of intense interest to
them. Elizabeth Browning was his devoted defender ; Browning
was alternately critical and condemnatory. Even 'the annexation
of Savoy and Nice' only momentarily shook her faith in him.
Browning summed up the situation by saying of Napoleon's part
in the Italian war that 'it was a great action but he has taken
eighteen pence for it, which is a pity.' They had agreed to write
of Napoleon and publish jointly. Elizabeth Browning's labours
resulted in *Poems before Congress*; on the annexation, Browning
dropped the project and destroyed what he had written. But he
came back to the subject, during that period when it delighted
him most to explore the intricacies of ambiguous souls whose
morality was 'pied' and intellects casuistical; and he produced
Prince Hohenstiel-Schwangau.

Both *Casa Guidi Windows* and *Poems before Congress* illustrate
the difficulty of lifting contemporary politics into poetry. Neither
these nor the aftermath in her posthumous *Last Poems* (1862)
have added to Elizabeth Browning's literary reputation.

It remains to notice the longest and the most ambitious of
her poems—*Aurora Leigh*, with its eleven thousand lines of
blank verse. It was the literary venture on which she staked
her fortune ; in her dedication of it to Kenyon, she calls it 'the
most mature of my works, and the one into which my highest
convictions upon Life and Art have entered.' The readers of
her time agreed with her; critics were unanimous, and their
praise was pitched high; the first edition was exhausted in a
fortnight, and a third was required within a few months.
Later readers have become much more temperate. It is a novel

in iambic decasyllables. The story is a thin thread on which are strung the opinions of the writer on all manner of matters— educational, social, artistic, ethical.

Elizabeth Browning's gifts were lyrical. She was essentially a subjective poet, in the sense that the events she described and the characters she drew were saturated with her own sympathies. All the characters in *Aurora Leigh* are entirely subordinate to the heroine, and the heroine, however little Elizabeth Browning intended it, is the unsubstantial shadow of herself. She had no dramatic or narrative genius. The world in which her characters move is always created on the pattern of her own inner life, for she dipped her brush in her own emotions. Her later poems show some improvement in technique, and some of them are enriched by her life in Italy and by the influence of her husband, which was very great : for it is not *Pippa Passes* only 'which counts for something in *Aurora Leigh*,' nor even *Paracelsus*, whose faith is paraphrased in hundreds of its lines. But they contain nothing equal to *Rhyme of the Duchess May, Cowper's Grave* and *The Cry of the Children.* If she is remembered permanently, it will be, as a poet, by reason of the expression she gave to a mother's love in *A Child's Grave at Florence*, and, even more securely, by the sublime passion of the love of wife for husband in *Sonnets from the Portuguese.*

The Italian period of Browning's life was comparatively barren. It has been suggested that this was due, in part, to the fact that the climate of Italy lowered his vitality; in part, to the unpopularity of his works. Moreover, he took to drawing, and to modelling in clay, copying masterpieces with intense pleasure. Only two publications of verse marked this period—*Christmas Eve and Easter Day* (1850) and *Men and Women* (1855). He also wrote at this time an essay on Shelley, by way of introduction to *Certain Letters of Percy Bysshe Shelley* (1852), which were afterwards found to be fabrications. The essay was evidently influenced by Milsand's article on Browning himself, in *La Revue des Deux Mondes.* It accentuates in the same way the distinction between subjective and objective poetry, and discusses Shelley's work with much skill and insight.

In *Christmas Eve and Easter Day*, critics discover clear evidence of the influence of Elizabeth Browning's devout Christian faith. Browning had been interested in religion all his life : for the ' atheism' which he caught from Shelley was as superficial and temporary as the vegetarianism. *Pauline, Paracelsus, Pippa*

Passes, all the principal poems of the early period bear witness to his sense of the profound significance of religion. *Christmas Eve* deals with contemporary attitudes towards Christianity—dissent, the higher criticism, Roman catholicism—with a characteristic preference for the first. *Easter Day* is more restrained and stern, more full of lyric beauty and more searching in its truth. It deals with the inner nature of the faith that is religious—religious and not epicurean or materialistic—not seeking its evidences in outward happenings or its worth in the complacency which it brings, the zest it gives to joy, or the bitterness it takes away from sorrow. Both poems are dramatic; neither is to be regarded as the poet's confession of faith; nevertheless, they express the profoundest of his spiritual convictions, which centred upon the most sublime of all religious hypotheses, namely, that of the omnipotence and omnipresence of a Christlike God, the divine power and work of love. *Saul,* especially the second part, which contains the prophecy of Christianity, *Cleon, Karshish,* bear witness to the same conceptions—the omnipresent wonder that transcends definition, and is yet the sole sure light whereby man can walk and find safe footing.

Elizabeth Browning's influence may be detected, also, in the poems which treat of love. The original *Dramatic Lyrics* (the *Dramatic Lyrics* as they stood before the poems transferred thereto from *Men and Women*) included *Cristina* and *In a Gondola,* and among *Dramatic Romances and Lyrics* there appeared *The Lost Mistress.* But the collection which included *A Woman's Last Word, Any Wife to Any Husband, The Last Ride Together, One Way of Love,* among many more, was certainly a richer rendering of the marvel of love than any of his previous works. It is probable that no single poet, in any country, so rendered the variety of its phases and the abundance of its power—its triumph, its failure; its victory over the world, its defeat by the world; its passion and poignancy; its psychical subtlety and its romance, and the immensity of its spiritual significance, whether in the life of the soul or in the outer cosmos.

Many of the poems in *Men and Women* of which the scene can be determined have reference to Italy. But it is doubtful whether his residence in Italy influenced Browning's choice of subjects to any great extent. 'He was deeply Italianised before he went to live in Italy.' To say nothing of *Sordello* and *Pippa Passes,* there was an Italian group in the original *Dramatic Romances and Lyrics,* which is almost as conspicuous as that of the original *Men and Women.* After *The Ring and the Book*, Italian subjects become both more rare and less important.

On leaving Italy, Browning settled in London. With the change of residence came a change of habit. His Italian life, quiet in the early years, had become gradually much more social. In Florence, in Rome and during their visits to London, the charm of Elizabeth Browning, and Robert Browning's own genius for noble friendship, brought them into intimate relations with the most gifted of their time. After her death, until the spring of 1863, he retired within himself, and his life, as he said, was 'as grey as the London sky.' Then, he thought that way of life morbid and unworthy, resolved to accept every suitable invitation and, thenceforth, his figure was familiar in the circles of the lovers of literature, although, except for a very few friends, all women, none ever saw of Browning more than 'a splendid surface.'

In 1863, he was much agitated by a proposal to publish a life of Elizabeth Browning, with letters. He turned savagely upon 'the blackguards' who would 'thrust their paws into his bowels,' and he destroyed the greater part of his own correspondence. But he preserved the letters that had passed between himself and his wife prior to their marriage ; with the result that hardly anyone, except, perhaps, Carlyle, protested more strongly against the intrusion of spies into his life's intimacies, and had the inner shrine more ruthlessly laid bare. He, however, freely gave to the public what had been intended for them. He republished Elizabeth Browning's prose essays on the Greek Christian poets and the English poets in 1863; and, two years later, made a selection from her poems, and expressed his delight at the popularity which made it necessary.

For three years in succession, he spent the summer months at Ste Marie, near Pornic, where he worked at his *Dramatis Personae*, published in 1864. Part of 1866 and 1867 was spent at Croisic, the name of which is linked with *The Two Poets of Croisic*, as he linked that of Pornic with *Gold Hair, Red Cotton Night-Cap Country* and the gipsy woman of *Fifine at the Fair*.

Browning was at the height of his power during this period. Nowhere is his poetic work so uniformly great as in *Dramatis Personae* (1864); and there is no doubt that *The Ring and the Book* is the most magnificent of all his achievements, in spite of its inequalities. Critics miss in *Dramatis Personae* something of the lightness and brightness and early morning charm of *Pippa Passes* and of some of his earlier *Men and Women*; and they find

in it, not any trace of the pathetic fallacy, yet a lingering echo of
the brooding sorrow for his life's loss.   It was later in the day; the
world was more commonplace; the outlook more desolate and
man's failure less tinged with glory; women were more homely,
love was less ethereal; and the stuff to be idealised through being
better known by a wiser love was more stubborn.   'The summer
had stopped,' and 'the sky was deranged.'   But the autumn had
come, bringing a richer harvest in *Dramatis Personae.*   The
significance of man's life, and of the clash of circumstance which
elicited it, was deeper as well as more grave.   The world's worn
look disappears when it is seen in the great context in which it
stands—'All we have willed or hoped or dreamed of good shall
exist,' says Abt Vogler.   Man has himself 'a flash of the will that
can,' for he can use its distraught elements of life to a moral
purpose, and weld them in a spiritual harmony—out of three
sounds make, 'not a fourth sound, but a star.'   *Prospice, Rabbi
Ben Ezra, A Death in the Desert,* even *Mr Sludge, 'The Medium'*
and *Caliban upon Setebos,* are strong with a controlled ethical
passion for what is real and true as things stand, and by interest
in the issues which are ultimate ; and, with this realism, natural
and spiritual, in both kinds, there is blended an imaginative
splendour which transfigures even 'the least of all mankind,'
when we 'look at his head and heart'; and

> see what I tell you—nature dance
> About each man of us, retire, advance,
> As though the pageant's end were to enhance
>
> His worth, and—once the life, his product, gained—
> Roll away elsewhere.

It is a permanent theme, its echoes are to be heard all the way to
Asolando—this wash of circumstance around man's soul which yet
maintains its mastery over all the play of the waves ; and nowhere
is it rendered more finely than in *Dramatis Personae* and its
Epilogue.

   The Edinburgh Review found it a 'subject of amazement
that poems of so obscure and uninviting a character should find
numerous readers'; and there were other critics besides Frederick
Tennyson who still thought Browning's poetry 'the most grotesque
conceivable.'   But the situation had, in truth, changed.   Browning's
admirers were no longer confined to pre-Raphaelites and 'young
men at the Universities.'   A second edition of *Dramatis Personae*
was called for within the same year as the first.   And the reception
accorded to *The Ring and the Book* was still more favourable.

At last, Browning was coming into his kingdom. It had taken long: so late as 1867, he spoke of himself as 'the most unpopular poet that ever was.'

There was an interval of four years between *Dramatis Personae* and *The Ring and the Book.* But the theme had interested him from the moment when he came upon the 'old, square, yellow book' on an old bookstall in Florence—the parchment-bound tale of the trial of an Italian noble for the murder of his wife. He saw its dramatic possibilities when he stood on the balcony of Casa Guidi, in June 1860, at night, watching the storm. But it lay long working in his mind, and the sorrow of the following year led him to abandon the idea of writing, and he suggested the subject to two of his friends. In September 1862, he recurred to it, spoke of 'my new poem that is about to be,' 'the Roman murder story.' He began to write it about 1864, and the poem grew steadily, for it became his crowning venture and he gave it regularly every day 'three quiet, early morning hours.' It was published in four volumes, the first of which appeared in November 1868; and the others during the three months following.

Many things concurred to make the story attractive to Browning. He had inherited a taste for tales of crime from his father; the situation was ambiguous and, as regards the priest and the girl-wife, it left room for a most beautiful, as well as for a sordid, explanation, and, therefore, it appealed both to Browning's love of argument and to his ethical idealism; moreover, opinion in Rome was divided, and the popular mind was on its trial; there was the possibility that the truth 'told for once for the church, and dead against the world, the flesh, and the devil'; and the story, in its essence, was not a common drab, but glorious—the romance of the young priest and Pompilia was 'a gift of God, who showed for once how he would have the world go white.'

It was inevitable that such a theme should set free all the powers of Browning's spirit; but it borrowed sublimity and a sacred loveliness from another quarter. For, undoubtedly, the 'poem which enshrined Pompilia was instinct with reminiscence.' 'With all its abounding vitality it was yet commemorative and memorial[1].' When he wrote of 'the one prize vouchsafed unworthy me'; of 'the one blossom that made me proud at eve'; of a 'life companioned by the woman there'; of living and seeing her learn, and learning by her, can there be doubt as to who lent to these utterances their pathetic beauty?

[1] Herford.

Nor is it fanciful to find in Caponsacchi something of the poet himself—more, perhaps, than in any other character he created. There was his own tempestuousness, much that a wise old pope could find 'amiss,' 'blameworthy,' 'ungainly,' 'discordant,' 'infringement manifold' of convention ; but there was also a 'symmetric soul within,' 'championship of God at first blush,' 'prompt, cheery thud of glove on ground,' answering 'ringingly the challenge of the false knight.' What are these qualities, with the ardour of a great love and the headlong and utter devotion of a large-hearted manhood, except the poet's own ? Caponsacchi's

> I am, on earth, as good as out of it,
> A relegated priest ; when exile ends,
> I mean to do my duty and live long,

is inspired by the manly recoil of Browning and his refusal to be crushed by his sorrow. But the dream of having his 'lyric Love' by his side has been broken ; and the bereaved poet is not perceptible in the 'drudging student,' who 'trims his lamp,' 'draws the patched gown close' and awakes 'to the old solitary nothingness.' The last words are a promise of this priest to 'pass content, from such communion'; and Browning would fain have come back into the world of men as if his wound had healed. But the truth breaks out—

> O great, just, good God! Miserable me!

There was, for both priest and poet, the rule in the world of a love that wrapped all things round about, and yet, somehow, also, there were sorrows that knew neither shores nor shoals.

To pass all the parts of this great poem under review is not possible, and to estimate the relative poetic worth of its several parts—*Caponsacchi, Pompilia, The Pope* and *Guido*—is not necessary ; there are kinds as well as degrees of perfection, and comparison is sometimes absurd. The possibility of justifying the structure of the poem as a whole will remain doubtful ; and the maccaronic speeches of the lawyers, and some parts of what Rome said, have no real artistic value. But the poem is unique in its excellence as well as in its defects.

During the six years which followed *The Ring and the Book,* Browning wrote nothing but long poems—with the exception of *Hervé Riel,* which was published for a charitable purpose. *Balaustion's Adventure* appeared in 1871. Balaustion had the

Alcestis of Euripides by heart, and, by rendering that 'strangest, saddest, sweetest song,' saves her own life and wins for the ship refuge in the harbour of Syracuse. Balaustion's character has the charm of Pippa; Hercules, re-created by Browning, is magnificent —with 'the gay cheer' of his great voice, heralding gladness as he helped the world, 'the human and divine, i'' the weary, happy face of him, half god, half man, which made the god-part god the more (a favourite and recurrent conception). In *Aristophanes'* *Apology*, Balaustion is reintroduced, and we have a second transcript from Euripides—and, with it, above all else, the incomparable portrait of Aristophanes. 'No ignoble presence': 'mind a-wantoning,' it is true, but 'at ease,' all the same, 'of undisputed mastery over the body's brood, those appetites.'

> A sea-worn face, sad as mortality,
> Divine with yearning after fellowship.

The transcribed portions of both poems have only secondary value; and the translation is said to be often tame, literal and even awkward. The *Agamemnon of Aeschylus* (1877) is said to be an even less acceptable rendering: 'exact' and unintelligible. It was undertaken on the suggestion of Carlyle and dedicated to him. One would like to know what mood Carlyle was in, when he gave his advice, telling Browning 'ye ought to translate the whole of the Greek tragedians—that's your vocation.' Browning was better left to sport in his own way, in his own element, like his 'King of Pride,' 'through deep to deep,' 'churning the blackness hoary.' There is ample evidence of his wide, intimate knowledge of the literature of Athens, and of his love of its methods; but his strength was not similar to that of the Greeks; and he cannot be said to have made a significant contribution either to the knowledge or to the love, in England, of the Greek drama.

As if Browning were under compulsion to squander the popularity gained by *Dramatis Personae* and *The Ring and the Book*, and with both hands, there appeared, besides these Greek poems, *Prince Hohenstiel-Schwangau* (1871), *Fifine at the Fair* (1872), *Red Cotton Night-Cap Country or Turf and Towers* (1873) and *The Inn Album* (1875). Either for its theme, or for the treatment of it, or for both theme and treatment, every one of these poems failed to please. *Prince Hohenstiel-Schwangau*, a monologue over a cigar, illustrated by connecting blot with blot on a 'soiled bit' of paper, is the mean and tortuous plea of a weak, possibly well-meaning, certainly discredited, politician. Its hero, Napoleon III, was hardly great enough to be tragical, or even picturesque. *Fifine at the Fair* shocked and alienated good people. It was supposed to be a defence of illicit love ; and its style was thought as turgid as its morality was false. *Red Cotton Night-Cap Country* is a novel in verse ; the story of a Paris jeweller and his mistress. It has been defended on the ground that, as a strong treatment of the ugly, it makes the ugly uglier ! More sanely it has been disapproved as 'versified special correspondence,' 'from which every pretence of poetry is usually remote.' *The Inn Album* once more deals with illicit passion, and, once more, is 'a novel in verse.' Its hero is all tinsel, and 'rag and feather sham,' irredeemably mean, smart and shallow, a cheat at cards, growing old amid his 'scandalous successes'—a figure, one might say, better let be by the poet. The heroine, the betrayed girl, is a genuinely tragical figure. And the tragedy is final, remorseless ; for she marries a parish priest who is unloving and unloved, dull, elderly, poor, conscientious, whom she 'used to pity' till she 'learned what woes are pity-worth.' Him, in an ugly, filthy village, sterile as if ' sown with salt,' she helps to drug and dose his flock with the doctrine of heaven and hell—the latter 'made explicit.' Much of this poem is powerful ; it contains one passage strangely Shakespearean in quality : that in which the elder lady describes her lost love, when its reality was questioned by her betrayer. As a whole, however, it cannot compare with *Fifine at the Fair*, either in range of reflective power, or in wealth of artistic splendour, or in the weight of the issues which are called forth. It was not without reason that Browning spoke of *Fifine* as ' the most metaphysical and boldest he had written since *Sordello* '; and not in all respects was Swinburne's dictum wrong—' This is far better than anything Browning has yet written.' Its main defect is that in it, even more than usual, ' Browning has presumed too much upon his reader's insight' and taken no pains to ' obviate confusions he would have held to be impossible had they occurred to his mind.'

His experience of his critics—'the inability of the human goose to do other than either cackle or hiss '—led him to banter them in *Pacchiarotto and how he worked in Distemper* (1876), which tells the whimsical tale of the artist who tried to reform his fellows. The poem is genial and boisterous and, in its rime, brilliant and absurd ; an instance of another of the poet's ways of Aristophanic wantoning. In *At the 'Mermaid'* and *House* and other poems in the same volume, the aloofness of the inner life, the deepest and real, is brought before us ; and how, in the last resort, the world of men, mingle with them as he might, was nothing but 'world without'—

> as wood, brick, stone, this ring
> Of the rueful neighbours.

He lived and he sang, and he was for 'one' only; for the rest of men, there was but his self's surface and the garb, and what it pleased him to dole.

The fact that, unmistakably, he speaks of himself, mingles and involves himself in his creations, shows that Browning's dramatic power was beginning to decline. The plea that the 'utterances' are those of 'imaginary characters' becomes less and less valid ; for the imagined characters are unsubstantial, the shadows thrown by the poet himself. But there is one theme which, change as life's seasons may, remains for him a perennial source of perfect song. In *St Martin's Summer*, where much that is green had turned sere, and the heart had lost its enterprise, in *Numpholeptos* and in other poems in this volume, love, which is now a memory of what was, and a wistful longing for what must yet be, retains all its mystic power and breaks into lyric poetry of unabated beauty.

In 1877, Browning visited the Savoy alps; and there his companion, Miss Egerton Smith, died suddenly, as she was making ready for a mountain expedition with him.

In the following year, *La Saisiaz* was published, a commemorative poem which states and tests the arguments for and against the immortality of the soul, and pronounces judgment. But the pronouncement, though affirmative, is not untinged with doubt, and it has the fatal weakness of being, at best, valid or conclusive only for the poet. Here, as elsewhere, there is a sophistic touch in Browning's philosophy; and it was not in the intelligence, but in the potency of love that he trusted. In the same volume as *La Saisiaz* there appeared *The Two Poets of Croisic*, in which, once more, the poet gambols, mocking, this time, at fame.

In the autumn of 1878, for the first time after the death of his wife, Browning went to Italy; and he repeated his visits every year until the close of his life. On his first journey, he stayed for some weeks at a hotel near the summit of the Splügen pass. *Ivàn Ivànovitch* and *Ned Bratts* were written here, and the volume entitled *Dramatic Idyls* (1879) contains these and *Martin Relph*, and *Pheidippides*, both magnificently told stories, the latter carrying the reader back to the tale *How they brought the Good News from Ghent to Aix*. The second series of *Dramatic Idyls* contained the dramatic stories of 'the foolishness,' which is love, of

Muléykeh's Arab owner, and Clive's confession to fear, with its startling turn. *Jocoseria*, published in 1883, contains two great poems, namely, *Ixion* and the lyric *Never the Time and the Place*— where longing love finds once more its perfect utterance. Then came *Ferishtah's Fancies* (1884) and *Parleyings with Certain People of Importance in their Day* (1887) and, finally, *Asolando* (1890). The garb of Ferishtah is eastern: he is a Persian sage; and the allegories and parables have, also, an eastern flavour. But Ferishtah is only a name, and the sage who speaks the wisdom of commonsense through his lips, illustrating his convictions regarding moral matters, pain, prayer, asceticism, punishment, by reference to common objects—the sun, a melon-seller, cherries, two camels, plot-culture—is Browning himself. The poems are simple, direct and pleasing; they contain a practical faith touched with theoretical doubt. The conclusions are all tentative and insecure, so long as the heart does not lead to them, and love is silent. The lyrics that intervene between the dialogues are exquisite.

Browning was seventy-five years old when he published *Parleyings*; and the 'importance' of the people with whom he parleys comes from the fact that they carried him back to his boyhood's industrious happiness in his father's library. There he learnt of 'Artistry's Ideal' from 'the prodigious book' of Gerard de Lairesse; and he remembered his mother playing Avison's grand march. The poems are vigorous, the learning displayed in them is immense and they abound in intellectual vitality; but the personages are as shadowy as they are voluble, and the poetic glory has left the grey.

Browning's health was becoming more uncertain, but he continued both his social life in London and his journeys south to the mountains and to Italy. In 1887, his son married, and bought the Rezzonico palace, Venice, and thither, for two summers more, the poet returned. He also went back (after forty years) to Asolo, and lived in a house there on the old town-wall; and the place which he had loved from the days of *Pippa* renewed its charm for him. He died at Venice, on 12 December 1889, and was buried in the poet's corner of Westminster abbey on the last day of the year.

He had not expected death, but, to the last, was full of projects, his courage unabated and his enterprise not weary; and his last words, the great *Epilogue* with which, in *Asolando*, he closed the collected gleanings of his genius, fitly express the faith which made his life heroic.

CHAPTER IV

MATTHEW ARNOLD, ARTHUR HUGH CLOUGH, JAMES THOMSON

EMINENT alike as poet and critic, Matthew Arnold holds a place of singular distinction among the representative writers of the Victorian age. His poetical work is much smaller in volume and less varied in interest and range than that of his two more popular contemporaries, Tennyson and Browning, but it reflects, along certain lines, even more faithfully than the poetry of either, some peculiarly significant tendencies of nineteenth-century thought. Arnold himself, at any rate, was convinced—and few poets have been surer critics of their own work than he—that he need not fear comparison with either Browning or Tennyson as an interpreter of even the 'main movement of mind[1]' in the England of his time. In his intellectual sympathies and interests, he was much nearer akin to Browning than to Tennyson. Like Browning, Arnold was largely a man of the world, though, unlike him, he studiously kept this side of his character out of his poetry. It is in his critical prose writings, and in his letters, disappointing though the latter may be from a purely literary point of view, that we discover the real Arnold—both the self-searching poet, with his

hidden ground
Of thought and of austerity within,

and the shrewd observer of men and movements, curiously sensitive to all 'play of the mind,' wherever and in whomsoever he found it. When, at a comparatively early period in his literary career, he virtually abandoned poetry for prose, he at once came into touch with a much wider public, and his letters frankly express the delight which he felt in having, at last, found an 'audience.' His poetry was the fruit of 'calm contemplation and majestic pains,' rather than of urgent and imperative impulse. There is a sense

[1] See letter to his mother, June 1869. *Letters*, vol. II, p. 9.

of freedom, and even of gaiety, about his prose which suggests a liberated spirit moving easily and happily in its proper element. And it was not only a delight, but a source of serious satisfaction, to Arnold to feel that, through his prose writings, he was able to exert a real influence upon the life and thought of his own generation. He was an ineffective public speaker; but his written excursions into regions where the popular speaker holds the field attracted as much attention and made as powerful an impression as the most sounding platform utterances of the day. His manner of preaching his new-found gospel had little in it of the fervour of the social crusader, and offered a marked contrast to the strident rhetoric with which Carlyle, for example, sought to impress his contemporaries. He himself defined his method as 'sinuous, easy, unpolemical'; but he employed it with deadly effect in undermining the 'forts of folly.' His banter and his irony often gave offence, and many of his readers found it difficult to put up with the Olympian air of superiority affected by a critic who took the whole conduct of life for his province. But there was no escaping the literary charm of prose discourses cast in a delightfully fresh and individual style, which, with all its mannerisms, retained the pellucid clearness and distinction of his poetry. Moreover, his later prose writings confirmed the opinion which his poetry, and a few early essays, had gone far to establish, that Matthew Arnold was the most brilliant literary critic of his time. Much of his social, political and religious criticism is, perhaps because of its ephemeral subjects, doomed, ultimately, to oblivion, although a good part of it can never lose its point or practical value while the temper and habits of the English people remain substantially what they are. His literary criticisms, however, will live as long as the best of their kind; and, in the combination of remarkable poetic achievement with illuminating discourse on the art of poetry and on 'the best that is known and thought in the world,' Dryden and Coleridge alone, among English writers, share his pre-eminence.

Matthew Arnold, the eldest son of Thomas Arnold, headmaster of Rugby, was born at Laleham on Christmas eve, 1822. His mother, who survived her husband more than thirty years, was a woman of great force of character, who had so much intellectual sympathy with her son as to make his letters to her the most intimate personal records of him that we possess. Matthew owed much to his distinguished father—his high sense of duty, his intellectual honesty, his austere moral ideals were abiding paternal inheritances; but, as his life and writings tended more and more to show, he was in some ways, and particularly in temperament, curiously unlike him. Matthew Arnold entered Rugby in 1837, where he remained until he won a Balliol scholarship at Oxford in 1841. Oxford, at that time, was agitated by the tractarian movement, and Newman was at the height of his extraordinary influence in the university. That influence does not seem to have had much, if any, intellectual or spiritual effect upon Matthew Arnold; but, like others of more or less note in the Oxford of his day, he fell under the spell of Newman's personal charm, of which he gives a vivid description in one of the latest of his public utterances[1]. Arnold, by temperament, was too anticlerical, and, probably, shared too strongly his father's pronounced hostility to the neo-catholic movement, to have any deep sympathy with Newman's teaching. In 1843, he won the Newdigate prize with a poem entitled *Cromwell*, but he disappointed his friends and tutors, a year later, by obtaining only a second class in *Literae Humaniores*. Like his friend Clough, however, who had met with a similar fate before him, he was consoled for his ill-success in the schools by the award of a fellowship at Oriel. Passionately though Matthew Arnold loved the 'sweet city with her dreaming spires,' even the attainment of this coveted academic dignity could not keep him at Oxford. Probably, as some of his admirers have suggested, the line of life that would have suited him best was that of a diplomatist[2]. A diplomatic career seemed to lie in his way when, in 1847, he was appointed private secretary to lord Lansdowne. The best thing, however, in the way of advancement which lord Lansdowne, then president of the council, could do for him was to appoint him to an inspectorship of schools. 'Though I am a schoolmaster's son,' Arnold long afterwards frankly told a meeting of teachers, 'I confess that school-teaching or school-inspecting is not the line of life I should naturally have chosen. I adopted it in order to marry.' That was in 1851, when he married Frances Lucy Wightman. The conditions of his official work were anything but favourable to the production of poetry; but nearly all Arnold's best poetry was written during the busiest years of his school inspectorate. As the years went on, he came to discover that even the drab task-work of school inspection had its compensations. He loved children, and he took a genuine interest in the welfare of teachers; moreover, in his journeys from school to school, he acquired that manysided knowledge of English life and character

---

[1] *Discourses in America.*
[2] G. W. E. Russell, *Matthew Arnold*, 1894, p. 49.

of which he made effective use in his social criticisms. He dwelt with 'the Philistines' in their tents, was constantly going in and out among 'the populace' and, on occasions, broke bread with 'the barbarians.'

In 1859, Matthew Arnold was appointed foreign assistant commissioner on education, and sent on a mission to enquire into the systems of primary education prevailing in France, Holland, Belgium, Switzerland and Piedmont. The immediate result of this continental visit was the issue, in 1861, of his *Popular Education of France*, of which the most permanently valuable part, the introductory essay, was subsequently republished under the title 'Democracy' in *Mixed Essays* (1879). In 1864 appeared a by-product of the same foreign mission entitled (not, perhaps, very appropriately) *A French Eton*, being an account of the general economy of a *lycée* at Toulouse. In 1865, he went abroad on a second educational mission, of which the published record appeared, in 1868, under the title *Schools and Universities on the Continent*. These volumes, and the *Reports on Elementary Schools*, edited after his death by Sir Francis Sandford, make up the sum of Arnold's official educational writings, and they all belong to the period of his poetical activity, which practically ended with the year 1867. To the same period, also, belong two other prose works which stand somewhat apart from the series of writings, beginning with *Culture and Anarchy*, which won for him his contemporary renown as a social and political critic. They are the delightful critical discourses *On Translating Homer* (1861) and *The Study of Celtic Literature* (1867), in which we find the essence of his prelections from the chair of poetry at Oxford, a post to which he was elected in 1857 and which he held for ten years. After 1867, Arnold wrote little poetry, and entered upon a career as publicist on social, religious and political subjects which led him somewhat far afield from the high road of literature. He soon became a controversialist whom the newspapers and magazines of the hour found it profitable to notice and to attack; his fame spread across the Atlantic, and, in 1883, led to the inevitable American lecturing tour which has been the not always happy lot of many popular English authors. Arnold's American experiences seem, on the whole, to have been fairly fortunate, and he himself set such store by his lectures in the United States as to tell one of his friends[1] that *Discourses in America* 'was the book by which, of all his prose writings, he most desired to be remembered.' In 1886, he resigned his school

---

[1] G. W. E. Russell; see his *Matthew Arnold*, p. 12.

inspectorship, and was awarded a state pension. He died suddenly at Liverpool on 15 April 1888. His life, in spite of uncongenial tasks and some sore domestic trials, was a peculiarly happy one, and the secret of its happiness was his serene temper and an inexhaustible interest in mundane things, evident throughout his letters to his friends and his family.

Arnold's first volume of poems was printed in 1849 under the title *The Strayed Reveller, and other Poems, by A.* This modest budget of verse, though it contained a few short poems not inferior in quality to the best of his subsequent work, attracted little public attention, and was withdrawn from circulation after only a few copies had been sold. The same fate befell his second published volume, *Empedocles on Etna, and other poems, by A.*, which appeared in October 1852. Dissatisfaction with the title-poem was the reason given by Arnold himself for the withdrawal of this second volume; but, fifteen years afterwards, at the instance of Robert Browning, he republished the poem. The sacrifice of *Empedocles*, however, seems to have been a kind of strategic retreat which enabled the poet, in the following year, to publish boldly, under his own name, a new volume, with a preface defining his views upon some of the prime objects and functions of poetry. This volume (1853) included many of the poems already printed in its two predecessors, together with others which are shining examples of his more elaborate and considered work, such as *Sohrab and Rustum* and *The Scholar-Gipsy*. In 1855 appeared *Poems by Matthew Arnold, Second Series*, a volume with only two new poems, *Balder Dead* and *Separation*, but containing a further instalment of republications, including some fragments of *Empedocles*, from the earlier volumes. In 1858, *Merope, a Tragedy*, composed as a sort of 'poetical diploma-piece' on his election to the Oxford professorship, was published. After an interval of nine years, his next, and his last, separate volume of poems—as distinguished from editions of his collected works—appeared under the title *New Poems*. In this volume, *Empedocles* made its reappearance in the company of such notable poems as *Thyrsis, Rugby Chapel, Heine's Grave, A Southern Night, Dover Beach* and *Obermann Once More*. During the last twenty years of his life, with the exception of a few occasional pieces of the quality of *Westminster Abbey* and *Geist's Grave*, Arnold produced nothing which added materially to his poetical reputation.

A survey of Arnold's poems in their chronological order brings into prominence two outstanding facts—the early maturity of his genius, and his steadfast adherence throughout to certain very definite ideals of poetic art and to a singularly melancholy philosophy of life. We note, at once, in the first small volume of 1849, the predominantly Greek inspiration of its contents, both in matter and in style. As the poet himself avows in a famous sonnet, the three Greek masters who, most of all, 'propped, in those bad days, his mind' were Homer, Epictetus and, especially, Sophocles —the latter a poet fulfilling Arnold's ideal as one whom

> Business could not make dull, nor passion wild;
> Who saw life steadily, and saw it whole.

The title-poem, *The Strayed Reveller*, is itself Greek in both subject and form, its rimeless and irregular metre being an attempt to reproduce the effect of the choric odes of Attic tragedy. *The Fragment of an 'Antigone'*—another experiment in unrimed lyric—*Mycerinus, The New Sirens, The Sick King in Bokhara* are all Greek either in subject, or in source, or in manner of treatment. Writing in 1867 of the Greek strain in Arnold's poetry generally, Swinburne said,

> Even after his master, this disciple of Sophocles holds his high place; he has matched against the Attic of the gods this Hyperborean dialect of ours, and has not earned the doom of Marsyas.

In his endeavours to attune our 'Hyperborean dialect' to Attic music, Arnold was plainly influenced by the example of Goethe —another of his life-long masters, alike in art and in his 'wide and luminous view' of life, who, for him, was 'the greatest modern poet, the greatest critic of all time[1].' Goethe's presence is felt in *The Strayed Reveller* volume, as, also, is that of the English master who

> laid us as we lay at birth
> On the cool flowery lap of earth.

The Greeks, Goethe, Wordsworth—these are the prime literary sources of Matthew Arnold's poetical inspiration; and we are in as close touch with them all in the poems of 1849 as we are in those of 1867. The Wordsworthian 'note,' as the poet himself might say, is clearly heard in *Resignation, To a Gipsy Child* and *Mycerinus.* Distinct echoes of *Laodamia* are caught in *Mycerinus,* while the grave movement of *To a Gipsy Child* is quite after Wordsworth's manner. But the influence of Wordsworth is most apparent in *Resignation*—at once a poem of nature and a cry

---

[1] Preface to the 1853 volume of poems.

from the depth of the poet's own soul. No poem, however, illustrates better than this last the essential difference between Arnold's feeling for nature and that of Wordsworth. There is a wide distance between the poet to whom, if he 'might lend their life a voice,' hills, streams, rocks, the sky, 'seemed to bear rather than rejoice,' and the seer who felt it was nature's 'privilege to lead from joy to joy' and who held the faith that 'every flower enjoys the air it breathes.' Perhaps the most original poem in the 1849 volume is *The Forsaken Merman,* which is remarkable alike for its pathos and its metrical skill, and was singled out by Clough in a review published in 1853[1]. Clough found *The Sick King in Bokhara* 'rather strained.' Other critics have found it dull, whereas one whose literary judgment was never far at fault— R. H. Hutton—held that Arnold 'never achieved anything so truly dramatic.'

With the volume of poems published under his own name in 1853, Arnold, as already stated, issued a preface expounding some of the main principles of his 'theory of poetry.' This preface, now easily accessible, deserves careful reading, as it is Arnold's first published 'essay in criticism,' remarkable alike for its ease and grace of style, which bears little trace of the marked mannerisms of his later prose, and for its clear exposition of a poetical creed to which its author, in the main, adhered, both in precept and practice, throughout his life. We find him definitely ranging himself as the apostle of a classical ideal of poetry, in opposition to the vagaries and excesses of the romantic school, of which England seemed to him then to be 'the stronghold[2].' And, more particularly, he denounces views like those of the critic whom he quotes as maintaining that

the poet who would really fix the public attention must leave the exhausted past, and draw his subjects from matters of present import, and *therefore* both of interest and of novelty.

Here is sounded the first note of that war-cry against the Philistines which he was destined, in later years, to send ringing through many grooves of the national life. When we examine the preface in the light of Arnold's own poetical practice, it may be urged that he failed in his attempts to exemplify, on any large scale, one of its main theses. *Empedocles* and *Merope* are his two most ambitious efforts to represent 'situations' after the

[1] *The North American Review,* July 1853. Republished in *Prose Remains of Arthur Hugh Clough,* edited by his wife, 1888.

[2] See preface to *Merope,* 1858.

manner of the ancients—the first, on his own confession, an unsatisfying achievement, the latter, in the opinion of the majority of even his admirers, a graceful, but somewhat ineffectual, academic exercise.

Of the contents of the volume of 1853, the poem which comes nearest to a practical illustration of the theories of the preface is *Sohrab and Rustum*, the most finished and successful of his narrative poems. The subject appeals, like the themes of classical tragedy, to 'the great primary human affections,' and is treated with a clearness and sustained elevation of style as closely approximating the Greek manner, 'the grand style,' as anything else to be found in later English poetry. The blank verse is handled throughout with subtle skill, and, in many passages, is reminiscent of Milton—particularly in the artistic use of the long simile and of recurrent parades of sonorous proper names. Arnold's similes, here, are, like Milton's, all after the Greek epic type, and the whole poem is thoroughly Homeric in manner and substance. The human interest of the 'episode'—for so the author describes his poem—centres in the tragic fate of the brave and gentle Sohrab, slain by the father who does not know him ; and in the delineation of no other character in his poetry does Matthew Arnold show a surer and more sympathetic touch. The well-known description of the Oxus at the close of the poem is no mere pictorial afterthought, due to Arnold's alleged *penchant* for 'effective endings,' but is as artistically right as it is intrinsically beautiful.

With *Sohrab and Rustum* much the most notable new contribution to the 1853 volume is *The Scholar-Gipsy*, perhaps the most charming, as it is one of the happiest in conception and execution, of all Arnold's poems. Its charm lies partly in the subject, naturally congenial to the poet, and partly in the scene, which stimulates one of Oxford's poetic children to lavish all his powers of description upon the landscape which he dearly loved. He was to return to the same natural scenery in *Thyrsis*, but, although, in the later poem, there may be one descriptive passage which surpasses anything to be found in the earlier, *Thyrsis* fails to give the impression of eager freshness and ease which are felt throughout *The Scholar-Gipsy*. The two poems are pastoral in form, but there is much less concession to artificial conventions in *The Scholar-Gipsy* than in its more consciously elegiac successor. What, however, gives their abiding charm to both is the vividness and the beauty of their pictures of nature, and the magic spell

cast by their haunting lines over Oxford and its adjacent fields
and hills. In *The Scholar-Gipsy*, the subtle glamour of all that
Oxford and its neighbourhood suggest to the eye and to the
memory is felt in glimpses of

> The line of festal light in Christ-Church hall,

of the 'Oxford riders blithe'

> Crossing the stripling Thames at Bab-lock-hithe,

of 'the warm, green-muffled Cumner hills,' 'the Fyfield elm in
May,' the 'distant Wychwood bowers,' Godstow bridge, Bagley
wood and 'the forest-ground called Thessaly.' In the latter part
of the poem, Arnold finds a natural opening for his characteristic
pensive moralisings upon

> this strange disease of modern life,
> With its sick hurry, its divided aims,

when men are but 'half-believers' in their 'casual creeds'—as contrasted with days when 'life ran gaily as the sparkling Thames,'
and when it was still possible for an 'Oxford scholar poor' to
pass through them nursing 'the unconquerable hope' and 'clutch-
ing the inviolable shade.'

Several poems from the withdrawn volume of 1852 were reprinted in 1853; but only two or three of the more important ones
can be noticed here. The most elaborate, and the finest, of these
is *Tristram and Iseult*, a poem which seems to reveal the author
in a peculiar mood of hesitation. He is here exploring the shores
of old romance as if afraid of making a firm landing and of boldly
occupying the fair country that opens out before him. The very
frequency of his changes of metre in the poem produces an impression of uncertainty and of a shrinking from the full challenge
which his subject gave him. *Stanzas in Memory of the Author
of 'Obermann'* is one of those personal and reflective poems
which are characteristic of Matthew Arnold's work, and which
give us the most intimate revelations of his soul. It is strange to
find a comparatively obscure writer like Sénancour classified with
Goethe and Wordsworth as one of the three puissant spirits who, in
'the hopeless tangle of our age,' alone seemed to the poet to
'have attain'd to see their way[1].' But it was a somewhat morbid
interest, after all, that the poet felt in Sénancour—

> A fever in these pages burns'
> Beneath the calm they feign;
> A wounded human spirit turns,
> Here, on its bed of pain.

[1] See Arnold's note, appended to the poem.

What, however, in this first *Obermann* poem is of most import are the brief passages which speak of Goethe and Wordsworth. Its sequel, *Obermann Once More*—written many years afterwards—is, as a whole, a more thought-compelling poem, not so much because of what is said about Sénancour as of what is revealed of Arnold's own attitude towards the religious thought of his time. In *Memorial Verses*—another poem included in the 1853 volume— we have the poet's elegiac tribute to his greatest English master, Wordsworth, and, incidentally, memorable summaries of the gifts of Byron and Goethe. Whether the critical estimate of Wordsworth embodied in these verses is complete or just at all points may be a matter of dispute; but no one can refuse to join in their felicitous parting note,

> Keep fresh the grass upon his grave,
> O Rotha, with thy living wave!
> Sing him thy best! for few or none
> Hears thy voice right, now he is gone.

A Summer Night gives us as moving and as artistically perfect an expression of Arnold's philosophy of life as anything to be found in his poetry. None of his poems opens in a finer imaginative strain, and in no other is the transition from the human interest suggested by the 'moon-blanch'd street,' and its opposite vision of the headlands and the sea lit by 'the same bright, calm moon,' to the central meditative passages more skilfully and yet naturally contrived. After comparing, in one of these passages, those who escape from this world's prison with its 'unmeaning task-work' to the tempest-tossed helmsman who clings to his 'spar-strewn deck,'

> Still bent to make some port he knows not where,
> Still standing for some false, impossible shore,

he ends up with a magnificent affirmation of the power and steadfastness of nature, as

> A world above man's head, to let him see
> How boundless might his soul's horizons be[1].

The so-called 'second series' of poems, which Arnold published in 1855, included only one considerable new poem—*Balder Dead*, a work which the poet thought would 'consolidate the peculiar sort of reputation he got by *Sohrab and Rustum*[2].' This poem, slightly longer than *Sohrab*, is cast in the same Homeric vein, and

---

[1] Cf. with this closing passage the entire poem called *Self-Dependence*, first published in 1852.
[2] *Letters*, vol. I, p. 47.

written in equally excellent blank verse. But the subject fails, somehow, to grip the reader as powerfully as does that of the earlier poem[1]. To the year 1855 also belongs his next important poem, *Stanzas from the Grande Chartreuse*, which was published in the April number of *Fraser's Magazine*. These verses, in which Obermann again appears, are among the most pathetic of Arnold's personal 'confessions' in verse. Nowhere else does he give us a clearer, or a more poignant, articulation of his feelings as a solitary, and all but forlorn, wanderer from all familiar folds of faith than in the lines where, of the Carthusian 'brotherhood austere,'

> Not as their friend, or child, I speak!
> But as, on some far northern strand,
> Thinking of his own Gods, a Greek
> In pity and mournful awe might stand
> Before some fallen Runic stone—
> For both were faiths, and both are gone.
>
> Wandering between two worlds, one dead,
> The other powerless to be born,
> With nowhere yet to rest my head,
> Like these, on earth I wait forlorn.
> Their faith, my tears, the world deride—
> I come to shed them at their side.

In 1858, a year after his election to the Oxford chair of poetry, Arnold published *Merope, a Tragedy*—with an elaborate preface, of which the most permanently interesting part is an exposition, admirably clear and concise, of some of the cardinal principles of Greek tragic art. *Merope* was not reprinted and included in his own authorised canon of his poetical works until 1885. As a drama, it lacks life; as poetry, it is certainly inferior to *Empedocles*. The rimeless choruses, upon which Arnold bestowed much pains, may, as he tells us, have produced on 'his own feeling a similar impression to that produced on it by the rhythms of Greek choric poetry'; but they fall flat on an uninstructed ear and, despite their effort after correctness of structure, give a much less vivid impression of the general effect of Greek choric measures than does the 'relaxed form' which Arnold wishes Milton had not adopted in *Samson Agonistes*.

The *New Poems* of 1867 included several by which Matthew Arnold is now best remembered, but none which can be said to excel the best of his previous work. They are, nearly all, of an elegiac or meditative character, and repeat the old familiar

---

[1] It is significant that the author, while including *Sohrab and Rustum*, left this poem out of his own *Golden Treasury* selection of his poems published in 1878.

melancholy strain.   Like *The Scholar-Gipsy, Thyrsis* is both an
idyll of the Oxford country and a plaintive protest against the
discordant spectacle

> Of men contention-tost, of men who groan.

The landscape is pictured, once more, in lines as exquisite as those
of the earlier poem, while no passage in all Arnold's poetry surpasses in beauty the two stanzas which contrast the 'tempestuous
morn in early June,' with 'the high Midsummer pomps' under

> dreaming garden-trees,
> And the full moon, and the white evening-star.

Rugby Chapel, again, is another professedly elegiac poem, which
is as much concerned with 'the cloud of human destiny' as with
the memory of the poet's father.   Though *Rugby Chapel* is
charged with intense feeling, its rimeless verse has about it something hard and rhetorical, which is felt still more in *Heine's
Grave*.   As a purely elegiac poem, *A Southern Night*, in which
Arnold laments the death of his brother, surpasses all the others
in tenderness and depth of feeling, and is not inferior to them in
poetical expression.   *Westminster Abbey*—a noble elegy on his
father's biographer and his own life-long friend, dean Stanley—and
three other poems were the only efforts in verse Arnold attempted
after 1867.   Of these last three, the poem on his dead dachshund
'Geist' is one of the most beautiful things of its kind in the language.

'The criticism of Dryden,' says Johnson, 'was the criticism
of a poet'; with even greater justice it may be said that Matthew
Arnold's poetry was the poetry of a critic.   Although it is the
fashion to call him the best of our elegiac poets, and although
his verse consists mainly of short poems, we do not instinctively
think of him as primarily, or pre-eminently, a lyric poet.   There
is scarcely one poem by him which is felt to be an outburst of
unpremeditated, careless lyric rapture.   There is, doubtless, an
'emotion of the intellect,' which finds as glowing utterance in
lyric poetry as the emotion of the heart; but it does not touch
us in quite the same way.   And it is just because of our consciousness of the predominance of the intellect over the heart,
even in his simpler and more moving poems, that we miss the
thrill which all really passionate lyric poetry forces us to feel.
Requiescat, the Switzerland poems, *Dover Beach*—to name a few
of his best known shorter pieces—are all either too 'lucidly sad'
or too palpably meditative to be classed as pure lyrics.   His
'second thoughts,' running always on the riddle of this painful
earth, cloud his vision and stay his utterance.   When he turned to

poetry, Arnold—capable though he was of being gay and light-hearted enough in his prose—seemed to surrender himself to a melancholy apparently so bred in the bone as only to be explained as something constitutional. This it was that, most of all, froze the genial current of his poetic soul. His limitations, however, to whatever cause they may have been due, have not been altogether to his disadvantage, for few poets, at any time, have produced so much which is so uniformly excellent in style. Lucidity was what he aimed at, above all things—classical beauty and truth of phrase and image, suggesting always, in his own words, 'the pure lines of an Ionian horizon, the liquid clearness of an Ionian sky.' This studied effort after perfection of form accounts largely, though not altogether, for 'the quality of adhesiveness' which Sir Leslie Stephen found in Arnold's poetry. It is poetry which, as the same critic adds, 'learns itself by heart' in many places. But it could not do this, had it not, over and above this formal excellence, qualities that touch the heart and stir the feelings. Lovers of poetry less reticent and restrained than Arnold's in the expression of emotion, less concerned with spiritual doubts and discords, and more abandoned in its indulgence in the more facile forms of sentiment, may find his poems cold, unsympathetic, even repellent. But those who look for the more abiding elements of poetical charm and power can never remain insensible to the intensity of feeling, 'the sense of tears in mortal things,' the heroically austere temper and, above all, the feeling for nature and her chastening influences, which they will discover in all his best poems. In his view of nature, Matthew Arnold is not, as we have seen, quite Wordsworth's disciple. For Arnold, nature's 'secret was not joy, but peace.' He loved her in her quieter and more subdued moods; he preferred her silences to her many voices, moonlight to sunlight, the sea retreating from the 'moon-blanch'd land' with 'its melancholy, long, withdrawing roar,' to the sea in tumult and storm. The sea—'the unplumb'd, salt, estranging sea'—was, for him, the one element in which he discovered the deepest reflection of his own melancholy and sense of isolation. But, above everything, what he worshipped in nature was her steadfastness and calm, ever teaching the lesson of *Self-Dependence.*

> And with joy the stars perform their shining,
> And the sea its long moon-silver'd roll;
> For self-poised they live, nor pine with noting
> All the fever of some differing soul.

By a strange irony, it was the lot of a poet who found these mighty consolations in the life of nature to 'pine with noting' the fever of his own soul to such an extent as to mark him out among the poets of the Victorian age as the one who articulates more distinctly than any other the cry of the *maladie de siècle*—the 'doubts, disputes, distractions, fears' of an 'iron time.' He has no certain spiritual anodynes to prescribe for those who suffer from this sickness beyond a stoical recognition of the paramount claims of duty, and an effort to live 'self-poised,' like the powers of nature, until we feel our souls becoming vast like them. But, in spite of these counsels of fortitude, we find the poet himself often possessed by a wistful yearning to 'make for some impossible shore'—'agitated,' as he says of Marcus Aurelius, and 'stretching out his hands for something beyond—*tendentemque manus ripae ulterioris amore.*'

Matthew Arnold's prose writings, mainly, were the work of his middle and later years[1]. They deal with, practically, the entire fabric of English civilisation and culture in his day; and they are all directed by one clear and consistent critical purpose. That purpose was to 'cure the great vice of our intellect, manifesting itself in our incredible vagaries in literature, in art, in religion, in morals; namely, that it is *fantastic*, and wants *sanity*[2].'

The main body of his purely literary criticism, with the exception of a few scattered essays, is to be found in the lectures *On Translating Homer* (1861), and *The Study of Celtic Literature* (1867), and in the two volumes entitled *Essays in Criticism* (1865, 1889). The most notable of these books, as illustrating Arnold's literary ideals and preferences—his critical method may be equally well studied in the others—is, undoubtedly, the first series of *Essays in Criticism*. Its appearance, in 1865, was something of a literary sensation, by reason of its style, the novelty and confidence of its opinions and the wide and curious range of its subjects. No volume of critical essays had before appeared, in England at least, on a collection of subjects and authors so diverse as the literary influence of academies, pagan and medieval religious sentiment, a Persian passion-play, the Du Guérins, Joubert, Heine, Spinoza, Marcus Aurelius. And the first two essays, in particular,

---

[1] It is a pity that no complete edition of Arnold's prose works has yet been published. In a selection of his essays issued by the Oxford university press in 1914, 'five essays hitherto uncollected' were included, the most interesting of which are, perhaps, a review, reprinted from *Macmillan's Magazine* for February 1863, of Stanley's *Lectures on the Jewish Church* and a short article entitled *Obermann*, written in 1869.

[2] Preface to second edition of *Poems*, 1854.

struck a note of challenge to all the popular critics of the day.
They proclaimed the appearance of a paladin bent, above everything,
upon piercing the armour of self-sufficiency and 'provinciality,' in
which the average English 'authority in matters of taste' had been
accustomed to strut with much confidence. Here, for the first time,
we come across verbal weapons to be repeatedly used with devas-
tating effect in a lifelong campaign against the hosts of Philistia.
The famous nickname 'Philistine,' borrowed from Heine, makes its
first appearance in this book—to denote the 'strong, dogged, un-
enlightened opponent of the chosen people, of the children of light.'
We now first hear, also, of 'the provincial spirit,' 'the best that is
known and thought in the world,' 'the free play of the mind,'
'flexibility of intelligence'—afterwards to be identified with Plato's
εὐτραπελία[1]—'prose of the centre,' 'the modern spirit,' 'criticism
of life' and other phrases destined, by reiterated use, to become
familiar. Although the author's weapons were mainly of his own
making, his way of using them, his adroit and dexterous methods
of attack, had been learnt from France. French prose, for
Matthew Arnold, was the 'prose of the centre,' the nearest modern
equivalent to 'Attic prose,' and the two contemporary critics he
admired most were Sainte-Beuve and Renan. In purely literary
criticism, Sainte-Beuve is his chief model; but his methods in
other critical fields were largely the results of his reading of
Renan. As early as 1859, he speaks of Renan as one 'between
whose line of endeavour and my own I imagine there is considerable resemblance[2].' The two resembled each other not least
in the adoption of a style, *lenis, minimeque pertinax*—'sinuous,
easy, unpolemical'—very unlike the 'highly-charged, heavy-shotted
articles' of English newspaper critics[3].

Arnold's knowledge and appreciation of French prose were
wide and peculiarly sensitive, and stand in curious contrast to his
lack of enthusiasm for, if not indifference to, French poetry.
France, 'famed in all great arts, in none supreme,' appeared to him
to have achieved her most signal triumphs in prose, but his
partiality to French prose led him to some strange vagaries of
judgment in his estimates of individual writers. Sainte-Beuve and
Renan, no doubt, deserved the flattery he paid both by imitating
them, but he has given an exaggerated importance to such writers
as the Du Guérins, Joubert and Amiel.

---

[1] In 'A speech at Eton,' *Mixed Essays*.
[2] *Letters*, vol. I, p. 111.
[3] See his essay 'Numbers' in *Discourses in America*.

When we turn from these eccentric preferences to the main principles of his literary criticism, we find, in his definitions of them, at any rate, much that is incontrovertible and a little that is open to question. 'Disinterestedness,' detachment, he tells us, is the first requisite in a literary critic—'a disinterested endeavour to learn and propagate the best that is known and thought in the world.' With this goes 'knowledge'; and no English critic is adequately equipped who does not 'possess one great literature, at least, besides his own.' Criticism in England was altogether too provincial. Nothing quite like this had been stated in English before, and no critic, in his practice, made so sedulous an effort as Arnold to convince his countrymen of their insularity, and to persuade them to acquire an European outlook in literature and art. When he becomes a little more particular in his definitions and says that 'the end and aim of all *literature* is 'a criticism of life[1],' and, again, that '*poetry* is, at bottom, a criticism of life[2],' he provokes a debate which, at one time, was pursued with considerable spirit and some acerbity—especially, as Sir Leslie Stephen has put it, by critics who were 'unable to distinguish between an epigram and a philosophical dogma.'

While little fault can be found with his standards and ideals, as a critic of poetry, some of his methods lie open to easy and serious objection. Their defects are inherent in the very qualities that give charm and individuality to the best of his literary criticisms. None of his works exhibits so well both the strength and the weakness of his methods as *The Study of Celtic Literature*—one of the most delightful of his books, consisting of a number of Oxford lectures directly inspired by an essay by Renan[3]. In his excursions into the Celtic wonderland, Arnold lacked one of the chief qualifications which he desiderates in a critic—knowledge. At least, he had no knowledge of a single Celtic tongue; and, though he wanders into by-paths of ethnology and philology, he has to rely upon the learning of others for evidence in support of his brilliant generalisations. But, even those who do know something of the Celtic tongues are among the first to recognise these lectures as a triumph of the intuitional method in their instinctive seizure of the things that really matter in Celtic literature, and in their picturesque diagnosis of the Celtic genius. The 'intuitional' process, however, has its dangers, and the passages in which

---

[1] *Essays in Criticism*, vol. I, 'Joubert.'
[2] See, especially, Introduction to T. H. Ward's *English Poets*.
[3] 'The Poetry of the Celtic Races.'

Arnold traces the Celtic 'note' in Shakespeare, Byron, Keats, Macpherson and the rest are about as adventurous an example of skating on the thin ice of criticism as anything to be found in our literature.

The first two of *Essays in Criticism*, semi-polemical as they were in their motive, and creating, as they did, a considerable stir among the Philistines, seem to have opened Arnold's eyes to his opportunities as a social critic. He became conscious, by degrees, of having something like a 'mission' to his countrymen, who soon came to speak of him as, pre-eminently, the 'apostle of culture' in the England of his day. It was the effect of *Essays in Criticism* that led to the composition by instalments, between 1867 and 1869, of the book ultimately called *Culture and Anarchy*, which may be termed his central work in criticism other than literary, containing, as it does, the quintessence of what he had already written, and of much that he was again to write, upon English life and character. Memorable phrases which he had already used are here effectively repeated and expanded; and new phrases and catch-words, with the same quality of 'adhesiveness' as the old, are paraded with the same imperturbable iteration. Some of these phrases, such as 'sweetness and light' and 'the Dissidence of Dissent,' are borrowed from wellknown sources, while other things, like the description of English public life as a 'Thyestean banquet of claptrap,' and the definition of 'the two points of influence' between which our world moves as 'Hebraism and Hellenism,' are the author's own. *Culture and Anarchy* is, if not a great, an undoubtedly stimulating, book, still capable of exerting a strong influence on young minds. In 1871, Arnold published another series of essays in social criticism under the title *Friendship's Garland*, perhaps the most mischievously amusing of his books.

It was, undoubtedly, the impression made in certain quarters by *Culture and Anarchy* that led Arnold into the somewhat perilous field of theological and religious criticism—in which his chief works are *St Paul and Protestantism* (1870), *Literature and Dogma* (1873), *God and the Bible* (1875) and *Last Essays on Church and Religion* (1877). Little need be said of these works here, constituting as they do, as a whole, the least valuable and enduring group of his prose writings. The most popular of them in its day was *Literature and Dogma*, a work bearing obvious marks of the influence of Renan, and an elaborate disquisition upon a text enunciated in *Culture and Anarchy*—'No man, who knows nothing else, knows even his own Bible.' The frequent flippancy, not to say levity, of tone which characterises his treatment of sacred subjects in this and other books, together with his too exclusively literary and 'intuitional' critical methods in dealing with problems of theological scholarship, aroused a good deal of resentment. No careful and dispassionate reader of his religious writings can, however, have any question about the sincerity and the seriousness of Arnold's motives. Some of his catch-phrases obtained a wide currency, and are, perhaps, destined to live among the most famous things of their kind coined by him. The definition of God as 'a stream of tendency, not ourselves, which makes for righteousness,' of religion as 'morality touched by emotion,' of ἐπιείκεια as 'the sweet reasonableness' of Jesus—these and other phrases have an epigrammatic quality which will prevent their being soon forgotten.

Sufficient has been incidentally said about the characteristics of Matthew Arnold's prose style to make it unnecessary to attempt here any elaborate estimate of its qualities as a whole. 'The needful qualities of a fit prose,' he himself has said, in a familiar sentence, 'are regularity, uniformity, precision, balance.' All these things, it may be said, Arnold's own prose has as markedly as that of any other modern English writer. The one pre-eminent virtue of his prose, as of his verse, style is its lucidity —we never miss, or doubt, his meaning. But the qualities which he enumerates—and clearness—may be found in prose styles which have little or no distinction; and distinction, in the strict sense of the word, Matthew Arnold's has. It is an unmistakably individual style, and, in spite of its obvious mannerisms and occasional affectations, is extremely difficult of imitation. It is a style which is not free from some caprices that 'prose of the centre' would avoid, but which, at its best, is about as near a fulfilment as is humanly possible of his own ideals of order and lucidity, with the added graces of ease, elegance and a grave rhythmical movement, the effect of which, like that of the best music, can be felt but never adequately described.

Their common connection with Rugby and Oxford, and the imperishable commemoration of their Oxford friendship in *Thyrsis*, inseparably link with the name of Matthew Arnold that of Arthur Hugh Clough. Clough was Arnold's senior by some four years, and their friendship was founded on a deep mutual respect for each other's character and intellectual powers.

'You and Clough,' Arnold writes to his sister Fanny in 1859[1], 'are, I believe, the two people I in my heart care most to please by what I write'; and, at the time of Clough's death, he speaks to his mother of his loss as one 'which I shall feel more and more as time goes on, for he is one of the few people who ever made a deep impression upon me[2].' The most elaborate tribute paid to him in *Last Words on Translating Homer* is well known : the 'admirable Homeric qualities' of *The Bothie* are there duly noted ; 'but that in him of which I think oftenest is the Homeric simplicity of his literary life.' The impression which Clough made on Arnold was largely due to the fact that they were both in the same 'movement of mind' in the England of their day. In any comparison, however, between Arnold and Clough, it should be remembered that, probably, the former has given us all the poetry that was in him, while Clough died young.

Arthur Hugh Clough was born in Liverpool on 1 January 1819. In 1828, he was put to school at Chester, whence he shortly afterwards went to Rugby. At Rugby, Clough became Thomas Arnold's ideal pupil, and he left the school, in 1837, with a great reputation and a Balliol scholarship. Like Matthew Arnold after him, he only took a second class in the Oxford schools, but so much was thought of him that he was soon made a fellow and tutor of Oriel. He resigned both fellowship and tutorship in 1848 because of his inability to subscribe any longer to the faith of the church of England. Few of the remarkable group of Oxford men who found themselves 'contention-tost' in the welter of the tractarian agitation were so dominated by a single-minded endeavour after truth as Clough. Most of his poetry is the record of the spiritual and intellectual struggles into which he was plunged by the religious unrest of the time. In 1854, he married Blanche Smith, who was a first cousin of Florence Nightingale; and, in the work of the latter during and after the Crimean war, Clough took the liveliest interest. His health, never at any time very strong, began to give way in 1859. After long and weary wanderings on the continent, he died at Florence on 13 November 1861.

The record of Clough's literary activity is mainly concerned with poetry ; he wrote but little prose of permanent value and interest, and that only in the form of scattered articles, which his wife collected and reprinted long after his death. His first poem to appear in print was the 'long-vacation pastoral' in hexameters,

---

[1] *Letters*, vol. I, p. 102.   [2] *Letters*, vol. I, p. 152.

The Bothie of Toper-na-Fuosich[1], composed immediately after he left Oxford—the liberation song of an emancipated soul. He had already written short poems, and these were, soon afterwards, published (1849), first in a volume called *Ambarvalia*, the joint production of Clough and his friend Thomas Burbridge, and, subsequently, in a separate form. These poems include several of the best of his shorter lyrics, such as *Qua Cursum Ventus* (recording the break of his friendship with W. G. Ward), *Qui Laborat Orat, The New Sinai, The Questioning Spirit, Sic Itur, Duty, The Higher Courage*—all poems which bear the marks of the spiritual conflict of his Oxford days.

During a visit to Rome in 1849, Clough composed his second hexameter poem, *Amours de Voyage*, and, in the following year, at Venice, he began *Dipsychus*. This latter poem, like *Mari Magno*—a series of 'modern' tales introduced and told in a manner reminiscent of Chaucer—'was not published,' as we are told in the collected edition of the poet's works, 'during the author's lifetime, and should not be regarded as having received his finishing touches.' The works recorded here, together with a number of other lyrics—of which the group entitled *Songs in Absence* are the most notable—and a few satirical and reflective pieces, constitute the sum of Clough's poetical productions.

Of few poets can it be said more positively than of Clough that his appeal is, and always must be, to a select and limited audience. His poetry can never be popular, not only because much of it is too introspective, but because the form of two of his most elaborate poems will remain a stumbling-block to the average English reader of poetry. 'Carmen Hexametrum,' says Ascham in *The Scholemaster*, 'doth rather trotte and hoble than runne smoothly in our English tong,' and his words are still true in spite of nineteenth-century efforts to establish that measure in our common prosody. Neither Matthew Arnold's advocacy of it as the fit medium of Homeric translation, nor Bagehot's description of it, in discussing Clough's hexameters, as 'perhaps the most flexible of English metres,' disposes of the hard fact that, to quote again from Bagehot, no 'consummate poem of great length and sustained dignity' has ever yet been written in it in English. To say, as one of his admirers does, that Clough's hexameters 'are unlike those of any other writer in any language and better than those of any other English author,' and that

---

[1] The more familiar title *The Bothie of Tober-na-Vuolich* was given to it afterwards.

he had in his mind a very subtle and consistent conception of the harmonies of the measure, is but to emphasise the charge that the poet was remote and required a specially instructed class of readers to appreciate him. But it will not do to dismiss him, as Swinburne, markedly appreciative of Arnold's Attic grace, did, as being no poet at all. In actual achievement, he is, indeed, but one of 'the inheritors of unfulfilled renown.' Time conquered him before he attained to full clearness of poetic utterance.

> When we have proved, each on his course alone,
> The wider world, and learnt what's now unknown,
> Have made life clear, and worked out each a way,
> We'll meet again,—we shall have much to say,

he sings in one of his most touching lyrics. But 'the future day,' on which he was to fulfil this covenant with readers of his poetry, never dawned for him. His later poems, however—particularly *Mari Magno*—show that he was gradually feeling after a mellower and a richer note. His brief married life was beginning to enlarge and to deepen his experience, and, had he lived to write more, his poetry would have embodied a more profound 'criticism of life.' It would certainly have become less self-centred and less preoccupied with the questionings and doubts of the solitary spirit.

These doubts and questionings form the substance of what was probably his most ambitious work, *Dipsychus*—a poem consisting of a series of dialogues between the poet himself and an attendant spirit, who is an obvious, though distant, relative of Goethe's Mephistopheles. Clough, like Arnold, was largely a disciple of Goethe; and the influence of *Hermann und Dorothea* is to be clearly seen both in the form and in the thought of *The Bothie*. But, both *The Bothie* and *Dipsychus* reflect far more of the intellectual atmosphere of Oxford and of the free open-air life of England than they do of either the art or the philosophy of Goethe. The best expression of Clough's own character and genius is, undoubtedly, to be found in the 'long-vacation pastoral.' The poet's humour tempers the hexameter with mercy, and gives it, in places, a semi-burlesque effect which is not without suggestion of the best uses to which the measure may be turned in English. The poem, however, is thoroughly serious in its main drift and purpose, dealing, as it does, with social problems which were then being eagerly discussed by the more thoughtful minds of the time, and, particularly, with the ideal of true womanhood. That ideal Clough himself finds in

Meanest utilities seized as occasions to grace and embellish;

and the whole poem is a protest against the conception of feminine grace and embellishment as consisting of vulgar decoration and intellectual insipidity. But the most charming features of *The Bothie* are its delightful pictures of nature, which show how fresh was Clough's enjoyment of natural scenery, and how deep and intimate was his communion with the very soul of the Highlands. Many discerning readers express a preference for some of Clough's shorter lyrics to everything else he wrote, and they are probably right. He wrote nothing so likely to keep his name and memory alive as the best of *Songs in Absence.* A host of readers, who know little else of his work, know him by *Say not the struggle nought availeth*; and, during the period of the greatest national stress ever endured by his countrymen, few lines have been more frequently quoted for consolation and hope than

> For, while the tired waves, vainly breaking,
> Seem here no painful inch to gain,
> Far back, through creeks and inlets making,
> Comes silent, flooding in, the main.

Although James Thomson, second poet of the name, belongs to no school, and defies classification with any poetic fraternity, his place in literary history is, perhaps, most appropriately fixed in proximity to the poets of doubt and of 'the sceptical reaction.' But he stands quite apart from his companions both in personal character and temperament and in the life-long struggle which he was condemned to wage with what might well seem to him a malign fate. In the poetry of the others, even the depths of their despair are not without gleams of something divine. But all that is most authentic and arresting in the poetry of James Thomson is absolutely 'without hope, and without God in the world.' It is the poetry of sheer, overmastering, inexorable despair—a passionate, and almost fierce, declaration of faith in pessimism as the only true philosophy of life. Here we have one who unequivocally affirms

> that every struggle brings defeat
> Because Fate holds no prize to crown success;
> That all the oracles are dumb or cheat
> Because they have no secret to express;
> That none can pierce the vast black veil uncertain
> Because there is no light behind the curtain;
> That all is vanity and nothingness.

The City of Dreadful Night, from which these lines are taken, is far from being all that is of account in the poetry of Thomson; he could strike other, and more cheerful, chords. But this poem is so

distinctively individual and sincere an utterance springing from
the depths of the poet's own feelings and experience, and is so
powerful and original a thing in itself, as to make it the one
supreme achievement in verse by which Thomson is, and probably
will be, remembered.

James Thomson was the son of a sailor and was born at Port
Glasgow in November 1834. While he was quite a small boy, a
sudden breakdown in his father's health brought the family into
very low circumstances, and forced them to seek better fortune in
London. At the age of nine, he was admitted to the Royal Cale-
donian Asylum, where he spent probably the happiest eight years of
his life. In 1850, he entered the military training school at Chelsea,
with a view to qualifying as an army schoolmaster. In 1851, he
was appointed teacher in a garrison station at Ballincollig, a village
near Cork, and here he met two persons who had no small influence
upon his subsequent career. One was a young girl, Matilda Weller
by name, for whom the poet formed a passionate attachment, and
whose early death appears to have left him wandering, on his own
testimony, in

a waste of arid woe
Never refreshed by tears.

At Ballincollig, he also met Charles Bradlaugh, then a trooper in a
regiment of dragoons, and it was mainly under his tuition that
Thomson became an atheist, and, subsequently, cast in his lot with
a small but intrepid London band of free-thinking journalists.
For several years during his chequered career as a journalist in
London, Thomson found in Bradlaugh a steadfast friend and bene-
factor. He was for some length of time an inmate of Bradlaugh's
household, and a constant contributor of prose and verse to *The
National Reformer*, in the columns of which *The City of Dreadful
Night* made its first appearance in 1874. Thomson's career in the
army ceased in 1862, when he was dismissed because of a somewhat
trivial act of insubordination. He afterwards became a solicitor's
clerk, then secretary to a mining company in America, a war correspondent in Spain, and, finally, a journalistic free-lance in London.
His later years, darkened by poverty and ill-health, largely due to
insomnia and intemperate habits, were spent in London, and he
died at University college hospital, under distressing circumstances, in June 1882.

Thomson was a man of genius who, in the blunt common phrase,
'went wrong.' Weakness of will, and some insidious inherited
malady, accounted much for his misfortunes than any vicious

propensity or deliberately perverse conduct. All his friends bear testimony to the genial and sunny side of his character; kind, courteous and chivalrous in his ways, he won the love and the esteem of those who came into closest contact with him. 'A man,' writes his editor and biographer, Bertram Dobell, 'could hardly wish for a better companion than he was; while as regards women there was a charm about him which invariably made them his friends and admirers.' But 'Melancholy, of... blackest midnight born,' marked him for her own, and, under her baleful influence, he fell a helpless victim to intemperance and disease. This is the first consideration to be taken into account in any judgment of Thomson's poetry. *The City of Dreadful Night*, he wrote to George Eliot, 'was the outcome of much sleepless hypochondria.' It is not the utterance of a sane mind; but, whatever one may think about the sanity of the poem, nobody can fail to recognise, and feel, its sincerity. Human life, on Thomson's experience and interpretation of it, was one long 'all-disastrous fight' against a blind destiny. The infinite pathos and the pain of the self-sacrificing souls who, throughout the ages, had 'striven to alleviate our lot,' did not seem to him to have 'availed much against the primal curse of our existence.'

It is strange to find that, of all English poets, the one who influenced this latter-day prophet of despair most was he who sang of the indomitable hope that

> creates
> From its own wreck the thing it contemplates.

Next to him, among his literary favourites, came, perhaps, Heine, many of whose lyrics he has finely translated, and the arch-optimist Browning. Thomson's admiration for Shelley is indicated by the pseudonym 'Bysshe Vanolis'—the latter part being an anagram of Novalis, another of his chosen authors—under which, using generally only the initials B. V., he wrote many of his contributions to *The National Reformer* and other periodicals. Of both Browning and Shelley he wrote some admirable prose critiques, which, with other things of the kind, attest not only Thomson's catholicity of literary taste and sympathy but his acute insight and sound judgment as a critic. His studies of Ben Jonson, Blake, John Wilson, James Hogg, Walt Whitman, Heine and others —many of them originally written for *The Secularist,* and for that most intellectual of tobacconists' advertising journals, *Cope's Tobacco Plant*—constitute a budget of prose criticism which even the leading lights of the greater reviews might have been proud to own. Nor is it fair to judge the range and variety of his poetical powers by *The City of Dreadful Night* alone. His collected poems form, in mere substance and extent, a very considerable literary legacy, and prove that he could sing in many a key. The two separate volumes of poetry published just before his death—*The City of Dreadful Night and other Poems* (1880) and *Vane's Story and other Poems* (1881 [1880])—contain nearly all his best work. In these volumes, poems like *To Our Ladies of Death*, a finely conceived little phantasy 'suggested,' in the author's words, 'by the sublime sisterhood of Our Ladies of Sorrow' in the *Suspiria de Profundis* of De Quincey; an oriental tale called *Weddah and Om-el-Bonain*; *Vane's Story*, a personal confession, well exhibit his range of interests and his skill as a versifier. Among poems otherwise published should be noted his tribute to Shelley (1861), and *Insomnia* (1882)—a fitting pendant, in its terror and gloom, to *The City of Dreadful Night*. As a lyric poet, Thomson ranks high, and every thoughtful reader of his lighter verse will have little patience with those who assert that the most depressing of his poems is his only title to literary distinction. Two poems, in particular, have often, and deservedly, been singled out as delightful examples of his lighter vein—*Sunday up the River* and *Sunday at Hampstead*, both 'genuine idyls of the people,' as his friend, Philip Bourke Marston called them, 'charged with brightness and healthy joy in living.' The weakness of most of Thomson's verse, with all his metrical skill and his astonishing command of rime, lies in its carelessness, not to say slovenliness, of execution, and in a constant tendency to fall into a hard and glittering rhetoric, reminiscent of Byron at his worst. When all is told, however, *The City of Dreadful Night*, with its 'inspissated gloom,' inevitably remains his most haunting and powerful production—a poetical monument well nigh unique in its sombre and awe-inspiring splendour. It is a poem that takes no account of such pleasant theories as Matthew Arnold's, that 'the right art is that alone which creates the highest enjoyment.' But he would be a bold man who denied the right of utterance, even in poetry, to feelings so intense and real as those which tore and tortured the heart of James Thomson.

CHAPTER V

THE ROSSETTIS, WILLIAM MORRIS, SWINBURNE
AND OTHERS

I

In 1848, a number of young artists and men of letters, united in opposition to conventional systems of artistic teaching, formed themselves into a circle to which they gave the name 'the pre-Raphaelite brotherhood.' The painters William Holman Hunt and John Everett Millais, who were originally responsible for the idea, were joined by five others. Of these, Dante Gabriel, originally called Gabriel Charles Dante, Rossetti, then in his twentieth year, was best fitted to express the aims of the coterie by his possession of the double gift of poetry and painting and by the power of a singularly masterful personality. Thomas Woolner, sculptor and poet, William Michael Rossetti, the younger brother of Gabriel, Frederick George Stephens and James Collinson were the remaining four. To these might be added the names of several sympathisers who, though in close communion with the brotherhood, were not of it. Among elder men, Ford Madox Brown became one of the most thorough exponents of its aims in painting. William Bell Scott and Coventry Patmore gave it their help, and it found an ardent champion in Ruskin, who used his persuasive eloquence to define pre-Raphaelism and vindicate it against the charges of mere imitation and relapse into medievalism.

The term 'pre-Raphaelite' implied merely a kinship of method with artists whose direct influence upon the work of the brotherhood was relatively small. Rossetti, though of Italian parentage and closely acquainted with Italian literature, was a Londoner born and bred, who had no first-hand knowledge of Italian art in its native country. Of him and his friends, Ruskin said that they 'imitate no pictures : they paint from nature only.' Their passion for rendering nature as she is, in obedience to their sense of truth, was instinctive : it was pre-Raphaelite only in so far as their practice found authority in the fidelity to nature of the later medieval painters, which was abandoned by the followers of Raffaelle. When, on 1 January 1850, the first number of *The Germ: Thoughts towards Nature in Poetry, Literature and Art* was published, the brotherhood formulated its artistic creed, in a manifesto printed on the cover of the magazine, as ' an entire adherence to the simplicity of art.' The contents illustrated a strict obedience to this principle. Graphic art was represented only by Holman Hunt's etching in illustration of Woolner's poems *My Beautiful Lady* and *Of my Lady in Death*; but Rossetti's poem *My Sister's Sleep*, afterwards subjected to much revision and alteration, successfully combined realistic description with pictorial effect, and his mystical prose narrative *Hand and Soul* gave evidence of his understanding of the spirit of the painters in whose work he found the closest response to his own ideals.

A creed held so earnestly as that of the pre-Raphaelite brotherhood easily lends itself to over-serious expression. Sonnets and lyrics, interspersed with didactic essays and laboured critiques, do not suffice as the material of a successful periodical; and the poetry of *The Germ* was too novel, its prose too conscientious, to attract general admiration. In the third number, its title was changed to *Art and Poetry: being Thoughts towards Nature*, and it was announced as 'conducted principally by artists.' After the fourth number, it ceased to appear. Apart from Rossetti's *Hand and Soul*, the style of which is remarkably mature and full of the romantic imagination and depth of colour noticeable in his paintings, the prose of *The Germ* is almost negligible. Its verse is by no means of equal value, and some of it was experimental work by persons of no special poetic talent. The eminence of some of its promoters and contributors is enough to give it historical value as an attempt to apply an extremely rigid canon to varying forms of art. But its literary importance is almost entirely due to the eleven poems by Rossetti himself and the seven lyrics by his sister Christina, two years his junior, which it contained. In the case of Rossetti, *My Sister's Sleep* was written in close adherence to the truth of detail demanded by the pre-Raphaelite creed. The subject, however, the peaceful death of a girl at midnight on Christmas eve, amid a quiet broken only by common sounds and the striking of the church clock, while the scene outside is bathed in cold moonlight, is invested with the mysticism and romance which were an inalienable part of Rossetti's thought. Conversely, *The Blessed Damozel*, the first version of which appeared in the second number of *The Germ*, applies realistic touches to a subject which is primarily mystical and romantic. His remaining contributions to *The Germ* were chiefly reminiscences of a tour with Holman Hunt in Belgium, and included six sonnets on pictures by Memling and other painters. *Pax Vobis*, now called *World's Worth*, written in the church of Saint-Bavon at Ghent, indicates, like the later *Ave*, Rossetti's sensitiveness to the charm of ritual and historical doctrine from which art has derived much of its highest inspiration.

During the ten years that followed the publication of *The Germ*, Rossetti published little poetry, devoting himself chiefly to painting. It was about 1850 that he met the beautiful Elizabeth Eleanor Siddal, who permanently inspired his painting and poetry alike. They became engaged to be married ; but, owing to want of money and to Miss Siddal's weak health, their marriage did not take place till 1860. In 1861, Rossetti published his first volume, *The Early Italian Poets*, rearranged, at a later date, under the title *Dante and his Circle*. This was a series of translations, including a prose version of *La Vita Nuova*, from Dante and his thirteenth-century precursors and from his friends and contemporaries. Meanwhile, Rossetti had contributed to *The Oxford and Cambridge Magazine* in 1856 three poems, *The Burden of Nineveh*, a new version of *The Blessed Damozel* and *The Staff and Scrip*. Of his influence over Morris and the other contributors to this publication more will be said later. Other poems written during this period were copied into a manuscript book, which, when his wife died in 1862, was buried with her. He died at Birchington near Margate on 9 April 1882 and was buried in the churchyard of the parish church.

Poems by D. G. Rossetti, his first volume of strictly original poetry, was published in 1870. Most of the contents of this book, which included some of the sonnet-sequence afterwards called *The House of Life*, had lain undisturbed in his wife's grave in Highgate cemetery since 1862, and it was with great difficulty that he was persuaded to consent to their disinterment, and the publication of pieces which were known only in oral versions. *Ballads and Sonnets* in 1881 completed *The House of Life*, and, among other poems, added *Rose Mary*, *The White Ship* and *The King's Tragedy* to his work. The volume of his verse, even when his translations are added to it, is comparatively small, and his productiveness was restrained by fastidious habits of revision, by which the text of whole poems such as *The Blessed Damozel* was materially altered.

The influences which formed Rossetti's style were complex. The elements of romance and mysticism in his nature were too strong to be curbed by the preciseness of delineation which his pre-Raphaelite creed required. Reference has already been made to the conflict between natural inclination and artistic principle in *My Sister's Sleep* and *The Blessed Damozel*. The setting of *The Blessed Damozel*, 'the rampart of God's house' over which the immortal maiden, in her longing for the lover whom she has left on earth, leans down towards 'the tides of day and night,' transcends the power of realistic narrative. For the contrast between 'the fixed place of Heaven' and the planets in time and space, for the procession of souls 'mounting up to God,' for the fluttering of the moon in the gulf below the golden rampart, simile has to be invoked. The boldness of imagination which likens the moon in space to 'a curled feather' comes dangerously near grotesqueness, so material is the image employed to define an object of transcendental vision. On the other hand, the comparison of the revolving earth to a 'fretful midge' is a master-stroke of daring; that of the mounting souls to 'thin flames' is absolutely unforced; and the phrase in which the Blessed Damozel sees

Time like a pulse shake fierce
Through all the worlds

is a triumphant attempt to figure forth the indescribable, which was kept without alteration through all the versions of the poem. In the later stanzas, which celebrate the joys of paradise, details are particularised with a clearness of sense and fullness of melody which give to every word a visible and audible value; but the power and beauty of the poet's work are at their height, not in the even flow of the rapture in which he translates heavenly pleasures into earthly terms, but in the occasional sublimity of the opening visions which defy direct description.

The Blessed Damozel is without a counterpart in English poetry; for the ecstasy of such poems as Crashaw's *Hymn to the Name and Honor of...Sainte Teresa* and *The Flaming Heart*, in which sensuous imagery is used to express celestial delight, is founded upon a definitely religious enthusiasm. Rossetti, on the other hand, although brought up in a religious atmosphere, and retaining a deep reverence for Christian tradition, regarded religion primarily from an aesthetic point of view. He was a mystic; but his mysticism did not take the form of a spiritual exaltation to which the beauty of earth is subordinate: it was a perception of the undefinable unearthly quality which adds an attraction to

earthly beauty, supplying, as it does, a glimpse of things distant
and unattainable. In this respect, the poet to whom he was most
nearly akin was Keats, whose sense of beauty of form and colour
he shared to the full. The influence of Keats is felt in many ways
in the poetry of the nineteenth century; but his profuseness of
detail appealed to no poets so thoroughly as to those whose
sympathies had been attracted by pre-Raphaelite doctrine. Such
poems as *The Eve of St Agnes* were the immediate ancestors of
the poetry of *The Germ.* The wild night through which Porphyro
came across the moors, the throbbing music, the carven angels on
the cornice, the moonbeams shining through the stained windows,
the wind-shaken arras in the hall, are described by Keats with an
accuracy and a sensuous appreciation of every detail which makes
the whole scene present to the reader, but, also, with an added
mystery which stimulates his sense of the romantic and unfamiliar.
Rossetti, however, was not successful in combining the magic
element with the purely descriptive side of his art in this way.
Powerfully affected as he was by Keats's methods of description,
his strength as it developed did not lie in informing old-world
stories of love and passion with a heightened charm of romance.
In *The Bride's Prelude,* an unfinished poem upon a singularly
painful theme, realistic description is used with a completeness
which excludes all mystery. The contrast between the glare of
the hot summer day without, and the half-darkness of the room in
which the bride and her sister await the wedding, the fitful sounds
breaking the silence amid which Aloÿse falters out her secret
to the horror-stricken Amelotte, are incidents which, felt and
pictured with a vivid intensity, stand out in relief from the
surface of a somewhat prolix story, of whose weaknesses Rossetti
himself became conscious as he proceeded. His imagination
needed a stimulus from the supernatural for complete success in
narrative. It was quickened by ballad-poetry and its tales of
witchcraft, love-philtres and such accessories of tragedy. The
directness and simplicity of the ballad were not within the range
of his genius, of which the love of ornament was an essential
quality ; but he achieved something of its swiftness and vigour in
The White Ship and *The King's Tragedy.* Although the supernatural plays no direct part in the story of *The White Ship,* the
fate which presides over the action is clearly expressed by the
thrice repeated stanza at the beginning, middle and end of the
poem, with its double refrain, a comment upon the insecurity of
earthly power. *The King's Tragedy,* on the other hand, is full of

sinister and foreboding incident to herald the fatal climax. Twice, by 'the Scotish Sea' and in the Charterhouse at Perth, the spae-wife warns the king of her recurring vision of the shroud that gradually envelops his phantom form, and, as the tragedy nears its consummation, the moonlit shield of Scotland in the window pane is blackened by an obscuring cloud.

Rossetti's highest achievements in giving dramatic effect to the blending of romantic narrative with supernatural atmosphere are *Sister Helen*, one of his earlier poems, and *Rose Mary*, which belongs to his later work. The subjects are, to some extent, complementary. In *Sister Helen*, the woman who works out her revenge by destroying the waxen image of her lover dooms her soul by her own act. In *Rose Mary*, the centre of the poem is the magic beryl into which the heroine's sin admits a band of evil spirits. Her resolute breaking of the beryl and the death of her body free her soul from destruction. The tale of *Sister Helen* is suggested rather than told. Each of the forty-two stanzas adheres to a rigid plan. The innocent questions of the little brother who looks out into the frosty night, gathering fear as each suppliant for the life of Keith of Ewern proffers his vain request beneath the windows of the gallery, are answered by the inexorable words of the sister, intent upon her false lover's doom ; while the wailing refrain, 'O Mother, Mary Mother,' echoing her words and thoughts with variations of hopeless pity, is the lament of an unearthly chorus awake to the catastrophe and powerless to avert it. Rossetti's use of the refrain is not here, as it is in *Troy Town* and *Eden Bower*, a mere metrical artifice: it is the crowning feature of the piece, and the highly artificial structure of the stanza is bent with entire success to the representation of tragic passion. In *Rose Mary*, the marvellous element becomes the subject of direct narrative. The outlines of the picture are less distinct : the imagination is left to fill in much that defies the power of words, and the story proceeds with a shadowy movement like that of the fire-spirits who, gyrating within the beryl-stone, end the first and second parts of the poem with songs of melancholy triumph, circling in a mazy rhythm linked by echoing rimes, and, cast out of their stronghold, close the third part with a hymn of anguish. As in Rossetti's later masterpieces of painting and in his short poem *The Card-Dealer*, so in *Rose Mary*, his interest in the mystical side of his composition leads to some obscurity of detail and meaning and is the very antithesis of his early preRaphaelite manner.

The chief qualities of Rossetti's narrative verse are pictorial and dramatic. The impressions which it conveys are most powerful when they act immediately upon the senses. While his language is often simple and vigorous, as in *The White Ship*, its vigour and simplicity are carefully meditated. His fertility in melodious phrase, as in *The Blessed Damozel* and *The Staff and Scrip*, lulls the reader in the enchantment of music and colour, and his strains frequently have a 'dying fall' which invests some of his lyrics, such as *The Stream's Secret* and *Love's Nocturn*, with a positive languor of sound. While, however, sensuous and decorative instincts play a large part in his poetry, and its dramatic effects depend largely upon circumstances remote from ordinary life, it cannot be judged on these counts alone. His life was passed in a world of imagination : its material limits were narrow and the circle of his friends was restricted. In spite of his up-bringing as the son of an Italian patriot, he had none of that political enthusiasm which often kindles the highest poetry. Of contemporary poets, Browning had the strongest influence upon him, exercised chiefly on the side of that spontaneous lyric beauty which led the young Rossetti to make a manuscript copy of *Pauline* for his own use. The monologues, *A Last Confession* and *Jenny*, in which he chose subjects from the life of his own day, exhibit something of Browning's influence. *A Last Confession*, which embodies a sombre tragedy, was written in blank verse full of vivid and beautiful description ; but its great merit is the inset lyric, which, written in Italian and translated into English by Rossetti himself with a skill recalling his earlier translations from Italian poets, gained enthusiastic praise from so good a judge of poetry as Swinburne. *Jenny*, conceived in a reflective mood and worked out with pre-Raphaelite attention to detail, is the one poem in which he showed himself alive to the pity and pathos of everyday life. Its subject gave rise to some unjust criticism on the part of those who regarded Rossetti as the master of the 'fleshly' school of poetry. No fair-minded critic, however fastidious, could take exception to the poet's moral attitude and his appreciation of the pathetic aspect of his theme; but the situation of the speaker of the monologue is one with which moral reflection is seldom associated.

If the greatest function of poetry is its power to interpret the permanent yet ever new phases of human thought and emotion, Rossetti was too enchained by material beauty to be in constant touch with the highest objects of verse. But, in the sonnets of

The House of Life, the record of the spiritual experience which transfigured his whole career from 1850 to his death, the exquisite craftsmanship that wrought music out of earthly form and colour was applied to a more abstract use. The sequence is a sequence only in name, for no connected story, such as ingenious historians endeavour to weave into Elizabethan sonnet-books, can be made out of it : each sonnet is, in Rossetti's phrase, a 'moment's monument,' numbering high tides of rapture and regret, whose sum is the impelling force of the poet's inner life. The rhythm and phraseology are moulded, to a great extent, by Rossetti's early practice in the translation of Italian sonnets and *canzoni*, which imparted an occasional archaism and mannered diction to all his work; nor could any English sonneteer whose theme was the passion of love be free from some debt to Shakespeare and the Elizabethans generally. But Rossetti's familiarity with Italian models brings *The House of Life* into competition with his sixteenth- and seventeenth-century precursors. His imagery and personifications of abstract qualities are not borrowed at second-hand, but come direct from the fountain-head of sonnet-poetry. The sequence has the further virtue that its theme is spontaneous and personal. The variations upon it are meditated and elaborate, but they are not embroideries upon an artificial groundwork or masterly simulations of passion, like those which were a second nature to poets during the vogue of the sonnet. It was characteristic of Rossetti that concrete manifestations of love should play a large part in his thought, and his warmth of expression in certain passages now removed from the collection was the chief object of the notorious attack by Robert Buchanan, writing under a pseudonym, to which Swinburne returned a scathing answer. But the keynote of his love-poetry, which is heard again in the dactylic measures of *The Song of the Bower*, is the union of the body and the soul, in which the impulses of the one are the outward symbol of the hidden emotions of the other. Throughout the series, Rossetti's mystical view of life asserts itself more exclusively than in any of his other poems, and the second part of it is a dreamland of thought through which the story of his loss is but vaguely implied. The visions which, for a time, are concentrated in one bodily shape retain their power after that shape has yielded to change and fate, and death itself at last is hailed with calmness as the child of life, surviving love and song and art and bringing ultimate consolation.

The work of Rossetti as a translator is hardly less remarkable than his original poetry. It is not confined to one language, and perhaps the most striking example of his power of transmuting the melody of one tongue into another is his version of Villon's *Ballade des Dames du temps jadis*. Italian, however, was as much his native language as English. His father had won distinction as a commentator on Dante, and one of his sisters, Maria Francesca, wrote a popular exposition of Dante which is still justly valued. His appreciation of the subtleties of English melody enabled him to present the more ductile cadences of Italian poetry in an approximately literal English form, full of softness and grace. It is curious that his English poem *Dante at Verona*, though it has a dignity which befits its subject, is frigid when compared with his other original compositions of equal importance. Dealing directly with Dante's own work, he translated his sonnets with the warmest sympathy and turned *La Vita Nuova*, the most intimate expression of the emotions of one of the greatest of poets, into English which gives pleasure for its own sake. The work of translating the lyrics of Dante's predecessors was achieved with equal skill and gave Rossetti excellent practice in metrical agility. These poems suffer from monotony of subject, and the devotion of the *gentil cuore* to the lady for whom alone it beats is at once an advantage and a drawback to Rossetti's translations—an advantage, because most readers will be content to take them on their own merits, without comparing them with the original; a drawback, because the most sympathetic student, with full appreciation of their beauty of phrase and variety of metre, is cloyed with the uniform sweetness of their prolonged descant upon one theme. The contemporaries of Dante are more interesting. Guido Cavalcanti had more than one string to his lyre, and, if it is difficult to take a lively interest in Cino da Pistoia and the elusive Selvaggia, the graceless Cecco Angiolieri is more of a human being and his Becchina is not a mere abstraction.

No more conclusive testimony to the magnetic attraction of Rossetti's personality could be found than his influence over the impetuous and restless temperament of William Morris. Morris, born at Walthamstow on 24 March 1834, had developed his love of medieval antiquity while at school at Marlborough, and had gone up to Exeter college, Oxford, in January 1853, a disciple of tractarianism and with the intention of taking holy orders. Here he formed his life-long friendship with Edward Burne-Jones, the two becoming the most prominent members of a circle, chiefly composed of schoolfellows of Burne-Jones from Birmingham and including the poet and historian Richard Watson Dixon[1]. In 1855, this group took the title 'the Brotherhood.' Contact with men of common interests but of some variety of taste enlarged Morris's sympathies. Under the guidance of Burne-Jones, he learned to appreciate Chaucer and Malory and was first introduced to northern mythology and epic. The contrast between the world of imaginative beauty in which he now found footing and the conventional hideousness of ordinary life gave definite shape to his imperfectly understood emotions. In the summer of 1855, Burne-Jones and Morris, returning from a tour in northern France and walking by night on the quay at Havre, decided to abandon their intention of taking orders and to devote themselves to art. At first, Morris studied architecture under Street. Under the influence of Rossetti's conviction that painting was the only art with a future in England, he changed his profession and pursued painting with characteristic ardour in the rooms at 17 Red Lion square, which were the birthplace of his ultimate career as decorative artist and furnisher. During his participation in the too hastily considered scheme for frescoing the walls of the Oxford Union, he met Jane Burden, whom he married in 1859. After his marriage with this lady, whose type of beauty, like that of Rossetti's wife, has become a permanent possession of English art, his substantial income enabled him to choose and build his home upon Bexley heath. The Red house, designed by his friend Philip Webb, was the forerunner of a revolution in domestic architecture, and its furniture and household appliances were designed in a spirit of revolt against the ugliness which contemporary taste approved. Out of this satisfaction of personal needs arose, in 1861, the formation of the firm of decorative artists, guided by the influence of Rossetti and known, at first, as Morris, Marshall, Faulkner and Co., which, in process of time, was entirely controlled by Morris himself and continued to be the chief practical business of his life. It is not too much to say that, by thirty-five years of ceaseless activity, from 1861 to his death in 1896, he effected an entire revolution in public taste. His love of medieval art and literature and his instinct for all that was beautiful in them were carried into practice in his workshops, and the contrast between the conditions under which the masterpieces of medieval art were produced and the

---

[1] See, *post*, chap. VI.

commercialism of the nineteenth century impelled him to his renunciation of distinctions of class and his fervent advocacy of the socialist cause as a master-workman. His voluminous poetry and prose, resorting for its inspiration to an elder day remote from the life around him, is, superficially, the work of a dreamer who seeks refuge from materialism in a world of visions. But, to Morris, his visions were capable of realisation and formed the inspiration of an eminently practical life. *The Earthly Paradise* was written during a period when the business affairs of his rising firm called for his unwearied attention. The active and the contemplative life were, in him, not mutually opposed but complementary. His periods of retirement to the beautiful manor-house at Kelmscott in the meadows by the infant Thames, which became his country home from 1871 onwards, recruited the energy of his London life in Hammersmith mall beside the busier and broader reaches of the same river, and, as we read his romances in verse and prose, we see in their imaginings the material which he worked into visible beauty in his textile fabrics and stained glass.

Morris's earliest attempts at poetry, unpremeditated lyrics in a highly original style, won the admiration of his friends at Oxford, who hailed him, rather prematurely, as a great poet. Some of his poems, with a series of remarkable prose tales, were printed, in 1856, in *The Oxford and Cambridge Magazine*, the organ of the Brotherhood, to which Rossetti also contributed. In this periodical, the earnestness of purpose which had been fatal to *The Germ* was even more marked. Financed largely by Morris, it ran its course of twelve monthly numbers with a decreasing circulation. Its contributors were animated by a noble sincerity. Among contemporary influences, the poetry of Tennyson and Browning, the critical philosophy of Ruskin and the chivalrous ideals of *The Newcomes* and *The Heir of Redclyffe* fostered their passion for truth in life and art. Their performances, however, are, for the most part, heavy reading, and there can be no doubt that, apart from Rossetti's imported contributions, the principal literary result of the Brotherhood's endeavour was Morris's first experiments in fiction. His rapid and heady style, similar to that of his early correspondence, is crowded with vividly imagined detail and flashes out again and again in phrases of picturesque colour. In *The Story of the Unknown Church*, he showed his kinship with medieval life and thought, of which he always wrote with a contemporary insight and accuracy seldom acquired by scholars and antiquaries.

The Hollow Land is the first example of his use of an atmosphere
for romance which, though medieval in its general features, can be
referred to no special age or century and became the characteristic
setting of his later prose tales. In the somewhat repellent story
entitled *Lindenborg Pool*, with a theme and setting which recall
the type of narrative associated with Edgar Allan Poe, he paid
his earliest tribute to the attractions of northern mythology.

Four of the five poems written by Morris for *The Oxford and
Cambridge Magazine* appeared in 1858, in the volume called *The
Defence of Guenevere and other Poems*. The contents of this book
are, from one point of view, hasty and unequal. The metre of
Morris's romantic lyrics suffers from overfluency and want of
restraint and is occasionally both weak and harsh. They lack
certainty of touch and completeness of finish ; many of them are
broken off suddenly with an effect of weakness which sinks to
bathos. Full of highly-coloured imagination, they express it in-
articulately and imperfectly in forms which waver between the
lyric and dramatic, in broken phrases and involved sentences.
Their virtue is their spontaneity, a natural, unlaboured gift of
poetry, asserting itself without any definite effort and producing
its treasures without consciousness of the mixture of precious metal
with alloy. They are the experimental work of a poet who has
found no absolutely suitable medium of expression out of many
which appeal to his taste. In the *terza rima* of *The Defence of
Guenevere*, the rugged elegiac stanzas of *King Arthur's Tomb*,
the dramatic blank verse of *Sir Peter Harpdon's End*, the varied
lyric measures of *Rapunzel*, the ballad metre of *Welland River*
and the recurrent refrains of *Two Red Roses across the Moon,
The Song of the Gillyflower* and *The Sailing of the Sword*, a spirit
intoxicated with the romance of the past is striving after a perfect
utterance of its sense of beauty. Morris's admiration of Browning
is, probably, responsible for the frequent intricacy of his style: this
influence had entire control of *Sir Peter Harpdon's End*, where
Browning's alternations of roughness and abruptness with smoothly
flowing passages are closely imitated. Yet, although in these early
pieces Morris was swayed by varying influences, there is none in
which his sensitiveness to the charm of colour and sound and scenery,
to all the beauty of the visible world, fails to find expression. He
is frequently spoken of as though he were a member of the pre-
Raphaelite school. His connection with it was indirect, and his
art had little in common with the accurate genre-painting which
it had been the immediate object of that school to promote. But

his truth of detail was pre-Raphaelite in the wider sense of the word and his realism was more thorough than the realism which became more and more a mere incident in Rossetti's verse and departed from his painting. Morris was more closely attached than Rossetti to the world around him; the most vivid landscapes of his poems belong to the English country to whose quiet moods he was perpetually alive. His love of romance has been attributed to his Celtic ancestry; but the sights and sounds amid which his gifts were developed were characteristically English, and, even in the lands of fantasy in which his later prose tales were laid, his best power of description was exercised upon the meadows and villages, the winding streams and chalk downs, the marshes and seaward flats of the parts of England that he knew best. More than Rossetti, too, he was awake to the sense of struggle in life, which is the animating power of the highest form of narrative. If it is wrong to count Rossetti merely as a languid aesthete, catching at the pleasurable moments of life and allowing its seriousness to escape unmarked, a similar estimate, which might easily be formed by a casual survey of Morris's preference for a bygone age, taken together with the archaisms of his style and his characterisation of himself as 'the idle singer of an empty day,' would be even more superficial. The echoes of the pain and suffering of the outside world are never silent in his enchanted world of fable ; they are the disturbing force of that tender and resigned melancholy in which his personages, acutely conscious of the shortness of life and the transitoriness of beauty, move to their appointed end.

This sense of the intimate connection between poetry and life, in which one becomes the best interpreter of the other, grew with advancing years. The practical and visionary elements in Morris's character drew more closely together, and, as the union progressed, his poetry grew in strength and purpose. Nine years after *The Defence of Guenevere*, he appeared, in *The Life and Death of Jason*, as a master of romantic narrative. His treatment of his classical subject was founded upon medieval practice. His master in narrative poetry was Chaucer : he employed the couplet, Chaucer's most perfect medium for story-telling, and, as in *The Knightes Tale*, he translated a tale whose nominal scene was the antique world into the terms of the age of chivalry. Nevertheless, while the form which he adopted was Chaucerian, the spirit of his story was different. Just as the couplet-form which he used, although derived from Chaucer, had passed since Chaucer's day under the influence of Dryden and Keats and had been moulded by them into the shape in which Morris received it, so no modern writer, however closely in sympathy with a past age, could wholly reproduce an attitude towards love and chivalry which the conditions of modern life have changed profoundly. The love of Palamon and Arcite for Emelye, devouring in its passion and tragic in its consequences, was the unavoidable duty of a medieval knight, a necessary part of the science of his profession. Morris's Jason and Medea submit to the dominion of a natural instinct apart from any code of manners, their delight in the present being tempered by foreboding of the future. Medea is not the queen of a court of love, who takes Jason's devotion as a conventional homage : she is a modern woman, surrendering all to her love and putting her fortunes in her lover's hands, with her eyes fully open to the risks which she willingly runs. In this respect, Morris comes nearer to classical antiquity than to his medieval model. His love-story is free from those constant touches of humour which link Chaucer to the modern world : on the other hand, his sense of the pathos of life is deeper than Chaucer's. The tale of Jason and Medea is informed by the spirit which fills Vergil's tale of Dido and Aeneas.

> With their love they fill the earth alone,
> Careless of shame, and not remembering death.

While that love is a temporary forgetfulness of the 'fury and distress' of life, its future is darkened by the haunting sense of satiety and decay, the Vergilian consciousness of *lacrymae rerum,* 'sorrow that bides and joy that fleets away.'

The same contrast between the setting of the poem and its inner spirit is obvious in *The Earthly Paradise,* a series of twenty-four tales in verse, two for each month of the year, published in three volumes between 1868 and 1870. They are bound together, in imitation of Chaucer, by a connecting link which forms the subject of the prologue. A company of wanderers, driven from their Scandinavian home by the great pestilence which overspread Europe in the middle of the fourteenth century, after long journeyings in search of the fabled earthly paradise, come, 'shrivelled, bent, and grey,' to 'a nameless city in a distant sea,' where Hellenic civilisation and culture have been preserved. Here, they find rest and hospitality, and twice a month they and their hosts meet at a solemn feast, at which a story is related. An ingenious medley of romance is thus provided. Twelve of the stories, told by elders of the city, come from classical sources ; the other twelve, told by the wanderers, are derived chiefly from medieval Latin, French and Icelandic originals, with gleanings from Mandeville and *The Arabian Nights*. The metrical forms employed throughout are Chaucerian, with those inevitable modifications which the progress of literary form had brought to pass. The prologue, the narrative links between tale and tale and eight of the stories themselves are written in the ten-syllabled couplet. Seven stories, six of which are told by the wanderers, are in the short couplet of *The Book of the Duchesse* and *The Hous of Fame*. The rest, with the short lyrics in which each month is introduced, are in the seven-lined stanza of *Troilus and Criseyde*. That all the stories should be equal in interest is not to be expected, and a few are written in a somewhat perfunctory spirit. Where, however, a tale, familiar and often told though it might be, really arrested Morris, he used all his power to adorn it with novel detail, and the success of *The Life and Death of Jason* is well maintained in *The Doom of King Acrisius* and *The Story of Cupid and Psyche*. The wanderers' narratives, to the tellers of which the noble prologue gives a more dramatic interest than to the placid elders of the undisturbed city, are naturally less familiar and have less to fear from competition than the classical stories. In one of these, *The Land East of the Sun and West of the Moon*, Morris taxed his narrative power to its utmost capacity by giving his romance the shape of a dream told within a dream at broken intervals. In all the stories alike, his command over his metre and rhythm is unfailing. He achieves no striking effects such as were promised by the irregular and faulty measures of *The Defence of Guenevere*. In *The Life and Death of Jason* he had settled down to a smooth and steady pace of reserved energy. To a sensitive ear his prosody lacks variety: in his disregard of the elision of vowels and his fondness for riming weak syllables there is a want of robustness, which, however, is thoroughly in keeping with the character of the old and worn narrators and their autumnal view of life. The interest which his stories excite, however, precludes monotony, while their consistent tunefulness, if it provides few individual passages which can be remembered for their own sake and involves a considerable amount of repetition of the same minor air, creates a harmonious atmosphere entirely appropriate to the waking dream in which they are set. From the purely poetic point of view, the most memorable passages of the poem are the interpolated lyrics in which, at the beginning of each month, Morris records his own delight in the changing English landscape, the verses in which he bids adieu to his accomplished task, and the occasional snatches of song introduced into the stories. To these last, as to the Christmas carol of *The Land East of the Sun and West of the Moon,* he gave a freshness and charm already heralded by the shorter lyrics in *The Defence of Guenevere* and 'I know a little garden close' in *The Life and Death of Jason.*

In the later portion of *The Earthly Paradise,* the pure romance of his earlier stories began to give place to a higher and stronger form of poetry. The transition to epic, with its prevailing theme of strife and suffering, is marked by *Bellerophon at Argos* and *Bellerophon in Lycia,* and still more strikingly, in view of later developments, by *The Lovers of Gudrun.* His feeling for the classical epic led to his translations of *The Aeneids of Virgil,* in 1875, and the *Odyssey* in 1887, the first of which, at any rate, showed an appreciation of the spirit and influence of the poem superior to its actual rendering of Vergil's individuality of style. His imagination, however, found its true home in the less trodden fields of the northern saga. *The Lovers of Gudrun,* a version of the Icelandic *Laxdaela saga* in heroic couplet, is the masterpiece of *The Earthly Paradise.* The habitual melancholy, with its emphasis upon the shortness of life and the bitterness of love, is apparent here, but without the romantic listlessness which besets it elsewhere. Kiartan, Bodli, Ospak, Gudrun are active living figures engaged in dramatic conflict befitting the stern and barren scene of northern legend. In 1869 and 1870, Morris had collaborated with Eiríkr Magnússon, in the translation of *Grettis saga* and *Volsunga saga,* and, in 1871, he reached an epoch in his life with his first visit to Iceland and the actual scenes of the events of the stories of Grettir, Gudrun and Burnt Njal, where 'every place and name marks the death of' the 'short-lived eagerness and glory' of this home of epic poetry. His literary work during the next few years included the morality *Love is Enough,* the structure of which, a play presented within a play, resembles the intricate method employed in *The Land East of the Sun and West of the Moon.* For this, he adopted a somewhat monotonous form of unrimed verse, more definitely archaic in form and spirit than any of his other work; but its unattractiveness is redeemed by occasional passages of description in which his love and knowledge of medieval art overcome all obstacles, while the long rimed measures of 'the Music,' the series of interludes by which the drama of Pharamond and Azalais is broken into parts and the amoebaean lyric of the emperor and empress with its answering refrains are, perhaps, his highest lyric achievements. *Love is Enough* was, however, merely a divergence from the channel which his verse had now marked out for itself. In 1875, he published his translation of the *Aeneid* and a small volume of translations of Icelandic stories which preluded his most ambitious poem, *The Story of Sigurd the Volsung and the Fall of the Niblungs.*

This epic in four books, founded upon the prose *Volsunga saga,* was published in 1876. Its story, in loftiness of theme and the completeness with which it is controlled by an overmastering fate, is at least the equal of the great Greek legends ; and, to tell it, Morris employed an anapaestic couplet of his own invention, with six beats to each line. This metre, which he afterwards used in his translation of the *Odyssey,* suited the natural ease and rapidity of his writing. The swinging cadences might easily become monotonous or slovenly; but the nobility of his story had so thoroughly taken hold of him that he never sacrificed dignity to swiftness of execution. With plentiful variety of movement, a stateliness appropriate to the theme is maintained throughout the whole of the poem. It has been questioned whether *Volsunga saga,* as a whole, is suitable for epic treatment. Morris himself closed his story with the death of Gudrun, the true consummation of 'all the death of kings and kindreds, and the sorrow of Odin the Goth,' without proceeding to the final incidents of the saga, but he introduced, in his first book, the whole grim episode of Sigmund and Signy and the monstrous Sinfiotli, which is purely preliminary to, and, in fact, a separate story from, the epic of Sigurd, son of Sigmund and Hiordis. That the book thus falls into two epics, a short and a long one, cannot be gainsaid, and there is a signal contrast between the inhumanity of the opening story, whose personages excite terror and repulsion but little sympathy, and the gentler aspect of its sequel, in which, superhuman though the actors are in stature and in spirit, their errors and woes are those of mortality. Morris, however, so managed the transition from the overture to the actual drama that the interest is not suspended or noticeably broken, and, before our concentration upon the fate of Sigmund is wholly diverted, we are carried away upon the tide of Sigurd's heroic youth. The episodes follow one another with unfailing vigour and freshness, and, in the climax of the story, the slaying of the Niblung kings, the slayers of Sigurd, in the hall of Atli, the death-song of Gunnar among the serpents and the vengeance and death of Gudrun, Morris pursued his theme triumphantly to the

end. If the chosen form of *Sigurd the Volsung* did not wholly
fulfil its promise when it came to cope with the Homeric hexameter, it was at least thoroughly adequate to an occasion when
Morris was free to deal with his story untrammelled by the
exigencies of translation.

After *Sigurd*, Morris practically abandoned poetry, save for the
Odyssey, and his last original book of verse was the collection of
lyrics and ballads, *Poems by the Way*, issued from the Kelmscott
press in 1891. His activities outside his artistic life during the
early eighties were devoted to the spread of socialism and to
enthusiasms closely connected with his love of beauty and his
attempt to realise the past in the present. His socialist propa-
ganda was marked by two romances, *A Dream of John Ball*,
remarkable for its vivid and beautiful medieval setting amid
English village scenery, and the Utopian *News from Nowhere*,
whose doctrinal aspect has earned it a fame out of proportion to
its actual merits. In 1889, when his political energy, though
not abated, had been somewhat disappointed by the intracta-
bility of those with whom he had associated himself, he returned
to pure romance with the prose story, interspersed with lyrics,
The House of the Wolfings. This was followed, in 1890, by
The Roots of the Mountains and, in 1891, by *The Story of
the Glittering Plain*. Morris succeeded in communicating his
own pleasure in these narratives to the reader; and the in-
definiteness of place and time in which they are set, contrasted
with the extreme definiteness of their imaginary topography,
gives them the vivid charm of fairy-tale. His mind still
ran upon the northern epic, and the scenes and personages of the
first three of these romances, so far as they belong to any
country at all, belong to the remote north of Europe. In *The
Roots of the Mountains*, the longest of the three, the self-contained life of a pastoral community threatened by the mysterious
barbarians of the neighbouring forest tracts, and its victory over
them with the aid of a warrior race from a distant valley, are
pictured with extraordinary completeness and sustained interest.
In 1892, Morris produced a translation of *Beowulf* in collaboration
with A. J. Wyatt, and, in 1891, he began, with Eiríkr Magnússon,
to produce a Saga library which included a version of the
Heimskringla. Amid the crowded interests of the closing years
of his life the production of magnificently printed volumes from
the Kelmscott press took the chief place, while his love of
medieval architecture prompted him to protest with increasing

vehemence on behalf of the Society for the Protection of Ancient Buildings, which he had founded in 1877, against destructive works of so-called restoration. Meanwhile, his leisure hours were occupied with prose romance of which the atmosphere was chiefly medieval. The brief *The Wood beyond the World* (1895) was followed, in 1896, by *The Well at the World's End*, a somewhat prolix tale, the interest of which, however, is continually revived by scenes and episodes of memorable clearness and beauty. Two more romances were published posthumously, *The Water of the Wondrous Isles*, the most fairylike of the series, and *The Sundering Flood*, which he finished less than a month before his death. In these later books, the attraction which he felt for the England of Chaucer's day is as powerful as it was in *The Earthly Paradise*; if their passages of adventure amid black mountains and 'perilous seas, in faery lands forlorn' belong to a world common to all lovers of the marvellous and romantic, the lowland country in which his heroes have their home, with its meadow-lands, its cities of merchants and its abbeys and priories, is the English country to which his imagination restored its fourteenth-century aspect, peopling it with feudal lords and their households, prosperous middle-class traders and the labourers who listened to the preaching of John Ball. Malory, equally beloved with Chaucer, had his influence on Morris's prose style, but the peculiar archaisms in which it abounds were natural to Morris's thought and were used with a vigour free from affectation. On 3 October 1896, the greatest master of romantic story-telling among modern Englishmen died at his London residence, Kelmscott house, Hammersmith, worn out by a life of unceasing work, in which he had endeavoured, with remarkable consistence and success, to realise and translate into practice for his countrymen the beauty of the visionary world of his prose and poetry. His love of the beautiful work of the past, material and imaginative, stood for him in the place of religious fervour, and his whole strength of purpose was dedicated to the reconstitution of modern life upon conditions similar to those under which such work, impossible in an age of mere competition for money, was produced. Read in this light, his writings are no mere pictures of an irrecoverable past painted with a dilettante regretfulness: they are a coherent revelation of his sources of inspiration in his combat with the torpor from which, like Ruskin and Carlyle, he, not the least of the three, strove to deliver the life of his day.

The dedication of *The Defence of Guenevere* to Rossetti tes
to the quickening power exercised over Morris by his associa
with that less prolific and more fastidious genius. To Rossetti, also,
was dedicated, in 1860, the first work of Algernon Charles Swinburne,
The Queen Mother and Rosamond, two poetical dramas written
in elaborate and intricate blank verse and containing incidental
lyrics in English and French. For the time being, the book
passed almost unnoticed. Swinburne, born in 1837, belonged to
a younger branch of the Northumbrian family of that name.
His youth, spent between the isle of Wight and the house of his
grandfather, Sir John Swinburne, at Capheaton in the country
between Morpeth and Bellingham, fired him with a passionate
enthusiasm for the sea and open country, which supplied his verse
with an inexhaustible theme. At Eton and Balliol college, Oxford,
he developed his inborn love of poetry, and, although he came into
close connection and friendship with Rossetti and his circle and
shared their love for medieval romance, it was with a taste already
formed for other types of verse that exercised little, if any, direct
influence upon them. To more than an ordinary Englishman's
pride in his country and her past achievements, his reading of the
Athenian drama revealed the meaning and value of the liberty
for which Athens and the England of Shakespeare had alike contended. His sympathy with republican freedom was learned from
Landor and Shelley and, last but not least, from Victor Hugo, who
shared with Shakespeare the shrine of his life-long idolatry. To
Victor Hugo's mastery over the forms of lyric and dramatic verse
he owed his most direct impulse: it is not too much to say that,
after a certain period, under the conviction that no man could
do more than Hugo had done, Swinburne's poetry became dominated by the ambition of following in his footsteps and ringing
changes on the themes already chosen by Hugo's manifold genius.
Of other French poets, Gautier and Baudelaire affected him with
their command of form and melody, and it was on this side of
his appreciations, open to sensuous impression, that Rossetti's
peculiar vividness of phrase and harmony of music appealed
to him. Daringly irreverent in his rejection of all conventions
that seemed to repress the freedom of the human spirit, he paid
humble and, at times, uncritical homage to works of human genius,
even when they were least in sympathy with his fervently held
and freely uttered creed of liberty. In the childlike frankness
of his denunciation of kings and priests he rivalled the outspokenness of Shelley, whose lyric copiousness and variety he even

surpassed. But, while Shelley, of the masters of English song, came nearest to him in point of time and the spirit of his verse, the cadences of his music were also founded upon the Elizabethans and Milton, and no influences moulded his phraseology so completely as the sacred literature, biblical and liturgical, of the religion whose professors were the objects of his tireless invective.

Atalanta in Calydon and *Chastelard* in 1865 and *Poems and Ballads* in 1866 won Swinburne celebrity and notoriety. *Chastelard*, the first of his three plays upon the life of Mary queen of Scots, is a romantic drama in the style of his two earlier works. *Atalanta*, classical in subject, was an attempt to reproduce the characteristic forms of Greek drama in a corresponding English dress. The dialogue, closely following the conventional order of Greek tragedy, is in the involved blank verse, copious and pregnant in its content and artfully varied in its music, for which he had already shown his capacity. In his choruses, he adopted rimed stanzaic forms, in which he gave proof of an unparalleled range of musical compass. While his subsequent poetry showed that his metrical agility was incapable of exhaustion, he never excelled the ringing melody of the famous hymn to Artemis, afire with the new-born passion of spring, the firm and rapid tread with which 'Before the beginning of years' proceeds to the melancholy assurance of its climax and the wavelike measures of the κομμός, weighted with the certainty of tragic doom, near the end of the poem. *Atalanta* is no mere archaic experiment : its structure is superficially Greek, and the old classical themes of controlling fate and divine intervention pervade its story; but the spirit in which it is written is the modern spirit of revolt against the religious acquiescence in the will of Heaven accepted by Greek tragedy. The cause which it pleads is that of 'the holy spirit of man' against the tyranny of 'the gods who divide and devour.' Its sympathy is with the beauty and strength of life and nature, and its burden is a complaint against 'the supreme evil' whose weapons are decay and death. It needs no reading between the lines to see that Swinburne's eloquence, in rhythms and periods which taxed all the resources of modern romantic poetry, arraigned the subservience of man, not only to the gods of ancient Greece, but to the religious ideals of his own day. Following Shelley's audacious reversal of the principles of good and evil, typified in *The Revolt of Islam* by the conflict between the eagle of tyranny and the serpent of freedom, he denounced the binding spell of creeds with a free appropriation of the august language of the charms with which that spell had been woven round the heart of the nations.

The atheism of *Atalanta* might pass unchallenged, so long as it was partly veiled by its antique setting; but *Poems and Ballads* not unnaturally shocked austere critics by its negation of conventional reticence. Not all the beauty of its verse can palliate Swinburne's waywardness in his choice of themes, and his attempt to acclimatise his *fleurs du mal* to English soil in defiance of prudery and philistinism created a prejudice against him in a society which had responded heartily to Tennyson's noble celebration of duty and virtue and welcomed the bracing quality of Browning's optimism. The subjects of *Laus Veneris, Anactoria, Faustine* and *The Leper* were sensual obsessions, marring and wasting life : their end, satiety and hopeless weariness of spirit, was the burden of *Dolores, Ilicet* and *The Triumph of Time*. No one could have felt more amusement than Swinburne himself at the plea occasionally made by his defenders that *Dolores* is a moral sermon, because it is full of the pain and bitterness of sensual indulgence. The spirit of *Poems and Ballads* is frankly pagan : the goddess, *hominum divumque voluptas*, to whose cult it is dedicated, is, also, our Lady of Pain : the inevitable escape from the barren pleasures of her worship and the revulsions of feeling which they entail is 'the end of all, the poppied sleep.' There are, naturally, two opinions upon the desirability of asserting such views publicly without suggesting a tonic remedy; but there can be no question as to the beauty of form in which the assertion was clothed. Swinburne's work, as a whole, suffers from the paucity of its contents; his rapid genius was too easily satisfied with returning to the same themes over and over again and reaffirming them with increased emphasis but little variety. But, in metrical skill and in the volume of his highly decorated language, he had no rival among English poets. The first of these qualities he preserved to the end ; the second was somewhat affected, as time went on, by the monotony, already noticed, of his favourite subjects, which became unequal to the strain put upon them by their constant changes of elaborate dress. In *Poems and Ballads,* however, as in *Atalanta,* his verse had lost none of its freshness, and his metre and rhythm adapted themselves freely to change of subject. The 'profuse strains of unpremeditated art' of the earlier romantic poets were not his ; but the constraint of form was a positive pleasure to him, under which he moved with unequalled freedom. The slow movement of *Laus Veneris*, and the sorrow-laden spondees of *Ilicet*, the impetuous haste with which the lover in *The Triumph of Time* flings away regretfully but unhesitatingly his past happiness with both hands, the forced lightness of *Faustine*, the swift anapaests of *Dolores*, full of reckless glorying in forbidden pleasure, the solemn affirmations and cowed responses of *A Litany*, the bird-notes of *Itylus*, mingling with magic skill the sweetness and sorrow of the nightingale's song, the careless innocence of *A Match*, are striking instances of his power of adapting sound to meaning. Characteristic features of all these poems are the use of alliteration and of words which, by community of sound and form, echo and are complementary to one another. The accusation of sound without sense has been brought by unsympathetic critics against poetry in which the charm of sound is remarkable. If Swinburne's wealth of language sometimes obscured his meaning with allusiveness and periphrases, his rhythm is an unfailing guide to the spirit of his words.

Poems and Ballads contained tributes of admiration to Landor and Victor Hugo, while *A Christmas Carol* and *The Masque of Queen Bersabe*, to say nothing of the constant use of imagery and phrase in *Laus Veneris* and other poems, were evidence of close kinship with the medieval romance beloved of Rossetti and his circle. There were signs, also, in this volume of the special enthusiasm which filled Swinburne's next books of verse. The spirit of liberty was abroad upon the winds. In 1867, the poet whose hymns of lust and satiety had dazzled the lovers of poetry with their youthful vigour sang the praise of Mazzini and Garibaldi in *A Song of Italy*. *Songs before Sunrise* in 1871 was a collection of poems written during the final struggle for Italian freedom. To analyse its characteristics would be to repeat what has been said already of *Poems and Ballads*. It includes much of Swinburne's best work, the majestic *Hertha*, the lament for captive Italy in *Super Flumina Babylonis* and the apostrophe to France in *Quia Multum Amavit*, whose strains sway and fluctuate at will between fierce scorn for the oppressor and tenderness for his victims, hope and comfort for Italy in her slavery, compassion for prostituted France. Where Victor Hugo's war music had led the way, Swinburne's clarion was bound to follow. It was difficult to enter a field so fully occupied by the author of *Les Châtiments*, and it must be owned that, when the clarion sounded a charge against Napoleon III, it made up for want of originality by an excess of shrillness. Nevertheless, the sonnets written at intervals during this period and collected under the title *Dirae* sound an individual note of abuse and add their quota to the imagery even of such poems as *L'Égout de Rome.*

After the achievement of Italian hope in 1870 and the fall of Napoleon III, which he hailed with savage delight in 1871, Swinburne had leisure to return to more purely artistic work. In the length and rhetoric of *Bothwell,* sequel to *Chastelard* and precursor of *Mary Stuart,* he followed the example of Hugo's *Cromwell.* This play, published in 1874, is a dramatic poem in which he pursued with close attention to historical fact his conception of Mary's character, defending her against the sympathisers who, in their anxiety to clear her of knavery, only succeeded in convicting her of senseless folly. Unfitted by its extreme length for the stage, *Bothwell* is yet a work of great dramatic power ; its sustained speeches, chief among them the great speech of Knox, are written in music which is susceptible to every change of tone, and tragic terror could go no further than in the scene at Kirk of Field where, before Darnley's murder, Mary is heard singing snatches of *Lord Love went maying,* the lyric sung by Rizzio to the queen and her ladies on the night of his death. As *Bothwell* followed *Chastelard,* so *Erechtheus,* in 1876, followed *Atalanta* with equal eloquence and with a somewhat closer relation to the inner spirit of Greek tragic form than its predecessor. The lyric choruses of *Erechtheus,* while they give less immediate delight than the enchanting music of those in *Atalanta,* have a more constant loftiness and majesty, and no passage of Swinburne's lyric work is more spontaneous and splendid than the apostrophe to Athens, the

> fruitful immortal anointed adored
> Dear city of men without master or lord,

which is an episode of the opening chorus. Athens is the true heroine of the drama ; love of country and hatred of slavery are its inspiring passions.

A second series of *Poems and Ballads* showed no falling off in melody, with a more chastened tone than that of the first volume. There is equal ease in Swinburne's handling of the music of enchantment in *A Forsaken Garden* and of the dignified choral harmonies of *Ave atque Vale,* his beautiful tribute to the memory of Baudelaire. In his translations of some of Villon's *ballades,* he acknowledged, with his usual generosity, his inferiority to Rossetti in this field : if, in choice of material, he was too often guided by the example of others in whose wake it was dangerous to follow.

it was, at any rate, with an admiration totally distinct from a desire to rival them. *Studies in Song* and *Songs of the Springtides*, in 1880, were full of love of the sea, the prevailing passion of his later verse. *By the North Sea*, a lyric symphony in seven movements echoing the rushing of the east wind and the chiming of sun-lit breakers beating upon a crumbling coast, was his highest tribute to the resistless power and eternity of ocean, the sense of which plays an animate part in the later *Tristram of Lyonesse* and *Marino Faliero*. A rather excessive ingenuity obscures the *Song for the Centenary of Walter Savage Landor* and the *Birthday Ode* to Victor Hugo: allusions to the works of these authors are woven into the substance of both poems with a skill that suggests an acrostic, and the short explanatory key which Swinburne found it necessary to add to them is an indication of his own uneasiness on this head. His own humour was quick to detect possible weaknesses in the fiery enthusiasm of his verse, and in the same year he parodied himself mercilessly and perfectly in the last piece of the anonymous *Heptalogia*.

Most lovers of Swinburne will agree that the *Tristram of Lyonesse* volume, published in 1882, is the crown of his mature work. The long romance in couplets which is the title-piece challenges comparison with the romantic narratives of William Morris. In the art of story-telling, Swinburne was Morris's inferior; but in the structure of his verse and the value which he gave to musical effects and the technique of vowel-sounds, elisions and alliteration, Swinburne was as careful an artist as Morris was negligent. The theme of *Tristram* is the glorification of lovers' passion. With Morris, such passion is apt to be a pining sickness which clouds mortal joy with an anticipation of its end: the love of Medea and Jason brings very little present enjoyment to the lovers. Swinburne's lovers are conscious of the disadvantages their passion involves and the pain inevitably mixed with it; but their apprehensions are drowned in the buoyancy of the moment, and they rush upon their doom with a resolution born of the conviction that the strife and suffering inherent in their abandonment to passion are no cause for wavering or regret. If disloyal in their human relations, they are the loyal votaries of a love in which they have found delight without weariness. The coming of fate finds them united:

> from love and strife
> The stroke of love's own hand felt last and best
> Gave them deliverance to perpetual rest.

Tristram of Lyonesse, the highest achievement of English couplet verse since *Lamia*, is the English epic of passionate love, which, recognising nothing in the world but itself, goes through fire and water for its own sake: it realises in dramatic narrative the theme of 'the Music' which forms the chorus to Morris's *Love is Enough*. But *Tristram* was not all that the book contained. In *Athens, an ode*, Swinburne worked out the comparison between the victors of Salamis and those who conquered the Armada, and poured forth his gratitude to the dramatists of the Athenian stage. His love of the great English dramatists was expressed in a series of sonnets, many of whose phrases remain in the memory side by side with those of Lamb's no less lyric prose criticisms. The sequence of lyrics *A Dark Month*, with which the volume concluded, was prompted by a child's death, and belongs to the class of exquisite and tender poems in which Swinburne, turning from his habitual tone of exalted and exhausting passion, followed the example of the author of *L'Art d'être Grandpère*. Such poems, in the year after the appearance of *Tristram*, stood in company with the Guernsey sequence and other spontaneous variations of an artificial form in *A Century of Roundels*.

In 1881, Swinburne had concluded with *Mary Stuart* the trilogy which *Chastelard* had begun. His devotion to this subject was expressed in the lyric *Adieux à Marie Stuart*, which, in one of its stanzas, sums up with sane precision the estimate of the queen expressed at length in his dramas. After this period the hues of autumn begin to tinge his verse. Ready as ever to assume graceful or majestic forms at will, his genius, though impelled to speak, had little left to say that was new. After *A Midsummer Holiday*, in 1884, he returned to drama in *Marino Faliero*, a subject which he felt had been handled unworthily by Byron. This drama followed the lines of the early plays in combining historic with poetic treatment without regard to suitability for the stage; but, as in *Bothwell*, powerful dramatic situations are achieved. Swinburne put into the part of the doge who conspired against the oligarchy of Venice his own passion for freedom and love of the sea and wind, the symbols of unchained liberty; and the contrast between his hero's monologue and the Latin hymn of the penitents, whose verses form intervals in it, is the contrast most congenial to him—that between the freed will of man and the will in bondage to custom and tradition. *Locrine*, his next drama, in 1887, was an original experiment in which each scene was presented in rimes of a recurring stanza-form: the design, beautiful from a lyric point of view, was, however, unfavourable to the presentation of character and retarded dramatic action. Two years later came the third series of *Poems and Ballads*. In its lighter pieces and especially in such ballads as *The Jacobite's Lament*, in which the calm melancholy of an exile like him who 'pined by Arno for his lovelier Tees' is touched with the passion of romantic sorrow, there is much of the accustomed freshness of spirit; but the chief effort of the volume, the poem written to commemorate the tercentenary of the Armada, shows fatigue, and the force which drives its galloping and thundering rhythms is more mechanical than that which, at a touch, set in motion the ardent measures of the choruses of *Erechtheus* and the ode to Athens. At the same time, the falling off noticeable in the later volumes, *Astrophel* and *A Channel Passage*, and his two last plays, *The Sisters*, a drama of modern life more ingenious in design than satisfactory in execution, and *Rosamund Queen of the Lombards*, is only the decline incidental to growing age. Loyal to his old enthusiasms, he was lover of freedom and patriot to the end; and the last poems of his life, though their insular tone may have astonished some of his old friends, gave utterance to his conviction that England, like Athens of old, was the safeguard of the world's liberty.

In addition to his poetry, Swinburne published from 1868 onwards several volumes of literary criticism. His *Essays and Studies* and *Miscellanies* bear the most striking testimony to his comprehensive knowledge and love of poetry and to his scholarly insight. Of his monographs upon individual writers, *A Study of Shakespeare* takes the first place, not merely as a panegyric in eloquent prose, but as the most stimulating and original contribution made by an English poet to the understanding of the greatest master of English song. His various essays upon the dramatists of Shakespeare's age, a subject always congenial to him, have the aspect of final pronouncements. His criticism, however, was too much charged with the white heat of enthusiasm to be always judicious: his praise, always lavish, was, at times, extravagant, and his condemnation of his *bêtes noires* knew no measure. His admirable estimate of Wordsworth in one of the most elaborate of his essays was the fruit of calm and measured judgment: no greater contrast to this could be found than the scorn poured, in the same essay, upon Byron, whose negligent trifling with the gift of verse and occasional vulgarity of execution were, to Swinburne, inexcusable faults without compensation. Thinking and writing in superlatives of praise and blame were natural to him. In the genius of Shakespeare,

Shelley and Victor Hugo, 'God stood plain for adoration': to write of their work was to express the most cherished tenets of a creed of which they were the deities. For those who failed when judged by his standard, who touched the shrine of song with unworthy hands, who misused or paltered with their talent, Swinburne had no mercy: they were the enemies of his creed, to be denounced with the energy of a fanatic. Thus, while his praise constantly glows with the rapture of lyric devotion and his blame draws freely upon the resources of irony and epigram, the unvaryingly rhapsodical tone of his prose, its over-copious periods and unrestrained vocabulary are not a little exhausting to his readers. The 'fury in the words' is not seldom out of proportion to the value of the words themselves, and the insight of the poet is dulled by the excessive protestations of the enthusiast.

When Swinburne died in 1909, England lost the most fertile lyric poet of the Victorian era, whose unequalled versatility in the use of lyric form was amazing in its brilliance. Receptive of manifold influences, classical, English and foreign, he reproduced them in a style which was wholly individual. With all his fiercely cherished prejudices and his unsparing condemnation of the dogmas and opinions held most sacred by his countrymen, few poets have been more catholic in their tastes or more ready to recognise and applaud sincerity of purpose in other men's work. An implacable enemy, he was the most devoted of friends; his cordial admiration for the work of his brother poets was as generous as the selflessness with which Scott praised his contemporaries. His earliest volume was inscribed to Rossetti; Christina Rossetti received the dedication of *A Century of Roundels*, William Morris that of *Astrophel*, Theodore Watts-Dunton, the constant companion of his later years, that of *Tristram of Lyonesse* and of later poems. The first series of *Poems and Ballads* was dedicated to Edward Burne-Jones, and the last volume of Swinburne's life bore an inscription to the joint memory of Burne-Jones and Morris, the painter and poet of old-world romance, united in life-long brotherhood. In return, his simplicity of character and the unswerving idealism to which he devoted his genius won the admiration and affection of all who knew him. All, indeed, who are aware that truth takes many and diverse forms and value the sincere expression of conviction more than a tame acquiescence in convention pay unconstrained honour to Swinburne's celebration of his ideals of liberty and justice, clothed in music which is borne upon the wings of the wind and wails and rejoices, now loud with delight in its beauty and strength and now threatening or plaintive in its anger or sadness, like the voice of the sea.

The first number of *The Germ* contained, as well as Rossetti's *My Sister's Sleep*, a sonnet by his brother William Michael and two lyrics by his sister Christina Georgina Rossetti. Christina, born in 1830, produced her earlier work under the pseudonym Ellen Alleyn. The two lyrics in question, *Dream Land* and *An End*, are the natural outcome of a mind that instinctively translates its passing dreams into music as faint and clear as the horns of elf-land, such music as is heard at its perfection in the lyrics of Shelley. A song, *Oh roses for the flush of youth*, in the second number of *The Germ*, has the same unsought grace. Together with this appeared the more elaborate *A Pause of Thought* and *A Testimony*, the second of these founded on the recurrent theme of *Ecclesiastes* and employing scriptural language with the skill and ease manifested by Rossetti in *The Burden of Nineveh* and by Swinburne in countless poems. Unlike her brother, whose sympathy with religion was purely artistic, and still more unlike Swinburne, whose attitude to the orthodox conceptions of Christianity was openly hostile, Christina Rossetti was, to the end of her life, a devout Christian, finding the highest inspiration for her song in her faith and investing Anglican ideals of worship with a mystical beauty. Her volumes of collected verse, beginning with *Goblin Market and other poems* in 1862 and ending with *New Poems*, collected in 1896, two years after her death, by her brother William, are permeated, even when they deal with subjects not primarily religious, with this devotional feeling. *Goblin Market* and *The Prince's Progress*, her two chief narrative poems, are both, in effect, allegories, the first obvious in its application, the second capable of more than one interpretation, of the soul in its struggle with earthly allurements. Her sequences of sonnets, *Monna Innominata* and *Later Life*, are filled with her sense of the claims of divine love over human passion. While her brother, in *The Blessed Damozel*, drew the picture of an immortal spirit yearning for the love it has left behind and translating the joys of heaven into concrete imagery, Christina Rossetti embodies the desire of the soul on earth to climb

> the stairs that mount above,
> Stair after golden skyward stair
> To city and to sea of glass,

and the heaven which she sees is the mystical city of *The Revelation of S. John*. In her *Martyrs' Song*, the blessed ones who 'lean over the golden bar' have no regret for earth : amid the welcoming angels, painted in verse that translates into words the visions wrought in tapestry and stained glass by Burne-Jones and Morris, they find 'the rest which fulfils desire' in the light of the divine presence. Such verse has a natural kinship with the religious poetry of the seventeenth century, and especially with George Herbert and Henry Vaughan, where their excessive ingenuity in metaphor gives place to spontaneous lyric fervour. The clear notes of Herbert's *Easter Song* and the calm rapture of Vaughan's 'My soul, there is a country' find their closest echo in Christina Rossetti's devout songs, and she adopted instinctively the free metrical forms of rimed stanza in which they clothed their thought.

While all her thoughts were drawn together towards one central ideal and her verse was ruled by the supreme conviction that

in la sua volontade è nostra pace,

she expressed herself with a variety of metre and rhythm and a musical power unequalled by any other English poetess. If she had less intellectual force and a more confined range of subject than Elizabeth Barrett Browning, who certainly, by virtue of her more liberal sympathies, makes an appeal to a wider audience, Christina Rossetti unquestionably had the advantage in melodiousness. *Goblin Market*, written in paragraphs of varying length with short lines and rimes binding them together at irregular intervals, is an example of a form which, adapted by a careless writer even with considerable imagination, might easily become mere rhythmical prose. While the language is of the most simple kind and the lines run freely into one another, the music of the rimes, half unheard, is, nevertheless, strongly felt. Whether moving in these lightly fettered cadences or in the stricter confinement of the stanza, her lyric verse is always remarkable for its combination of strength and seriousness of sentiment with simplicity of expression. Mystic though she was, her thought never found refuge in complicated or obscure language, but translated itself into words with the clearness and definiteness which were among the aims of the pre-Raphaelite associates of her girlhood. In such short bursts of song as *A Birthday*, simile and coloured phrase came to her aid, without effort on her part, to adorn a *crescendo* which rises to a climax of innocent happiness. Her

A Christmas Carol cannot be matched among Christmas songs for its union of childlike devotion and pathos with pictorial directness : Morris's 'Outlanders, whence come ye last?' and Swinburne's 'Three damsels in the queen's chamber' are not less beautiful and are more elaborately pictorial, but they are designedly archaic in style and are without her earnestness and concentration of feeling. It is true that there are poems by Christina Rossetti in which her sense of the necessity of simplicity is too apparent, either in the intrusion of too homely words or in occasional metrical weakness. Her ballads of everyday life, such as *Maude Clare* and *Brandons Both*, inevitably recall, to their own disadvantage, the successes of Tennyson in the same field. On the other hand, where her imagination pursued a higher path, as in the allegorical visions of *A Ballad of Boding*, the note which she sounded was clear and unfaltering. In the third of her *Old and New Year Ditties*, the famous 'Passing away,' she showed herself no less capable than Swinburne of wedding appropriately majestic music to her theme, varying the cadence of her verse upon the groundwork of a single sound, the passing bell which is heard at the end of each line, and gradually relieving the melancholy of her opening passage, until, in the last notes, new hope is heard. The range of her verse was, naturally, somewhat limited by her preoccupation with religious subjects. Contemporary movements touched her lightly, and it was seldom that, as in the two poems entitled *The German-French Campaign*, she referred to them. If this aloofness from the world precludes her from an uncontested claim to the position sometimes given to her as the greatest of English poetesses, no religious poet of the nineteenth century, even if we take into account the brilliant but more turbid genius of Francis Thompson, can be said to challenge comparison with her whose 'shrine of holiest-hearted song' Swinburne approached with reverent admiration of her single-heartedness and purity of purpose.

To the group of poets treated in this chapter may be added Arthur William Edgar O'Shaughnessy, who was born in 1844 and died in 1881. His working life, from 1861 to his death, was spent as an assistant in the British museum, chiefly amid surroundings far removed from the themes of his verse. He was a friend of Rossetti and of Ford Madox Brown and married the sister of another poet, Philip Bourke Marston. French poetry, however, was the prevailing influence which guided his sensitive and highly uncertain talent, and the English verse to which his own is most nearly related, though at a considerable distance, is that of Swinburne. In the three volumes which contain his best, as well as his weakest, work, *An Epic of Women, Lays of France*, founded on the lays of Marie de France, and *Music and Moonlight*, he frequently adopted lyric forms which Swinburne had used in *Poems and Ballads*. Sometimes, as in the were-wolf story, *Bisclavaret*, which is in the stanza of *The Leper*, this justifies itself; but *The Fair Maid and the Sun*, in the stanza of *Laus Veneris*, is merely pretty, and the obvious following of *Dolores* in *The Disease of the Soul* is a signal failure. O'Shaughnessy, with a temperament which induced him to overload with sensuous imagery the verse of *An Epic of Women*, a series of lyric episodes with a too ambitious title, had little of the gift of self-criticism. The easy and graceful stanzas, 'We are the music-makers' and the echoing melodies, with their reminiscence of Edgar Allan Poe, of *The Fountain of Tears* are worthy of their place in most of the modern anthologies. Occasional pieces, too, have the sudden magic effect of which Beddoes's lyrics hold the secret. The story of *Chaitivel* in *Lays of France* contains a song in the pleasant and effortless stanza of which Samuel Daniel's *Ulisses and the Syren* is the best English model. All these pieces, if they do not belong to the highest class of poetry, have their own charm and furnish abundant proof of their author's keen appreciation of musical sound. On the other hand, his ear in the poem called *Love's Eternity* was hopelessly at fault and the versification is positively slovenly. A lover of verse, with a somewhat restricted range of theme and without strikingly original methods of treatment, O'Shaughnessy's 'heaven-sent moments' were few. His higher flights, as in *An Epic of Women*, were restricted by excess of heavy ornament; on lower planes, he moved more easily, but his tripping measures were hampered by faults of harmony and little affectations of phrase. The substance of his best pieces is immaterial, and their value is their mellifluous sweetness of sound. As such, they are casual triumphs in a field of which he never obtained perfect command.

II

EDWARD FITZGERALD

As one who found the freest current for his delicate and impressionable genius in the translation and adaptation of the works of others, Edward FitzGerald stands as far aloof from the ordinary activities of the literature of his day as his life was remote from that of the world in general. He was the third son of John Purcell, of Bredfield hall, Suffolk, where he was born on 31 March 1809. When, in 1818, Mrs Purcell's father died, the family assumed his name and arms. At king Edward VI's school at Bury St Edmunds, which he entered in 1821, Edward FitzGerald was a contemporary of James Spedding, John Mitchell Kemble and William Bodham Donne. The friendships thus begun were continued at Cambridge, and afterwards. For Spedding's scholarship, FitzGerald cherished an affectionate admiration, with some regret at its devotion to a purpose with which he had no sympathy, and the series of letters to Fanny Kemble, the last of which was written less than three weeks before his death, recalls his friendship with her brother. He entered Trinity college, Cambridge, in February 1826. Tennyson did not come up till 1828, and does not appear to have met the 'Old Fitz,' addressed, many years later, in the proem to *Tiresias*, until they both had left Cambridge; but, of Tennyson's immediate contemporaries, Thackeray, W. H. Thompson and John Allen, afterwards archdeacon of Salop, were among FitzGerald's intimates at Trinity. He took an ordinary degree in 1830. After a short visit to Paris, where he had already spent some time with his family in his early boyhood, he returned to England and gradually settled down to a quiet life in his native county, which, with the course of years, became practically that of a recluse. Its uneventful story of commerce with books, varied by an occasional visit from a friend, brief journeys to London, becoming rarer and more distasteful as time went on, and boating expeditions on the estuary of the Deben, is told in his letters, a series extending over fifty-one years and remarkable for their naturalness of style, vivacious humour and keen literary criticism, strongly tinged with the individual prejudices of an independent student unswayed by public opinion. He made his home, first at Boulge near Woodbridge, and afterwards at Woodbridge itself. Woodbridge was also the home of Bernard Barton, the friend of Charles Lamb; after Barton's death in 1849, FitzGerald married his daughter and aided her in the publication of a selection from Barton's poems, writing a short biography which forms its preface. Out of a correspondence upon the topography of the battle-field of Naseby, where FitzGerald's father owned property, arose a friendship with Carlyle, while among men of letters with whom he exchanged views in later life were Lowell and Charles Eliot Norton. He died on 14 June 1883 at Bredfield rectory near Woodbridge, while on a visit to George Crabbe, the grandson of a poet for whose memory FitzGerald's devotion was expressed in his *Readings from Crabbe*, compiled in 1879.

Of work which was entirely original, FitzGerald left little. The charming verses, written at Naseby in the spring of 1831 under the influence of 'the merry old writers of more manly times,' and printed in *Hone's Year-Book* under the title *The Meadows in Spring*, were thought, at their first appearance, to be the work of Charles Lamb and were welcomed by their supposed author with good-humoured envy. Diffidence of his own powers and slowness in composition prevented FitzGerald from rapid publication. It was not until 1851 that the dialogue *Euphranor* appeared, a discourse upon youth and systems of education set in the scenery of Cambridge, amid the early summer flowering of college gardens and 'the measured pulse of racing oars.' Its limpid transparency of style was not achieved without an effort: in 1846, when FitzGerald was writing it, he alluded to his difficulties with the task in a letter to his friend Edward Cowell, and its ease and clearness, like those of Tennyson's poetry, appear to have been the fruit of constant polish and revision. This was followed in 1852 by *Polonius*, a collection of aphorisms, 'wise saws and modern instances,' with a humorously apologetic preface. Meanwhile, probably some years before the publication of *Euphranor*, he had been attracted to Spanish literature, in which Cowell, a master of many languages, gave him some assistance. In 1853, he published *Six Dramas of Calderon*, free translations in blank verse and prose in which he endeavoured, by methods fully explained in his preface, to reproduce the substance of the selected plays, while suppressing such details as seemed otiose or foreign to English thought. Following the general course of Calderon's plots and selecting the essential points in his dialogue with much skill, he had no hesitation in diverging, especially where he was tempted by soliloquies, from the text and in altering portions of the action to suit his own

taste. One has only to compare the soliloquy of Don Juan Roca
in *The Painter of his own Dishonour* at the sight of the sleeping
Serafina with the original passage to see how the mental argument
in Calderon, with its direct summary of the facts of the situation,
is transmuted by FitzGerald, with added imagery, into language
of indirect reflection and allusion, in which such facts are taken
for granted without reference. Although he had little taste for
the elder English dramatists, apart from Shakespeare, his verse,
always lucid and free from the turbidity in which their style
was frequently involved, has much of the flow, the tendency to
hendecasyllabic lines and the fondness for radiant and brightly
coloured simile and metaphor characteristic of Beaumont, Fletcher
and Massinger. Such qualities made FitzGerald's translations
eminently readable for their own sake. In spite of their cold reception by critics who preferred something more literal, he was able
to write in 1857, 'I find people like that Calderon book'; and, about
1858, he began translations of the two most famous of Calderon's
dramas. *Such Stuff as Dreams are Made of* and *The Mighty
Magician* bear only a general resemblance to their original.
FitzGerald regarded Calderon as too closely tied to the conventional requirements of the Spanish stage ; the machinery which
bound the main and secondary plots together, provided theatrical
situations and introduced the inevitable *gracioso* with his antics
and proverbial or anecdotal philosophy, creaked too audibly to
please him. Therefore, he confined himself to the main story of
both plays, heightening or tempering the situations as suited his
taste, reducing the part of the *gracioso* in one case and practically
eliminating it in the other. He justly considered that there was
'really very great Skill in the Adaptation, and Remodelling of'
The Mighty Magician : the part of Lucifer, Calderon's Demonio,
is, on the whole, more effective than in the original, where, at any
rate to an English reader, it is somewhat lacking in imaginative
power, and for the frigid, if forcible, dialectic of the scene in which
Cipriano uses the tempter's art against him and extorts his admission of the superior power of the *Dios de los cristianos*, FitzGerald
substituted a more impassioned dialogue rising to a more dramatic
climax. Similarly, in *Such Stuff as Dreams are Made of*, the
contrast between the philosophic and brutal elements in the
character of Segismundo is softened so as to give more consistency
to his bewilderment amid his sudden changes of fortune, and to
lead up to the climax with a greater show of probability ; but
it was the extreme of licence to transfer the famous soliloquy

at the end of the second act of *La Vida es Sueño* from Segismundo to his gaoler and to depress it to a less prominent position in the play.

The *Agamemnon* of Aeschylus and the two *Oedipus* tragedies of Sophocles were also adapted for English readers by FitzGerald with considerable freedom. *Oedipus at Thebes* and *Oedipus at Athens* were works of the last years of his life, and he was content to supply the choruses from Potter's translation. But the work which has given his name its most enduring celebrity was the *Rubáiyát of Omar Khayyám*, of which the first edition appeared in 1859. The stimulating influence of Cowell led him to take an interest in Persian poetry. In 1855, he began his version of the *Salámán and Absál* of Jámí, the first poem which he read in the original, and, in 1862, he completed *A Bird's-eye View of Faríd-Uddín Attar's Bird-Parliament*. These, however, were mere experiments. With the detached quatrains of Omar Khayyám, each a poem in itself linked to the rest by community of thought and subject, he felt a closer sympathy. During a visit to Bedfordshire in May 1857, he read over Omar 'in a Paddock covered with Butterflies and 'brushed by a delicious Breeze, while a dainty racing Filly of W. Browne's came startling up to wonder and snuff' about him, as he turned quatrains into medieval Latin rimes and found his author, one of the 'lighter Shadows among the Shades, perhaps, over which Lucretius presides so grimly,' breathe 'a sort of Consolation' to him. The result of these ruminations was an English poem of seventy-five quatrains founded upon the selection and combination of *rubáiyát*; reproducing the form of the original but weaving its isolated pieces into a continuous train of thought. A new edition, in 1868, in which the stanzas were increased to 110, completely remodelled the poem of 1859, to the disadvantage of the bold imagery of the opening quatrain, but, in other respects, with great felicity; and this, after further but less drastic alterations, which rearranged and reduced the stanzas to 101, formed the basis of the later editions of 1872 and 1879. A comparison of FitzGerald's poem with earlier and later translations of Omar into more literal prose and verse proves the extreme freedom with which he handled his original, transferring thoughts and images from their actual context to clothe them in a dress which is entirely his own. At the same time, his main object, as in the case of Calderon, was to present, in a connected form intelligible to English minds, the characteristics of Omar's thought, his pondering upon life and death, the eternal mysteries

of the whence, why and whither of man and the influence of
external and irresponsible power upon him, and his resort to the
pleasures of the moment as a refuge from the problem. He did
not shirk the freer speculations of his author : 'I do not wish
to show Hamlet at his maddest : but mad he must be shown,
or he is no Hamlet at all.' Characteristically avoiding audacious
expressions which have been regarded by some students of Omar
as the esoteric utterances of an ultra-refined mysticism, he gave
a turn to the culminating stanza preceding the *coda* of the piece,
the appeal to heaven to take, as well as give, man's forgiveness,

> For all the Sin wherewith the Face of Man
> Is blacken'd,

which suggests an impiety undiscovered by other translators, but
not out of keeping with the tone of some of the numerous *rubáiyát* omitted by him. FitzGerald habitually concealed his own
thoughts on the mysteries which perplexed Omar ; and the
warmth of religious enthusiasm which he infused into the somewhat formal atmosphere of *El Magico Prodigioso* might, considering its gratuitous copiousness, quite as reasonably as a single
stanza of his *Rubáiyát,* be taken to express his convictions.
Apart from the question of its contents, the singular beauty
and perfection of phrase in the *Rubáiyát* and the dignity and
melodiousness of its rhythm have earned it a permanent place
among the masterpieces of English lyric poetry. Its stanza was
a novelty which others, like Swinburne in his *Laus Veneris,* were
not slow to borrow. It is not FitzGerald's only claim to eminence,
for *Euphranor* and the translations from Calderon, to say nothing
of his letters, must always appeal to those who love polished simplicity of style. But, in this one instance, his genius, which needed
external literary stimulus for complete expression, responded so
naturally to the call as to clothe its original in a form attractive
not merely to the connoisseur in style but to all who recognise the
true relation of poetry to human life.

CHAPTER VI

LESSER POETS OF THE MIDDLE AND LATER NINETEENTH CENTURY

In taking up, and endeavouring to complete, the chapters on poets[1] who, though not in general opinion attaining to the first rank, have, at one time or another, enjoyed some considerable amount of esteem or who, in that calculus of criticism which disregards popularity, have deserved such esteem, the method pursued will be, as it has been on former occasions, systematised, to some extent, though avoiding arbitrary classification. The number of verse-writers who fall to be mentioned, as representing the middle and later generations of the last century, is very great: and, even after careful sifting and the relegation of some to the bibliography and others to silence altogether, will amount to a round hundred. But it is not necessary to present them in a mere throng or in simple catalogue, alphabetical or chronological, though, after some grouping, the last named method may become necessary.

We may take, first, three very remarkable, though, in themselves, most dissimilar, representatives of the curious class which, attaining, for a time, and not always losing, popularity of the widest kind, is demurred to by critics and sometimes succumbs totally, sometimes partially, to the demurrers. These are Macaulay, Martin Farquhar Tupper and Philip James Bailey. The last named will lead us, naturally enough, to a fairly definite group of which, in a way, he was the leader: the so-called 'spasmodics' of the mid-nineteenth century. That name or nickname, invented by Aytoun, will, in the same fashion, introduce a numerous, and, in some cases, excellent, class of satiric and humorous writers, in whom the century, until quite its close, was specially rich. As a contrast, the equally remarkable section of 'sacred' poets, headed by Keble

---

[1] The poets excluded by the specification of this chapter are Tennyson, the Brownings, Matthew Arnold, Kingsley, the Rossettis, William Morris, Swinburne, James Thomson and O'Shaughnessy. For these, see *ante* and *post*.

and Newman, may succeed these; and then we may take up the great body of verse-writers of the other sex, though their 'prioresses,' Elizabeth Barrett Browning and Christina Rossetti, are denied us[1]. One or two smaller groups may present themselves for treatment together; but the bulk of our subjects, though sometimes admitting what may be called linked criticism, will have to follow mainly in chronological order[2].

The case of Macaulay's poetical work is a very peculiar and a very instructive one in the history both of poetry and of criticism; in fact, in the history, properly so-called, of literature generally. The poems included in *The Lays of Ancient Rome*, though partly printed at earlier dates, were collected and issued at a time when poetry had, for years, sunk out of the popular esteem which it had enjoyed during the first quarter of the century; and was only, for the younger generation, rising again at the call of Tennyson. Criticism was in a very similar position—the almost simultaneous deaths of Coleridge, Hazlitt and Lamb having left no prominent representatives of it except the scattered utterances of Coleridge's son and the senescence of Leigh Hunt, the rather untrustworthy and eccentric survivals of 'Christopher North' and De Quincey and a *numerus* of very inferior and haphazard reviewers who had not yet felt the influence of the new examples of criticism to be set in the fifties by George Brimley and Matthew Arnold.

This combination of long disuse of appetite with an almost entire want of guidance in taste goes far to explain, though, except in Macaulay's case, it is required to excuse, in very different degrees, the immense, and by no means ephemeral, popularity of *The Lays of Ancient Rome*, *Festus* and *Proverbial Philosophy*, far asunder as are the positive poetic merits of these books. In the case of *The Lays*, the public was fortunate in what it received and, whatever may have been said by later criticism, was justified in its reception thereof. That, in his singularly constituted, and, perhaps, never yet quite adequately mapped-out, mind, Macaulay had secret places, where lay concealed springs of poetry of purer kinds than that which he allowed to flow freely in *The Lays*, is proven, as finally as fortunately, by the exquisite classicism of *Epitaph on a Jacobite*, which Landor could not have bettered, and the romantic strangeness of *The Last Buccaneer*, which suggests an uncanny collaboration

---

[1] See *ante*.

[2] The strictly prosodic aspects of the more important of these will be found in some cases dealt with in the next chapter; but it may be difficult entirely to exclude glances at them here, where, indeed, place has been expressly reserved for them.

of Macaulay's two contemporaries Praed and Beddoes. But his
Lays themselves are far finer poetry than Matthew Arnold and some
other critics have been willing to allow. They belong, indeed, to a
wide-ranging class of verse which includes masterpieces like Gray's
Elegy and things certainly not masterpieces like *The Minstrel*
and the poems of Mrs Hemans, not to mention, for the present,
more modern examples—a class which seems deliberately to set
itself to give the public just the sort of poetry which it can well
understand and nothing more. In the better examples of this
poetry—to which *The Lays*, though they may not attain to the
height of Gray, most certainly belong—there is no sacrifice of
poetry itself. Anybody who denies that name to the larger part
of *The Battle of the Lake Regillus* and the best part of *The
Prophecy of Capys*, with not a little elsewhere, had best be met
by the silence, the smile and the not too obvious shrug, which
are suitable to Ephraim when he has irrevocably announced his
junction with idols. And they have the special merit (belonging
to the best of their class) that liking for them, acquired, as it is
probably most often acquired, early, will mature into liking for
greater poetry still. *The Lays*, in a certain, and only a certain,
sense, may be milk for babes; but good milk is a great deal
better than tainted meat and unsound wine. The babes can go on
to relish such meat and wine as the author also showed that he
knew how to produce when he wrote how the broken heart by
the Arno thought of 'the lovelier Tees' and how

> the crew with eyes of flame, brought the ship without a name
> Alongside the last Buccaneer.

Therefore, in this case, the unshepherded, and for long almost
ungrassed, public went not wrong ; but it is impossible to say the
same of its somewhat earlier divagation in favour of Martin
Farquhar Tupper. *Proverbial Philosophy*, to this day, is and will
probably always remain, one of the chief curiosities of literature,
perhaps the supremest of all such things in its own special class.
The author, from the combined and direct testimony of persons
who knew him at different times of his life, was by no means
a fool, when he had not a pen in his hand. In his other books of
verse, which are numerous, it is possible, as, for instance, in *The
Crock of Gold*, to discover passages, or even poems, of passable or
possible poetry of a not very high kind. These volumes were not
much bought; and, no doubt, were, as wholes, not very much worth
buying. But *Proverbial Philosophy*, which made his reputation,
which sold in unbelievable numbers and which has sometimes earned

for him the title 'The People's Poet Laureate,' is such incredible rubbish that it would almost justify the obloquy which has come upon 'early Victorian' taste if it were not that even the loose and unregimented criticism of that period itself would have none of it. It furnished the subject of one of the most brilliant of the *Bon Gaultier* parodies and skits (see *post*) a few years after its appearance; the very schoolboys (not to mention the undergraduates) of its date seem, from not untrustworthy testimony, to have been taught by their still uncorrupted classical education to revolt against it; and the present writer can give personal evidence that, by the middle of the fifties or thereabouts, it was a hissing and a scorn to all who had any sense of literature, or were ever going to have it. But the great middle, or lower middle, class here, and, still more, in America, steadily bought it till much later; and nobody can refuse it rank as a 'document' of what myriads of people thought might be poetry in the beginning of the second third of the nineteenth century.

As such, it can never wholly lose its position; and it would be rash (considering the extraordinary changes of superficial and ephemeral taste which are familiar to the historical student) to say that it can never recover something, at least, of what it has lost. But it would certainly be surprising if it did, especially as, since its time, other examples of popular rubbish have secured, and yet others are, at intervals, likely to secure, equal vogue with the same class of readers. In it 'there be truths,' unfortunately always presented as truisms. There is—if not, as lord Foppington sarcastically observed of his lost bride and actual sister-in-law, 'a *nice* marality'—a sound one enough. There is an unflinching adoption of the proverbial form with its strange popular effect. But, over the whole, platitude broods with wings that drop the deadliest tedium : one waits in vain for any phrase that shall give light to the gloom or life to the stagnation; at times, the dullness ferments itself into sheer silliness after a fashion which exasperates instead of relieving. A faint amusement at such an impossible thing ever having been thought possible may support the reader for awhile; but sleep or the relinquishment of his task can be the only 'happy ending' of such an adventure.

But, even thus, not quite enough has been said for present purposes about *Proverbial Philosophy*. An 'interlunar cave' of poetical matter for people to fix their eyes on will do much ; and an almost entire want of authority in criticism (though, as has been said, even the usually feeble critics of the day would not stand *this*), will, perhaps, do more. But the inexorable 'historic estimate' has something to add. Tupper (no doubt in the most unconscious way in the world) had hit on the fact, corroborated by that poetical history of which he had probably not much notion (his attempts at transversing Old English poetry prove it), that, in poetic *interlunia*, irregular rhythms acquire a certain phosphoric light. *Proverbial Philosophy* is written in a sort of doggerel which, sometimes coming very close to what some call the 'accentual' English hexameter[1], more often strays into a vaguely rhythmical, but quite unmetrical, stave reminiscent of *Ossian* and Blake, perhaps, and pretty certainly not without influence on Whitman. The intolerable imbecility of the statement of the matter,

> pay quickly that thou owest;
> The needy tradesman is made glad by such considerate haste;

the infantine egotism of such things as this,

> I never forced Minerva's will, nor stole my thoughts from others,

(where one feels instinctively that Tupper never came within finger-tip reach of Pallas, and that, if he never stole his thoughts from others, it was, at least, partly because he never knew what was worth stealing)—these things are, or ought to be, balanced, if not compensated, by the reflection that the form, chiefly through Whitman's transformation, has been largely used since ; that the principle of it—the revolt of rhythm against metre—is very much alive at the present day; and that Martin Farquhar Tupper— impossible as he is to read, except as a sandwich of somnolence and laughter; probable as it is that the reading may be inter- rupted for ever by a paroxysm of utter repudiation of the book to the second-hand stall or the dustbin—is, in literary history, not a mere cypher. He teaches lessons amazingly different from those which he thought he was teaching; and he utters warnings which never, in the slightest degree, entered his own head. These lessons and warnings have been partially disclosed in the remarks just made; there is no room for more of them. Let it only be added that, if an adventure of the kind of this *History* be again undertaken 'a hundred years hence,' though it is possible that Tupper may be omitted or merely glanced at, the popularity of certain verse- writers of present or recent days will probably form the subject

---

[1] In the very first paragraph there are two examples—one of the spondaic, one of the regular dactylic, form of this :

Corn from the | sheaves of | science with | stubble from | mine own | garner,
These I com|mend to | thee, O | docile | scholar of | Wisdom.

The Alexandrine and the fourteener occur, also, and practically the whole wanders round these centres.

of remarks not very different from those which have appeared here. And it is not quite so probable that, in these new essays of dullness, there will be found any formal originality or impulse from the historical point of view to supply such a solace or set-off as has been pleaded here for the heavy and silly sin of *Proverbial Philosophy*.

The third member of this trio, though somewhat closer, in some ways, to Tupper than either he or Tupper is to Macaulay, and almost, though not quite, sharing the oblivion which has engulfed *Proverbial Philosophy* and has not engulfed *The Lays of Ancient Rome*, is, perhaps, the most difficult of the three to estimate aright. Philip James Bailey, when, at the age of twenty-three, he wrote *Festus*, in its original form, had the full benefit of that comparatively dead season, in poetry and criticism, which has been spoken of above. Editions by the dozen in England and by the score in America (where men, at that time, were desperately busy 'getting culture') came at his call as they came at Tupper's; but the nature of the call was itself essentially different, and (as it is almost safe to say never happened in the case of *Proverbial Philosophy*) contemporaries of undoubted poetical competence, from Tennyson himself to Westland Marston, were ready to welcome Bailey as a brother. He had, in fact, as Macaulay had not attempted to do in his principal work, and as Tupper, if he had ever attempted to do it, had obviously and ludicrously failed to do, in an old-new way—effective if not perfect—struck that vein of 'strangeness' which, from Aristotle downwards, all the greatest writers have recognised as more or less necessary to poetry. As being so, it had been a main source of the earlier romantic triumphs; but the great poets of that time had not found it necessary to labour this vein extravagantly or exclusively, though some signs of doing this were obvious in the group who, in a former chapter[1], have been called 'the intermediates.' Bailey drove what pickaxe he had straight at this vein and never thought of limiting his extraction from it. He was almost immediately followed by some notable persons who will be dealt with next under their nickname 'spasmodics'—and it is by no means unarguable that both Tennyson and Browning showed signs of slight infection—while the creed of 'strangeness for strangeness' sake' has never wanted adherents up to the present day, and it now has quite a company of them. Every now and then some generous member of this community makes a plea—with due stridency and gesticulation—for *Festus*: and it is doubtful whether any critic

[1] See vol. xii, chap. v.

endowed by nature with some catholicity of judgment has read
the poem without seeing its merits, especially in its original form.
But the defects even of that form, and, still more, of the later transformation, can, at the same time, escape no such critic.

To give any account of *The Lays of Ancient Rome* in detail
would be absurd, for everybody knows them ; to give any account
of *Proverbial Philosophy* in detail would be as impossible as to
do the same to a bale of cotton wool; but something of the kind is
necessary—and, in fact, from what has been said, must be seen to
be at least very desirable—in the case of *Festus*. As originally
planned, and as its name indicates pretty clearly, it is a variant
on the Faust story. The hero neither succumbs wholly to diabolic
temptation, as in the Marlowe version, nor is saved by the *Ewig-
weibliche*, as in Goethe ; but he has an accompanying tempter in
Lucifer himself, and he has a whole harem of Gretchens, none of
whom he exactly betrays, and one of whom, Clara, he eventually
marries, though a sort of battle of Armageddon, followed by the
consummation of all things, interrupts the honeymoon. In the
enormous interim, Lucifer, for purposes not always obvious, personally conducts Festus about the universe—and all the universes ;
foregathers with him in merely mundane societies both of a mixed
ordinary kind and also of political-theosophical studentry, and
once creates a really poetical situation (which the author, unable
to deal with it even at first, spoilt further in the incredible
processes to be described immediately) by himself falling in love
with a girl whom he has thought to use for ensnaring Festus.
Usually, the tempter indulges in speeches of great length, replied
to with tenfold volubility by Festus, who might have claimed (as
Joanna Southcott is said actually to have done) to have 'talked
the devil dead,' inasmuch as Lucifer himself at least once cries for
mercy. The whole concludes with the complete defeat of the
spirit unfortunate ; but with more than a hint of an *apocatastasis*
—of an assize in which he will share.

It is quite possible that this argument, so far as the strict
Festus of 1839 is concerned, may be slightly contaminated by
later insertions, for the writer has read the poem in more versions
than one, as, indeed, is necessary, owing to the unparalleled processes (above alluded to) which Bailey adopted towards it.
Between 1839 and 1850, *Festus* had a comparatively fair field
opened to it ; but, by the latter year, Tennyson had thoroughly
established himself, Browning was there for those who could like
him and others had come or were coming. *The Angel World*, a sort

of satellite of *Festus*, was not received cordially ; *The Mystic* and *The Spiritual Legend* (1855) still less so ; and, when an entirely new poetical period had thoroughly set in, the *Universal Hymn* in 1868 least of all. No one but a very curmudgeonly person quarrels with a parent, poetical or other, for standing by his unpopular children. But the way in which Bailey acted towards his was without precedent, and, one may hope, will never be imitated. He stuffed large portions of the unsuccessful books into what was becoming the not very popular body of *Festus* itself, which, thereby, from a tolerably exacting individuality of 20,000 lines or thereabout, became an impossible sausage of double the number.

The earlier eulogists of *Festus* dwelt almost wholly, and their more recent successors, after a very long gap, have dwelt partly, on a supposed magnificence of subject—the ways of God being justified to man on the basis of what is called universalism. This, it would be quite out of place here to discuss, though, perhaps, one may, without too much petulance, repeat that perambulation of the universe or universes in blank verse shares the drawback of that medium, as immortally urged by Thackeray, that it is 'not argument.' The person who succeeds in reading *Festus*, even in the original, much more in the later, form, 'for the story,' 'for the argument,' or for anything else of the kind, must be possessed of a singular prowess or of a still more singular indifference and insensibility.

The form requires some notice. It is, perhaps, more eccentrically blended, and the elements of the blend are more strangely selected and associated, than is the case with any other long poem which has ever attained, as *Festus* has done, both popularity and critical acceptance of a kind. The greater part of it, as indicated above, is couched in a curious loose blank verse, neither definitely individual nor clearly imitated from anybody else ; but marking a further stage of the pseudo-dramatic 'blanks' of the 'intermediates.' It drops, occasionally, into couplet or into semi-doggerel anapaestics—generally bad—while it is, in one part frequently, in others sometimes, interspersed with lyrics of extraordinary weakness. Bailey's 'spasmodic' pupils (see below) were to redeem their faults and frailties by occasional bursts of genuine lyric of high and (as lyrics go) new quality. But his near namesake Haynes Bayly himself could give the author of *Festus* points and beat him in a pseudo-Mooreish, twaddling-tinkling kind of melody, which never (so far as it is safe to use that word in connection with an author so voluminous and so difficult to pin down in printed form as Bailey) attains any clear lyrical colour, passion or 'cry.' On the other hand, in the blank verse itself there are occasionally to be found—and this was probably the cause of the original recognition by brother poets and has always been the handle seized by later eulogists of ability—passages of extraordinary brilliancy, in diction, versification and (with a slightly rhetorical limitation) general literary appeal. Sometimes, these are merely lines or short fragments; sometimes, more sustained and substantive pieces of accomplishment. They rarely have, as the common phrase goes, 'much to do with anything' and are usually 'purple patches' in the strictest sense—purple enough, but, also, patchy enough. They are acceptable for their own beauty and they acquire additional interest from the point of view of the historian; because, it was certainly *Festus* and its imitations which, coming, as they did, just at the time when a critical 'instauration' was beginning, set Matthew Arnold, Bagehot and others against detailed ornament of treatment not demonstrably connected with the subject. It is probable that this somewhat barbaric jewellery had not a little to do with Bailey's popularity and with that which, for a time, at least, rewarded his followers next to be treated. It will be best to postpone some general remarks on it till they have been dealt with, but others may be interposed here.

The central point in Bailey and in these others who, though they can hardly be called his disciples and form a very loose 'school,' have this centre in common with him, is a kind of solidifying or, at least, *centripetalising* of the loose and floating endeavours towards something new and strange which we found in the 'intermediates.' None of these can stand by himself in individual quality, like Tennyson and Browning; none of them can, by an effect of scholarship and poetic determination, reach the eclectic individuality of Matthew Arnold; they have not even virility of genius enough to work in a definite school like the later pre-Raphaelites. But, by a certain gorgeousness or intricacy of language, by a scrupulous avoidance of the apparent common-place in subject; by more or less elaborately hinted or expressed unorthodoxy in religion or philosophy; and, above all, by a neurotic sentimentalism which would be passion if it could, and, sometimes, is not absolutely far from it, though it is in constant danger of turning to the ridiculous or of tearing its own flimsiness to tatters— by all these things and others they struggled to avoid the obvious and achieve poetic strangeness.

The most usually quoted names in the group are those of Sydney Dobell, Alexander Smith and the two Joneses, Ernest and Ebenezer, each of whom deserves some special notice here. But some community of character, both in the respects noticed above and, sometimes, also, in a sort of vague political unrestfulness, may be observed in others, such as William Bell Scott and Thomas Gordon Hake, who, after showing 'spasmodic' signs, became, as it were, outside pre-Raphaelites later.

The most 'occasional' poet among the semi-official spasmodics, as we may call them, was, probably, Ernest Jones, son of a soldier of distinction, a king's godson in Germany, presented at court in England, and a barrister, but a violent chartist agitator, a two-years' prisoner for sedition, an industrious journalist and lecturer, later a not unsuccessful practitioner in his profession, a frequent candidate for parliament and, at last, just before his death, a successful one, after a fashion. This brief biography does not sound very promising ; but, as a matter of fact, Jones was not a bad poet. Even his *Songs of Democracy* redeem their inevitable clap-trap with less spitefulness than Ebenezer Elliott's (though Elliott was a prosperous, and Jones a very unlucky, man) and by an occasional humour of which the Sheffield poet was incapable. It is impossible for the bitterest reactionary who possesses a sense of that inestimable quality not to recognise it in *The Song of the Lower Classes*, with its mischievous, ricketty, banjo-like quasi-refrain of

We're low—we're low—we're very very low!

And, when Jones would let politics alone—politics which, on whatever side the subject be taken up, seldom inspire any but the satiric muse—he could, as in some of his pieces on the Crimean war and in others, more general, such as *The Poet's Parallel*, show real poetic power.

His namesake, Ebenezer, was also bitten with the chartist mania, having some excuse in the facts that his circumstances, never very bright or prosperous, became steadily worse, while, though never quite in Alton Locke's straits, he was so like him in his infirm health and in other ways, that, if dates and other things did not make it extremely unlikely, there might be suspicions of his having been taken as a model, to some extent, by Kingsley. *Studies of Sensation and Event* (1843), his only substantive published work, shows a quite unmistakable poetic faculty, though undeveloped (he was only 23) and never fully to be developed (for he died in 1860 and the interval had been sterilised by ill-health, domestic misfortune and office work). But it appeared in that disastrous interval of poetic taste and poetic criticism which has been more than once mentioned, the only cheerful side of which is the hard discipline it gave to the two great capacities—great enough to meet and withstand and conquer it—of Tennyson and Browning. Ebenezer Jones had no such greatness—would probably never have attained it even if circumstances had been more favourable; and they were not favourable at all. But *The Hand* and *Rain* and *The Face*—these are the stock extracts, but it is as silly to neglect as it is degrading to rely on stock matter—have something that is not like other people, and is poetry. The ill-success of his first book and the possibly unfortunate, but certainly unusual and respectable, variety of 'poetic irritability' which seems to have determined him, in consequence of that ill-success, to destroy what unpublished verse he had and write little more, prevented him from being much more than a promise of a poet. Such posthumous work as we have shows little new merit. But, in the circumstances, it would be a vulgar error to expect such merit, and an error even more vulgar to cancel the praise due to the promise. Judging by that, Ebenezer Jones might have been at least as good a poet as most of those mentioned in this chapter; and there is hardly a case in it in which the phrase *Dis aliter visum* is at once more obvious and more explicable.

Alexander Smith and Sydney Dobell are persons and poets of what we may call more substantive character than those whom we have been mentioning after Bailey. It is true that, in both cases, pleas in arrest of definite judgment—things troublesome to the critic but not negligible by him—exist. Both suffered from bad health, and, though fortune, in the more vulgar sense of the term, was kind enough to Dobell, it was not till rather late, and in a very moderate fashion, that she was kind to Smith. Yet, these external circumstances cannot, as in the case of the Joneses, be allowed to leave historical judgment uncertain. Both Smith and Dobell had sufficient opportunities of showing the best that was in them; and they must be presumed to have shown it. It is a 'best' which, sometimes, has undoubted, and not unplentiful, good in it; it has flashes of a quality to which Southey's ingenious glovemaker must have allowed his most complimentary label, 'the real best'; but it never holds this quality for long, and it is full of the 'spasmodic' flaws—extravagance of conception and diction, a sort of Byronism metamorphosed, imitation of other poets which, sometimes, goes near to plagiarism, an inequality which exceeds the large limits allowed to poets and, worst of all, that suggestion of ineffective and undignified effort—of the 'ginger-beer bottle burst,' to borrow a phrase from Smith himself—which is the universal mark of the spasmodic beast.

Alexander Smith, though the younger of the two, deserves, for more reasons than one, the earlier mention. His *Life Drama* appeared in the same year as Dobell's *Balder*; and was, perhaps, the last book which profited—if the result can be called profit—by that depression in poetry itself and in criticism of poetry which had characterised the second quarter of the century. It was greeted at first with the wildest hosannas; and men now old, but not old enough to have shared in, or refused, the welcome, may remember how the bookcases of friends ten or twenty years older than them-selves contained the volume with obvious marks of those friends' youthful admiration. But fortune was just about to turn her wheel. The far greater poetic powers of Tennyson and Browning were, at last—the former in all but actual possession, the latter in comparatively near expectance, of recognition. The new criticism was cutting its teeth and—in the somewhat ill-conditioned fashion of youthful animals—was ready to fix them in something. Smith was accused of plagiarism from Tennyson himself and others; *City Poems*, his second book, containing some of his very best work, was a failure; and *Edwin of Deira* (1861), though rather better received than *City Poems*, might, without much loss, have remained unwritten. In his later years, Smith wrote some ex-cellent prose, especially of the miscellaneous kind, collected in books called *Dreamthorp* and *A Summer in Skye*[1]. But he died early, and it is more than doubtful whether, if he had lived longer, he would have done much more in verse.

It is evident that he had early absorbed a great deal of the new poetry from Wordsworth to Tennyson, and that he was re-turning it in a fashion sufficiently, if not masterfully, dissimilated. Hence, the charge of plagiarism[2], from which he can be victoriously cleared on almost every point—not least so on the famous passage about 'the bridegroom sea toying with the shore,' on which Kingsley founded a not very clear-sighted diatribe against what was then

---

[1] See *post*, chap. xv.

[2] The presence of constant suggestion in him from others cannot be denied, and, curiously enough, it is even more obvious and much more teasing in his prose than in his verse, there being less originality of form to carry it off. *Dreamthorp* is a pleasant book enough for an uncritical reader : the critic cannot read it without incessant reminders of Lamb, Hazlitt, De Quincey, Carlyle and others clanging in his ears, and disturbing his enjoyment.

modern poetry. It is evident, likewise, that he had taken pretty severely the 'spasmodic' measles—the nineteenth-century joint revival of fifteenth-century 'aureation' and seventeenth century 'metaphysicalism'—with a fresh neurosis of *Weltschmerz,* and so forth. But he could write beautiful passages, if not a beautiful poem, and he had a real lyrical gift. He might sue for citizenship in poetry on the strength of *Barbara* alone; and no fairly selected jury of poets or critics could deny it him. Perhaps he has nothing else so solidly good; but he has other pieces not far inferior in the lyric way, and the small blank verse passages, above referred to, would, if collected, make a notable sheaf. In substance, fable, matter, as well as in poetic temper, *A Life Drama* resembles *Festus* and *Balder*; but it has the advantage of being infinitely shorter than the former and infinitely less pretentious than either.

And yet there are grounds for holding Sydney Dobell the greatest poet of the group. He, like some others, has been more unfortunate in his eulogists than in his detractors, for to say that *Balder* 'contains beauties *beyond the reach of* any contemporary poet' (the competitors, be it remembered, including, to mention nobody else, Tennyson, Browning and Matthew Arnold) is so monstrous an exaggeration that it may recoil not more on its author than on its subject. But the critic who indulged in this aberration of enthusiasm palinodes it in the same sentence with such terms as 'preposterous' and 'chaotic,' while, in others, we find charges of 'dull verbiage,' 'outrageous extravagance,' 'mere inanity,' 'obscurity,' 'pretentiousness,' 'sentimental and sonorous claptrap' and the like. The *indignité,* to use the old tag once more, is not much more exact than the *excès d'honneur.* A purely private education, very bad health and (though he was a man of business for parts of his life) recluse habits fostered in Dobell an evidently congenital incapacity for self- and other criticism. *The Roman,* his first book, is, admittedly, a mere rhetorical utterance of the 'Italomania' common at the time; *Balder,* with some fine passages, though none of his finest, has more of the 'burst ginger-beer bottle' quality of the spasmodics than any other poem by any other author; and *England in Time of War* contains a good deal of rubbish, with some things as different from rubbish as it is possible to conceive. Of Dobell's two masterpieces, *Keith of Ravelston*[1] and *Tommy's Dead,* as of a considerable number of passages, if hardly another complete

---

[1] Not so entitled, though generally so called. It is part of another poem *A Nuptial Song.*

poem, in his other works, though it is, as has been said, absurd to put them 'beyond the reach' of others, it might truly enough be said that, in those others, nothing exactly like them is actually found. There is, in them, an idiosyncrasy of strangeness—a faculty of inspiring and surrounding sometimes the very simplest words with an *aura* or atmosphere of poetic unfamiliarity—which thing whosoever possesses, he passes as a poet without further question. None of Dobell's fellows—not even Elizabeth Barrett Browning— who is a sort of she-spasmodic of the nobler kind—actually has it in the same way or in the same degree. But it must be allowed that no other poet brings so vividly before us the faults which Kingsley (with the spasmodics clearly in mind) has attributed to his Alton Lockes and his Elsley Vavasours; while none enables us so thoroughly to understand the way in which Matthew Arnold, at this very time, was plying the new critical weapons he had forged against extravagance, caprice, the subordination of the general fashioning of the poetic garment to its decoration with purple patches or tinsel trimmings and the like.

We may turn, in logical connection as well as rhetorical contrast, from these poets who, though they were not all entirely destitute of humour, undoubtedly owed most of their faults to the want of its chastening influence, to another group composed of writers of verse, not always purely humorous, but, at its and their own best, mainly so. And we may, with special propriety—again logical as well as chronological—begin with the coiner of the name 'spasmodic'—William Edmonstoune Aytoun.

As in most, if not in all, cases, the possession of the faculty of writing light verse was accompanied, in Aytoun, by no inconsiderable command of serious poetry. The style of his chief efforts, in this latter—ballad-romances of Scott's type—has not retained much popularity; but no one whose taste in poetry is free from mere caprice, or mere prejudice, can deny unusual merit to *The Island of the Scots* and to more than one or two other passages of *Lays of the Scottish Cavaliers*. Still, Aytoun's best work was, undoubtedly, of the comic or tragi-comic kind. Although *Firmilian* and the pilot-article on it in *Blackwood* at once attracted the popularity they deserved, and have received honourable mention from almost all critics and literary historians of competence who have mentioned them since, it may be doubted whether the full intrinsic and historical importance of the piece is now, or, indeed, has ever been, sufficiently recognised. In general scheme a rather close parody of *Balder* and *A Life Drama*, with an extra dose of melodrama in action, *Firmilian* not merely administers the castigation of laughter to these pieces and to their authors, not merely, in its burlesque of extravagant statement, phrase and conceit, reaches back to Bailey and to the Byronists, if not even to Byron himself, but positively anticipates spasmodic productions yet unborn. Even *Maud*, not to appear till a year later, is galled in its weaker parts by this audacious and prophetic satire; so is some then unpublished work of Mrs Browning. In fact, it would not be very difficult to make a chain of spasmodic instances up to the present day which cannot escape the mirror of Aytoun's parody.

If it be urged that *Firmilian* requires for its full appreciation rather more knowledge of past literature than most people can be expected to possess, that plea cannot avail as regards the famous and delightful *Bon Gaultier Ballads* which Aytoun, some years earlier, wrote with Theodore Martin. *Ta Fhairshon* and the parody of *Locksley Hall* have probably been the most popular pieces; but it may, perhaps, be questioned whether *George of Gorbals*[1]—a burlesque both of the metre and the manner of Mrs Browning—is not the best of all. Aytoun's scholarship, his mastery of phrase and metre, his sardonic humour and, behind it, that blend of romance and passion, without which so-called humorous verse is apt to be merely funny or merely horse-playful, made it difficult for him to go wrong; while his powers in criticism and in satiric prose-narrative were hardly less.

The historical influence of two such books as *The Ingoldsby Legends* and *The Bon Gaultier Ballads*, following, as it did, on the exceptional development of satiric verse of the lighter description from *The Rolliad* onwards through Canning and his group to Moore and others with Hood and Praed following[2], is greater than has always been allowed for. Among the numerous sources of amusement provided by a certain recent tendency to regard early and mid-Victorian things as characterised by dull conventionalism alternating with silly sentimentality, there is hardly

---

[1] The subject of this, otherwise *The Rhyme of Sir Launcelot Bogle*, matters nothing, but it is curiously difficult to trace it to anything actual. Aytoun's partner, interrogated on the subject late in life, declared that he had forgotten, if, indeed, he ever knew; and venerable citizens of Glasgow (the scene) have been unable to do more than assign it to some unchronicled municipal squabble. Not thus unknown should be the facts that suggested

'Nay! tarry till they come' quoth Neish 'unto the rum—
They are working at the mum
And the gin!'

[2] For these, see, *ante*, vol. XII, chap. v.

any one which is so much of a *fons Bandusiae* as the memory of these two books, of Thackeray's light verse and of the enormous popularity of at least the first two collections. For, at least, twenty years past there has been no 'master of the laugh' who has produced anything approaching them. In fact, there have been pessimists who have held that, since the departure of 'C. S. C.' and 'J. K. S.' and the comparative desertion by W. S. Gilbert of the pure lighter lyric unconnected with the stage, the gloomy assertion of Théodore de Banville, much earlier justified in French,

> Mais à présent c'est bien fini de rire

has transferred itself to English.

Certainly, however, no such thing was true from 1830 to 1890 or even a little later; and we must briefly survey here the bearers of that torch of laughter which some very grave and precise persons have not hesitated to indicate as one of the most triumphant and idiosyncratic possessions of humanity at large and of English humanity rather specially.

The first group or sub-group to be noticed should consist of the earlier mid-century 'Bohemians,' whom, however, we can discuss here only in part, Maginn and 'Father Prout'[1] being reserved for other divisions; Thackeray himself rising higher; and others for other reasons being, also, excluded. Here, however, may be mentioned Percival Leigh[2], a great contributor to *Punch* in its brilliant second early period ; and W. J. Prowse, 'Nicholas,' who died young and took little care of the work which his short life and his weak health enabled him to do, but whose talent has appealed very strongly to some good judges and can hardly be denied by any. *The City of Prague*—which has sometimes been attributed to others, particularly to James Hannay, but which is really by Prowse—wants only a very few revising touches to make it a masterpiece. With one of such touches, so slight that the reading is a common one in quotation, and can be constructed out of the printed poem itself, we get the stanza:

> Though the latitude's rather uncertain,
> Though the longitude's possibly vague—
> The people I pity who know not the city—
> The beautiful city of Prague

---

[1] See, *post*, vol. xiv.

[2] Not to be confounded with his junior, H. S. Leigh, who was himself a writer of some talent in light verse.

—a thing of much sweetness. But the wisest sojourners in Bohemia have admitted that its capital is not a good city to abide in; and we shall find that the best of the group now under mention were only visitors of the spiritual Prague, if even that. More of a scholar than Prowse was Mortimer Collins, who frittered away, if not in actual idleness yet in hasty and desultory work, talents perhaps greater than anyone else of the class, except Maginn, possessed. He left, however, some charming love-poetry, as *To F. C.*, and some brilliant satiric verse, as *The British Birds*.

The author of one of the most original books of comic verse ever written, Edward Lear, though he was a great traveller, had not much to do with Bohemia. An artist he was in more than one sense and in more than one branch of art; but none of his artistries led him Prague-wards, just as the fact that he owed not a little to patronage did not, in the least, subject him to any of the trials, or tempt him into any of the revolts and excesses, of Bohemia's uglier elder sister Grub street. Severe critics in the arts of design have admitted him to be an excellent draughtsman: it would be a sufficient and final testimony of the hopelessness of a literary critic if he failed to find in Lear a super-excellent writer of an almost unique kind.

The delightful *Book of Nonsense* (the form of the verse of which was long afterwards senselessly vulgarised and, in fact, prostituted, in newspaper competitions under the equally sense-less name 'Limerick'), taking, perhaps, a hint from the im-memorial nursery rime, combined sense and nonsense, after the specially English fashion, in a way never known before; while his somewhat longer poems—*The Owl and the Pussy-Cat*, the famous *Jumblies* and others—readjusted the combination in a fashion almost more delectable still.

Frederick Locker (who, late in life, on the occasion of his second marriage, took the additional name Lampson) was one of the few English writers who have devoted themselves wholly to what is called 'verse of society.' The advantage of official or private means—sufficient at all times and, latterly, large—made it possible for him entirely to avoid the hack-work which is nowhere more perilous to perfection than in this particular department; and his total production is, comparatively, small. It is included chiefly in the frequently reprinted and much altered volume *London Lyrics*, to which has to be added the most remarkable and too little known book called *Patchwork*, a sort of olio or

macédoine slightly resembling Southey's *Omniana* and consisting
of prose and verse partly original partly not. But Locker made
the very best use of his leisure, and has left practically nothing
that is not perfected and polished up to the limit of his own
powers. These powers, no doubt, had certain limitations. He had
pathos—or he could not have displayed his humour to such advantage; but this pathos seldom reached poignancy, as may be
seen by comparing those two remarkable pendants, his *To My
Grandmother* and Oliver Wendell Holmes's *Last Leaf.* His rigid
abstinence from all major notes may be thought to show something of what is opprobriously called 'sparrow-hawking.' But,
though these be, in a certain sense, truths, they are very unjust
objections. A man has a perfect right to choose and define his
own business; and the only question is whether he has done it
well. Locker did his supremely well. His extraordinary urbanity
and ease have been admitted by fellow-craftsmen from whose
judgment there is no appeal, as well as by quite disinterested
critics. He is, perhaps, the only instance of a poet who was perpetually altering and retouching his verse without ever spoiling it.
His obvious and, indeed, avowed model was Praed ; but, except in
some very early pieces, perhaps, where he was following too
closely, one would not often mistake or mis-ascribe work of the
two. The same is the case—and still more so—with Prior. Moreover, the enjoyment of his work is constantly heightened by the
sense, for those who have some knowledge of literature, of what
he has escaped. The dangers of this light, easy verse are very
much greater than anybody who has not studied it very carefully
may think. Vulgarity, of course, is the worst of all; but, of this,
there was not a trace in Locker. Triviality is a subtler danger ;
and, as, perhaps, no two people entirely agree upon what is trivial,
it is difficult to speak positively about it. Perhaps, Locker sometimes approached it in pieces like *Our Photographs*, but much
less often than any save the very princes of the craft of light verse.
From that 'inept laughter' (which is different from triviality and
which the Latin tag justly stigmatises as the ineptest thing in the
world) Locker was perfectly free. His form, if never quaint and
not often exquisite, is surprisingly adequate. And, lastly, not only
does he possess the almost indefinable air of good breeding, but he
adds to it something more indefinable still, the quintessence of that
widely varying quality which, in its different lower forms, is called
'slyness,' 'archness,' and which, in its better shape, the eighteenth
century, with a slight difference from the modern use of the word,

called 'dryness.' This quality, perhaps, is nowhere shown in such perfection as in the prose anecdote *My Guardian Angel*, to be found in *Patchwork*; but, in different degrees, it suffuses almost the whole of his verse. He rises highest, perhaps, in *My Neighbour Rose*, the finale of which contains something that indicates a possibility of entirely serious verse of a high kind from him. But, for anyone who can enjoy this class of poetry, it is very difficult to go wrong with Locker.

We may close this survey of lighter nineteenth-century verse with notice of three or, perhaps, four most remarkable 'university wits[1].' Of the first three, one belonged wholly to Oxford, one wholly to Cambridge and a third—the eldest, as a matter of fact, and the most widely known—to both. This was Charles Stuart Calverley (born Blayds), a man who, in consequence of a disastrous accident, suffered severely for years and died in middle age; who, in consequence, partly, of this, did not do much work; but who made the initials C.S.C., by which he was usually known, early familiar and, to the present day, famous for the expression in verse of a scholarly wit unsurpassed in its own kind. Comparing notes with younger readers one may pretty well assure oneself that the intense enjoyment caused to the undergraduate mind by *Fly Leaves*, in 1866, was not a mere matter of contemporary partiality and congruity; while Calverley's translations from Greek and Latin yield to none in fidelity or in finish. He has, perhaps, attracted most popular attention as a parodist; and not very wise exception has been taken to the 'bitterness' of his exercise in this kind on Browning. Better balanced judgment will see in it, as in all Calverley's work in parody, nothing but fair play if not, also, positive good nature. Scarcely the most extravagant line but could be paralleled from Browning's actual work somewhere or other.

Nor did this most scholarly of humorous poets and least pedantic of scholars require the canvas of an original on which to embroider his thoughts and fancies; for many of his best things are quite original themselves. He had eminently the faculty of giving to a word a ludicrous aspect, by unobtrusive pun or otherwise, or of getting a secondary comic effect from a simple phrase, as in

> The ladies *following in the van*

of one of his lightest things and

> We're not as tabbies are

---

[1] See, also, *post*, vol. XIV, the chapter on university journalism.

in his noble apology for tobacco.   His considerable critical faculty was inadequately, but clearly, shown in his *Remains*; he was a student of the theory of verse, as well as a skilled practitioner in it; and it is evident that, with better luck, he might have produced a great bulk of valuable work in various kinds.

Henry Duff Traill had a longer life than Calverley, though his, too (in this case directly), was cut short by an accident.   But his time, almost from the moment of his leaving Oxford, was occupied by journalism; and of the immense quantity of this which he produced very little ever found its way into permanent and acknowledged form.   This little included, however, two volumes of satiric verse (*Recaptured Rhymes* and *Saturday Songs*) of very high quality indeed.   Traill was almost, if not quite, as deft a parodist as Calverley; and the most enthusiastic admirer of Rossetti who has any sense of humour cannot fail to enjoy his caricature of the Rossettian sonnet.   But his great excellence was as a political satirist in verse—a department in which he came very close to Canning and, perhaps, even surpassed Moore.   *The Ballad of Baloonatics Craniocracs* (a satire on the philological and historical arguments used in regard to the war of 1878), and *Laputa Outdone*, on the arguments for the miscellaneous extension of the franchise, are masterpieces of their kind.   But Traill had a strong inclination—which circumstances did not allow him to indulge—towards more serious or wholly serious poetry, and examples of each of these may be found in *An* Enfant Terrible and *The Age of Despair*.   Some who knew Traill well, and the press of the last third of the century fairly, have held that no greater talent than his, both in verse and prose, was diverted into, and swallowed up in, the gulf of anonymous writing.

The youngest and the shortest-lived of the three, James Kenneth Stephen, who, like Calverley, established himself in literature by his initials, had his chances marred in a manner even worse than that from which Calverley suffered, by his early death and the illness which preceded it.   The variety and brilliancy of the talent shown in *Lapsus Calami* and the other too rare waifs of J. K. S.'s short life were altogether exceptional.   Time and chance, with which no man can strive, arrested their development, but not before they had shown themselves unmistakably.

It would be difficult to pass over, in this survey of university wits, the verse included in the ever delightful *Alice in Wonderland* and other pieces of Charles Lutwidge Dodgson, otherwise Lewis Carroll.   In some respects, and those important ones, it comes

nearer to Lear's than to any other by the approximation to
nursery rimes; he wrote pure nonsense sometimes; the use of
jargon in proper, and, indeed, in common, names and so forth. But,
it is, in others, not far from Calverley's—the two men, indeed, were
born close together and must have been actual contemporaries at
Oxford before Calverley migrated. Dodgson's academic vein, however, was mathematical not classical, and there is something of the
manipulation of symbols in his systematical absurdity and the non-
sensical preciseness of his humour. Some, indeed, of his collegiate
and private skits were actually mathematical in form. But the
public joy which he gave to grown-up people quite as much as, or
even more than, to the young, was scarcely analysable; for it
arose from all sorts of springs of wit and humour combined or
alternated. The mazy but not entirely unplanned jargon of *Jabber-
wocky*, and the sense married to nonsense, without the slightest
grotesqueness of language, in *The Walrus and the Carpenter* are,
each in its kind, supreme. His later book *Rhyme? and Reason?*
contained some things that were not in his proper vein, and *Sylvie
and Bruno* unwisely set at naught the Aristotelian warning against
shifting from kind to kind. But the comparative unpopularity
of *The Hunting of the Snark* was not quite justified. It may
be a little too long for its style; but some things in it are of
its author's best quality, and the subtle distinction between 'Snark'
and 'Boojum' is but too true an allegory of life and literature.

At the other extremity of the scale of poetry in subject, but,
like the last group, largely academic in character, we may find
another company of singers wholly or mainly in the difficult and
debated department of sacred verse. The number might be made
very large if persons who have written a creditable hymn or two (or
even twenty) were included. But this is impossible. John Keble,
cardinal Newman, archbishop Trench, Frederick William Faber,
Isaac Williams, John Mason Neale and, perhaps, as representatives
of a school different from any represented by these and specially
numerous during the nineteenth century, Wathen Mark Wilks Call
and Thomas Toke Lynch, must suffice in this place, though, in the
account of poetesses, some names may be added. The author
of *The Christian Year*[1] has, of course, gained as well as lost
by the facts that, in a certain sense, his book was the manifesto
and the manual at once of a great religious movement, which was
enthusiastically supported and bitterly opposed, that it marked the
beginning of an epoch of English church history which has not yet

[1] See, *ante*, vol. XII, chap. XII.

closed and that, however earnestly critics may inculcate the
principle of not judging by any agreement or disagreement with
an author's opinions, and however honestly they may endeavour
to 'reck their own rede,' the majority of mankind will always be
more or less influenced by that most natural but most uncritical
doctrine, 'I must take pleasure in the thing represented before
I can take pleasure in the representation.' On the whole, it is
very doubtful whether, despite the enormous popularity of his
book, well deserved and well maintained, Keble has not lost more
than he has gained in the general estimate of him as a poet. Very
large numbers—perhaps the vast majority—of those who have
admired the book have been too much impressed and too much
affected by their agreement with its temper and teaching to care
much about critical examination of the merits or demerits of its
expression. On the other hand, it is an equally natural tendency
in those who disagree with the doctrine to try if they can find fault
with the music. With charges of bigotry, narrowness and the like,
we have, of course, nothing to do. But other accusations, of 'tameness,' of unfinished and obscure expression and the like, concern us
very nearly. One of the most agreeable of literary anecdotes, to
which there is a supplement more delightful than itself, tells how
Wordsworth, admiring the book which owed much to him and
to which he himself, in his later work, perhaps owed something,
declared that 'it was so good that if it were his he would rewrite
it.' The addition (fathered on Pusey) is that he actually proposed
to Keble collaborative rehandling. If Pusey really said this, it
must be true, for, though he had quite humour enough to invent
it, his sense of veracity was of the strictest.

It is said frequently, and with some plausibility, that allowances
and explanations are inadmissible in the judgment of poetry—
poetry is poetry or it is not. As regards what may be called
'pure' poetry, that, no doubt, is true; but, as regards what may,
with equal justice, be called 'applied' poetry—verse with a special
object and purpose—it is not. In cases of this kind, you have to
discover, more or less accurately, what the poet meant to do before
you can decide whether he has done it. In Keble's case, we could,
without very much difficulty, conclude what he meant to do from
his actual work in verse; but, fortunately, we have an invaluable
external assistance. His Oxford *Praelections*, as professor of
poetry, are not now, as they were till very recently, locked up in
their original Latin from general perusal; and nobody who had
any right to call himself a critic ought to have been ignorant of

them while they were. If, to them, be added his posthumously
collected critical essays in original English, the clearest possible
notion of his attitude can be obtained. He has left descriptions
of poetry—one in English, one in Latin—the second of which is
rather a rider to, than a variant of, the first. This first, evidently
starting from Wordsworth's, but greatly improved on it, runs thus:

> The indirect expression in words, most appropriately in metrical words, of
> some overpowering emotion or ruling taste or feeling, the direct indulgence
> of which is somehow repressed.

To this he adds, in his Latin comments, starting from Aristotle
and Bacon, but, again, improving upon the former and correcting
the latter, that it is *subsidium benigni numinis*—the 'assistance
of the Divinity—in purifying passion. Now, when the original
emotion, taste, feeling, passion, were all religious or ecclesiastical,
and the poetry itself an assistance—a *subsidium*—for their expression, but not, in any way, an end in itself, it would, naturally,
follow that this expression must be, in many ways, conditioned,
and, in fact, limited. Ornament, as the rubrics have it, will be
but a 'decent tippet' for the subject; no far-sought or far-brought
curiosities of rime, or rhythm, of fancy, or conceit, will be cared
about; in fact, 'stimulus' itself (see the Taylorian[1] context quoted
in the last chapter of this kind), though not neglected, will be
subordinated to edification.

Yet, it may be boldly asserted, and safely argued, that Keble
is not 'quotidian,' while the defects in form which have been urged
against him have altogether escaped the notice of some critics
rather apt to be over- than under-critical in that matter. Indeed,
it may be very strongly suspected that an antecedent notion about
the probable dullness and not improbable clumsiness of all religious
poetry has, in some, if not all, cases invited an injurious application
of it. *The Christian Year* has, perhaps, nowhere the astonishing
and rocket-like soar and blaze of more than one seventeenth
century religious poet, or the quieter, but hardly less unique, glow
of some later nineteenth century sacred verse-writers. The great
motto of the school in conduct and faith, 'quietness and confidence,' is extended to Keble's verse. But the quietness never
becomes tameness, and the confidence never passes into rhetoric.
The poet with whom he comes into nearest comparison is, of course,
George Herbert; and, though Keble has not Herbert's seasoning
of quaintness, he has other merits to make up for the absence of
this, and he sometimes rises to a grandeur which Herbert hardly

[1] *Ante*, vol. XII, chap. v, p. 97.

ever attains. The book has been so long and so widely known that its best things are, as it were, sifted and laid out beforehand; and it would be mere coxcombry to attempt to specify others. The *Evening Hymn*, which has the peculiar placid piety noted by Thackeray in Addison's similar work, with a more than Addisonian unction, has been, also, the most popular of all; but, perhaps, the best—certainly those where the asserted quality of grandeur shows most—are *What went ye out to see* (third Sunday in Advent), *See Lucifer like lightning fall* (third Sunday in Lent), and best of all *O for a sculptor's hand* (second Sunday after Easter), with its almost Miltonic phrasing and moulding of the magnificent words of Balaam. Nor should *Red o'er the forest peers the setting sun*—the only thing in the manner of Gray's *Elegy* that has ever come near the *Elegy* itself—be unnoticed.

It is not quite an idle question whether, if Newman had been more secularly minded, or even if, retaining his actual temper, he had taken seriously to poetry, he would or might have been a very great poet. That *Lead, Kindly Light* (it is, perhaps, rather a misfortune that it is not more generally known by its actual title *The Pillar of Cloud*) is poetry and great poetry in one poetical way can only be denied by those (they have been known) who, not out of mere idle paradox but, exercising such intellectual faculties as they possessed, have made the same denial in the case of *Dies Irae*. That, in another way, and looking rather at choice and grasp of subject than at isolated poetic phrase or musical cry, *The Dream of Gerontius* is poetry, and even great poetry, is equally certain. That the two or three fragments of early light verse show great faculty in that way likewise is true. On the other hand, there is the fact that, in the not very small volume entitled *Verses on various occasions*, composed during a long life, though there is 'nothing base,' there is, also, nothing at all, except the things already mentioned, which is above the level of *The Christian Year*, and nothing, with the same exceptions, equal to Keble's best things. There might be two different explanations of this: one is furnished by the rather curious, but, apparently, quite frank and genuine, preface to the volume. Surprise at critics having discovered merit in your work is a not very uncommon affectation; but it is not one of which Newman, considering both his faults and his virtues, is likely to have been guilty; and he says he felt it. But he goes on to make the much more curious excuse for republishing all his verse, that he really does not himself know whether it is good or bad, and is of opinion that there is no criterion of poetry at all. In another man, this statement would probably be like the former, an affectation, or else a mere whim. But Newman's mind, as is well known, was rather over-furnished with logic, and extremely under-furnished with the historic sense; and, no doubt, he meant what he said. To one who did mean it, poetry must, necessarily, seem an altogether inferior thing—supplying 'the harmless pleasure of verse-making' (his own words) and, perhaps, the equally harmless pleasure of verse-reading, but not σπουδαῖον—not serious. It was almost impossible that, from a man so minded, much poetry of any kind should come: we have only to be thankful that, as a matter of fact, *The Pillar of Cloud* and *The Dream of Gerontius* actually came.

The most noteworthy of the numerous writers of verse whom the tractarian movement and the powerful example of *The Christian Year* raised up were Isaac Williams, Frederick William Faber and John Mason Neale[1]. The *odium theologicum* which excluded Williams from the Oxford professorship of poetry was exceptionally unjust, for his combined claims as poet and scholar far exceeded those of his actual opponent, Garbett, or, indeed, of any likely candidate; and he has scarcely had full justice done to him since. But it may be admitted that *Lyra Apostolica* (of which he was part-author), *The Cathedral* and his other works show him as a sort of 'moon' of Keble—always a dangerous position, and specially dangerous here, because Keble's own poetic light had more of the moon than of the sun in it. His characteristic is certainly not strength; but the grace and scholarship and purity of his verse can hardly be missed by any impartial student of poetry. Faber (who followed Newman, not Keble, at the parting of the ways) had, possibly, the greatest specially poetical power of the whole group. It is well known, both from a certain rather ungracious anecdote and from his general expressions on the subject, that Wordsworth was exceedingly chary of the title of poet; yet, he told Faber that, by his devoting himself to orders, 'England lost' one. In the principal book of his younger, and still Anglican, years, *The Cherwell Water Lily,* and in most of his other work, the possibility rather than the certainty of such a development, to any great extent, may be noted. The verse—which shows the influence not merely of Wordsworth himself but of Scott—is fluent, musical and possessed of something like, with a nineteenth century difference, what the eighteenth century called 'elegance'; but, still more, it wants strength and concentration. Later, if he

---

[1] See, *ante,* vol. xii, chap. xii.

did not exactly acquire these, he displayed something which unfavourable critics have labelled 'meretricious,' a term which itself
gives a grudging recognition of a kind of beauty. The label is
unfair and undiscriminating. The famous hymn *The Pilgrims of
the Night* has, certainly, a feminine quality; but even Aristotle has
admitted that the feminine is not always the bad. The singular
piece entitled *The Sorrowful World* comes, sometimes, near to
consummateness. But, in his later years, at any rate, Faber gave
himself no elbow-room and, in his earlier, he had not come to
full powers.

The third of this group, Neale, was, also, a member of another
—larger, in itself, but still very small—of those curious and
extremely beneficent writers of whom Edward FitzGerald is, perhaps, the chief, and who, without showing any great talent for
original poetry, have an extraordinary faculty of translating or
paraphrasing verse from other languages. His life, though not
long, was, after he left Cambridge, almost entirely leisurely; and
he devoted his whole leisure to hymnology and other ecclesiastical
study and writing. His original verse has, perhaps, been sometimes
too contemptuously spoken of; but, at its best, it is second-rate.
Some of his translations are really marvellous—not merely as compositions, but when taken in close connection with their originals.
Of the millions (the number is certainly not exaggerated) who, in
the sixty or seventy years since its appearance, have known
Jerusalem the Golden, probably not more than hundreds are
really acquainted with its source, the *De Contemptu Mundi* of
Bernard of Clugny or Morlaix, though the earlier publications
of this by Flacius Illyricus and Polycarp Leyser were always more
or less accessible to scholars; though archbishop Trench had
included extracts of it in his *Sacred Latin Poetry* before Neale
took it in hand; and though it has been several times printed
since. Nobody accustomed to medieval Latin and capable of
recognising poetry could fail to see the extraordinary beauty of
the best parts of Bernard's work. Its form, however—dactylic
hexameters, unbroken except for the final spondee, with internal
rime in each line and end rime for each couplet—though managed
without the least effort and with wonderful effect, is not only
rather difficult in itself and in Latin, but would, in English, not
so much (as the stock-phrase goes) 'court,' as ensure, disaster.
Neale neither attempted the impossible by trying the metre itself
nor endeavoured to come near it by employing anapaests or any
English swinging measure. He boldly transposed the rhythm

altogether into the shortened iambic 'common measure' of seven, six, seven, six, rimed only on the shorter lines. And he got out of this a rhythmical effect which, though in mere scheme and prosodic analysis as different as possible from the Latin, provides, in English, a parallel if not an identical effect of panting and yearning music, with diction and imagery to match. As pieces of craftsmanship for the expert not less than as providing popular satisfaction for the multitude, *Jerusalem the Golden* and its companions have few equals. Nor was this Neale's only, though it was his greatest, triumph. For others, we may be content with noting *The day is past and over* and *Art thou weary, art thou languid*, which show hardly less command of rhythm, language and general atmosphere inspired by, rather than simply taken from, the originals.

Trench[1] himself has much more extensive and direct claims to appear here than those—not in themselves unimportant—given by the volume just referred to; and, unlike most of the poets recently mentioned, he wrote miscellaneous, as well as sacred, verse. Like many, if not most, of his exact contemporaries, he was very much under the influence of Wordsworth, personal as well as poetical, and his sonnets in a Wordsworthian fashion are among his best work. One of his best known things, the verses on the battle of the Alma, is marred by a certain monotony in the long trochaic metre which he adopts. The remarkable poem on love (love divine, in the first place, but not without a reference to human) has, on the other hand, a distinct individuality of metre. Trench's wellknown work in popular linguistics had some bearing on the study of poetry; and there is no doubt that the selection, already quoted, of medieval Latin verse had a very much fuller result than that with which it has been credited. Yet, he was, perhaps, born just a little too early. It is surprising to find, in the very context more than once referred to, that he—a fervent admirer of Latin hymns and author of an early and remarkable tractate on accentual Latin poetry generally—while extolling the matter of Bernard's poem, positively abuses the 'inattractiveness,' 'awkwardness' and 'repulsiveness' of the metre. It was neither Latin nor English, neither orthodoxly Vergilian nor orthodoxly Miltonic—it was strange and new, and Trench could not put himself in a mood to hear it gladly. Something similar may have cramped him in his own production. He is, putting the sonnets above mentioned aside, best when he is pretty definitely

---

[1] See, *ante*, vol. XII, chap. XII.

echoing the seventeenth-century divine poets, and the short piece *Lord! many times I am aweary quite* is not unworthy of Vaughan.

All the writers of sacred poetry just mentioned professed throughout their lives one or another—sometimes more than one—form of orthodox Christianity. But free thought, undogmatism, unorthodoxy, or whatever it pleases to call itself, also produced a number of verse-writers too large to be dealt with here except by sample. The best sample of them, moreover, A. H. Clough, is not within our jurisdiction here[1]. We must, therefore, confine the representation of the class to two writers only, W. M. Wilks Call and Thomas Toke Lynch.

Call was a Cambridge man and, on leaving college, took orders; nor was it till he was near the half-way house of a rather more than ordinarily prolonged life that what are politely called 'difficulties' made him give up his duties. He never returned to them; but the type (a not uncommon one) of his dissidence may be gauged by the fact that, in one of his best poems, having made the refrain

I praise thee, God!

he altered 'God' to 'World' and afterwards altered it back again. Eloquent, also, is the compliment which an admiring critic of, perhaps, his best known thing, the prettily sentimental and pathetic *Manoli*, published in a popular magazine, that it 'illustrates the saddening idea that the collective welfare is too frequently purchased by the suffering of the individual'—on which, as a theme for poetry, one would like to have heard Matthew Arnold, himself no fanatic of dogma. But Call had some poetical gift, and *The Bird and the Bower* shows it. Lynch was an Independent minister and carried his independence somewhat far even in the opinion of his brethren. But he also had a not inconsiderable power of writing hymns and nondescript lyrics which warble in the precincts of hymnody proper.

Yet another class may be made, though space forbids lengthy discussion of its members, of the numerous, and sometimes very interesting, translations of classical and other languages who flourished during our period. It is possible that none of them achieved anything that was such a classic in itself as Cary's *Dante*; and certainly none approached the unique originality and poetic merit of FitzGerald's *Omar Khayyám*[2]. But the

---

[1] See, *ante*, chap. iv.　　　　[2] See, *ante*, chap. v.

Aristophanic versions of Thomas Mitchell and John Hookham
Frere, who belonged partly to the earlier nineteenth century,
were of singular vividness and vigour; and they were followed
by the Vergilian renderings of the two Kennedys, Rann and
Charles Rann (father and son), and of John Conington; by the
Catullian of Robinson Ellis; by the numerous attempts from the
versions of Lord Derby and F. W. Newman onwards, in all sorts
of metres and all manner of styles, to storm the impregnable fort
of Homeric quality (the best poetry, if the farthest in reproduction of character, being, perhaps, the Spenserian *Odyssey* of
Philip Stanhope Worsley); and these are only a few specimens
of the great library of verse translation produced during the time.
Indeed, few poets of that time, whether among those noticed
in this chapter or among the 'majors dealt with elsewhere,
abstained wholly from translation. Whatever opinions may be
held *in petto* about the necessary limitations, or the equally
necessary licences, of such translation in itself, it may fairly claim,
in the nineteenth century, to have escaped one almost fatal
danger which had pursued it in the eighteenth. The immense
variety of poetic metres and styles which was now common and
almost obligatory gave no excuse for, and, indeed, definitely pro-
hibited, the reduction (in a special sense) to a common measure
not particularly suitable to Latin, hopelessly unsuited to Greek
and of doubtful application to modern foreign languages, which
had prevailed earlier. Among the innumerable compilations and
anthologies of recent years one does not remember any wholly
composed of nineteenth-century translations in verse from different
modern languages. It might not be ill worth doing.

It was observed of the poetesses noticed in the last chapter of
this kind[1] that they increased largely in numbers during the early
part of the nineteenth century. Ten years before the death of
Mrs Hemans, Dyce had been able to fill a respectable volume
with applicants of older date for the position of 'Tenth Muse,'
but the remaining three-quarters of the century were more prolific of these than the whole earlier range of English literature.
The popularity of Mrs Hemans herself and of Miss Landon were far
exceeded by that of Mrs Browning; and, just as Mrs Browning
died, Miss Rossetti began. The works of these two, as well as
those of Emily Brontë, George Eliot and one or two others, fall,
for various reasons, out of our flock, but a very considerable
number remain—in only one case, perhaps, to be noticed last of

[1] Vol. xii, chap. v.

all, exhibiting a quality which marks the ticket 'lesser' as rather ungracious, but in all entitled to challenge a place here with the masculine minorities.

The eldest of the whole group, a lady born just within the century and nearly ten years older than Tennyson, though she made no public appearance with verse till just on the eve of his volumes of 1842, was Caroline Archer Clive, author of the powerful novel *Paul Ferroll* and its, as usual rather less powerful, sequel *Why Paul Ferroll killed his Wife*. A sufferer from lameness and weak health, it was not till 1840, the year of her marriage, that she gave to the world the quaintly titled book *IX Poems by V*—the latter symbol being, by those who were not in the secret, sometimes interpreted as a number, not an initial. They attracted much attention and high praise; but Mrs Clive did not allow herself to be tempted into over-production, and the complete edition of her poems which appeared years after her death scarcely exceeds two hundred pages. There is, however, hardly a page that is not worth reading, though, of the two longest pieces, *I watched the Heavens* and *The Valley of the Morlas*, which fill nearly half the book, the latter is better than the former, and neither has quite the poetic value of the shorter constituents. The dates of the compositions are scattered over quite forty years; and, with rare exceptions, exhibit a singular freedom from any of the contemporary influences which might have been expected to show themselves. Indeed (and this is made less surprising by the early date of her birth), there is a certain eighteenth-century touch of the best kind in Mrs Clive's work; although hardly a poem, as it stands, could have been written except in the nineteenth. The general tone (though at least the last half of her life seems to have been quite happy) is of a sober and utterly unaffected melancholy. The most striking piece in subject—it is not quite the most perfect in execution, though it does not fall short of its own necessities—is one suggested by a friend's statement that, at a great court ball, when invitations were issued by hundreds, scores of the proposed guests were found to be dead. The completest, in union of matter and form, are *Hearts Ease*, *Venice* and *Death*; but few will be found unsatisfactory, unless the reader's nature, or his mood, be out of key with them.

Some others must be more briefly noticed. Sarah Flower Adams—the conjunction of whose wellknown piece *Nearer, my God, to Thee* with Newman's *Lead, Kindly Light* as the most poetical of nineteenth-century hymns is not more hackneyed than

correct—wrote nothing else equal to it, and wasted most of her
poetical efforts on *Vivia Perpetua*, one of the class of curiously
sterile closet plays formerly noticed in connection with *Philip
van Artevelde.* Of two sister Sheridans, alike beautiful and witty,
Lady Dufferin (the Helen of Tennyson's *Helen's Tower*) wrote
some pretty songs. Her sister, Mrs Norton (as she is still
almost invariably called, though she was Lady Stirling-Maxwell
before she died) may be said, at one time, to have shared
the popularity first of Mrs Hemans and L. E. L. (whom, though
with less gush, she somewhat resembled) and, latterly, of
Mrs Browning. But her poems have not worn well, and one of
the latest and (as some held) best of them, *The Lady of
La Garaye*, was found singularly wanting at the time by then
younger tastes. It is to be feared that the amiable muse of
Eliza Cook will never, unlike the lady in *Comus*, escape from
that 'Old Arm Chair' which contrasts, fatally for itself, with
Thackeray's 'cane-bottomed' rival. On the other hand, it is
doubtful whether, except among the numerous friends of her
famous family, Fanny Kemble has had, at any time, the reputation she deserves as a poetess. It is difficult, indeed, to name
any single poem by her which is, as it were, a diploma piece;
but she is scarcely ever commonplace, and, while one would be
prepared to find a following of 'J. M. K.'s' friend by 'J. M. K.'s'
sister, her work is, on the contrary, full of puzzling passages which
suggest Tennyson only to *un*suggest him. But her long life,
despite its intervals of leisure, was frittered away between acting,
an unfortunate marriage, public readings and recitations, travels
and the accounts of them, autobiographic writings and a variety
of other things of interest but of no great value.

All the ladies just mentioned were born in the first two
decades, and most of them in the first decade, of the century;
but, about 1820[1] and in the years following, another group of
poetesses arose. The two eldest, Menella Bute Smedley and
Dorothy (Dora) Greenwell, were members of families otherwise
distinguished in literature, and their own names are worthily
inscribed on the columns which invidious satire long ago
grudged to lesser poets; but there is some lack of inevitableness

---

[1] In 1820 itself was born Anne Evans, sister of a poet to be noticed later (see, *post*,
p. 199). Her health was weak and her life not long, but she possessed, as is not very
common, skill in music as well as in poetry, and made the two work together.
Roses and Rosemary has few superiors in these 'double honours,' and among her
other poems more than one or two, especially the sonnet *Pevensey and Hurstmon-
ceaux*, possess unusual qualities.

about their work. Dinah Craik (born Mulock) is herself more distinguished as a novelist than as a poet. But the mild genius of Adelaide Anne Procter, daughter of Barry Cornwall, had something attaching about it which justified the use of the substantive just applied, though the adjective must be kept in view. Very recently, an Austrian monograph on her, though it was possibly prompted by the zeal of religious sympathy (she joined the Roman catholic church rather late in her short life), may have startled some of its readers who remembered Adelaide Anne Procter's work as ' a book that used to belong to a fellow's sisters '—to borrow an admirable phrase of Thackeray about something else. The fancy which Dickens had for her verse is not to be too much discounted by personal acquaintance, though that existed; for he accepted her poetry in *Household Words* when he did not know it was hers; and, though he certainly was not what one would call 'nothing if not critical,' especially in poetry, he always knew what would please the public. Pretty music and, at one time, magnificent public singing may have had something to do with the vogue of *The Message*, but it retains a charm for some who are not mere sentimentalists and who never were specially musical. And she had no small power of verse narrative—among numerous examples is the version of the beautiful story of St Beatrix, here called Sister Angela, which was given to 'Belinda' in a Christmas number of *All the Year Round.* Now, verse narrative, save in the very different hands of William Morris, has seldom been satisfactorily handled since the first half of the nineteenth century.

With the chief singer of the other sex, born in 1830, Christina Rossetti, we are not here concerned[1]; but she had, as close contemporaries and sisters in art poetic, two writers, one of whom obtained a great, though hardly sustained, notoriety, while the other is one of the most notable instances of the fact that, while judging any kind of literary worker from first appearances is rash, and judging a poet in this manner is rasher, to judge poetesses from single specimens is, perhaps, rashest of all. The person first referred to was Isa Craig, afterwards Mrs Knox, the victress in the rather foolishly devised public competition for an ode to celebrate the centenary of Burns. 'Six hundred' is the conventional Latin equivalent for our equally conventional 'a thousand,' and Miss Craig actually had more than six hundred rivals. Her ode, if the adjudicators were competent, showed no very considerable poetical power

[1] See, *ante*, chap. v.

in this large body. It is respectable but nothing more. She did better things—the best, perhaps, being *The Woodruff*, though this itself comes in most unlucky comparison both in title and in subject with Dante Rossetti's *Wood-spurge.* On the other hand, if we had nothing of Jean Ingelow's but the most remarkable poem entitled *Divided,* it would be permissible to suppose the loss, in fact or in might-have-been, of a poetess of almost the highest rank. Absolutely faultless it is not; a very harsh critic might urge even here a little of the diffuseness which has been sometimes charged against the author's work generally; a less stern judge might not quite pardon a few affectations and 'gushes,' something like those of Tennyson's early work. It might be called sentimental by those who confound true and false sentiment in one condemnation. But the theme and the allegorical imagery by which it is carried out are true; the description, not merely plastered on, but arising out of, the necessary treatment of the theme itself, is admirable; the pathos never becomes mawkish; and, to crown all, the metrical appropriateness of the measure chosen and the virtuosity with which it is worked out leave nothing to desire. Jean Ingelow wrote some other good things, but nothing at all equalling this; while she also wrote too much and too long. If, as has been suggested above, this disappointingness is even commoner with poetesses than with poets, there is a possible explanation of it in the lives, more unoccupied until recently, of women. Unless a man is an extraordinary coxcomb, a person of private means, or both, he seldom has the time and opportunity of committing, or the wish to commit, bad or indifferent verse for a long series of years; but it is otherwise with women.

The period of the forties was somewhat stronger in the number, if not in the quality, of the poetesses it produced. Harriet Eleanor Hamilton-King is best known by her respectable, but tedious, *The Disciples*—a sort of Italomaniac epic influenced in spirit, perhaps, by both the Brownings and written in a blank verse not unsuggestive of *Aurora Leigh.* Her shorter poems are rather better; but, like most of the lesser poetesses of this particular time, she not only, in a famous phrase, 'could be very serious,' but thought it her duty to be this rather too exclusively. One of her companions, indeed, Emily Pfeiffer, rather unnecessarily excused herself for want of proficiency in the for some time popular pastime of rondeaux, ballades and so forth, on the ground that 'the burden of meaning lay too heavily on a woman singer's heart' for her to excel in these trivialities. The same lady is also reported to have explained that she considered it her duty to go on writing poetry after her husband's death because he had a high opinion of what she wrote before it. There have, no doubt, been great poets capable of such innocent egotism and want of humour; but Emily Pfeiffer could scarcely claim their excuses. The compassionate sonnet, which will tolerate and, to some extent, ennoble all faults except triviality and carelessness, enabled her to do her most tolerable work; the rest was mostly negligible. Another very serious poetess was Augusta Webster, who, again, represents a strong Browning influence both from husband and wife, and who, owing, perhaps, to this, sometimes made fair experiments in lyrical metres. Her blank verse, however, of which she was very prolific in forms non-dramatic, semi-dramatic and dramatic, sometimes employed Robert Browning's licences without his justifications, and, at others, became unspeakably monotonous. To the forties, also, belongs Sarah or 'Sadie' Williams—a short-lived singer in both divine and human fashions, of which a remark made already, and to be repeated in reference to other writers, is again true—that they show a certain diffused poetic power which is hardly concentrated in any single piece; Isabella Harwood, who wrote not a few closet dramas under the pseudonym 'Ross Neil,' in blank verse, better than that of most of her companions mentioned here; and the various and sometimes almost brilliant talent of 'Violet Fane'—Mary Montgomerie Lamb, Mrs Singleton by her first marriage and Lady Currie by her second.

A poetess who has scarcely received the credit she deserved was Margaret Veley, whose scanty but excellent verse will be found in a posthumous collection prefaced by Sir Leslie Stephen and entitled *A Marriage of Shadows and other Poems*. The author was a novelist also, but, in that department too, was not voluminous; and she died in rather early middle age. It is particularly interesting to compare her work with that of Mrs Clive ('V')[1], because the strong resemblance between them, in general, brings out the difference between the first and second halves of the century. Both in thought and expression of a similar attitude, and in formal and verbal utterance, Margaret Veley's melancholy is vaguer and fainter than her senior's; her metrical devices and her vocabulary are more elaborate; she is sometimes rather more obscure and more deliberately artistic, though the elaboration and deliberation are not in the least affected. Her art, in fact, is, though

---

[1] Anne Evans (see *ante* and *post*), who came between them in time, might, with advantage, be joined in the comparison.

not consciously, more sophisticated. But her accomplishment is various and almost great. Her chief work, *A Japanese Fan*, is really something of a positive masterpiece of quiet ironic passion, suitably phrased in verse. The title poem of her book and *The Unknown Land* deserve an honourable place among the phantasmagorias in irregular Pindaric which have formed a great feature of later nineteenth-century poetry; while, among definite lyrics, *Michaelmas Daisies* may stand as a representative document for the survey of the subject of this chapter with which it should conclude.

Some, mainly younger, poetesses must be mentioned more briefly, though most of them obtained, and one or two of them deserved, reputation as such. Mathilde Blind, daughter of a wellknown German refugee, wrote much verse in unimpeachable English, showing strong literary sympathies and correct versification. Any competent critic in the future will be able to see at once that she wrote in the last quarter or third of the nineteenth century, and did good 'school-work' in its styles—work agreeable enough to read. Over-estimation may be thought to have been the lot of the two ladies, Miss Bradley and Miss Cooper, an aunt and a niece, who had the curious fancy of writing in collaboration under one masculine name, Michael Field. Their work, which was most commonly tragic drama, but included lyric, received very high praise from reviewers, from the appearance, in 1884, of *Callirrhoe*, a piece on which the influence of Landor was evident in style as well as subject. Others have failed to discover much in the joint work which goes beyond the standard, already noticed, of nineteenth-century closet drama, or, in the lyrics, much more than the half machine-made verse which usually comes late in great periods of poetry. There was, perhaps, something more to be made of two others, who both died young and of whom the second died not happily, Constance Naden and Amy Levy. Miss Naden's work is a little overloaded by its sometimes very serious subjects, pantheistic philosophy and the like, though, at times, it is also comic. But already (she died at thirty-one) she showed signs of that internal fire which melts and recasts subject according to the poet's idiosyncrasy. Amy Levy, dying still younger, achieved even less, but gave occasional evidence—especially in a short and very simply languaged poem on the waltz—of a passionate and almost triumphant intensity not common.

But the most remarkable poetess, after Elizabeth Barrett Browning and Christina Rossetti, of the later and latest nineteenth century, was one of whose poetical capacity few people, except personal friends, had any opportunity of judging till the century itself was nearly closed; while her death, not long after its actual close, was the first occasion of extensive eulogy and collected publication of her poems. Then, the name of Mary E. Coleridge became widely divulged, and her poems (printed in a fairly full collection, besides some remarkable prose essays) were, for a time, quite eagerly bought. The eulogists, in some cases, were of the highest competence, but not quite always so; and the chorus of compliment, in some cases, had its frequent, if not constant, effect of arousing something like the feeling of the historical or legendary Athenian in regard to Aristides. But it is recorded that one critic, who, by accident, had known nothing of her work and was somewhat inclined to revolt against this chorus, having gone to a public library and obtained her poems, opened them at a venture in three places, and read the poems on which he chanced. He then shut the book, returned it to the librarian and immediately ordered a copy from his bookseller, in obedience to the law which ordains that true poetry shall never (cases of necessity being excluded) be read except in a book belonging to the reader. Nor did the complete reading contradict—on the contrary, it confirmed and intensified—the impression derived from these *sortes Coleridgianae.* It is not, of course, to be expected that everyone will—and it would be unreasonable to insist that everyone should— agree with the estimate implied in this anecdote. There are, in particular, two objections to Mary Coleridge's verse which cannot be merely dismissed—as we have dismissed others in these historic reviews of poetry—with a simple 'disabling of judgment.' One such objection might be derived from the almost unbroken gloom of the general atmosphere[1]; the other, from the frequent use (and, as some may call it, abuse) of the parabolic method—employed with such complication that an imaginative interpreter, whose 'cocksureness' is not equal to his imagination, may wisely decline to be certain of the special *moralitas* to be adopted. An objection of the first class is sometimes met by the retort sarcastic, 'Oh! you want the universe to be universally regarded through a horse-collar,' but this is obviously idle. The house of mourning deserves its bards at least as well as the house of mirth, and is likely to get poetry of a higher class out of them. There are poems and

---

[1] It will have been noticed that this characteristic, not uncommon in poets, is specially common in poetesses. They prolong their attendance on the school of suffering, even after they have attained the strain of song.

poem-books of all kinds, from *In Memoriam* to *A Little Child's Monument*, which, even in recent times, justify a statement hardly needing any justification. But, when a collection of poems, written on no common subject, and at periods apparently extending over more than five and twenty years, is something like a cypress-grove, a certain morbidity of temperament may be not unfairly suggested. And, on the other hand, the person who is quite sure of the exact intention of such a poem as *Unwelcome*—

We were young, we were merry, we were very very wise,

with all its welcome strangeness, and its quaint urbanity of rhythm, may, perhaps, rather be commiserated on his certainty than complimented on his acuteness. Let the reader, however, prepare himself for a garden of Proserpine rather than of Adonis, for a region if not exactly of 'mystery' at any rate of 'enigma'— the words come from Mary Coleridge's most distinguished eulogist— and he will, if he have any taste for poetry, find no further difficulty and a great deal of delight. When she did not publish quite anonymously, she seems to have generally adopted, from George Macdonald, the signature Ἄνοδος—which, evidently, means, in the two writers[1], not so much (as it has been inadequately translated) 'wanderer' as 'wayless one'—a person who is not only not travelling by a definite road to a definite goal, but who hardly sees any road before him at all. In fact, the influence of that most unequal genius[2] who produced *Phantastes* and *The Portent* and *Lilith* was evidently much stronger on Mary Coleridge than the mere adoption of the pseudonym would show—though her shorter life, her greater poetical and critical gift and the absence of any temptation to produce hack-work all told in her favour.

She is said to have refrained from publishing her poems herself and to have objected to others publishing them, at least in her lifetime, out of ancestral reverence—for fear of dishonouring the shade of S. T. C. As a matter of fact, there is more of the 'Estesian' character in her than there is in Hartley or in Sara, while her pure originality is, perhaps, also greater than that of either of these kinsfolk. She was only unlucky in her time. It has been observed more than once—Matthew Arnold himself, though he sometimes exemplifies the feature poetically censured, might be cited in critical support of the censure—that mere discouragement, mere quest, as it were, of a stool to be melancholy upon,

---

[1] In Greek itself, the word is used of places not persons, and is simply our ordinary 'pathless.'

[2] As to his own poems, see *post*.

and remonstrances, from that *cathedra* when it has been found, with the arrangements of the universe—though by no means an unpoetic mood, is apt to become monotonous in its expression. Since Byron and Shelley, in their lower and higher ways respectively, until the present day, we have had a very great deal of it. But the unavoidable monotony of the key can be overcome by the variety and idiosyncrasy of note, and this is most eminently true of Mary Coleridge. Others may have lent her fiddles to play, melancholy or mysticism; but, in Latimer's famous phrase, her rosin is her own—borrowed from, and, as yet, borrowed by, none. To specify pieces from the nearly 240 poems found in her collected poems is at once very difficult and rather idle, for, as has been said above, the merest chance-medley will serve in the case of readers likely to care for her, and there is hardly a poem in the book which will not displease or weary others. For those who must have specimens, *The Other Side of a Mirror, A Difference, He came unto His Own and His Own received Him not, The Witch,* (a worthy progeny of *Christabel*), *A Day-dream* and *On the Arrival of a Visitor* may serve. And it may, perhaps, be added that it will be found useful to read her in close connection with canon Dixon (see *post*), whose work may not impossibly have influenced hers. The connection, at any rate, struck the present writer independently; and it adds a somewhat interesting touch to the mental map of the poetry of our time.

We must now turn from groups aggregated according to subject, style, sex and other joint characteristics to the large number of individual poets who do not seem to lend themselves, without arbitrary classification, to such grouping. In their case, chronological order is almost the only one possible; though arrangement by decades may be convenient[1].

The first batch thus to be formed consists of men the eldest of whom were born in the same year with Tennyson, while none of them was younger than Browning. Tennyson's contemporaries were two poets as much contrasted in every possible way as could well be—Richard Monckton Milnes, known, during the latter part of his life, as lord Houghton, and Thomas Gordon Hake, glanced at above. Milnes, always widely known in society and, to some extent, in politics, was, also, at one time, almost a

---

[1] This form of grouping may seem artificial; but only to those who have not taken the trouble to notice, or who are unable to understand, the subtle influence of the spirit of even narrowly separated times which literary, like other, history shows to have been exerted on persons born within them.

popular poet. Lord Houghton (who also possessed an admirable
prose style, and whose services in editing Keats were important in
quality and still more important in time) was not a poet of the
'big bow-wow' tone, but he was neither a twitterer nor a yelper.
A critic's attitude towards *Strangers Yet* and *The Brookside* now,
and for the greater part of the last twenty years, may be compared,
from the higher and wider historic standpoint, with its counterpart, the attitude of eighteenth-century critics towards 'the metaphysicals.' If, as they saw nothing but 'false wit,' 'awkward
numbers' and so forth, in the one case, he sees nothing but sentimentality and 'jingle,' in the other, then we can class him and
find him wanting. These two famous, or once famous, songs and
other poems by the same author belong to their own division of
poetry only. But that division is not the lowest, and these
themselves rank high in it.

The contrast just made might almost have been supplied,
so far as kinds of poetry go, without exploring further than
Houghton's own contemporary, Hake, who sought for depth
even at the cost of obscurity, for strangeness at the cost of
broken music and for quaint thought and expression at the
cost of attraction and grace, risking, also, the charge of posturing
and jargon-making. He never could have been a popular poet,
and neither when the somewhat younger spasmodics caught the
public ear, for a time, with verse not wholly dissimilar, nor when
the work of poets nearly a generation younger than himself, such
as Dante Rossetti, created a taste for poetry still more like
his own, did he become so. His best things—*Old Souls, The
Palmist* and great part of *Maiden Ecstasy*—have what has been
called a 'fortified' character : they require, save in the case of
exceptionally qualified or exceptionally exercised persons, either
to be taken by storm or sapped with elaborate approaches.
Now, about poetry of this kind, there is not only this difficulty
but another, and an even more dangerous one—that composition
of it tempts imitation of a merely specious kind and measure.
For the last half century a great deal of verse has been written
suggesting the speech which an acute critic of the last generation,
G. S. Venables, put in Carlyle's mouth—

> I will be strange and wild and odd,

but not possessing root of thought or fruit of beauty enough to
support and to carry off the strangeness and wildness and oddity.
This is not quite true of Hake : but it might seem to be true.

Very different, again, from either of these was their (slightly) junior, Sir Francis Hastings Doyle, who, rather late in life, became professor of poetry at Oxford, and justified his election by lectures, somewhat exoteric, indeed, but singularly acute and sensible. Sir Francis could write verse of various kinds which was never contemptible, but his strong point was the very difficult and dangerous kind of war poetry, in which, putting *The Charge of the Light Brigade* aside, he surpassed every other writer between Campbell and a living poet. Whenever he came near this great and too often mishandled subject, his genius seemed to catch fire ; and, in two almost famous pieces—*The Red Thread of Honour* and *A Private of the Buffs*—in the first especially, that curious inspiriting and exciting quality which all songs of what Dante calls *salus* (war and patriotism)[1] should have, and which they too often lack, is present in almost the highest degree.

Another small group of poets born before 1820, the youngest of whom was not Browning's junior so far as years go, may be formed of three men, each of whom exercised other arts or professions besides poetry—Alfred Domett, William James Linton and William Bell Scott. Domett, as probably many people know who know nothing else about him, was the Waring of Browning's vivid and grotesque poem. He fulfilled his poet's apparent expectations of his doing something respectable by becoming prime minister of New Zealand. But, when he returned to England and published a long poem, *Ranolf and Amohia*, it must be confessed that not a few who eagerly read it as the long-expected work of 'Waring' himself, experienced considerable disappointment, which has not been removed by subsequent perusal. Others praised it highly ; and even Tennyson, who, though not as grudging as Wordsworth in his estimate of other poets, was not mealy-mouthed, granted it intellectual and imaginative subtlety and 'power of delineating delicious scenery.' But he confessed that he found it difficult to read ; and this it certainly is. The story fixes no hold on the immediate interest or the later memory; the characters are outlines only ; and, though the descriptions are certainly often beautiful, they do not exactly charm and are frequently interrupted and spoilt by flatnesses of phrase like

> Where they a small canoe had found
> Which Amo settled they might take,

the last line of which would have been a triumph for the most disrespectful and audacious parodist of Wordsworth or of Crabbe.

[1] *De vulgari eloquentia*, book II, chap. II.

Before he went to the colonies, Domett had written minor verse of merit, some of which was published in *Blackwood*, with boisterous eulogy from Wilson. *A Christmas Hymn* with the refrain 'Centuries ago' is the stock selection of these for praise. It has merit, but no consummateness.

The other two, W. J. Linton and W. B. Scott, were artists as well as poets; and Linton had very much the advantage in both his professions. The excellence of his engravings is universally known; his skill in verse, translated and original, less so. Linton was essentially—in the original Greek, not in the modern, sense—an epigrammatist: that is to say, not a wit but a writer of short poems on definite subjects, finished off in a manner suggesting the arts of design as well as those of poetic expression. In perfection of these things—which may, of course, be called toys or trifles, and which are certainly miniatures—he yields only to Landor; and, while even his best things have not Landor's supremacy when he is at his best, Linton avoids the austere jejuneness which characterises some of the greater writer's trifles, and suffuses his own with more colour, shadow and light. Such apparently slight things as *Epicurean* and *A Dream* need no slight skill—as anybody who tries to imitate them will find.

Of Linton's at one time friend (for W. B. Scott had a habit of quarrelling, whether it was exercised in this instance or not), it is difficult to find anything more complimentary to say than that his verses, to use Browning's words of something else, 'intended greatly.' He put forward various theories of poetry; affected considerable contempt of others; and always, whether writing in a way somewhat like Hake or in a way somewhat like Rossetti, tried to be different and difficult. Unfortunately, he very seldom succeeded in being good; and, perhaps, never in being very good. His ballads really deserve the name (unjustly given in some other cases) of Wardour street work; his elaborate efforts in the greater ode are pretentious and hollow. A little prettiness in lyric and a little picturesqueness in sonnet he did, sometimes, reach; but, on the whole, his execution was emphatically a failure[1] whatever may have been the merit of his aims and his theories.

The most noteworthy of the poets who were born between Browning's birth-year and the ten years' later date 1822 were Aytoun and Bailey, who have been already noticed in this chapter,

[1] Anyone to whom this judgment seems harsh should read *The Sphinx*, Scott's most highly praised poem, and think what Rossetti or James Thomson the second would have made of it.

and Matthew Arnold, who falls out of it. But there were others not negligible, especially Aubrey de Vere, Thomas Westwood and Charles Mackay, who were all born in 1814. The son of one verse-writer of merit and the brother of another, Aubrey de Vere possessed connections, different from those of blood, with two groups interesting, directly and indirectly, in literature. He was a personal disciple of Wordsworth and, perhaps, chief of all Wordsworthians pure and simple; and, also, he was one of the Anglican group who were not satisfied *tendere in Latium*, but who made the full voyage and found the waves irremeable. There may be something to attract, and should be nothing at all to repel, the true critical approach in any or all of these circumstances; but, when the critical judgment is directed solely to his work, its summing up cannot be wholly favourable. He wrote both longer and shorter poems; the former, on a considerable variety of subjects—preferably legendary, the legends being supplied by Irish early poetry, hagiology, the classics and so forth. They seldom fail to command respect and esteem[1]; but, alas! they still seldomer transport—the one thing needful. Of all the numerous attempts to English in verse the famous epic duel of Cuchullain and Ferdia, De Vere's, if the most elegant, is the flattest, the most devoid of local colour and temporal spirit; and his lyrics, though sometimes pretty, are never anything more.

Westwood was one of the members, though the youngest, or nearly so, of Charles Lamb's circle; but he did not publish till much later and, in middle life, was a good deal occupied with business. His most ambitious thing, *The Quest of the Sancgreall*, is, unfortunately, post-Tennysonian in more senses than that of date. Latterly, he took much interest in the literature, as well as in the practice, of angling, and wrote some good fishing songs. Once, in the little piece called *Springlets*, he reached charm; in some others, he was near it.

Less polish but somewhat more vigour than is to be found in these writers characterised the verses of Charles Mackay—a long-lived and hard-working journalist and man-of-letters-of-all-work. A good deal of it is in the mixed vein of sentiment and what may be called 'rollick,' which was popular in the second third of the century. The song *O Ye Tears!*, which was once a favourite, requires either more simplicity, or more art, or more of both, to make it capital; but that adjective may almost be applied to the

---

[1] It may be worth mentioning that Landor, who, though not a jealous critic, was very sparing of admiration for poetry, bestowed it unsparingly upon De Vere.

Cholera Chant (quoted and justly praised by Kingsley in *Alton Locke*), and others of his lyrics are above the average. There are reasons for believing that if he had led that life of concentration on poetry which seems to be, if not quite universally, in a very large majority of cases, necessary to produce poetry in perfection, he might, like others mentioned in this chapter and the last of its kind, have been more than a lesser poet. But journalism and bookmaking, though they may favour the production of verse, are not usually favourable to the quality of poetry.

The first writer of poetic importance between 1820 and 1830 was Matthew Arnold[1]; but the years immediately succeeding the decade added to the list a fair number of poets who were to be of note, especially Coventry Patmore, William Allingham, Francis Turner Palgrave, George Macdonald and the very remarkable writer known as a poet chiefly under the name of Johnson and as a prose writer under that of Cory. To this group some, perhaps, would add the rather younger Gerald Massey, whose birth drew towards the thirties, William Caldwell Roscoe, Thomas Woolner and Walter Thornbury. But none of these excite either personal enthusiasm or a sense of historical importance in some minds[2]. Thornbury's ballads are spirited, but too often, if not always, give one the depressing feeling that if Macaulay, Maginn, Thackeray and Aytoun had not written neither would he; and they constantly sin by exaggeration. Gerald Massey's considerable bulk of war, love and miscellaneous poetry has, sometimes, been commended on the ground that he was a self-made man, sometimes on the other ground that, like Eliza Cook, he appealed to strictly popular and uncultured tastes. But nothing that the present writer has read of Massey's work seems anywhere near poetic 'proof.' Roscoe, coming of a family distinguished (not merely by the historian) in letters, had his work ushered to the world with strong recommendations from a well-known critic, Richard Holt Hutton, who was his brother-in-law; but it has no 'inevitableness' whatever and no very special poetic qualities of any kind. Thomas Woolner, the sculptor, was a member of the early pre-Raphaelite group and had many literary friends outside it. His *My Beautiful Lady* was received with a round of applause which did not last very long, and has seldom been echoed since. His blank verse suggests an imitation of

---

[1] See *ante*, chap. IV.

[2] Some would rank above them all an eccentric poet of rather wasted talent, Arthur Joseph Munby, who wrote verse at intervals from the time of his leaving Trinity college, Cambridge, in 1851, till his death, all but sixty years later. Nor would this estimate lack arguments to support it.

Tennyson, conditioned by an attempt to give roughness and originality to phrase, and generally unsuccessful; his lyrics are unimportant. Whether Allingham deserves to be given any higher place than these is very doubtful. He had the fluency and ease of verse which has been again and again noticed as common in Irish poets; and some of his lighter songs and ballads, such as *Lovely Mary Donnelly,* are really pretty. But he has been allowed by patriotic and competent critics to be dull, tame and uninventive; one of his best shorter things, *Up the Fairy Mountain,* borrows its first and best stanza from one of the most beautiful of Jacobite ballads and entirely fails to live up to it; while he constantly indulged in banalities like

> A thing more frightful than words can say.

Not thus can the others mentioned above be dismissed. Coventry Patmore, though a recent and comparatively accidental coterie admiration has sometimes exalted him too high, was a very remarkable poet in more ways than one. That he was one of the few poets who have given careful attention to the mechanism of poetry is the least of these ways; nor were his prosodic speculations, though interesting and ingenious, very happy. It is of more importance that his actual verse was not only of great merit as a whole, but of two kinds exceptionally different from each other. The kind of criticism—scholastic, in the worst sense only—which has never been absent when there was any criticism at all, and which has recently been present to an intolerable degree, would, no doubt, if it had the chance, decide that the same person could never have written *The Angel in the House* and *The Unknown Eros,* though the last part of the first named work, *The Victories of Love,* might be a saving stepping-stone to a few brighter spirits.

The Angel in the House first appeared in 1854 and may be said to be—like Matthew Arnold's nearly contemporary work in one direction and that of the spasmodics in another—a kind of half-conscious, half-unconscious revolt against both Tennyson and Browning, but especially against the former. Revolt, indeed, may seem too fierce a word for the mild domesticities of Patmore's poem; some critical stand might even be made for the contention actually made, that it is a direct development of more than one of Tennyson's poems, especially *The Miller's Daughter.* But development itself has, in the language of the *Articles* as to another matter, often something 'of the nature of' revolt; it

indicates, at any rate, want of complete satisfaction. The poem
contained, even at the first, much very pretty verse ; as it went
on, it was to contain not a little that is positively beautiful. But
its ambling versification—somniferous to some of those whom it
did not merely please, and positively irritating to others—the
deliberate banality of the subject; and the equally deliberate
adoption of language outgoing even Wordsworth, even Crabbe,
in its avoidance of poetic diction, though they conciliated a large
part of contemporary taste, produced a by no means conciliatory
effect upon another part which, in the long run, has prevailed.
When a man writes

> Our witnesses the cook and groom,
> We signed the lease for seven years more,

it is not unreasonable to think that Apollo, if he thought it worth
his while, must have twitched the poet's ear rather sharply and
that attention should have been paid to the twitch. The scornful
allusion 'idylls of the dining-room and the deanery,' though its
author, Swinburne, was courteous enough not to name the idyllist,
expressed a good deal of the younger and youngest opinion of
the time. Many years later, after changes of family, faith and
circumstance, Patmore produced a book of odes, entitled *The
Unknown Eros*, which, as was said above, might, but for certain
evidence, have seemed the work of an entirely different person.
Instead of the regular and too often monotonous flow of the
Angel poems, abrupt Pindaric measures were tried, challenging,
and sometimes attaining, splendour but, at the same time, risking—
and sometimes falling into—harshness and dissonance. The simple,
almost lisping language was changed, likewise (indeed, some hint
had been given of this in *The Victories*), into a grandiose diction,
sometimes violent and bombastic, but, at other times, really grand ;
and the subjects, instead of being those of ordinary and domestic
prattle—'personal talk' of the most commonplace kind—were
always elevated or deeply pathetic, at least in intention. It
was as if someone who had threatened to sink to the level of
Ambrose Philips had changed his models to Donne, Vaughan,
Milton, even Aeschylus. It is true that, as Patmore had seldom
fallen into actual silliness, so he rarely rose to actual sublimity;
but he did reach it sometimes and often came very near it. And
it must be admitted that such a combination of parts and scales
in poetry is a curious and, perhaps, a unique thing.

George Macdonald, better known as a novelist than as a poet,
but author of a good deal of verse, some of it exquisite, some of it

worthless and a great deal of it unimportant, is, also, rather an exceptional figure. Like Patmore, he was a critic, though not to the same extent a formal critic, of poetry; and, like Palgrave, who is to follow, he was an accomplished anthologist. Of his two main achievements of any size, *Phantastes* and *The Portent*, the latter, though of extraordinary goodness, is entirely prose and not very long; the former is a mixture of prose and verse, including Macdonald's masterpiece, and one of the miniature masterpieces of the century, in the stanza beginning

Alas! how easily things go wrong,

while scores of scraps hardly less good may be picked up out of his various writings. Unfortunately, the ideal which he set before himself, in his more poetical books, where verse and prose are mixed, was a dangerously eclectic (some critics would call it a rococo) model. It combined or tried to combine the supernatural and the natural, the romantic and the grotesque, allegory and passion, sentiment and philosophic religiosity. The two chief divisions of literature from which it might be thought to draw illustration or, at least, suggestion were English Caroline poetry and the work in prose and verse of the German romantic school from Tieck and Novalis to Chamisso and Fouqué. Now, mixed work of all kinds, of this particular kind especially, requires either absolutely heaven-born, though not necessarily universal, genius, which goes right and avoids wrong instinctively in its own way, or an almost equally supernatural spirit of self-criticism to avoid or to correct the dangers. With neither could Macdonald be credited, though he certainly had genius and was not destitute of critical power. The consequence is that his verse, like his prose, but more annoyingly so, is marred by constant incompleteness and inequality; by triviality, now and then; at times, by a suspicion of pose; at others, by other bad things. Few writers of his time, except the very greatest, have more diffused poetry about them; but few, also, are more uncertain in catching and concentrating it.

It is probable—though it will be rather unfair—that Palgrave's name will always be thought of rather as that of a dispenser—a '*promus* of elegancies'—in poetry than as that of a poet. The goodness of *The Golden Treasury* is certainly extraordinary; it is not rash to call it unmatched. No such epithets could be applied to the compiler's own verse, though this is not by any means contemptible. Intimate friend as he was of Tennyson, his shorter pieces are Wordsworthian rather than Tennysonian. But it would be a pity if the longer *Visions of England* ceased to be read. In the first place, they were one of the earliest expressions of that historical-patriotic poetry of which much has been produced since; and which, while some of it has been good, has certainly done good, even in its weaker examples. In the second, the book, though there are few 'jewels five words long' in it, shows a poetic imagination much superior to the poetic expression with which it is united.

Exquisiteness and idiosyncrasy, rather than fullness, magnificence and force of general appeal, were the characteristics of the work in verse (his prose was singularly nervous and virile) of the author of *Ionica*—the double-edged punning title of the poems of William Johnson, otherwise Cory. They have been rebuked for 'modern paganism'; but that does not much concern us, and it may be remembered that some have found traces of this quality even in Wordsworth himself. Johnson, whose object was to keep as much of the tone and style of the Greek anthologists as could be saturated with nineteenth-century temper and tone, could not have avoided the appearance of modern paganism if he would. In the inevitable, and, indeed, quite legitimate and instructive, comparison with Landor, it is this which chiefly distinguishes Johnson. Landor is Hellenic generally, but not definitely pagan ; nor is he, strictly speaking, modern unless the eighteenth century be called modern Johnson is late-Hellenic with intensely modern touches. The best of his few verses are exceptionally familiar to all who are likely to like them, and who have not missed them by chance. The most familiar and, perhaps, most general favourite, the short translated epitaph on Heraclitus, has been objected to (perhaps finically, perhaps not) because, in English, the first line

> They told me, Heraclitus, they told me you were dead

would, rather, raise expectation that the tidings were false. *Mimnermus in Church*, another great favourite, is, perhaps, a little overdosed with modernity. *An Invocation*, disclaiming any wish for the society of Greek nymphs and preferring that of Greek shepherds, has some excellent verse in it, though anybody is certainly at liberty to prefer the dryads as a subject of personal wish for their resurrection.

The next decade, from 1830 to 1839, besides yielding the major names of Swinburne, the greater Morris and James Thomson the younger, was peculiarly fertile in poets of the second rank, some of whom stand very high in it. The best of all were, probably, Thomas Edward Brown and Richard Watson Dixon—indeed, there are those who would deny the limitation of 'second' or 'lesser' to Dixon. They may, therefore, be treated first, Dixon being taken out of chronological order, and should be followed by Sebastian Evans, Robert earl of Lytton (better known as a poet by his pseudonym Owen Meredith), Sir Edwin Arnold, Sir Lewis Morris, Sir Alfred Lyall, Roden Noel, Alfred Austin, lord de Tabley, Thomas Ashe and Theodore Watts[1]. One or two of these had, in their day, great popularity, whether deserved or not; one held the perilous premiership of the laurel; several occupied important positions outside poetry and even outside literature altogether. But they all have an interest of a peculiar kind historically, because they may be said to be the first group born to the full influence of Tennyson and Browning, whose appearances, as poets, coincided with, or very slightly preceded, their own births.

Thomas Edward Brown—author of *Fo'c'sle Yarns* and a good many other volumes of verse, collected and enlarged from MS matter after his death—is not the easiest of the minor poets of the later nineteenth century to survey with what has been called a 'horizontal' view. Living, for the greater part of his life, within what he certainly regarded as the 'black purgatorial rails' of schoolmastership, he made of not a few of the boys who emerged from the black-railed fold fervent disciples and fast friends, whose voices, including the very forcible and peremptory one of W. E. Henley, were loudly raised in his favour. Except the short and remarkable yarn *Betsy Lee*, he published nothing till he was over fifty; but, later, he made his verse more accessible. Nor could others, personally impartial, fail to discern in his work, not merely when it was collected, but as isolated examples came before them, a quite uncommon tone frequently, and, sometimes, a suggestion of something more behind which might become not merely uncommon but supreme.

---

[1] To these, some would add Richard Garnett, best known as a librarian and, next best, as a literary critic, editor, biographer and historian, but, also, a very skilful writer of verse; David Gray, one of the numerous beneficiaries, and not the least deserving of them, by the fund of pity and praise always open for poets, actual and possible, who die young; Herman Charles Merivale, who, at least, must have a line of mention for certain charming lyrics and sonnets, especially, in the latter kind, *Thaisa's Dirge*; and John Nichol, professor of English literature at Glasgow, whose principal work was done in prose, but who wrote a closet drama *Hannibal*, of no low rank in the *Philip van Artevelde* class, and some lyrics which were both scholarly and graceful.

On the other hand, a thorough critical examination of his work, conducted, so far as possible, with full allowance to himself for his time and complete absence of what may be called 'temporal prejudice' on the part of the critic—assisted, likewise, by a careful consideration of the special claims put forward for him, and guarding almost more carefully against prejudice arising from any particular statement of these claims—is not facile. One may be repelled by some of these statements of claim, although Brown is not responsible for them. There are to be found expressions about him which would be exact enough, though a little enthusiastic in their exactness, if made about Dante. And Brown is not Dante.

What he is, is excessively difficult to define without those limitations and reservations which are apt to revolt uncritical minds; but, with not too much indulgence in them, it is possible enough. About his general poetic kind, there is no difficulty at all : every one who has appreciated him has seen that he is of the mystics—of the company of his namesake Sir Thomas in prose, of Vaughan, Blake and, to no small extent, Wordsworth in verse. But, with this mysticism, he combines a vivid and, sometimes, almost familiar realism of expression and choice of subject, which Wordsworth did not reach and which none of the others attempted. In this combination, having much less power of expression than of thought, he sometimes breaks down. He is often strangely destitute of sheer clarity, as in *The Peel Life Boat*, a defect which, probably, prevented its appearance in Henley's *Lyra Heroica*. It seems to have been commissioned for this book; but Henley, who, with all his admiration for Brown, was, as an editor, utterly autocratic and quite free from respect of persons, must have seen that it wanted the indefinable 'that!' In his narrative poems, the following now of Tennyson now of Browning is so unmistakable and so continuous as to be teasing; and the 'unconventionalities' in diction and thought which have largely caused his popularity, such as it is, and his relatively greater influence, are not safe from very damaging comment. The outburst against his 'Englishwoman on the Pincian' which concludes *Roman Women* is only the 'platitude reversed' of Tourguénieff's pitiless and fatal epigram on later nineteenth-century *esprit*—and as conventional itself as the conventionalities it objurgates. The satire on commonplace orthodoxy in *A Sermon at Church on Good Friday* is as stale as its subject, and in hopelessly bad taste. One could find many other faults in Brown.

His dialect pieces—agreeable in one or two instances—force on one by their bulk the fact that the lingo itself is not a real dialect, but an ugly and bastard *patois* or, rather, jargon of broken-down Celtic and the vulgarest English. His 'idylls,' such as *Mary Quayle* and *Bella Gorry*, are fine and affecting stories. which would have been much better in prose.

And yet Brown is a poet—and, at times, much more than a minor poet. No one who knows what poetry is can turn the leaves of the most convenient and accessible selection-collection of his poems—that in *The Golden Treasury* series—with any fair attention and remain in doubt of this. The remarkable *Opifex*, in which he confesses the limitations of his own powers, justifies his claims in poetry; and there are dozens of other lyrics which will appeal—some to some tastes and some to others—but all to those fortunate ones to whom all poetry that is poetry is welcome. *White Foxglove* in one vein ; *The Sinking of the Victoria* in another; *Risus Dei*, and, as comments on it, in the poet's extremer style, the *Dartmoor* pieces, in a third ; *The Prayer*, perhaps likely to be the most popular of all with the most different people—and the most seventeenth-century in tone; *The Schooner*, an early instance of the modern violent style, but a fine one ; others too many to mention occur as specimens. And one great thing may be added to the right side of Brown's balance-sheet—that he is singularly free from monotony—in fact, he might have lost in freshness of appeal if he had gained in formal mastery of expression.

A much greater poet at his best than Brown, like him most imperfectly known or knowable during his lifetime and nearly contemporary, still only accessible in selection and probably never to be studied in completeness (it is believed that he destroyed much of his work) was Richard Watson Dixon, canon of Carlisle for many years, a strenuous worker in the two northern dioceses, an ecclesiastical historian of the first rank, and an early member of the original literary offshoot at Oxford of the pre-Raphaelite brotherhood. Brown was not exactly 'a man of this world,' but he was very much more so than Dixon ; and, while Brown largely took the Wordsworthian side of poetry, Dixon was wholly on the Coleridgean. He published several volumes most of which are extremely difficult to obtain ; and the reader who cannot easily frequent large public libraries must judge him from *Mano*, his longest poem, from the so-called *Last Poems* and, best of all, from the *Poems* selected and prefaced by or under the

supervision of the present poet laureate—to which volume one
would gladly see added all or most of what has not been selected
there but is still available. In this case, the editor has been
a more austere man than Henley was in regard to his friend—
pronouncing his poetry not to be defended against charges of
inequality, poor and faulty passages and, above all, want of
finish. Each of those charges may, undoubtedly, be advanced,
and, to some extent, supported. And even Mary Coleridge, a
great champion of Dixon and probably, as has been said above,
not a little influenced by him, admitted, in nine probable readers
out of ten, a first feeling of 'disappointment'—though she
promised them a change first to 'surprise' and then to 'ecstasy.'
But, if not in every tenth, in some proportion or other, the
unpleasant first step will be happily escaped, unless the reading
begins with *Mano*, in which case there is some danger that the
surprise will be rarely, and the ecstasy never, reached. That
longest and most ambitious of his attempts contains beautiful
passages ; and, even as a whole, it leaves an impression of
somewhat reluctant and extorted esteem. But there is too much
history in it ; the history, moreover, is of a period (the tenth and
eleventh centuries) which is difficult to make interesting unless
it is treated with a purely romantic neglect of history itself ; the
characters hardly grasp the reader ; and the audacious attempt
to use *terza rima* for a really long poem in English fails, as it has
always failed and as it probably always will fail. *Love's Consolation*—much shorter, but still extending to some 400 or 500
lines—is a beautiful but incoherent pre-Raphaelite dream, the
expression of which too often follows those early Keatsian lapses
which the greater pre-Raphaelites avoided.

It is only as a lyric poet that Dixon shows his full power; but,
sometimes, in this capacity, his command over strangeness and his
ability to transport are all but supreme. It was said above that
Brown has a Blake-like quality ; but Dixon's *Fallen Rain* is
Blake himself, not a *pastiche* or an imitation but a poem, Blake's
authorship of which, if it had been found anonymous with a
possibility of its having been somehow saved from Tatham's crime,
no one would have doubted for a moment. As it is, the resemblance is almost bewildering. *The Feathers of the Willow* has been
recognised by almost all competent critics who have come across
it as unique in its peculiar exemplification of the combined
pictorial and musical appeal of poetry. Less perfect, because
longer, but, as being longer, somewhat more imposing and varied,

is *To Shadow*, a poem, in parts, more like Beddoes than it is like
any other poet, but, again, absolutely free from plagiarism or even
suggestion. Perhaps the greatest of all—to use the superlative
and the adjective itself carefully—is the *Ode on Advancing Age*.
In form, this is of the most apparently irregular Pindaric, though
every apparent irregularity may be justified on the strictest
prosodic principles. But this form is not in the least intruded,
so as to obscure; it is, on the contrary, suited in the highest degree—
as, also, are the diction, the imagery and the whole body and garment
—to the strange spirit of the piece. Everyone knows Lamb's
description of the two great dirges in Shakespeare and Webster
as, the one of the water watery, the other of the earth earthy.
No other poet in any passage occurring to the memory of the
present writer, has, in the same way, saturated a piece of verse—
itself almost a dirge—as Dixon has done here with the melancholy
essence of sea and shore and sea-birds' cry, or with any similar
conjuring of scene and sound and atmosphere. These, perhaps, are
Dixon's very best things ; but there are many others not far short
of them, while for passages of sheer word-painting none of his
friends surpassed him. There has been some discussion on the
point whether he can be called a Wordsworthian or not ; and
a settlement of this, perhaps, is not much to be hoped for, because
the genuine impressions of what is and is not Wordsworthian differ
in competent critics more widely than is the case in regard to the
essential quality of any other poet. But it is, at least, a testimony
to absence of monotony in a writer that, with an entire freedom
from mere imitation, he should suggest Wordsworth at one time
and Keats at another, while the lyrics specially cited above are
quite different from both and belong, in an equally independent
manner, to the traditions of Blake or of Coleridge. On the whole,
Dixon may be allowed to be not an easy poet to understand, and
one in respect of whom it is necessary, in critical slang, to 'get the
atmosphere' before appreciation is possible. No doubt, this is
what Mary Coleridge meant. But, when it has been achieved, or,
in the fortunate cases where the reader drops into the proper place
and attitude at once, there is not likely to be much quarrel as to
the quality of the poetry.

Sebastian Evans, who was born in the same year with Brown,
but whose favourite subjects were nearer Dixon's, was a younger
brother of the well-known antiquary Sir John Evans and also of
Anne Evans, whose verse has been noticed already[1]. She was a

---

[1] See p. 177.

friend of Thackeray and, for some time, an inmate of his house, where she may have derived the suggestion of one of the least unsatisfactory definitions of humour ever attempted—'thinking in jest while feeling in earnest.' Her brother Sebastian was himself possessed of the quality; but (which may surprise some who do not possess it) he was, among a variety of pursuits—art, literature of other kinds, journalism, politics—an enthusiastic medievalist, as was shown in his poetical and other writings, from the early *Brother Fabian's Manuscripts* to his late presentation of *The High History of the Holy Graal*, including the part to be found in French and Welsh but not in Malory or in most modern adaptations of the story. The thinking in jest and the feeling in earnest of his sister's words are both present in Evans's poetry; and they find frequent expression which, if not exactly consummate, is distinct and attractive. Of the rather numerous attempts at retelling the story of St Brandan and Judas his, if the most deliberately quaint, is one of the most original; and *Shadows* is a poem which would not disgrace the signature of any poet.

Three charges—heavy and, if fully substantiated, damaging if not even damning—have been brought by some against Robert, second lord and first earl Lytton, viceroy of India and author of a long series of books in various kinds of verse. It is the opinion of others that they cannot be fully substantiated; and that there are in 'Owen Meredith,' as he called himself at first, especially in his earliest and latest work, counterbalancing merits which have been too much disregarded by critics. But dangerous defects, laying him open to the charges referred to, cannot be denied. The first and vaguest is something like a repetition of accusations constantly brought against his father—accusations of unreality, affectation, pose, theatricality and so forth. That he does not always avoid the suggestion of such things may be granted: that he was able to avoid them and frequently did so may be affirmed. With regard to the second charge—that of plagiarism, a somewhat similar position may be taken up. There is, undoubtedly, a good deal more echo of other men's work in 'Owen Meredith' than was either necessary or wise. But, as this echoing was always of work generally known, the writer could never possibly hope to escape detection or to pass off what was not his own as his own—which is the essence of plagiarism—and the habit, in fact, was only an incident or item of the third count, which cannot be denied at all, and which really contains within itself almost everything that can justly be said against lord Lytton as a poet. This concerns his enormous, and almost fatal, fluency. He did not live to be an old man ; and his life was full of vocations and avocations of all kinds. Yet, the bulk of his work in verse would be unusually large for a man who had as little else to do as Wordsworth or Tennyson, and who had lived as long as either. It was said that, even when he corrected his work, he was sure to recoup himself for any omissions by manifold insertions ; and he had a fancy for extensive verse-novels, such as *Lucile* and *Glenaveril.* His really brilliant satiric-epic-fantasy *King Poppy*, which was posthumously published after he had been writing and rewriting it for twenty years, would be much better if it were half the length. Yet, from the early *Wanderer* to the again posthumous collection of lyrics called *Marah*, which contains some of his very best work, there is constant evidence that, when some invisible mentor seized him and forced him to concentrate his powers, they were equal to the composition of real poetry of a high class. The piece variously called *Astarte* and *Fata Morgana* in *The Wanderer*, and that entitled *Selenites* (though a slight licence is taken with the quantity of the word) in *Marah*, are, perhaps, the very best of all; but there are scores nearly as good. *A Love Letter*, which has been the most general favourite and which opens admirably, would have gained by losing half its forty-two stanzas. For those who do not insist upon lyric, not a few passages and some pieces in *Chronicles and Characters, Fables in Song* and *After Paradise* ought to give a satisfaction which, if they have, up to the time, only thought of lord Lytton as a flashy Byronist, born out of due time, will surely make them change their minds.

Whether Edwin, later Sir Edwin, Arnold can be called a more popular poet than lord Lytton is a question which might occasion logomachy ; but he certainly escaped the unfavourable criticism which, in this way and that, 'Owen Meredith' attracted. Although we do not now write *Arts of Preserving Health* or discussions of the sugar cane in verse, there has never failed a public for poetry which, as the naïve phrase goes, 'tells you something'; and *The Light of Asia*, Sir Edwin's best known poem, gained vogue as an easy version of what some said was a very exoteric Buddhism Despite active employment, first in educational matters and then in journalism, he produced a good deal of verse on many different subjects and in many different forms. Some of it obtained considerable praise, while, on the other hand, there are critics who are seldom able to perceive true poetry in anything that Sir Edwin wrote—his blank verse appearing to them fluently insignificant and his lyrics, with one remarkable exception[1], lacking life, wanting in intensity and in anything but rather commonplace music.

There was, however, never so much difference in his case between the public and, at first, a few, but, latterly, nearly all, critics as occurred in the case of Lewis Morris, who, also, was later knighted. Lewis Morris has been called 'the Tupper of the later nineteenth century'; but the comparison is unfair in both ways, except so far as it concerns the just mentioned difference between public and critics, and the extraordinary vogue of more or less worthless verse. The historic circumstances of the two are curiously and distinguishingly different. Tupper, as has been said above, obtained his popularity in a dead season of poetry with matter of, at least, unusual form. Lewis Morris, on the other hand, began when poetry, especially through Tennyson's work, had again been popularised, and even when new movements in advance had stimulated the appetite but, in some cases, had shocked or puzzled the taste of the average reader. The French, if one remembers rightly, long ago manufactured out of Defoe's masterpiece a *Robinson des enfants*. Lewis Morris set himself to be a *Tennyson des enfants*, and was justified of a considerable number of the grown-up children whom he addressed. *Songs of Two Worlds*, which first appeared in three series, and the more ambitious *Epic of Hades* which followed, deserved the title of perfect works of art in one sense only perhaps; but they certainly deserved it in that. They hit the object at which they were immediately aimed; though, beyond all doubt, their success helped to provoke in others a reaction of taste which has dominated the last thirty years and more and which has most curiously and uncritically affected the popular estimate of Tennyson himself. Often, when one reads uncomplimentary remarks on *Idylls of the King*, one thinks that the critic, by some mistake, has come upon a copy of *The Epic of Hades* with a wrong lettering on the back.

The means by which Lewis Morris hit the vulgar and some, at first, of those who should not have come under that designation, were the strictest 'propriety' of subject and expression, a modern and liberal tone towards questions of politics, religion and philosophy; an entire avoidance of all obscurity, preciousness or eccentricity of language; and the observance, respectable till it

---

[1] This is the poem called *He and She*, the subject being a living husband who sits by the side of his dead wife and implores spiritual communion. It has been very highly admired by some; and, though not without flatnesses here and there, really has something of the intensity and the music generally denied to his poetry above.

became distressing, of an absolute smoothness of versification. He was great at truisms in morality, and, indeed, in everything. He could draw fairly pretty pictures, though, when you examined them, you found that there was scarcely ever a touch of real nature or original wit in them, that the colours were those of the tenpenny-halfpenny box and the outlines stencilled. He had, sometimes, a faculty—which, in a satirist, would have been admirable—of writing things which looked like poetry till one began to think of them a little[1].

A pleasant and popular person, with a great many friends both in Oxford and in London, Lewis Morris secured fairly favourable views at first. But unbiassed censors, especially of a slightly younger generation, began to revolt before many years had passed; and, not content with a rough reception of his later works *Gwen, The Ode of Life, Gycia, Songs Unsung* (a dangerously suggestive title), went back to the earlier *Songs* and *The Epic* and did their best to demonstrate the poetical nullity of the whole work. That work, for a good many years, has been available in a single volume, and everybody can form his own opinion on it. It may be warranted to do nobody any harm; if, by some curious chance, a little savage on a desert island read it knowing no other poetry and liked it, this would be a rather good sign in him.

A very different poet was Sir Alfred Lyall[2] who, both during, and after, a brilliant career in the Indian civil service, wrote verses, few but fit, in a style very much his own, though Browning must have had considerable influence on his way of poetising thought if not of framing expression for it. The spirit of the opening poem of his *Verses written in India, The Old Pindaree,* has inspired others to an extent much greater than its debt to earlier poets. *Theology in Extremis* (his other most famous poem) is of the 'problem' order, the speech or meditation of an Englishman in the mutiny who, though a freethinker, will not purchase his life by uttering the Mohammedan formula. Most, however, are rather studies of Indian, than of English, nature; and the situation between

---

[1] For instance, in an imposing Pindaric (that old refuge-bag of poetic wind that is not of the spirit), he writes of nature or the world

Unchanging she
Alike in short-lived flower and ever-changing sea.

A paragraph or stanza which ends with 'sea' always has a certain conjuring effect in English, and 'flowers' are useful to the poet as well as to the poetaster. But a minute's reflection will show that there is no real antithesis between the brief life of the flower and the 'ever-changingness' (which, no doubt, is itself the most unchanging thing in the world) of the ocean.

[2] See, also, vol. XIV.

the two is sometimes strikingly put, as in *Badminton*, the half parodied, half serious *Land of Regrets* and the sombre *Retrospection*. From one critical point of view, indicated already, one might call Sir Alfred's poetry rather 'applied' than 'pure'; and, from another, it might seem the work of an exceedingly clever and scholarly man of the world rather than of a poet. It is, no doubt, essentially 'occasional'—anecdotes, situations, reflections, brief characters thrown into verse-form. But there is always distinction in it, generally music, often really poetic expression of thought.

That Alfred Austin hardly deserved to be made poet laureate is a proposition which very few persons, whatever their personal or political attitude towards him, are likely to deny now, and which, in after times, nobody at all, except out of mere whim, is likely to dispute. But, as in other cases, the penalty of the error fell unfairly on himself. It could not be said of him, as we said of Pye, that he was not a poet at all; but it could be, and was, said that, though a really vigorous and accomplished writer of prose, and a tolerable master of unambitious form in verse, his poetical powers were of the most mediocre kind. He began with cheap satire in an exploded style; and, though he fortunately abandoned this, neither his longer nor his shorter poems possessed pathos, power or beauty enough to give them much attraction even for a time or to keep them in memory after their writer's death. Browning's nickname 'Banjo Byron,' in the exceedingly ill-mannered and not extraordinarily witty attack prefaced to *Pacchiarotto*, was not very happy; for, though Austin was a professed admirer of Byron, he cannot be said to have copied him much except in satire, where Byron himself was a copyist. He could keep up poems of some length like *Prince Lucifer* and *The Human Tragedy* without being so tame as Lewis Morris, and he could come rather nearer to vigour and passion in lyric than (with the exception here noted) Edwin Arnold. So that, had only the three been available, his appointment would have been fully justified.

Only that indefinable something which constantly and mysteriously interferes in the history of poetry prevented the Cambridge poet, Roden Berkeley Wriothesley Noel, from attaining a rank in his art which would have taken him out of this chapter. As it is, there are none of his contemporaries who, to the present writer, seem to have come so close to majority, except his two close contemporaries at Oxford, R. W. Dixon and lord De Tabley. This 'something' may, perhaps, be connected with two other things which have unfavourably conditioned many poets during the nineteenth century—undue voluminousness of work, and an undue influence of ' the printed book '—not, as in the case of ' Owen Meredith,' running into anything that even an unfavourable judge could call plagiarism, but communicating a sort of *aura* of secondhandness—a faint suggestion of reminiscence and *pastiche*. Of these two failings, the latter may almost be disregarded; at certain times (and they are usually not times of small things in poetry), it is almost inevitable. The bulk of the work and the causes or constituents of that bulk—undue fluency to start with and subsequent inability to compress or distil that fluency into something stronger and more forcible—is a more serious objection. Roden Noel's most remarkable single book, *A Little Child's Monument*—a collection of episodes on his own son Eric, who died at five years old—equals, for intense reality of feeling and general adequacy of expression, anything of its kind. But pure personal lamentation unrelieved by digression and, as it were, episode, is, of all kinds of poetry, and, perhaps, of literature, that which should be kept from undue expatiation and prolongation. The book contains most beautiful things ; but the comment 'something too much of this' must force itself upon the least cynical of readers. The same fault is observable in *Livingstone in Africa*, but is even more noticeable there because there is no depth of passion even to attempt to carry it off. He, perhaps, shows at his best in pieces like *A Vision of the Desert, The Water Nymph* and *The Boy*. Here, though there is not the slightest imitation, and the subjects, especially in the second-named poem, are quite different, there is a suggestion of Darley's masterpiece *Nepenthe*; but the very mention of that poem implies a certain incoherence, a wealth and almost spilth of imagery and sound flung abroad 'as boys fling nuts.' In this and other aspects, Roden Noel has been compared to Shelley, but no critic can fail to discern the difference between them. The intensity and mastery of Shelley always unify, for the time and in the poem, his prodigality of image and colour and symphonic arrangement; this can hardly be said of Noel. The Land's End poem, *Thalatta*, wants, like much of the rest, carding and thinning and winnowing; but the study is a really fine one, and some of the shorter love-poems, as well as of the individual constituents of *A Little Child's Monument*, escape almost all censure. Now, to make a pardonable repetition, he who can write without banality of the sea and of love and of death is a poet.

But, perhaps, the most interesting subject of analysis, for one who would master the riddle—if it be a riddle—of later nineteenth-century verse which did not 'attain unto the first three,' or the first half-dozen, is the already mentioned lord de Tabley, who, succeeding to the title rather late in life, had been known, when he began to write after leaving Oxford, under the pseudonyms 'Preston' and 'Lancaster,' and, later, while still a commoner, by his own name John Byrne Leicester Warren. His literary history (he was also a scientific botanist, an authority in numismatics and, altogether, a man of very wide culture) was curious. He did not publish any verse till he was nearly thirty; then, during about twelve years, he issued no less than seven volumes, with a novel or two; then, for nearly twenty more, he contributed nothing at all to literature, and, at last, after his accession to the title and just before his death, published two volumes of selected poems which, if they did not secure an adequate recognition of his powers, did awake, in younger critics, something like what a few of their elders had vainly striven to bring about earlier, a sense of undue neglect.

It was, undoubtedly, unfortunate for him that his period of earlier poetic appearances exactly coincided with the appearances of Morris, Swinburne and Rossetti, who were not only, in different ways, undoubtedly, greater poets than himself, but poets great in a more popular fashion, though not a more vulgar one. *Philoctetes*, in particular, his first really important work, came, in the most unlucky fashion, just after *Atalanta in Calydon*; and, though its author was at no time in the very slightest degree an imitator, still less a plagiarist, the similarity of classical subject (there was no other), and the quieter and more purely scholarly character of Warren's piece, made a certain 'occultation' inevitable. The last of the series, *The Soldier of Fortune*, published ten years later (the ill-success of which has been thought to be the reason of its author's long abstinence from poetry), is an extreme instance of an error frequent in the subjects of this chapter. Among the few people who have read it through—it is now believed to be a very difficult book to obtain—there can have been little difference of opinion as to the merit, not merely of individual passages, but as to the remarkable presence in it of what the Greeks used to call by the difficultly translatable word *dianoia*, 'thought,' 'mental temper,' etc. But it is too long— enormously too long—and not sustained in its length by varied incident or story. The two late selected volumes, however, make it inexcusable for anyone who cares for poetry to remain ignorant of the merits of what they contain. It is almost safe to say that in these contents there is hardly a poem which is not really a poem.

When a historical critic gives such a judgment in such a case, he is bound to explain, if he can, the reasons which have made the general estimate of the poet different. Two of these reasons, applying to the original reception of lord de Tabley's poetry, have been given: two others may be added. As he was distinctly unfortunate in the time of his beginning, so he was, at least partly, in that of his reappearance. The younger generation (to its credit) did him more justice than the elder, with rare exceptions, had done. But, still, they were a younger generation, and he represented an elder: his ways were not their ways; so that respect, rather than enthusiasm, was excited. Lastly, it must be admitted that, except for sworn lovers of poetry, Warren's poetry may be said, in the common phrase, to want 'a little more powder.' It is apt to be too scholarly and quiet for the general taste, which wants strong flavour, luscious sweetness, lively pastime, exuberant force and the like. But, after this admission, the judgment given will still stand.

Something more than a neighbourhood of birth-years connects Thomas Ashe with Noel and de Tabley, though he was certainly inferior to both of them as a poet. He, too, began with a classical drama, *The Sorrows of Hypsipyle*, which, at the time, tempted some who read it, though they knew the danger and deception of these closet dramas, to expect not a little from him. After leaving Cambridge, he was, for the greater part of his not very long life, a schoolmaster and, latterly, a working man of letters; but he never left off verse-writing, and divided his practice between longer poems, such as the drama just mentioned, a narrative piece on the story of Psyche—often told but so charming that nobody but a blockhead could spoil it wholly—and lyrics. The general impression of Ashe's work is that given by much modern poetry, namely, that compression, distillation—any of the metaphorically allied processes which, without importing actually foreign qualities, bring out and bring together those which exist in a too diffused condition—might have made of him a poet of real value. In further comparison with some of his near contemporaries, he takes far higher rank; for, in almost his least good work there is always what analysts call a 'trace' of poetry. But the trace rarely rises to a distinctly appreciable, and, perhaps, never to a high, percentage.

To this decade, likewise, belonged Theodore Watts, in the later years of his life known as Watts-Dunton, a solicitor, a sonneteer and the author of a novel, *Aylwin*, which had a great popularity for a time, as well as a frequent, a voluminous and a highly serious critic of poetry. He was, and, no doubt, still more will be, best known from the generous and faithful friendship and hospitality which he showed to the poet Swinburne. Only coterie enthusiasm could regard him as being himself a very noteworthy poet[1], but he had cultivated his natural gifts that way by much frequentation, not merely of Swinburne but of the Rossettis and others, and some of his sonnets are not unworthy of his society.

The notable poets born in the forties who can be noticed here are rather fewer in number than those of the previous decade[2], but they are of more uniform merit; and, once more, they introduce, as a group, new influences of the highest importance from a historical point of view. Almost all of them felt early, and most of them felt from the beginning of their poetical career, the great new impulse of the pre-Raphaelite movement, in development, in revolt, or in simple agreement or difference. In chronological order they include John Addington Symonds, Robert Buchanan, Frederic Myers, Gerard Hopkins, Andrew Lang and William Ernest Henley[3].

The defect of Symonds in verse is the same as that which is notable in his prose, and a variety of one which has been, and will

---

[1] He was, at any rate, a better one—he certainly belonged to a better school—than his namesake Alaric Alexander Watts, who might have been noticed in the last chapter on this subject, but most of whose work belonged to the earlier part of this. The elder Watts was unlucky enough to provoke the wicked wit of Lockhart and to live (with perversion of his second name) in the 'singing flames' of

I *don't* like that Alaric *Attila* Watts,
His verses are just like the pans and the pots, etc.

The pans were neatly enough polished, and the pots were quite clean; but they were turned out by mould and machinery, and there was very little in them. Their author was an industrious and ingenious, though not very fortunate, journalist and book-maker, and his principal collection *Lyrics of the Heart* (1850), besides serious things very much of the kind suggested by the title, contains the earlier-written alliterative *amphigouri*,

An Austrian army awfully arrayed,
which has had an unexpected illustration in very recent times. Alaric 'Attila' was a very harmless person, but not a very meritorious poet.

[2] Partly for the comfortable reason that some of the best of them are still alive.

[3] There might be added, in a sort of second division, Cosmo Monkhouse, a remarkably unpretentious poet whose work was not seldom above his pretensions; George Augustus Simcox, a scholar who, late in life, met a still mysterious fate on the Irish coast, and who, much earlier, had published some distinguished verse; and Samuel Waddington, a special student of the sonnet and no mean practitioner in it, as well as in other forms of lyric verse.

be, noticed frequently among all his contemporaries, but it was more prejudicial in verse than elsewhere. In his principal prose work, *The Renaissance in Italy*, it certainly made itself felt; but the abundance of the subject matter and the obligation which every scholar (and Symonds was a scholar) feels to do his subject the fullest justice possible in mere information counterworks it to a considerable extent. The poet, of course, does justice to his subject, as he may, but he is less, if at all, under the control of pure fact. The result on Symonds was too often unfortunate. In his translations, the necessary attempt at fidelity acted sometimes as cold water to keep his ebullience down; in his original poems, it is almost always unrestrained. A similarity of title and title-suggestion (though there is no copying on the English poet's part) makes Gautier's *La Chimère* and Symonds's *Le jeune homme caressant sa Chimère* worth comparing. Both have beauty; but that of the French verse is heightened by brevity, by discipline of phrase and (within even the narrow limits) by increasing concentration and final poignancy of feeling and expression; while the English steeps itself and washes itself out in endless lusciousness of fancy, and incurs the charge of what Keats called (and had, of all poets, the right to call and to condemn) mawkishness[1].

That, at least, is a fault which could not be charged against his junior by a year, Robert Buchanan. A novelist, a dramatist, a miscellaneous writer of all sorts, Buchanan underwent to the full the drawback and the danger (here often pointed out) of such divagation; and his temper, rather than his genius, exposed him to another set-back. He was quite entitled to attack the pre-Raphaelite school if he wished to do so; but his unluckily pseudonymous assault (if it had been anonymous it would hardly have mattered much, and if it had been signed nothing at all) on the 'fleshly' school of poetry combined the violence of Esau with the disingenuousness of Jacob; and, though some of those whom it attacked were magnanimous enough to forgive it, it could not be easily forgotten. It ought to be said, however, that Buchanan showed no bad blood in regard to open counter-attacks on himself, and his verse, as always, is entitled to be judged without regard to this misadventure, after the dues of history are paid. His verse, though produced rather in the earlier than in the later part of his career, was voluminous, and it was exceedingly unequal; but it has, what many of his contemporaries lacked,

---

[1] Symonds's theories of versification, like those of Patmore, may be best noticed in the chapter on nineteenth-century prosody.

a certain sincerity sufficient to atone for an occasional imitation which he shared with them. *Ratcliffe Meg*, one of his most commonly praised poems, is rather a close approach to success than an attainment of it. But *The Vision of the Man Accurst*, *The Ballad of Judas Iscariot* (perhaps the best of the numerous attempts on the subject) and some passages on awe-inspiring aspects of the scenery in the Coolin and Coruisk districts of Skye, are poetry.

A sharp difference of specific quality, if not of general poetical merits, again meets us when we turn to Frederic Myers. He was early distinguished, even at school and still more at Cambridge, by the unusual idiosyncrasy of his verse, an idiosyncrasy the more, not the less, remarkable that he had recently felt, and very strongly felt, the influence of Swinburne. Myers afterwards became an inspector of schools and interested himself in other matters; so that he did not produce much poetry. What he did, from his prize-poem, *St Paul*, onward, was distinguished both in choice and treatment of subject and in character of form; but the distinction of form was certainly by far the greater. A good critic now living is said to hold that he could always tell any verse by Myers, though he might have no external knowledge of the authorship, by its peculiar rhythm; and, though this may be an exaggeration, it is an exaggeration of a truth. Myers's lyrics are not very individual in substance and, perhaps, never consummate; but his blank verse, his heroics and especially his use of the decasyllabic quatrain with feminine rimes in the first and third lines, are certainly fingered in a singularly original manner.

Originality, not confined to form or to a single cast of thought, appeared in Andrew Lang, in connection with whose work must be surveyed a curious episode, affecting a large number of verse-producers for no small period of years in the history of English poetry. Lang's own work in verse, in point of bulk, was an infinitesimal part of an enormous productiveness in literature— journalism of many kinds, especially reviewing and miniature essay-writing, historical discussion on the larger, and also the smaller, scale, studies in folklore and in other branches of scholarship, translation, editing, what not, all permeated by an individuality not so much of mere form as of general style and attitude, which was not exceeded by that of any writer, greater or lesser, in his time[1]. This immense production began before he left Oxford, and continued for more than forty years till his death. As usual, his

---

[1] See, also, *post*, vol. XIV.

poetical work, for the most part, belonged to the earlier time, though he never lost grip of the lyre. It comprised one long poem, *Helen of Troy*, some early imitations and translations chiefly of French poetry, and a considerable body of lyric, partly, but by no means wholly, in special forms to be presently noticed. In humour, which never turned to horseplay, and always showed the vein of feeling referred to in Anne Evans's definition; in a certain touch of melancholy, which never became affected or morbid; and in a command of 'numbers'—music in language and rhythm—which, though it could manage the most complicated measures, never enslaved itself to them or relied on them, Lang's verse could stand the severest tests. He chose to liken his poetry to grass of Parnassus—wild flowers at the foot of the mount only—but such things as the *Ballade of his Choice of a Sepulchre*, and as the great sonnets entitled *The Odyssey* and *Colonel Burnaby* know nothing of the lower slopes. Only, in Lang's case, as in many others, but, perhaps, more than in any, there is to be lamented the dissipation—in the strict, not the transferred, sense of the word—of his powers. It may safely be said that hardly any great poet has ever achieved his greatness in the course of varied avocation by daily work, literary or other, unless, like Shakespeare, he happened to be a dramatist, where the poetry, if not of the essence of the journey-work, is, so to speak, inextricably connected with it, so that the writer passes from one to the other with no sense of change or rupture. It may, in particular, or it may not be, possible to write, but, as a matter of fact, no man has written great poetry on a large scale and in bulk while he was perpetually called off to go to a newspaper office and 'get a subject'; to go home or to his club to write on it; to visit a library to look up facts for a book of another kind; to write a chapter or a page of that, and the like. Every known example shows that dame Oiseuse is as much the portress of poetry as she is of love. *Helen of Troy*, though, in parts, very beautiful, is not an achieved poem as a whole. If the author could have been shut up for a year or two in a fairly comfortable prison it might have been[1].

[1] A few lines must be given to a contemporary of Lang at Oxford who was, to a greater extent than is usual, a poetical might-have-been. Gerard Hopkins was not only much let and hindered in writing poetry, but never published any, and all we have consists of fragments issued as specimens from MSS. But these fragments show that he not merely might have been, but was, a poet. Unfortunately, an ingrained eccentricity which affected his whole life, first as an undergraduate and then as a Jesuit priest, helped these accidents. He developed partially acute, but not generally sound, notions on metre; and though, quite recently, broken-backed rhythms like his have been often attempted, the results have scarcely been delightful. In his

This question, however, does not touch the other and more general one referred to above. Much of Lang's work is couched in the strict metrical forms which, by the operation of a slightly different temper and language, arose in northern France after the downfall of Provençal poetry in the south, were widely cultivated there from the thirteenth to the fifteenth and even sixteenth centuries, were imitated by English poets such as Chaucer, Gower, Lydgate and others of the time, but never with us achieved anything like the effect attained by French poets from Lescurel to Villon. They were still largely written in the earlier French renascence, but were turned out of favour by the *Pléiade*; were occasionally, though rarely, attempted in English[1] during the seventeenth century, but died away almost entirely later. These forms— ballade, rondeau, roundel, triolet, virelai, chant royal—may, loosely, be said to belong to the same general class as the sonnet, but are much more artificial in their structure; the keys of all being first the use, under more or less intricate laws, of the refrain, and the repetition of one or more lines at statutory intervals; and, secondly, the observance of regularly recurrent rimes. The effect, especially when the poet is skilful enough to make this kind of *carillon* express sense as well as mere sound, is, sometimes, extremely beautiful; but, obviously, it is likely to become monotonous, tedious and purely artificial.

The revival of these forms in English depended upon an easily discoverable train of causes. The French romantic movement of 1830, and earlier, eagerly and naturally fed itself upon old French patterns, and some writers of its second generation, especially Théodore de Banville, had already managed the forms with singular grace. Now, in turn, the interest in these modern French poets created among younger English writers and critics by the pre-Raphaelite school, especially Swinburne, was very keen; and the result was practically unavoidable. Who first accomplished an English ballade or triolet is rather an idle question[2]; what is important is that the forms were adopted by many eager and skilful verse writers—at least three of the chief of whom, Austin Dobson, Edmund Gosse and the present poet laureate—are still alive, besides Lang, Henley and many others down to the merest

own case, though the process of appreciation is most like the proverbial reconstruction of a fossil beast from a few odd bones, it shows that they belonged to a poet.

[1] For instance, by Patrick Carey.

[2] There are, of course, roundels in Swinburne's *Poems and Ballads* (1866) and ballades in Rossetti's *Poems* (1870). But neither of these distinguished persons played quite the rigour of the game.

poetasters, who must needs try the trick of the time. This fancy continued during the seventies and earlier eighties in some force, lasted yet longer with diminished vogue and is not absolutely out of fashion even now, though examples are not common[1]. The present writer, as one who was prepared for it almost before it arose, who welcomed it eagerly, who preserves some of its results in his own private and unprinted anthology of preferred poetry, but whose acquaintance with it has 'come to forty year' and more, may, perhaps, be permitted to give his opinion about it, briefly, because it is, as was laid down above, a distinct and noteworthy episode in English poetic history.

There can be no doubt, then, that, originally, these forms were of great benefit to French poetry. The danger, at various times, and not least when the heroic part of the middle ages, on the one hand, and the folk song part, on the other, ceased, has been an easy skipping quality—a sort of recitative not far from prose. The firmer outline and the definitely concerted music of these refrain pieces was a great corrective to this. But, when they came to be applied to a perfected poetic language like nineteenth-century English, which, whether in blank verse, in couplet, in stanza, or in miscellaneous lyric measures, had learnt how to combine the greatest variety with the most serried force, the maximum of rhetorical, with the maximum of strictly poetical, music—certain things were almost bound to follow. The results achieved were, in some cases, as has been more than admitted, really beautiful. It would be improper to quote living writers here, but the two others named above supply unquestionable examples. The very piece cited above as a masterpiece by Lang is a ballade. But, from itself, a curious side-deduction may be made. In all the best French examples, the ballade form impresses itself inevitably ; you may read Lang's poem, and hardly notice that it is a ballade at all. In short—and the same, more or less, is the case with the best exercises of still living poets—the poem gains little from the form, unless the poet has put in poetry enough to make it independent of any form in particular. The fact seems to be that English is somewhat intolerant of measures which are too regularly and intricately concerted. Bacon's old and often repeated sarcasm, 'you may see things oft as good in tarts,' applies here.

At the same time, with fire enough in the inside—and, fortunately, there are numerous cases of this—the things can

---

[1] Ernest Dowson was, perhaps, the last of its best younger practitioners.

be subdued to the poet's most serious purpose excellently well. And, for playful purposes, whether half tender or wholly burlesque, these forms are unsurpassable. There are dozens of Lang's pieces, some of them never yet fished up from the depths of old periodicals, which are perfect in these ways.

To sum up, these artificial forms may be very useful and can be charming in various respects. But it is difficult, unless they are very freely treated, to get rid in them of a certain exotic and constrained air ; and, unless they are undoubted successes, they are apt to be intolerable.

General appreciation of the poems of William Ernest Henley has not, perhaps, been helped by coterie admiration, however generous and eager. But they occupy a peculiar and, in their way, a commanding position among their fellows. Henley tried the artificial forms, as has been mentioned above ; but they did not entirely suit his touch. The best, by far, is the splendid and quite serious rondeau, *What is to come?* which concludes his own collection of them under the sub-title (itself a half confession) *Bric-à-Brac.* Next to it, but much lower, may come, in the lighter kind, the ballade which opens the set *I loved you once in Old Japan.*

But, with him, it was a case of 'Not here, O Apollo,' and the poems by which he obtained, and will keep a place, in English poetry, as well as the most characteristic of those which may not have so fair a fate, are markedly different. Henley, from a rather early period, was a student not merely of modern French light literature and poetry but of French art; and these influences probably brought it about that he was almost, if not quite, the introducer of impressionism into English verse. The extremely striking *Hospital Verses,* written during a long sojourn in the Edinburgh infirmary—where the skill of Lister did what was possible to minimise an affection of the limbs which left Henley a cripple—are entirely of this class. When restored to comparative health, he took to journalism, and, for nearly twenty years, was an active and, for the whole of the rest of his life, an occasional contributor or, more frequently and preferably, editor —an occupation for which he had remarkable talents. His actual production, however, was never very large, though, both in verse and prose, it was exceedingly characteristic ; and his abstinence from the excessive collar-work to which most tolerably successful journalists and working men of letters are tempted gave him time to write as much poetry as, probably, he would have written in any case—his bad health and his not long life being duly considered. Henley's main characteristic in life and letters alike was masterfulness ; and it should be left to individual taste and judgment to decide whether a quality which almost as often leads men ill as well instigated more or less than it injured in his case. It certainly led him to violence and eccentricity of form and expression ; and (though this affected his prose more than his verse) to a rather perverse adoption and propagation of opinions, not so much because he held them himself as because former writers had held the opposite. It may be doubted whether he gained much by his fondness for rimeless measures ; or by his symbolist, and almost futurist, if not Blastist (for Henley was singularly anticipatory of later developments in the fringes of literature), adoration of 'speed.' But, *In Hospital* can at no time be read without admiration ; and very beautiful things will be found among the, again characteristically, but, in a way, unfairly, entitled *Echoes*. There are echoes (all but the greatest poetry of the period is an echo, though a multifarious and often a beautiful one) of old ballads, of standard verse, of modern singers as various as Tennyson and Emily Brontë and Swinburne. But, even in these, as, for instance, in the best known of his verses except, perhaps, the portrait of Stevenson, *Out of the Night that covers me*, Henley almost always contrives to blend an original tone ; and, sometimes, the echo is so faint, and derivable from so many separate sources, many, even, so doubtfully present, that the title becomes a mere polite or ironic apology. Such pieces are *In the Year that's come and gone*, *Love, his flying feather*, and, at least, the beginning and end (for the middle is not so good) of the splendidly swinging ballad with the half refrain

> I was a king in Babylon
> And you were a Christian slave,

with not a few others. In his later books, *The Song of the Sword, Hawthorn and Lavender, London Voluntaries, Rhymes and Rhythms*, including his admirable 'England ! my England ![1],' he sometimes allowed the violence which has been noticed to remain unchastened, if he did not even lash it up ; but this violence never sprang, as it often does, from weakness, but only from an erroneous theory, from a naturally fervid temperament and, beyond all doubt, very largely from the irritation of harassing disease. Of him, the old parable is surely justified as to the

---

[1] *Pro rege nostro.*

union of sweetness and strength, though the other combination of sweetness and light may not always have been present.

The dividing year of the century produced two poets, neither of whom can receive extended notice here but who are worth study both intrinsically and historically.

Philip Bourke Marston, who, from infancy, was threatened, and long before his early death struck, with blindness, had domestic afflictions which aggravated this greatest of personal ones. These, no doubt, influenced the verse of which he wrote not a little ; nor, perhaps, in any case, would he have been a poet of great intensity, while his actual production was, in Henley's phrase as to his own, much 'echoed.' But, some of his work, especially of his sonnets, is beautiful ; and the frequent wailing of his verse never turns to whining—a too natural and common degeneration. The other, Robert Louis Stevenson—as full, despite some counter-influences, of buoyancy as Marston was lacking in it—found his principal and abiding vocation in prose, not verse ; but, in the latter form, did some remarkable work, entirely, or almost entirely, free from that 'sedulous aping' which he frankly acknowledged in prose and which does not always improve his more popular and permanent tales and essays. *A Child's Garden of Verses* is, perhaps, the most perfectly natural book of the kind. It was supplemented later by other poems for children ; and some of his work outside this, culminating in the widely-known epitaph

> Home is the sailor, home from sea,
> And the hunter home from the hill,

has the rarely combined merits of simplicity, sincerity, music and strength.

Slightly younger than these two, but, as it happened, a friend of Philip Marston, came Herbert Edwin Clarke, whose verse, though always well received by competent critics, had, perhaps, less effect on the public—even such part of the public as reads poetry—than that of any writer of anything like equal merit noticed in this chapter. This might have been partly due to the fact, glanced at in other cases, that his first books, *Poems in Exile* and *Storm-Drift*, appeared at an unlucky time (1879—82), when there was a great deal of verse of relative excellence, but, so to speak, 'held under' by the eminence of the leaders, old and new ; partly to the pessimism which was displayed in some of the poems. Owing, it is believed, to discouragement, and, also, to business occupation, Clarke did not write much for some years, and his later volumes, *Poems and Sonnets* and *Tannhäuser and other Poems*, though, apparently, rather more widely read, came into competition, as such competition goes, with a new flight of verse, some realist, some ultratranscendental, beside which it may have seemed out of fashion. But those who read poetry for its own sake will scarcely fail to find it in all his books. Of his earlier work, three poems (which may be conveniently found together in the useful thesaurus to be mentioned in the bibliography)—*A Nocturn at Twilight, A Voluntary* and *Failure*—give different aspects of his verse in very high quality. *By the Washes, Chant d'Amour* and certain of his latest sonnets, should, also, be sought for. And there may be reckoned to Clarke one signal merit—that, putting a few scattered passages of Tennyson aside, his is the only poetry which has done justice (he was to the manner and matter born, at Chatteris in Cambridgeshire) to the strange and unique beauty of the fen-country, with its command—unequalled save at sea and very different from that given by the sea—of level horizon and unbroken sky.

The remarkable sonnets of Edward Cracroft Lefroy—poems of a style rather older than their date, and singularly free from pre-Raphaelite influence—the precocious achievement of Oliver Madox Brown, in whom that influence was naturally very strong; and the somewhat epicene touch (acknowledged long after it had been recognised by some under the for a long time well-kept pseudonym Fiona Macleod) by William Sharp, can receive no extended notice here. But two poets, born towards the close of the fifties, Francis Thompson and John Davidson, are too notable, both intrinsically and historically, not to receive as much as can be given. With two yet younger, but, also, now dead, they may close our record.

The eldest of the group, John Davidson (in whom some fairly sober critics have seen the best poet, not now living, who belonged to the second half of the last century by birth), was not a very early producer and, for a time, confined himself chiefly to unclassified dramas, *Scaramouch in Naxos, Bruce, Smith,* showing great ability, but too inorganic to establish a reputation. Coming to London when he was a little past thirty, he fell into a better vein of chiefly lyric poetry, which, fortunately, he continued to work, but to which, unfortunately, he was neither able nor, indeed, wholly willing to confine his energies. Attempts at novel-writing, which showed the ill-organised character of his early verse with the same kind of promise; miscellaneous journalism, which was wholly against grain or collar (whichever metaphor be preferred); and a barren rebellious pseudo-philosophy, which had its root in temper not in intellect, partly called him away from the muse, partly spoilt his sojourns without her. He was, to some extent, saved from uttermost need by a small civil list pension, but could not reconcile himself to life (he also thought himself to be threatened with cancer), and committed suicide by drowning. His work, which has a faint resemblance to that of Robert Buchanan, but with much more genius and accomplishment on one side, and to Henley's, with less leisurely deliberation on another, is, necessarily, rather unequal ; but, from the early *Fleet Street Eclogues* to the posthumous volumes, 'splendid gleams' are never wanting, and some pieces give a full and steady light throughout. There is, therefore, hardly any part of Davidson's poetical work which does not deserve to be read. The blank verse of the early plays possesses a singular originality ; while, chaotic and 'topsy-turvified' as is the matter, it wanted but a little more art to be triumphantly carried off by the form, and may still be so with a little allowance—no more than reasonable—in the case of any who know poetry when they see it. Of one modern kind of ballad— that which does not aim at being a *pastiche* of the old kind, but at telling a story lyrically in a fairly simple and ordinary kind of verse—Davidson was a master, and nearly a great master. The *Ballad of Heaven* is, though, perhaps, he did not mean it to be so, one of the best. His miscellaneous lyrics, where his greatest strength lies, are not poetry for everyone. There is violence—uncritical, but pathetic because not in the least merely affected; there is attempted vulgarity, though it was as impossible for Davidson to be really vulgar as it has been easy for some poets of higher rank in certain ways. There is frequently mistake—that is, say, the poet attacks things that he does not understand and, therefore, makes a mere windmill charge at them. But there is no mere copying or echo ; there is a strange command of poetic music and always 'the gleam.' *Kinnoull Hill, For Lovers, London, The Lutanist* may be mentioned in a sort of random choice out of many of his best poems ; but, as was said before, he must be read as a whole.

A curious complement-contrast is supplied by Francis Thompson, Davidson's close contemporary from birth to death, and, with him, almost completely representative of the main tendency of poetry among men who had reached, but not more than reached, middle life before the twentieth century began. Thompson, like Davidson, suffered from poverty and ill-health, though this last was partly caused, as it was not in Davidson's case, by imprudence on his part. But, during the latter years of his life, he was 'taken up,' both in person and in reputation, by benevolent persons in a powerful coterie. He was very much more of a scholar than Davidson, and was always, or almost always, as definitely devout as Davidson was the reverse ; nor, though, as has been said, he had had losses and privations, did he make these much of a subject for poetry. The two are thus, in many ways, different ; but, for that very reason, the representative character assigned to them in regard to the poetry of the latest years of the century is the more complete.

It has been said that Thompson had strong classical leanings; he was, also, very much under the influence of Caroline poetry, especially that of Crashaw, and, in more recent styles, of Coventry Patmore (the Patmore of the *Odes* not of *The Angel in the House*), a definite suggestion from whom he at least once quite frankly acknowledges and whose poetry was, perhaps, present with him oftener than he knew. His most famous poem, *The Hound of Heaven*, is, like others of his pieces, irregular Pindaric of a thoroughly seventeenth-century kind. The opening stanza is undeniably fine ; it is the best following of Crashaw in his *Sainte Teresa* vein that has ever been achieved, and the rest is not too unequal to it. But the anticipated pre-Raphaelitism of the Fletchers has been called in to blend with Crashaw's often extravagant, but seldom too gaudy, diction ; and the result, too often, approaches the fatal 'frigidity.'

> Across the margent of the world I fled,
> And troubled the gold gateway of the stars,
> Smiting for shelter on their clangèd bars—
> Fretted to dulcet jars
> And silvern chatter the pale ports o' the moon

makes one think rather of Benlowes (and of Butler upon him) than of Crashaw. Thompson sometimes played undesirable tricks with rime and diction, as in 'able' and 'babble' and as in the, certainly 'gritty,' lines

> Wise-unto-Hell Ecclesiast!
> Who *siev'dst* life to the gritty last.

But his following of the 'metaphysicals' sometimes resulted in quite charming results. *The Inconstant* need not have been disowned by any captain of the Caroline crew, and the following led him through pieces that have less of the *pastiche* about them, like *Absence*[1], to some that have hardly any, such as *Penelope*. Whether he ever became entirely free from his various imitations and attained the true *mimesis*—the creation or re-creation of something after his own image and not other people's—whether the clothes of gorgeous language and an elaborate imagery in which he swathed himself did not prove as much a hamper as a help are, perhaps, questions for individual decision. But that he is on the right side of the dividing line is certain.

The last pair of all our company once more supply, between them, a representative contrast; but it is of a very different kind. Ernest Dowson and Richard Middleton, who both died about the age of thirty, though there were some dozen years between their births, reproduce once more a situation which has been already noted twice in surveying nineteenth-century poetry. As, at the beginning, there were those who had partially, and, later, those who had fully, shared the influence of the great romantic school from Wordsworth to Keats; as, later, there was a similar division among those who felt the power of Tennyson and Browning; so, now, was it with regard to the school of Rossetti and Swinburne. Both Dowson and Middleton represent the poetry of youth—and of youth which has been brought up from the beginning on the theories of art for art's sake and enjoyment (literary and other) for enjoyment's sake. Both have had the benefit of that 'Marcellus allowance,' as it has been called, which is earned by early death; and, in consequence of sympathy from these various sources, both have been extravagantly praised. The extravagance, however, may be thought to have been far better justified in Dowson's case than in his companion's. He wrote little, his life being, undoubtedly, shortened by habits destructive of health, peace and power of mental exertion. His work may be injured to some tastes, though not to all, by its being largely in the artificial forms noticed above. Dowson was an excellent French scholar. His verse is exquisitely finished and curiously appealing. His most famous poem, *I have been faithful to thee, Cynara, in my fashion*, is couched in unusual, but quite defensible, metre and has singular music and 'cry.' A little more virility would have made it a very beautiful poem, and it is actually a beautiful one. Something else, and no little thing, may be said in Dowson's favour. There is scarcely a single poem in his scant hundred and sixty pages of largely and loosely printed verse which, when one has read it, one

---

[1] This is quite different from the poem of the same title sometimes ascribed, and sometimes denied, to Donne.

does not want to read again, and which does not leave an echo of poetry, fainter or less faint, in the mind's ear.

Richard Middleton, latest born of all the writers who can be mentioned in this chapter, was only twenty-nine when he died; and he is said to have written little, if any, verse for some time before his death. The actual volume which contains what he did write (for the most part, if not wholly, reprinted from periodicals) has, no doubt, what may be called the exterior character of poetry. There is a good deal of especially Swinburnian *pastiche* in it, though, also, there is something that is not. But it may be said to present rather another catching, and, to some extent, condensing and uttering of the general poetic *aura* of the period, than any very strong idiosyncrasy. The searcher of the perilous ways of poetry can see behind him many Richard Middletons of former ages, each with that age's differential chances. But, in most cases (not, of course, in all), they had later chances of showing their power if they had it. He had no such chance, and, apparently, might not have taken it if he had. He is not, in what he has actually left, an unequal poet; one may almost say, without paradox or unfairness, that it might have been better if he had been, as there would have been more chance of discovering where his strength lay. A good sense of form; a fair command of picturesque language; a decidedly 'young' expatiation in sensuous imagery and fantasy; a still younger tendency to 'shock'—these and other familiar things occur throughout his work. But their fermentation was not over; and a critical palate can hardly judge what was likely to have been the achieved flavour of the wine. As it is, it leaves (in this respect contrasting most unfavourably with Dowson's) hardly any flavour at all or any reminiscence. The very name Cynara calls up the sad tune and burden of the celebration of her to anyone who has once heard it: that of Middleton's Irene— though we have two poems about her—touches no chord at all.

It would be a pity to leave this *chorus vatum*, comprising more than a century of persons and extending, in point of time of poetical production, over more than seventy years, without some general remarks, which need be neither forced nor perfunctory, and which certainly need not indulge in the rhetorical *fioriture* too often recently associated with criticism. Colour on colour, whether it be bad heraldry or not, is bad history. We have regimented our poets, to some extent, as to classes differenced by subject, by sex and other considerations; but it has been freely acknowledged that the greater number are rebels to any such process. It does not, however, follow that they are a mere throng, or that the general poetical production of the last two-thirds of the nineteenth century (and, in some cases, a little of the twentieth) affords no symptoms to the systematic student of literary history. It may, therefore, be briefly considered from this point of view.

A theory—or, if that be too dignified a term, at least a notion—glanced at above suggests that the commanding and protracted influence of the two greatest poets of the period, Tennyson and Browning, especially that of Tennyson, has not, on the whole, been favourable; and an extension of this idea might urge something similar, as regards the later time, with respect to Swinburne and Rossetti. It was, however, also hinted, on the former occasion, that this theory will not stand examination. In order that it might do so, it would be necessary to establish the fact that the lesser poetry of 1840—1900 was, generally and individually, worse than the lesser poetry of the period immediately preceding it. Now this, as it may be hoped the dispassionate examination of these two periods, in chapters of some length, has shown, is far, indeed, from being the case. In the second place, granting, for a moment, and for the sake of argument merely, that there was such deterioration, it would have to be established that it was due to these influences—a more difficult task still. The influence of Tennyson may have been apparently disastrous on such a writer as Lewis Morris; but to say that Tennyson's influence produced the badness, or, rather, the nullity, of Lewis Morris's verse would be not so much uncritical as purely absurd. Perhaps those who hold the view referred to may contend that it is not so much definite imitation that they mean as a certain overawing and smothering influence—that the lesser poets of the period felt like Cassius in regard to Caesar, as petty men in the presence of the colossus Tennyson, and dared not show their real powers. To this, again, it can be answered that there is no evidence of it whatever, and that, if they did so feel, they must have been a feeble folk from whom no great poetry could be expected in any circumstances[1].

Brushing all this, and other fantasies, aside and 'taking the ford as we find it,' there is, beyond all question, in this long period and among this crowd of lesser singers, an amount of

[1] As a matter of simple historic fact, revolt of one kind or another from Tennyson is, from the days of Matthew Arnold, downwards, much more noticeable than servile imitation of him. It is, perhaps, permissible and even desirable to add that this summing up is strictly directed at, and limited to, the actual subjects of the chapter. No innuendo is intended as regards poets who are still living.

diffused poetry which cannot be paralleled in any other age or country except, perhaps, in our own land and language between 1580 and 1674. At no period, not even then, has the standard of technical craftsmanship been so high; at none has there been anything like such variety of subject and, to a rather less extent, of tone. Nor can we exactly charge against these writers, as, it was claimed, we might against the 'intermediates' of the earlier century, an uncertainty of step or object—an obviously transitional character. If a fault can be found with this poetry generally—and it is a fault which, as the detailed criticism offered above should show, presses lightly on some, though heavily on others—it is a want at once of spontaneity and of concentration, which results in a further want of individuality. And this may be regarded as due, not to the imitation of this or that contemporary poet, but to a too general *literariness*—to what has been called 'the obsession of the printed book.' These poets, as a rule, have read rather too much; and, if the reading has polished their form, it has sometimes palled and weakened their spirit.

We may extend the ungracious task of the devil's advocate a little further, partly returning upon and collecting points hinted at already. In, perhaps, no period of poetry has there been, even allowing the proper average for gross bulk of production, so large a number of first books of verse which have excited the hopes even of experienced and somewhat sceptical critics, only to disappoint the hopes and confirm the scepticism by subsequent failure—or, at any rate, failure to improve. At no time—this point, no doubt, is, in many cases, pretty closely connected with the last—has there been such a dissipation, in the waste and evaporating waters of mere journalism or journey-work, of powers which might well have ripened into more generous and lasting wine of poetry. And, even in the case of those who have never left their first loves, there has seldom been produced such a bulk of what we have here several times in individual cases, unconcentrated work—poetic negus, as one might designate it—sweet and spiced and pleasant to the taste and fairly comforting, but watered and sophisticated. Undoubtedly, these things are very largely due to those very circumstances which have just been mentioned—to the positive inability of a large proportion of the poets concerned to indulge that engrossing and exclusive disposition of the muse which has been often noticed; perhaps to some general conditions of the time—social, political, religious and other; certainly to that over-literariness which has been admitted. Yet, these allowances and explanations are still allowances and explanations only. They do not remove or alter the fact.

Nevertheless, these poets have given us a pretty extensive paradise of sometimes very dainty delights to wander in and feed upon; and it should be not impossible to play the Parkinson to some of its classes of flower and fruit—the Paterson to its main roads and places. The whole region is dominated by the two general principles of the earlier romantic movement, the increased and ever increasing appeal to the senses of the mind; the ingemination of varied sound; and the multiplication of varied form and colour. A second notable thing, connected closely with the first, is the prevalence of lyric in the widest sense, including sonnets, ballads, odes, short poems of more or less single situation, emotion or thought, and the like, in whatever form. The closet drama and the long poem are, of course, attempted and even sometimes with a certain popularity, if only for a time; but never with entire success to the satisfaction of critical judgment by any poet surveyed in this chapter. 'Songs and sonnets,' in the old acceptation, are your later nineteenth-century poet's only—or, at least, his chief and principal—wear and ware. Further, there are curious strains or veins of poetic manner which emerge at the beginning and continue to manifest themselves until, practically, the end. One is the 'spasmodic,' which has never been without representatives, for better for worse, from Bailey to Davidson. The style most opposite to this is the quietly classical, having its most powerful exponent outside our list in Matthew Arnold, but represented not unworthily in that list itself. A most prominent feature is that revival and extension of aureate language which was one of the main objects of the pre-Raphaelites, and has never had, not even in Rossetti sixty years since, a more audacious practitioner than Francis Thompson, who died but the other day. We have noted, too, in the last twenty or thirty years, a kind of what has been called 'violence'—a development in one direction of the spasmodic association itself with the so-called 'realist' tendencies of the time. The artificial forms practised by no mean poets for a considerable period must, also, keep their place, whatever it be, in history.

But the attraction and the charm of poetry—though it is a vulgar error to suppose that they are in the least injured or lessened, palled or withered, by applying to them historical and analytic considerations—are, after all, independent of these. 'Is there good and delightful poetry here?' that is the question; and it can be most unhesitatingly answered 'There is.' A new Johnson or Anderson or Chalmers, containing all the works of all the poets noticed in this chapter would be a vast collection—one would have to be, or to employ, a very skilful and industrious 'caster-off' to estimate its extent. It would certainly far exceed the twenty-one volumes of Chalmers and might come near the scores or hundreds of the *Parnaso Italiano*. Some volumes or parts of volumes (which need not be again indicated) would be seldom disturbed and rapidly left alone again by the few disturbers. But, on the whole, an astonishing amount of poetic pleasure would be available in the collection—some of it for all, and all of it for some, who care for poetry. This chapter, perhaps, is already too long; but it may be permitted to lay a little final stress on the remarkable absence, in the period and production considered as a whole, of monotony. The very excess of 'literariness' which has been admitted escapes this condemnation (easily applicable to some other times), because of the immense extent of the literature from which suggestion has been taken. Classical literature, and medieval, foreign of all nations and languages in modern times—history, religion, philosophy, art of all times and kinds—have been drawn upon, as well as the never-ending resources of nature and of life. Neither, it may be confidently affirmed, despite the admissions which have been required, has this vast variety of subject and of form failed to meet an at least fairly corresponding diversity of talent and even of genius in the poets dealing with it.

CHAPTER VII

THE PROSODY OF THE NINETEENTH CENTURY

In the last chapter on this subject[1], we confined ourselves strictly to the prosody and the prosodists of the eighteenth century proper, postponing not merely the remarkable developments which took place at the close of that century, but, also, certain phenomena of actual versification, some of which appeared when the century was little more than half over. These designed omissions must now be made good, as necessary preliminaries to the account of the prosody of the nineteenth—in fact, as practically the first section of the history of that prosody itself. In many, if not in all, cases, refer- ence to the notices of the several poets (and, sometimes, the prose-writers) referred to will enlarge and comment what is here given; the present summary is strictly confined to its own title.

The important occupants of that vestibule or antechamber of the subject above referred to are *Ossian*, Percy's *Reliques* and the poems of Chatterton and Blake. From them, we must proceed to the various signs of prosodic upheaval shown, at the extreme end of the century, in the ballad verse of Southey and Coleridge, with the tendency to rimelessness, and to the imitation of classical metres, of which the same poets are the chief, but not the only, or the first, exponents. It will, next, be necessary to survey the chief prosodic developments of nineteenth century poetry itself in its two great divisions, and to follow up in each of those divisions the account of treatises on the subject. The matter to be dealt with is extremely voluminous, and the account of it cannot, it is feared, be very short.

The four books or 'works' mentioned above as holding the first place are not merely of importance, individually and as a group, for intrinsic character and as influences on others; they are, also, curiously combined and cross-connected in themselves. For,

---

[1] *Ante*, vol. xi, chap. xi.

Ossian undoubtedly influenced Blake's 'prophetic' writing: and Percy, as undoubtedly, influenced both Chatterton's and Blake's verse. As a whole, they may be taken, from our point of view, not merely as influences, but even more remarkably as symptoms of the growing discontent with the limited practice, and almost more limited theory, of prosody in the century wherein they appeared. But the several constituents of the group illustrate this discontent in curiously different ways. *Ossian* and Blake's *Prophetic Books*, the latter deliberately and explicitly, revolt against the 'fetters,' the 'mechanism,' of poetry, which was, certainly, never more fettered or more mechanical than in their time. They carry this revolt to the point of intentionally discarding the uniformity of metre altogether, and of preferring the variety of prose-rhythm, subject to divisions less rhythmically continuous, but somewhat more parallel to each other than those of prose proper. They do not, however (and Macpherson fails here specially), succeed in doing this without including large proportions of imbedded metre, which constantly produce regular lines, often regular couplets and not seldom actual stanzas—occasionally, even, suggestive of something like rime. Blake's greater power in actual poetry commonly saves him from this; but, on the other hand, it tempts him to make his rhythmical staves more like loosened and enlarged variations on certain kinds of verse—especially the 'fourteener.'

The lesson of *Reliques*, felt strongly in spirit, and partly in form, by almost all later poets of the century, was not, in its most important prosodic point—the licence of substitution in ballad-metre—perceived or, at least, boldly adopted by anyone (except Chatterton and Blake again) till quite the close of the period. Even then, a lover of English verse like Southey's friend Wynn protested against that poet's innovations, in this respect, as faulty; and such pusillanimity accounts for the painful sing-song of most ballad imitation from Percy himself, through even Goldsmith, to Mickle—a sing-song which gave its main point to Johnson's disrespectful parodying of the ballad. But Chatterton saw the truth and followed it; Blake saw it and followed it still further and more boldly; while Burns's practice—inherited, not, indeed, from Percy but from Scots originals—came to reinforce the movement.

It would appear difficult for some people, even yet, to perceive either the importance or the novelty of these examples of substitution (or admission of trisyllabic feet) in English poetry. The great prevalence, during the last hundred years, of a purely

accentual system of prosody disguises the importance—for it
suggests that, supposing you get your requisite number of accented
syllables in a line, the rest may, as it has been put, be 'left to take
care of themselves.' The absence of attention to historic facts
disguises the novelty. But it is difficult to think that anyone with
a delicate ear can, when his attention is called to it, fail to perceive
that the difference between 'Like a rogue for forgery' and 'Like
rogues for forgery' is much greater than that between singular
and plural only; or to see how much rhythmical gain there is in

> The wild winds weep
> And the night is a-cold,

compared with

> The wild winds weep
> And night is cold,

though in each case the number of accents is exactly the same.
And it is almost as difficult to conceive how anybody with a
logical mind can fail to see the force of Shenstone's almost timid
championship of what he calls 'the dactyl' in the first half of the
century, or of Wynn's distinct protest against it some sixty years
later, taken with its actual absence between these dates in the verse
of almost every poet except those named.

The revived fancy for rimelessness and for classical metres
which the extreme end of the century saw runs in a curricle
rather with the Ossianic hybrid verse-prose than with the new
use of substitution; but it is quite as much a sign of discontent
with the favourite metres and metrification of the century as
either. It also, of course, had precedents—though, perhaps, not
very happy ones—to plead in English, though the immediate
stimulus was, possibly, German. Frank Sayers[1] was able to muster
(and might, even, have further strengthened) a tolerable body
of such precedents for his rimeless stanzas; and English hexameters, sapphics and the like could bring forward undoubted,
though rather dangerous, ancestry. But it is nearly certain
that disgust with the tyranny of the stopped rimed couplet, and
craving for a change—the most decided change possible—was the
chief agent in the matter. The rimeless Pindarics were to produce
two remarkable poems of some length and of no small merit in
Southey's *Thalaba* and Shelley's *Queen Mab*; little good came, as
little good has ever come, of English classical forms. But, as
direct or indirect protests, both have a value which is not to be
neglected.

When the actual turn of the tide took place, in the very closing

---

[1] See, *ante*, vol. xi, pp. 179, 180.

years of the century, it was impossible that some attention should not be paid to the theoretical as well as to the practical aspect of the turning. Whether Southey and Coleridge talked on the subject, during that meeting at Oxford which was only less fateful than the subsequent meeting of Coleridge and Wordsworth, there is not, it is believed, any documentary evidence to show. Both, certainly, became, very shortly afterwards, champions of substitution in practice ; and Southey's already referred to profession of faith on the subject is much earlier than any similar pronouncement that we have by Coleridge. There are, in addition to Coleridge's long known metrical experiments, and the famous note on the metre of *Christabel*, further and only recently published exercises by him ; and it would be possible (and worth while) to arrange a considerable cento of scattered remarks on the subject from Southey, at all periods of his life up to the very eve of the failure of his powers. Even Scott, the least ostentatiously theoretical of poets or of men of letters, has some. But Wordsworth chose to speak as if he believed that prosody, like reading and writing, 'came by nature'; the remarks of Landor, from whom something might be expected, are few and disappointing; and, generally (and not at all disappointingly), the greater and even the lesser agonists in the romantic battle obeyed the precept 'Go and do,' without reasoning much on the manners and theories of the doing. We shall be able, therefore, without difficulty or impropriety, to separate the practice from the principles, if not from the dealers with principle, and that not merely in regard to the first half of the century. For it so happens that one of the most important turning-points of English prosodic study, Guest's *A History of English Rhythms* (1838), coincides nearly enough with the definite, though not as yet generally recognised, establishment of a new era in poetry, by Tennyson's volumes of 1842 and Browning's *Bells and Pomegranates* (1841 ff.).

Perhaps the importance of Bysshe's *The Art of English Poetry* cannot receive a better completion of proof than by showing that the general characteristics of the prosody of 1798—1830 are simply anti-Bysshism. Whether or not it is probable that any poet of mark thought of Bysshe is quite immaterial ; though it is likely that Coleridge, and pretty certain that Southey, knew him. The point of importance is that, not merely the theoretical observations of Coleridge and Southey, but their practice, and the practice of the whole group (with exceptions proving the rule, as aforesaid) goes directly against the principles first formulated by Bysshe. He had

said that English verse was to be strictly measured by syllables;
they disregarded the syllabic limitation continually, and, in some
cases, deliberately refused—in almost all neglected—the aid of
'elision.' He and the whole eighteenth century after him had limited
the preferred orders of our verse to two or three groups only; the
poets now under discussion made their lines of any number of
syllables they liked, from one to fourteen or fifteen. He had
distinctly barred stanza-writing as obsolete; they, in many if not
most cases, preferred any stanza to the couplet. The effect, and, in
some instances, the expressed effect, of his rules, had been to snub
triple time; to insist on middle pauses; to deprecate overlapping
of couplet if not even of line. In every one of these respects, more
or fewer of them—in one or two all—adopted practices diametrically
opposed to his laws. If ever in prosodic history there was a case
of 'taking the "not" out of the commandments and putting it into
the creed,' that case occurred as regards the new nineteenth century
poetry and the old eighteenth century formulas.

No good, however, has ever yet come of a merely negative
revolt, and the anti-Bysshism of poets from Wordsworth to
Keats had quite definite and positive objects. These objects may
be described briefly as, in the first place, the liberty to use any
form which might suit the poet's subject and temper, and, secondly,
the special selection of forms and the special adaptation of them
when selected, to the new varied appeal to ear and eye, mental as
well as bodily, and not merely to the pure understanding.

The difference is susceptible of being put to a test which, to some
readers, may seem too mechanical, but which has a real cogency.
Run the eye over a fairly considerable number of pages of any
eighteenth century poet. In the long poems, with the very rarest
exceptions, you will find the regular outline of the couplet or of
blank verse; in the great majority of the short ones, symmetrical
sequences of sixes and eights in various, but still few, arrangements. Apply the same process to poets of the earlier nineteenth
century. In long poems, you will, of course, still find a very
considerable proportion of blank verse; but that of the heroic
couplet will be greatly reduced; Spenserian and other stanzas, with
octosyllables, regular or irregular, will constantly obtrude themselves; and more eccentric outlines still will not be wanting. But,
when you come, in turn, to the collections of shorter pieces, all
attempts at a few rigid specifications will have to be thrown to the
winds. Length and grouping of line become, at first sight, absolutely
'at discretion,' or, as the older critics would hold it, 'indiscretion.'

And, when you examine the lines themselves, the arrangement of rimes and so forth, you find that what the eighteenth century prudishly called 'mixed' measure and sparingly allowed licence to —that is to say, substitution of trochee for iamb—gives way or is extended to what it would have thought the most lawless and promiscuous debauchery of indulgence in iamb, trochee, spondee, anapaest, dactyl and (you may sometimes think) even in other combinations of quantity or stress.

For detailed accounts of prosodic characteristics of greater poets recourse must be had to the chapters concerning them; but a brief juxtaposition of these characteristics from the general prosodic point of view can hardly fail to be of use. Crabbe and Rogers, as survivals, require next to no notice ; but it is noteworthy that Campbell, who belongs to the same general school and is even definitely eighteenth century in his longer poems, adopts measures of distinct idiosyncrasy, and decidedly nineteenth-century character, for his great battle songs. Landor, not, perhaps, by any unnecessary connection with his 'classicality' of one kind, is, also, distinctly classical in his neglect or refusal of frequent substitution in line, as well as in his sparing use of varied outline in line-group. But he had a definite, though surely a mistaken, idea that the variations of English verse were, comparatively, few ; and a corresponding belief, of which he very satisfactorily availed himself, that those of prose were much more numerous. Wordsworth, Coleridge, Southey and Scott, among the first group, Moore, Byron (classical as he would have liked to be), Shelley and Keats, among the second, took almost every possible advantage, though in varying degrees, of the new scale ; and we might add some remarkable instances from the minors of a generation slightly younger, though still older than that of Tennyson and Browning, such as Hood, Darley, Praed, Beddoes and Macaulay[1].

Wordsworth, as might be expected, allows himself less freedom than any of the others, yet his own range of metre is considerable. The great *Immortality Ode* would, by itself, supply large, if not exhaustive, texts for dealing with new methods ; and the handling of his best blank verse embodies, to the full, that constant shifting of the values and cadences of the line by alteration of pause, by insertion of words of special weight or colour and the like, against which Johnson had partially protested, but which the joint study of Shakespeare and Milton is, of itself, sufficient to suggest and to authorise. Nor is it necessary to point out, at any

[1] See, *ante*, vol. XII, chap. V and this vol. chap. VI.

length, that the mere revival of the sonnet—especially its adoption
in the forms which do not consist of regular quatrains and a final
couplet—is a 'sign of profession and mark of difference.' It was
not for nothing that the late seventeenth century and nearly
the whole of the eighteenth were shy of the sonnet. Its great
scope as a metrical unit, the intricate arrangement of its rimes,
the close-knit structure of successive lines and the absolute impossibility of maintaining a middle pause right through without
destroying the whole principle of the form, were enough to set
any eighteenth-century writer against it, quite independently of
vain imaginations about the unadjustable differences between
English and Italian, the paucity of rimes in our language, or the
artificial, trivial character of the thing in itself.

Coleridge was certain to be interested in this matter; and,
whether the famous introductory note to *Christabel* be a satisfactory statement of the nature of the *Christabel* metre or not—
whether his notion that the principle was new can or cannot be
reconciled with his undoubted knowledge of previous examples
thereof—the statement itself remains one of the most important
and epoch-marking, if not epoch-making, in the history of the
subject. Even when we make the fullest allowance for his
peculiarities in the way of not doing things, it is extraordinary
that, in the welter of individual utterances that we have from him,
there is not more on the matter. If he had only indicated to
his nephew the exact grounds of his remarkable dissatisfaction
with Tennyson's prosody, we might have had more to go upon.
But it is now known that, in addition to the pretty numerous
metrical experiments which have long been in print, he made
others of a much more interesting character, directly on the lines
which Tennyson himself pursued; and some of them, if not all,
have already been published. They all show—as does *Christabel*,
whichever side be taken in the accent *v.* foot battle about it; as
do other pieces of his strictly English versification; and, as do even
those very pretty and most remarkable dodecasyllabic hendeca-
syllables of the 'old Milesian story'—that his natural ear, assisted
by his study more especially of Shakespeare, had made him
thoroughly—if not, to himself, explicitly—conscious of that principle
of substitution which, more than anything else, and almost by itself,
strikes the difference between the old (or rather middle) prosody
and the new, and which *The Ancient Mariner* and *Christabel*,
each in its way, were to beat, inextricably, into the heads of the
next three generations.

Although Southey never reached any point near the heights of Coleridge in poetical practice;. although, except in parts of *Thalaba, Kehama* and a few shorter poems, his actual prosodic touch is somewhat blunt; there are very few poets who have shown so direct a knowledge of the root of the matter in theory, and still fewer technical prosodists who have been able to put their theories into anything like such poetic practice. The possible cento of remarks from his letters and works has been referred to above. It was he who, first of all English poets, gave precision to Shenstone's vague hankerings after 'the dactyl'; and indicated a more scientific system than Coleridge's rough and ready indication of accents as all that mattered, by remarking to Wynn, in the letter above referred to, that 'two syllables may be counted as one: they take up only the time [*that is, the technical time*][1] of one,' and justifying his principles and practice not merely from the balladists but from Milton. It is quite clear that he had arrived at the secret simply through his wellknown early, extensive and accurate reading of English poetry.

So, again, whatever may be thought of his rimeless verse, and of his classical verse, they are, at any rate, testimonies of the strongest kind to his prosodic 'curiosity,' in the Johnsonian and good sense. And there is to be added to his credit, in the case of each, that he avoided the great prosodic danger of irregular rimelessness (the constant drop into blank verse), and that, if he did not cure, he saw, the diseases of the English hexameter. His blank verse is not, as a rule, masterly, and he was much too fond of writing it ; but, if it never, at its best, approaches anything like the best of Wordsworth's, it never, at its worst, comes near the flatness of Wordsworth's average. And—once more specially to his credit from the present point of view—he knew the dangers that he dared. He perceived, as none of its numerous enemies in the eighteenth century had perceived, and as too few of its less numerous friends had seemed to perceive, that instead of being an easier, blank verse is, in fact, a much more difficult, metrical vehicle than rime, whether in couplet or stanza; and he had the combined insight and frankness to point out that it had the special drawback of setting the weakest parts of the composition in the clearest lights. The loss of his intended review of Guest, which, by reason of his interest in, and knowledge of, the subject, would, probably, have extended to the length of a long pamphlet or short book, may almost be set beside those other losses of the

[1] Bracketed passage in italics inserted by the present writer.

prosodic works of Jonson and Dryden which have been noticed formerly.

If Southey is the poet from whom we should most expect such studies, Scott is certainly the one from whom we should expect least; yet the omnipresence, expressed or 'understood,' of the matter is visible in him also. At least one remarkable evidence[1] of study of the shortcomings of eighteenth-century versification occurs in his prefatory discourses, and, as to practice, he stands almost in the very first rank. It may be true (and he, according to his habit, acknowledged it himself with more than generosity) that his meeting at Rose's with specimens of the unpublished *Christabel* had a great effect upon, if it did not actually determine, the metre of *The Lay of the Last Minstrel*. But Coleridge's erroneous idea that the principle of this metre was new blinded his own eyes (as it has less excusably blinded those of others since) to the real state of the case. Scots dialect had (and Burns is a sufficient, and, in the circumstances, much more than sufficient, example of this) preserved the principle of substitution better than had southern English; and Scott's own wide and unrivalled acquaintance with romance, combined with his knowledge of Spenser and of Shakespeare, would have put a far inferior poet in a position to understand and work out the powers of the equivalenced octosyllable. Moreover, *The Lay* and its successors avail themselves of variety in treatment of this much more than does *Christabel*, and somewhat more than *Christabel* and *The Ancient Mariner*, even when combined, can be said to do.

But Scott's contribution to, and his exemplification of, the new principles of prosodic variety were far from being limited to his voluminous and various experiments in the manipulation of what his contemporaries would persist in calling 'Hudibrastics,' though the metre had existed in English for nearly five hundred years before *Hudibras* appeared. His best exercises in blank verse were confined to those extraordinary 'old play' fragments where, in editions in which the real Simon Pures have not been distinguished from the others by commentatorial labour, it is almost impossible to tell (except from actual personal knowledge of the older texts) which is genuine Elizabethan and which is wholly or mainly Scott's own. He evidently did not care much for the stopped heroic couplet; and, though he must have known it from his

---

[1] Introduction to *The Lay of the Last Minstrel*, on the possibility of cutting down the usual heroic to octosyllables by the omission of otiose epithets. It is characteristic that Scott disclaims all originality in this suggestion.

seventeenth-century reading, he did not try the enjambed. But his Spenserians are much better than is generally thought; and his command of 'fingering' in lyrical measures—both complete pieces and scraps—is a really wonderful thing, which cannot be (as it has been, by some, in Moore's case) dismissed as merely due to following of music. That he caught the best and rarest cadences of the ballad in a hundred different instances (the finest of which are, perhaps, the girl's song at Ellangowan and Elspeth Cheyne's ballad of the Harlaw) may be thought, though with doubtful sufficiency, to be accounted for by his acquaintance with original ballad literature. But no one before him, from the unknown author of *Mary Ambree* downwards, had put into the serious anapaest, continuously used, anything like the varied fire and colour of *Bonnie Dundee* and *Lochinvar*; the metre of the unapproachable *Proud Maisie* is very rarely, if, as an accomplished thing, ever, to be found in the old ballad; and there are not a few others that might be cited. Moreover, it has to be remembered that the enormous popularity and consequent diffusion of Scott's verse scattered the seed of these varied measures to an unequalled degree.

With respect to Moore, on the other hand, the debt to music, though it may be exaggerated, certainly exists. It has been a critical observation, ever since dispassionate reviewing came into occasional existence, that the rhythm of Irish poets, though sometimes a little facile and jingly, is usually varied and correct; whether this, in its turn, has something to do with any general musical attitude need not be discussed. In his longer poems, Moore, perhaps, shows the correctness rather than the variety; and he has a considerable liking for that heroic couplet to which, as we have seen, no one of the greater elders born in the same decade with himself was much inclined. In fact, there is no metre like this for poetical satire; and it need hardly be said that Moore is a very expert satirist in verse. But it is when we come to his lyrics that the strength of his prosodic power, its exemplification of the new variety, colour and outline, and, withal, its direct connection with actual 'setting,' are clearly seen. Most of these, as is well known, are definitely adjusted to certain musical airs; and it is probably not rash to say that Moore (who, it must be remembered, was a skilled composer as well as practitioner of music) never wrote a lyric without an actual or possible accompaniment sounding in his ears at the time. But it is greatly to his credit that this has not resulted either (as has been too frequent with others) in mere facile sing-song, or (as has not been unknown) in mechanically rhythmical but spiritless stuff, in which the whole burden of charm is left to the musical setting itself. And no ear that is an ear can possibly deny, even if it tries to discount, the sound-charm of not a little of Moore's lyrical work. Also, he has a *virtuosity*, in this respect, which it is difficult to discover anywhere else. Some of the airs to which he composed 'words' are, as he most frankly confesses (accompanying the confession with a really unnecessary apology), so odd and 'catchy' that it is necessary to violate at least eighteenth-century laws to get their equivalent in metre at all. The once enormously popular *Eveleen's Bower* and the less known but much more beautiful *At the mid Hour*[1] are capital instances. But Moore has conquered the difficulty by an extension certainly—but only by an extension at least occasionally licensable—of those laws of equivalence and substitution which, perhaps, he himself doubtfully approved and, in theory, may have hardly comprehended.

The great differences which exist as to the merits of Byron as a poet fortunately need not affect estimate of his prosody in the very least. His expressed—and, probably, to, at least, some extent, his real—tastes were for eighteenth-century norms; and he wrote heroic couplet of the orthodox type with acknowledged expertness, while his blank verse, which, on occasion, could be very fine, was an interesting variety, not, perhaps, too fancifully to be called an unrimed heroic with a certain, but not large, admixture of the newer style. For his Spenserians he went, as he has practically confessed, rather to Beattie than to Spenser or even Thomson, and the result was not altogether fortunate; the metre, in his hands, losing that flow as of mighty waters meandering, eddying, sweeping, 'without noise or foam,' which is its proper character, and attaining in exchange, at best, a somewhat declamatory construction and intonation. He could manage the continuous anapaest well, but not consummately, as may be seen by comparing *The Assyrian came down* with *Bonnie Dundee* or *Young Lochinvar*. His continuous octosyllabics, whether pure or mixed, have, at their best, a greater intensity than Scott's, but lack variety. Still, if reservations have to be made on some of these heads, it must be admitted that this is a remarkable tale of metres to be achieved without what can be fairly called a failure in a single case; while it has to be added that some of the lyrics actually attain the peculiar 'fingering' which is necessary to complete success.

---

[1] 'At the mid hour of night, when stars are weeping I fly.'

But Byron's greatest metrical triumph is, assuredly, to be found in the octaves of *Beppo* and *Don Juan*. He had, of course, Frere before him as a pattern; and, also, he had the Italians who had been patterns to Frere. But, patterns are of curiously little use in prosody; and each consummate practitioner is, in fact, a new inventor. For light narrative and satiric running commentary, as well as for description of the kind required, this octave of Byron simply cannot be excelled. At any rate, it never has been; and, despite his vast popularity and the consequent fact that the pattern was long in everyone's hands, it has scarcely ever been equalled and very rarely even approached.

The prosodic variety of Shelley is immense; there is, perhaps, hardly a poet—certainly there was none up to his time—who has written so consummately in so large a number of measures. But, one of the most interesting points about him, and about the contrast which is constantly presenting itself between him and Keats, is the peculiar character of his following of others. That this following should appear in his early and curiously worthless apprentice-work might be expected; but in the later and larger poems—not in the smaller—there is to be found one of the strangest compounds of imitation and originality that meets us in the entire range of prosodic study. *Queen Mab* follows *Thalaba*, and declares the following in the very opening stanza with that astonishing *naïveté* which is one of Shelley's great characteristics. But, although he had, by this time, hardly got out of his novitiate, the necessity for him to become unlike everyone else, even in apparent endeavour to be like them, appears; and the total effect of the *Queen Mab* stanza is utterly different from that of Southey's arrangements. The same, in a more remarkable degree, is the case with *Alastor*, where the blank verse is obviously Wordsworthian in suggestion, but acquires even more obviously a colour entirely its own; and with *The Revolt of Islam*, where the Spenserians pretty certainly start with a touch of Byron, but transform themselves into something not much more like *Childe Harold* than *Adonais* itself was subsequently.

It is possible, of course, to take exception to some of the devices (such as the large employment of double rimes in *Adonais*) by which Shelley impresses his own mark on these famous old measures; but it is not possible to fail to discern in them the most perfect products yet of emancipated prosody. And, when we turn to his shorter poems, it is still more impossible to discern even suggestion from any previous model, while the variety is

innumerable without a single failure to produce beauty. There
are those who hold that, in one or two places, Shelley outsteps
even the large room given by the new prosody and passes off
lines—and beautiful lines—which no principle of mere substitution
of equivalent values will justify. The present writer doubts this
very much. Very rarely can you trace Shelley's exact processes,
even when you can trace some origin and discern the difference
of his result; but that result, at least after the date of *Alastor*,
if not, prosodically speaking, after that of *Queen Mab*, can almost
always be justified on the new principles which have been and will
be sketched in this chapter. And, where it cannot, it is, at least,
fair to remember that his text, if not exactly corrupt, can in very
few cases be said to have undergone definitive revision at its
author's hands.

In the case of Keats, the results of prosodic study of his methods
are curiously different. In him, we have, not a poet who catches
up a suggestion and in whose mind that suggestion transmutes
itself, one can hardly tell how, but a 'sedulous ape' of a glorified
kind who takes a definite model and works on that model in a way
the processes of which can be traced with tolerable exactness. In
the early pieces, as one would expect, the workmanship is crude and
the hand uncertain. But, in the three longest poems, *Endymion,
Lamia* and *Hyperion*, the prosodic process is perfectly distinct,
and in *Isabella, The Eve of St Agnes* and *The Eve of St Mark*
and the odes and smaller poems hardly less so, though there are, as
a rule, even more striking examples of the completed fusing of the
various elements. As a prosodic example, *Endymion* is not the
least remarkable. Leigh Hunt had, indeed, ventured to revive the
heroic couplet by recourse to the overlapped form of the seventeenth century. Keats may have followed Hunt. But, at least
some of the not very numerous persons who are familiar with the
Jacobean and Caroline originals feel pretty sure that Keats knew
them too. He has, to some extent, imitated their vices[1]; but he
has attained a constant sweetness which is nowhere in *The Story
of Rimini*, and an occasional strength which is seldom found in
Chalkhill or in Chamberlayne.

He himself, however, knew that he had let this sweetness
become cloying and had occasionally, at least, turned softness into
flaccidity; and he set to work to tone up his strings. He did this by
arduous, and evident joint, study of the prosodies of Milton and of
Dryden. In the first place, he still clave to Dryden's form-couplet.

[1] For which see, *ante*, vol. VII, chap. IV.

The result was the fine verse of *Lamia*, with triplets and Alexandrines restored, and with a good deal of Miltonic phraseology. But it was almost impossible that this should not attract Keats to Milton's metre as well as to his phrase: and so there was *Hyperion*. Yet, no one of the three poems is open to the reproach, constantly and sometimes justly urged, against work which shows the existence of a model—of being a mere imitative exercise. The poet has infused sufficient of himself into all of them, and hardly the dullest critical ear could fail to distinguish a specimen of *Endymion* from *Pharonnida*, of *Lamia* from any of the *Fables*, or even of *Hyperion* from *Paradise Lost*. The octaves of *Isabella* show less definite following; and, perhaps, despite some extremely beautiful things, less individuality in the success; but the two *Eves* again show us something of the earlier phenomenon. Spenser had now been so often and so variously imitated, and the peculiar combination of character and adaptability in the metre had been so freely shown, that the finished poem, from this point of view, is less surprising than it is beautiful. But the unfinished *Eve of St Mark* is, again, a most remarkable prosodic study. Its octosyllable is usually traced to Chaucer; but, to the present writer, Gower seems to be much more in evidence and the way in which Keats flushed Gower's too frequently insignificant flow with colour and spirit, undulated its excessive evenness, stocked the waves with gold and silver fish and paved the channel with varicoloured pebbles, is, indeed, a marvel. In the odes and smaller pieces it is still more difficult to separate study of the prosody from praise of the poetry; but, in *La Belle Dame sans Merci*, at least, the modification of the ballad lesson would take a whole paragraph to display it fully.

Not less indicative of the course of prosodic events is the group of poets, in one way minor in another transitional, discussed in an earlier chapter[1]. They were by no means all of one literary school or sect. Beddoes and Darley were what their slightly younger contemporaries in France would have hailed with joy had they known them, *romantiques à tous crins*; Hood was not quite that, but a decided follower of the earlier and more sober romantic school, deriving straight from Elizabethan literature. Praed was an accomplished classical scholar, of the type of Canning and Frere but with more lyrical gift; and Macaulay the same, with, perhaps, something of a taste more 'classical,' in the transferred sense, and, thus, less romantic than any of the others.

---

[1] See, *ante*, vol. XII, chap. V.

Yet, even he, and much more the rest, would give a sufficient text, even without any of the greater poets just dealt with, for illustrating the present discourse. The adoption of the metre of the *Lays* for their subject would, in fact, be enough; still more the execution. But the contrast of Macaulay's two best poetic things—*Epitaph on a Jacobite,* at once stately and pathetic, with its firm memory of Dryden and Pope, fretted and chased with touches very different from theirs; and *The Last Buccaneer,* one of the uttermost stretches of the new prosodic licence, perfectly justifiable, indeed, but justifiable only so—marks his prosodic character far more unmistakably.

Only brief reference can be made to Praed's equally exquisite manipulation of the old three-foot anapaest of Gay and Byrom and Pulteney, of Shenstone and Cowper and Byron[1], into the metre of the *Letter of Advice*; to the triumphant irregularity of *The Red Fisherman* bettering Southey's instruction; and to other things by him. The too little remarked skill of Hood, not merely in what may be thought the deliberate acrobatism of his comic pieces, but in *The Haunted House,* in *The Bridge of Sighs* and in more than one or more than half a dozen of his songs, requires no long comment. But these two, like Macaulay, are specially valuable for the purpose, because no one can decline to accept them—though some still decline to accept the authors of *Death's Jestbook* and *Sylvia*—as formal and duly qualified representatives of their period in English literature. Yet, it will be exceedingly difficult for the recusants, unless they adopt some of the purely arbitrary doctrines of the prosodists to whom we are coming, to deny to Beddoes and Darley perfect prosodic correctness of the new kind. Both were, no doubt—Beddoes to a proven certainty—influenced by Shelley; and both carried even further the liberty of combining lines of almost any length into stanzas of almost any shape. We have glanced at the danger of this process—shown by the old 'Pindaric' writers *ad nauseam* and by some of the present school, with Southey occasionally among them—that is to say, the construction of merely mechanical aggregations of line which have no symphonic effect. But, neither Darley nor Beddoes can be charged with this; and we can turn from them to theoretic dealers with subject, as from almost typical examples of its practice.

After what has been said of the professional prosodists of the

---

[1] An intermediate between Cowper and Byron, very likely to have been known to the latter, has been recently noted by W. P. Ker in that curious person Charlotte Smith, who gave Scott the name 'Waverley.'

last years of the eighteenth century, no experienced reader will expect much from those of the early nineteenth. Nor will such a person be in the least surprised to find that the lessons of the practice of the new school of poets exercised very slow influence on 'prosodic' critics, even when they were not indignantly or scornfully rejected by them. One of the chief counts in Croker's indictment against *Endymion* in *The Quarterly*, when nearly a fifth of the century had passed, was that 'there is hardly a complete couplet enclosing a complete idea throughout the book.' Nearly ten years later, when all the greatest poetry in varied form of the first school had been written and, on the eve of Tennyson, Crowe, himself a small poet, public orator at Oxford, and a very amiable and scholarly writer, denounced, in his *Treatise on English versification*, the combination of short and long lines, and stigmatised contemporary verse, generally, as 'slovenly.' Nor, though it is impossible wholly to omit, would there be much good in dwelling upon the prosodists of the nearly forty years between Fogg[1] and Guest. Walker, of the famous dictionary, writing towards the end of the eighteenth century, sneers at the whole subject, but practically repeats what Bysshe had said at the beginning, that a line has so many syllables, and *ictus* in such and so many places. Lindley Murray, of the still more famous grammar, is muddled and inadequate, with some terrible scansions, but, perhaps, deserves to be saved from utter condemnation by his remarkable phrase, 'We have all that the ancients had; and something they had not'; which, though a little oracular, is perfectly true, and might easily be expanded into a sound system of prosody.

John Warner's *Metronariston* (1797) is a remarkable book, dealing partly with classical, partly with English, prosody, and is well worth the study of specialists; but it is not easy to give brief account of it. Steele's[1] notions, after lying for some time neglected, attracted attention from three writers: Odell, a Cambridge man; the revolutionist and elocutionist Thelwall; and Richard Roe of Dublin. Of these, Odell deals with the subject chiefly *a priori*, his starting-points and methods being either musical or phonetic; and Roe is an intensified Odell. But Thelwall goes farther than either of them in the direction of repeating and exaggerating Steele's impossible scansions. One will do:

To | momentary | consciousness a|woke.

The hexameters of Southey's *A Vision of Judgment* naturally

---

[1] See, *ante*, vol. XI, chap. XI, p. 250.

caused not a little discussion ; in fact, if what was written on them were taken with the renewed discussions about the time of Longfellow's *Evangeline,* and with the third stage of the controversy reached in more recent years, the whole of this chapter could easily be occupied by summary and criticism. A writer in *The Edinburgh Review* not merely disapproved of the English hexameter as such, but expanded the reasons for his disapproval into a general anathema on equivalence, and a reaffirmation, in the strongest terms, of the old belief, not merely in the allowableness, but in the necessity, of pronouncing 'feath'ry' and 'wat'ry.' Another enemy of the verse, but, in this case, a friend of the versifier, Tillbrook of Peterhouse, was almost the first to show real acquaintance with earlier prosodists from Elizabethan times downwards, but did not treat his subject quite in the right way.

Some others, Herbert, Gregory, Blundell and even such better known names as Hookham Frere and Payne Knight, must be only names for us here. But not in such silence or quasi-silence, nor with the slight notice accorded to others in the last two pages, can we pass Edwin Guest, master of Gonville and Caius college, and first historian of English rhythms in any sense worthy of the title. In comparison with him, all his predecessors, even Mitford, are merely fumblers with history; while the enormous majority of them never attempt the historical method at all, and show constant ignorance of facts vital to their subject. Guest knows, uses and, in selection, cites the whole range of English poetry from Caedmon to Coleridge, and, though he supplies no positive evidence of knowledge of younger contemporaries such as Tennyson, there are hints in his work which, if they do not directly suggest such knowledge, are, at least, not inconsistent with it. And he applies this knowledge, in the whole of his second volume and in part of his first, with such industry and such method that, subject to a reservation—unfortunately rather a large one—to be made presently, it would be difficult to conceive, and a great deal more difficult to execute, a more thorough conspectus of the forms of English poetry up to *circa* 1830, continuously illustrated by specimens of every age and more particularly from those departments of Old and Middle English verse which, in his time, were largely inaccessible, and which, even now, are not to be found in every library of fair size.

Unfortunately—and there is no undue begging of the question in the use of the adverb, since Guest himself, revising his work some time after he had begun and even printed part of it, made large admissions; while, even those who share part of his views hardly in a single case adopt the whole—this laborious, excellently arranged and almost exhaustively informed survey was made under the influences of some of the most arbitrary assumptions and some of the strangest prepossessions that ever affected a work of scholarship. We must not include among these the doctrine that English prosody is wholly accentual and syllabic; for that doctrine, in part or whole, has been and is shared by many, though it seems to others partly erroneous and wholly inadequate. Nor, though there may be more doubt here, is his system of 'sections' (starting with *three*, and possibly extending to *eleven*, syllables), in place of the 'feet' which he will not admit, incapable of defence, though the same remark applies to it. The influences that injure, if they do not spoil, his work for all but very discreet users of it are different.

The first of them was an extraordinary idea—utterly at variance with that historic view which, in other respects, he took so well— that the laws of Old English verse must govern those of modern. The second (again absolutely unhistorical and, to do him justice, apparently the subject of misgivings on his part before he published the book) was that, during the Middle English period, there was no blending, but merely the intrusion of an alien versification, and that 'the rhythm of the foreigner' (*i.e.* that of the vast majority of English verse, since Chaucer at least) is an unclean thing.

These two huge assumptions were partly necessitated, partly accompanied, by the strangest arbitrarinesses of minor judgments: such as that no two adjoining syllables can be accented; that the adjective ought to be always more strongly accented than the substantive; that accented rhythm implies a fixed caesura or pause; that no more than two unaccented syllables can come together, and so forth. And these, in their turn, result in such verdicts on particular verse as that Milton has no business to write

The Cherub Contemplation;

that Shakespeare's

Dead
Is noble Timon,

is 'opposed to every principle of versification'; and that Burns's

Like a rogue for forgery

'has very little to recommend it.'

In other words, Guest may be described, by borrowing an old formula, as 'indefatigable in collecting and arranging examples, not trustworthy in judging them'; and it may be questioned whether his book has done more good or harm, especially since its republication in 1882 after his death. But, for the present, we may leave it and its earlier or later successors for treatment hereafter and return to the actual prosody of the second great period of the nineteenth century, that of the strictly Victorian division of poets.

Between the prosodic practice of the later and larger part of the nineteenth century and that of the earlier, there is no such difference of principle as had prevailed between the earlier practice and the orthodox prosody of the eighteenth, so that, despite the number and importance of Victorian poets, we shall be able to treat them here more shortly than their teachers. But there are still three, not ill-marked, shades of division—the last of them as yet not clearly determinable but, possibly, of great importance—between the stages of this Victorian poetry itself; and there is at the opening, and not there only, a phenomenon which, though once more not at all surprising when duly considered, is certainly remarkable. Moreover, the actual prosodists of the sixty years are an almost formidable multitude, belonging to various prosodic nations and speaking, as it were, different prosodic languages; so that we shall have to give them more room as we give the poets less. And the most logical order of arrangement will be to deal with the special phenomenon above referred to first; to take the theorists next and to end with the sweeter mouths of the poets themselves.

The point to start with is the fact that, though we can, it is believed, prove the general identity of method in the verse of 1798—1830, this was not by any means generally recognised, and the absence of recognition was, undoubtedly, at the root of the prosodic confusion of tongues which has succeeded. It has been mentioned, and cannot be mentioned too often, that Coleridge 'could hardly scan' some of Tennyson's verses; that he thought the younger poet 'did not very well know what metre is,' and wished him 'to write for two or three years in none but well known and correctly defined' measures. Now, at the present day, there is not the slightest difficulty, not merely in scanning Tennyson's metres throughout, even in the unfinished forms in which Coleridge saw them in 1833, but in perceiving and proving that they proceed wholly on that very same principle of equivalence which accounts for *The Ancient Mariner* and *Christabel*. Fifteen years later, and half a dozen after the definitive exhibition of Tennyson's genius and method in the 1842 volumes, a critic by no means despicable and far from generally hostile, William Smith, uttered a wail of agonised despair over the 'Hollyhock' song— every principle and almost every line of which can be defended and paralleled from Shakespeare—as outlandish 'ear-torturing' and altogether metrically indefensible and unintelligible. Bearing these things in mind, and bearing in mind, also, the strange paralogisms of Guest, rather less than midway between Smith and Coleridge, we shall not be unprepared to find that neither the return to the study of Elizabethan poetry, nor the great practice of the first romantic school, nor the strictly historical, though unfortunately misdirected, enquiries of Guest himself, saved the prosodists of Victorian times from all sorts of contradictory will-worships, of which the best thing that can usually be said is that one often exposes the faults of another.

For at least twenty—indeed, one might almost say for thirty— years after Guest, prosodic study in England was, though not wholly, mainly devoted to the vexed question of English hexameters, which, already revived seriously[1] by *A Vision of Judgment*, was made active a second time in 1841 by Longfellow's *Children of the Lord's Supper*, and, a few years later, by the immense popularity of his *Evangeline*. Generally, prosodic study, even when not directly concerned with this question, was still very largely classicalised. One of the curiosities of the subject is Evans's *Treatise of Versification* (1852), where the author, slightly to our surprise, busies himself with a subject which he frankly declares to be wholly unsatisfactory. No one acquainted with the classics 'can possibly feel any satisfaction with blank-verse'; 'an evil genius has always presided over our lyric poetry'; English poetry generally is 'deficient in richness and

---

[1] The main stepping-stones between the collapse of the Elizabethan efforts and Southey's attempt may be conveniently arranged thus:

Later seventeenth century. Some specimens by *Robert* Chamberlain (not the author of *Pharonnida*) in 1638; and by a very obscure person named Hockenhull in 1657; with, between them, both example and discussion by the famous mathematician, John Wallis, in his *English Grammar* (1652).

Eighteenth century. An anonymous work entitled *Greek and Latin Measures in English Poetry* (1737), which is thought to have supplied Goldsmith with the grounds of his recommendation of English hexameters (and sapphics—Watts's? for Cowper's were not then known) in his 16th *Essay*. Some references in the prosodic work of Tucker and Herries (see *ante*, vol. XI). Last and most influential, William Taylor's rendering of German, in the last decade of the century, which acted directly on Southey.

variety of sound.' The quotations will probably be sufficient, but it must be owned that they are interesting. The names of O'Brien, Latham, Dallas, lord Redesdale, Sydney Walker, Masson, may be mentioned as helps to those who wish to work up the subject thoroughly, but they can receive no detailed discussion here.

On the other hand, the hexameter controversy requires some careful general notice, but few of the combatants can be individually dealt with. It was, perhaps, unavoidable—though the present writer frankly admits that it does not seem to him to be really so—that this controversy should be, if not exactly confused with, almost inextricably joined to, the old accent *v.* quantity battle. As this is one of the somewhat numerous discussions in which it seems impossible to arrange a set of terms which the combatants will accept in the same sense, it is pretty hopeless ; but the matter can, perhaps, best be dealt with by a series of short propositions presenting the views of various parties, reproduced, so far as possible, in uncontroversial language, if not as to the whole question (for there are hardly any two persons who agree on that), yet as to its general subject and constituent parts.

First, as to the metre in itself :

I.   There are those who, like the writer in *The Edinburgh Review* above referred to, altogether deny the possibility or, at least, the legitimacy of it in English on the simple ground that we have no quantity.

II.   Others, and, in fact, the vast majority, whether they like or dislike the result, admit the possibility of the verse ; but dispute whether its constituent feet are to be connected with a view only to accent, as in the verse of Southey, Coleridge, Longfellow and some of Clough's ; or by quantity, determined in various ways (see *post*) but non-accentually.

III.   A very few have maintained that the combination of dactyl and spondee is practically impossible, or, at least, a cacophonous jingle in English, and that, though good verses simulating the hexametrical form can be, and have been, produced (as especially in Kingsley's *Andromeda*), they are always really five-foot anapaests with *anacrusis* (initial syllable or syllables outside the first foot) and *hypercatalexis* (ditto after last ditto). This view seems not improbably to have been held, though it is never clearly expressed, by Campion and other Elizabethans ; it was formulated in relation to Greek by the eccentric John Warner, was deliberately championed and exemplified by Swinburne and was long ago independently arrived at by the present writer, whose conviction of its truth has grown stronger and stronger.

As to the construction of it :

I. Southey, who bestowed considerable pains (see his *Preface*) on the theory of the matter, came to the conclusion that spondees were scarcely available in English, and contented himself with trochees as a substitute—a licence of no great importance to those who hold that a very large number of syllables are 'common' in our tongue. He also claimed, but did not really often exercise, the right to begin the line with a short syllable, which can hardly be so well allowed[1]. The result was a cantering measure, rather 'ungirt,' if not actually ricketty, with a special tendency to break itself, not into irregular halves as a hexameter should, but into a rocking-horse rhythm of three parts, two feet in each, yet sometimes providing fine lines, which, however, always suggest the anapaestic arrangement above referred to. This metre was, in turn, taken up by Longfellow, who made it rather more tunable as a whole, but even looser and more ricketty.

II. On the other hand, strict believers in quantity, as necessitating either long-vowel sound or 'position,' revolted against the acceptance of stressed syllables as 'long,' and began in various ways to meet their own difficulty. Some met it by selecting for their long syllables such as combined stress with one or both of the other qualifications; and the most successful examples of this plan are Tennyson's experiments—of which, however, he himself saw the futility.

But yet others, including some persons of unquestionable scholarship and talent, not to say genius—Spedding, Cayley, Calverley, Clough in his later experiments, and others down to the late W. J. Stone, with the support of the present poet laureate—determined either to neglect accent, or (in some cases basing themselves on certain theories as to practice in the ancient languages) to pit quantity against it, and to produce verses which should scan by the first in the teeth of the second. The novelty and startling character of these proceedings, and the undoubted abilities of some of the practitioners, have given, at different times, a certain amount of vogue to the system. As usual, nothing will be attempted here beyond presenting a selection of the fruits for judgment of the nature and merits of the tree. If the examples given below are possible and euphonious English verses of

---

[1] Frere, and one or two others, went further, and postulated an *additional* ('anacrustic') syllable at the beginning.

hexametrical, *i.e.* dactylic-spondaic rhythm, then that system is admissible : and if not, not[1].

For some years, on each side of the very middle of the century, attention was chiefly directed to this question; but, by degrees, it widened, and the last forty or fifty years have been the most fertile in prosodic study of any similar periods in English literary history. A remarkably original, in some respects very acute, but, in others, slightly chimerical, student of the subject (who, like most persons of this blend, has exercised much influence lately) was Coventry Patmore, author of *The Angel in the House.* He, next to Tillbrook and Guest, and rather more than the latter, took full cognisance of previous prosodic theory, and his later poetical work (the earlier was rather facile, metrically speaking) showed good knowledge of poetic practice. But he was somewhat given to what the eighteenth century, with its usual practical wisdom, would have called 'airy notions.' It is mostly from him that a rather favourite modern fancy of a sort of eternal fisticuffs between the law of metre and the freedom of language[2] is derived, though the hexameter controversies also started this. He held very singular theories as to pauses and pause-endings, and, on the whole, his prosody may be described in the terms of the modern scientific foes of Bacchus as rather a stimulant than a food.

Towards the close of the sixties—perhaps owing to the great developments of actual poetry during that decade, perhaps not— a remarkable number of prosodic works appeared. In the single year 1869 came Edward Wadham's *English Versification*, with an entirely new terminology of a most fantastic character, not much knowledge of the history of the subject and a certain return to the eighteenth-century views about trisyllabic feet ; R. F. Brewer's *A Manual of English Prosody* (since republished and renamed), which is a useful magazine of fact, but does not show much grasp of the subject from any point of view; a shorter,

---

[1]   Dons, undergraduates, essayists and public, I ask you.

                                (*Hexameter*—Cayley.)

     They, of Amor musing, rest in a leafy cavern.

                                (*Pentameter*—Clough.)

     Is my weary travel ended? much further is in store.

                                (*Hexameter*—Stone.)

[2] This, after the old manner, was taken up by the Germans and passed back again to us; so that these 'conflict' theories have very recently assumed great prominence. That a contrast, rather than a conflict, between rhetorical and metrical arrangement is, in some cases, observable, cannot be denied, and is often very interesting to trace. But to elevate it into a principle is, probably, a very great mistake; and would certainly, if insisted on too much, lead to a new prosodic chaos.

equally practical and sounder book, *The Rules of Rhyme,* by the younger Thomas Hood; and the prosodic part of Abbott's *A Shakespearian Grammar,* in which strict syllabic, and strict accentual, doctrines are combined in the most peremptory fashion. In the next few years there were added Sylvester's *The Laws of Verse,* a book somewhat abstruse in appearance but very lively and suggestive in fact; the prosodic section of Earle's *Philology of the English Tongue,* and, a little later, the work of Henry Sweet, both of them specially devoted to the sound value of words and syllables; and (another starting point of much subsequent writing) J. A. Symonds's *Blank Verse,* an interesting but somewhat anarchical tractate which denies the possibility of scansion on any scheme. Meanwhile was begun and carried on the most elaborate of all treatises on English pronunciation, that of A. J. Ellis, which includes an extraordinarily intricate and minute scheme, extending to forty-five different items, of syllabic value from the point of view, single and combined, of pitch, force, weight, length and strength.

Later still, and in the last quarter of the century, may be noticed Gilbert Conway's *Treatise of Versification* (1878), written on uncompromising accentual principles, and reverting to such pronunciations as 'int'resting,' 'am'rous,' 'del'cate'; the characteristic eccentricity of Ruskin's *Elements of English Prosody* (1880); and parts of two most interesting books by the late Edmund Gurney, very strongly musical in system. These last, like two later works by persons of distinction, the first in philosophy, the second in physical science, Shadworth Hodgson and Fleeming Jenkin, were largely influenced by the republication of Guest in 1882; and they all represent the attempts of men of distinguished ability in certain specialised ways to theorise on prosody. They are all, in the highest degree, ingenious and suggestive, and one is loth to apply to them the obvious terms which are often used in regard to excursions from the outside into technical subjects; but they certainly suggest somewhat insufficient acquaintance with the facts and the history of the matter. No such suggestion can be made in respect of J. B. Mayor's *Chapters on English Metre* and *A Handbook of Modern English Metre,* books in the highest degree valuable for their general view of the subject and specially for their criticism of Guest and of not a few of the writers just mentioned.

Only three more prosodists can be individually noticed here. In 1888 appeared an anonymous treatise (or part of one, for the promised continuation never appeared) entitled *Accent and Rhythm explained by the law of Monopressures*. This doctrine, which was afterwards taken up and applied by Skeat, rests the whole prosodic matter on, and practically confines it to, a physiological basis—speech being regarded as only possible in jets governed by the glottis. No examination of this can be given here, but the objection brought against it that these jets, if they exist, must be 'the raw material of prose and verse alike' seems almost fatal of itself and could be carried a great deal further. A year later appeared the most important book by a poet on poetics that has ever been issued in English, Robert Bridges's *Prosody of Milton*, which, later much expanded, has almost become a treatise of stress prosody, while the actual history of the subject was, for the first time, set before the public with full bibliographical and large, if not exhaustive, critical detail by T. S. Omond.

Before concluding these remarks, or as an appendix to them, it may not be impertinent to sum up very briefly the chief points of the prosodic system from which (though it is believed without prejudice to other views) they and the whole of their predecessors in the prosodic chapters in this *History* have been made. For it is a constant—whether in all cases or not a quite well justified—complaint that writers on prosody do not make themselves clear —that the reader does not understand what they mean. The principle of the system—drawn from no *a priori* ideas as to metre or rhythm, to quantity or to accent, but from simple observation of the whole range of English poetry—is that it can, from the time of the blending of romance and Teutonic elements in Middle English, be best accounted for by admitting 'feet' corresponding —as, indeed, all such things, whether called 'feet,' 'bars,' 'groups,' 'sections' or anything else, must, of mathematical necessity, correspond—to those of the classical languages, but composed of syllables the contrasted metrical quality of which (called for similar convenience 'length' and 'shortness') is not arrived at in exactly the same way as in Greek or in Latin. There, length depended usually on vowel quantity or on 'position,' technical 'accent' having nothing to do with it; though 'stress' could have exceptional effect on what was called *arsis* and *thesis*. In English, all these act, but, in the case of vowel-value and position, with a much lesser and more facultative effect; while accent acquires an almost unlimited power of lengthening syllables and can be disregarded with impunity in few cases. With a reasonable accentual system which, objecting to the word 'quantity' for this or that extraneous reason (such as that 'quantity' implies 'time'), formulates its arrangements with the substitution of 'accented' and 'unaccented' for 'long' and 'short,' there need be no irreconcilable quarrel; though such a system may be thought cumbrous and open to a constant danger, which has often become disastrous, of unduly neglecting the unaccented syllables, and their powers of affecting the integral character of the accent-group. But, with any system which simply strides from accent to accent, neglecting or slurring other syllables, still more with any which would have sequences of similar lines to be composed of discretionary bars or sections varying like the rhythm clauses of prose, it may be admitted that no concordat is possible; nor any with those yet cruder systems which, starting from a purely syllabic basis, would, as did Bysshe and (partly) Johnson, either force extra syllables into unnatural coalescence or forbid them altogether as illegitimate. Nevertheless, an endeavour has been made to prevent colouring the actual history unduly with opinion; and, as it would hardly be possible to find anyone who can write on prosody without holding prosodic opinions of some sort, serious objection to the method adopted can hardly be taken.

As noted above, the history of the practical prosody of the last two thirds of the century may be taken in three stages, the last of which may be said to be still existing and, as has rarely happened in our history, owes something directly to preceptist studies. In the first, from the thirties to the sixties, the ever-developing genius of Tennyson and Browning developed, in its turn, as has been partly observed already, the prosodic enfranchisement of the first romantic school, with definite, if not always with conscious, reference to that school's work. On almost every poet of the time (except men who practically belonged not merely to the last generation but to the last century), the lesson of equivalence taught by Coleridge had its effect almost unresisted, though sometimes not fully understood, and nothing can be stranger than Coleridge's own inability to recognise that in, for instance, *The Dying Swan*, this lesson is simply exemplified—that you can expound it out of his own mouth. The blank verse of Wordsworth, on the other hand, had very great influence on Browning, less on Tennyson, who may be said almost to have developed a fresh variety of his own straight from Milton, but with very strong idiosyncrasy of blend. Metrically, the influence of Keats on him, strong in other ways, was less perceptible than that of Shelley, which, in those same other ways, is not so noteworthy as it is on Browning

Nobody, indeed, before Matthew Arnold (and he only to relinquish it) adopted the enjambed couplet of *Endymion*. But the so-called 'irregular' lyric forms of both these great and too early removed poets exercised the widest power, not merely in respect of abstract form, but in directing the principal efforts of both their successors towards lyrical poetry. If anyone demurs to this, let him perpend the striking lesson of the first and second editions of Tennyson's *Princess*, the first without, the second with, lyrical insets.

These two great poets continued, the one for nearly, the other for more than, sixty years, to multiply examples of their metrical, as of their poetical, powers. Towards the close of his career, Tennyson perhaps exaggerated that free admission of trisyllabic feet which he had made the differentia of his blank verse; and Browning, in the same vehicle, undoubtedly carried to excess the almost pedestrian looseness of his style. But, by this time, each had made excursion into almost every principal province of English metre, and in no one excursion had failed. The charge of over-sweetness in 'numbers' brought against Tennyson was merely a crotchet; that of over-discord brought against Browning had more apparent, and even real, justification, but, on the whole, was a mistake. And it is difficult to know where to look for other examples of a metrical system—for it was really the same in both despite its apparent 'differences of administration'—justified by such entirely novel displays of craftsmanship as Tennyson's in the anapaests of *The Voyage of Maeldune* and Browning's in the Alexandrines of *Fifine at the Fair*, each written half a century after the writer's first appearance as a poet.

The younger and lesser verse-writers of this time cannot be reviewed here[1]; but the prevalent tendency need not be better illustrated than by the example already glanced at, in part, of Matthew Arnold. His wellknown classicism and anti-Tennysonianism might have been thought likely to lead him to discard variety of rhythm, and did, indeed, produce a somewhat stiffer if statelier form of blank verse in *Sohrab and Rustum*. But his best and best beloved poems—*The Forsaken Merman, The Scholar-Gipsy* and its sequel, the two *Nights* and others—are all in carefully and, for the most part, originally 'researched' metres, while, in *Tristram and Iseult*, he alone, between Keats and William Morris, tried and tried most successfully the enjambed heroic couplet, and his wellknown experiments in unrimed (but not in

---

[1] Some remarks may be found in the chapter specially devoted to them.

the ordinary restricted sense 'blank') verse, from *The Strayed Reveller* onwards, are characteristic of his time.

The school which made its appearance (the work of its eldest member Dante Rossetti being accidentally held back except in fragments) towards the close of the fifties cannot be said to exhibit any general change from the prosody of Tennyson and Browning, though it exhibited some very interesting minor developments. The most peculiar of these, which was chiefly taken up and worked by rather younger men, and which produced some very charming work, was the revival of the artificial forms of verse —ballades, rondeaux, roundels, and so forth—which had been the favourite occupation of French poets from the thirteenth century till well into the sixteenth, and which, in the late fourteenth and fifteenth, had been pretty largely practised in England. This revival, however, after some years died off, chiefly, as it seems to the present writer, because no poet had cared or dared, save in a very few cases, to ease off the syllabic rigidity of the originals into that equivalence which is the soul of English verse. But Dante Rossetti himself, perhaps at the call of his Italian blood, wrote sonnets in the more favourite Italian forms with an effect only matched by those of his sister Christina; and showed, besides, remarkable mastery of English measures, ballad, and other. William Morris, besides reviving not merely, as has been said, the overlapped Keatsian decasyllabic couplet, in *The Life and Death of Jason*, but the hitherto unfollowed octosyllabic of *The Eve of St Mark*, used both, and especially the latter, with extraordinary effect in *The Earthly Paradise*. In *Love is Enough*, he tried a bolder and, in most judgments, less successful archaism by reviving alliterative and rimeless movements; but, later, in *Sigurd the Volsung*, he adjusted this and the old rimed fourteener (in fact, the *Gamelyn* metre)[1] into a really splendid metre for narrative purposes.

Meanwhile, Swinburne combined the widest exercise in prosodic practice with not a little definite theorising on the subject. The most important result of the latter was his distinct formulation of the doctrine that spondaic-dactylic measures in English have a tendency to pass into anapaestics; it would be impossible to analyse his practice fully in any space possible here. In metrical 'virtuosity,' it may be doubted whether he has ever had a superior, and the immensely long lines in which, latterly, this tempted him to indulge, though seldom, if ever, actual

---

[1] See, *ante*, vol. II, chap. VII.

failures, have too much of the *tour de force* about them. So, too, the extreme fluency of language, which was often charged against him, had a tendency to make both his blank verse and his couplets too voluble. He may be said, indeed, to have combined, in a very curious fashion, the characteristics of both Tennyson and Browning in blank verse. But his more compassed and studied exercises in this were frequently admirable; while a finer example of a peculiar kind of couplet—again blended of stop and overlap—than the opening of *Tristram of Lyonesse* it would be difficult to find. It stands as a sort of contrast to the other remarkable blend in Tennyson's *Vision of Sin*. But the sharper and more fretted outline of lyric was what was wanted to bring out Swinburne's prosodic power to the full, and no poet has ever exemplified those general principles which have been kept in view during this chapter as he did. The variation of the Praed metre into that of *Dolores*, and of FitzGerald's quatrain in *Laus Veneris*, together with the elaborate and triumphant stanza of *The Triumph of Time*—these are only three out of scores, or almost hundreds, of experiments which, however daring, never fail in bringing off the musical and rhythmical effect.

This remarkable blend of sureness and freedom in rhythm may be said to be the full result of the successive processes which have been pointed out above in reference to the late seventeenth, the eighteenth and the nineteenth century respectively. The period in which Dryden and Pope ruled drove out—if, possibly, by too severe a tariff of penalty and restriction—the indulgence in uncertain, if not positively arrhythmic, caprices, which had marred not merely the fifteenth but (after a premature resipiscence from Wyatt to Gascoigne) the magnificent accomplishment of the late sixteenth and early seventeenth centuries. Then, the Shakespeares and the Miltons did as they would, but always did right; others, not always much less than great, did as they would and frequently did wrong. So, English verse had to return into the go-cart and stayed there for a century and a half. Then it got free, and arose, and walked and flew. But, about the time of which we are now specially speaking, there began, partly in the realms of prosodic discussion, partly in those of poetic production, and, now and then, in quarters where the dissidents could both sing and say, a revolt against even qualified regularity. The different schemes which have been glanced at above of scansion by systems of irregular stress in corresponding lines; by 'bars' of varying, and in none but a very loose way, equivalent length; and so forth, could not but suggest something very different from that general identity as opposed to variety of rhythmical arrangement which had hitherto been taken as the great differentia of verse as compared with prose. And verse to match the theory was, almost a generation ago, composed and has been since attempted on methods of increasing 'impressionism'; some recent examples being admittedly intended to be read like prose, without any regard to supposed antecedent forms of correspondence, or mainly to illustrate the theory, noticed above, of a sort of prophetical cockpit-fight between quantity and accent, metre and rhetoric, and, perhaps, other pairs also, which may be left to suggest themselves.

> But what success the efforts met
> This story will not say—*as yet,*

to alter very slightly the famous and much discussed phrase in *Cadenus and Vanessa*. To some tastes, this success has not been great; the good verse produced being always scannable by the old methods and that recalcitrant to those methods being, to such tastes, not so good. But the whole principle of these prosodic chapters has been to take good English verse at every time and exhibit its characteristics of goodness without attempting to dictate. If anyone continues to apply that rule to the present and future efforts of English poets, he is not very likely to go far wrong.

CHAPTER VIII

NINETEENTH-CENTURY DRAMA

THE drama in the nineteenth century was much affected, as drama always must be, by social conditions, and by theatrical conditions which social development brought about. When the earlier years of the century had passed, and the fall of Napoleon had relieved England of much danger and anxiety, the less educated and the uneducated parts of the population began to improve in manners and in mind; and one of the means of refinement of which they showed a desire to avail themselves was the drama. Hitherto, to a very great extent, the theatre had been the amusement of educated classes only. The pit was still occupied by the acutest critics, members of the professional or the higher commercial classes. The people had not yet begun to take any wide or keen interest in the drama. The nineteenth century saw the influx of the populace into the theatre. And the populace, though ready to have its taste improved, brought with it its love of sensational incident and of broad humour. Not for it the elegant, if rather bloodless, tragedy, and the fine comedy, of high life, which had been the educated theatre-goers' staple fare. Caring nothing for poetry or for the subtler shades of feeling, it needed a hearty kind of play, full of excitement and written in expressive, high-flown language; it needed stories of passion, or terror, or lively fun. And, little by little, the demand created the supply. The nineteenth century saw the drama become, for the first time since the days of queen Elizabeth, a popular amusement. For the most part, educated classes and the higher ranks of society ceased to attend the theatre. It needed the attraction of some famous actor—Kemble, the two Keans, or Macready—to draw them back to what had been their special province; and, until some years later than the middle of the century, the creation of any drama of high quality was dependent upon the fame of some great actor who could draw refined and educated people to witness it.

Even so, it was presented under theatrical conditions that gave it small chance of a fair hearing. The theatre was still under the control of the court; and the only theatres which the court, as represented by the lord chamberlain, recognised were the two 'patent' houses, Drury lane and Covent garden, and the theatre in the Haymarket. But the increasing number of theatre-goers rendered these three insufficient for the public need. The patent houses, and especially Drury lane, were enlarged until they reached a size in which no drama of any delicacy or subtlety, none, indeed, which was not spectacular and, in some manner, violent, could be thoroughly effective. A quarter of the audience could neither see nor hear; many of the rest could neither see nor hear well.

A theatre of enormous size had been no bar in Athens to the existence of a noble drama; but, in nineteenth-century London, the conditions were different. Plays were not, as will be seen, a vehicle for religion : religion chose to regard the theatre as an enemy, and the theatre took what was, on the whole, a very mild revenge. Moreover, since James I had turned the Globe and Blackfriars company into an appanage of his court, the whole tendency had been to divorce the drama from the national life. The great size, therefore, of Drury lane and of Covent garden meant that these were no fit places for the representation of the plays enjoyed by educated classes; and, considering the growth in importance, volume and interest of the novel, it is not surprising that educated classes stayed away from the theatre, except when it was occupied by the fashionable Italian and French opera and ballet, and left the drama almost entirely to the new class of theatre-goers, drawn from the people. Meanwhile, the demand for theatrical entertainment on the part of the populace, and of the man of average refinement and intelligence, could not be satisfied by three theatres only. In defiance of the law, other theatres sprang into existence. By many undignified shifts, these theatres succeeded in avoiding sudden extinction at the hand of the lord chamberlain, and in increasing their number and importance. But dramatists who wrote for them were, necessarily, ill-paid, and the drama which they produced was, necessarily, ephemeral. For not only was every such theatre liable to be closed at a moment's notice; each work of dramatic art had to masquerade as something other than a play—to be interspersed with music or dancing or exhibitions of performing animals—in order that its producers might persuade themselves, or the lord chamberlain, that they were not breaking the law. Not till the year 1843 did the Theatre Regulation act legalise the position of 'illegitimate' houses. To these disabilities must be added the deterrent effect of the lord chamberlain's power to forbid the performance of plays on the grounds of seditious, blasphemous or immoral matter in them. The effect of this power was to prevent the drama from concerning itself with any of the subjects about which intelligent people think and feel; and this restriction militated against the production of good plays long after the act of 1843 had given the public the right to have practically as many theatres as it liked in which to develop the kinds of dramatic production which it required.

Under these conditions, the plays of the first half of the century were not likely to be endowed with much merit; and, in this period, we reach the low-water mark of the English drama in quality, together with a great increase in quantity. The death of tragedy; the swift decline of the romantic or poetical drama and the coarsening of comedy into farce are scarcely outweighed by the rapid growth of an honest and fairly spontaneous, but crude, domestic play suitable to the taste of the new theatrical public. Theatrical conditions, rather than social, prevented the amalgamation of the popular drama with the existing drama into a national drama that should, like that of Shakespeare, satisfy the tastes of refined and homely alike. On the one hand, the 'legitimate' play declined into 'lugubrious comedy and impossible tragedy,' and the poetic play found itself wholly dependent upon the popularity of some great actor to restore it to brief semblance of life; on the other hand, there came into existence a vigorous school of little artistic merit, lacking the finer qualities which the great Elizabethans had contrived to combine with the homelier.

'Sophocles and Shakespeare,' wrote G. H. Lewes, 'are as "sensational" as Fitzball or Dumas; but the situations, which in the latter are the aim and object of the piece, to which all the rest is subordinated, in the former are the mere starting-points, the nodes of dramatic action'[1].

In *The London Magazine* for April 1820, Hazlitt 'proved, very satisfactorily, and without fear of contradiction—neither Mr Maturin, Mr Sheil, nor Mr Milman being present—that no modern author could write a tragedy.' The age was 'critical, didactic, paradoxical, romantic,' but not dramatic. The French revolution had made of the English a nation of politicians and

---

[1] G. H. Lewes, *On Actors and Acting* (1875), p. 15.

newsmongers; and tragedy, being 'essentially individual and concrete, both in form and power' was irreconcilable with this 'bias to abstraction' in the general. There had hardly been a good tragedy written, he declared, since Home's *Douglas*. Nevertheless, tragedy was written in considerable quantities. It was a favourite exercise with men of letters, whether or no they possessed any power of dramatic invention. Wordsworth tried his hand at tragedy; Coleridge, Godwin, lord Byron, Mary Russell Mitford, Disraeli and many others, whose writings are dealt with elsewhere in this work, composed tragedies, some of which were produced upon the stage, while others remained polite exercises in a literary form. The present chapter will touch upon the minor tragedians, of whom the three mentioned in the quotation from Hazlitt given above are the first to call for notice.

Richard Lalor Sheil, who is more famous, perhaps, as politician than as dramatist, first came before the public with *Adelaide; or, The Emigrants*, a tragedy of the French revolution, which was produced in Dublin in 1814 and at Covent garden, where it occupied the stage for one night only, in 1816. The savagery of Hazlitt's attack upon this tragedy in *The Examiner* may be due, in great measure, to his resentment of the author's endeavour to 'drench an English audience with French loyalty' to the house of Bourbon. In spite of this, Hazlitt's condemnation is scarcely excessive, though there are passages of modest merit in the verse. Sheil's second tragedy, *The Apostate*, produced at Covent garden in 1817, met with more success. A tragedy of the Moors in Spain, this piece pleased Hazlitt a little better, because it contained a passage on the horrors of the inquisition; but he is just in his strictures, that the tragic situations are too violent, frequent and improbable, and that the play is full of a succession of self-inflicted horrors. It is effective stage-work, if far from being fine tragedy; and the versification has an appearance of vigour which, possibly, might conceal from the hearer, though it cannot from the reader, its essentially commonplace character. There are lines in it which amused even its first hearers—notably the heroine's exclamation: 'This is too much for any mortal creature!' Sheil's next tragedy, *Bellamira; or, The Fall of Tunis* (produced at Covent garden in 1818), is the best of his original plays. The language is purer and less extravagant, though by no means free from sound and fury; but Leigh Hunt, in *The Examiner* for 26 April 1818, was right in censuring

the tendency to mistake vehemence for strength, the impatience of lowness for the attainment of height, and excessive tragic effect physically over-powering for real effect at once carrying away and sustaining.

In other words, *Bellamira* is, again, a telling piece of stage-work, and an inferior piece of dramatic art. Sheil was more successful as dramatic artist in his next play, *Evadne; or, The Statue,* produced in 1819 ; but, here, he had the advantage of a foundation taken from Shirley's play, *The Traytor.* It may seem strange that a play of 1631 connected with the Italian renascence should be able to steady a dramatic author of the early part of the nineteenth century ; but so it was. Sheil altered the plot, dispensing, among other things, with the slaughter at the close of *The Traytor* ; and, in adapting the play a little more closely to the tragic ideals of his own day, indulged less freely than was his wont in extravagance of incident or language. Hazlitt took *Evadne* for the text of the last of his lectures on the dramatic literature of the age of Elizabeth ; and Leigh Hunt found the 'truly feminine and noble character' of Evadne 'a delightful relief from the selfish and extravagantly virtuous wives who have been palmed upon us of late for women.' *The Huguenot,* written in 1819, but not produced till two or three years later, shows a return to the aim at violence of effect, and an appeal through strangeness of scene and incident to emotions which the nature and sufferings of the characters could not arouse by themselves. And that its failure on the stage was ascribed by the author and others to the absence of Eliza O'Neill from the cast shows how dependent the drama had become upon the popularity of this or that player. After the failure of *The Huguenot,* Sheil gave up play-writing ; but previous to its production he had written *Montoni* (produced in 1820), a poetical drama founded on the French, and remarkable for some of Sheil's wildest extravagance in incident and for some of his best verse ; had adapted Massinger and Field's *The Fatall Dowry*; and had revised *Damon and Pythias,* a tragedy by John Banim, which turned out a better piece of work than any play written by Sheil alone.

Hazlitt's last lecture on the dramatic literature of the age of Elizabeth is largely concerned with German influence on the tragedy and romantic drama of his day. That influence can be clearly discerned in the plays of Charles Robert Maturin, an Irish clergyman, whose three tragedies—*Bertram; or, The Castle of St Aldobrond ; Manuel*; and *Fredolfo*—were produced in London in the years 1816 and 1817. *Bertram* was a famous and successful play in its time. It was brought to the notice of Edmund Kean by Walter Scott and Byron ; it was the object of an attack by Coleridge in *The Courier,* which, in its turn, roused a notorious attack by Hazlitt on Coleridge. The ridicule of *The Anti-Jacobin* had not opened the eyes of the public to the shortcomings of the drama of Kotzebue; and Coleridge's translation of *Wallenstein* appears to have had no corrective influence on taste. Maturin's *Bertram*, with its gloomy 'Byronic' hero-villain, its strained sentiment, its setting in castle and monastery and its attempt at the portrayal of frantic passions, has all the vices of a vicious order of tragedy. Nothing, to the modern reader, seems real; nothing inevitable. In Hazlitt's words: 'There is no action: there is neither cause nor effect....The passion described does not arise naturally out of the previous circumstances, nor lead necessarily to the consequences that follow.' This is true, also, of *Manuel*; and *Fredolfo*, 'a piece of romanticism run mad,' shocked the first and last audience that ever saw it with a display of villainy which even that age could not stomach. Maturin, in later years, admitted that his acquaintance with life was so limited as to make him dependent on his imagination alone (and he might have added the imagination of other dramatists) for his characters, situations and language. He was, however, a better poet than Sheil. For all his excess in physical horror, his verse shows sensibility and has some beauty.

The plays of Henry Hart Milman, afterwards dean of St Paul's, reveal a taste somewhat surer; although, in *Fazio*, a tragedy published in 1815 and produced in London in 1818, there is plenty of false fire. Milman took inspiration rather from Fletcher or Massinger than from Kotzebue or 'Monk' Lewis; and *Fazio*, at least, is a very lively drama, if not a good tragedy. It is a tale, placed in Italy, of robbery and supposed murder, of splendid harlotry and devoted conjugal affection; and its acting qualities kept it on the stage nearly all through the nineteenth century. It has another title to remembrance: from it, Hazlitt drew a speech which he hurled at the head of Coleridge in the attack referred to above. Milman's other plays show less of false taste and less of theatrical merit, being, for the most part, dramatic poems rather than stage-plays. *The Fall of Jerusalem* (1820) and *The Martyr of Antioch* (1822) are both founded upon a legitimately conceived struggle between two passions or ideas. *Belshazzar* (1822) contains some good lyrics. *Anne Boleyn* (1826), Milman's last dramatic composition, was, also, his poorest. He cannot, perhaps, be accused of misrepresenting facts and characters so grossly as some later historical dramatists; but his anxiety to state a good case for protestantism against Roman catholicism mars the dramatic quality

of the play. In this connection, the plays of Henry Montague
Grover are worth mention. Grover, in 1826, published a play on
the same subject, Anne Boleyn, in the preface to which he hints
that Milman had made unacknowledged use of his manuscript.
Such a complaint is not uncommon among dramatic authors.

Meanwhile, there had arisen a tragedian who endeavoured to
purge tragedy of the extravagance with which the influence of
German romanticism had affected it. James Sheridan Knowles,
said Hazlitt,

> has hardly read a poem or a play or seen anything of the world, but he hears
> the anxious beatings of his own heart, and makes others feel them by the
> force of sympathy.

Save that Sheridan Knowles had read Shakespeare to such good
purpose that contemporary critics accused him of borrowing everything from Shakespeare, Hazlitt's remark is just. Knowles 'kept
his eye on the object,' and abstained from seeking effect from wild
and whirling words that had little or no connection with the subject
and the characters. His situations arise out of the characters and
the circumstances. A sympathetic imagination and an instinctive,
rather than acquired, reverence for the principles of dramatic
composition make his work, in the main, just, sensible and moving ;
and he delineates natural feeling with much simple understanding.
To this simplicity, he owes the few things in his work which come
near to genius—speeches, like Virginius's remark to his daughter :

> I never saw you look so like your mother
> In all my life![1]

which might well seem almost 'low' to an audience accustomed to
Sheil and to Maturin, but which impress the reader with their truth.
Such moments are rare ; for, though Knowles's language brings
relief from the towering nonsense of his immediate predecessors,
it varies between triviality and excessive, sometimes ridiculous,
decoration ; and his verse is pedestrian. When the plot was given
him by history, he could handle it clearly and effectively. In his
comedies, of which an account will be given later, he proved himself
unable to spin a comprehensible tale ; but his chief tragedies and
plays—*Virginius* (1820) ; *Caius Gracchus* (produced in 1823,
though written before *Virginius*) ; *William Tell* (1825) ; and *The
Wife* (1833)—are clearly constructed and full of situations at once
effective and inevitable. Supported by the acting of Macready and
Helen Faucit, Sheridan Knowles succeeded, for a time, in restoring
tragedy at once to its proper dignity and to a good measure of

[1] *Virginius*, IV, 1.

popularity in the theatre; but the taste for it, poisoned by the excesses of the romantics, was all but dead. The fine plays of Richard Henry (or Hengist) Horne were never produced on the stage. *Cosmo de Medici*, a tragedy in five acts, published in 1837, is a well-built, well-written piece of poetical drama, in which two brothers fall with perfect naturalness into a fatal quarrel; the murderer's attempt to conceal the half-involuntary deed is acutely imagined, and the only questionable episode is the somewhat theatrical death of the father after he has executed the offender with his own hand. *The Death of Marlowe*, a short play published in the same year, has a curious and beautiful intensity in the execution of the theme; and Horne's other plays, *Gregory VII* (1840) and *Judas Iscariot* (1848), are works of power and some grandeur, born out of due time.

The age, becoming more and more critical, scientific and unemotional, fell, more and more, out of touch with tragedy. It was almost certainly the desire to bring tragedy back to the business and bosoms of men that induced John Westland Marston to attempt a verse-tragedy of contemporary life. *The Patrician's Daughter* (1842) tells the story of an able politician of humble birth, who is 'taken up' by an aristocratic family for political ends, and then treated with contumely when asking for the hand of the daughter of the house. He takes his revenge by rejecting the lady (something in the manner of Claudio in *Much Ado about Nothing*) when her family has found it necessary to offer him her hand in exchange for his support; and the insult kills the girl, who had loved him all the time. The plot, in one place, runs thin; the humiliation of the hero is accomplished by means of a commonplace of stage-craft, one of those misunderstandings or misrepresentations which a moment's calm enquiry would have cleared up. But Marston was a poet and a scholar; his mind was richer, his social knowledge greater and his poetical faculty more highly trained than those of the other tragedians mentioned in this chapter. He wrote sense, and he understood character. And he showed considerable courage in writing what was so near to a political play as *The Patrician's Daughter*. 'The play,' as he said later, 'represents a period when the fierce class animosities excited by the first Reform bill had by no means subsided.' It is a manifesto for neither aristocracy nor democracy: indeed, it exposes the particular danger on each side, on the side of the patricians, pride; on the side of the plebeian, the tendency to 'indulge a passion in the belief that he was vindicating a principle.'

But, considering the strictness of the censorship and the heated state of public feeling, Marston went as near as anyone dared to writing a poetical play about the actual life of his time; and the favour with which the play was received ought, it would be imagined, to have inspired others to follow his example and win for tragedy a new vigour. Nothing came of it; and this opposition between the haughty, heartless world of high life and the meritorious poor became a favourite subject of other kinds of drama than tragedy. Marston's other tragedies in verse, *Strathmore* (1849) and *Marie de Méranie* (1850), were the last of their kind that deserve consideration from the student of literature. The drama was soon to develop along lines more suited to the age. With the retirement of Macready and Helen Faucit, the succession of great actors who had inspired dramatists with the desire to write poetical drama came to an end, and was not to be renewed. Thus, Marston's exciting and romantic *Life for Life* (1869), his equally romantic and slightly Byronic *A Life's Ransom* (1857) and others, had no successors worthy of comparison with them in the ordinary traffic of the stage.

The first half of the nineteenth century was a period of very brisk dramatic activity. The pressure of the public demand for theatrical entertainment caused prolific production. The comparatively low state of public taste and the insecurity of tenure of unlicensed theatres caused that production to be of little value. The kinds of drama were many—comedy, farce, extravaganza, burlesque, opera and melodrama; and authors, many of whom were attached to certain theatres and paid fixed salaries to produce whatever kind of play might be wanted, wrote in haste dramatic pieces of all sorts. Under these conditions, originality in plot could scarcely be expected. Stories were snatched from all sources[1]; especially from French and German drama and from French and English novels. The works of Scott, of Dumas and of Dickens were especially favourite hunting-grounds for plots; and the law of copyright then offered no protection to the novelist against the playwright. The period exhibits a confusing jumble of trivial aims and poor accomplishment; from which may be extricated two principal characteristics—the degradation of comedy into farce, and the growth of what is now known as melodrama. The name, melodrama, was taken from the French *mélodrame*, which, as in English, meant a play of sensational

---

[1] John Oxenford, more distinguished as dramatic critic than as playwright, made a play out of Pope's *The Rape of the Lock*.

incident and broad humour, interspersed with songs and dances. In England, the musical adjuncts were introduced not only to please public taste but, largely, in order to evade the law by presenting a stage-play in the guise of a musical entertainment. In character and content, melodrama was very various. It included the operas of Isaac Pocock and Henry Bishop; the adaptations of Fitzball; the wild imaginings of Shirley Brooks; the nautical drama made popular by T. P. Cooke, the actor; the equestrian drama of Astley's; the domestic drama of Tom Taylor; and the Irish drama of Dion Boucicault. In Taylor and Boucicault, it had practitioners of skill and sense; at the opposite extreme were authors of blood-curdling pieces performed at the outlying theatres. To the composition of this heterogeneous mixture, many strains contributed. So far as it had any descent from English tradition, it may be traced back to the fairy plays and spectacles of John Rich. These were melodramas, inasmuch as they were opera without operatic singers; but the musical element was destined to give way to the dramatic. By the time of *The Miller and his Men* (1813), the author, or, rather, the adapter, Pocock, is as important as the composer, Bishop; and, before long, the music disappeared altogether, as it had disappeared from the French *mélodrame*, leaving the sensational incidents and the broad humour unrelieved. The romantic movement, which had produced *The Mysteries of Udolpho* and the works of 'Monk' Lewis, contributed not a little of the sensational element; and the new theatrical public brought with it the taste for horrors which continued to be stimulated and fed by ballads and broadsheets. The French drama of incident and sensation, which had come into being after the revolution— the drama of Pixérécourt, of Caigniez and of Cuvelier de Trye —lent something; shows and spectacles, performing animals and acrobatic exhibitions, with which licensed houses recouped themselves for their losses over 'legitimate' drama, flowed, at the Surrey theatre, at Sadler's wells, or at Astley's, into the stream; and, by the middle of the century, melodrama had taken a form which has scarcely been altered since. Melodrama divides human nature into the entirely good and the entirely bad, the two being bridged by an uncertain structure based on the possibility of reform (in minor personages only) by sudden conversion at a critical moment of the action. That is to say, incident and situation, not character, are its aims. It allies itself boldly with the democrat against the aristocrat. To be rich and well-born is, almost inevitably, to be wicked; to be poor and humble is all but a guarantee of virtue. These characteristics did not become crystallised all at once; they grew by degrees through works of a large number of playwrights, some among whom may be particularised.

Isaac Pocock, the author of *The Miller and his Men*, took the subject of his melodramas, which, in his own day, were called librettos, but are practically plays, almost entirely from French or German drama and English novels. His earliest melodrama was *Twenty Years Ago*, produced in 1810. *The Magpie or the Maid?* (1816) was taken from the French, *The Robber's Wife* from the German. Defoe contributed the source of *Robinson Crusoe* (1817); and from Scott he took the subjects of *Rob Roy Macgregor; or, Auld Lang Syne* (1818) and *Montrose; or, The Children of the Mist* (1822), besides dramatising, it is recorded, *Woodstock, Peveril of the Peak, The Antiquary* and *Old Mortality.* Edward Ball, afterwards Fitzball, one of the most prolific among the prolific authors of his day, compiled a great number of dramas and librettos for operas, nearly all of which were founded upon borrowed plots. William Thomas Moncrieff, at one time, was manager of Astley's circus, to which he furnished at least one very successful equestrian drama, *The Dandy Family*; and he won fame by supplying Drury lane with a romantic melodrama called *The Cataract of the Ganges; or, The Rajah's Daughter,* which gave the national theatre an opportunity of displaying upon its stage not only real horses but, apparently for the first time, a real waterfall. Moncrieff is best known by his *Tom and Jerry,* an adaptation for the stage of Pierce Egan's[1] *Life in London*; but he drew, also, upon the novels of Dickens for the plots of several plays. With the dramas of Douglas William Jerrold we come to work far more reasonable and not wholly unreadable. His comedies will be considered later; among his dramas, the most famous is the still enjoyable *Blackey'd Susan; or, 'All in the Downs,'* founded upon Gay's ballad. Helped by the acting of T. P. Cooke, this admirable piece of popular drama was received with great favour at the Surrey theatre, and has been the subject of several adaptations, burlesques and pantomimes. The dramas of John Baldwin Buckstone, most of them written for the Adelphi theatre, are the origin of the familiar term, 'Adelphi melodrama.' They are extravagantly sentimental, and they are written in the turgid 'literary' language with which the taste of the day demanded that the memories and tongues of the players should wrestle. But they are well constructed, frequently with borrowed plots; and are

[1] See, *post,* vol. xiv.

not so violent in incident as to be ridiculous. *The Bear-hunters; or, The Fatal Ravine* (1829) has a quite exciting story; and both *The Green Bushes; or, A Hundred Years Ago* (1845) and *The Flower of the Forest* (1849) kept the stage till the end of the century. In the American-born William Bayle Bernard, a mind of very different calibre turned to the trade of dramatic composition. Bernard was a scholar and a sound critic, although those of his 114 plays which survive in print would scarcely lead the reader to believe it. But he relied largely upon his own invention, and had a purer standard of prose than his contemporaries, a neat wit and some notion of characterisation. His domestic drama, *Marie Ducange* (1837) and his 'fireside story,' *The Round of Wrong* (1846), are among the best of his pieces. He composed also a romantic drama, *The Doge of Venice* (1867), and made an adaptation of the story of Rip van Winkle (1832). *The Passing Cloud* (1850), a drama in verse and in something that is neither verse nor prose, at least shows some independence of aim. Joseph Stirling Coyne, an industrious adapter from the French (of which he was reputed to know less than he knew about the tastes of the London audiences) and Charles William Shirley Brooks, who, in date, belongs to the last half of the century, but, in spirit to the first half, also deserve mention among the authors of popular dramas.

The writer who gave to melodrama its distinctive formula, and set it upon a path of development which, in time, was to draw it far apart from drama of serious interest, was Dionysius Lardner Bourcicault, better known as Dion Boucicault. This prolific author of plays was a master of dramatic construction. His plots were seldom of his own invention; the incidents never. He borrowed from near and far, and his special skill lay in weaving multifarious incidents together into a swiftly-moving and exciting plot, and in writing dialogue that is nearly always fresh and racy. His characters are never human beings, but always representatives of some one quality. That, however, does not prevent him from filling his dramas with sentiment, not grossly exaggerated, which may appeal to a mixed audience as recognisably human. Before him, there had been no dramatic author so cunning in the discernment of what elements are desired in a popular play, and in the mixing of the ingredients. Before the works of Sardou were introduced to English audiences, the influence of Boucicault's very different compositions had become almost as tyrannous as the dramatic construction of Sardou was to prove itself; and, to Boucicault's influence, largely, must be attributed a conception of the necessities of dramatic form

which was destined to hamper the efforts of later dramatists and to
cause, for a while, a split between two schools of drama and dramatic
criticism. At the same time, there is more 'nature' in Boucicault's
drama than in that of his predecessors. This is due, in great measure,
to the humour and suggestiveness of his dialogue, which often
bears a close resemblance to natural speech; and this especially
in his famous Irish dramas, such as *The Colleen Bawn, Arrah-na-
Pogue* and *The Shaughraun*. Boucicault thus occupies a position
at the turning-point between the purely theatrical drama of the
first half of the century and the more naturalistic drama which
was to put forth a bud while he was at the height of his career as
dramatist. In some of his adaptations, such as *The Corsican
Brothers* and *Louis XI*, he belongs entirely to the footlights;
through much of his work gleams the false dawn of a coming
day. It cannot be said that there was any improvement, later in
the century, on the melodrama of Boucicault. The type remained
fixed, and subsequent examples showed merely variation in detail,
though Pettitt and other authors contrived to treat the familiar
material with vigour. The new impulse was to reach the drama
through another channel. Meanwhile, a small amount of superior
work was being produced outside the region of comedy, though in
sporadic fashion. Both Sheridan Knowles and Westland Marston
wrote dramatic pieces of merit besides their tragedies and comedies.
The next playwright to show something of their calibre was
Tom Taylor. Like his contemporaries, Taylor seldom trusted to
his own invention for his plots. He collaborated with Charles
Reade and others, and he took his stories from French drama,
from the works of Dickens and from other English novelists; but,
in *Plot and Passion* (1853), *Still Waters Run Deep* (1855), *The
Ticket-of-Leave Man* (1863) and other plays, he proved himself
both a capable playwright, from the theatrical point of view, and
a fairly keen observer of human passions. His construction is
solid and careful; and he wrote, for the most part, without
affectation or extravagance; so, though much of his dialogue
seems stilted to the modern reader, it is not without some
resemblance to nature; while his *Arkwright's Wife* (1873) is a
domestic drama almost 'naturalistic' in language, achievement and
spirit, though sensational in incident. Taylor's best work lies in
his series of historical dramas: *The Fool's Revenge* (1869), which
was founded upon Hugo's *Le Roi s'amuse*; *'Twixt Axe and
Crown* (1870), founded upon a German play; *Jeanne Darc*
(1871); *Lady Clancarty* (1874); and *Anne Boleyn* (1875). His

treatment of history is fairly respectful; his language, whether in prose or verse, is more direct and forcible than that of some of his successors in this field; and Taylor fills in his historical outlines with warmth and movement. With Taylor, rather than with Boucicault, still less with Webster, should be classed Watts Phillips—and that in spite of such plays as *Lost in London* or *The Woman in Mauve*. The best examples of his work, such as *Camilla's Husband* (1862), though leaning to the sensational side and ingeniously constructed according to the ideals of the contemporary theatre, have some flavour in them of human nature, which, added to the comparative simplicity of their dialogue, entitle Phillips to consideration. *The Dead Heart* (1859), which, possibly, owed something to *A Tale of Two Cities*, is Phillips's most famous play, because of its spectacular qualities; but, as dramatic art, it is not fairly representative of his ability. In the field of historical drama, Taylor's eminence was shared by William Gorman Wills. For Wills, historical truth had no charms. His caricature of Oliver Cromwell in *Charles I* (1872) must strike anyone who has seen or read that play not only as ridiculous, but as a sacrifice of dramatic for theatrical effect; and, to judge from contemporary criticism, his treatment of John Knox in the unpublished *Marie Stuart* (1874) was no better. As a deviser of theatrical scenes and situations, Wills had power. His taste was thoroughly commonplace, his language trivial or extravagant. But he could fit eminent actors with telling parts, and was useful as librettist to the scene-painter and stage-manager.

Thus, drama grew up to take the place of tragedy. For the most part, it was melodrama: at first, violent and coarse; later, somewhat refined, and crystallised into a definite form. The stage grew more insistent in its demands, and less suitable either to poetical or to naturalistic drama. Character was sacrificed to situation, and art to artifice. With the exception of certain respectable historical plays, and a moderate amount of domestic drama contributed by Taylor (with or without Charles Reade), Marston and Phillips, little survives in print that is likely to tempt anyone to read it except for the purposes of historical study.

The comedy of the period, for the most part, is as remote from dramatic art and from nature as is the drama. During the first half of the century, comedy, as distinct from farce, is represented only by Sheridan Knowles, Douglas Jerrold, Marston, Tom Taylor and Boucicault. Practically, the only attempt to carry on the tradition of English high comedy was a work of Boucicault's youth, *London Assurance* (1841). On the modern stage, this play is classed among 'old comedies'; and it has some affinity, as a whole, with the work of the elder Colman, while portions are obviously due to Goldsmith and Sheridan. But the coarsening of the types and forcing of the situations show how far from his models Boucicault's work fell. The comedy of Sheridan Knowles is more original in type; but his plots are more confusing than even Congreve's. Indeed, the plot of *The Hunchback* (1832), a pompous and heavy play, has never yet been satisfactorily explained. *The Beggar's Daughter of Bethnal Green* (1828) looks back to Elizabethan domestic comedy, with which Knowles was probably not acquainted. Its story is simpler than those of his other comedies, and it is written with freshness and skill in dramatic expression. Douglas Jerrold relies much upon extravagance of 'humour.' The characters in his comedies are less human beings than personifications of this or that peculiarity—family pride, valetudinarianism, or what not; and the misunderstandings and complications which go to make up his plots are nearly always flimsy. But he handles his materials with ease, and, now and then, makes his 'humours' very amusing—Dr Petgoose, for instance, the domineering doctor in *The Catspaw* (1850); Miss Tucker, the spitefully humble companion to the heroine in *Time Works Wonders* (1845); best of all, perhaps, the true-blue Briton, Mr Pallmall, in a clever and amusing comedy, *The Prisoner of War* (1842). Pallmall

quarrelled with some French dragoons, because he would insist, that the best cocoa-nuts grew on Primrose-hill, and that birds of Paradise flew about St James's.

In defence, he pleads that his motive was patriotism:

They abused the British climate, and I championed my native air. As a sailor isn't it your duty to die for your country?...As a civilian, it is mine to lie for her. Courage isn't confined to fighting. No, no—whenever a Frenchman throws me down a lie—for the honour of England, I always trump it.

Marston was not at his best in comedy. His most successful attempt was *The Favourite of Fortune* (1866), which, doubtless, was amusing when acted, but is pale in the reading. The character of Mrs Lorrington, the rich and vulgar widow, demands expression by a comic actress. It is little more than an outline, waiting to be filled in. A match-making mamma, a young man of fortune, who hides a Byronic heart and a noble nature under a disguise of phlegm, are more clearly imagined and expressed; but the play, as a whole, is lifeless. The comedy of the time was, in fact, dependent upon the stage and the actor. In order to compete with more popular forms of drama, it was obliged to coarsen its lines, and to avoid all subtlety of character and development. The political and social history of the period was not such as to produce the atmosphere in which fine comedy grows freely. The rich and leisured classes became the butts, rather than the models, of a swiftly developing democracy ; in the drama of the time, serious and humorous alike, they are nearly always exhibited in opposition to honest poverty. And the predominance of the actor helped to make broad and simple characterisation and theatrical effect more valued than truth to life or fineness of understanding and expression.

Meanwhile, there was very great activity in another branch of comic drama, the farce. The lavish playbills of the time always concluded with a dash of fun, the original object being to relieve the horror inspired by the violent drama ; and the fun chiefly enjoyed by the new public of theatre-goers was farcical fun. The demand brought into being an innumerable number of short comic pieces of broad and bustling humour. Adelphi 'screamers' became, under J. B. Buckstone, as famous as Adelphi dramas. In many of these plays, the imagination of the reader can still supply the personal drollery of some comic actor and the ceaseless physical movement which were necessary to their effect. One of the earliest and best of the farce-writers was John Poole, most famous as author of *Paul Pry* (1825). Several actors have found in *Paul Pry* a fine field for their talent or their peculiar personality. From the reader, the play cannot draw a smile, unless his imagination endow the figure of Paul with the voice and face and personality of some comic actor whom he has seen. Granted this effort, the fun of the thing is still fresh ; and so is that of *'Twixt the Cup and Lip* (1827) and of *Lodgings for Single Gentlemen* (1829). Among the most eminent of other writers of farce were Pocock and Moncrieff, who both wrote farces for music, Stirling Coyne, who betrays in farce a genuine sense of fun, and James Robinson Planché ; and no one produced more successful or more amusing farces than John Maddison Morton, a son of the dramatist Thomas Morton, and an industrious adapter of plays from the French. His most famous work, *Box and Cox* (1847), was founded upon two French vaudevilles ; but it still reads like an original and single creation. These farces all depend upon some marked and simple oddity in the chief character, upon complicated misunderstandings or broadly ridiculous situations. There is very little comedy in them; but their hearty fun is clean and seldom absolutely silly. Early in the second half of the century, the popularity of farce waned, to some extent, under the increasing taste for burlesque. The example had been set chiefly by Planché, a dramatic author with a wide knowledge of drama, ancient and modern, a lively sense of humour and a wit that was by no means merely verbal. Those were days in which the gods and goddesses of Greece and Rome were more familiar to the public than they are now; and Planché liked to make them characters in his various and spirited dramatic work. Mythology and fairy lore were generally in favour; Shirley Brooks wrote a burlesque, *The Exposition* (1851), in which the Scandinavian gods pay a visit to the great exhibition. Planché's principal successor in this field was Henry James Byron, a prolific author of dramatic pieces of many kinds. To judge from contemporary estimates, Byron's wit consisted chiefly of puns; and of puns there are plenty in his published comedies and plays.

During Byron's career, the drama became affected by an influence which proved to be more important than the positive achievement of the writer who exercised it, Thomas William Robertson. By the middle of the nineteenth century, the drama had become all but wholly stagey. Broad farce, theatrical comedy and machine-made melodrama, written in doggerel verse or cumbrous and showy prose, were produced in enormous quantities; but playwrights had not yet learned how to make use of the freedom and the comparative security conferred upon them by the act of 1843. Most dramatists were still, practically, in the position of writers retained by this or that theatre, to compose whatever the manager might demand of them; and the tyranny of the actor was still paramount. Twenty years separated the passing of the act from the first distinguishable effect of its provisions, which is to be found in the plays of Robertson. Robertson began his work as dramatic author much as did all the men of his time. He adapted plays and knocked off trifles of many kinds. A play called *David Garrick*, which he made out of a novel of his own composition, founded upon Mélesville's three-act comedy, *Sullivan*, brought him into notice in 1864; but *David Garrick* belongs wholly to the drama of the first half of the century. Robertson's proper achievement begins with *Society* (1865), which, after being rejected by many managers, at last found a home at the Prince of Wales's theatre. In *Society*, he made a distinct attempt to introduce naturalism into the drama. To a modern reader, the tone of the play does not seem very natural, unless it be contrasted with the purely theatrical plays that preceded it; but it bears evidence that the author observed life about him, and endeavoured to reproduce it. The result is a commonplace of nineteenth-century drama—a picture of tender and sentimental youth in a setting of worldliness and cynicism. The plot is bald and crude; and these qualities, though they have no merit in themselves, at least distinguish the play from others, which depended entirely upon the spinning of intrigue. But the dialogue is natural—or, if unduly smart, as in Robertson's favourite device of antiphonal, or echoing, speeches, it is not tainted with the display familiar in the contemporary drama. The characters behave, on the surface, like people of their day; the atmosphere which the author endeavours to create is the atmosphere of the life going on outside the walls of the theatre. Though, to modern readers, the psychology of *Society* and other plays by Robertson may seem childish, his presentation of manners and his reliance upon nature rather than upon plot or violence were signs of the emancipation of the drama from a long tyranny. Thanks, largely, to the manner in which the play was presented by young actors fully in sympathy with the author's naturalistic aims, *Society* achieved a success which encouraged Robertson to go further along the same path. *Ours* was produced in 1866; *Caste* in 1867; *Play* in 1868; *School* in 1869; and *M.P.* in 1870. Both *Ours* and *Caste* show an advance on *Society* in Robertson's peculiar province of manners, though his plots remain crude and his characterisation elementary. *School*, which was partly founded upon the *Aschenbrödel* of Benedix, is a very pretty idyll, lacking the quality of ease which is to be found in Robertson's best work. *Play* is a feeble piece of work, and *M.P.* was written when the author was practically dying.

Robertson's direct influence was not so strong as it might have been, because, soon after his death, another and an opposed influence cut clean across it in the taste for the plays of Sardou. The French literature which Robertson enjoyed was that of Alfred de Musset and George Sand: the drama of Sardou had reduced romanticism, for others, to a mechanical trick, and the English public fell once more a victim to the wholly unnatural 'well-made play.' This was a return to the drama of the first half of the century; with the only difference that Sardou was an accomplished craftsman, whose work was all but proof against bungling adaptation, whereas preceding adaptations from French or German and the

few original English plays were almost all the work of bunglers.
It needed a stronger influence than that of Robertson's delicate
and naïve little pieces to arouse in England the demand for
dramatic truth and good sense. Meanwhile, however, the work
of Robertson had its effect upon certain playwrights of his time,
upon Byron, for instance, and upon James Albery, a successful
dramatist, none of whose pieces have been printed. In comedy
and domestic drama alike, Byron showed himself lacking in
originality, in taste and in dignity. His humour, though not coarse,
is mean; his plots are at once complicated and puerile; and his
characterisation is purely theatrical. Nevertheless, he deserves
mention among dramatists of the latter half of the century
because of an undeniable cleverness, and a shrewd ingenuity
in the management of familiar materials, which distinguish such
pieces as *Cyril's Success* (1868), *Our Boys* (1875) and *Uncle Dick's
Darling* (1869); and because, also, of certain flashes of homely
verisimilitude which are due to the influence of Robertson. That
influence having failed to produce any marked effect, there was no
other yet at work. The 'artistic revival' of the eighteen-seventies
found expression rather in the mounting of plays and in stage-
decoration than in the quality of the drama produced; and it was
not until the influence of Ibsen, however reviled by its opponents
and misunderstood by its very champions, had percolated into the
theatre that the English drama made any noticeable effort to
burst the chains of outworn tradition and a constricted view of
the province of dramatic art.

   One other dramatist demands notice, perhaps the most brilliant
of his century, but almost wholly unrelated, in his mature work, to
the drama of his age. The earlier pieces of William Schwenck
Gilbert were burlesques and other such trifles. In 1870, he began
a second period with *The Palace of Truth*, a poetical fantasy,
adapted from a story by Madame de Genlis and undoubtedly
influenced by the fairy-work of Planché. This period included
other plays in verse: *The Wicked World* (1873); *Pygmalion and
Galatea* (1871); and *Broken Hearts* (1875). These plays and
others of their kind are all founded upon a single idea, that of
self-revelation by characters who are unaware of it, under the
influence of some magic or some supernatural interference. The
satire is shrewd, but not profound; the young author is apt to
sneer, and he has by no means learned to make the best use of
his curiously logical fancy. That he occasionally degrades high
and beautiful themes is not surprising. To do so had been the

regular proceeding in burlesque, and the age almost expected it;
but Gilbert's is not the then usual hearty cockney vulgarity. In
Pygmalion and Galatea, and, still more, in *Gretchen* (1879), a
perversion of part of the story of *Faust*, the vulgarity is cynical
and bitter. And, in Gilbert's prose plays, the same spirit may be
found in greater degree. He could be pleasantly sentimental, as
in *Sweethearts* (1874), without sacrificing his cynicism altogether;
but *Engaged* (1877), a farcical comedy, compels the reader to
laugh in spite of an exceedingly low conception of human nature.
Gilbert was not at his ease in prose. He writes it pompously and
with an inartistic display, which was inherited, to some extent,
from his predecessors in dramatic writing. His true province was
verse, and especially light verse; and, in the third period of his
activity, he found the perfect medium for his genius in comic opera
of an original kind. In *The Bab Ballads*, he had already shown
his skill in metre; and, when all is said, an extraordinary skill in
the writing of songs is the most remarkable feature of the comic
operas which began with *Trial by Jury* in 1875 and ended with
The Grand Duke in 1896. Gilbert was a metrical humourist
of the first water. His lyrical facility and his mastery of metre
raised the poetical quality of comic opera to a position that it had
never reached before and has not reached since. Moreover, the
skill was used in the expression of truly humorous ideas. The
base of Gilbert's humour is a logical and wholly unpoetical use of
fantasy. It carries out absurd ideas, with exact logic, from premiss
to conclusion; or it takes what passes in daily life for a matter of
fact or of right and shows what would happen if this were pushed
to an extreme without regard to contrary influences and considerations. The difference between the shrewd, neat satire and
fine workmanship of Gilbert's operas and the vulgar inanities of
the comic opera of his early days was, unfortunately, too wide for
any contact to be established. Gilbert remains alone, a brilliant
and original genius, whom it is obviously hopeless to imitate, and
on whose example no school could be founded.

CHAPTER IX

THACKERAY

Of all English novelists whose fiction has been founded on a perception of the comedy of life with its alternations of the ridiculous and the pathetic, none has met with more adverse criticism than Thackeray. The versatility of his work as novelist, essayist, writer of humorous trifles, rimester and draughtsman causes some difficulty in forming a coherent judgment upon his total achievement. At once satirist and sentimentalist, he combined two points of view the relation between which is invisible to many eyes; and, in both capacities, he worked with a refinement which does not make for general popularity. In the wide field of action which his novels cover, in the generous proportions of their construction and in the great variety of their personages, he bears a superficial resemblance to his contemporary Dickens; and the two novelists have become the object of a traditional contrast in which Dickens's colossal power of fantastic creation and more direct appeal to popular sentiment, as opposed to Thackeray's minute observation of everyday peculiarities and more elusive humour, has, perhaps, gained the vote of the majority. No such competition, however, is really possible between two writers whose view of life and artistic methods were, fundamentally, different. The true criterion of Thackeray's, and of his great contemporary's, work, upon their own merits is the exactness with which they reproduced the contradictions and variations of the comedy of which they were the amused and sympathetic spectators.

The family of Thackeray was of Yorkshire origin, and one of its branches was settled at Hampsthwaite on the Nidd, seven miles above Knaresborough, until within a few years of the novelist's birth. His father, Richmond Thackeray, was grandson of Thomas Thackeray, headmaster of Harrow and archdeacon of Surrey, whose youngest son, William Makepeace, had entered the service of the East India company, and had married Amelia,

18—2

daughter of colonel Richmond Webb. Richmond, the second son of this marriage, entered the same service. He married Anne Becher, and William Makepeace Thackeray, their only child, was born at Alipur near Calcutta on 18 July 1811. Richmond Thackeray, who, at this time, held the office of collector of the twenty-four Parganas, died in 1815 : his widow not long afterwards married major Carmichael-Smyth, and outlived her famous son, dying in 1864.

Thackeray, a child of six, was sent to England in 1817. Among his earliest impressions were a distant sight, at St Helena, where his boat touched, of Napoleon walking in the garden of Longwood, and the spectacle of the national mourning for princess Charlotte on his arrival in England in November. His home was with relations, chiefly at Hadley, near Barnet, where Peter Moore, member of parliament for Coventry, husband of one of his great-aunts, was lord of the manor. He was sent to school first at Southampton, where he was near Fareham, the home of another great-aunt, Miss Becher; then, at Walpole house, Chiswick mall; and, from 1822 to 1828, at Charterhouse. His school-days were not altogether happy. He loved Walpole house no better than Becky Sharp loved the seminary of which it became the prototype ; while his memories of Charterhouse, as it appears in his writings, were certainly softened and transfigured by the passage of years. He amused his schoolfellows with his ready gifts of caricature and parody; but the temperament which criticises its surroundings with an exceptionally acute sense of their relative values is not often congenial to the atmosphere of a public school, and Thackeray had the self-consciousness and desultory tendency which are its dangerous entail. He left Charterhouse without distinction, and, before entering Trinity college, Cambridge, read, for a few months, with his step-father at Larkbeare in Devon. The neighbouring town of Ottery St Mary, the native place of Coleridge, the church bells of which ring melodiously in some lines of Lamb's *John Woodvil*, became the Clavering of *Pendennis*, and Exeter provided the original for the cathedral city Chatteris, where Arthur Pendennis lost his heart to Miss Fotheringay.

In February 1829, Thackeray went to Cambridge, and remained at Trinity college for a year and a half. *Pendennis* contains chapters founded upon this part of his life with a characteristic mixture of fact and fiction. Its story of extravagance and failure is, of course, overdrawn; but he seems to have done little work and spent money freely, and he went down in June 1830 without waiting to take a degree. His talent for riming and parody was exercised in two ephemeral university papers, *The Snob* and *The Gownsman*. *The Snob* of 30 April 1829 contained his burlesque upon the subject set for the chancellor's medal for English verse, *Timbuctoo*. Critics who foresaw the genius of Tennyson in the poem which won the medal could hardly have prophesied eminence for the author of these facile couplets, which begin happily and are brought to an end neatly, but, otherwise, are not noticeably above the ordinary level of clever parody. Although Thackeray's career at Cambridge was not academically successful, the friendships which he made among his contemporaries there had a lasting influence upon him. His special affection was reserved for William Henry Brookfield and Edward FitzGerald; but Tennyson and other members of one of the goodliest brotherhoods of which the world holds record remained his life-long friends, and the ideals of life and conduct to which Tennyson dedicated his verse, fostered among that 'band of youthful friends,' came to a maturity hardly less noble in *Esmond* and *The Newcomes*.

After leaving Cambridge, Thackeray spent a year abroad, living at Weimar from September 1830 to the following summer. Here, he laid in a stock of impressions of the life of a small German court upon which he afterwards drew freely. Schiller's poetry filled him with enthusiasm, and he met Goethe, of whom he drew two sketches. Pleasant, however, as he found his residence in Weimar, Paris, where he had joined FitzGerald for a stolen holiday at Easter 1830, was his first and most enduring love. In the autumn of 1831, he began to read law in the Middle Temple; but, on coming into £500 a year on his twenty-first birthday, he left London for Paris. His small fortune soon disappeared, partly in a bank failure. He appears to have been relieved of the rest by a gentlemanlike card-sharper, from whose society he gained some compensating advantage in material for the portraits of Deuceace and other members of the same profession. These misfortunes compelled him to live by his wits. He was divided, for a time, between his talent for easy and fluent writing and his love for drawing. In May 1833, he became proprietor of a weekly paper, *The National Standard*, and wrote or drew regularly for it for a few months. The venture, however, was a failure: after a fitful existence, the paper came to an end in February 1834. Thackeray had already returned to Paris in the previous October, with the intention of studying art. His fondness for painting was of use to him in the casual journalism on which he soon embarked, and, in *The Newcomes*, he reverted with affection to this period of his life. But his studies had no serious outcome. His natural gift of humorous draughtsmanship, however, was illustrated, in March 1836, by a series of eight caricatures of ballet-dancers, published under the title *Flore et Zéphyr*, by Théophile Wagstaff, the first of many names under which the future Michael Angelo Titmarsh and Mr Snob disguised himself. On 20 April of the same year, he married Isabella Shawe at the British embassy in Paris, apparently on the strength of his appointment as Paris correspondent to *The Constitutional*, a new radical daily, published by a company of which his step-father was chairman. His letters to this paper, signed T.T., began in September 1836 and continued till February 1837. *The Constitutional* lived little longer, and Thackeray, deprived of his salary of £400 a year, took up his abode in London at 15 Great Coram street, and began to write miscellaneous reviews and stories for the newspapers and magazines.

Before 1837, he had been an occasional contributor to *Fraser's Magazine*, and he has been credited with the authorship, as early as 1832, of a story called *Elizabeth Brownrigge*, printed in the August and September numbers for that year, which dealt ironically with the career of the notorious criminal who

> whipp'd two female prentices to death
> And hid them in the coal-hole.

There is no conclusive evidence for attributing this performance to Thackeray, although its tone bears a general likeness to that of the series of works of fiction which began with *The Yellowplush Correspondence*. His criticisms, as a reviewer, if not profound, were readable. Carlyle thought his review of *The French Revolution* in *The Times* of 3 August 1837 'rather like' its author, 'a half-monstrous Cornish giant, kind of painter, Cambridge man, and Paris newspaper correspondent, who is now writing for his life in London,' and supposed that it was 'calculated to do the book good.' A book which suited Thackeray's humour better was a manual of etiquette, *My Book, or, The Anatomy of Conduct*, by one John Henry Skelton, which he reviewed in *Fraser* for November 1837, writing under the disguise of Charles James Yellowplush, a footman whose social experience made him an exigent critic of manners, while his observations were clothed in an effective garb of judicious mis-spelling. During succeeding months, Mr Yellowplush regaled his readers with his reminiscences of service. The device of mis-spelling was by no means new, and Yellowplush's methods are too consistently ingenious to bear comparison with the well-feigned illiteracy of Win. Jenkins's spelling in *Humphry Clinker* ; but, whereas the errors of Win. Jenkins belong to pure farce, Yellowplush is a chronicler of tragedy. Eight years later, in *Punch*, his successor 'Jeames,' the speculator in railway stock and perjured lover of Mary Ann Hoggins, was the subject of an episode which is farcical from beginning to end; but the Yellowplush of *The Amours of Mr Deuceace* is the shrewd spectator of a social drama which, with all its mirth-provoking incidents, derives its motives from the most selfish and sordid qualities in human nature and culminates in the misery, appalling even to the callous flunkey, of its one approximately innocent personage. The detached point of view of the narrator and the outward eccentricity of form which he gives to his story are the artistic foil to its base passions and enhance the effect of those scenes in which the veil of irony is dropped for a moment.

Yellowplush bade a temporary 'ajew' to the world in August 1838, in his original character of literary critic, to which the household of a reputable baronet was more congenial than the precarious service of Deuceace and lord Crabs. In this last paper, he satirised with genial mischief Bulwer's sentimentality and grandiloquence. He returned to the same theme in 1840, with a diverting criticism of the flowery language of Bulwer's play, *The Sea-Captain*. Meanwhile, Thackeray had adopted a new disguise. Major Goliah O'Grady Gahagan, a new Münchausen, began to contribute his *Historical Reminiscences* of a life of adventure, adorned with much ingenious distortion of Hindustani terms, to *The New Monthly* in November 1838. Gahagan was succeeded by Ikey Solomons, junior, who lent his name to *Catherine*. Solomons, however, unlike Yellowplush and Gahagan, had no personality of his own. The narrator of *Catherine*, which appeared as a serial in *Fraser*, was Thackeray himself, bent upon demolishing a pernicious abuse of sentiment, but nervously anxious to preclude any misunderstanding of his object. His attempt was to ridicule 'with solemn sneer' the vice of ennobling crime in fiction, to which Bulwer's sophistries and Ainsworth's gift for writing a readable novel had given some popularity. Fielding's *Jonathan Wild the Great* supplied a model in which the baseness of criminal life was exposed in a mock-heroic strain, maintained with merciless thoroughness. Thackeray failed in the essential quality which such writing demands. His irony is incomplete : it is overcome by his own indignation with his characters, and is interrupted by quite unnecessary assurances that he is holding them up for contempt. Naturally, the reader whose prejudices he feared to shock sees no point in this vacillation between two opposite treatments, equally unpalatable, of a revolting subject ; while, to the elect who can relish the severe medicine of *Jonathan Wild*, his attempts to sugar his draught to the general taste are inartistic and ineffectual. Moreover, in these efforts he invested the worthless character of Catherine herself with a spurious pathos, foreign to his intention, but closely allied to that abuse against which he protested. He was far more successful when, somewhat earlier, he allowed the complacent Stubbs to relate his own autobiography in *The Fatal Boots* ; while the vulnerable point of the literary apotheosis of burglars and murderers, its want of humour, which the intermittent moralising of *Catherine* failed to touch, was reached several years later with less effort and less expenditure of pen and paper in *George de Barnwell*.

In 1840, the failure of Mrs Thackeray's health necessitated her separation from the society of her husband and their two infant daughters. This calamity curbed his ironic mood ; and it is about this time that the interplay of satiric wit with the tenderest pathos which, henceforth, was never absent from his work, begins to be noticeable. Something of this had already been discoverable in Yellowplush's instinctive compassion for the deformed Mrs Deuceace ; but her fidelity to her husband was animal, and she had none of the qualities of Caroline, heroine and victim of *A Shabby Genteel Story*, which Thackeray contributed to *Fraser* in 1840. Long afterwards, Caroline's mature simplicity of character, enriched with sound common sense, shone more brightly in *The Adventures of Philip*. In the earlier story, she plays a passive *rôle* amid her unattractive surroundings, the shabbiness of which is enhanced by the intrusion of the crapulous lord Cinqbars and his Oxford friends. These devotees of pleasure belong to a class which Thackeray satirised freely, partly, no doubt, for the benefit of the middle-class reader. Their foibles, however, although strongly emphasised, are not caricatured, and George Brandon, the villain of the piece, is not without his moments of generous sentiment. While Thackeray was fully alive to the distresses of the virtuous Caroline, his appreciation of contrast enabled him to draw her drunken father, her odious mother and step-sisters and the conspirators who wreck her happiness, with gusto and even with sympathy ; just as Yellowplush, while able to pity Mrs Deuceace, was equally able to admire the guile of her husband. Similarly, in *The Great Hoggarty Diamond*, written for *Fraser* in 1841, the simple pathos of the struggles and bereavements of Samuel Titmarsh and his young wife is balanced by the antipathetic portraiture of Mrs Hoggarty and the swindling Mr Brough. It is not un-natural that, to enhance the effect of Brough's subtlety, the honesty of his victims should be so freely underlined that it bears some relation to credulous stupidity. There is a humour, keenly apparent to Thackeray's temperament, in the precarious existence of rascals who live upon intrigue and subterfuge, which is wanting in the sorrows and trials of more straightforward natures. Of his personal preference for virtue, there can be no question ; but, while his virtuous characters are not seldom insipid, his scoundrels, with few exceptions, are singularly amusing.

The pseudonym of Michael Angelo Titmarsh, which was assumed by the author of *The Great Hoggarty Diamond*, and had been first used in 1840 for *The Paris Sketch Book*, also appeared, in 1841, on the title-page of *Comic Tales and Sketches* as the name of the editor of *The Yellowplush Correspondence, Major Gahagan* and other previously published stories. In *Fraser* of June 1842, Thackeray took the name George Savage Fitz-Boodle. For the *Confessions* of this middle-aged clubman, a younger son without a fixed profession, he drew freely upon his German experiences, and autobiography may have been mingled with farce in these records of misdirected affection. The impressionable Fitz-Boodle supplemented his reminiscences of German damsels in *Men's Wives*, a series of which the longest and most important member was *The Ravenswing*. Unequal and hastily written as is this story, and although its most laughable incident, the evening ride of Mr Eglantine beside the carriage which took Mrs and Miss Crump and Mr Woolsey home from Richmond, is, confessedly, not wholly original, it contains one of Thackeray's most diverting adventurers, captain Howard (or Hooker) Walker, the promoter of the scheme for draining the Pontine marshes, while the portrait of the British composer Sir George Thrum anticipates the best chapters of *The Book of Snobs*. In January 1844, Fitz-Boodle, playing the part of editor, began to supply *Fraser* with the remarkable auto-biography called *The Luck of Barry Lyndon*, Thackeray's most substantial work of fiction before *Vanity Fair*. An Irish adven-turer, Redmond Barry, fallen upon evil days, tells the story of his

life, his calf-love for his cousin Nora, his flight from home after
a duel in which he is deluded into believing that he has killed his
man, his career as a soldier of fortune, his meeting with his uncle
the chevalier de Balibari, his desertion from the Prussian army,
his wanderings as a gamester, his flirtation and marriage with the
wealthy lady Lyndon, his miserable married life and his final
defeat at the hands of the woman whom he has beguiled and
ill-treated. Apology forms no part of this record : like Stubbs in
The Fatal Boots, Barry is satisfied with himself and disgusted
with a world in which he has been the sport of chance. Nor does
he leave us altogether disgusted with him : if he is impudent, he
is, at any rate, no coward, and he and his uncle the chevalier are
the most companionable people in a society whose prevailing
passion is cold selfishness. They are genuinely attached to each
other : the old rascal is proud of the young one, and, while Barry
himself richly deserved his fate, it is a relief to know that the
chevalier, at last, was able to devote himself to the practice of
piety in the Minorite convent at Brussels. It is only towards the
close of the book and after the death of his spoiled child, which
provokes a sincere outburst of grief, that Barry altogether forfeits
our sympathy. While he quite convinces us that 'if any woman
deserved a strait-waistcoat, it was my Lady Lyndon,' his frank
disclosure of his brutality to that vain and selfish woman and her
son leaves him without excuse. If, in *Catherine,* Thackeray felt
his subject too disagreeable for consistent irony, he felt that
Barry Lyndon was too entertaining a scoundrel to be made
wholly detestable. The revelations of his conduct as a husband,
possibly intended as an antidote to the easy-going narrative of
his earlier career, occur at a point where the story has already
reached its height. The tragedy of the ducal court of X—— displays Thackeray's powers of telling a story with a historical
complexion at their best ; and, after this digression is passed, the
tale of Barry's misdeeds is resumed with less energy and more
prolixity.

The period 1840—4 produced, also, *The Paris Sketch Book*
(1840), *The Irish Sketch Book* (1843) and Thackeray's earliest
contributions to *Punch. The Paris Sketch Book* was a *réchauffé*
of miscellaneous tales, criticisms and essays with a general bearing
upon French life and manners. Their chief recommendation is
that easy and simple style which Thackeray used without effort,
taking his reader at once into his confidence. Success in conversation owes much to diplomatic precaution, and it is possible

that Thackeray remembered this fact too well. At all events, his frequent exhibitions of impatience and even disgust at French characteristics which may irritate or shock the Briton are somewhat forced. He protests too much, as if to assure his public that a liking for Paris has not shaken his insular convictions. Personal prejudice, however, is clearly visible in such articles as *The Fêtes of July* and in *The Second Funeral of Napoleon*, published separately in 1841. Emotional display roused his sense of the contrast between sham and reality. Victor Hugo's poetic appeal to Louis-Philippe on behalf of Barbès struck him merely as a theatrical flourish of rhetoric : it quite escaped him that the spirit which dictated it was as natural to a Frenchman as it was foreign to English ways of thought. George Sand's utopian visions offended his commonsense, although he admired her 'exquisite prose.' As a critic of literature, his appreciation was always limited by considerations which have little bearing upon purely literary merit, and it is not surprising to find that the French novelists of manners whom he selected for his approval were by no means of the first class. We are invited to the perusal of long extracts from Charles de Bernard, 'without risk of lighting upon any such horrors as Balzac or Dumas has provided for us.' It is strange to think that anyone could have preferred these easily written, but somewhat insipid, passages to the 'horrors' of *Le Père Goriot*, *Béatrix*, *Eugénie Grandet*, or *Le Curé de Tours*, from all of which it would have been possible for Thackeray to select.

The Irish Sketch Book, a consecutive record of travel in Ireland, contains much delightful observation of the ways of a people in whom Thackeray found abundance of material for his novels, and is full of picturesque and accurate appreciation of Irish scenery. Thackeray's sense of natural beauty and his skill in describing what he saw were not mingled with any high poetic feeling, but are often overlooked in the contemplation of the human interest which overshadows the other qualities of his work. His Irishmen—captain Costigan, Redmond Barry and the Mulligan—are not the most creditable members of their nation. But, while their weaknesses are enlarged upon to the verge of caricature, they are treated with considerable sympathy. It amused Thackeray to be with them : he enjoyed their good-humour, even where their generosity gratified itself at the expense of others ; and, far from disliking them, as those who miss the point of his humour are apt to argue, he leaned too readily to the amiable error into which Englishmen habitually fall of regarding Irishmen as pathetic repositories of unconscious humour. His observations on the state of the country are tinged with that patronage which the inhabitant of a land of progress carries into benighted and backward districts, and Irishmen, witty themselves and ready to be the cause of wit in other men, are able to appreciate them at their true value.

Thackeray began to contribute to *Punch* in July 1842 with *Miss Tickletoby's Lectures on English History*. This dispiriting beginning was followed by a long succession of contributions, some trifling and indifferent, others, such as the revival of Yellowplush's mannerisms in *Jeames's Diary* (1845) and the parodies of *Mr Punch's Prize Novelists* (1847), brimming over with ludicrous invention. *A Legend of the Rhine*, written for Cruikshank's *Table Book* in 1845, was the first of the mock-heroic medieval tales which include *Barbazure* and the inimitable *Rebecca and Rowena*. A tour to the east in 1844 was recorded in *Notes of a Journey from Cornhill to Grand Cairo* (1846), a medley, after the manner of *The Irish Sketch Book*, of pleasant observation and criticism of men and countries, with much lively description. During 1846 and the beginning of 1847, he wrote for *Punch* the papers entitled *The Snobs of England, by one of themselves*, afterwards published as *The Book of Snobs*. But, while the *Snob* papers were approaching completion, the monthly numbers of *Vanity Fair* were beginning to appear from the office of *Punch*.

On the covers of *Vanity Fair*, the Titmarsh of the *Sketch Books*, the Jeames and Mr Snob of *Punch*, used his real name. His Protean changes of pseudonym may have had the effect of obscuring the reputation which his miscellaneous work deserved, and it was not until the new novel was well advanced in its serial course that it arrested popular interest. Much of the mass of writing which Thackeray had produced during the ten years which preceded *Vanity Fair* was purely fugitive : much is even flat and poor in quality. But he had acquired practice in a style which, allowing for its impatience of minor correctnesses of phrase and for some looseness of construction, is the perfection of natural ease. The history and literature of the eighteenth century exercised a spell over him which lent an attraction to *Barry Lyndon* over and above the adventures of the hero. The combination of character-drawing with narrative and genial comment in *The Book of Snobs* traced its ancestry directly to *The Spectator* : the familiar tone of these essays, in which the barrier of literary convention is broken down and Mr Snob talks at his ease with an audience of average education, is that of the eighteenth-century essayists, smooth and graceful. It would be useless to claim any eighteenth-century author as definitely the parent of a style which was Thackeray's birthright: his kinship to the writers of this period was one of predilection and natural sentiment. In Fielding's tolerant view of life he found the closest response to his own feelings, his appreciation of generosity and hatred of meanness. Just as he fell short, however, of Fielding's pitiless consistency of irony, so, in his confidences to his readers, he had less of the assured superiority with which Fielding 'seems to bring his arm-chair to the proscenium and chat with us in all the lusty ease of his fine English.' Fielding makes himself at home with us with a condescension which we welcome, treating us to conversation and criticism which are free from all extremes of passion and senti-mentality, and judging character upon the broad basis of its merits without insisting upon casual detail. Mr Snob, on the other hand, runs the risk of being dismissed as an intruder. He constitutes himself the critic of a society of which he assumes that snobbishness, 'the mean admiration of mean things,' is the master passion. No detail escapes his eye. The hospitality of the Ponto household is not sacred to him: he dissects with unsparing minute-ness the pretentiousness which sacrifices comfort to position. The sherry is marsala, the gin hollands, the groom who acts as footman has dirty hands and smells of the stable. Not that Mr Snob is blind to the pathetic aspect of these subterfuges. It is im-possible, nevertheless, to dwell, however lightly and amusingly, upon such trifles without a feeling of contempt; and this feeling is a constant corrective to pathos. While he anatomises snob-bishness, its characteristic signs delight and feed his humour. He may assail it with invective or cover its victims with sympathy, but the pettinesses which he uncloaks and condemns are essential to his amusement.

In *Vanity Fair*, the influence of Thackeray's long apprentice-ship to fiction is felt in the sureness of touch with which he describes the manners of a large and various group of *dramatis personae* and unites the diverse elements of the story. His ability to reproduce the life of a special period never flags: the scene never changes into dullness or inactivity; and long practice in the anatomy of social eccentricities and familiarity with special types of character are apparent even in the least important figures of his stage. The book was planned and written more carefully than his later novels : it has more unity and less tendency to digression, while following his usual plan of a chronicle extending over a considerable period of years. All the groups which compose its world—the Crawleys, the Sedleys, the Osbornes, lord Steyne and his led captains, even the O'Dowds—are united under the dazzling influence of Becky Sharp. She gives the book the cardinal interest which is wanting in all but one of its successors ; and, even in *Esmond,* that interest belongs, not to a single character, but to the mutual relations of a group of persons. From the first chapter it is evident that, if the amiability of the tale is to be the monopoly of the fortunate and beloved Amelia, the despised and scornful Becky will supply its dramatic excitement. Their temperaments develop upon inevitable lines. Amelia, with less than the average amount of intellect and with virtues that are mainly negative, is the foil to Becky, who, with cleverness and courage as her only virtues, wins more sympathy than she deserves because these qualities are conspicuously lacking in Amelia. Her cleverness, it is true, defeats its own ends ; but her disasters bring her courage and resource into play, while Amelia becomes irritable and capricious under misfortune. Becky plays her game without a confederate : her husband, so long as he trusts her, is merely her blind agent. She overdoes her part in her initial experiment with Jos Sedley. At Queen's Crawley, her diplomacy again overreaches itself, and she snatches at a clandestine marriage with a younger son, when, by waiting a little, she might have married the father. After her marriage, she engages out of pure mischief in a pointless *liaison* with Amelia's coxcomb of a husband. Her conquest of a reluctant society, a feat of generalship achieved by the exercise of personal attractions and a ready wit, is rendered useless by her disastrous relations with lord Steyne. So brilliant has been her career up to this point that we could well be spared the history of her later wanderings and her final assault upon Jos Sedley's fortunes, with the dark suspicion which clouds its success. Her cause, all through, is her own selfish comfort, but the resourcefulness with which she champions it compels admiration. Those who are alive to the conventional limitations of Thackeray's world beside the primitive unrestraint of the world of Balzac's prodigal imagination contrast her, to her disadvantage, with her contemporary, Valérie Marneffe. The answer to their objections is Becky's confession that she could have been a good woman with five thousand a year. In spite of her hereditary drawbacks, which Steyne coarsely flung in her face in the hour of their joint discomfiture, her ideal is a discreet respectability, and her intrigues are the means to the attainment of an assured position. Madame Marneffe was entirely free from any such ideal: in her most prosperous days, there could have been no question of her unfitness for the saloons of Gaunt house; and the decorous twilight of Becky's retirement at Cheltenham would have been impossible for the woman whose last aspiration was *à faire le bon Dieu* with the methods that had enchained her mortal lovers. Further, while Becky fights her own battle and Rawdon Crawley and the watchdog Briggs are only pawns in her game, Valérie is a deadly weapon employed by the diabolical intelligence of Lisbeth Fischer, to whose part in the story she is always secondary. To admit, however, that Becky admires and covets the blamelessness of the British matron is not to give her credit for a possible attainment of disinterested virtue. Sincerity is alien to her nature. The only genuine tears which she is recorded to have shed came from her disappointment that she had married Rawdon and missed a shorter cut to fortune; and her only charitable act, the disclosure to Amelia of George's infidelity, was prompted more by her irritation at Amelia's obtuseness than by any desire to give the patient Dobbin the reward of his long devotion.

Vanity Fair is 'a novel without a hero,' and neither the virtues nor the vices of its characters are of a heroic order. They are, for the most part, selfish people, bent upon following their pleasures, if they can afford them, or devoted to the task of keeping up appearances if they cannot. Money and rank mean everything to Mr Osborne, with his pompous parade of dull cynicism, to the elder Sir Pitt, who, from a consciously cynical point of view, affects to disregard them, to his needy brother and sister-in-law at the rectory, to his genially malicious sister at Brighton and to his intolerable son, the would-be statesman and stupid tyrant of his household. With rank as its only asset, the house of Bareacres can ruin its creditors with impunity. Lord Steyne's rank and wealth excuse his vices to a lenient world. Upon this point, the analyst of snobbery laid almost excessive emphasis. The spectacle of earthen pots competing in the same stream with stouter vessels is attractive to the critical onlooker, and the progress of so finely wrought a masterpiece as Becky, fatal to objects of less well tempered clay, must be arrested by a collision to which it can offer no resistance. Against lord Steyne's invulnerable hardness and selfishness, aided by their external advantages, Becky cannot hope to compete successfully. It was her greatest mistake and misfortune that she could not keep out of his way. It has become customary to contrast Steyne unfavourably with Disraeli's more urbane portrait of lord Monmouth in *Coningsby*, principally because the same nobleman suggested both pictures. Beyond this historical identity there is not much ground for the antithesis. Steyne plays a part in *Vanity Fair* which could not have been played by Disraeli's accomplished patron of the arts and profound man of the world, the connoisseur, not the slave, of passion. It was necessary to make him something of a monster, to exaggerate his callous sensuality, to accentuate his repulsive features and his hoarse 'brava.' At the same time, it cost Thackeray some trouble to reconcile the satyr whose vices meet with poetic justice in the famous scene with Becky and Rawdon, and the tyrant who bullies his wife and daughter with a vulgarity more suited to Mr Osborne, with the nobleman of birth and breeding who played some part in the history of his time, and, even in the hour of his decay, sat at prince Polonia's table, 'a greater prince than any there.' The irony with which his death is recorded, with the full parade of his honours and titles, is stinging enough in the vehemence with which it pours scorn upon greatness without goodness ; but it reminds us, also, that Steyne's position, in the eyes of the world, could hardly have been achieved without some qualities to compensate for the insolent debauchery which has been offered hitherto for our exclusive contemplation.

While humour, at its best, is as keenly conscious of the pathos, as of the ludicrous aspect, of life, the humourist's sense of the ludicrous, as we have seen in the case of *The Great Hoggarty Diamond*, is apt to check his unreserved appreciation of the pathetic. A betrayed and suffering Clarissa was beyond Thackeray : the Little Sister of *Philip*, his nearest approach to this type of character, has an appreciation of comedy which goes far to compensate her for her misfortunes. Where his virtuous personages are without a sense of comedy, they are without heroic qualities. They submit too readily to circumstances : they lay themselves down willingly to be passed over by the less scrupulous. It may be suspected that Thackeray originally intended to make Amelia as consistently lovable as her schoolfellows found her. But, as the character developed, it resisted all his efforts to conceal the growing distaste which he felt for its insipidity, and he took no pains to protect her against the inevitable contrast with Becky. As a family, the Sedleys, who live easily in the sunshine, offer no resistance to misfortune ; and Amelia, widowed and reduced to a narrow existence, loses her charm. When Thackeray mentions her with affection, it is with the perfunctory appreciation which the conscientious person feels it right to pay to deserving characters with whom he is out of sympathy. No good intentions can conceal that she is stupid. With regard to her long-suffering admirer Dobbin, while Thackeray rated his constancy and self-effacement at their full value, he laid excessive stress upon his awkwardness and shyness. It is one thing to be reminded that the unpolished Dobbin is of more sterling worth than the graceful George Osborne, that he is a gentleman and Osborne is not ; but the contrast is pressed home too hard. The very name Dobbin is against any exalted exhibition of heroism ; and, while it is honest William's fate to feel too deeply, his outward man is always getting in the way and affording material for the satire or impatience of less obtrusive and more superficially accomplished people. Again, lady Jane Crawley has too much of the silly simplicity of the animal alluded to in her maiden name. She rises to the occasion when her brother-in-law needs her help, but her conduct in that famous scene is strikingly at variance with her usual passivity, and the transformation which it works upon the brutalised Rawdon is almost as surprising as one of those passages in Beaumont and Fletcher or Massinger, where the pure heroine confounds the ruffian of the piece by an unexpected assertion of her persuasive influence. When she follows up this action by daring to defy Sir Pitt, she is less of a ministering angel and more of a woman ; but, even then, her show of temper is hardly in keeping with the abnormal docility with which she bears the yoke of her marriage to a fool. Thackeray's susceptibility to the inherent beauty of the common relationships and duties of daily life is declared in many passages of exquisite prose, which turn the laughter of one moment into the tears of the next ; but, in dealing with characters which depend for their life upon their capacity for such sentiment, he was hampered by the uncomfortable consciousness that it is from similar material that the cheap effects of sentimental fiction are produced. And the sentimental reader, feeling this restraint and failing to see the open dislike of mere sickliness and lachrymosity which causes it, attributes it to a persistent tendency to underrate goodness, and dismisses Thackeray as a cynic laughing in his sleeve at qualities of which this type of critic can appreciate only the unreal shadow.

The objective and impartial nature of Thackeray's character-drawing must be clear to any reader of *Vanity Fair* who watches

the effect upon himself of the gradual unrolling of the careers
of its principal personages. They come before us like the casual
acquaintances of ordinary life: we may feel instinctive affinities
or repulsions, but we suspend our judgment till we get to know
them better, with the consciousness that the novelist is in the
same position as ourselves. As he writes, his characters discover
themselves to him: he becomes the interpreter of events which
lie beyond his conscious control. If this is obvious in *Vanity
Fair*, it is even more obvious in *Pendennis*, the opening number
of which was published in November 1848. Ostensibly a biography
of Arthur Pendennis, written in the third person by himself, its
interest lies not so much in the hero, whose importance chiefly
depends upon the close resemblance of his early career to Thackeray's own, as in the world of individual types which passes under
his eye. Pendennis is a careless young gentleman, quite satisfied
with himself and the world, running out of one escapade into
another with the assurance that all will come right in the end,
and fully aware that, in the event of bankruptcy of fortune or
reputation, he has the fund of his mother's and cousin's affection
to draw upon. Thackeray's early Bohemianism and humorous
appreciation of follies of which, doubtless, he had had his own share
tinged the portrait with leniency, but Pendennis is so sure of his
position as a lord of creation that only his talent as a chronicler
preserves our patience with him. Of the persons most intimately
concerned with him, his mother and Laura, perhaps, fill more space
than their individualities actually claim. It is a foregone conclusion that, even though the early admiration of the little girl
for her patronising cousin gives way to criticism of the spoiled
darling who takes his mother's love as his unquestioned birthright,
Laura will be ready, eventually, to take him to her heart. She is,
however, natural, not without charm and a faithful portrait of
maidenly propriety without a shadow of prudish insincerity.
By the side of Blanche Amory, that bundle of diverting affectations
mingled with shrewishness and sinister vulgarity, Laura does not
suffer the eclipse into which Amelia falls by the side of Becky.
Helen, on the other hand, is inconceivably good. Only her British
prejudices, which occasionally provoke her into human annoyance,
save her from a perfection unattainable by human nature. Her
patience, indeed, is not so extraordinarily tolerant as that of
Adeline in *La Cousine Bette*, whose incurable habit of forgiveness
is almost a vice, nor, in an atmosphere whose moral values are
pitched in a more normal key, has it to face trials so colossal; but it

is so unvarying that her son was almost justified in regarding it as a fair object for provocation. The wisdom of motherhood is sacrificed to Helen's saintly forbearance : in a mother less super-human, resentment might have added its embittering force to affection, but Helen continues to idolise her son. The society of his sister-in-law must have been an intolerable strain upon major Pendennis, the one person who is capable of making the debonair Arthur thoroughly ashamed of himself—for Laura's efforts are discountable in the certainty of her eventual condonation of the prodigal. The major is the leading portrait of the novel. He is the first person who appears in it, and, from the time when he intervenes in his nephew's love affair with Miss Fotheringay, his worldly wisdom is at hand to provide the wayward Arthur with help from a more practical, if less innocent, point of view than that of Helen. His philosophy of life, founded upon the contemplation of a society of which his friend lord Steyne was a chief ornament, is not exalted; but its cynical expression does not prevent a respect for less worldly ideals, not without some surprise at those who prefer them, from intruding into his conduct and conversation. As ambassador and mentor he displays consummate tact. He knows his part too well to treat his pupil as a mere child or to show his apprehensions to the opponents whom he has to disarm by conciliation and adroit flattery. His prompt recognition of the shrewd Foker as a man of the world at once enlists the services of that connoisseur in human nature, whose own philosophy is doomed to suffer defeat under the killing glances of Blanche Amory. The attempt of Morgan to blackmail the major, although, in itself, a somewhat theatrical episode, the object of which is to help in unravelling the complications of the chief characters, brings out conclusively the major's ability to fight his own battles.

Plot is a somewhat negligible quantity in *Pendennis*, and the part played by the ruffianly Altamont, Amory, or Armstrong, in bringing the story to a satisfactory conclusion, is purely conventional. The Clavering household, whose unstable fortunes he threatens, is our means of communication with the Chevalier Strong, the most gallant and lovable of Thackeray's adventurers, and with the Begum, an excellent study in innocently vulgar amiability; but the debauched and hysterical Sir Francis is too contemptible to be interesting, and Blanche's poses are too patent to have been tolerable in real life. Blanche, however, is prolific in amusement, and Thackeray devoted himself to enlarging upon her traits with that power of ludicrous invention which he exercised upon the objects that diverted him most. It was at this time that he was beginning to produce his *Christmas Books,* and the types described and drawn by pen and pencil in *Mrs Perkins's Ball* and *Our Street,* with mingled truth and extravagance, are to be recognised over and over again in his longer works. Without the fixity of plan with which Balzac created a coherent world in *La Comédie Humaine,* Thackeray liked to allow the characters of one novel to move across the scene of another and to invest them with the bond of interest in a common society. This was done casually and without strict attention to accuracy, and, as time went on, with much less inventive power. The variety and freshness of *Pendennis,* however, are remarkable. While it includes a character so extravagant as the French cook Mirobolant, with his ideal passion for Blanche and his consecration of his art to her virginal allurements, it introduces us, also, to the premature sage Harry Foker, in his flowered dressing-gown, 'neat, but not in the least gaudy,' to the genial and disreputable Costigan, who was to rouse colonel Newcome's indignation at a later day, to the forlornly faithful Bows, to captain Shandon, who, modelled upon Thackeray's knowledge of the versatile Maginn, presided over the inception of Pendennis's *Pall Mall Gazette,* and to George Warrington, scholar and humourist, concealing the tragedy of his life and, somewhat ineffectually, his noble tenderness and selfishness beneath a gruff uncouthness of exterior.

The *History of Henry Esmond,* published in 1852, is connected with *Pendennis* by the very slight bond of its hero's relationship to George Warrington. Thackeray had already displayed his predilection for history in *Barry Lyndon* and in the historical setting of portions of *Vanity Fair.* In *Esmond,* he applied his powers to a drama of the close of the seventeenth and beginning of the eighteenth century, with a wide knowledge of the social and literary history of the age. He was guilty of a certain number of anachronisms; for, while Scott's lordly inattention to chronology was not acceptable to Thackeray's idea of the historical novel, his conscientiousness did not carry him to the length of verifying his references with the painful care of George Eliot. But he had an advantage over other writers of historical fiction in the fact that his style adapted itself admirably to the art of telling a tale of the past in language suited to the supposed time of action. The love of Esmond for Beatrix, his gradual disillusionment, his recognition of the love that may be his for the asking, are told in language that is no mere attempt to recover the vanished graces of an archaic literary form, but is Thackeray's own spontaneous English, always akin to that of his eighteenth-century models, and wrought by his vivid imagination of the past into conformity with the style of his chosen period. Esmond, even in using the third person, has a difficult story to tell; for the situation on which his narrative is founded is a change of sentiment in a heart as honourable as that of Dobbin, and it is further complicated by the fact that his marriage with lady Castlewood, after his long devotion to her daughter, is not that retreat upon a sure stronghold which Pendennis, after his flirtation with Blanche, made to the willing Laura, but is the true reward of his deserts. Thackeray's complete sympathy with his hero enables Esmond to tell the story without affectation or egotism: it even surmounted the dangers of the delicate experiment of making daughter and mother the successive objects of the same man's love. His restrained humour, which allowed him to smile compassionately at Esmond's infatuation for Beatrix, endowed him with the double gift of seeing life through Esmond's eyes and from his own point of view at the same time; and, where Esmond must, of necessity, exercise reticence at the risk of being misunderstood, Thackeray's appreciation of the position suggests those touches and turns of phrase which reveal the truth. If Esmond was misled by the fen-fire of Beatrix's attractions, there are few of his readers who, on the first sight of Beatrix descending the staircase, candle in hand, in all the splendour of her young beauty, have not fallen under that spell. And its removal, as he awakens to her heartlessness and mercenary ambition, is told with a warmth of sentiment, far removed from sentimentality, which carries the reader with it. This story of love and self-sacrifice, set in an atmosphere of history which has its unobtrusive influence upon the plot, is the most perfectly conceived and carried out of Thackeray's novels. The style, if more carefully studied than usual, shows no abatement of its charm. Seldom in English literature has the emotion founded upon the ties of relationship and friendship in everyday life, and hard to describe because it is natural and common, been touched so skilfully or with such truth to nature as in the gentle gravity of Henry Esmond; and even the most intransigent sceptic, with *Esmond* before him, is forced to confess that its 'cynical' author had visions of a world of which meanness and pretentiousness were not the ruling passions.

During the period from 1847 to 1852, Thackeray reached the

height of his fame. *Vanity Fair* had brought him into sudden renown, and, from that time, he shared with Dickens the pre-eminence in contemporary fiction. In 1846, after six years of living in lodgings, first in Jermyn street and afterwards at 88 St James's street, where most of *Vanity Fair* was written, he made a home for himself and his daughters at a house in Young street, Kensington, from which he moved, in 1853, to 36 Onslow square. Until 1852, he continued to be a frequent contributor to *Punch*, and, at this time, his ingenuity in writing light verse, abounding in quaint rimes and ludicrous conceits, was freely exercised. If *The Ballads of Policeman X* are not poetry, they are, at any rate, some of the most spontaneous expressions in rime of the humour which can find food for merriment in the prose of ordinary life ; and Thackeray's more serious verse, unambitious of the higher achievements of lyric poetry, embodies a kindly philosophy, fostered by his favourite Horace, which touches the deeper chords of feeling lightly and gracefully. From Christmas to Christmas appeared the series of books beginning in 1847 with *Mrs Perkins's Ball*, in which Mr Titmarsh commented, with the aid of his pencil, upon the eccentricities of his social surroundings. In 1850, the same guile-less author took his readers abroad in *The Kickleburys on the Rhine* and excelled his earlier *Legend of the Rhine* in *Rebecca and Rowena*, to which Richard Doyle supplied the illustrations. The versatile Michael Angelo himself, however, illustrated the last and best of *Christmas Books, The Rose and the Ring* (1855), a perpetual joy to the 'great and small children' to whom it was dedicated. Fresh from the writing of *Pendennis*, Thackeray, in 1851, succumbed to the temptation of lecturing. His lectures entitled *The English Humourists of the Eighteenth Century*, first delivered at Willis's rooms in the summer of that year, and in America, at the end of 1852 and beginning of 1853, were, financially, very profitable. As criticism, they can hardly be said to do justice to the literary side of their subjects : they are simply Thackeray's impressions of men whom he judged through their works as he judged the characters of his novels. The simple rule of life which he laid down with earnest emphasis in the epilogue to *Dr Birch and his Young Friends,*

Who misses, or who wins the prize ?
Go, lose and conquer as you can:
But if you fail, or if you rise,
Be each, pray God, a gentleman,

is not, however, a safe criterion for the impartial estimate of literary worth. Thackeray's severe condemnation of Swift is more than unjust : his disgust with Sterne's indecency and habit of pose naturally obscures his discernment of the qualities which made *Tristram Shandy* an influence far beyond the bounds of England; while the author of *Joseph Andrews* and *Tom Jones* needs no defence because he shared the habits of his age. The moralist was too prominent in his second series of lectures, *The Four Georges,* delivered in the United States and London in 1855 and 1856. Thackeray could not fail to be interesting in his dealings with the eighteenth century. But the memory of George IV had not yet passed into the remoteness of history, and, by training and conviction, Thackeray belonged to the party which had seen in 'George the Good, the Magnificent, the Great' an object for savage detestation ; and, if the loyalty with which Scott bent before his august patron in his lifetime was extravagant, it was, at any rate, mingled with an appreciation of his princely tastes and qualities to which Thackeray was blind.

Meanwhile, *The Newcomes* had run its serial course from October 1853 to August 1855, under the ostensible editorship of Pendennis, domesticated with his Laura and fortified by personal experience in the task of piloting stormy youth to the sheltered haven of middle life. The habit of digression is more confirmed in *The Newcomes* than in any previous work; but one can hardly blame the desultoriness which elaborated the sympathetic portrait of Florac and strayed from the main current of the story to enlarge upon the wiles of the duchesse d'Ivry. The manifold happenings of the novel have their centre in the fortunes of Clive Newcome, and the device by which these are saved, the discovery of a will in a book, is mechanical. But Clive himself is much the least interesting member of his family : his excellent instincts, frequent errors and alternations of mood between gaiety and sulkiness excite sympathy, but the character is a type of which Thackeray had written much under other names, and its individual strength is not enough to obscure the fact that it exists for other purposes than its own sake. The contrast between the stately Sir Brian and the agricultural Hobson, the oblique references of Mrs Hobson in Bryanstone square to lady Ann in Park lane, the impecunious Honeyman's devices for his own precarious comfort, and the devotion of his admirable sister to the comfort of others, are individual traits of a stronger kind than any which Clive possesses.

The unpleasant Barnes is too much of a monster : his brutality, amounting to insanity, is somewhat overdrawn to balance the virtues of the more deserving branch of his family. His maternal relations, however, his grandmother lady Kew and his cousin the earl, play a more natural part in the tale. Kew, faults and all, is honourable and lovable, and lady Kew is the most perfectly drawn of Thackeray's worldly and cynical old women, sometimes almost terrible in their disregard of scruple and in the tyranny with which they alleviate the dreariness of their old age. But, if lady Kew is intimidating, she is, at all events, a more pleasant object of contemplation than Clive's vulgar mother-in-law, Mrs Mackenzie, whose transformation from a scheming but commonplace widow of some attractions in her better days to the compound of harpy and fury of her days of adversity makes some of the later chapters of the book intolerably painful. As for her daughter, the ill-fated Rosey, perplexed between her mother's violence and Clive's moodiness, her individuality is that of the light-hearted nonentity of ordinary life, who needs the stay of a perfect devotion to support her through the troubles she is incapable of meeting on her own account.

But the colonel and Ethel are the two portraits on which the fame of *The Newcomes* rests. Ethel, if her artistic presentation is less striking than that of Becky Sharp and Beatrix, redeems Thackeray from the charge of inability to draw a good woman. Amelia was inferior and insignificant, Laura was shadowy, Helen could have been effectual only as an angel and even lady Castle-wood was better suited to another sphere than a troublesome world which tried her temper. Ethel is perfectly adapted to our planet : she has her caprices and contradictory moods, all the capacity for making mistakes and inflicting unconscious injury which belongs to pride and high spirits. The trouble which she can cause to others is fully atoned for by the unhappiness which she can inflict on herself; and the period of trial through which she passes strengthens a nature too true and honourable to be deluded and spoiled by flattery and by ambition of the mere externals of success. Colonel Newcome's character, on the other hand, is free from the complications which beset Ethel. From the evening when he rebuked old Costigan at the Cave of Harmony to the last scene when 'he, whose heart was as that of a little child, had answered to his name, and stood in the presence of the Master,' his attitude to the world is perfectly simple. It cannot be said that he is drawn entirely without blemishes. He had knowledge of the world, and the trustfulness which survived this knowledge is sometimes incredible; in his period of financial success, he runs the risk of being condemned as ostentatious. It was a dangerous experiment to put so guileless a chevalier in the position of a promoter of a fraudulent company; and it might be argued that his martyrdom at the hands of Mrs Mackenzie is a cruel expedient adopted to enhance the effect of a nobly pathetic climax. However this may be, the colonel's simplicity, detestable to Barnes Newcome, mere quixotism in the eyes of Sir Brian and Hobson, wins the instinctive respect and love of all who, like Ethel, Martha Honeyman, Florac and the erratic Frederick Bayham, are capable of generous emotion. His character responds to those ideals which were the contemporary theme of the poetry of Tennyson; it awakened the enthusiasm, expressed by Burne-Jones, of the young band of poets and artists who were producing *The Oxford and Cambridge Magazine*; and it endowed English literature with the most lifelike picture of a man governed in all his actions by an absolutely direct sense of honour and duty, with a complete absence of self-consciousness.

In July 1857, Thackeray followed colonel Newcome's example by standing as a liberal candidate for a seat in parliament. The electors of Oxford rejected him by 67 votes, thereby doing probably little disservice to politics. His best work in letters had been done, it is true. His fund of invention was not inexhaustible, and, in his early journalistic work, he had shown a tendency to repeat himself, even in his fertile gift of coining appropriate names for his humorous types. *The Virginians*, appearing in serial parts from November 1857 to September 1859, was a chronicle of the descendants of Henry Esmond, the American Warringtons to whom Pendennis's friend traced his ancestry. There is no falling-off in the matter of style. Thackeray wrote as freely as ever, dropping, with all his accomplished ease, from narrative into reflective digressions, which, if they interrupt the story, are, themselves, as lightly broken off in turn. The general construction, however, is even more careless than usual, and there are portions of the book in which the situations are so prolonged that action seems to hang fire altogether. The brothers George and Harry Warrington are spectators, as their grandfather had been, of stirring historical events; but the elements of history and fiction are less successfully blended than in *Esmond*. Washington and Wolfe are felt as excrescences upon the story: that one is the friend and adviser of Madam Warrington and the other the intimate of the father of Theo and Hetty Lambert is not enough to give them an indispensable connection with the chief actors. The exigencies of the historical setting are so severely felt that the concluding chapters are little more than an appendix devoted to the American war of independence. Moreover, while the grandsons of colonel Esmond are two very pretty young men, united, even when outwardly opposed, by a firm bond of sincere affection, it must be owned that Harry, with some of George's brains, would have been less of a blockhead, and George, with a compensating quantity of Harry's insouciance, would escape the imputation of being something of a prig. Theo and Hetty are charming examples of a type which Thackeray, devotedly attached to his own daughters, drew with tender affection. But, without the family of Castlewood, *The Virginians* would be a pale and fatigued performance after *Esmond* and *The Newcomes*. After Harry, standing upon the bridge at Castlewood, has seen his cousins return to their home in their coach-and-six, followed by the chariot that bore the baroness Bernstein, 'a stout, high-coloured lady, with a very dark pair of eyes,' and has received their dubious welcome to the house of his ancestors, the long digression in which the antecedents of his visit to England are related finds us impatient to know more of the children of the boy to whom Esmond had unswervingly resigned his own rightful inheritance. The sins of the fathers have overtaken the children : lord Castlewood is a polite swindler, his brother Will is a boor and blackleg, while his sisters have achieved a notoriety conspicuous even in an age tolerant of scandal. Nevertheless, the fortunes of this doomed household awaken interest and pity. Lord Castlewood retains his breeding and has not wholly renounced acquaintance with the virtues which he does not practise ; while lady Maria's frustrated attempt to ensnare her young and susceptible cousin with her autumnal attractions, and her eventual infatuation for the actor whom she marries are the theme of a comedy with a strong element of pathos. But the presiding genius of the house, malignantly open-eyed to its faults, sardonically resigned to the destiny which she has chosen of her own freewill, but determined that the grandson of the man whose love she has rejected shall not be condemned to share the limbo of vanished fortunes and ruined reputations which is her own refuge, is baroness Bernstein. At the end of *Esmond*, Beatrix had made her choice, and the baroness, after many years, is still Beatrix, with her beauty gone and ambition defeated, but with her intelligence sharpened and with an undisguised consciousness, quite distinct from remorse, of the relative value of the lot which she has renounced and the risks which she has preferred. Her influence is the most powerful factor in determining the course of events in *The Virginians*, and, with the moving scene in which she passes out of life, revealing in her delirium the hopes and fears which had agitated her at the crisis of her youth, the real interest of the book is over.

The first number of *The Cornhill Magazine*, under Thackeray's editorship, was published in January 1860, containing the first instalment of *Lovel the Widower*, a short story closely akin to Thackeray's early essays in fiction, and the first of *Roundabout Papers*, discursive essays in which his genius for embroidering a fabric of mingled satire and sentiment upon a ground of casual reminiscence surpassed itself. Thackeray had not the unworldliness of Elia, nor had his style that magical kinship to poetry and that power of giving new currency to the gold of the past which place that most lovable of essayists above all rivals ; but the man of the world who unburdens himself of his wisdom with colloquial ease, commenting upon the contradictions and humours of everyday life with a sympathy born of self-knowledge, wins the affection even of those who are a little afraid of his keen criticism. His last complete novel, *The Adventures of Philip*, was contributed in serial instalments to *The Cornhill* of 1862. For the subject of this, he returned to the characters of *A Shabby Genteel Story*. The deceived Caroline re-appears as the Little Sister, the hero of the story is the son of her seducer, whose shiftiness and heartlessness have not grown less with years, and the Tom Tufthunt who performed the mock marriage of Caroline to Brandon attempts, as the drunken blackmailer Tufton Hunt, to wreck the peace of the leading characters. As in *The Newcomes*, the urbane influence of Pendennis checks the whirlwind of the hero's passion. No one, however, who has known Clive Newcome will find much that is new in Philip Firmin, whose bearishness and tactlessness, however, are individual outgrowths of a mercurial temperament. The cousin of the piece, unlike Ethel, is fundamentally heartless and fickle ; and Philip finds his happiness, where Clive missed it, in the incidental lady of the drama. While his mother-in-law, Mrs Baynes, is as great a virago as Mrs Mackenzie, he has not to endure the martyrdom of a poverty-stricken life under the lash of her tongue ; and Charlotte is more nearly related to Theo and Hetty Lambert than to the inane Rosey. With all these qualifications, it is impossible to feel that the book contains a new character : the old pieces are arranged upon the board in a new formation. The story drags rather slowly through its appointed length of twelve monthly numbers, and ends with a theatrical device, the discovery of a will in the lining of a family chariot, which relieves Philip, as a somewhat similar discovery relieved Clive, from all financial cares. But, in *The Newcomes*, this event is redeemed by the true climax of the book, the colonel's death, and to this recovery of interest *Philip* affords no parallel.

Thackeray's last work of fiction, *Denis Duval*, was left unfinished at his death. The incomplete story was printed in *The Cornhill* during the first half of 1864. Its close relation to historical events resembles that of *Esmond* : in this instance, the chief actors, introduced through the medium of a tragic episode, as skilfully told as the court drama in *Barry Lyndon* and intrinsically even more piteous, were intended to work out their fortunes in the French revolution. Denis is his own autobiographer : writing in the evening of his days, he looks back upon the past with something of Esmond's subdued humour and pity for the blind striving and wasteful passions that wear out human life. While Thackeray struck out no new line for himself in *Denis Duval*, he showed no sign of the exhaustion of power which is evident in *Philip* ; and the last work that came from his hand is vigorous in conception and embodies his matured view of life with unabated clearness and simplicity.

In his later years, Thackeray began to feel heavily the strain of the hard and continuous labour with which he paid toll for fame and comfort. In February 1862, while still occupied with *Philip*, he moved into a house in Palace green, Kensington, which he had rebuilt upon a scale compatible with somewhat luxurious ideals of living. Here, he proposed to devote himself to what he intended should be his greatest work, a history of the reign of queen Anne. But *Denis Duval* came in the way of his new plan, and, before *Denis Duval* was far advanced, its author died suddenly in the early morning of the Christmas eve of 1863.

Thackeray's life is entirely bound up in his literary work. Its great catastrophe took place before he had achieved fame and social success, and, while it affected him deeply, did not check his appreciation of the fullness and gaiety of existence. To his contemporaries, who saw the redoubtable satirist at work in his clubs, where it was his habit to write daily in the heart of the life which he described, he appeared a cool man of the world, ready to meet their advances with an easy and, sometimes, formidable politeness.

The notorious character-sketch, written by Edmund Yates in 1858, which brought about the rupture of friendly relations between Thackeray and Dickens, expressed, with malicious resentment, the bewilderment provoked by his superficial conversation and the suspicion with which persons of less alert intelligence regarded the apparent contradictions in his writings. The misunderstanding still exists, and in more than one form. There are those, on the one hand, who complain that Thackeray was heartless and cynical, because he lacked a cheerful faith in the general excellence of human nature. Others, who, from a different point of view, seem to regard a genius for satire as precluding a sincere appreciation of goodness, condemn his use of sentiment as a mere concession to contemporary ideas of propriety. It is, indeed, true that his range of character was limited compared with that of Dickens and Balzac, and that the sentiments and actions of his people are far more restrained by the conventions of their age and country. But, if this be equivalent to the confession that he had less imagination and invention than his two greatest contemporaries in fiction, it also implies that he kept more closely than they to the observation of the life that lay immediately beneath his notice. His appreciation of the comedy of manners was accurate and conscientious : he brought to his work an historic faculty which not only enabled him to vary his operations by re-creating with astonishing freshness the manners of a past age, but made his novels, where they dealt with his own times, important landmarks of fiction in its relation to contemporary manners. Even where his characters were most akin to himself, he was able to watch them from a detached and critical point of view, impatient of extravagance and improbability. Combining sympathy with criticism, he recognised that the puppets of his stage possessed a higher value for themselves than for the impartial spectator, that what is petty and laughable in its relation to life at large is of serious importance to the individual. No one has seen this double aspect of life more clearly than Thackeray. Conscious of his own share in the imperfections of humanity, he was unable to regard his fellows with an Olympian indifference. He varied continually between the two points of view, different and yet hard to distinguish. His sense of human littleness now had the upper hand, to be succeeded, without a pause, by a revulsion of feeling, in which the laughing philosopher trembled on the brink of tears. These apparent contrasts and sudden variations are the perplexing quality of his work to the reader who prefers the ludicrous and pathetic elements of life to be divided into distinct chapters, or, at any rate, to be isolated in parallel columns. The balance which Thackeray holds may not always be even: at times, his satire and irony may seem wanting in sympathy, his pathetic passages excessive in their demand upon the reader's emotions. But, when these sides of his art in its relation to human nature are examined as a whole, it is found that, like their prototypes in life, they meet so closely that there is no line of demarcation between them. And this sense of the humour of life, of the proportion in which its elements are mingled, is conveyed by means of a style, not, indeed, free from mannerisms and imperfections, but endowed with a flexibility that responds at a touch to the demands of gravity and gaiety alike, and with a freedom of flow that brings the novelist into unstrained communication with his readers.

CHAPTER X

DICKENS

THERE is a point in the consideration of the subject of the present chapter which, though of the most obvious to uncritical, as well as to critical, appreciation, is, perhaps, worthy of more attention in respect of criticism proper than has usually been given to it. This point is the immense popularity of Dickens, as it is vulgarly called, or (as it may be put in a form more critically useful) the immense amount of pleasure which he has given to a number of people who, from the very vastness of that number, must, necessarily, have included individuals and whole sections of readers of the most various tastes, powers and qualifications. Except Shakespeare and Scott, there is, probably, no other English writer who can match him in this respect. Now, mere popularity, especially of an ephemeral kind, of course, proves nothing as to merit ; and, though it is never exactly negligible to the critic (for he must satisfy himself as to its causes), he can scarcely allow it to affect his judgment. But very long-continued popularity is in a different case ; and popularity which has been attained in the case of very dissimilar classes and individuals, and, therefore, by very dissimilar appeals, is in a different case again. These latter kinds of popularity not only cannot be neglected, but they cannot, without danger, be slightly recognised by the critic, and, especially, by the historical critic.

It may be said, perhaps, that Dickens's popularity has not yet had time, as Shakespeare's has, to vindicate itself by the test of long continuance and some vicissitudes. More than a century has, indeed, elapsed since his birth and nearly half a century since his death : but instances could be produced of reputations which, after towering for at least as long, have dropped to a much lower level, if they have not fallen altogether. Complaints, undoubtedly, are, sometimes, made that his atmosphere is becoming difficult to breathe ; and, though the lungs which feel this difficulty are probably rather weak, their complaint must be registered. But, in regard to the other point, there is no possibility of rational and well informed doubt. It is probably safe to say (here making no exception at all and giving him no companions) that no author in our literary history has been both admired and enjoyed for such different reasons; by such different tastes and intellects; by whole classes of readers unlike each other. He is 'made one with Nature,' not, indeed, by a Shakespearean universality—for there are wide, numerous and, sometimes, unfortunate gaps in his appeal—but by the great range and diversity of that appeal. The uncritical lover of the sentimental and the melodramatic; the frank devotee of mere 'fun'; the people who simply desire to pass their time by witnessing a lively and interesting set of scenes and figures; the respectable yearners for social and political reform; the not quite so respectable seekers after scandal and satire on the upper and wealthier and more accomplished classes: these and a dozen or a hundred other types all fly to Dickens as to a magnet. And—what is most remarkable of all and most unparalleled in other cases—the very critics who find it their duty to object to his faults most strongly, who think his sentiment too often worse than mawkish, and his melodrama not seldom more than ridiculous; who rank his characters too close to 'character *parts*,' in the lower theatrical sense; who consider his style too often tawdry; his satire strained, yet falling short or wide of its object; his politics unpractical and, sometimes, positively mischievous; his plots either non-existent or tediously complicated for no real purpose; who fully admit the quaint unreality of his realism and the strange 'some-other-worldliness' of much of his atmosphere—these very persons, not unfrequently, read him for choice again and again. In fact, neither the uncritical nor the critical lover of Dickens ever tires of him, as both often do of some writers whom they have admired. Some of his books will, of course, in different cases, be read oftener than others; but, generally, the Dickens quality, mixed and diverse as it is, never loses its attraction for anyone who has once felt it. The road to Eatanswill is never hard or hackneyed; the company of Mrs Gamp never ceases to be as delightful in fiction as it would be disgusting (especially supposing her to be on duty) in real life.

It results infallibly from these facts that the quality in question must, as it has been called, be extraordinarily 'mixed.' The simpler kinds of genius never attain to this result. They being of a 'higher' (to use the question-begging but unavoidable word) strain, may create a higher satisfaction, and, as we flatter ourselves, appeal to a higher order of mind ; but this, of itself, means limitation. And it follows that mixed genius of the Dickens kind requires a corresponding variety of analysis to understand itself, its causes and its manifestations.

The influence of life on literature, commonly exaggerated, may be easily exaggerated here ; but it counts solidly, if not in a manifold fashion. Dickens's biography is familiar from one great storehouse, Forster's *Life,* and from many smaller monographs of varying merit, nor does it require full handling here. Born in the lower, rather than the upper, middle class, and sunk, by family misfortune, at one time, to the very level poignantly described in *David Copperfield,* he acquired, in his interrupted schooldays, a very limited amount of regular education and never enjoyed David's subsequent 'advantages.' But he knew something of the school groundwork usual at that time, and, on his own account, developed a keen and most fortunate fondness for the great classics of English fiction, original or translated—Smollett, perhaps, most of all, but, also, Fielding ; *Don Quixote,* as well as *The Arabian Nights.* After all the sordid but, eventually, genial experiences which, later, reflect themselves in his books—the childish schooling which provides some of the most charming themes of his Christmas stories ; his father's prison in the Marshalsea ; the dismal shabby lodgings at Camden town and in Lant street and so forth—he got no nearer Copperfield's dignified articled position in Doctors' Commons than a boy-clerkship in a solicitor's office and a reportership in the Commons itself. But this last gave him a sort of hold on the fringe of journalism, if not of literature, and he soon fastened that hold on the garment itself. More varied and important reportings ; *Sketches by Boz,* at first mainly imitative but, even then, in part, noticeably original, led to the great chance of *Pickwick,* which was taken greatly. After the success of *Pickwick,* the aspect of his life presented as sharp a contrast to its earlier phase as the often cited one which is shown by the two parts of a portrait in a picture-cleaner's windows, or the advertisements of a certain soap. It was, if not exactly all dark, at any rate all shabby, grimy and obscure before : it was all bright now, except for certain domestic inconveniences late in his career. He never had any more money troubles ; he never had any lack of popularity ; he worked hard, indeed : but he was a 'glutton for work' and could choose his time, place and manner of doing it after a fashion which deprives work of all, or nearly all, its worrying effect. He found, in addition to his original and independent work as novelist, two occupations, that of editor and that of public reader, both of which were very profitable, while the former of them gave exercise to his busy and rather autocratic temper, and the latter furnished an outlet to the histrionic faculty which was almost as strong in him as the literary. He died, it is true, in middle age only; but after a full, glorious and, apparently, on the whole, happy life, not, indeed, without some preliminary illness, but without suffering from that terrible lingering failure of faculties which had beset Scott and Southey and Moore in the generation immediately before him. Fame and fortune after the very earliest step, and far earlier than in most cases, had, in almost all respects, been equally kind to him.

Not the least of these respects concerns the exact relations of his life and his work; though qualifications begin here to be necessary. The hardships and vicissitudes, the enforced self-reliance of his youth, confirmed, if they did not originate, the unflinching, undoubting adventurousness which enabled him to turn out book after book—most of them utterly unlike anything that had been seen before, and hardly one of them, even at its worst, showing that fatal groove-and-mould character which besets the novelist more than any other literary craftsman. His almost immediate success, and the power of taking his own line which it conferred, removed the slightest temptation to follow fashions in any way. Neither kind of influence could have been better contrived to nurse that indomitable idiosyncrasy which was his.

At the same time, neither, as it will at once be perceived, was likely to contribute the counterbalancing gift which idiosyncrasy requires—the gift of self-discipline and self-criticism. 'Self-sufficiency,' unfortunately, has two meanings; and those who, in early life, have to learn it in the one and better sense are too apt to display it later in the other and worse. That the qualities of what the Italians have denominated the *selfelpista* are not always wholly amiable or admirable is a truism. Their dangerous side is not likely to be effaced when the severer struggle is over almost before the man has reached full manhood, and when, thenceforward, he is almost as much 'his own master' as if he were born to independence and several thousands a year. And these qualities themselves are well known, especially on the ethical side, though they have seldom had such an opportunity of developing themselves on the aesthetic and literary as they had in Dickens's case.

Arrogance, 'cocksureness,' doubtful taste, undue indulgence in 'tricks and manners' (one naturally takes his own words to describe him), a general rebelliousness against criticism and an irresistible or, at least, unresisted tendency to 'do it again' when something has been found objectionable—these things, and a still more general tendency to exaggerate, to 'force the note,' to keep one's own personality constantly in the fore-ground[1], are among necessary consequences of the situation. If a man of this stamp is, for his own good fortune and the world's, endowed with a great inventive genius, it would, according to some critics, be actually possible to forecast, and it certainly is, according to, perhaps, safer and saner views, not at all surprising to find, a result of work such as that which Dickens has actually given. Let us follow the method of these latter critics and examine the work itself with the least prolix but most necessary preface as to the historical circumstances in which he began.

To understand his position thoroughly, it must be remembered that, when he began to write, Scott had been dead for some years and Jane Austen for nearly twenty ; that no one had yet seriously tried to fit on the mantle of the latter in the domain of the domestic novel; that Scott's had been most unsuccessfully attempted by men like Ainsworth and James ; that new special varieties had been introduced by Bulwer, Marryat, Lever and others ; but that nothing of absolutely first class quality had been achieved. The most popular novelist of Dickens's younger manhood was, however, none of these, but a man who produced work not so good as that of even the worst of them—Theodore Hook. That Hook's novels, as well as Leigh Hunt's essays, had immense influence on *Sketches by Boz* few critical readers of the three will deny ; and that the habit of the essayist as well as that of the novelist clung to Dickens, much better things than *Sketches*—such as *The Un-commercial Traveller* and not a few oddments up to the very close of his career—remain to attest. Both, as well as his earlier

---

[1] Dickens's way of doing this is curious and easy to feel, though not so easy to analyse. He is not always drawing 'costume'-portraits of himself, like Byron : it is difficult to think of one of his characters (for Copperfield is only so in childish externals and literary success later) who is at all like himself or could have been meant for himself. He does not 'meditate himself' before our eyes as, in different ways, do Fielding and Lamb and Thackeray. And yet, in most of the books (*Pickwick* is the great exception and, perhaps, this is not the least of its merits), there is a constant and, sometimes, an uneasy feeling of the showman behind the curtain. We are not allowed to forget all about him and to 'amuse ourselves frankly,' as Émile de Girardin said to Théophile Gautier, about the other matter of style.

favourite, Smollett[1], were his masters in the comparatively little used art of minute description of 'interiors' and 'setting.' Hook gave him the tone of caricature and extravaganza: Hunt that of easy intimate talk.

But he added to these 'the true Dickens,' and it is difficult, even for those who hold, with the greatest tenacity, to the historical view of literature, to believe that this true Dickens would not have made its way without any patterns at all, though it may be that they gave that mysterious start or suggestion which is sometimes, if not always, necessary. What is certain is that they hindered almost as much as they helped; and that some of the faults of the later and greater books are not unfairly traceable to their influence; while it was some considerable time before he got free from relapses into mere bad imitation of them. To appreciate this, it is necessary to pay more attention to the early *Sketches* than has sometimes been given to them. Dickens himself wisely refrained from re-printing any of them except the Boz division, which, though it is the earliest, contains, also, by far the best work. But the student, if not the general reader, must submit himself to the perusal not merely of these, but of *Sketches of Young Gentlemen, Sketches of Young Couples* and *The Mudfog Papers*, which the ruthless resurrectionists of literature have unearthed. There is, indeed, hardly anything that is good in these; the best of them are weak copies of papers by Hunt and others of the older generation; survivals of the old stock 'character'; newspaper 'Balaam' (as the cant phrase then went) of the thinnest and dreariest kind. Yet, some, if not all, of them were written after *The Pickwick Papers* and alongside of the greater part of the earlier novels. They—or, rather, the critical or uncritical spirit which allowed him to write them—account for the clumsy and soon discarded framework of *Master Humphrey's Clock*: and their acceptance of the type by one who, in his better moods, was one of the most individual and individualising of writers, never quite effaces itself from his work to the very end; while, in the *Mudfog* group, at least, the habit of exaggerated and overdriven irony (or, rather, attempt at irony) which, unfortunately, was to increase, is manifest. These things, though, as has been pointed out, not exactly novice-work, are such obvious 'slips of the pen' on a large scale that one is almost

---

[1] Attempts have been made to deny the connection, chiefly on the ground that Dickens was of the order of Abou ben Adhem, and 'loved his fellow men,' while Smollett did not. This, if true, could be of little or no literary importance: and, as a matter of fact, Smollett, though possessed of a savage pen, seems to have had habits the reverse of uncharitable.

ashamed to speak of them seriously. Yet, after all, they form part
of the *dossier*—the body of documents in the case—which every
honest historical critic and student has to examine.

There is very much better matter in the Boz *Sketches*
themselves, though their immaturity and inequality are great,
and were frankly acknowledged by the author himself, whose fault
was certainly not excess of modesty. The patterns are even more
obvious; but the vigour and versatility are far greater, and the
addition to the title 'illustrative of everyday life and everyday
people' is justified in a fashion for which Hunt had not strength
enough, which Hook's inveterate tendency to caricature and *charge*
precluded him from attaining and which the lapse of nearly a
century throws out of comparison with Smollett. The best of them
are real studies for the finished pictures of the novels; and the
author rarely attempts the sentimentalism, the melodrama and
the fine writing which were to be snares for him later. There
are not many things more curious in critical enquiry, of what may
be called the physiological or biological sort, than the way in
which 'Our Parish' shows the future novelist. It is, to a large
extent, made up of studies of the type kind above described and
not commended; but these are connected, if not by any plot, by a
certain community of characters, and even by some threads of
incident; and, accordingly, things become far more alive and the
shadow of the coming novelist falls on the mere sketch-writer. The
scenes are still Leigh-Huntian in general scheme; but they are drawn
with a precision, a *verve* and an atmosphere of, at least, plausible
realism which Hunt could not reach. Of the 'Tales' (so called),
Dickens himself was rather ashamed; and no wonder. None,
perhaps, has the merit of Hook's best short stories, such as *Gervase
Skinner*; the subjects are, sometimes, thin for the lengths; and
a certain triviality is not deniable, especially in the longer efforts
about boardinghouse society and the like. But the teller can, at
other times, tell; conventions pass, now and then, into vivid touches
of, at least, low life; there is, occasionally, fun which does not
always mean mere horseplay; there is, almost always, the *setting*
of the scenes adapted to show up whatever incident there may be[1].

Still, neither in the larger, earlier and better, nor in the
smaller, later and worse, collection of these *Sketches* is there
anything of that 'true Dickens' which is a more remarkable —
idiosyncrasy than even what Browning meant when he used the

[1] The 'Parliamentary Sketch,' especially the admirable description of 'Bellamy's'
is, perhaps, the best of all; but this is not a tale.

words. It is, again, a curiosity of historical criticism to note that, while in Thackeray's nearly contemporary and similarly 'Hookish' attempts, such as *The Professor*, there are immature, but quite perceptible, traces of the special quality which was to need seven years' hard labour and constant failure to mature it, there is in Dickens's big volume of early sketches hardly anything of the astonishing 'quiddity' which was to reveal itself at once in *The Pickwick Papers*. There are some of the externals ready; there is something of the framework and machinery—of the 'plant'; more than something of the sentiment, opinion and the like; but nothing whatever of the strange phantasmagoric spirit of life[1] which was now, apparently, by a sudden daemonic impulse to be breathed into what had been hitherto simply puppets. It has been complained, with what justice we may consider later, that Dickens's folk, at their greatest and best, are not exactly, in the Falstaffian phrase, 'men [and women] of this world.' But, up to this time, they had been trying to be so and had been more or less pale copies of such. They now become conscious living beings of a world of their own; varying, of course, in power, gift, appeal, like creatures of any world, but seldom without flashes of their peculiar life; while, at times, and at their best, they are creations and such creations as had never been seen in literature before and have never been seen since, whether anything like them has been seen in this life or not. And it adds to the curiosity that the actual opening of *Pickwick* itself promises little or nothing of this. The club scene and debate with their stock machinery; the parody, smart enough but rather facile and rather overdone, of parliament and the like might easily have been a Boz sketch. The second chapter opens with another parody of Fielding which promises little more. But the journey from Goswell street to the Golden Cross (though this, too, links itself with the 'red cab' driver in *Boz*) is big with quite new suggestions and possibilities; and even before Jingle elbows himself in, still more when he takes further root (though he, too, is Hook's debtor to an extent which few people know) we are in the new world—never (not even in *Hard Times*) to be entirely shut out of it until death performs the ungracious office and leaves *Edwin Drood* not half told.

Whether Dickens was himself conscious of this sudden and, as it were, miraculous transformation nowhere (speaking under correction) appears. But he has, in a way however circular and

---

[1] Producing those ἀπόρροιαι or 'effluences' of humanity happily described by Lewis Campbell, see, *ante*, vol. XII. p. 220.

cryptic, registered the time of its occurrence in the famous phrase 'I thought of Mr Pickwick,' when telling how he brushed aside the proposals of his publishers for what was, in fact, a stale competition with the already popular Mr Jorrocks, and substituted his own. As has been hinted, there are signs of his not having 'thought of Mr Pickwick' in the full sense quite at once—signs which are not entirely accounted for by, though they are not inconsistent with, his equally wellknown apology about the salient absurdities of a man's character being noticeable first. Probably, Seymour's death relieved him rather of something like a clog than (as was suggested, illiberally but inevitably, at the time and denied by him with his usual over-sensitiveness) of an inconvenient suggestion of the general idea. At any rate, how it happened we do not and cannot know ; that it happened, we know and ought to be truly thankful for. There is no book like *Pickwick* anywhere ; it is almost (extravagant as the saying may seem) worth while to read the wretched imitations of it in order to enjoy the zest with which one comes back to the real, though fantastically real, thing. The diversity of Dickens's clients is nowhere better illustrated than in the case of this, his first, and, as some think, his greatest, book. Those much to be commiserated people, on the other hand, who do not like it may be said to consist of two classes only—classes each well worth the consideration of the historical student of literature. The first, which has existed from the beginning and must always exist, consists of those who cannot relish pure fun— fantastic humour which cares nothing for probability, consistency, chronology (the chronology of *Pickwick* has long been a favourite subject for the amazement of the serious and the amusement of others) and is not in the least afraid of invading those confines of nonsense which Hazlitt proudly and wisely claimed as the appanage and province of every true Englishman. For these, of course, nothing can be done. They may or must be looked at (whether with humility, respect, contempt, pity or thankfulness matters little) and passed.

These, however, are a constant body at all times. The other class varies much more with times and seasons, and is, therefore, of greater historical interest. It consists of those who feel, not exactly a critical or rational objection to the author's methods and results, but a half aesthetic and half intellectual incapacity to adjust themselves to his means, his atmosphere and what is sometimes called his *milieu*. These persons appear (for what reasons, educational or other, it would be irrelevant to enquire) to be particularly numerous just now. The combination of near and far in Dickens ; the identity of places, names and so forth, by the side of the difference of manners, habits and, to some extent, speech, seems altogether to upset them. They cannot 'see' the spencer-wearing, punch-drinking, churchgoing world of seventy or eighty years since. This certainly argues what Dryden, in discussing a somewhat similar matter, calls a singular 'heaviness of soul'— a strange inability to transport and adjust. One can only hope— without being too certain—that it will be outgrown, and that these persons (some of whom, at least, would be not a little offended if they were assumed not to like Homer or Vergil, Dante or Shakespeare, because the manners of the times of each were different from ours) may, at last, consent to allow the characters and the atmosphere of Dickens to differ from those of today, without declining, in consequence, to have anything to do with them. But, for the time, they may be nearly as hopeless as the others.

It cannot have taken many people of any competence in criticism very long to discover where, at least, in a general way, the secret of this 'new world' of Dickens lies. It lies, of course, in the combination of the strictest realism of detail with a fairy-tale unrealism of general atmosphere. The note of one or the other or both is sometimes forced, and then there is a jar : in the later books, this is too frequently the case. But, in *Pickwick*, it hardly ever occurs ; and, therefore, to all happily fit persons, the 'suspension of disbelief' to adopt and shift Coleridge's great dictum from verse to prose fiction, is, except in the case of some of the short inset stories, never rudely broken. Never, probably, was there a great writer who knew, or cared, less about Aristotle than Dickens did. If he had spoken of the father of criticism, he would probably have talked—one is not certain that he has not sometimes come near to talking—some of his worst stuff. But, certainly, when he did master it (which was often), nobody ever mastered better than Dickens, in practice, the Aristotelian doctrine of the impossibility rendered probable or not improbable.

As yet, however, nothing has been said of his conversation, though something of what has been said above applies to that, too. Conversation had always been one of the main difficulties of the novel. The romance, with some striking exceptions, had not indulged much in it ; and the novel, till Dryden and Addison and Steele and Swift created something of the kind, could find no good conversational style ready to its hand. Even after them—after the great eighteenth century groups, after Scott, after Jane

Austen—there hung on the novel a sort of conventional lingo, similar to that of the stage and, probably, derived from it, which was like nothing ever used by man in actual speech—as heavy as frost, but far from having any depth of life at all. Dickens himself was very long in getting rid of this, if he ever did; and some of the worst examples of it are in the speeches of Nicholas Nickleby and his sister in a book which was not begun till *Pickwick* was nearly finished. But, in *Pickwick* itself (some of the inset stories again excepted[1]), this lingo hardly ever appears, being ousted, no doubt, to some extent, necessarily, by the prevailing grotesque, and by the fact that a very large part of it is 'in the *vulgar* tongue' with the adjective underlined. But, even when neither of these cathartics of book-made and stage-made lingo was present, the characters almost invariably talk like human beings.

The mention of the word character brings us to another and still more important aspect of our 'true Dickens.' It has been said that even the very rudimentary connection of character and incident which is observable in 'Our Parish' had stimulated, to some extent, the author's actual novel-writing faculty; the infinitely more complicated interconnection of the same kind in *Pickwick* seems to have stimulated it still more. Story of the more technical kind there is, no doubt, little; though there is more than has been sometimes allowed, for the intended exploration of England provides a sort of beginning, the Bardell imbroglio and its sequels provide a really distinct middle and Mr Pickwick's retirement and the marriage of his younger friends give us as much of an end as most novels contain. But the interest is really in the separate scenes and not in the connection of them, except in so far as the same characters reappear. Nay, it is scarcely extravagant to say that the interest of the scenes is largely due to the fact of the same characters appearing in them.

Yet, these characters themselves, with the possible exception of the hero, can hardly be said to be in any way developed by the different situations. They remain the same; not now exactly types, though Mr Snodgrass, at least, is not very far from 'the poetical young gentleman[2]' who seems actually to have succeeded him in production. But they are always 'humours,' in the Jonsonian sense. Only late in his career, in *Hard Times, A Tale of*

---

[1] These insets (which gradually disappeared) were, of course, mere legacies from eighteenth century practice. And this inheritance was by no means always *damnosa*. The two tales told by the bagman in *Pickwick* are among the very best of English short stories.

[2] In *Sketches of Young Gentlemen*.

Two Cities, Great Expectations and, perhaps, *Our Mutual Friend*, did Dickens attempt anything like a character at least apparently prepared to stand analysis and to achieve or suffer development. Even then, he never went far; it was, frankly, not his business.

But, here, in *Pickwick* once for all, and as no one had done before him, he displayed the power of imparting, not, indeed, the complexity, variety and depth of life, but a certain—to stoop, for once, to paradoxical phrase—'external intensity' of it[1]. The characters of *Pickwick* are not, perhaps, in any one instance, like anyone that we have actually met or shall probably meet, but (the insets once more excluded) they are not puppets. The worst treated in this way is the unfortunate Mr Winkle, who is wanted so often for the horse-play and pantomime business, and is devoted to it so early, that it seems a little incongruous when a girl like Arabella is made to reciprocate his affection. Yet, to us, he is not a mere puppet; and, from the duel scene to that where he manages to get the better of Dowler, he is alive with the strange Dickensian life, if not with the quintessence of it. It is easy to say that the characters furthest from him, the truest 'servants of Quintessence,' the two Wellers, are impossible, that they could not be. The only reply is that they are; and that, this being the case, their possibility is a mere 'previous question,' a phantom from which we pass to the order of the actual day. Nor is there (once and always excepting the insets and not all of them) any part of the book where this mimetic actuality does not prevail. Improving immensely upon the lines of Defoe and Smollett, and adding to them an imagination of which Defoe had nothing and Smollett not very much, Dickens by this time creates, in a fashion unprecedented and unparalleled, his characters and their surroundings. The personages may be psychologically rudimentary, and often put into exaggerated comic or tragic action; the scenes may be curiously destitute of beauty (Dickens can make a place comfortable just as he can make it horrible and ugly, but he never makes it exactly beautiful; in fact, when he merely tries to describe beauty, as in *Pictures from Italy*, he cannot do it); they may be open to criticisms of all sorts; but, in their own order of logic, they never fail to be what the critical man of a later day calls 'convincing,' though with a conviction which has nothing to do with

---

[1] At the moment of writing, an illustration occurred, not, indeed, from *Pickwick* but from *Nicholas Nickleby*. The keeper of Mrs Nickleby's mad lover ' shook his head so emphatically that he was obliged *to frown to keep his hat on.*' Almost everybody has done this; very few people can have noticed that they do it; Dickens registers it.

evidence. They are, in their own way, real: and there's an end of it. The 'swarry' at Bath is open to a hundred cavils; but it is as real, if as artificial, as the Roman remains there, and likely to be as solid, when it is equally out of date and fashion.

The originality of this method of construction could, of course, never be exhibited again as it is in *The Pickwick Papers.* Whether its power was ever better shown, so far as presence of merits with absence of defects is concerned, is a question, perhaps, of opinion mainly; but that it was capable of almost indefinite extension in range was clear. Strict realism (from which, except in his Christmas books and stories, Dickens never departed) in main subject and in what may be called detail of setting, with audacious *dis*realising in treatment, were of its essence. But he had tendencies and characteristics which, though visible even in the immature work, and not quite obscured in *Pickwick* itself, had been kept down in the first group by the fact of its being hackwork, and, in *Pickwick*, by its general scheme of cheerful extravaganza. The not quite immediate, but speedy and immense, success of *Pickwick* made it possible for him to write more or less as he liked; and, unless he had been more or less than human, he must have been slightly intoxicated with the wine of his own achievement. He continued, for some time (in *Bentley's Miscellany,* chiefly), to write the slight things noted above; but, before *Pickwick* itself was finished, he began to compose, and within a short time of its completion he had published, two elaborate novels of a much closer construction, and (as some would say) of a much more ambitious character than *Pickwick* itself. In these works, he allowed very large scope to the tendencies above mentioned—that towards sentimental pathos; that towards melodrama; and that towards carrying out political-social purpose of a reforming kind. These were *Oliver Twist*—the shorter, the earlier published, but, perhaps, not the earlier begun—and the much longer, the more varied and, with some strands of melodrama, the less serious, *Nicholas Nickleby.*

The Pickwick Papers, as everybody knows, were issued in monthly numbers, a revival of an old, if not exactly time-honoured, fashion which was coming in at the moment, and which was maintained in popularity through the adoption of it by Dickens, by Thackeray and by others for a full generation. All his books, indeed, appeared either in this manner or as contributions to periodicals, the monthly *Miscellany* already mentioned, and the famous weekly papers, *Household Words* and *All the Year Round,* which he

edited later. He never, on any occasion, issued a work as a whole.
It is doubtful, however, whether this piecemeal method of publication exercised on his writing either the mischievous influence
with which it has been credited and which it certainly seems to
have had in some cases, or, indeed, any particular influence at all.
For, whatever else Dickens was, he was certainly a man of business,
and not likely to neglect his business in whatever form it presented
itself, especially when that form was of his own choice. *Oliver
Twist,* which succeeded *Pickwick* as a book, came out in *Bentley's
Miscellany.* It has been more differently valued at different times
than, perhaps, any other of the whole list; and the revival, some
twenty years ago, of a fancy for grime-novels should have been in
its favour. But it is doubtful whether, in good judgments, it has ever
been, or ever will be, put in the first class of Dickens's work. The
author's general quarrel with society as it is or was; and that
particular and personal sympathy with neglected or persecuted
childhood which was to leave such striking marks on almost all his
books, here first lay a distinct, and, to some tastes, a rather
cramping, hand on his creative powers. Sentiment and melodrama
both have the reins flung on their backs; and, though the comic
power refuses to be suppressed altogether, the book is too short and
too little varied to give it fair play. Oliver himself, save in the one
sublime, but early and never repeated, moment of his demand for
'more,' is totally uninteresting except from the point of view of
sheer compassion; the other good characters lack even that virtue
and are, therefore, uninteresting *simpliciter*. But, whether the
high-flavoured crimes of the goats have interest enough to make us
forget the insipid virtues of the sheep is, of course, the point of
difference. The tragedy of Nancy is a real tragedy, for it springs
partly, at least, from a human and forgivable frailty; but it is
awkwardly introduced at first and it is some time before Nancy
herself becomes, in any way, a sympathetic character. Moreover,
the unbroken sordidness of the whole scene and setting makes one
apt to revise unfavourable opinions of certain once orthodox critical
notions as to 'dignity' of subject. Charley Bates and the Dodger,
with Bumble (in the middle division), do what they can to temper
disgust; but it is not quite enough. The progress of Sikes from
the murder to his self-execution is, indeed, fine (Dickens had a
singular mastery of *travel*, in all its phases, tragic, comic and
neutral), nor can he, even earlier, be said to be an impossible ruffian.
Fagin is some way further from reality; and a pithy observation
attributed to the late G S. Venables, that 'Dickens hanged

Fagin for being the villain of a novel,' might be extended over the Jew's earlier history. Noah Claypole is merely, and his Charlotte is much too frequently, disgusting. But the greatest blot on the book is Monks, the first of the scarecrow scoundrels whom Dickens was always too fond of putting on the stage, to be followed—in more or less detail, and with more or less inclination towards the partly verisimilar and the wholly incredible—by Ralph Nickleby and Barnaby Rudge's father and Jonas Chuzzlewit, and to leave traces of himself even on the Carker of *Dombey* and the Rigaud of *Little Dorrit*.

The faults of *Oliver Twist,* and the tendencies and methods which brought about those faults, reappear in *Nicholas Nickleby.* But the book is on a very much larger scale; it is very much more varied in scene and character; and almost all the new elements as well as the reversions to Pickwickian ways are sheer gain. It would, indeed, be amazing—were there not many examples of similar blindness in life and literature—that Dickens, whose portrayal of the weakness of the stage and its population makes one of the most delightful features of the book, should (obviously without the least consciousness of what he was doing) have put beside the Crummleses and in fuller and more constant presence a stage-acting and stage-speaking hero in Nicholas; a stage-heroine in Kate; a stage-villain in Ralph, and a second ditto combined with a stage bad fine gentleman in Sir Mulberry ; a stage silly aristocrat with a few better touches in lord Frederick; stage supers in Pyke and Pluck and the Wititterlys and others : almost all these, moreover, being of a very inferior stage kind. Yet, even this part provides one atoning comic moment when lord Frederick pronounces Shakespeare 'a clayver man,' and a really fine, if distinctly melodramatic, finale in the duel and the scene more immediately leading up to it. Luckily, too, this element is practically merged in, altogether overweighted and counter-influenced by, 'metal more attractive.' The sordid misery and brutality of Dotheboys hall, unlike things of the same general class in *Oliver Twist,* are not too long dwelt on, are enlivened with excellent comedy and afford opportunities for more than one exhibition of the most refreshing and least mawkish poetical justice[1]. Mrs Nickleby atones for her son and her daughter and

---

[1] Four and twenty years after the book appeared, two Oxford undergraduates, tramping toward Barnard Castle, stopped at a little inn and, half in joke, asked about the truth of Dotheboys hall. ' True ! ' said the innkeeper, ' why Fanny Squeers was sitting, last market-day, in the chair you've got ! ' Whereat, the occupant promptly jumped out of it—a double testimony to Dickens's realism.

her brother-in-law and a whole generation of stage Nicklebys twenty times over. The more sentimental 'facets,' as they may be called—the Smike part and the Cheeryble part and Madeline's sufferings from her again too histrionic papa—may appeal differently to different persons; but the liberal provision of other matter should reconcile reasonable doubters. Mr Crummles and those about him remain, like all the best things in Dickens, joys unspeakable and inexhaustible for ever; and they are not ill-seconded by the Mantalinis, the Kenwigses and others, especially Newman Noggs, who is, perhaps, that one of Dickens's avowed grotesques who has had least justice done to him. The book, in fact, has regained and displayed, in more variety than *Pickwick*, if less uniformity, that quality of abundance, of 'God's plenty,' to use a famous phrase, of production without reproduction, and variation without obvious mechanical effort, which only the greatest 'makers' in verse and prose possess.

This 'ebullience of creative' faculty (to borrow once more from Coleridge, though from a less admirable phrase) is, how-ever, notoriously subject to boiling over ; and it certainly does so in the misplaced ingenuity of the framework which, for a time, enshrined, and very far from adorned, the next two books *The Old Curiosity Shop* and *Barnaby Rudge*. There are two explanations, though they can hardly be called excuses, of the mistake of *Master Humphrey's Clock*. One is that Dickens (whose strong sense of his predecessors is never to be forgotten, though it often is) had not freed himself from that early difficulty of the novelist—the nervous idea that, in some way, he ought to account to his readers for the way in which he got his information. The other is that the period of publication—weekly not monthly—suggested the necessity of some vehicle to excuse and convey the actual works. However, this framework soon proved itself (as it was bound to do) not merely a superfluity but a nuisance ; and Dickens (who, if he was not a perfect critic, was, as has been said, a born man of business) got rid of it. The 'transient, embarrassed [and still more em-barrassing] phantom' of Master Humphrey still hinders, without in the least helping, the overture of *The Old Curiosity Shop* ; with the actual text of *Barnaby Rudge*, it, fortunately, does not interfere at all. In the more recent reprints of Dickens's mis-cellaneous remains, the reader may, if he choses, read so much of the framework as was actually written ; but, except for critical purposes, he had much better not. The belated club machinery of the *Tatler* tradition works to no satisfaction; and the inset tales (with the possible exception, to some extent, of 'Gog and Magog') take us back to the level of the *Sketches*. The frequently falsified maxim as to the badness of sequels has, perhaps, never been more thoroughly justified than in the unfortunate resurrection of the Pickwick group[1]; and the additions to them are wholly uninteresting. For one good thing, it taught him never to reintroduce his characters—a proceeding successful enough with some other authors, but which the very stuff and substance of his own form of creation forbade.

But, if the attempted, and, fortunately, abortive, husk or shell was worthless, the twin nuts or kernels were very far from being so. *The Old Curiosity Shop*, like all Dickens's novels without exception[2] save *The Pickwick Papers*, contains a tragic or, at least, sentimental element ; at the time, that element attracted most attention and it has, perhaps, attracted most favourable or unfavourable comment since. On the vexed question of little Nell, there is no need to say much here. She ravished contemporaries, at least partly because she was quite new[3]. She often, though not always, disgusted the next age. That wise compromise for which there is seldom room at first has withdrawn the objections to herself, while, perhaps, retaining those to her grandfather, as (except at the very last) an entirely unnatural person, especially in speech, and one of Dickens's worst borrowings from the lower stage. But it has been, perhaps, insufficiently noticed that, except in her perfectly natural and unstage-like appearances with Kit, with Codlin and Short and elsewhere, she could be cut out of the book with little loss except of space, taking her grandfather and her most superfluous and unsatisfactory cousin Trent with her. There would remain enough to make a book of the first class. The humours of the shop and the pilgrimage are almost, if not quite, independent of the unhappy ending. We should not lose Codlin and Short themselves, or Mrs Jarley, or other treasures. The Brasses —close, of course, to the Squeerses and even to the Fagin household, but saved, like the former, if not like all the latter, by humour—Quilp, an impossibility, equally of course, but, again, saved

---

[1] The very Wellerisms, with the rarest exceptions, are quite inferior ; you may often see as good in the actual imitations, such as G. W. M. Reynolds's *Pickwick Abroad*.

[2] *Our Mutual Friend* is not one, though the tragedy is partly simulated and partly minor.

[3] Sterne and his school may be objected. But Dickens had quite a different manner of handling the pocket-handkerchief from that of 'the gentleman in the black silk smalls.'

from mere loathsomeness by a fantastic grotesque which is almost *diablerie*; and, above all, Dick Swiveller and the Marchioness would abide with us as they do. There have been some, it is believed, who regard the prodigal son of Dorsetshire (that small but delightful county bred the Dorrits, too, but cannot be šo proud of them; and, though it has had important offspring in literature since, has been unfairly merged in 'Wessex') as one of Dickens's choicest achievements, while the Marchioness herself (would there were more of her!) is simply unique—the sentimental note being never forced, the romantic pleasantly indicated and the humorous triumphantly maintained.

Barnaby Rudge, independently of its internal and detailed attractions, has a special interest for the student as a whole book. It may seem strange that Dickens had not, like almost all his contemporaries and immediate predecessors in novel-writing, attempted the historical novel, which, in the hands of its creator Scott, had shown itself to be a royal road to praise and profit. The reasons why he had not are speculative, and, though more than one could easily be alleged[1], there is no room here for mere speculation. The fact that he attempted it now is a fact, and to be registered with the companion fact that, except in *A Tale of Two Cities*, he never attempted it again. And these two facts, taken with the character of the particular books, suggest that, in the kind, as a kind, he did not feel himself at home. It is certain that the historical events and personages in *Barnaby Rudge* are not the main source or cause of the interest, though they are, with a skill which the author did not often show elsewhere, constantly made the occasion of it. That the actual Gordon riots, though described with splendid vigour and with a careful attention to documentary detail which sometimes suggests Macaulay and sometimes Carlyle, were somewhat exaggerated in presentation was to be expected, and matters but little, especially as the tale is most powerfully told. But, once more, the chief attraction of the book is in the comic or heroi-comic accessories. Barnaby is, of course, Smike endowed with some more heroic qualities; and Hugh stands to Barnaby, with a melodramatic addition, very much as Barnaby does to Smike. Gashford rings up once more the unwelcome *eidolon* of the stage villain, and lord George is ineffective, while the tragedy part connected with Barnaby's father and the Haredales were much better away. But the Vardens and Sim

---

[1] As, for instance, want of knowledge of past times and, hence, want of sympathy with them. See, *post*, on *A Child's History*.

Tappertit and Miggs and old John Willet (a little overdone perhaps) are of the best Dickens quality. Even Dennis, who stands to Squeers very much as Hugh to Smike and sometimes shivers on the brink of caricature, can be accepted as a whole. The blot on the book is Sir John Chester, who is not only, once more, 'of the boards,' merely, but, also, is an abiding proof of the author's weakness in historical psychology. Lord Chesterfield had some real, and more assumed, foibles, common in his time, and he was a man of no high passions and few great actions. But he was a man (as even Horace Walpole, who hated him, admits) of singular weight and wits; not a few of his letters show real good nature and good feeling under fashionable disguises; he might have been a great statesman, and he was quite a human being. His double, here, is little better than a puppet, and a puppet 'made up' wrong.

The great attractions, however, and the smaller defects of the book in detail, subordinate themselves, in a general view of Dickens, to the question of the total result. Was this substitution of the more ambitious and unified style an improvement on the rambling chronicle of humour and incident, comic mainly, sometimes serious, which had formed the staple of his earlier books? Opinions will, of course, differ, but that of the present writer inclines to the negative answer. There is, certainly, no falling off in it as regards power; on the contrary, there are variations and additions in this respect. But, on analysing the satisfaction derived from it, one finds that the sources of this satisfaction fall apart from each other almost as much as in the more disconnected chronicles of the earlier books. There is still no 'total impression,' but a succession of situations, incidents, utterances, which excite amusement, suspense, pity, terror and other kinds or phases of interest. To so remarkable an extent is this the case that, in almost all Dickens's books, if you take the appearances of one character and put them together in what the eighteenth century would have called a 'history,' with as little inclusion of their companions and surroundings as possible (the thing has once or twice been tried by injudicious meddlers), a great deal of the interest is lost. The successive situations form, as it were, separate *tableaux*, to which all the persons and circumstances contained in them are necessary, but which refuse to combine in any strict sense, preferring merely to follow one another.

Almost immediately after the completion of *Master Humphrey's Clock* (or, rather, of the two novels for which it had long been nothing but a mechanical sort of cover, or even label), Dickens undertook, in the spring of 1842, his journey to America—the first of a series of longer or shorter visits to foreign countries which became frequent and exercised a great influence, both direct and indirect, on his work. This particular voyage produced *American Notes* as an immediate, and *Martin Chuzzlewit* as a not long delayed, consequence.

In the *Notes*, their author may be thought to have been a little oblivious of the sarcasm[1] contained in his own Mr Weller's suggestion that Mr Pickwick should escape from the Fleet in 'a pianner' to America and then come back and 'write a book about the Merrikins as'll pay all his expenses and more if he blows 'em up enough.' But, though the subjects of the description probably disliked even more the subsequent utilisation of his experiences in the novel, the extra-severity of which, to some extent, they had provoked by their complaints[2], this latter was much more legitimate; and *Martin Chuzzlewit*, undoubtedly, is one of Dickens's greatest successes. A hint has been given above that, here again, the present writer cannot acknowledge true tragedy in Dickens. Jonas may not be an absolutely impossible creature, but his improbability, as he is presented, is so great, and his ethical-aesthetic disgustingness is so little palliated by actual touches of nature or of artistic power, that he becomes intolerable to some people, and has upon the book the same effect as might be produced by a crushed black beetle between its actual leaves—that of an irrelevant and intruded abomination. His father is of the Ralph Nickleby and Gride order, with too slight a difference; and Mercy, like others of Dickens's mixed characters, is not mixed 'convincingly.' But, once more, all this could be cut out with perfect ease and then you may say 'Here's richness' indeed. There is, in the bulk of the book, and in the majority of its characters, an intensity of *verve*, 'a warmth of imagination which excites the composition of the writer,' only to be found in *Pickwick* earlier and never surpassed, and seldom, even in *David Copperfield*, equalled later. Martin himself, whether unreformed or reformed, may have too much of the stock quality which clings strangely to nominal heroes; his grandfather may have some of the old touch of the theatrical tarbrush;

---

[1] This, no doubt, was aimed at Mrs Trollope. Marryat had not yet written.

[2] The indignation, though natural, was scarcely wise. There are, on the whole, more compliments than reproaches; the real sting does not come out till *Martin Chuzzlewit* itself, and no 'institution,' except the sore place of slavery, is seriously attacked. As a book, *American Notes*, though amusing enough, perforce lacks the peculiar fantastic attraction of the novels; and, perhaps, in it, the tendency to exaggerated description, which, later, was to be, sometimes, almost disastrous, first displays itself.

Tom Pinch may want a little disinfecting of sentimentalism
for some tastes. But the Pecksniffs, Mark Tapley, Mrs Gamp,
'Todgers's'—any number of minorities display the true Dickens,
once more, *in excelsis*. Whether the American scenes were, at
the time, over-coloured in fact is, now, merely a historical question.
That they justify themselves artistically few competent judges will
deny.

Between *American Notes* and its second crop in fiction, Dickens
had begun the remarkable series of Christmas books which,
probably, gave him almost as much popularity, in the strictest
sense of the word, as any other part of his work. Beginning in
1843 with *A Christmas Carol*, they continued annually through
The Chimes, The Cricket on the Hearth, The Battle of Life and
The Haunted Man for five years and only ceased when the
establishment of *Household Words* changed them to Christmas
stories of smaller bulk which, in that paper and in *All the Year
Round*, were scattered over the rest of his life and produced some
things perhaps of greater literary value than the 'books.' The
division, though partly, if not wholly, accidental in origin, is a real
one ; and the first batch only had better be noticed here, reserving
the 'stories' for subsequent criticism.

Dickens himself, in the brief later preface to the collected
Christmas Books, describes them as 'a whimsical kind of masque
intended to awaken loving and forbearing thoughts.' In later
days, ignorant and hasty writers have, sometimes, credited him with
creating the popular notion of Christmas as a season of enlarged
heart, and, also, waistcoat. Scores and hundreds of passages from
all ages of our literature refute this folly ; and the simple fact
that Washington Irving wrote *Bracebridge Hall* when Dickens
was at the blacking manufactory is enough to expose its gross
ignorance. But the idea of Christmas as a season of good feeding
and good feeling was congenial to all Dickens's best characteristics,
though it may have slightly encouraged some of his weaknesses.
The fanciful supernatural, too, for which influences (chiefly, though
not wholly, German) had already created a great taste, was
thoroughly in his line, and he had used it in some of the inset
stories of *Pickwick* and elsewhere not without effect. Of the five
actual books, only one *The Battle of Life* can be called a positive
failure ; it is, indeed, probably the worst thing that Dickens, after
he came to his own, ever did in fiction except *George Silverman's
Explanation*. Some have found his true quality in Britain, the
gloomy footman, and it may, at least, be conceded to them that it is

difficult to find it anywhere else. *The Chimes* and *The Cricket on the Hearth* have been great favourites, though, to some tastes, the first is almost fatally injured by dull stock social satire—lacking all real sting of individuality in Sir Joseph Bowley and alderman Cute and others ; while *The Cricket,* with some refreshing chirps in Tilly Slowboy and elsewhere, does not, to some tastes, seem quite 'to come off.' The first 'book,' *A Christmas Carol* and the last, *The Haunted Man* are, by far, the best and the *Carol* is delightful. We must, of course, grant—as we must grant to Mrs Barbauld in the case of *The Ancient Mariner*—that its story is 'improbable'; there is scarcely another objection that can be sustained against it except in the eyes of those to whom all sentiment and all fairy tales are red rags. *The Haunted Man* is more unequal and some-times commits the old fault of 'forcing the note.' But the Tetterbys are of the first water ; they are, indeed, better than the Cratchits, their parallels in the *Carol* ; the good angel Milly is managed with an unusual freedom from exaggeration or mawkish-ness ; and, in the serious parts, unequal as they are, there are touches and flashes of a true romantic quality which Dickens often attempted but less often attained.

The years which produced these by-works produced, also, not a little else. *Martin Chuzzlewit* itself overran a considerable portion of them, and a long visit (two visits, indeed) to Italy resulted in the *Pictures* from that country originally published in *The Daily News,* which Dickens nominally edited for a week or two but quickly relinquished. He had, thus, no time during them for more than one new attempt at fiction on the great scale. *Dealings with the Firm of Dombey and Son,* the title of which posterity, in general, has wisely cut down to the last three words, if not even to one, *Dombey,* is of importance in more than size. In the first place, it marks a very important transition in the handling of scene and personage, especially the latter. For reasons obvious enough, partly from his biography and partly from the character of the work itself, his drawing of actual society, except as concerns the middle, lower and lowest classes, had been very vague. Mr Pickwick is 'a gentleman retired from business' and, as some of his less discreet admirers almost petulantly insist, he possesses all the moral qualities of gentlemanliness. Nor are his actions, nor is his general behaviour, inconsistent with that status. But his 'atmosphere' is certainly not quite that which we know not merely from other novels but from letters, biographies, indisputable documents of all sorts, to have been that, not merely of the upper ranks, but of the upper

middle and professional classes at the time. The superior personages of *Oliver Twist, Nicholas Nickleby, The Old Curiosity
Shop* and *Martin Chuzzlewit* (*Barnaby Rudge,* definitely dealing
with the past, here falls out) partake of the same vagueness when
they are not purely theatrical. But, in *Dombey,* Dickens has more
or less shaken off the theatrical, and, apparently, is endeavouring to
observe the actual manners and character of society. Dombey is,
at least, meant to be an actual city man of quite the highest class.
Dr Blimber and Major Bagstock, however obviously caricatured,
are meant to retain the general character of an officer who has
emerged from real barracks, a clergyman and schoolmaster who is
no shadowy angel like the good clergymen of *Pickwick* and *The
Old Curiosity Shop,* no fantastic tyrant like Squeers in the past
and, to some extent, Creakle in the future, but a rational, if somewhat pedantic, individual who has passed through a university and
taken orders himself and is preparing other persons for the same
or similar occupations. Even the Dombey servants, though, of
course, comically heightened, are nearer to the actual population
of London areas than ever before. It is true that Dickens has (to
avail oneself of the dictum of the dictionaries that '*dis-* is used at
will to form words' and to coin one much wanted in English) 'disdamaged' himself most freely in this respect. Cousin Feenix,
though almost the first 'aristocrat' whom he represents as a
thoroughly good fellow, is, of course, all but burlesqued ; Mrs
Skewton is, at least, much exaggerated, and, as for Edith, she is
completely 'out of drawing,' as is, by common consent, her villain-
lover Carker, who once more belongs to the tribe of Monks, save
that, unfortunately, he is much less shadowy. Even in the characters
not yet mentioned, the element of exaggeration and caricature
comes in to some extent. Susan Nipper, though we should be very
sorry if she had not, has it ; Toots has it to the utmost possible or
impossible extent ; Captain Cuttle (and great would be the loss)
could not exist without it ; even Miss Tox has it in no slight
degree. He has further relieved himself in the old directions by
doubling, in the sentimental way, with more detail, the part of
little Nell with that of little Paul and, in the melodramatic, by
the retribution of Carker. But, at the same time, *Dombey* remains
his first attempt at painting actual modern society—his first to
'disfantasy,' so far as he could, the atmosphere, and to be not
merely realist but real. General remarks as to his success will come
best later, but the point of departure should be marked.

About a year after the close of *Dombey,* and a few months after the issue of *The Haunted Man*, the time having been also partly occupied by the composition of his favourite and (as some think) greatest book, *David Copperfield*, Dickens also undertook the new and very important adventure of editing *Household Words*, a weekly periodical which very soon justified its title and which, with its sequel *All the Year Round*, he carried on for more than twenty years till his death.

The two (though he by no means discontinued the method of monthly issues for the bigger novels which would have overloaded a weekly paper) contained, thenceforward, a great deal of his own work; they caused a, perhaps, rather beneficent change of the Christmas books into shorter Christmas stories and they undoubtedly enriched popular literature with a great deal of good work besides his own. Dickens was a decidedly despotic, and a rather egotistic, editor; and work of the very highest merit, off his own special lines, would have had little chance with him. But he succeeded in attracting and training a remarkable number of competent writers who could, more or less, fall in with those lines. The short story and the short miscellaneous essay which had already made lodgments in the monthly magazines found open house in these weekly ones; and, though a great many of the contributions have been more permanently and accessibly enshrined in collected *Works* of himself, of Wilkie Collins, of Collins's less known but, perhaps, even more gifted brother Charles, of Mrs Gaskell and of others, there must remain a considerable residuum on which it is rather surprising that the active reprinters of today have not laid hands. It is certain that there are few luckier 'finds' on a wet day in a country house, or, still more, a country inn, than a volume of *Household Words* or *All the Year Round*.

The *opus majus*, however, above glanced at, was given to the world in the old monthly form by itself, though its first part did not appear till a month or two after the first number of *Household Words*. Of his own interest in *David Copperfield*, the author has made no secret—hardly any of the autobiographical reasons of that interest. But, to all 'men of feeling,' in something more than the sense of Sterne and Mackenzie, the main appeal of the book must lie in a fact which Dickens could not be expected to indicate —which, probably, he did not consciously recognise. Copperfield is not only partly what Dickens was, but, to a much larger extent, what Dickens could not be and would have liked to be. The early sufferings and the early successes were there; but the interval between them had no counterpart in fact. The liberal education at the Wickfield's and Mr Strong's which succeeds the Murdstone and Grinby purgatory, the position at Doctors' Commons and the society which it opened, the other 'liberal education' of the successive loves, 'calf' and real, for Miss Shepherd, Miss Larkins, almost Rosa Dartle, Dora and Agnes, very different from the shadowy and unfelt amorosities of the earlier books ; the true boy's worship of Steerforth—whatever reserves may be made as to Steerforth himself —and the rest, had been denied to him or very partially given hitherto : now they flourished. From this 'lived' or 'would-have-been-lived' character of the book comes its unique freedom from what has been unkindly but intelligibly called the pantomime character of much of the author's work. Even Mr Dick, much more Miss Betsey, is free from this, and it only appears (if there) in mere side-sketches like that of 'Hamlet's Aunt,' of no importance to the story. Nobody, save those unfortunate persons before referred to who are untouched by the comic spirit altogether, can say 'Let us have no more of this foolery' to any part of *David Copperfield* ; though the comic spirit is sufficiently present, from Mr Chillip's first appearance at the Rookery to his last in the coffee room. On the other side, the position is, perhaps, a little more assailable. Although there was, perhaps, no reason for making Dora quite so silly in life, it must be an excessive, and, probably, rather an affected, cynicism which finds her death mawkish. But it may be allowed that the triangle of Dr Strong, his wife and her admirer is handled rather unintelligibly, and that Uriah Heep, though not to be spared, has a little too much of the old type villain about him. Few people now consider Rosa Dartle an entire success, and the whole Steerforth and little Em'ly business is open to the other old charge of melodrama. But Mr Micawber (though the success may have been obtained a little in the teeth of the fifth commandment) is an unsurpassed triumph ; most of the pure comedy is first rate ; the chapter 'I Fall into Captivity' has, in anything like its own kind, no superior in fiction ; and, almost throughout, the reality of interest felt by the author exalts all his powers and keeps down all his foibles. There is, in short, hardly any possibility of denying that *David Copperfield* is Dickens's most varied and, at the same time, most serious and best sustained effort—one to be accepted 'with all faults' on its side and with all gratitude on the reader's.

As Dickens had never before attained to such an equable combination of the various elements of his power and skill, so he never attained to it again ; though some would make a partial exception for *Great Expectations.* Nothing that he did later, except (and this is not invariably allowed) his last and unfinished work, failed to contain something of his best; nothing, perhaps (except that and *Hard Times*), was without something of his very best. But the total results were much more unequal; and they began to show, in a degree far greater than had appeared in the earlier work (though there had been something of it there), the 'obsession' of social and, to some extent, of political purpose. For a year or fifteen months, after the close of *David Copperfield* in 1850, Dickens gave the public nothing except *Household Words.* But, in the spring of 1852, he began *Bleak House,* which occupied the rest of that, and most of the next, year. It illustrates most strikingly, and, perhaps, more valuably than any of its sucessors, the remarks just made. Most of the comic, and some of the serious, parts are 'true Dickens' to the very *n*th; and it is, perhaps, one of the most interesting of all, except in the character of its quasi-heroine and part narrator, Esther Summerson, who is one of the most irritating of Dickens's unconscious angels. But the overdone onslaught on chancery and the slighter, but still constantly attempted, satire on parliament, the aristocracy and so forth, become, at times, almost insufferable, and the author's determination to take things seriously provokes a corresponding and retaliatory disposition to take seriously in him things that one hardly notices in the earlier books. Of the too famous Skimpole matter one need not say much. Macaulay, in one of the very latest entries of his diary, has expressed the judgment of most people who have impartially examined the matter. Nobody dreams of imputing to Leigh Hunt the worst rascalities of his *eidolon,* such as the selling of Jo. But Dickens himself afterwards admitted that he took 'the light externals of character' from this veteran of letters— then still living and his friend—and everybody knew that some such not very light characteristics—reckless running into debt and complete neglect of obligation—were common to the fictitious and to the actual personages. The fault of taste, to call it no worse, was very grave; but, as no one but a foolish partisan would maintain that good taste was Dickens's strong point, there need be no more said[1].

Other things of a different kind should be noticed because, as has been said, they become stronger and stronger features— not for the better—in Dickens's general work henceforward. Not to

---

[1] The taste of the Boythorn-Landor pendant in portraiture may not have been perfect; but, at any rate, there was nothing offensive in it.

mention many minor improbabilities, the reason for Mr Tulkinghorn's persecution of lady Dedlock, on which the whole plot turns, is
never made apparent or plausible. The divulging of the secret could
do neither himself nor anybody else any earthly good; he certainly
was not looking forward to be bought off; and the actual revelation
would have been most likely to damage very seriously his character
as a sort of living Chubb's safe for such matters, not to mention that
silence gave him continuance of power over his victim[1]. One might
add to this the quite illegal hunting of Jo by the police (which
would have got them into considerable trouble if it had ever come
before a magistrate) and the entire presentation of some characters,
especially Mr Vholes. For the 'spontaneous combustion' business,
Dickens had (as Marryat had had before him) the excuse of some
quasi-scientific authority; and there is so much that is good in
the book that one is loth to speak anything but good of it. But
it certainly does show a 'black drop'—or two black drops—of
quarrelling excessively with the world and of over-emphasising
scenes and characters.

These drops continued to spread and to ink the water for some
time, if not for ever, afterwards. The year 1854 was a rather disastrous one in Dickens's annals. It saw the production in book form
of two works, both of which had previously passed through *Household Words*. Of the deplorable *Child's History of England*,
it is not necessary to say more than that it is, perhaps, the capital
instance of a man of genius, not tempted by the wellknown 'want
of pence,' or by anything except his own wilfulness, going far out of
his way to write something for which he was (in everything but the
possession of narrative faculty) absolutely disqualified. But *Hard
Times*, the other fruit of that year, cannot be passed over quite so
lightly. The book has had its admirers; and for at least one
thing that it gives us—the Sleary group—some readers, at any
rate, would put up with even worse company. There is certainly
genuine pathos—whether overdone or not is, perhaps, a matter of
taste—in the Stephen and Rachel part, while (a thing which has
sometimes escaped even laudatory critics) Louisa, though she is
made the cause or occasion of some of the least good parts of the
book, is more of a real live girl of the nineteenth century than

---

[1] If anyone urges lady Dedlock's disregard of his wishes with regard to
Rosa as a provocation, it can only be said that this is utterly inadequate.
Mr Tulkinghorn may have been as fond of power as he was of port wine; but he
ought to have been as good a judge of the one as the other, and to have known that
he would lose more than he gained by making disobedience to an arbitrary caprice an
unpardonable sin.

Dickens ever achieved, except in the more shadowy sketch of Estella in *Great Expectations*. But these good things, comic or pathetic or analytic, are buried in such a mass of exaggeration and false drawing that one struggles with the book as with a bad dream. There are, unfortunately, many such young whelps as Tom Gradgrind, and many such cads and curmudgeons as Josiah Bounderby; but Dickens has made Tom nothing but a whelp and Bounderby nothing but a curmudgeon and a cad. Now, that is not the way in which the actual Creator makes people; or, if He very occasionally does so, these exceptions are not to be used in art by His imitators in fiction. The elder Gradgrind, on the whole, and especially towards the end, has more verisimilitude; but he himself, for a long time, his school and the society of Coketown generally, with Mrs Sparsit and her visions about Louisa in particular, have got hopelessly into the world of ugly and preposterous fantasy—a world where, to adapt the classical myth, Phobetor reigns, his sway untempered by Icelus—upon which Dickens was too often tempted to draw. The book seems to have been rather popular with foreign critics, partly because it has a certain unity of plot and action, and, perhaps, also, partly because it gives a picture of England unfavourable, indeed, but rather consistent with the continental view of us. But it is difficult, from the standpoint of comparative and impartial criticism, not to put it lowest among Dickens's finished novels.

His work as editor—which, like all his work, he took the reverse of lightly—and, perhaps, some of the inevitable revenge which nature exacts for the putting forth of such power as he had shown for nearly twenty years, rather slackened Dickens's production after this; and it was not till the close of 1855 that he began to send *Little Dorrit* on its usual year and a half, or rather more, of serial appearance. This novel has been even more variously judged than *Hard Times*; indeed, judgment of it has been known to vary remarkably, not merely as between different individuals, but as formed by the same individual at different times. Probably the general result, at first reading, has been unfavourable. Not merely the tiresome ' crusade ' element, which had made its appearance in the books immediately preceding, but the tendency to dwell, and thump, upon particular notes not always very melodious or satisfying, which, more or less, had been apparent throughout, are unluckily prominent here. And the newer feature—that is to say, the attempt at a rather elaborate plot which adds little or nothing to the real interest of the story—

appears likewise. Carker's teeth, in *Dombey*, are excusable
and almost negligible beside the trivial, tedious and exasperating business of Pancks, with his puffings and snortings, and
the outward and visible signs of hypocrisy in his employer
Casby. That employer's daughter Flora[1] is so exceedingly
amusing that one does not care to enquire too closely into
her verisimilitude; and 'Mr F.'s aunt' is one of those pure
extravaganzas of the author who justify themselves offhand.
But the Circumlocution office is merely a nuisance of a worse
kind in literature than even its prototype in life; the soured
blood and shabby state of the Gowans as human fringes of
aristocracy might have been hit off admirably in a few touches,
but are spoilt by many. The absence of that calming and restraining
influence which has been noted in *Copperfield* is felt in every part
of the book except the pure extravaganzas just referred to. The
Marshalsea scenes, which, again, are autobiographic (for Dickens
the elder had been immured there), escape partially because there
is much of this fantastic element with a great deal of real 'business.' But the Dorrits themselves, especially when the father is
released; that unpoetical and dismal 'House of Usher' where
the Clennam family and firm abide (of all deplorable heroes
Arthur Clennam is, perhaps, the most deplorable); the contrasted Merdle household with its stale social satire ('Bar' and
'Physician' escape best); the old toy-theatre villains Rigaud and
Flintwinch (Affery saves herself with Mr F.'s aunt, and one would
like to have heard a conversation between them); even the
Meagles family and the puppet Tattycoram and the 'villain*ess*'
Miss Wade—all these come under the same curse of fundamental
unreality which derives hardly any benefit from the fantastic
energy expended by the author. And yet it is one of the most
remarkable testimonies to Dickens's really magical power that,
when the faults have become familiar and, thus, cease to tease
much, *Little Dorrit* remains almost as *re*-readable as any but the
very best of its companions.

These faults, however, could not escape notice, and they

[1] Unfavourable critics of Dickens from other than purely literary points of view
have, sometimes, declared that Flora is Dora grown old, and that both had a live
original. It is sufficient to say that the evidence produced for this is quite insufficient;
and that, if it were true, Dickens would have made an artistic blunder almost greater
than the ethical one, and extremely improbable. Flora may have been attractive
enough as a girl, and if Dora had lived she might have lost much of her attraction.
But, had she lived, she never could have become Flora; and Flora never, at any time of
life or fortune, could have been Dora.

suggested (unless *Bleak House* and *Hard Times* had done it before them) to Anthony Trollope a rather smart scenario-parody of Dickens's manner in *The Warden*. But the completion of the book brought many other matters to give Dickens's mind new turns. He had already bought, but had not yet settled in, his famous country house, Gadshill place; in the spring of 1858, he was separated from his wife—a fact which requires no comment here; the separation was the indirect cause of his giving up *Household Words* and starting *All the Year Round*; and he thought of, and began, the 'readings' of his own work which brought him in large sums of money; created for him a new kind of popular reputation; enabled him to display his singular histrionic faculty; but, also, beyond all doubt (combined, as they were, with unbroken, though not quite such abundant, production of original work), put a strain upon his nervous system which had a great deal to do with his comparatively early death.

In the new paper, he used his energies in a more strictly literary, and a much more permanently delectable, fashion, starting off with an elaborate historical romance, *A Tale of Two Cities*, and contributing to it, from time to time, exercises in his own earliest kind but of much greater power, variety, originality and artistic value. He put them forth as reports entitled *The Uncommercial Traveller*, under which form they were separately published, in successively enlarged collections, during the remainder of his life. Sometimes, but not too often, he made them the vehicle of his social-reform purpose; sometimes, they were sketches of scenes and manners in the style of the earlier 'eye-witness' papers of *Household Words*, to which Charles Collins had been a main contributor; sometimes, more or less fantastic pieces; but, almost always, good. *A Tale of Two Cities* belongs to quite a different type, in almost all respects, from that of any of his previous novels, save that, like *Barnaby Rudge*, it has a historical subject. It would seem as if he had intended to leave out the comic element altogether; and, though, for him, this was nearly an impossibility, there is certainly very little, except in the grim-grotesque of the body-snatcher Jerry Cruncher and his family; the grotesque, if not grim, ways of the faithful Miss Pross; and a very few other touches. Taking for canvas *The French Revolution* of his friend Carlyle (for whom he had a strong admiration), he embroidered upon it a rather strictly constructed, but not very richly furnished, story of action and character, bringing in a victim of the *ancien régime*, a wicked example of it (unfortunately, as much a caricature as is Sir John Chester, in Dickens's most nearly allied book), a younger aristocrat, who would fain atone for his family's crimes and who loves the victim's daughter, who nearly falls a prey to the vengeance of 'the people,' but who is saved by the self-sacrifice of his rival, a ne'er-do-weel barrister. In contrast to all this, we have some leaders of 'the people' themselves, especially a much overdone wine-shop keeper and his wife—a still more exaggerated *tricoteuse* of the guillotine. The book has been said to be more of a drama than of a novel, and it has been actually dramatised more than once—recently, it would seem, with considerable success. Even as a novel, it has been highly praised by some good judges. To people not acquainted with Carlyle's own book, and even to some who are, the vigour of its sketches of the oppression and the terror might, no doubt, carry it off sufficiently ; and the character of Sydney Carton is altogether of a higher type than any other that Dickens ever attempted. But the rival for whom Carton sacrifices himself is entirely uninteresting ; Lucie Manette, the heroine, has little more attraction than any pretty and good girl, so labelled, might have ; and even her father's sufferings and madness are doubtfully treated; while the mannerisms of expression are stronger than ever, and the glaring high lights and pitchy shadows weary more than they move.

There are, however, those who admire *A Tale of Two Cities* sincerely, and who think but little of the novel which followed it through the paper and in publication ; while there are others who take up the *Tale* more seldom than any other of Dickens's books, and who consider *Great Expectations* one of his very masterpieces, putting it with the 'wild freshness of morning' in *Pickwick* and the noonday completeness of *David Copperfield* as an 'evening voluntary' of the most delightful kind. It is not faultless. The mannerism and the exaggeration of all the later books sometimes break through, and the grime of the heroine's parentage is not only unnecessary but ill-managed. That obsession of feeble satire as to rank and respect to rank, which was one of Dickens's numerous forms of his own 'king Charles's head' disease, comes in, and melodrama is not far off. But he had never done anything, not even in *Copperfield* itself, so real as 'Pip,' with his fears, his hopes, his human weaknesses and meannesses, his love, his bearing up against misfortune. Never did **he** combine analysis and synthesis so thoroughly as here. He has given Estella little space and some unattractive points, so that some do not like her; but others see in her at least the possibility of a heroine more thoroughly real and far more fascinating than any in Dickens. Joe Gargery has conciliated almost everybody, and his alarming wife, Pip's terrible sister, does not require her punishment in order to conciliate some. The Havisham part may seem extravagant, but is not so to all; and Trabb's boy and Mr Jaggers and Wemmick and yet other persons and things garnish a delightful feast.

He never did anything so good again; and, though he had nearly ten years to live, he did not, in the way of actual literature, do very much at all. The fatal 'readings' were filling his pocket and draining his powers; editing took much of his time; he travelled a good deal, and even he began to find that 'his chariot wheels drave heavily'[1]. In 1865, he had a serious illness, with threatenings of something like paralysis, which was certainly not staved off by the great railway accident of that year on the South Eastern railway, in which, though he sustained no visible injury, he was severely shaken. But, in these years, with all his other employments, he managed, besides two or three smaller things— the powerful if slightly melodramatic *Hunted Down*, the almost worthless *George Silverman's Explanation*, the charming *Holiday Romance* as well as not a few notable Christmas stories—to finish one long novel, *Our Mutual Friend*, and to plan and begin another, *The Mystery of Edwin Drood*. This latter appeared as a fragment between his return from that quest of suicide, as it may be called—his second journey to America, in 1868, to read himself into twenty thousand pounds and almost into his grave— and his actual death in 1870, the interval being occupied by further readings at home which brought eight thousand pounds more, and the death warrant. He had added to his early selections the murder scene in *Oliver Twist*, which he read with an intensity described by those who heard it as almost frightful, and not such as would have been particularly wholesome for a young man in full strength. He was a man of nearly sixty, broken down by five and thirty years of varied work, much of it of a kind most trying to the brain, and actually threatened, for the last five, with

---

[a] One instance of his exceedingly nervous temperament, confessed by himself, may have found sympathy in others who had not his qualification of genius or of energy. If he had an appointment, say at mid-day, he could not work with any comfort in the earlier morning.

cerebral and cardiac disease. It is only wonderful that the two burning ends of the candle took so long to meet.

Of *Edwin Drood* itself, little need be said here. It has, through one of the numerous oddities of the human mind, received a great amount of attention, repeatedly and recently renewed, simply because it is unfinished ; but, of intrinsic attraction, it has, for some critics, little or nothing except its renewed pictures of the beloved city of Rochester, first drawn and latest sketched of all Dickens's 'places.' But the Christmas stories of the two weekly papers and his last considerable and complete novel, *Our Mutual Friend*, require longer notice. Like, but even more than, *The Uncommercial Traveller* articles (which he continued during most of this time), the 'stories' contain some of Dickens's most enjoyable things. He had begun the substitution of collections only partly written by himself for single, and singly written, 'books,' twenty years earlier, in *Household Words*, and his con- tributions there included the pathetic story of 'Richard Double- dick' in *The Seven Poor Travellers*; some vigorous stuff in *The Wreck of the Golden Mary* and 'The Island of Silver-store[1]'; and, above all, the unsurpassable legend of child-loves told by the 'Boots at the Holly-Tree Inn.' But, in the *All the Year Round* set—nine in number—the general level of Dickens's own stuff was even higher, except, perhaps, in the last, *No Thoroughfare*, which he wrote in conjunction with Wilkie Collins, but where the disciple's hand is more evident than the master's. The framework of *The Haunted House* (as, indeed, of most of the sets) is his, and admir- able, while 'The Ghost in Master B.'s room' is one of the best of his numerous half humorous, half sad reminiscences of his own youth. In *A Message from the Sea*, we have, for the first time, actual collaboration in these 'stories' with Wilkie Collins, and would rather have Dickens alone. *Tom Tiddler's Ground* im- proves, and, with *Somebody's Luggage*, we reach, in Dickens's own part, something like his quintessence in the case of Christopher the waiter. It persists in the twin appearances of *Mrs Lirriper*, and is partly upheld in *Doctor Marigold's Prescriptions*, but whether or not it is in full force at *Mugby Junction* is a point on which men may differ, though, in the child Polly, he is, as usual, at his best. On the whole, too, his part in this batch of Christmas numbers (they contain much excellent work of others) is practically never bad and sometimes first rate.

To reverse this sentence almost directly and say that *Our*

[1] In *The Perils of Certain English Prisoners*.

Mutual Friend is sometimes nearly bad and never quite first rate would be excessive; but it is only a very harsh and sweeping statement containing something not far from the truth. The illness and the accident above mentioned, no doubt, conditioned the book to some extent unfairly for the worse; but its main faults are scarcely chargeable upon them. It has been justly and acutely remarked that, though Wilkie Collins was, undoubtedly, Dickens's pupil, the pupil had a good deal of reflex influence on the master, not always for good[1]. The plot of *Our Mutual Friend* is distinctly of Wilkie Collins's type, but it is not managed with the cat-like intricacy and dexterity, or with the dramatically striking situations, which were Collins's strong points. In what may be called the central plot within a plot — the miser-and-tyrant metamorphosis of Mr Boffin—the thing is in itself so improbable, and is so clumsily and tediously treated, as to suggest throwing the book aside. The whole Veneering society, barring a few of the 'inimitable' touches to be noticed presently, is preposterous, disagreeable and dull. It was, indeed, interesting, not long ago, to find a critic of the younger generation candidly admitting that, to him, Eugene Wrayburn had been, if he was not still, a striking, if not an ideal, figure. But, as the strangest mistakes are constantly made about the relations of life and literature, especially as to 'mid-Victorian' matters, it may be well to put on solemn record here that, among well-bred young men of 1865, Mr Wrayburn, in, at least, some of his part, would have run great risk of being regarded as what had been earlier called a 'tiger,' and what, somewhat later, was said, like the tiger, to 'bound.' The good Jew Riah, and the spirited but slightly irrational Betty Higden, have failed to move even some who are very friendly to Dickens's sentiment. Still, the book is saved from sharing the position of *Hard Times* by its abundance of the true Dickensian grotesque, a little strained, perhaps, now and then, but always refreshing. The dolls' dressmaker is, perhaps, a distant relation and inheritrix of Miss Mowcher, but she is raised to a far higher power; in fact, one almost wishes that Dickens had not chosen to make her happy with a good scavenger. Her bad child-father is, in literature, if not in life, excused by his acts and sayings. Some have been hard on Silas Wegg; the present writer, admitting that he ends appropriately in the slop cart, does not think him out of place earlier. Rogue Riderhood would be ill to spare; and

---

[1] The present writer intends no injustice to Collins's powers, which were great. But, unluckily, nearly all his faults and some, even, of his merits, tended to aggravate Dickens's own failings.

so, at the other extremity of class and character, would be Twemlow, the single soul saved out of the Veneering group, except Boots and Buffer as supers. These and some others flit agreeably enough in the regions of fantastic memory to make one willing not to dwell on the darker side further than to observe that, though some of the right-grotesquerie saves the other members of the Wilfer family, Bella, for a long time, is merely an underbred and unattractive minx, while, after her reformation, she joins the great bevy of what, in the sacred language of the Bona Dea, it is whispered, are called 'Lady Janes'—mechanical lay-figures, adaptable to various costumes, in this case that of the foolishly affectionate bride and young mother. As for her husband, except in his account to himself of the attempt to drug or drown him, which is rather well done, it is impossible to feel the slightest interest in the question whether he was drowned as well as drugged, or not.

It is, therefore, not improbable, to speak in the manner of the 'gelid critic,' that, even had Dickens been less reckless of his failing health, and had that health given him a fuller span of life, no further masterpieces would have been added to his tale; and, so, the story of his work need not be affected by that sense of possible injustice to future achievements which, occasionally, besets such things. The system of survey which has been actually adopted may seem to some too pedestrian—too much of a mere inventory. But it has been adopted quite deliberately and with an easy choice of other plans of a more generalising and high-flying character. And it may be possible to justify the choice in the few remarks of a more general kind which will close the chapter.

The survey of Dickens, then, is, perhaps, best conducted in the way of a catalogue, yet of a *catalogue raisonné*, precisely because his inspiration itself is, after all, mainly an inspiration of detail. Those who feel his special charm most keenly and most constantly do not, as a rule, find it in actually close-woven stories like *A Tale of Two Cities* and *Hard Times*, or in books with an ostensibly elaborate plot, like most of the later ones. The term 'phantasmagoria'— which, though it does not, perhaps, please some of the more fanatical Dickensites, is often attached by critical admirers as a label, but a label of honour, to his work—almost expressly excludes definite scenes, acts, plays or even trilogies or cyclical sequences of the more sharply separated and elaborately planned kind. 'The Shapes arise,' to borrow an excellent phrase from Whitman; the scenery rises with them; they play their part; and they pass. Shapes and scenes alike are of extraordinary number and variety; they very seldom, as has been said above, merely repeat each other, though there are some natural family likenesses among them; they are grave or gay, tragic, comic or grotesque. Sometimes, especially at the first, they are of somewhat too familiar or 'stock' character; sometimes, especially at the last, their rising, action and passing seem to be accompanied by more effort, somewhere, than is compatible with the keeping of the vision. But, on the whole, the spring never dries up; the Great stream of people hurrying to and fro never ceases or breaks. Astonishingly devoid of what may be called subject-tautology as the books are, various as are ever their themes, there is a relationship of continuity between them which hardly exists anywhere else. There must be more than one person living who has read Dickens through night after night and week after week as if the whole were one book—a thing (*experto crede*) almost impossible to do with some novelists and a terrible task with all but two or three. The reason why it is possible easily in his case is that you do not read merely for the story—of which, sometimes, there is as little as the knife-grinder had to tell, or for the characters, who rarely excite any passionate interest—but for the Dickens quality of fantastic humour, which may come at any time and is seldom absent long.

But, if this seem an exaggeration, something closely connected with it and referred to briefly already is not: and that is the unique *re*-readableness of Dickens. In this, he surpasses, for those who can taste him at all, even Scott; and he surpasses, also, others whom, in some cases, the same readers would put on a level with him or above him in total literary rank. It may, possibly, be the case that the very superiority of total effect, and the deeper draught of character found in these latter, require the lapse of some time in order to get the table of the mind ready for fresh impressions; while Dickens's crowd of flitting figures and dissolving views always finds a fresh appetite. If you like them at all you will like them always.

How far this bears on the still vexed question of their 'reality' will, probably, be decided by foregone opinion. 'How is it possible that things not fully real should exercise such power?' some may ask, and others may answer, that it is precisely the fantastic element—the contrast of real and unreal—which keeps the charm effective. *David Copperfield*, in its characters, is, undoubtedly, the nearest throughout to persons whom we have met and feel it quite likely that we might meet. Pip, who, to some extent, is David's younger brother, perhaps comes next. It would be hard to find them many companions.

There are other points in Dickens of which some treatment may be expected, but on which it does not seem necessary to say much. Some peculiarities of his earlier style—especially his most unlucky fondness for blank verse imbedded in the more impassioned passages of his prose—have been more than enough rebuked. His irony was seldom happy; first, because he had not the command of himself which irony requires, and, secondly, because, in strict wit, which irony requires still more, he was by no means so strong as he was in humour. His irony, moreover, was almost wholly exerted in the political-social passages where he was never at his best. His politics and his sociology themselves are hot ashes at which there is no need to burn discreet feet or fingers. Certainly he, perhaps more than anyone else, started that curious topsy-turvyfied snobbishness—that 'cult of the *lower* classes'—which has become a more and more fashionable religion up to the present moment.

The more excellent way is to concentrate attention on those purely literary qualities which have given to English literature one of its greatest and most unique figures and contributions of work. He has constantly been compared to Balzac, and the comparison has some solid foundations. But it must be a strange taste which would take in exchange even the great Frenchman for our English Dickens. Of the faults—ethical and aesthetic—of the national character he has plenty : prejudice, party spirit, aptness to speak without sufficient information, lack of criticism, insubordination to even reasonable rules in art and literature, exaggeration, extravagance, doubtful taste. The French themselves, since their romantic transformation, have, at least, pretended to like Dickens; but a criticism on him by Voltaire would be very precious. On the other hand, he has many, if not quite all, of the virtues on which we most pride, or, at least, used to pride, ourselves —courage, independence, individuality, imaginative freshness and activity, which does not disdain to approach the diviner kinds of nonsense, humour, in some, if not all, of its quintessences, kindliness, the sense of comfort and cheerfulness and home. And all these good and bad things he put together for our literary use with an unstinting fertility of device, a daemonic energy, an actual power of artistic creation in certain kinds, to which there is, perhaps, no parallel in our literature and certainly none in any other.

CHAPTER XI

THE POLITICAL AND SOCIAL NOVEL

DISRAELI, CHARLES KINGSLEY, MRS GASKELL, 'GEORGE ELIOT'

OF the four eminent novelists whose names are placed at the head of this chapter, the first three are representative rather of a period than of any school, properly so called, of English prose fiction; while the fourth, whose works, in a sense, complete the cycle of imaginative literature here brought under review, stands, in purpose and in method, as, to some extent, she does in point of time, away from the rest. Yet, the novels of all of them, as well as those of many authors of lesser note who were their contemporaries, had certain notable features in common which were more or less new to English fiction, and which warrant a consideration, side by side, of writers between whom, singly and severally, there was a great and unmistakable diversity of genius.

With Disraeli and Kingsley, as, in a measure, with Bulwer Lytton in certain of his works, and with one or two other writers before them, the English historical novel, which had reached the height of its glories in Scott, and, through him, had come to be imitated in almost every other modern literature, changed into the political (though both Disraeli and Kingsley, the one in passing and the other with conspicuous success, also essayed the older kind of fiction). At the same time, they, and the two women writers whose names are here associated with theirs, were led to give attention to a number of social questions of pressing political significance. Simultaneously and, in part, as a natural result of the expansion of the choice of themes, the new kind of novel, even more distinctly than the historical novel before it, supplemented and enlarged the range of subject on which earlier English fiction, culminating in Richardson, had concentrated its efforts. The treatment, in artistic form, of the experiences of individual men and women, and of the reaction of these experiences upon their thoughts and feelings, had intimately connected English fiction with the philosophy of Rousseau, and with its unparalleled influence upon his generation. Now, the novelist went on to deal with the life and doings, and the intellectual and moral condition, of whole classes of men and women; till, at last, in the stories of George Eliot above all, it became difficult to decide whether the interest of the reader was more widely and effectively challenged by the leading figures in front of the scene or by those which made up the surroundings, constituted the atmosphere, or—to use a word for which we have no satisfactory English equivalent—formed the *milieu* of the action[1].

From the point of view of literary history, these changes, to which the application of the comparative method would find it easy to suggest analogies, connect themselves with the inevitable reaction against the tendencies of the romantic school, which, for some time, had been approaching superannuation. The rights of individual fancy, taste, opinion and belief to go each its own way and pursue each its own subjective course of development had prevailed, with readers of novels, so far as to allow their heroes and heroines the prerogative of an interest enhanced by the very fact of their isolation. The effects of this and other cognate characteristics of the romanticism which had long held the field had begun to show themselves in imaginative literature at large by an increased monotony, by occasional self-satire, by the weakening of poetic forms and by the predominance of lyric over dramatic or epic treatment of literary themes.

Against all this, a reaction, in any case, must have arisen in every branch of English literature, and, most of all, in that which, more than any other, had come to supply the intellectual and imaginative sentiment of the largest body of readers. But there were forces at work in the life of the nation which were certain to cooperate with this reaction, and to impart to it a force beyond that of a literary movement pure and simple, which spends its strength till superseded in its turn.

The literature of English fiction in the period with which these chapters are chiefly concerned, and the beginning of which may be dated from that of the fourth decade of the century, was, in the first place, more and more intent upon dealing with things as they actually were. This realism corresponded to the political and social

---

[1] See, as to what he calls the *Milieuroman*, Dibelius, W., *Englische Romankunst* (Berlin, 1910), vol. II, p. 338.

changes which had given the nation, as a whole, wider and readier opportunities of observing the different parts of its own organism and, thus, of better understanding and appreciating the various aspects and interests of its own life. In the course of the period beginning with the death of George IV (1830), and the passing of the Reform bill (1832), and, even more distinctly, from the accession of queen Victoria (1837) onwards, society, whatever its habits or desires, was no longer able to fence itself round, within limits mainly determined by personal descent and connection with landed property. There was a great movement upwards, as there had been in the Tudor days ; and, while the metropolis, with its predominant commercial interest, was becoming, far more than it had hitherto been, the real capital of the country, other large towns, more especially in the manufacturing districts of the north, were growing into what only one or two of them had been before, real centres of popular life. Much to their own benefit, though, not necessarily, in the same degree, to that of other classes, the court, nobility and wealthier gentry were living under a new light of publicity—a publicity increased by the twofold growth of locomotive facilities and of the public press—and institutions which, for many a generation, had been mainly appropriated to the use of the privileged classes, the universities in especial, were more freely opening their doors. The great professions, including that of the church, were, at the same time, being popularised; and, though the Reform bill had not brought to the popular chamber a representative body of pure radicals of the type of Felix Holt, it was becoming an assembly through whose proceedings and their motive causes a good deal of daylight was allowed to shine.

All this, unmistakably, facilitated the process by which the English novel of the generation which entered into its prime in 1830, or thereabouts, devoted itself very largely to a critical examination of the various classes comprising the nation—however ingeniously this criticism might be interwoven with the narrative of the fictitious experiences of imaginary personages. As a matter of course, it often turned into satire ; but its primary purpose was to exhibit, or, at all events, to seem to exhibit, an actually existing state of things, in lieu of the old romantic pictures either of the present or of the (still more easily misrepresented) past.

In the second place, the condition of affairs in this country during the years 1830 to 1850 (in which fell the greater part of the new productivity of the English political and social novel) was

one of constant ferment, of great fears as well as of high hopes, of
terrible sufferings and of ardent efforts for better things. The
prophet of this period was Carlyle, who proclaimed the message of
an idealism no longer satisfied with the old aims and methods
of a political philosophy which, in fiction, too, had not been left
unrepresented. Here, it was taught with premeditated emphasis,
by a writer so successful in her work that the sage was himself
fain to declare her 'the only instance he knew of clear activity
being compatible with happiness.' But Harriet Martineau, though,
besides her justly celebrated *Illustrations of Political Economy*
(1832—4) and *Illustrations of Taxation* (1834)—confessed hybrids
of directly didactic purpose in innocently narrative form—she
published two novels of ordinary length and an effective series
of short tales for the young, collected under the title *The
Playfellow* (1841)[1], cannot properly be classed among English
novelists, and will be more fitly spoken of among historical and
political writers, in whose ranks an honourable place is her
due. Indeed, in that brief *Autobiographical Memoir* where
Harriet Martineau tells, with a frankness so frank as to have no
humour in it, the story of her own life up to the time when she
believed it to be drawing to its close, she states that

none of her novels or tales have, or ever had, in the eyes of good judges, or
her own, any character of permanence. The artistic aim and qualifications
were absent—she had no power of dramatic construction; nor the poetic
inspiration on the one hand, nor critical cultivation on the other, without
which no work of the imagination can be worthy to live[2].

Such candour disarms; and her further admission that, in some of
her political economy tales, perhaps her best achievement in
fiction, the plot which she was elsewhere unable to create was
furnished by the doctrine which she desired to enforce, may readily
be accepted as part of the disclaimer.

[1] Of her two novels, *Deerbrook* (1839) and *The Hour and the Man* (1841), the
former offered her an opportunity of expressing an opinion on most subjects under
the sun; but the conversations contain much that is felicitous as well as true, and
the insight into character, chiefly from an educational point of view, is remarkable.
The Hour and the Man, which calls itself 'a historical romance,' consists of a judicious
selection of historical facts, skilfully adapted to the conception of the characters introduced, and especially of that of the hero, Toussaint Louverture. The popularity of
The Playfellow tales—especially of the first of them, *The Settlers at Home*, still endures;
though *Feats on the Fiord* is not quite so good as its name, and *The Peasant and the
Prince* ('Louis XVII'), largely based on Mme de Campan's memoirs, is, in more
ways than one, too *doctrinaire* for maturer readers. *The Crofton Boys* successfully
insists on homeliness as an element in the life of both school and family.

[2] *Autobiographical Memoir* in *Harriet Martineau's Autobiography*, with *Memorials
by M. W. Chapman* (3rd edn, 1877), vol. III, pp. 482 sqq.

In the field of fiction, with which alone we are at present concerned, no agency on behalf of the new idealism, and of the resolve to set right by speedy action what was out of joint in the social condition of the people, could approach in effectiveness that of Dickens, who was able to touch chords of popular sentiment with a masterhand that had no equal. Both these writers, and, with them, a group of young men, partly clergy, partly barristers and university scholars, who took pride in ranging themselves under the moral and intellectual leadership of Frederick Denison Maurice, pressed upon the nation the necessity of continuous effort on behalf of the suffering and struggling working classes, as entitled to a share in the blessings of human life as well as in the privileges of citizenship, and thus became the leaders of a movement which has been given the name of 'interventionism[1].' Their endeavours were most memorable while they were most needed, and while the material sufferings of the working classes embittered their sense of their political grievances. About 1846, a time of greater prosperity began to set in ; and, in 1848, chartism came to what seemed a rather abrupt end; but the mid-Victorian age, and the tranquil enjoyment during its course by the middle class of an assured predominance in English political and social life, can hardly be said to have begun much before 1851, the year of the festival of peace—the first great international exhibition.

This period, then—from about 1830 to about 1850—is that to which the great body of the literary work of the first three eminent novelists discussed in this chapter belongs. With Dickens, as has been already pointed out, their relations are more or less close, while Thackeray holds aloof from 'novels with a purpose,' be that purpose conservative or socialist[2]. For the eager productivity of these writers and of those who shared in their endeavours, it would not be easy to account, had they not been under the influence of the spirit of the times in which they lived and had their being. Instead of contenting itself with the new inheritance of political rights into which it had entered, their age was ready to recognise that a social regeneration must follow, and prepare the ground for further political progress. The new reformers must be men and women arguing not from theories but from facts, writers whose sympathy with the people proceeded from a study of its

---

[1] See, more especially, the important work of L. Cazamian, *Le Roman Social en Angleterre* (1830—1850) (Paris, 1904), in which he discusses the idealist and interventionist reaction against the individualism of the utilitarians and of the Manchester school, as the adherents of earlier political economy are persistently called.

[2] See *A Plan for a Prize Novel* (cited by Cazamian).

actual condition, and who refused to remain deaf to the unanswerable grievances, and blind to the unendurable lives, of town and country. Before relief came, in the latter part of this period, it had seemed as if a revolution more like the first than the second French revolution must break out in England, and as if 'the two nations' at home would be ranged in warfare, the one against the other. Such, deep and serious, was the nature of the problems faced by the 'young England' of Disraeli, by the disciples of Maurice, from whose earnest ranks Charles Kingsley stood forth in bright literary panoply, and by tender-hearted women whose hearts went out, like Mrs Gaskell's, to their neighbours in the great industrial towns, while to George Eliot's critical but sympathetic intelligence these questions were familiar traditions. The genius of none of these writers, was absorbed by their social or political interests; and of each of them this chapter will speak as distinguished by what was individually the writer's own. But the influence of their times was upon them all—times in which, amidst great political storm and stress, the spirit of England stood high and her soul renewed itself in the struggle onward.

A quite unique place in the history of English fiction will be universally allowed to be held by Benjamin Disraeli, once called the younger—in recognition of his learned father, who is still remembered as one of the lesser lights of critical antiquarianism—and afterwards the wonder of the world under his title the earl of Beaconsfield. W. F. Monypenny, in a *Life* of very high merit which he has not lived to complete with his own hand[1], justly observes that 'novels may not be read for biography, but biography may be used to elucidate novels,' and it is only from this point of view that, in the following rapid survey of Disraeli's principal writings, reference will be made to the events of his life, the most striking of which form part, for better or for worse, of our national history.

Nothing that Disraeli ever did, said or wrote was done, said or written without self-consciousness; everything worked together in the scheme of his life, between the private and public aspects of which it is often difficult to draw a line, and which stands freely self-revealed in his books as it does in the extraordinary story of his career. He became a writer when very young; his earliest book, though not the first production of his pen[2], appeared in

[1] Monypenny, William Flavelle, *The Life of Benjamin Disraeli, Earl of Beaconsfield*, vols. I and II, 1804—46; 1910—12. Continued by Buckle, G. E., vol. III, to 1855. In this volume, the analysis of *Tancred* is by Monypenny.

[2] See bibliography.

1826, when he was in his twenty-first or twenty-second year, and was afterwards reckoned by himself among 'books written by boys.' The earliest literary training which he received was that which, like Vivian Grey, he sought for himself in his father's library— hence, the wide, though superficial, knowledge of books which he had not time to supplement in later life, his resolute adherence to the literary heroes of his youth (Byron and Bolingbroke above all[1]) and, also, the ineradicable imperfection of his spelling of French, the only language except his own with which he attained to any degree of familiarity. Oxford and Cambridge remained unknown to him, and he made bold, at times, to treat them in his books with a touch of more or less friendly scorn.

During much of the earlier part of his life, he was burdened by debt; and the pressure of such a burden is nowhere more forcibly depicted than in a passage of *Henrietta Temple*, though, at times, his buoyant nature may have led him, like Fadredeen in *Tancred*, to believe in indebtedness as a stimulant of genius. Partly because of these difficulties, against which he gallantly struggled, he was not a great traveller, though, like Contarini Fleming, he made the grand tour; and among his most notable literary achievements are the pictures in the same novel, and in *Tancred*, which, like those in *Eothen*, appreciatively reproduce the humours as well as the splendours of the near east.

Disraeli's literary masterpieces have an irrefutable claim to be included in a chapter on the political and social novel of his age; but it would be an error to suppose politics to have been, from the first, the main element of his fiction any more than it was the chief interest of his early personal career. *Vivian Grey* (1826), written from an experience developed by a vivid imagination out of conversations to which the youthful author had listened at John Murray's dinners, contains no serious political thought, for 'the New Union' has no purpose beyond that of faction; and, when Disraeli wrote *Contarini Fleming* (1832), his dream, as Monypenny points out, was to acquire fame through literature, just as the hero of this romance purposed to 'devote himself to the amelioration of his kind' by authorship. There can be no doubt that, as, indeed, the author himself indicates, the conception of his novel owed something to *Wilhelm Meister*; but, except in the imitation of the character of Philine, only in a very general way. Disraeli's

---

[1] As to Byron, see, especially, *Venetia*, and Sidonia's expatiation, in *Coningsby*, on the text 'Genius when young is divine.' Bolingbroke was, of course, Disraeli's political ideal as well as one of his literary exemplars.

next novel, *The Young Duke* (1830), although containing some
pungent political criticisms, deals almost exclusively with the
world of fashion ; and, if it professes to supply the reader with
something very different from the ordinary type of fashionable
novel as defined in the course of the story[1], certainly keeps whatever may be its special purpose well in reserve. *Alroy* (1833) and
The Rise of Iskander (1835) are historical, or quasi-historical,
romances of a more or less conventional type. *Henrietta Temple*,
which rightly calls itself 'a Love Story,' and *Venetia* (both 1837),
with its topsy-turveydom of literary portraiture and reminiscences,
have nothing to do with political or social problems; nor was it
before *Coningsby, or The New Generation* (1844) and *Sybil, or The
Two Nations* (1845) that the author deliberately sought to concentrate the attention of his readers on the treatment of such matters.
He declares that, in the frenzied period of the Reform bill, thirteen
or fourteen years before the publication of these cognate if not
twin novels, he took occasion ' to intimate and then to develope to
the first assembly of his countrymen that he ever had the honour to
address the convictions which he expounds in these works[2].' Two
or three years after that historic date—in 1835—he had, in the
Vindication of the English Constitution which he addressed to
the sympathetic ear of lord Lyndhurst, enunciated, with extraordinary gusto, his views on the three estates of the realm, on
the difference between governing for a people and governing for
a party, on the enormities of the whigs and on the enduring
significance for the national welfare of the church and the
house of lords. This animated essay was followed by *Letters of
Runnymede,* which, after appearing in *The Times,* were published
in 1836 with a brief congenial diatribe *The Spirit of Whiggism,*
but which their author never acknowledged. Modelled, in form,
upon the letters of Junius, they outdid their predecessors in
scurrilous violence, but lacked that calm assumption of self-evident
superiority which gave to the earlier diatribes so much of their
authoritative tone. They were dedicated, as a whole, to Peel, whom
the time had not yet come for attacking, but were individually, for
the most part, addressed to the whig leaders, for whom no method
of abuse seemed out of place[3].

[1] ' Take a pair of pistols and a pack of cards, a cookery book and a set of new
quadrilles, mix them up with half an intrigue and a whole marriage, and divide them
into three equal portions.'

[2] See *L'envoi* to *Sybil.*

[3] To the same period belong a number of contributions to *The Times, The Morning
Post* (June 1834), the short-lived *Press* and *Fraser's Magazine,* all of which were

In Disraeli's two great political novels, and, in a measure, in
their companion romance, *Tancred, or The New Crusade* (1847),
he fully developed the revised tory creed. Equally removed from
the 'stupid' and stagnant toryism of the Liverpool era, and from
the colourless conservatism proposed by the party without principles which followed Peel after the passing of the Reform bill,
the new generation represented by the young England party
makes open war upon political radicalism and utilitarian philosophy,
upon the coldblooded whigs who have allied themselves with these
tendencies, upon the middle classes, the merchants and the manufacturers who profit from their ascendancy, upon the cruelty
of the new poor law (against which, in parliament, Disraeli had
voted with a small minority) and upon the unimaginative and un-
aesthetic impoverishment of the life of the peasantry[1]. Contempt
is poured upon the existing system of government, which a 'heroic'
effort must be made to overthrow, instead of continuing to depend
on 'a crown robbed of its prerogative, a church extended to a
Commission, and an aristocracy that does not lead[2]'; and the
heart must thus be taken out of chartism, the fondly trusted
gospel of the second of the 'two nations' into which the English
people is divided. In *Sybil*, we seem to be nearing the thought
that, in the emancipation of the people, the idealism of the church
of Rome will lend powerful aid, and, in the earlier part of *Tancred*,
we are treated to an excursus on the English church and its
defects, which might seem to tend in the same direction[3]. But
the defects of that church, we learn, lie not only in the mediocrity
of its bishops, but, primarily, in its deficiency in oriental knowledge,
and, thus, with a note that Tancred began to doubt 'whether faith
is sufficient without race,' we pass into another sphere of Disraeli's

unacknowledged and some of which have only recently been discovered to be his.
A selection from these articles, which illustrate their author's genius for invective—
some of them in a way which, perhaps, he might prefer not to be too closely remembered—has been reprinted with the *Runnymede Letters* by Hutcheon, W., under the
title *Whigs and Whiggism*, covering the period from the passing of the first Reform
bill to the year 1841.

[1] Cf. Cazamian, L., *Le Roman Social en Angleterre* (1904), pp. 334 ff.

[2] *Coningsby*.

[3] The Roman church had an irresistible attraction for Disraeli, though the anti-
papal agitation of 1850 caused him to abandon the 'tractarian' tendencies of his
'young England' days. His admiration for the Roman system may be traced in a
phase of the experiences of Contarini Fleming, in the influence exercised upon the
young duke by Mary Dacre, and, *passim*, in *Henrietta Temple*, as well as in *Sybil*.
In *Lothair* and *Endymion*, the admiration is not extinct, but has passed into an
ironical stage. The movement for protestantising Ireland is mentioned with scorn in
Tancred.

political and historical philosophy, which concerns itself with the question of race. Here, we are scarcely any longer in the region of practical politics, but, rather, in that of semi-occult influences such as are best demonstrated by the esoteric knowledge and prophetical certainty of Sidonia, or illustrated by the traditional tale *Alroy*. The inner meaning of *Tancred* may be veiled, but its courage, as a declaration of faith in the destinies of the Jewish race, must be described as magnificent. Disraeli's last two novels —*Lothair* (1870) and *Endymion* (1880)—are, of course, full of political passages and invaluable to the historical and political student as containing the *obiter dicta* of a statesman to whom the world of contemporary politics was as familiar as the boards of the stage are to its veteran protagonists. But these books have no longer any political purpose; the writer looks on the contentions of ultramontanism and Mazzinianism from the outside, and the very motto of *Endymion*[1] betrays the unimpassioned spirit of the observer for whom political life no longer has any secrets.

Among those secrets is the mysterious action of personal character, on the paramount importance of which Disraeli (who never shrank from repeating himself) again and again descants. He possessed a wonderful insight into the motives that actuate men not only in their public doings, but in the shaping of their lives, or in the leaving of them to be shaped by circumstances as the agents of Providence. Thus, when he worked with special care and elaborated his presentiments, he could place on his canvas figures typically true and yet highly original, such as Monmouth in *Coningsby*, the selfish aristocrat of whom Carabas, in *Vivian Grey*, is merely a first sketch and Montfort, in *Endymion*, a more delicate part-copy, the omniscient Sidonia, Rigby, the embodiment of official meanness, and the radiant Mr Phoebus. All these have in them features of actual individuals well known to fame[2]; but they are, at the same time, types worthy to stand by the side of the best remembered in English fiction; and the same may be asserted of a few others who are types only, such as the immortal Tadpole and Taper. In many of the characters which crowd his pages, Disraeli was content to introduce contemporaries under a more or less thin disguise, without, on the one hand, working them out with fullness or, on the other, aiming at photographic exactitude. It is not of much importance whether

---

[1] *Quidquid agunt homines.*

[2] In Sidonia, these features are, of course, purely external; and the author goes out of his way to make Sidonia appear at the ball of baroness S. de R—d.

Disraeli hit upon this device unassisted, or whether he borrowed it from a popular novelist of a rather earlier day, who had personal experience of political life, Robert Plumer Ward[1]. In Disraeli's novels, the real personages introduced are all recognisable by those acquainted with the social history of the age, even if they cannot attest the likeness on the strength of personal intercourse or even of a deprecatory *vidi tantum.* Such are, among a multitude of others, the delightful Mirabel in *Henrietta Temple*; the almost equally delightful St Aldegonde in *Lothair*, who re-appears as Waldershare in *Endymion*; besides Coningsby himself, lord Henry Sidney, Sir Charles Buckhurst, Eustace Lyle in *Coningsby*; Vavasour in *Tancred*; Monsignore Catesby and the cardinal, and, at the other pole, Mirandola, in *Lothair*; and prince, afterwards king, Florestan in *Endymion*. As a rule, all these are touched with equal humour and a kindliness, or, at least, gentleness, in accordance with the obvious demands of good taste; but there are a few notable exceptions. The character of Rigby in *Coningsby* has already been mentioned; and it remains, so far as we are aware, unknown why Disraeli should have displayed so vitriolic a hatred of Croker as is displayed in this portrait—unmistakable, at all events, in the account of him as a man of letters, the author of slashing articles, full of detail constantly incorrect. Here and there, in his political novels, Disraeli gives piquancy to his array of *dramatis personae* by introducing among them actual personages, such as lord (John) Russell, who intervenes in the action of *Sybil* and whose character is not unfairly drawn in *Coningsby*. But no such treatment is accorded to Sir Robert Peel, whom Disraeli hated with a bitterness that can only be accounted for by the fact that the great minister, on one occasion, had behaved to him with undeserved generosity. In return, he is assailed in *Coningsby* (though, in the same work, a recognition is accorded to his courage), insulted in *The Young Duke* and held up to scorn in *Tancred*. Disraeli's spite against Goldwin Smith, in the character of the Oxford professor in

---

[1] A perusal of Ward's *Tremaine; or the Man of Refinement* (1825) can hardly fail to suggest to readers of Disraeli's best known novels some similarity in style and treatment—more especially in the way of introducing characters and recalling, in an easy fashion, as if treating of familiar circumstances, their antecedents and surroundings. But the resemblance does not go deep; and the story of a tired man of pleasure and fashion, led gradually by the influences of friendship and love, but, also, by sustained argument in moral theology and philosophy, to a nobler view of life and its duties, takes the reader out of Disraeli's sphere of thought and experience. Very ample and very polite, the style of *Tremaine* is, at the same time, easy and attractive, and the success of the book is not surprising.

Lothair, was, perhaps, provoked, and certainly requited ; but it is really too inept to have deserved notice. Could his equally violent, if not equally pointless, caricature of Thackeray, as St Barbe in *Endymion,* have been merely the result of annoyance at the happy parody of himself as a prize novelist in *Scaramouch*?

Hardly less captivating than the likenesses of prominent contemporaries introduced by Disraeli into his novels are the apophthegms which he puts into their mouths or delivers on his own account. His earliest work, *Vivian Grey,* is full of these; but, as they come to us in more mellowed form from the lips of Sidonia, they seem laden with wisdom. Where epigrams cannot conveniently be coined, mere phrases have to do their duty, and no audacity is too great to fill them with sound. The author of *Vivian Grey* was able to produce an equivalent of diplomatic phraseology, as it were, from his inner consciousness ; and, like the master of diplomatic speech in the period of European congresses, he could always find a formula, even when his purpose was mainly negative.

It may, perhaps, be added that the names of Disraeli's personages are generally chosen with great felicity. In this respect, he has few equals except Thackeray, who, however, occasionally condescends, as Dickens avowedly seeks, to raise laughter by his inventive power in this respect. It is not often that Disraeli unbends so far. Not that he was wanting in the imitative humour which could reproduce, with lifelike correctness, the talk between two young sporting dukes at Doncaster, the vaunts of G. O. A. Head at Manchester and even the rodomontade of Chaffing Jack, the keeper of a music-hall in a small manufacturing town, who, indeed, has in him something of the volubility of Alfred Jingle. Though he loved hyperbole, and though it would be easy to cite passages, even in his later works, which must be called grandiloquent, and others which are wholly artificial, even in the inversion of their sentences, yet, the favourite form of Disraeli's humour was irony, in which, both as a writer and as a speaker, he excelled all his contemporaries. The earliest manifestations of this gift will be found in the short stories or sketches, beginning with *Popanilla* (1827), and including *Ixion in Heaven* (1833), pure burlesque, though almost Lucianic in its urbanity, and *The Infernal Marriage* (1834), a little lengthy, but containing some good political banter. The gift was carefully cultivated, and is abundantly exhibited in all Disraeli's later works. Sarcasms like 'the old ideal, to do nothing and get something' are as plentiful with him as leaves in Vallombrosa, and whole episodes —such as the diplomacy of the prime minister of the Amsarey in *Tancred* and the Roman plot for the conversion of Lothair—are conceived in this vein, with equal delicacy and malice.

'Thought and passion,' Disraeli writes in *Henrietta Temple*, 'are required in a fine novel, besides the descriptive accessories.' The intense energy of his nature, the strength of his will and the consistency of his purpose did duty for the primary ingredients. When their flow might have seemed to slacken, imagination, wit and extraordinary quickness of insight did the rest. His power of construction was considerable; *Coningsby* and *Sybil* in different ways, are interesting as stories, and the turn of the narrative in *Lothair* (by the appearance of Mr Phoebus) is very deftly contrived. On the other hand, not only *Vivian Grey*, but *Tancred*, lacks an ending, and *Endymion* (it must be confessed) a hero. Yet, with all their combined effectiveness and particular brilliancy, his literary gifts were limited in their range; notwithstanding his extraordinary power of writing dialogue, he had no essentially dramatic gifts, while the feebleness of his lyrics is manifest in both *Henrietta Temple* and *Venetia*, though, in the latter novel, they are introduced as the productions of a second Byron. His blank verse was not much superior, though it found its way into some of his prose. The merits of his style are confined to his prose, though estimates have differed as to the work or works in which it attained to its highest excellence. He himself thought that *Contarini Fleming* was the perfection of English prose, and his biographer considers that this novel shows him at his best as a prose-writer. But, to us, the *afflatus* of the latter part of his favourite *Tancred* appears stronger, and its effect more stimulating. The vividness, subtle humour and attractive lightness of his general prose style seem to have reached their height in *Coningsby* or, perhaps, in *Sybil*, where his historical and other excursuses begin to have a value of their own, something like that of the openings of Fielding or the digressions of Thackeray; but none of his earlier works exhibits the exquisite finish of style which, in his latter days, he knew how to impart to *Lothair* and to *Endymion*. In the former of these, at all events, his genius for depicting the conflict of great ideas had not deserted him.

Of Disraeli's contributions to literature outside the field of prose fiction, very little needs to be said here. He took himself very seriously in writing *The Revolutionary Epick* (1834), of which he states himself to have conceived the idea on the plains of Troy; but the fragment of a blank verse poem which remains consists partly of commonplace rhetoric, partly of a faint reflection of the influence of *Childe Harold*, with a troublesome interference of the allegorical element. *Count Alarcos, a Tragedy* (1839), though not without telling points, has neither reality of passion nor strength of style. Quite at the beginning of his career, Disraeli incurred and escaped the chance of settling down into journalism; but he withdrew from the Murray-Lockhart scheme of *The Representative*, and had no share in the production of that short-lived journal (1825). So late as 1853, he returned to journalism, as the founder and guiding spirit of a weekly journal called *The Press*, for which he wrote the opening leader *Coalition*, and which he did not sell till 1866. To his published political writings proper, no further reference is needed; but it may be well to note that, in his 'political biography' of lord George Bentinck, Disraeli essayed a kind of writing of which there are not many examples in English literature, namely, the life of a statesman designed, primarily, to illustrate the nature and value of the political principles by which it was animated, and only secondarily the character and qualities of the man himself. How far he was successful in fulfilling the former purpose must largely depend on political opinion and sentiment; but, of the purpose itself, even without the guidance of a recent editor of the book, no doubt can remain; and the work is almost as much an attack upon Peel as a panegyric upon the protectionist leader. The personal touches, so far as the hero of the story is concerned, are effectively introduced, though the elegiac note at the close, with its three Greek quotations, is strained. On the other hand, a scene or two in the narrative—Peel in a reverie, and the same statesman in the hour of final defeat—as well as some incidental touches—O'Connell in decay, and the duke explaining the motives of his policy to the press—are worthy of the author at his best. His own self he more or less effaces, tactfully, in the biography of his friend, but he finds room for a chapter on the Jewish question, in which both were at one.

The life of Charles Kingsley is outspanned at both ends by that of lord Beaconsfield; it was, in its outward circumstances, as simple and modest as the career of his senior was world-embracing in its notoriety. But, in the writings which have secured to the one and to the other a place in every history of English literature, they dealt, each after his own fashion and in his own spirit, with many of the same social problems of the age of transition which, in this and other European lands, set in with the fourth decade of the nineteenth century. Though, in heart as well as by profession ever since he had grown into manhood, a country parson, and yet, also, an author whose full-fledged imagination felt at home alike in the oases of the eastern desert and amidst the waters of the western main, Kingsley, if any man, was always the same in his life and in his writings, and the latter can never be dissociated from the experiences and conditions of the former. For what was most vital in his books was inspired by the ideas and purposes which determined the essential course of his life, and took immediate shape under the impulses which created them. Kingsley, in the words of one of the most just as well as most affectionate of his critics—Max Müller—always 'did his best at the time and for the time.' He disliked being called a muscular Christian ; but he would not (at least in his own day) have repudiated the title of a militant apostle. Deliberation was not less foreign to his nature than were afterthoughts ; and, though he was not given to inner self-contradictions, even self-consistency he held of small account as compared with the duty of declaring that which was in him. He was, it may confidently be added, wholly devoid of either literary or other personal ambition, properly so called, and was quite conscious of his powers as forming part of himself. But what he had in view was the end. In the same letter[1] in which, when, on the very threshold of his career as a writer, he acknowledged the weight of his wife's advice that he should write no more novels, and allowed that, as a matter of fact, he had no more to say, he declared that, while God had bestowed on him

a certain artistic knack of utterance (nothing but a knack), He had done more; He had made 'the Word of the Lord like fire in his bones' giving him no peace till he had spoken out.

It is partly because of these characteristics and partly notwithstanding them, that his life and works appear fused together like the bronze in the statues of those Greek heroes—a Perseus or a Theseus—in whom he loved to trace the congenial features of Christian chivalry.

Charles Kingsley, who described his own talent as 'altogether hereditary,' owed many enduring impressions to the scenes and

---

[1] See *Charles Kingsley, his Letters and the Memories of his Life*, edited by his wife (here cited as *Letters and Memories*, the 4 vol. edition, 1901—2), vol. I, pp. 188—9.

associations of his boyhood, his father's livings on the edge of the
fens and in north Devon, his mother's West Indian descent, and
his schooldays at Helston under Derwent Coleridge. He afterwards
entered King's college, London, of which, in his manhood, through
the intervention of Frederick Denison Maurice, he had nearly
become a professor. Thence, he passed to Magdalene college,
Cambridge, and, after taking a good degree, into the active service
of the church, to which, as an undergraduate, he had resolved on
devoting his life. He became curate at Eversley on the borders
of Windsor forest, and, after a very brief interval, was, in 1844,
appointed rector of the parish—an office which became an integral
part of his life and which he held till its close.

Yet, it was not likely that either his care for his parish, or his
happy home life, should confine his interests within the circle of
the chalkstreams and firtrees of his Hampshire home. At an
early date, he was led to enquire into the condition of the working
masses and into the problems suggested by it, above all to
those called upon by their profession to minister to the poor.
The writings of Carlyle, which, in this period, were reaching
the height of their power, were among the earliest of these
influences; but it should be noted that Kingsley strongly
deprecated being considered 'in any wise in theology as a follower
of Carlyle.' In 1844, Kingsley made the acquaintance of
Maurice, who soon became 'the Master' to him and to a band
of fellow-teachers and workers. When the year 1848 drew near,
from which, in England, also, much was expected and much
feared, Kingsley had come to be frequently in London, and, in
this and the following year, he held a professorship of English
literature in Queen's college, Harley street. More or less under
Maurice's guidance, he and the friends with whom he was
more especially associated—John Malcolm Ludlow and Thomas
Hughes above all—were preparing to play their part in the movement for social reform into whose broader and deeper channel
they hoped that the angry chartism of the day might be
merged.

That, after he had plunged into the struggle, his name speedily
became prominent among those engaged in it, was, in no small
measure, due to the reputation which, in this fateful year, he had
rapidly acquired by his earliest published literary work. When he
declared that, previously to this, he had not written five hundred
lines in his life, he, of course, meant in verse, though, even in that
form, he can hardly but have perpetrated, in blank or rime, other

juvenilia besides *Hypotheses Hypochondriacae*[1]. His lyric gift awoke early; but its best remembered fruits belong to a date rather later than his one dramatic work. *The Saint's Tragedy* (1848) had been designed neither as a drama nor for the public eye— still less, of course, for the stage, from which he had an inherited aversion, and which he found it difficult to judge equitably[2]. The work, which was to have been followed by a biographical essay on St Teresa, had been begun in 1842, and it was not until five years later that it took shape as a drama. Kingsley's own introduction to this dramatic poem shows it to have been written with the definite purpose of liberating his soul on the subject of the medieval conception of saintship—or religion in its loftiest phase—as a condition of mind and soul detached from human affections even of the strongest and the purest kind. As a drama, *The Saint's Tragedy* cannot be said to be powerful, although the character of the heroine is both deeply conceived and consistently elaborated through an action of which the interest grows more and more intense as it proceeds. The blank verse of the play, on the whole, is adequate, but, in one or two lyrical passages with which the dialogue is interspersed, the mixed metre is not very happily managed; while the prose strives too perceptibly after colour.

It was, as has been said, in the year of the publication of *The Saint's Tragedy* and that in which there appeared in *Fraser's Magazine*, as first of the large number of contributions made by Kingsley to periodical literature, a paper[3] not wholly alien in thought to his dramatic poem, that he and his fellows first bethought themselves of making a sustained attempt to meet the chief trouble of their times. During the decade which preceded the transmission to the house of commons, on 10 April 1848, of 'the people's charter,' that document had become, as it has been well put[4], 'the banner of the working classes round which millions gathered'; and, on the securing of its 'points' of political reform, the mass of English workmen had resolved to concentrate for the present their efforts towards ameliorating their social condition and obtaining their desired share in the government of the country. At the same time, while primarily directed to the

---

[1] For this, see *Letters and Memories*, vol. I, pp. 31 ff. *Psyche, a Rhapsody*, which follows, is in prose.

[2] See his essay *Plays and Puritans*.

[3] *Why should we fear the Romish Priests?*

[4] By Kaufmann, M., in *Charles Kingsley, Christian Socialist and Social Reformer* (1892).

gain of the charter, the general movement named from it stood in close relation to those projects of social change which, of late years, had, in a great part of Europe, come to occupy the minds of working men and those in sympathy with their claims. These projects had been urged with increasing persistency since the Reform bill and the French July revolution seemed to have established the ascendancy of the middle classes in England and in France. Thus, the avowed object of the Working Men's association, founded in London in 1836, was to bring about, by means of the equality of political rights which the charter would secure, a full enquiry into the social grievances of the working classes. Both country and town were concerned in these grievances: the decline of agriculture and the approaching extinction of small landholders, the troubles of the towns, more especially those in manufacturing districts, and of London, the lowering of wages owing to immigration from the country and from distressed Ireland, the sudden developments of machinery, the sufferings of those employed in sweated trades, the pressure of excessive hours of work in factories upon men, women and children and the insanitary conditions of their daily life, while left unprotected against the inroads of infectious disease.

These were some of the causes of a movement which deeply stirred all men and women of the age with thoughts and feelings to spare for concerns outside their own doors and apart from their immediate cares and interests, and which led not a few of them to believe that England was on the eve of a social crisis incalculable in its results. And it was to meet, so far as in him lay, the demands facing him, that Kingsley and his friends went forth—stimulated, no doubt, to quick action by such words and wishes as those of F. D. Maurice, who hailed in him another 'Thalaba, with a commission to slay magicians and put the Eblis band which possesses our land to rout.' He and his associates proposed, in the first instance, to obtain the goodwill of the working classes, whom their efforts were, above all, to bring to believe in the brotherly sympathy and aid offered to them. Their social grievances were not to be gainsaid or the sufferings to which they were subject minimised ; and, again, the risk was to be cheerfully run, on their behalf, of being decried as identified with their cause—chartists with the rest of them. On the other hand, working men were not to be encouraged in the delusion that political concessions would, of themselves, assure social reforms—or, in other words, that the 'points of the charter' went far enough and struck at the root of the matter.   Support and advice of this sort was to be given by word and pen, in tracts and contributions to journals written for perusal by the workers, or in their interest, and by the spoken word on platforms, in lecture-halls and in the pulpit—which last, on one occasion, was used by Kingsley, with the consequence of his being temporarily interdicted from preaching in London[1].

It was on the very morrow of the *coup manqué* of 10 April 1848, when the storm had blown over, though, as it seemed, only for the moment, that Kingsley is found entering heart and soul into the scheme set on foot by Maurice, to bring out a new series of *Tracts for the Times*, addressed to the higher orders, but on behalf of the working classes—'if the Oxford tracts did wonders,' Maurice asked, 'why should not we?' The design (as well as that of converting the then existing *Oxford and Cambridge Review* into an organ of the opinions of Kingsley and his friends, including James Anthony Froude[2]) was, however, exchanged for the scheme, more directly to the purpose, of *Politics for the People*, a series of tracts, addressed to the working classes themselves. To the 'Workmen of England,' Kingsley spoke his first word in a placard signed 'A Working Parson,' posted all over London on 12 April, urging them to aim at 'something nobler than the Charter and dozens of Acts of Parliament'—'to be wise, and then you *must* be free, for you will be *fit* to be free.' To *Politics for the People*, of which the first number appeared on 16 May, he contributed a series of papers under the pseudonym Parson Lot (a name adopted by him in humorous commemoration of a gathering of friends and fellow-workers in which he had found himself in a minority of one[3]). They were partly admonitions, friendly but outspoken, to trust to a better guidance than that of political animosity, partly endeavours to direct attention to the great opportunities for action open to those who would set their shoulders to the wheel, or exposures of the abuses that needed and admitted of reform. About the same time, he wrote papers for *The Christian Socialist*[4], and *The Journal of Association*, and for

[1] See the account of the incident in *Letters and Memories*, vol. II, pp. 29—32.

[2] As to the beginnings of the lifelong intimacy between Kingsley and Froude, see Paul, Herbert, *Life of Froude* (1905), chap. III.

[3] See Hughes, T., prefatory memoir in his edition of *Alton Locke* (2 vols. 1881), where is also reprinted the tract *Cheap Clothes, and Nasty* (1851). Several of Parson Lot's papers are reprinted in *Letters and Memories*, vol. I, pp. 171 ff.

[4] It was in *The Christian Socialist* that the story of *The Nun's Pool*, which had been refused admission to *Politics for the People* and which seems to have fascinated Kingsley, was, after some hesitation, inserted. See Kaufmann, *op. cit.* p. 147.

a penny *People's Friend*—all of which periodicals owed their
origin to this season of eager effort. He also produced a number
of tracts and pamphlets, of which *Cheap Clothes, and Nasty,* one
of a series on Christian socialism, with its fierce attack on the
ruthless application of the principle of competition, brought down
upon him the ire of W. R. Greg in *The Edinburgh Review*;
while *The Friends of Order* was, rather, a defence of himself
and his fellows as combatants on the side of society against
anarchy. In general, amidst all the vehemence of controversy,
the 'foul-mouthed, ill-tempered man,' as he half-ironically called
himself, not only repeatedly exhibited the virtue of self-control,
which was part of his manliness, but, also, asserted the right of
individual judgment, which was dear to his love of freedom.
Neither the teetotal movement, nor, in the long run, the
agitation for the rights of women, could reckon him among its
champions. On the other hand, certain lines or branches of
social reform were advocated by him from first to last with un-
abating vigour—and, among them, he always conceded to sanitary
reform the place to which the virtue which it has in view is pro-
verbially entitled.

To Kingsley's sermons at this period of his life we need not
specially return. But, unlike most of his fellow-workers, Kingsley
possessed, besides the gifts of an orator and a moralist, the strong
imaginative faculty which made him a poet. This faculty, like
most of his other gifts, he kept under restraint; and, while he
rarely cared to use it without a definite purpose—moral or practical,
or, more frequently, both—neither pleasure nor profit induced
him to wear it out. This showed itself even with regard to the
form of imaginative composition which he now came to essay.

The first of his novels to be planned and begun was *Yeast,
a Problem*; so that, though *Alton Locke* was published a year
sooner as a whole, *Yeast* has an undoubted right of precedence.
Both works sprang—not, indeed, in full panoply, for the one was
hardly more than half-finished, and the other bears many marks of
haste—from a brain overwrought by the interests and labours
which it had shared; both were contributions to the solution of
England's pressing social problems, in country and in town, by
a writer to whom they came directly home, and who, while able to
sympathise with those oppressed whether by material or by spiritual
difficulties, could not, in either case, accept any answers irreconcilable with the religious convictions which formed the anchorage
of his own mind.

Yeast began to appear in *Fraser's Magazine* in the fateful year of revolutions, 1848; but the proprietors of that journal, though generous friends both to Kingsley and to his ideas, took fright, and, while they induced him to cut this novel short, declined to publish its successor. Moreover, Kingsley had overstrained his powers of work, and had been obliged to take refuge in his beloved north Devon in the midst of the production of *Yeast*. It did not appear as a book till 1851, without the new conclusion which he seems, at one time, to have intended to supply in a second part, called 'The Artists' and not absolutely alien in conception, perhaps, to the second part of *Faust*[1]. As it stands, the story, if judged by literary canons, must be allowed to exhibit some glaring defects. One of these is the weakness of its plot, which not only, as in a novel of the twentieth century, leaves everything unsettled at the end, but really hinges on the pusillanimous laches of a quite secondary personage. *Yeast* is far less successful than *Alton Locke* in adjusting the intermixture of narrative and declamation, and does not even scorn a boisterous transition such as: 'Perhaps, reader, you are getting tired of all this....So we will have a bit of action again.' The opening ' bit of action,' however—the run with the hounds—is so superlatively fresh and free that the reader may be excused for desiring more of the same kind. Yet, the centre of gravity of the book lies in the dialogues between Launcelot and the personages who exercise a varied influence upon his manly and noble, but roving and ungoverned, nature—the man of the world, Bracebridge, Launcelot's proud love, Argemone, and, above all, the philosophically observant keeper, Tregarva; and it is through the last named that Launcelot is brought to take cognisance of the question of the relation of classes in England and to seek to understand the real wants of the labouring poor. The treatment of this theme naturally suggests a comparison, from this point of view, of *Yeast* with Disraeli's *Coningsby* (published only four years before Kingsley's story was begun) and its successors by the same hand[2]. Although written from totally diverse standpoints, the earlier having an unconcealed party purpose to which the later was altogether a stranger, they came to much the same conclusion, well formulated by Leslie Stephen, as the acceptance of the same ideal of society: the few for the many, not the many for

---

[1] Kingsley was a great reader of Goethe, without entering very profoundly into the spirit of his genius.

[2] The similarity between the characters of Sidonia and Barnakill is too obvious to have escaped notice, though Kingsley had not read Disraeli's book when he wrote his own.

the few. Kingsley's utilitarian millionaire is not a caricature, nor
is his great remedy of sanitary reform a mere item in a party
programme. Contrariwise, his high-church curate on the way to
Rome stands almost alone among his types of clergymen in its
blank ugliness. The background of the degenerate weakness of
the rustic labouring class, its desperate acquiescence in its miserable
lot and its dogged blindness to the necessity of self-help ('Why
save the farmers' rates?') is painted with genuine power. As for
Launcelot, the process by which he has to work out his own
salvation ends, so far as the story goes, in a half-mystical, half-
ironical prognostic of the destiny of its chief personages; but for
Tregarva there remains a process of purification by faith as well
as by love.

Alton Locke, Tailor and Poet, was published in 1850, in the
midst of great social unrest, and a strong strain upon its author due
to his exertions towards meeting some of the causes of this widespread popular perturbation. Carlyle, to whose goodwill there lay
a strong appeal in the convinced impetuosity of the book, relieved,
in the character of Saunders Mackaye, by a humour which his
brother Scot pronounced 'nearly perfect,' nevertheless judged it
'definable as *crude,*' and averred that the impression made by it
upon him was that of 'a fervid creation still left half chaotic'; yet,
though *Alton Locke* ends in dreamland as *Yeast* dissolved itself
into a Utopia, it has attracted two generations of readers as a true
picture of the travails of a fellow-man. The hero is a poet as well
as a tailor, but a poet who, instead of wandering about like
Contarini Fleming (or, for that matter, Elsley Vavasour) in search
of themes and experiences worthy of his powers, finds them in
daily life and common things—a democratic poet, if you will, who
suffers severely when, after recognising that he has genius but has
been left without its rights, he swerves from the straight line
prescribed to him by his task in life. The direct bearing of the
attack upon the abuses of a typical town trade, from a picture of
whose conditions the narrative starts, was attested by its effects,
more especially in the partial adoption of the system of association
—on behalf of which, as Kingsley emphasised in 1854, working
men themselves failed to take sufficient trouble. The story,
throughout, exhibits a direct reference to facts: the dependence
of working men on the charter, the dubious ways of demagogy in
the matter of journalism and at meetings and so forth. On the
other hand, the picture of Cambridge—even of Cambridge as it
might strike a working-tailor on a casual visit—seemed, to the

novelist, at a subsequent date, to call for revision. Apart from those touches in Saunders Mackaye which came home to Carlyle, there is little humour in the book; for this, the writer was too fully absorbed in his theme and incensed by the grimness and cruelty of some of its aspects. Conceived, as it was, in a white heat, it was met, on both sides, with an unmitigated condemnation, showing that its earnestness of purpose was wholly misunderstood; and it remains, of all its author's books, that which shares with Mrs Gaskell's *Mary Barton* the credit of having come straight from the heart of a witness of the conflict who could not, when the fire blazed, remain a bystander.

When, in 1851, Kingsley began the publication, once more in *Fraser's Magazine*, of *Hypatia, or New Foes with an Old Face*, which did not appear in book form till 1853, he may be said to have written, with full consciousness of his literary powers, the only novel from his hand which, he believed, might endure. In his case, this consciousness came at a time when the ardour of youth still urged him on from venture to venture. Thus, when he turned from the social to the historical novel, the transition was made with extraordinary self-confidence by means of a work dealing, as its sub-title indicates, with spiritual and intellectual questions which had stirred bygone ages as they were stirring his own, and intended to convey lessons to the living with the aid of the experience of the past. The period in the history of the world chosen by him to show how wisdom without faith is as salt which has lost its savour was one to which he was long attracted by the greatness of the issues determined in it—the period of the downfall of the western empire, of which Africa was claimed as part, and the transformation of the western world by Teutonic immigration. The only course of his Cambridge professorial lectures published by him deals with the main aspects of this general theme, and, in a short series of lectures which he delivered at Edinburgh in the year of the publication of *Hypatia*, he sought to trace the history of civilisation, thought and religion at Alexandria, the chief theatre of the action of his novel[1]. Its special end is to depict the antagonism between an aggressive church and a decrepit empire, and, at the same time, to draw the lessons to be found in the struggles of a school of philosophy devoid of regenerative power. One of the new foes with an old face who reappear here is

---

[1] The lectures on *Alexandria and her Schools* (1854) reach down to the conquering advent of Mohammedanism, for whose founder and early leaders sympathy is expressed. The preface rushes patriotically into the eastern question of the day.

scepticism—an attitude of mind which Kingsley treated briefly, but with considerable skill as well as effect, in an essay, centring in a 'Platonic' dialogue, published about this time (1852), under the title *Phaethon, or Loose Thoughts for Loose Thinkers.* It is one of the freshest and brightest of Kingsley's lesser productions, and imbeds in the familiar surroundings of English country life and scenery a perfectly lucid and self-consistent argument against the complacent scepticism of a class of thinkers who were after-wards to form part of the large army of agnostics. In the novel, even the man of the world Raphael, saturated with intellectual experience, who forms a contrast to Philammon, the simple monk of the Laura, is led by the grace of divine love to a better mind.

The learning brought to bear upon the course of the narrative of which Hypatia, historical in the outline of the portrait, is the central figure, is ample enough to warrant the high praise bestowed upon 'Kingsley's masterpiece' by Bunsen[1], who had himself drunk deeply from the sources of the narrative. For the rest, *Hypatia* was, as *Yeast* had been before it, denounced as 'immoral'; but, in the present case, the charge was, manifestly, the invention of sheer perversity. The book has its flaws: the noble self-reliance of Hypatia is belied by her blind submission to Orestes; and Bunsen was probably right in complaining of the Goths being presented too exclusively 'in the drunken mood in which they appear as lawless and blood-sucking barbarians, and chronic berserkers.' But the brilliancy and glow of the whole picture, as it changes from quay and market to lecture-hall and amphitheatre, till, at last, it subsides into the solitude of the remote temple whence it took its start, is almost as notable as is the lifelike truth of the characters, taken from nearly every class and sect of the seething world-city.

The winter of the Crimean campaign (1854—5) and the following spring were spent by Kingsley, who was profoundly moved by the events of the war, in Devonshire; and the twofold influences of time and place, as well as the leisure imposed upon him by his wife's illness, account for the main result of his literary activity[2]. In 1855 was published the most successful of all his novels, *Westward Ho! or the Voyages and Adventures of Sir Amyas Leigh, Knight of Burrough, in the County of Devon, in the*

---

[1] *Memoir of Baron Bunsen by his Widow* (1868), vol. II, p. 309.

[2] Besides this, he found full opportunity for his natural history studies. *Glaucus, the Wonders of the Sea Shore,* which appeared in 1855, was developed out of an article in *The North British Review.*

reign of Her Most Glorious Majesty Queen Elizabeth, with a characteristic double dedication to rajah Brooke and the bishop of New Zealand (George Augustus Selwyn). The book breathes the spirit of martial heroism and naval enterprise typified by the Elizabethan age and the county of Devon ; but it is also animated by a, more or less, aggressive patriotism, of which Kingsley found no difficulty in 'rendering' the supposed autobiographical expression 'into modern English.' The novelist had a special gift of opening his stories in a vivid and stimulating way ; but, in the present instance, there follows a second opening, where Amyas, whom, in the first pages, we met, as a boy, vainly intent upon sailing with the luckless John Oxenham, reappears on his return from a voyage round the world with Drake. And so we are launched into the story, which is carried through with inexhaustible *verve*, but, also, with something beyond mere vigour and high spirits. The book is written by an Englishman for Englishmen—and by a protestant for protestants. Such Elizabethan stumbling-blocks as the penal laws are got out of the way without much trouble, and we are not allowed time to criticise the antithesis between the man who does right according to prescript and the man who does right by the spirit of God that is in him. Amyas, whose heart never quailed, whether before armada or before inquisition, deemed Parsons and Campion fair game, and the massacre of Limerick a painful necessity ; and, if his editor is almost visited by a feeling of compunction as to the whole quarrel with Ireland, he is able to suppress this qualm by means of an honourable mention (in a note) of the gallant conduct of Irish officers and soldiers in the Crimean war. The whole story, however, is too good, and the end, when Amyas, after throwing his sword, whose the vengeance was not to be, into the waters, returns home blind, is too tragic, to invite criticism of details. If not as notable a literary performance as *Hypatia*, *Westward Ho!*, too, is a masterpiece after its kind, and will live as such in the literature of English fiction.

In *Two Years Ago* (1857), Kingsley once more returned to contemporary life, dealing with such of its moral difficulties and of its material evils as more particularly came under his cognisance. The main teaching of the book may, perhaps, be said to be that the processes of Providence are to be read by him who runs in both the happiness and the unhappiness of which the world around us is full—in the beauty of nature, and in the power granted to human action to set right much of the wrong wrought by human sloth and self-indulgence, and that, consequently, man is called upon for faith and hope and the self-devotion of love, thus receiving the one answer for which pure and honest spirits are, consciously or unconsciously, in search. Had it not been for the force of some of the character-drawing in this novel, especially for the figure of the hero of the tale, Tom Thurnall, and for the vivid picturesqueness of the writing, both in passages of pure description and in the highly wrought episode of the storm, *Two Years Ago* would probably not have excited much interest as a story. The main plot, on the whole, is too transparent, and the advent of the cholera has been too fully prepared to tell strongly when it actually breaks out[1]. The Crimean war has no real bearing on the narrative, though Tom's imprisonment forms the turning-point of his inner life. The by-plot of Marie's (Cordifiamma's) love adventures has, as Kingsley confessed, no organic connection with the story; and the introduction, which dates two years after the action itself, throws no new light upon it. Nor are the lesser characters as interesting as is usual with Kingsley. The poet, Elsley Vavasour, who seems to be intended as a contrast to the downright Tom, is a mere caricature of what is most contemptible in a self-conscious and effeminate man of the pen. The moraliser of the argument, major Campbell, is not the less a shadowy figure because Kingsley drew him from life, and because he shares with at least two other characters in the story that passionate love for nature and the study of nature without which, to its author, life was colourless. Claude and Sabina are, as he told his critic George Brimley[2], only 'two dolls' with whom he had been playing, 'setting them to say and do all the pretty *naïve* things anyone else is too respectable to be set about, till I know them as well as I know you.'

Kingsley's belief that the true task of the age was self-sacrifice in the cause of suffering humanity—not talk but work, albeit not to be brought home to the national conscience without a great deal of talk—and his conviction that sanitary reform and what it implied was the most pressing of its needs, were in harmony with some of the noblest impulses of the era of Florence Nightingale and her contemporaries. But, of the vehemence of his earlier denunciations of existing social evils there is not much to be found in *Two Years Ago*. He has a kindly eye for helpless guardsmen, and even something more than this for well-meaning

---

[1] So far back as 1849, Kingsley had preached at Eversley three remarkable sermons on the cholera, which were published in the same year under the title *Who causes Pestilence?*

[2] *Memories and Letters*, vol. III, p. 44.

high-church curates ; and the general note of his social philosophy is optimism. To Christianity, he steadfastly looks as to the crowning grace of all, and, in a corner of his heart, there lurks the belief that, in the crises as well as in the general conduct of life, a gentleman is not a gentleman for nothing.

After *Two Years Ago*, Kingsley but once returned to the novel; for the project which he entertained of writing a story on the subject of the Pilgrimage of Grace was abandoned by him in 1858, after part of the book had been written[1]. His last completed novel, *Hereward the Wake*, was not published till 1866, with a dedication to Thomas Wright, to whose researches the author warmly acknowledged his indebtedness. It is one of the least read of his historical romances, and there is no reference to it in his biographical memorial. But it is a work of much vigour and freshness, and hardly inferior to *Westward Ho!* in the picturesque vividness of its setting; for the homeliness of much of the scenery (the fens are not all sunsets) finds a compensation in the truthfulness of the picture, familiar to Kingsley in his childhood and in his later days[2]. Nor is the characterisation less forcible, to whatever extent the reader may feel further removed from the followers of William and Harold than from the lieges of queen Elizabeth. On the other hand, the earlier of the two novels more successfully unites the personal with the historical interest called forth by it, and less encumbers itself by critical references to its sources. Thus, it comes about that the earlier part of the book, which tells of Hereward's strange adventures by flood and field as an outlaw before the landing of William, is more attractive than the later, in which the story becomes involved in that of the conquest itself and deals not only with the climax of the hero's career, the defence of Ely, but, also, with his rather inglorious exit. In Torfrida, the author of *Hereward* draws a fine and impressive female character such as is wanting in *Westward Ho!* and the figure of Martin, faithful to her even more than to her wayward hero, is, likewise, admirable. 'But as with Napoleon and Josephine, so it was with Hereward and Torfrida.' This analogy, like the less dignified remark that 'if tobacco had been known then, Hereward would have smoked all the way' to Crowland, fails to impair the historical veracity of

---

[1] See *Memories and Letters*, vol. III, pp. 59—62. The effort could not but have been interesting, since the heroes of the story, Robert and Christopher Aske, were 'both good Romanists,' though, as Kingsley points out, they knew nothing of the Jesuits.

[2] One of Kingsley's *Prose Idylls* (1873), treating of the fens, was a reproduction of his article on the subject in *Good Words*, 1 May 1867.

the romance ; the danger of a professor of history indulging in imaginative literature lay in a different direction.

The causes of the great popularity of Kingsley's novels as a whole, and of the attraction which they exercised upon a very large and diversely composed body of readers, are not far to seek. The strength of his imagination could throw its brilliant light both upon material taken from his own age and scenery with which he was familiar, and upon past periods of history known to him only from books, and lands and seas seen by him only with the mind's eye, while his descriptive power enabled him to reproduce them not so much with abundance of detail as with graphic distinctness of touch. These gifts made his fiction real to all who, like himself, were interested in the world and its inhabitants, in the life of nature with all its secrets and in human life with all its longings. But he wrote, as he made no secret that he wrote, for other ends than that of giving pleasure, or of stimulating sympathy with the things with which he sympathised himself ; he also meant, not only in those παραβάσεις, as he calls them, which go direct from author to reader, but by the whole current of his stories, to enforce certain ideas and principles, or the meaning of certain spiritual tendencies and movements of which those ideas formed part. In the correspondence with George Brimley to which reference has already been made, he observes that, in the modern novel, if it is to be a picture of actual life—and this was an end which, with his hatred of unreality, he always kept in view—'you must have people talk, as people do in real life, about all manner of irrelevant things,' but you must

take care that each man's speech shall show more of his character, and that *the general tone shall be such as never to make the reader forget the main purpose of the book.*

There could be no better description of the novel with a purpose— the *Tendenzroman*—which artistically conceals its moral, religious, political, or social aims, and gives pleasure without losing sight of its didactic object. It remains not the less a hybrid, even when the artist's satisfaction in his work from time to time overpowers the sense of his commission as a teacher. To Kingsley, this commission, as he believed, came from the same authority as that which he obeyed as a minister of religion and which he followed in taking upon himself what he held to be part of his ministerial duty, the task of social reform. All the manifold activities of his life— his work as a parson, professor, writer, poet—he sought to fuse in these works of fiction, together with his memories of 'the Berkshire chalkstreams and the Devonshire coast,' and of the town alleys where he 'preached his Gospel of godliness and cleanliness, while smoking his pipe with soldiers and navvies[1].'

Apart from his novels and his solitary tragedy, Kingsley's contributions to pure literature were by no means numerous. He wrote a considerable amount of miscellaneous verse[2]—some of it so excellent as to make it intelligible that he should, at times, have thought poetry the branch of composition for which his genius preeminently qualified him. Of the larger poems, *Andromeda* tells the familiar myth, with, perhaps, excessive elaboration, in not unharmonious hexameters—a metre to the English form of which he gave much consideration ; the poet would not have been himself had he not made his poem a tribute to the sea and even to the

Silvery fish, wreathed shell, and the strange lithe things of the water.

His own favourite poem seems to have been *St Maura*, which had satisfied Maurice. There are other legends, sagas and ballad-romances of slighter pretensions ; but the best of all are the quite short ballad-songs, some of them imbedded in his novels, which reveal their depth of feeling in a few words, of which the cadence persistently haunts the ear—such as *The Sands of Dee*, *The Three Fishers* and maybe one or two more.

In 1860, Kingsley was appointed regius professor of modern history in the university of Cambridge, an office which he held during nine years. He was as deeply gratified by the circumstances of his appointment as he was afterwards depressed by the responsibilities of a chair to which, from first to last, he never failed to devote the best of his powers. But they were not suited to many sides of the work, and could not be made to suit them. That, with many other things, he quickened, among his hearers, the interest in historical studies is indisputable. The publications connected with his tenure of the professorship are few. Besides the modest inaugural discourse on the human interests of history, printed (1860) under the title *The Limits of Exact Science as applied to History*, he published, in 1864, a course of lectures entitled *The Roman and the Teuton*. The subject, always particularly attractive to him, called for a close examination of evidence, in such enquiries, for instance, as that into the character of later imperial administration. The modest disclaimer 'I am not here to teach history—no man can do that ; but to teach you to teach it' will

---

[1] See Max Müller's preface to the 1875 edition of *The Roman and the Teuton*.

[2] Collected in vol. XVI of the 19 vol. edition of his *Life and Works*.

not prevent the conclusion that, as a historian, he was not equal
to his task, and this, not because of inaccuracies, partly disproved,
partly shown to be exaggerated, but, chiefly, by reason of his want
of insight into historic method. His historical essays published in
1873[1], of course, lay less open to this objection. In the last of these,
Kingsley was found ready to accept without hesitation the authority
of Froude; and it was a second review of the same *History* that
drew him into the controversy with Newman, which, inasmuch as
it gave rise to *Apologia*, belongs, rather, to an estimate of the works
of that writer. Kingsley's breakdown in the fray was due to his
original blunder of basing on evidence in part unfortunately chosen
and in part left vague the statement of a general conclusion on a
question not admitting of debate from two totally different points
of view. He was by nature neither dogmatical nor obstinate, as,
indeed, a candid examination of this controversy will itself suffice
to show. His lectures entitled *The Ancien Régime*, delivered at the
Royal Institution in 1867, have been left behind by later research.
During the last six years of Kingsley's life (1869—75), in which,
after resigning his Cambridge chair, he successively held canonries
at Chester and at Westminster (the latter from 1873), he was more
or less relieved from the necessity of work with his pen; but it
was never idle. Nothing further, however, need be said here of
his sermons, of which there are many volumes, from the *Village
Sermons* of Eversley to those delivered in Westminster abbey :
most of them are distinguished not only by an incisive brevity, but,
also, by a skilful, as well as courageous, choice of social or ethical
topics, and all of them breathe a spirit of generous humanity[2],
as well as of true piety. Among the writings which testify to his
love of natural scenery and its associations, the *Prose Idylls*, varying in theme from the home counties to the fens and the Pyrenees,
are, perhaps, the most delightful ; and the same appreciative spirit
accompanied him across the sea on a three months' visit in 1869, to
the West Indies, recorded in *At Last* (1871)—a happily chosen title
—which tells the story of a life's longing satisfied. He paid another
visit to the new world, in the year before he died ; but its literary
memorial deals with monuments and lessons of the old[3]. To an
earlier year (1863) belongs *The Water-Babies, a Fairy Tale for a
Land-Baby*, written in a happy vein of humorous fancy, while

---

[1] *Plays and Puritans, Sir Walter Raleigh*, review of Froude's *History*.

[2] See, by way of example, the sermons on David, whom he once playfully declared
his 'favourite hero.'

[3] *Lectures delivered in America in* 1874 (1875).

the didactic element introduces itself without insistence, as it should in a story meant for children and not for the grown-up people in the back seats.

Kingsley's life and literary career reflect and represent a restless age. He belonged to a band of courageous and clear-sighted men who, with Maurice at their head, tried to understand their countrymen and to lead them to a better time. Kingsley was gifted, like few of them, with a strong imagination and the power of direct and striking, as well as fervent and sympathetic, expression ; and, thus, he, more than any one of his companions, imparted to the most popular literary form of his times that quality of earnestness which associated it indelibly with the great social endeavours of the age.

Of Maurice's followers in the efforts for social reforms which marked the middle years of the century, Thomas Hughes was the only writer besides Kingsley who gained for himself an enduring name in the literature of fiction. And this, virtually, by a single work, *Tom Brown's School Days* ; for its continuation from no point of view equalled it in merit, and most of the author's other works were biographical. Hughes, like Kingsley, made no secret of the didactic purpose of his extraordinarily successful story, which was first published, anonymously, in 1857. 'He wrote,' he said, 'to get the chance of preaching, and not for any other object'; and the keynote of the story was the defence of earnestness in schoolboys as a brighter renewal of what, in former days, used to be called seriousness. The value of this quality, as the master quality of a boy's character and life, and of those of the man into whom he is growing, is set forth not only in the experience of the commonplace hero (for this commonplaceness is indispensable in an exemplar), but, also, in the personality of the man in whom he recognises his ideal. Rarely, if ever, has a great school been so identified with a great man as Arnold has become identified with Rugby; and, since Hughes's tale contributed to this result not less unmistakably than Stanley's *Life*, the one has as good a title to his statue by the playing-fields as the other has to his in the chapel of the school. Though there are passages in the book which may be fitter for men than for boys, that charge can, certainly, not be brought home to it as a whole ; and its close (written by the author in circumstances of deep personal distress) gives solemnity as well as unity to the story, though it begins with scenes of admirable humour and is, what few school histories succeed in being, a true picture of school life and of boys' nature.

The present seems the most appropriate place for speaking of the chief contributions to British fiction of Elizabeth Cleghorn Gaskell, a writer of rare charm and, though no one knew better than herself the limits prescribed to her creations, possessed of true powers of both pathos and humour. For, although she preferred to exercise those powers chiefly in tracing the interplay of personal affections and passions, the influence of character upon character, the genial impulses of the soul and the shy sorrows of the heart, and the all-healing love which rises above self, they were, it is certain, first set in motion when her mind was brought to bear upon the social problems and troubles around her. In these, her loving nature was drawn, by personal affliction of its own, to take a sympathetic interest; and *Mary Barton*, written to beguile a mother's grief for the loss of her infant son, her first book and that by which her literary reputation was at once established, may justly claim to rank among the most notable of the social novels of the age.

Mrs Gaskell was described by one of the most faithful and gifted of her and her daughters' friends[1] as

like the best things in her books; full of gracious and tender sympathies, of thoughtful kindness, of pleasant humour, of quick appreciation, of utmost simplicity and truthfulness, and uniting with peculiar delicacy and refinement a strength of principle and purpose and straightforwardness in action such as few women possess.

But her life was led in conditions of great tranquillity and almost unbroken happiness, and, after her death, the remembrance of her was preserved by the perfect love of those whom she had left behind her and to whom her wishes were law. She desired that no set biography of her should be attempted; and it is thus from her writings only that later generations are likely to gather much beyond the outward facts of her existence. Those who knew her or hers may indulge the belief that in those writings are to be found more than one experience that came very near home to her, transmuted into kindly lessons of resignation and of charity to all men[2].

Mrs Gaskell was born on 29 September 1810, in what is now

---

[1] Eliot Norton, in a letter to J. Russell Lowell, written in 1857. See his *Letters of Charles Eliot Norton* (2 vols. 1913), vol. i, pp. 171—2.

[2] A remembrance of the loss of her boy, already noticed, is traceable in *Mary Barton*, *Lizzie Leigh*, *Ruth*, *Cranford*, *Mr Harrison's Confessions*, *Cousin Phillis* and, doubtless, in other of her stories.

known as 93 Cheyne walk and was then called Lindsay row, Chelsea. Her father, member of a Berwick-on-Tweed family 'in which ran a strong love of the sea,' was a man of original ability, in turn unitarian minister and (after an interval of schoolmastering and farming) keeper of the treasury records[1]; her maternal grandfather was a descendant of the wellknown Lancashire and Cheshire family of Holland, who farmed his own land at Sandle bridge in the latter county. William Stevenson may be fairly set down as the original of minister Holman in *Cousin Phillis*, and the intimate and enduring connection of the Cheshire Hollands with Knutsford suggested an infinitude of personal and local reminiscences of that town and its vicinity under the *aliases* of Cranford, Duncombe (in *Mr Harrison's Confessions*) and Hollingford (in *Wives and Daughters*). At Knutsford (which thus became part of herself), most of Elizabeth Stevenson's girlhood was spent; the rest was divided between London, Newcastle-on-Tyne (where she resided in the house of a unitarian minister, William Turner, who is said to have suggested some features in the beautiful character of Thurston Benson in *Ruth*) and at Edinburgh (as humorously recorded in the introduction to *Round the Sofa*). In 1832, she married William Gaskell, then and to the end of his life, minister of the Cross street unitarian chapel in Manchester and an accomplished scholar, with whom all the rest of her life flowed on in perfect unison. The circle of friends of which she now became part and of which, in time, her house, 84 Plymouth grove, was to be looked upon as a chosen centre, was one of social as well as intellectual distinction; yet it was as a 'greater Manchester,' in more than the local sense of the phrase, that she learnt to love the place, till, even on her holidays in Wales, and, afterwards, on the Neckar, in Italy and in her favourite France, she could look back, like Mary Barton on the railway to Liverpool, 'towards the factory-chimneys, and the cloud of smoke which hovers over the place, with a feeling akin to *Heimweh*.' And it is not too much to say that what, from the first, helped to bind her to the city which, for more than fourscore years, was to be her home and that of her daughters, was the care for the poor of which she and they never lost sight. Several years before she began *Mary Barton*, she and her husband printed[2] the first (and, as it proved, the only) one of a projected series of versified *Sketches*

---

[1] His mother, Mrs Gaskell's paternal grandmother, was cousin, once removed, of tne author of *The Seasons*.

[2] In *Blackwood's Magazine* for January 1837 (vol. XLI, no. 255).

among the Poor, 'rather' as she confidentially put it to her friend
Mrs Howitt, 'in the manner of Crabbe, but in a more seeing-beauty
spirit.' The influence of Crabbe, tempered in the fashion which
this passage indicates, is, as will be seen, traceable in some of her
published writings.

Mary Barton, a Tale of Manchester Life, was written in
1845—7[1], when there was still great distress in the manufacturing
districts, and when the abolition of the corn laws was only beginning to exercise its remedial effects; and it was published in
1848, when the political and social fabric of this country stood
unshaken, though not unmoved, by the convulsions of the continent.
When, or just before, Mrs Gaskell was beginning her story,
Disraeli had published *Coningsby* and was preparing to follow
it by *Sybil*; but Mrs Gaskell was unacquainted with either of
these works, though she might have given them at least as
friendly a reception as was accorded to the later of them by her
contemporary George Eliot[2]. It is, however, clear that Mrs
Gaskell's story was concerned with a rather earlier period of
British social history—the years 1842—3; and this was recognised by the most powerful, though not by the most violent,
among its critics[3]. The troubles of these years really dated from
the series of bad harvests which had begun so far back as 1837,
and which had led, in 1838, to the great chartist meeting on Kersal
moor, Manchester, and, in the following year, amidst continued
distress, to the rejection, by a large parliamentary majority, of
a monster chartist petition, agreed upon by a national convention
of working men's delegates. It cannot be said that (though, as
John Barton and other less prejudiced observers noted, royal
drawing-rooms and other social functions were not suspended)
these occurrences made no impression even in London; but, at
Manchester and elsewhere in the manufacturing districts, there
ensued much agitation and violence, and, when, in 1840 and 1841, the
distress among the working classes continued and, in the following
year, reached its height, a great part of Lancashire fell into a
condition approaching to riot, though the queen's speech stated

---

[1] The conjecture that the short and powerful story *Lizzie Leigh,* of which the
first portion appeared on 30 March 1850, in the first number of *Household Words,* was
written, in part at least, before *Mary Barton,* is plausible, but unproved. Probably,
the reproduction in it, with a different relation, of the Esther episode was unconscious.

[2] *George Eliot's Life,* by Cross, J. W., vol. I, p. 104.

[3] Greg, W. R., speaks of 'such periods as 1842'; *The Manchester Guardian* of
28 February 1849 refers to 'this morbid sensibility to the condition of factory
operatives, which has become so fashionable *of late* among the gentry and landed
aristocracy.'

that the sufferings and privations of the manufacturing districts
had been borne 'with exemplary patience and fortitude.'   After
another petition—this time bearing more than three million sig-
natures—had been rejected by a sweeping majority of the house
of commons, a wild riot broke out at Manchester, and a general
strike was for a few days enforced.

It was the impression of these events, and of the efforts which
followed to allay the almost unprecedented sufferings, as well as
the perilous excitement, of the working classes, especially in the
manufacturing districts, which was upon Mrs Gaskell when she
wrote her 'tale of Manchester life.'   For it should not be overlooked that, if the preceding years had brought with them sore
suffering and savage wrath, 1842 and the years immediately
following, at all events, were full, not only of charitable effort, but
of legislative endeavour to find remedies for the existing condition
of things ; that, in a word, the conscience of the country was
awake, and the system by which things (including wages) were left
to right themselves had been definitely put on its defence.   This
is the point of view from which the authoress of *Mary Barton*
addressed herself to the problem of the early forties, which she
did not so much as profess to understand in all its economical
bearings ; and this is what the eminent political and economical
thinker who was the sternest critic of the book failed to see when
he tried to shift the chief blame for the patent evils of the situation
from the masters to the workmen, and, more especially, to the
ex-workmen 'who form the acting staff of trades' unions and
delegations[1].'   Mrs Gaskell's panacea—the bringing-about of a
good understanding (in every sense of the term) between masters
and men—had only begun to be put into operation in the period
with which *Mary Barton* deals ; and even to these beginnings she
pays a tribute, though not in a particularly decisive form[2].

Still, it is obvious enough that, in *Mary Barton*, there is no
very manifest intention of holding a careful balance between the
two sides[3], and that, as was inevitable, the sympathies of the

---

[1] Greg, W. R., *Mistaken Aims and Attainable Ideals of the Working Classes* (1876),
reprinted from *The Edinburgh Review*, April 1849.   See, also, *Essays in Political
and Social Science*, vol. I, 1853.

[2] *I.e.* in that of improvements effected by, or due to the mind of, the elder Carson
'which submitted to be taught by suffering.'

[3] Against the quite improbably cruel behaviour of the younger Carson in caricaturing
the unhappy workmen delegates might be set the much less improbable but infinitely
more heinous fact of his murder—especially when it is borne in mind that the actual
murder which probably suggested this incident was occasioned, not by private
vengeance, but by a wish to intimidate the masters of a district near Manchester.

reader are engaged on the side of those who have 'to stint in things for life.' The writer did not plead their cause as deserving, or deprived of, particular rights; chartist, or even democratic, dreams were far away from her mind; she and many of the working men and women would probably even have disagreed as to the protection which the law should give to wives and children[1]. But she thought that the men should be treated 'as brethren and friends' by their employers, and that, so long as this remained untried, there could be no desire for peace and, consequently, no hope of better things.

It is impossible to go back here upon the controversy to which the publication of *Mary Barton* gave rise; it did not weaken the force of her appeal for sympathy with those who needed it; but, if unjust to the main motive, it was almost inevitably provoked by the actual effect, of her book. That her own sense of justice and the magnanimity inspired by it became aware of this is shown by the novel which, six years later, she published under the title *North and South*, and apart from which, in justice to the writer, *Mary Barton* ought never to be judged. In 1854, the great remedial legislation of the abolition of the corn laws had borne its full fruits; the agitation for the charter, though not extinct, had cooled down, and working men in the manufacturing districts had begun to appreciate the value of association and the uses of combination. On the other hand, the more intelligent of the masters, too, could not but better discern the necessity, and the more conscientious of them the duty, of establishing with their men relations which no longer ignored their necessary dependence upon one another. This, so far as the question of factory labour came to be treated in it, was the general conception of *North and South*, the story which, curiously enough, appeared in *Household Words* immediately after Dickens's *Hard Times*, though written in absolute independence of it. The critic who had condemned, while admiring, *Mary Barton* blessed *North and South* altogether. But Mrs Gaskell had neither wished to receive, nor intended to make, an *amende honorable*. The social teaching of the two novels is perfectly self-consistent; and, though it did not solve the difficulties of the problem to which it addressed itself, in no later phase of that problem has the spirit of Mrs Gaskell's message been left aside with impunity.

Mary Barton, which, besides, as was inevitable, surpassing

---

[1] Old Alice is against the employment of married women in factories; but poor Mrs Davenport denounces the law keeping children from factory work.

all later works of its author in the spread of its popularity at home, has been translated into many foreign tongues, reveals more of her distinctive literary qualities than is common with first works. But it was written in conditions and with thoughts of its own. The working men and women who appear in it (including both hero and heroine) are not only true Lancashire, but living human beings. The plot is admirably clear, and rises to a climax of dramatic power rare, but not unparalleled, in Mrs Gaskell's later stories. Curiously enough, it is here that her humour, more or less repressed in the earlier part of the novel, for the first time comes freely to the front, in the old boatman and the *gamin* Charley. But the story was not conceived in cheerfulness, and, as its scene lies in humble homes, repeated appeal to the impressiveness of deathbeds (on which Maria Edgeworth remarked) seems not unfitting. On the other hand, it is full of strong passion, and of the tenderest of pathos, and is steeped in that feeling of neighbourly love which we are almost induced to deem the best privilege of the poor.

The success of *Mary Barton* speedily brought Mrs Gaskell into near relations with the grand masters of the branch of literature in which she had herself taken a leading place, and more especially with Dickens, who showed her, as a writer in *Household Words* and *All the Year Round*, and in many other ways, the highest consideration and regard. She wrote much for him during the greater part of her literary life, but hardly ever, either in her contributions to his Christmas numbers or in her occasional papers, anything unworthy of preservation, as illustrating her freshness of thought, power of observation and delicacy of sympathy. Unlike many of her fellow-contributors, she cannot be said to have fallen, except quite occasionally[1], under the spell of his manner or mannerism. Her own English style was always of singular purity; neither north nor south had marred it by 'provincialisms[2]'; and it is not by chance that one of her favourite writers[3] was Mme de Sévigné, whose style was wholly natural and perfectly pure. Whatever Mrs Gaskell's theme—a page of homely life, a tale of adventure or even of crime, or one of those mysterious

[1] Perhaps the most striking instance of an unconscious imitation of Dickens is to be found in both some of the pathos and some of the fun of the delightful *Mr Harrison's Confessions*. And see, *post*, as to *Cranford*.

[2] The best writers must have some little habitual flaw of diction; Mrs Gaskell's use of the verb 'name' is the only one that is recurrent in hers.

[3] The design of writing Mme de Sévigné's life occupied Mrs Gaskell in her last years.

supernatural experiences which had an irresistible fascination for her—the lucidity and delicacy of the style never fail the teller of the story.

After, in *The Moorland Cottage* (1850), which is full of simple charm, and has additional interest as containing the germ of not a few characters and situations in her later works[1], she had produced her second separately published story, Mrs Gaskell contributed to *Household Words* (1851—3), in a series of papers republished (1853) under the collective title *Cranford*, what (all questions of preference or predilection apart) must be described as the most original of all her works. The literary derivation of this inimitable prose idyll, that grew out of itself into a whole from which nothing is to be taken away and to which (as it proved) nothing could safely be added[2], is a question admitting of discussion : but this discussion may easily be carried too far. Crabbe and Mary Russell Mitford, Galt and Maria Edgeworth, and even Jane Austen, influenced the choice and limitation of theme to some extent, and Dickens was not wholly a stranger to the method of treatment[3]. But the interweaving of truth and fiction, and the proportioning of the elements of pathos and tenderness to those of humour and even of fun, were wholly the author's own. '*Cranford*,' says lady Ritchie[4], 'proves the value of little things, of the grain of mustard-seed,' and 'reveals the mighty secret of kindness allied to gentle force.' Thus, the intimate record of the human lives and souls sheltered by a sequestered little Cheshire home became a favourite of the English-speaking world ; and the gentle and shrinking Miss Matty takes her place among the true heroines of our domestic fiction.

In the same year as the collected *Cranford*, appeared a novel of a very different type—*Ruth*[5]. This book caused a controversy in its way almost as violent as that excited by *Mary Barton*— W. R. Greg, more in sorrow than in anger, censuring its 'false

[1] Maggie, above all, is Molly in germ, even in her attachment to her chosen solitary seat.

[2] One attempt was, not very successfully, made; another, on a larger scale, one may think fortunately, remained a passing fancy. *Mr Harrison's Confessions* and *Wives and Daughters* use the same background, but each in its own fashion. One or two passages in the latter story come rather close to *Cranford*, but are not, perhaps, so good as the rest of the book.

[3] The reference to *Pickwick* was removed from one passage of the text, but left standing in another.

[4] *A Discourse on Modern Sibyls* (read to the English Association, 1913), p. 8.

[5] The name of this novel was probably (though, of course, not certainly) suggested by one of Crabbe's *Tales of the Hall*.

morality,' and F. D. Maurice, Charles Kingsley (after a more or less *a priori* fashion), Florence Nightingale and others ranging themselves on the side of the defence. *Ruth* treats a wholly ethical problem, or, rather, two problems which the course of the story almost tempts the reader to confound. The plea for Christian forgiveness of sin following on repentance is unanswerable; but the incident on which everything is made to turn in the progress of the plot cannot be pronounced a happy conception. The value of the virtue of truthfulness was always present to Mrs Gaskell's mind, and there are few of her stories but, in one way or another, help to illustrate it[1]. But, in *Ruth*, though the lie is told for the wronged woman rather than by her, the trouble which it brings forth fails to strike the reader as inevitable, and the compassion evoked by a story of the deepest pathos is, therefore, not without reservation. Other exceptions might be taken to the working-out of the plot (especially as to the part played in it by a very unattractive Lothario); but the beauty of the central figure remains, and the pity of her fate, tenderly softened by the ministering love of those around her.

Of *North and South* (first published as a complete work in 1855) we have already spoken, and can only note further that, to its picture of the differences between masters and men, it adds, with great constructive skill, the contrast indicated in its title, and another contrast of wider sway and deeper import. If Margaret's prejudice against manufacturers is, perhaps, a little stubborn for her time of day, her virgin pride is not less true to nature than Thornton's tenacity; and the true crisis of the story—Margaret's farewell to her brother[2]—is not less dramatic than the earlier scene of her defence of Thornton against the mob. After the crisis, the story begins to drag—it was, like *Hard Times*, the first brought out by its writer in weekly instalments. That it should remain one of the finest, if not the finest, of her achievements, must, therefore, be allowed to show an extraordinary mastery of the art in which she had rapidly come to excel.

Yet, at this very time, she turned aside from this to another

---

[1] Thus, in tragic fashion, *Sylvia's Lovers*, and, in a more genial vein, *Wives and Daughters*, where Molly's truthfulness lies at the very core of her nature, in contrast with her stepmother's equally characteristic 'falsity in very little things.' The rather casuistical problem of the white lie recurs in *North and South*.

[2] The story of Frederick is a variation of that of Peter in *Cranford*; Mrs Gaskell's interest in the subject of reappearances, as well as in that of disappearances (on which she wrote a separate paper), was, no doubt, due to the disappearance in his youth of her brother John, a lieutenant in the merchant service.

field of composition in which she was a novice. Mrs Gaskell's *Life of Charlotte Brontë*, to which she devoted the whole of the year 1856 and which was published, in two volumes, in the following year, is a possession for ever, and while, in the words of Charlotte Brontë's father, the work had been done 'in such a way as no person but the writer could have done it,' no later treatment of the same theme, critical, controversial, supplementary, or retouching, will ever in any sense supersede it. Even were the present the most appropriate place, it would be impossible to notice here—quite apart from all discussion of details, whether of statement or of omission—cavils concerning the entire method and spirit of treatment adopted by the biographer, more especially in the earlier portions of the book[1]. No more spontaneous honour, it has been said[2], was ever offered by one woman of genius to another than when Mrs Gaskell wrote the life of her friend; and the time cannot be distant when those who care most both for the fame of Charlotte Brontë and her sisters will be the readiest to acknowledge what it owes to the generous and truthful record that made them enduring memories.

But the strictures passed upon passages of this biography gave much pain to its author, and for some years she published little of importance. *My Lady Ludlow*, which was reprinted with several other tales in the pleasantly introduced collection *Round the Sofa*, in 1859, after appearing in *Household Words* during the summer months of the previous year, cannot be reckoned among her best stories; though some of the characters, from the highbred *châtelaine* to the acute little poacher's son, are admirably drawn, the machinery, for once, does not move easily. Mrs Gaskell found herself and her wonderful power of narrative again in *Sylvia's Lovers* (1863), a perfect story but for a certain lengthiness and excess of ἀναγνώρισις towards the close[3]. The terrors of the press-gang, a remarkably lucid account of which, after the time-honoured manner of Scott, introduces the story, serves as a background to a domestic drama of extraordinary power, strengthened in its hold upon the mind by the

---

[1] Cf. Reid, Sir T. Wemyss, *Charlotte Brontë* (1877), and the observations on it, of Stephen, Sir L., 'Charlotte Brontë,' in *Hours in a Library*, 3rd series (1879), pp. 338 ff.

[2] By lady Ritchie, *op. cit.* A generous welcome was given to this biography at the time of its appearance by George Eliot, who had admired *Ruth*, but thought it strained.

[3] The *motif* of Philip's return to his wife reappears in Mrs Gaskell's short tale *The Manchester Marriage* (1859). Both this and *Sylvia's Lovers* were earlier in date of publication than *Enoch Arden* (1864).

graphic art that brings the grand 'Monkshaven' seascape and the rough times of the great naval wars vividly before us[1]. *Sylvia's Lovers* can certainly not be called a political novel; but it is a historical novel in the broader sense in which *The Heart of Midlothian* may be thus described, and worthy to be named with that masterpiece as a tale of passion and anguish that goes straight to every human heart. 'It was,' Mrs Gaskell said, 'the saddest story I ever wrote'; and she poured into it all the infinite pity of which her loving nature was capable. The canvas of the story is full of figures, instinct with life and truth, including Kester, her single male example of a class always a favourite in British fiction, but never drawn with more affectionate humour than by Mrs Gaskell, whom her own domestic servants adored.

It would not be easy to point to a more signal instance of the power of genius to vary both the forms in which it presents its creations, and the effects which these presentments produce, than is furnished by a comparison between *Sylvia's Lovers* and its successor *Cousin Phillis*. This short story first appeared in *The Cornhill Magazine*, in 1863—4, and was printed, as a whole, in the following year. In it, Mrs Gaskell once more tells the tale of a broken heart—broken by abandonment. But, this time, it is no seeming tragic destiny which has swept down upon the course of love—only an everyday cruelty of fate which, in this instance, was not even intended by its agent. *Cousin Phillis* is an idyll only, but one of the loveliest, and, in plan and in setting, one of the most finished, of its kind. If minister Holman, who quotes Vergil on his way home from farm-work and evening hymn, stands forth like one of the patriarchal figures in *Hermann und Dorothea*, the sweetness and the sadness of Phillis herself remain with us as an incomparable memory of love and loss—undisturbed by any happy ending.

One of Mrs Gaskell's novels has still to be noted here, which, though nominally unfinished, has, by many judges, been held to be in execution the most perfect of them all. *Wives and Daughters, an Every-day Story*, was, like its predecessor, first printed in *The Cornhill Magazine*, where it appeared from August 1864 to January 1866. Most of the story had been written during a happy holiday at Pontresina, on a visit to Mrs Gaskell's intimate

---

[1] Crabbe's story of Ruth in *Tales of the Hall*, already mentioned, may have suggested the first idea of a tale of impressment to Mrs Gaskell; but this part of the plot of *Sylvia's Lovers* is based on a historical episode of Whitby life of which she had carefully studied the facts.

friend Mme Mohl at Paris and at Dieppe. Before the publication of its last, but uncompleted, portion, Mrs Gaskell died, quite suddenly, but surrounded by many of those she loved best, at Holybourne near Alton in Hampshire, in a country-house which she had intended to present to her husband on the completion of her novel. This had been all but reached when death overtook her, while in full enjoyment of her powers, which had never been exerted with more delightful mastery and assured effect than in her last work. To describe *Wives and Daughters* as in its author's later manner is, however, a criticism of doubtful import. It was, rather, that some of her literary gifts—especially the humour which she had richly displayed in so early a work as *Cranford*—had now mellowed into a delicious softness, and that, even in depicting the serious conflicts through which the souls of men and women have to pass in this troubled existence, she had learnt the value of 'the subdued colouring—the half-tints of real life,' which George Eliot had desiderated in *Ruth*[1]. *Wives and Daughters*, thus, instead of being called in Mrs Gaskell's later manner, should be described as Mrs Gaskell's manner itself in perfection. Above all, its irony is inimitable. This enables the writer to furnish in Mr Gibson a fresh type of simple manliness —the type which women most rarely succeed in realising—quite different from that of Thornton in *North and South*, yet deserving a place by its side, and, among the female figures, to contrast with the true-hearted Molly and the irresistible Cynthia, the wholly original personality of Clare—second wife, stepmother, *ci-devant* governess and the embodiment of unconscious shallowness. She is certainly not a 'woman of feeling'; neither, however, is she a woman without feelings; for 'if Mrs Gibson had ever felt anything acutely, it was the death of Mr Kirkpatrick,' her first husband.

In Mrs Gaskell's hands, the social novel, which, in *Mary Barton*, she had essayed with extraordinary success, had thus developed into a form of fiction which she had made entirely her own. The power of finding full expression for the human sympathy within her, which had given force to her earliest work, had grown and been refined as it grew, till, in her latest, she had produced one of the most exquisite examples in English fiction of the pure novel of character.

In far different fashion from the reflection, in the writings of Mrs Gaskell, of her calm life, happy in itself and in the home

---

[1] *Life*, by Cross, J. W. (edition 1902), vol. i, p. 247.

where it was led, the experiences of the woman of genius who consistently signed her writings with the pseudonym George Eliot send their often refracted rays across the pages of her chief prose fictions. She was too thorough an artist to copy out into them either her own personality or that of any of her kinsfolk, friends or acquaintances; 'there is,' she wrote about *Adam Bede*, 'not a single portrait in the book, nor will there be in any future book of mine[1].' Moreover, her spirit, like that of her favourite heroines, was too lofty to allow her to complain of troubles or exult in happiness which she was conscious of owing, in part at least, to herself. And it was with her life's work, rather than with its outward events, that her mind was occupied, as she looked backward or forward during its course; 'the only thing,' she told her husband when urged by him to write her autobiography, 'I should care much to dwell on would be the absolute despair I suffered from of ever being able to achieve anything[2].'

The first twenty-one years of Mary Ann Evans's life—she was born 22 November 1819—were spent in the commonplace surroundings (on the border, though, of Shakespeare's forest of Arden) of a rather remote half manor, half farmhouse, on a great Warwickshire estate of which her father was agent. He must have been a notable man, and of his strong character some features are held to have passed into both Adam Bede and the high-minded and humorous Caleb Garth in *Middlemarch*. At Griff house, the companion of Mary Ann's childhood, before 'school parted them[3],' was her brother Isaac, just as Tom was Maggie's in the golden hours which never came back till the very last. To the associations of her early youth[4] she steadfastly clung, true to her belief in the formative influence of such remembrances upon the active, as well as the contemplative, passages of life. By her elder sister's marriage, she became, at an early age, the head of her widowed father's house, and thus soon acquired a self-reliance which had been fostered by her acknowledged superiority over her schoolfellows and companions. Though her reading seemed to her

---

[1] See *George Eliot's Life, as related in her Letters and Journals*, arranged and edited by her husband, Cross, J. W., vol. I, p. 486. This book, though its editor disclaims the functions of a biographer, is executed with great tact and ability. The references to it as *Life*, etc., in the present chapter, are to the reprint uniform with the Warwick edition of George Eliot's *Works*.

[2] *Life*, etc., vol. I, p. 29.

[3] See the charming 'Brother and Sister' in *Poems* (Warwick edition, vol. IX, pp. 578—589).

[4] See 'Looking Backward' in *The Impressions of Theophrastus Such* (vol. XII, pp. 23—43).

fragmentary, it was already assuming proportions which, in the end, were to make her a kind of Acton among Englishwomen of letters. In the meantime, she passed, alone, through the phase of absorption in religious and even ascetic ideas—which was intensified by the example of an aunt whose self-sacrificing devotion afterwards suggested that of Dinah Morris in *Adam Bede*—and then reached a recognition of the claims of the individual intellect to freedom of enquiry. The liberating influence, in her case, had been that of Charles Bray, a manufacturer at Coventry, into the immediate neighbourhood of which she had now removed with her father, and of his wife. Bray had recently (1841) published *The Philosophy of Necessity*, and his brother-in-law, Charles Hennell, was author of *An Inquiry concerning the Origin of Christianity* (1838), to the German translation of which a preface had been contributed by Strauss[1]. It was thus that Mary Ann Evans was led to take over from Mrs Hennell the laborious undertaking of an English translation of the celebrated *Leben Jesu*, which ultimately appeared, early in 1846, with a preface by the author.

The ethics of her inner life, as disclosed by her correspondence about this date, are those to which she afterwards gave repeated expression in her maturest works. There is nothing paradoxical in her description of herself, working at her desk till she felt 'Strauss-sick,' with a crucifix placed before her eyes, more familiar to them than it was to Romola's in her younger days. Her purpose was not to spread doubts and difficulties—she detested what she called 'the quackery of infidelity,' and even in Buckle she found only a mixture of irreligion and conceit. The ground was to be 'good,' *i.e.* well-prepared, into which she desired to 'sow good seed, instead of rooting up tares where we must inevitably gather up the wheat with them.' Yet, for freedom of enquiry, no effort, no struggle seemed sufficient to her. Such she was when, shortly after she had passed her thirtieth year, she may be said to have begun her literary life. After death had ended her father's long illness, during which she had been his devoted nurse, finding time, however, occasionally to work at her translation of Spinoza's *Tractatus Theologico-Politicus*[2], she rested, for a time, at Geneva, and, in 1850, took up her abode in London. Few men or women

---

[1] In 1852, Mary Ann Evans contributed an analysis of Charles Hennell's book to John Chapman's *Catalogue* of his publications (see *Life*, etc., vol. I, pp. 76—82). Hennell's unmarried sister Sara, author of *Thoughts in Aid of Faith*, was long one of her favourite correspondents.

[2] Neither this, nor a translation by her of Spinoza's *Ethics*, seems ever to have been published.

have ever entered upon a life of letters better fitted for it than she was. Enthusiastic—enthusiasm, she said, is necessary 'even for pouring out breakfast'; sympathetic—it was in her 'wonderful sympathy,' the two men to whom she was in succession most closely united agreed that 'her power lay[1]'; sincerely religious, though she had left both the creeds and practices of religion behind her[2]; equipped like very few writers laden with learning either of the schools or self-acquired; and possessed of a power of work such as only belongs to a lifelong student: so she set herself to her task.

Though she was to become one of the foremost of Victorian novelists, it was still some years before she essayed, or probably thought of essaying, a work of fiction. The political or politico-social novel was then, as has been seen, in the ascendant, and, in problems directly affecting the political life of the nation, her own experience and training had not hitherto been such as to awaken in her a special interest. The Reform bill agitation and its consequences were only impressions of her girlhood; in the party contentions which followed on the close of the whig *régime* she had no concern, and, on this aspect of politics, as even her latest novels show, she always looked coldly and quite from the outside. She had no sympathy with 'young Englandism' except in so far as she loved and respected the movement 'as an effort on behalf of the people,' and, curiously enough, the future authoress of *Daniel Deronda* sternly averted her eyes from 'everything specifically Jewish[3].' But Carlyle's *French Revolution* had not failed to appeal to her very strongly, and when, in London, the horizon of her intellectual interests widened and her powers of sympathy, which knew no distinction of class but were most at home with her own, had full play. She was much attracted by the novels of Kingsley, between whose genius and his faults she drew a drastic contrast[4].

At first, however, the influences under which she fell were not those of writers anxious to guide public feeling in political and social questions. Before settling in London she had been a temporary member of the Bray household at Coventry, and had there come to know some notable thinkers; it was thus natural enough that, in 1850, she became a contributor to *The Westminster Review*, which was then being taken over (from

---

[1] *Life*, etc., vol. I, p. 326.

[2] Her religious position is well characterised in Storr, V. F., *Development of English Theology* (1913), pp. 361—2.

[3] *Life*, etc., vol. I, pp. 138—9.   [4] *Ibid.* p. 246.

John Stuart Mill) by John Chapman, as an organ of advanced
theological and philosophical thought, and, to a considerable
extent, of the teaching of Comte and his followers. In the
following year, she became associated with Chapman in the conduct
of the *Review*, and, although she shrank from being put forward
as editress, it is clear that, before long, she bore the chief burden
of the office. Herbert Spencer, one of the leading lights of the
circle to which she now belonged, among other friendly offices,
introduced her to George Henry Lewes, who, at that time, was
editor of *The Leader*. Attracted by the extraordinary intellectual
vivacity and quickness of sympathy which, together with brilliant
scientific and literary gifts, distinguished Lewes, she formed a
union with him. His own home had, for some time, been broken
up; on his three sons, she bestowed the kindliest maternal
affection. He showed to her, as well he might, unsurpassable
devotion, and watched over her literary labours, and the fame
they brought her, with unremitting care. But, even after she had
become famous, her life with him long remained isolated, except
for the admirers of her genius whom he brought to their house.
It would be surprising if, especially in her earlier works, a tinge of
melancholy, which generally tended to take the nobler form of
renunciation, were not perceptible; but the personal trials of her
life never, as the whole series of those works shows, even momentarily overthrew the balance of her moral judgment. And this is
of the greater importance as applied to her writing, inasmuch as
she never ceased to regard it as the most responsible among the
activities of her existence. 'Writing,' she declares, soon after she
had first attempted fiction, 'is part of my religion, and I can write
no word that is not prompted from within[1].'

Besides a translation of Ludwig Feuerbach's *Essence of Christianity* (1854)[2], she was now at work on a variety of subjects brought
into her hands in the way of journalistic duty; and it is curious
that it should have been an article (of the superior 'smashing'
kind) on *The Evangelical Teaching of Dr Cumming*[3] which first
convinced Lewes of 'the true genius in her writing[4].' It was about
this time that they spent three weeks at Weimar (his *Life of
Goethe* was then on the eve of publication), going on thence to
Berlin—an experience of great value as well as interest to her.

---

[1] *Life*, etc., vol. I, p. 375.
[2] This is the only publication of Mary Ann Evans published under her own name.
[3] Reprinted from *The Westminster Review* in vol. XII, pp. 419 ff.
[4] *Life*, etc., vol. I, p. 311.

It cannot be said that her hand as an essayist was heavy—even against *Theophrastus Such* this charge cannot fairly lie ; but, the slighter the texture of her work, the more arduous she seemed to find the process of unloading her learning within its limits. When, in her novels, she essayed short introductory or discursive passages after the example of Fielding or Thackeray, ease was the one quality which she could not command. On the other hand, whatever she wrote, even, as it were, in passing, was invariably lucid ; and no pen has ever better than hers illustrated the truth of her own assertion: 'the last degree of clearness can only come by writing[1].'

At last—when 'we were very poor[2]'—her companion discovered the hidden treasure, or insisted on its being brought to light. Like a born novelist, she thought of the title *The Sad Fortunes of the Rev. Amos Barton*, almost before she had shaped the subject of the story in her mind ; but she was speedily in the midst of it and had resolved on its forming the first of a series to be called *Tales from Clerical Life*. *Amos Barton*, the first part of which appeared in the January 1857 number of *Blackwood's Magazine*, was followed, in the course of the same year, by the two other tales of the series, *Mr Gilfil's Love Story* and *Janet's Repentance*. All three bore the signature George Eliot—a name chosen, almost, at random and thus admirably adapted for giving rise to the widest variety of wild conjecture. Even Thackeray thought the author a man ; but Dickens was sure of the woman. Both great novelists were warm in their admiration, as, also, were Bulwer Lytton, Anthony Trollope and Mrs Gaskell—a pleasant testimony to the generous temper of literary genius in the Victorian age. We pass by the more doubtful tribute of admiration offered by an impostor whose impudent pretensions to the authorship of *Scenes*, and, afterwards, of *Adam Bede*, were not quashed until nearly two years had passed.

Notwithstanding the just and discerning applause with which the first appearance of George Eliot as a writer of fiction was greeted, it would not be difficult to show that, in *Scenes of Clerical Life*, her style and manner as a novelist were still in the making ; but what she still had to learn was so speedily learnt that not much needs to be said on this head. In after days, she laughed at herself for being—or at her critics for thinking her— 'sesquipedalian and scientific' at all costs ; and, on the very first

---

[1] *Life*, etc., vol. i, p. 334.
[2] See *Letters of C. Eliot Norton* (1913), vol. i, p. 307. Cf. *ibid.* p. 316, as to her social isolation at this time.

page of the first of these tales, the walls of Shepperton church are described as 'innutrient,' like the bald head of the Rev. Amos Barton. As this example indicates, the taste of the phraseology is not always perfect; and the artifices of style are not always original[1]. The humour, at times, is inadequate, and, at other times, forced: the group of clergy over whom Mr Ely affably presides at the book-club dinner in *Amos Barton* includes one or two very unfinished sketches, while the talk at the symposium in the Red Lion, in *Janet's Repentance*, is too cleverly stupid[2]. Moreover, in this last and, by far, most powerful of the three stories, the construction is seriously at fault; for Dempster does not, as had obviously been intended, die a ruined man, and (which is of more importance) Janet's recovery from her craving for drink is not harmonised with her deeper spiritual repentance. What, then, accounts for the effect produced by these *Scenes* when they first appeared, and still exercised by them on the admirers of George Eliot's later and maturer works? In the first place, no doubt, the gnomic wisdom, which generally takes the form of wit, is as striking as it is pregnant[3]; but, again, occasionally it has the lucid directness which, rather than mere pointedness, is characteristic of the Greek epigram[4], and, yet again, at times, it lurks in the lambency of unsuspected humour[5], while it may rise to the height of a prophetic saying or a maxim for all time[6], or pierce with poetic power into the depths of tragic emotion[7]. The examples of these varieties of expression given below have been taken almost at haphazard from *Scenes of Clerical Life*, and no attempt will be made, easy though it would be, to multiply them from this or later works. But they may be regarded as sufficiently illustrating a feature in the imaginative writings of George Eliot which must be acknowledged to be one of their most distinctive characteristics[8]. Yet,

---

[1] An ill-placed Sam-Wellerism in *Janet's Repentance* (p. 581) exhibits both faults.

[2] Surely Mr Dempster, even in a simulated access of rage, would hardly have talked of 'the asinine virus of dissent.'

[3] 'Though Amos thought himself strong, he never felt himself strong' (*Amos Barton*). 'The Countess intended (ultimately) to be *quite* pious' (*ibid.*).

[4] 'Animals are most agreeable friends. They ask no questions; they pass no criticisms' (*Mr Gilfil's Love Story*).

[5] 'The boys thought the rite of confirmation should be confined to the girls' (*Janet's Repentance*). 'A friendly dinner was held by the Association for the Prosecution of Felons' (*Mr Gilfil's Love Story*).

[6] 'Trust and resignation fill up the margin of ignorance' (*Janet's Repentance*).

[7] Tina is compared to a poor wounded leveret, painfully 'dragging its body through the sweet clover-tufts—for it, sweet in vain' (*Mr Gilfil's Love Story*).

[8] The reader desirous of an anthology of *Wise, Witty, and Tender Sayings of*

even the brilliancy of the writing—and no other epithet would suit it—allows itself to be overlooked, as the sympathetic power of the writer, and the catholic breadth of her principles of moral judgment, impress themselves upon the reader. *The Sad Fortunes of the Rev. Amos Barton,* though hardly more than a sketch, teaches a lesson, devoid of any subtlety or novelty, that it is neither the cloth nor the respectability of the man himself (and Amos was 'superlatively middling') that entitles him to goodwill, but the human anguish of his experiences—the pathos of an ordinary soul—as he is left with his children by the deathbed of his poor, beautiful, patient Milly[1]. *Mr Gilfil's Love Story* is of hardly more solid structure—a vision of the past, illustrating the beautiful simile of the lopped tree which has lost its best branches —but a true reflection of the tragedy of life with its unspeakably cruel disenchantments, softened only by fate's kindness in the midst of unkindness. And *Janet's Repentance* deals, as George Eliot herself put it[2], with a collision, not between 'bigoted church-manship' and evangelicalism, but between irreligion and religion. It is not perfection that makes Tryan a true hero any more than, as we are reminded in a fine passage, it made Luther or Bunyan; nor is it in what he achieved, but in the spirit in which he sought to achieve, that lies the value of his endeavour. The atonement of Janet, an erring woman as he had been an erring man, but whom his influence saves from herself, is told with the same power of sympathy; and, while Tryan dies with her love in sight, there remains for her a life which has become a solemn service. The humanity of both these stories, and of the last in particular, as exhibiting the blessed influence of one human soul (not one set of ideas, for 'ideas are poor ghosts') upon another— this is what came home to the readers of George Eliot's first book as already something more than promise.

Before *Scenes of Clerical Life* had reached a speedier close than the authoress had, at first, intended, and before the book, as a whole, had come into the hands of the great novelists by whose side she was soon to take her place, George Eliot had begun her new story, *Adam Bede.* A considerable part of it was written at Dresden, and it was finished by November 1858. The germ of this novel, the reading of which, Dickens said, 'made an epoch in

---

George Eliot is referred to the collection under that title by Alexander Main (1872), for whom she had much personal regard.

[1] She is surely not called Amelia without intention. George Eliot, as has been pointed out, was a reader of both Fielding and Thackeray.

[2] *Life,* etc., vol. i, p. 370.

his life,' and which, like the firstfruits of some other authors of
genius, is, by many of the lovers of George Eliot, held unsurpassed
in original power by any of its successors, was a story of terrible
simplicity. Her aunt Elizabeth Evans, methodist preacher at
Wirksworth, had told her of a confession made to her by a girl in
prison, who had been convicted of the murder of her child, but had
previously refused to confess the crime. On the foundation of
this far from uncommon anecdote of woe, the authoress of *Adam
Bede* raised a structure of singular beauty and deep moral significance. The keynote of the story—the belief that the divine spirit
which works in man works through man's own response to its
call—dominates the narrative from first to last. It is sounded by
Adam Bede in an opening scene of singular originality and force,
in which he is introduced with his brother Seth in the midst of
their fellow-workmen ; and it is the text of a full exposition of his
views on religion in the middle of the story, where it 'pauses a
little,' and Adam is represented as 'looking back' upon the experiences of his life and their illustration of the truth : 'it isn't
notions sets people doing the right thing—it's feeling.' And it
connects itself with the altruism which, though Adam does not
attain to it at once or till after sore trial, since nothing great or
good drops into our laps like ripe fruit, George Eliot exemplified
in this, as in other of the most grandly conceived characters in
her stories, and, thus, as it were, superinduced in her readers—
by making them

better able to imagine and feel the pains and the joys of those who differ from
themselves in everything but the broad fact of being struggling, erring,
human creatures[1].

While the ethical spirit of the narrative thus, throughout, maintains
the same high level, and while, with true moral strength, is contrasted
the weakness which neither beauty can excuse nor kindliness of
disposition cover, the awful gulf that separates act from thought,
and passionate longing or yielding languor from guilt and its
inevitable consequences, opens itself before our eyes, and we
recognise, in the results of human deeds, an ἀνάγκη far stronger
and more resistless than what men call fate.

Viewed from another point of view, it is little short of wonderful that so new a writer should have satisfied so many demands of
the novelist's art. The descriptive power which George Eliot here
exhibits, though the scenery and surroundings depicted by her are
associated with ancestral rather than personal reminiscences, is very

---

[1] *Life*, etc., vol. I, pp. 487—8.

fresh and vivid : the Staffordshire village and the Derbyshire neighbourhood have an element of northern roughness effectively mixed with their midland charm.   And the signature of the times in which the story plays is alike unmistakable—more especially in its treatment of the religious life of an age which was but faintly lit up with the 'afterglow of methodism,' and in which the new revival of church feeling had not yet made old-fashioned parsons like Mr Irwine feel uncomfortable.   But it is in the characters of the novel themselves that the author's creative power already appears at its height in *Adam Bede,* and that she gives proof of that penetrating perception of the inner springs of human action which, without exaggeration, has been called Shakespearean. Adam Bede himself is no Sir Charles Grandison of the class to which he belongs, but an example of a high-souled working man who has taught himself the duty of self-sacrifice, till, like the ploughman of old, Adam Bede brings us nearer to a conception of the divine mission which a fellow-creature may help to carry out. He is throughout contrasted, in no harsh spirit, with his younger brother, who is cast in a slighter mould, but whose humility has a beauty of its own.   The kindly rector, whose shrinking gentleness is defended almost without a touch of irony, and his godson, whose good resolutions are almost an element of his instability, the coldly selfish squire, the savagely sympathetic schoolmaster—all are more or less novel, and all are true, varieties of human nature.   Among the women, Dinah and Hetty sleep, separated only by a thin wall, in the Poysers' house—but, on the one side of it, there abides an innate selfishness which thinks itself born for the sunshine, on the other, the loving minister of comfort which will not be rejected at the last.   With Mrs Poyser herself and the family over which she holds sway, we enter into another sphere of George Eliot's creative genius.   Among all the groupings invented by her, the Poyser family has remained unsurpassed as a popular favourite, and such scenes as the walk of the family to church, or their appearance at the young squire's birthday feast, are pure gems.   Mrs Poyser herself, though universally admired, has, perhaps, not always been quite justly appreciated.   She is, above all things, a great talker, the value of whose talk should by no means be estimated only by that of the 'proverbs' by which it is adorned.   Indeed, since we have it on George Eliot's own authority, that ' there is not one thing put into Mrs Poyser's mouth that is not fresh from my own mind' —in other words, that Mrs Poyser's sayings are not, properly speaking, proverbs at all—they should be regarded merely as the

spontaneous decorations of an eloquence which can rely on powers
of exposition superior to all resistance, and merely on occasion,
when moved by didactic purpose, is fain to heighten the effect of
its colouring by means of these gnomic jewels[1].

The construction of the story is skilful and close, and, with
logical firmness, bears out the principle laid down by Adam Bede,
that 'you can never do what's wrong without breeding sin and
trouble,' as well as his later reflection : ' that's what makes the
blackness of it ... *it can never be undone*[2].' The only exception
that can be justly taken to the self-developing course of the narrative is concerned with its concluding portion. As was frequently
the case with the Victorian novel, the conclusion of *Adam Bede*
is long drawn-out—in this instance, probably, with the design of
reconciling the reader to Adam's second love, for Dinah, and to his
marriage with her. It is not so much as affecting any previous
notion of Dinah that this ending is unfortunate, or because we are
sorry for Seth, or even because the whole episode, intrinsically, is
not very probable. But could a deep and noble nature such as
Adam Bede's have forgotten his love for Hetty, while she was still
suffering for guilt which, as he well knew, was only half her own?
And if (as is not very clear from the closing pages) she had already
passed away, could she have been dead to Adam ? ' Our dead,' as
we read in a passage of the novel which seems to breathe, as it
were, the remorse of humanity, ' are never dead to us till we have
forgotten them[3].'

Adam Bede had been finished little more than three months
when a new story, ' a sort of comparison picture of provincial life '
was already in George Eliot's mind ; and, within a year from that
date, the story in question was already completed (March 1860).
The Mill on the Floss may not be the greatest of its author's
novels ; but it was that into which she poured most abundantly
the experiences of her own life when it had still been one of youth
and hope ; so that none of her books appeal with the same directness to the personal sympathies of her readers, at least in its earlier
and more simply developed parts : it is the *David Copperfield* or
the *Pendennis* among the products of her literary genius

---

[1] Cf. *Life*, etc., vol. I, p. 463, and *Adam Bede*, p. 119.   [2] *Ibid.* pp. 150, 641.
[3] *Adam Bede*, p. 152. Strangely enough, the relation between Adam and Dinah,
which, according to the ordinary laws of fiction could only end in their ultimate union,
was not suggested to George Eliot by Lewes till she had made some progress with the
story. His argument (for which see *Life*, vol. I,, p. 447) does not remove the blot (if it
be one), which was pointed out by Bulwer Lytton as the single thing, besides the dialect,
to be found fault with in *Adam Bede* (*ibid.* p. 526).

Although she was fain to acknowledge the truth of Bulwer Lytton's criticism[1], that 'the epic breadth into which she was beguiled by love of her subject in the first two volumes' caused a want of fulness in the preparation of the tragedy reached in the third, yet, the nobility and beauty of Maggie's personality has to be made fully manifest before we can absolve her for giving way, even momentarily, to her passion for Stephen ; and a long ending, such as goes far to mar the effect of certain other of George Eliot's works, would hardly have enhanced the expiatory solemnity of its perfect close.   Maggie's is the earliest in the sequence of George Eliot's heroines *par excellence*—Romola, Dorothea, Gwendolen being the others.   None of them brings home to us with more intense force than Maggie Tulliver the conflict waged by the great imaginative aspirations of the soul, which never abandons them though it cannot command their fulfilment, and the purifying influence of these aspirations.   For, with her, as with the rest, of whom, though with features wholly her own, she is a sort of prototype, the escape from hopeless battling or prostrating collapse lies one way only—that to which she is, as it were, accidentally led—the way of self-sacrifice.   If she stumbles on the threshold of her better life, it is that she may fully learn the truth of Philip's saying that there can be no renunciation without pain, and she has to pass through a struggle far harder than her early yearnings and strivings before she conquers.   After this, she can await the end, whatever judgment may be passed upon her by her brother, who cannot go beyond knowing that he is in the right, or by all the gossips of St Ogg's, who cannot rise above the certainty that she is in the wrong.   When the end comes, it finds her in the midst of tempest and destruction as a bringer of reconciliation and peace, and the novel closes, in perfect harmony with its opening, as a story of trusting love.

In *The Mill on the Floss*, George Eliot had already displayed an amplitude of exposition—both in the delineation of manners and in the analysis of their significance—which could not but, from time to time, seem exacting even to the warmest admirers of her genius.   Mr and Mrs Tulliver, in some ways, are a kind of inversion of the Poysers, and, though of a feebler personal texture, not less true to nature and nature's humorousness.   But Mrs Tulliver's sisters must be pronounced frequently tedious, and the enquiry into the motives of ordinary doings by ordinary people is, at times, trying.   Still, in *The Mill on the Floss*, the background remains a background only, and there is no dissipation of the interest which never ceases to centre in 'sister Maggie'—as the whole story was intended to have been called, till its present name, breathing the very spirit of English romance, and hinting vaguely at the tragic course of the homely story, was, in a happy moment, substituted.

After the completion of this novel, which was dedicated to Lewes, the authoress left England in his company for a few months' holiday, which she spent mainly in Italy. In Florence, which aroused in her a stronger interest than even Rome itself, she began to think of *Romola*; nor is it possible that this theme could have grown in her mind without the aid of the *genius loci*. But, after her return, although she continued to carry on an extensive course of reading for the sake of this book, she did not actually set to work upon it for nearly a twelvemonth further. Wholly absorbed as she was, at this time, by her literary work, and holding aloof from any wider social intercourse, she was able, by 1861, to complete for publication another story, totally different in its associations from that upon which her mind had already become primarily intent. *Silas Marner*, though it can hardly be said to fall under the category of short stories, extends to no great length, and, in construction and treatment, shows a perfect sense of proportion on the part of the writer. Indeed, competent judges have pronounced it, in form, George Eliot's most finished work, while none of her larger novels surpasses it in delicacy of pathos. The life of the solitary linen-weaver, driven out long ago, by a grievous wrong, from the little religious community to which he belonged, and doomed, as it seemed, to a remote quietude rendered bearable only by his satisfaction in his growing pile of gold, is suddenly changed by the theft of his treasure. The young spendthrift who has done the deed vanishes; and the mystery remains unsolved till it is cleared up with the unravelling of the whole plot of the story. Nothing could be more powerfully drawn than the blank despondency of the unhappy man, and nothing more beautifully imagined than the change wrought by the golden-haired child who takes the place of the gold by his hearth and in his heart. The tenderness of fancy which pervades this simple tale, and the brightness of humour which, not so much in the symposiasts of the Rainbow as in the motherly Dolly Winthrop, relieves the constrained simplicity of its course, certainly assure to *Silas Marner* a place of its own among George Eliot's works.

'I began *Romola*,' she writes[1], 'a young woman—I finished it an

[1] *Life*, etc., vol. II, p. 88.

old woman.' In whatever sense this saying is to be accepted, it shows how she had consciously and consistently contemplated this work as a labour of years, and how she had been led to the writing of it by something besides a vast variety of study in political and ecclesiastical history, in theology, in political philosophy, in humanistic and artistic lore and in illustrative literature of all kinds. Yet, it is a supreme prerogative of genius to be able to master its material by becoming part of what it has transformed; and George Eliot was never more herself, and never displayed her most distinctive intellectual qualities and moral purposes with more powerful directness than in this, the most elaborate, as well as erudite, of all her literary productions. *Romola* is one of the most real and lifelike of her prose fictions, and, from this point of view, too, shows itself altogether superior to a novel which it is difficult not to bring into comparison with it, Charles Kingsley's *Hypatia*, published about ten years earlier. Both works exhibit the movement of actual life, as well as of deep feeling; but *Romola* is not less distinguished from the older work by its greater variety and vividness of illustrative detail, than it is by the profounder depth of the human emotions, belonging to no age or scene in particular, which it calls up. For, although *Romola* may fairly be called a historical novel, it is something at once different from, and more than, this. The book has a right to be so described by virtue of the exhaustive view which it offers of the Florence of its period, of the men who helped to make or mar the fortunes of the republic, of the traditions, usages and notions of the city, of the humours of its festivals and the charms of its gardens, of the types of *signoria, mercato*, the world of learning and letters and the cloisters of San Marco. The actual historical personages introduced—Machiavelli, king Charles VIII and the rest—are not mere lay figures, but careful studies; and Savonarola himself towers before us, with the wellknown facial features in which a likeness, not without reason, has been discovered to George Eliot's own, while his eloquence is reproduced from his own written discourses. The lesser figures with which the canvas is crowded—the talkers in the barber's shop and the rest—are, to say the least, as concrete and as lifelike as are any of George Eliot's English townsfolk or villagers; indeed, she says herself[1] that her desire to give as full a view of the medium in which a character moves as of the character itself actuated her in *Romola* just as strongly as it did in *The Mill on the Floss* and

---

[1] See her letter in reply to R. H. Hutton's criticism, *Life*, etc., vol. II, pp. 96—7.

in her other books ; but that the excess of this was, naturally, more perceptible in the former instance. The wonderfully fine proem almost leads us to suppose that it is the opening to a historical novel, of which Florence itself will prove to be the main theme. Yet, the whole of these surroundings, to use George Eliot's word, form only the 'medium,' or *milieu*, of the action— of Savonarola himself as well as of his beloved Florence ; and the action itself is, once more, the struggle through which fate, circumstance, place, time and the individualities—her father, her husband and the rest—brought into contact with her own individuality compel a noble-natured woman to pass before she can reconcile herself to her lot in the consciousness of having striven for what is great and good. The evolution thus accomplished is a process of which the human interest pervades, but at the same time transcends, all its rich political, religious and literary envelopment. The piety of Romola, her maiden devotion to the service of her father and the studies which he loves, cannot, we know, circumscribe the life of one created, like herself, for the performance of the highest duties of womanhood. And so she falls in love with Tito—beautiful and clever and gifted with the adaptability which belongs to the lower scholarship, as it does to the lower statesmanship, of life, and which, if combined with an unflinching and unyielding 'improbity' of purpose, often comes near to brilliant success. There may be points and passages—beginning with his mock marriage to Tessa—in which the cruelty of Tito's selfishness is beyond bearing ; but the hardening of his heart is told with fidelity to nature. It may be added that, although the construction of the story is not open to the charge of artificiality (and the Baldassare by-plot is quite in accordance with historical probability), fateful meetings and lucky escapes from meetings are too liberally distributed over the surface of the action. But, as the novel runs along what, apart from mere details, may be truly described as its majestic course, Romola herself rises to the height of the problems which she is called upon to confront—problems of public and private duty, which her spiritual guide, Savonarola, refused to allow her to treat as distinct from one another. The hopes and fears of her fellow-citizens may shrink from the friar, when his position, gradually undermined, begins to give way ; when the plague takes the heart out of the people ; and when the church drives him out of her communion ; but neither plague nor papal thunder has terrors for her free and exalted soul, and she has not ceased to trust in the prophet because he has become rebel. In her personal experiences, she passes through a not dissimilar evolution. The tragic sorrow of her utter isolation seems, at last, to have descended upon her hopelessly, and, through the blue waters, she drifts away from all that was near and dear to her. But, like her boat, her lofty soul finds its way into harbour. To the villagers among whom she landed she left behind her the legend of the beneficent Madonna's visit; to herself, there remained the resolve to hold herself on the highest level of self-sacrifice possible to her, tending the children of her twice faithless husband, and leaving all else in the hands of God. Thus, while Tito had fallen, because, of the earth earthy, he could not, with all his beauty and learning and wit, rise above himself, Romola stands erect, though with bowed head. The variegated brilliancy of the setting which dazzles us in this wonderful novel thus melts, at its close, into a soft diffusion of the purest light.

Not long after the completion of *Romola*, George Eliot and George Henry Lewes had established themselves at The Priory, Regent's park. But, though the effort had been extraordinary— she had, as she wrote some ten years later, written the book 'with her best blood, such as it is, and with the most ardent care for veracity of which her nature was capable[1]'—she had no intention of resting on her laurels. 'The last quarter,' she writes in January 1865, 'has made an epoch for me, by the fact that, for the first time in my serious authorship, I have written verse.' The earliest mention in her correspondence of *The Spanish Gypsy*, early in September 1864, characteristically records that, while already engaged upon the play, she was 'reading about Spain'; but, before, in the beginning of 1867, she took a journey to that country, she had been persuaded to give herself a respite, producing, in the interval, the one volume novel *Felix Holt, the Radical* (1866). In some respects, this book holds an isolated position among her works, and, practically, alone warrants her being placed among eminent English writers of fiction who, in their novels, have treated political, as well as social, topics. Her consciousness of this direct purpose is shown by her having, after some hesitation, consented to follow up the publication of the novel by that of an *Address to Working-Men* issued in the name of its hero[2]. As was her wont, she

---

[1] *Life*, etc., vol. II, pp. 438–9.

[2] This address, printed in *Blackwood's Magazine* for 1866, able as it undoubtedly is, must, from the point of view of its probable effect on the audience or public contemplated, be confessed to be, in the first instance, too long; in the second, too full of figures and illustrations borrowed from popular science, general history and other, in

had prepared herself for her political novel by a solid course of reading, which included, besides the worthy Samuel Bamford's *Passages from the Life of a Radical,* such guidance as Mill's *Political Economy* and Harriet Martineau's version of Comte's *Système de Politique Positive.* On an examination, however, of her story itself, it will not be found to convey any political teaching of further purport than that which, a decade and a half earlier, Charles Kingsley and his friends had sought to bring home to the British working man. The secret of true reform is not to be found in any particular measure or programme of measures, whether it call itself Reform bill[1], people's charter or any other name of high sound; but it lies in the resolve of the mass of the people—in other words, of the working classes—to learn to think and act for themselves. This kind of radicalism, though far from being either vague or visionary, is that of an idealist; and, as such, the principles of Felix Holt are presented in this story, in contrast with the toryism of the Debarrys and the colonially clearsighted opportunism of Harold Transome. For the rest, the political philosophy of Felix Holt has not very much to do with the story, except as part and parcel of the manliness of character by which he secures his place in the heart of the heroine. The plot by which the contrasts in her fortunes and in those of the other personages of the story are developed is more melodramatic in its course than is usual with George Eliot; and, whether its legal machinery be perfect or otherwise, the general impression left on the reader is not one in which excellences of detail combine into a satisfactory total effect. Thus, and because of the lack of a female character comparable in interest to those standing forth in her other books, *Felix Holt* cannot be held entitled to rank with the finest of them.

The Spanish Gypsy, not completed and published till 1868, fills no such place in the sum of George Eliot's literary work as it does in her literary life as regarded by herself. The poem, of which the subject was first, more or less vaguely, suggested by an *Annunciation* of Tintoretto at Venice, is, in form, a combination of narrative and drama, with a considerable admixture of lyric; but, though thus suggesting a certain spontaneity of composition, it is artificial in the result, and, to put it bluntly, 'smells of the lamp.' The reader becomes oppressed, not only by the lore

themselves, suitable sources; and, finally, too obviously wanting in the balance of earnest encouragement which no popular oratory of the kind can afford to spare.

[1] Cf. the passage on the Reform bill, *Life,* vol. II, p. 152.

poured into the dramatic mould, but by the great amount of guidance bestowed upon him—the characterisation of characters, and the like—and is left cold by the solution of the problem whether racial duty has claims 'to high allegiance, higher than our love?' Some of the descriptive passages, above all the popular festival in which the acrobat-conjuror figures with his monkey Annibal, before the lady Fedalma is herself moved to join in the dance, have the brilliant picturesqueness of scenes in *Romola*; nor, of course, are we left without the sententious comments of a highly intelligent chorus.

George Eliot, now at the height of her literary reputation, was still to produce two of her most important prose fictions, and was able to suit her methods and forms of composition to her own preferences. The great length, and the production, in large instalments, of *Middlemarch, a Study of Provincial Life* (1871—2), and of its successor *Daniel Deronda*, were not unacceptable to a generation which, compared with its successors, 'lived when the days were longer (for time, like money, is measured by our needs).... We later historians,' she adds, speaking of Fielding, 'must not linger after his example, and if we did so, it is probable that our chat would be thin and eager, as if delivered from a camp-stool in a parrot-house.' This she says by way of humorously excusing herself for abstaining from those digressions which were not really very congenial to her; but, at the same time, she was conscious that the fullness with which she treated her proper themes might, at times, seem exacting. Yet, whatever may be thought of this increasing amplitude of treatment in her latest novels, accompanied, as it was, by a certain falling-off in the freshness and variety of accumulated detail, her incomparable power of exhibiting the development of character is here found at its height. This development, in which time, contact and purpose alike have their share, may show itself, as she writes in the preface to *Middlemarch*, in the epic life of a St Teresa; but it also shows itself in many a latterday life; and, if it is worth studying, analysing, following on to its results at all, must be best worth the effort if this is made with relative completeness. At the same time, *Middlemarch*—the same cannot, with equal confidence, be asserted of *Daniel Deronda*—is an admirable example of constructive art, and, in this respect, may challenge comparison with the consummate workmanship of *Romola*. The story flows on without constraint; but Dorothea never sinks out of her primary place in our interest; as her ideals never abandon her, so, her consistent shaping of her conduct in accordance with them never ceases to command our sympathy. Her great original blunder in allowing herself to be wooed and won by Mr Casaubon, whose ultra-academical pedantry and 'archangelical method of exposition' she mistakes for marks of real superiority, was all but unavoidable by one to whom, as to herself, an ordinary marriage was impossible (ordinary men may be consoled by the fact that Sir James Chettam is one of the best drawn gentlemen in George Eliot's gallery of characters). But, although her mistake is cruelly revenged upon her, after her very submissiveness to duty has deepened her husband's delusion as to his own value, it fails to debase her. As she gradually comes to love Ladislaw, she is protected by the lofty purity of her mind from acknowledging her feeling to herself too soon or from giving way to it after she has confessed to herself both her passion and its hopelessness. She is made happy in the end; but she has been true to herself from first to last. Side by side with Dorothea's experiences of life and its trials we have those of Lydgate, who has matched himself unequally with smiling commonplace and has to descend from his own level[1]. The whole story, with its double plot, is an admirable social picture as well as a profound study of human character ; the episode of the political reform struggle, with the inconsequent Mr Brooke as its central figure, is more satirical in treatment than is that of Lydgate's efforts for medical reform ; and, though ample in its framework and even finding room for a purely humorous character in the person of Mrs Cadwallader, the novel is far less diffuse than some of its predecessors.

Daniel Deronda (1876), the last of George Eliot's works of prose fiction, though, as is not to be denied, it brought some disappointment to the ever-widening congregation of her admirers, both in matter and style, maintains the high standard of *Middlemarch* ; and, in the character of Gwendolen, offers one more variety of the high-spirited and high-souled woman whom the experience of life trains to resignation—a resignation of little worth if it comes without pain. She passes, imperiously self-centred, through childhood and girlhood ; nor is it till after she has quickly shaken off the honest proffer of a boyish heart that she steadies herself to meet the first real trial—the imminent marriage proposal of Grandcourt, great by his calm acceptance

---

[1] The experiences of Lydgate were, probably, in part, suggested by those of the young doctor in Harriet Martineau's *Deerbrook*, to which Kingsley's *Two Years Ago* may, also, have been indebted.

of his great position in the world. His character, however, is
better conceived than executed; for, while we have to take his
high-breeding on assurance, his brutality thrusts itself pitilessly
upon us. A secret which makes Gwendolen pause on the brink
of acceptance causes her to go abroad to escape Grandcourt
(who follows her very slowly) and to be brought face to face
with Daniel Deronda. Gradually, he becomes a kind of higher
admonition—for he is too detached to fill the office of good angel
—in her life. His own, from his early days onwards, has been
enveloped in a mystery to the solution of which the reader looks
forward with tempered interest. It proves, in the end, to be a
racial problem—though a less violent one than that of *The
Spanish Gypsy*—with which we are invited to deal; and the haze
of Disraelian dreams hangs round this part of the story, till, at
the close, it leaves us face to face with the familiar project of
the restoration of a national centre to the Jewish race. The
attempt to constitute this Semitic mystery an organic part of
the story of Gwendolen and her experiences, which culminate
in her unhappy marriage with Grandcourt and his tragic death,
cannot be deemed successful. After she has grown accustomed
to rely absolutely on nothing but Deronda and his 'Bouddha-like'
altruism, she finds herself, at last, as her woman's nature cries out
in a moment of despair, 'forsaken' by him, so that he may fulfil
his destiny, which includes his marriage with Mirah. But the
candid though severe critic[1], who goes rather far in his suggestion
that this ending may 'raise a smile which the author did not
intend to excite,' is within the mark when he adds that 'no words
of praise can be too warm for the insight displayed by the book
into the complex feelings of modern character' or 'for its delicacy
and depth of delineation of sentiment.' Among the subsidiary
personages of the story, one is wholly new and original—the
musician of genius, whose single-minded devotion to an art which,
for George Eliot, always had a unique fascination, rises superior
to his personal grotesqueness. Thus, almost in spite of itself,
Daniel Deronda remains one of the great achievements of its
author's genius.

Between the inception of *Middlemarch* and the completion,
some seven years later, of *Daniel Deronda*, George Eliot wrote
some pieces of verse which must not be passed by without
mention. *How Lisa loved the King* (1869) is a very charming
treatment of a subject taken from Boccaccio, and previously—

---

[1] See *Letters of C. Eliot Norton* (1913), vol. II, p. 64.

so susceptible is a truly pathetic theme of repeated successful
adaptation—dealt with very happily in at least two plays of
note[1]. George Eliot's poem is specially interesting by virtue
of its graceful form—rimed couplets which suit themselves to the
delicately fanciful argument as if they had come from the pen
of Leigh Hunt. If this delightful little effort has in it just a
trace of artificiality, it is not on that account the less suited to
the conscious refinement of the renascence age.

Of about the same date, and conceived in no very different
mood, is *Agatha* (1869), a pretty picture of still-life and genial
old age, further softened by religious influence. Slightly later
(1870) is *Armgart*, which consists of three dramatic scenes, telling
a story of artistic triumph, followed by bitter disappointment and
renunciation. Here, may possibly be found the germ of some of
the Klesmer speeches in *Daniel Deronda*. To the same year, also,
belongs *The Legend of Jubal*, a more considerable poetical effort,
which treats with great breadth what are really two distinct *motifs*.
One of these is a tribute to the power of music in the form of
an account of its origin and first spread; the other is the old story
of the return of the inventor of the art after a long absence to the
scenes of its beginnings, where he has been forgotten and is treated
with ignominy, but consoled by the honour in which his art is
held. The theme, no doubt, in more respects than one, suited
George Eliot, and inspired her to one of her finest poems.

She afterwards wrote certain other pieces in verse[2]—some of
them lyrics not devoid of charm, and one of them, more especially
The Minor Prophet, in a vein which might be thought not wholly
unlike that of some of the characters in verse by Robert Browning,
but that his power of dramatic condensation is wanting. They
are full of brilliant turns of thought, and the poet had acquired
a mastery of metre which made her delight in putting her ideas
into a form well suited to gnomic utterances. In prose, she
produced nothing further of importance[3]. *The Impressions of
Theophrastus Such*, of which the publication was postponed to
1879, on account of George Henry Lewes's death, was much read

---

[1] *Decameron*, x, 7. The plays are Shirley's *The Royall Master* and Alfred de
Musset's *Carmosine*.

[2] They are collected, with those mentioned above, in the volume of *Poems* forming
vol. XI of the Warwick edition.

[3] *The Lifted Veil* and *Brother Jacob* (both printed with *Silas Marner* in vol. VI of
the Warwick edition) go back to the years 1859 and 1860 respectively. The former
is a study of clairvoyance as, at once, a gift and a curse, hardly less improbable than
it is painful. *Brother Jacob* is a rather sordid tale of nemesis.

when it came out, and the success of the book, which, in a more than ordinary sense, was one of esteem, sent a ray of consolation into her retirement.   The satire of the modern Theophrastus directs itself chiefly to the foibles and vanities of the literary class—a class to which no authors ever more thoroughly belonged, and took pride in belonging, than George Eliot and the lost guide and companion of her labours, but as to whose weaknesses her own single-mindedness of purpose and freedom from all pretence or affectation supplied her with a safe standard of judgment. But this series of essays falls short of the collections offered by the Greek moralist, and by the most successful of his modern imitators, whether French or English, not only in variety, but, also, by the absence of what might have been expected from George Eliot herself, had she still been at the height of her power—namely, evidence of the plastic or formative gift which tradition asserted Theophrastus to have carried even to the extent of mimicry.   The work is, explicably enough, devoid of gaiety—an element which, though not indispensable, can ill be spared altogether in a book of this sort.

Quite late in her life, a personal happiness for which it is not presumptuous to say that her heart had yearned, came to the gifted woman of whose writings we have briefly spoken, in the form of marriage.   In May 1880, she gave her hand to John Walter Cross, in recognition of a chivalrous devotion measurable only by those who knew him well.   But the dream was a short one.   On their return from a continental tour on which Cross had fallen ill at Venice, she, in her turn, was prostrated by sickness, and, before the year was out, on 22 December, she passed away.   Of no greater woman of letters is the name recorded in English annals, and of none who had made the form of composition finally chosen by her as her own so complete a vehicle of all with which she had charged it.   George Eliot's novels speak to us of her comprehensive wisdom, nurtured by assiduously acquired learning, of her penetrating and luminous wit, furnished with its material by a power of observation to which all the pathetic and all the humorous aspects of human character lay open and of her profound religious conviction of the significance of life and its changes as helping to better the human soul brave and unselfish enough not to sink before them.

CHAPTER XII

THE BRONTËS

WHEN Mrs Gaskell published *The Life of Charlotte Brontë*, she was forty-seven, and had already written *Mary Barton*, *Cranford* and *Ruth*. In six years, there were to follow *Sylvia's Lovers* and that story in which is embalmed the charm of all things fading—*Cousin Phillis*. The biography was worthy of its author. Here was presented, not less truthfully than exquisitely, all that it was essential to know of the sad story of Charlotte Brontë's life, and, interwoven in its texture, and consummately in place, the beautiful piece of prose in which Ellen Nussey told of Anne Brontë's death. It was surprising that this masterpiece, at its first appearance, should have been marred by indiscretions of revelation, relating, in part, to the father of the sisters, to whose paternal care the book paid tribute, and who was still alive, an octogenarian. The explanation was, partly, that Mrs Gaskell was a novelist whose first obligation was truth to character, and who was interested in the subordinate personages of her narrative mainly in so far as they illustrated the figure of its heroine; and, also, partly, that the task she had set herself—to tell soon and fully Charlotte Brontë's life-story—was not one that could possibly have been executed without giving some temporary offence. Yet, the main lines of the story were seized and held with the unerring hand of genius, and, in the amended version, we now possess a book that, both in its candour and in its restraint, remains the true record for posterity.

Of the substantial accuracy of its picture of the Brontë household, there is no longer any question. Some of the original domestic details now banished from the volume may not have been correct; but such stories as attached themselves to Patrick Brontë do not gather round a man of unexacting character. His custom of dining alone in a house with two sitting-rooms is sufficiently significant. 'No one,' writes Mary Taylor to Ellen Nussey, a year after Charlotte's death, 'ever gave up more than she did and with full consciousness of what she sacrificed.' Family affection for his offspring, on the one side, of course, there was, and, on the other, deep filial piety and that cherishing fondness which springs from piety ; but it is a main element in Charlotte Brontë's later history that talk in the lonely house must often have been 'but a tinkling cymbal.'

Patrick Brunty or Brontë, as, at Haworth, he came finally to write the name, was, so far as we know, a pure Irishman. He was born in Emdale, county Down, in 1777, and, in 1802, presumably with the aid of some slender savings, he entered St John's college, Cambridge. After taking his degree, he held various curacies, settling down finally, in 1820, in the incumbency of Haworth. But the troubles of life were not over ; for, in less than two years, his always delicate wife, Maria Branwell, whom he had married in 1812, had died, leaving him the care of six children, Maria, Elizabeth, Charlotte, Patrick Branwell, Emily Jane and Anne, of whom the eldest was eight and the youngest not yet two years of age. In this difficulty, his wife's sister Elizabeth Branwell took up her residence with him at Haworth, remaining there as mistress of his house till her death. Thus was the household constituted till Charlotte Brontë was twenty-six.

For so large a family, the house in the graveyard was a confined habitation : it stood at the top of the steep and drab village, its front windows looking on the church and the graves, and its back on the wide-stretching moors over which the tiny girls loved constantly to ramble. Their father was not a learned man ; but he knew enough to teach infants, and it was a mistake that, in order to provide them with more systematic instruction, he should have sent four of them to a clergy daughters' boarding school. This was an absurdly cheap subsidised institution, for no other was within his means ; and the disastrous experiment, afterwards forming the basis of the account of Lowood in *Jane Eyre*, came to an end within a year. Charlotte Brontë believed that the precarious health of her two elder sisters had suffered from the experience. In any case, the first tragedies of her home were the early deaths of the much-loved Maria and Elizabeth.

The household, thus reduced in numbers, remained at Haworth for the next six years, occupied with reading, rambling, household management and, above all, with literary invention ; and it was not till 1831, when Charlotte was nearly fifteen, that she was again sent to a boarding school, this time to Miss Wooler's at Roe Head, where she made the acquaintance of Ellen Nussey and Mary Taylor, who became her lifelong friends. Miss Wooler was kind and competent, and eighteen fairly happy months of pupilage resulted, three years later, in Charlotte's returning as an instructress, while Emily and Anne also became pupils in the same school. But Charlotte was not born to be a teacher of young girls, and, after another interval of three years, she returned to Haworth, fretted in mind and spirit. Yet, something had to be done to replenish the family exchequer on which the one, and thoroughly unsatisfactory, brother was beginning to make a series of claims. Emily had attempted and failed to live the life of an assistant schoolmistress under peculiarly exacting conditions, and there was nothing left for Charlotte and Anne except to become governesses in private families. But, though the gentle Anne was, apparently, a good governess, retaining one post for four years, the experiences of neither of the pair met their wishes, and it occurred to Charlotte and Emily that they should qualify for the three setting up school by themselves. For this, some knowledge of foreign languages was indispensable, and, in February 1842, the two sisters, aged, respectively, twenty-five and twenty-three, had found their way as pupils into a foreign school, the pensionnat Héger, rue d'Isabelle, Brussels. The short year spent there was made especially interesting on account of the lectures of the professor of literature, Constantin Héger, a man of thirty-three who, obviously, added to some of the usual Napoleonisms of the *professeur des jeunes filles* (Napoleonisms to which Charlotte Brontë was not blind) a genuine force of character, something of the genius of exposition and a touch of that ironic or semi-humorous malice which is the salt of personality. But this brightening episode was not to last, and, in eight months, the sisters were hurrying home too late to attend the deathbed of their aunt Branwell.

The home was reorganised, Emily being left to keep house. Branwell, who had failed in several occupations, found a post as tutor in the same family where Anne was governess, and Charlotte Brontë allowed herself to be tempted to return to Brussels, in January 1843, as instructress in English. She was now verging on twenty-seven, and at Brussels were the surroundings that had broken the dull monotony of her life. Hitherto, this monotony had been endurable; henceforth, it was no longer so. As she taught in the school of the Hégers, at times instructing Constantin Héger and his brother-in-law in English, and hearing from him constantly of the high things in literature and life, there was set up that *rapport* of intelligence, and, more than this, that interplay where soul responds to soul, of which, hitherto, she had known nothing. In a year, she was back in the lonely house, herself now twice lonely 'for remembering happier things.' All had not gone well in her absence : the brother was hastening down a career that ended in an early grave ; the plan of a school had come to nothing ; the tone of the communications she sent to her adored professor, too *exalté*, led to the ending of all communication ; and in the letters she wrote to Brussels in these barren years we can hear the cry of a stifled heart. In March 1845, she writes to Ellen Nussey :

I can hardly tell you how time gets on at Haworth. There is no event whatever to mark its progress. One day resembles another: and all have heavy lifeless physiognomies.... There was a time when Haworth was a very pleasant place to me: it is not so now. I feel as if we were all buried here. ... Write very soon dear Ellen.

There was one way of escape and one only—for 'the imagination is not a state,' as Blake tells us, 'it is the human existence itself.'

Yet, this relief was not found at once, nor was the unconscious attempt to supply it at first successful. In the poems which, with others by her sisters, were published in 1846 and in her first serious attempt at a novel, *The Professor*, traces of a recent loss are too evident, the transcription of emotional experience is too literal. The substance of the art-work is not yet just a number of things that had happened, ready for the free handling of the artist. The authoress is, obviously, trying to solve a riddle in her past, and it was not till 1847, when *Jane Eyre* was published, that, though still carrying her burden of experience, she found relief in imagination. The love-story which Charlotte Brontë tells in *Jane Eyre* is a more beautiful one than that which Mrs Gaskell has pictured in *Cousin Phillis*. It is finer because it is as innocent and yet it is not withered. In *Jane Eyre*, it dances before us dignified with the joy of living. Here, at last, the artistic problem solved itself, freely, without effort almost, the tangle of the real and the ideal, as it were, merely unrolling. In the midst of her care for her ageing father, now threatened with blindness, with the *Poems* fallen dead from the press and the little light she had known a memory only, the vision came to her, as it came to Thackeray, for 'behold, love is the crown and completion of all earthly good.'

Some concession, doubtless, had to be made to the requirements of the prevailing art of fiction. As novels were understood in the middle of the nineteenth century, they were always love-stories in the common or vulgar sense. You did really fall in love with someone and want to marry. The love in question was by no means simply a great and noble affection, an overflow of being, rather the contrary. There had to be a basis which people could understand. Esmond had really to marry lady Castlewood, though, of course, in that instance, the love of which Thackeray wrote was not a love that dreams of marriage. These things happen in fableland, or, at least, they thus happened in the fableland of the midcentury.

What Charlotte Brontë had to tell was a tale of the heart's realisation through another, and of the loss of what seemed to be realised. Because it was a novel she was writing, the loss had not to be final, but, because it was a story of loss, there had to be a bar. 'The plot of *Jane Eyre*,' writes Charlotte to Mr Williams in the autumn of 1847, 'may be a hackneyed one. Mr Thackeray remarks that it is familiar to him, but having read comparatively few novels, I never chanced to meet with it, and I thought it original.' Charlotte Brontë's possible forgetfulness, if she had seen the story, and Thackeray's dim memory are equally explicable. The tale of actual and intended bigamy which Sheridan Le Fanu contributed to *The Dublin University Magazine* in 1839 was just one of those stories eminently adapted for floating in the back of the mind. In the strange fictions of Le Fanu, the reader's feelings are sympathetically and deeply moved without his either seeing the actual occurrences face to face or believing them to be real. The atmosphere, which is, generally, charged with suggestions from the supernatural, has something of smoke in it and our memory of the stories is often but the memory of a dream. But that Le Fanu's tale suggested the plot of *Jane Eyre* is decidedly possible[1].

If so, Sir Leslie Stephen's query why the pleasing Rochester should have embarked on an intended bigamy is sufficiently answered. The original hint was a story of bigamy, and Charlotte Brontë altered and softened it to meet her purpose, like Shakespeare, moulding (but not entirely reversing) her plot, to make it correspond more nearly with her characters. If, on the contrary, she had not read Le Fanu's tale, one must admit that, with no hint to constrain her, she was guilty of one inconsistency of invention. There was, perhaps, another reason. Odd

[1] See appendix to this chapter.

as it may seem, the fact that Rochester had bigamous intentions took away any impropriety from Jane's reception of unrealisable advances on his part. Not that it greatly matters; for all this was merely machinery and was only of value as enabling Charlotte Brontë to give her outflow of heart a wholly fictional setting.

So novel, indeed, was this outflow that even Mrs Gaskell feels herself obliged to begin the long chorus of apology for occasional coarseness in the novel. There was never any need for it. *Jane Eyre* was a unique Victorian book because in it, whatever the age might think it right to say, it was made plain to the most unwillingly convinced that purity could be passionate and that a woman could read the heart. The scene in the garden with Rochester, the equally touching farewell and the joy of final meeting—these are love passages which truly introduced 'a new vibration into literature.' 'Childish and slender creature! It seemed as if a linnet had hopped on my foot and proposed to bear me on its tiny wing.'

But this was in the domain of the ideal. In Charlotte's home itself—except for her own book, and even of this there had been coarse criticism—there was nothing of attainment. *Wuthering Heights* and *Agnes Grey*, the works of her sisters, had passed without recognition. Anne, in her child's morality, was labouring at a task unsuited to her talent and fine observation[1], while Branwell, her text, was drugging himself to death upstairs. The opening chapters of *Shirley*, begun in the first excitement of success, with their hard and not very legitimate characterisation of neighbouring curates, were lying on Charlotte Brontë's desk. Reality, with its harsh surroundings, was not, after all, to be escaped from, and 'Ferndean', with its conquering triumph, had been but a castle in Spain. It was, therefore, in a mood of disillusionment that, after the *bravura* of the first chapters, the new story was continued, and very soon, coming nearer, though with hesitating steps, to the past, it is subdued to the mood. A great artist speaks again, and for the last time exquisitely, in the beautiful story of Caroline Helstone's unavailing affection. Who, then, was Caroline—Ellen Nussey or Anne or Charlotte—and who was Robert, as distinguished from Louis Moore? It does not matter; we are listening to a tale of feeling.

In September, Branwell died, and, before the end of the year, when the main story was nearly finished, Emily. By June of the next year, with the death of Anne, Charlotte was alone.

To understand Charlotte Brontë's masterpieces, it should be

[1] *The Tenant of Wildfell Hall.*

remembered that they were only compulsorily three-volume books. *Jane Eyre* was eked out with the St John Rivers addition, and, when, after Anne's death, Charlotte took up her pen to write the third volume of *Shirley*, the interest is shifted. The second plot of Louis Moore and Shirley was not an afterthought, but it reads like one. More vivid, doubtless, than the earlier part, it is far less full of meaning. In short, the recurrent tutor and pupil story, a story that will insist on being told whether consonant or not, is, here, but an addition. There are other weaknesses in *Shirley*. Caroline's affair ends happily—perhaps a necessity of mid-Victorian fiction—Mrs Pryor, though useful to the heroine as a confidante and a fair copy of the life, is amateur's work, beneath the colour of the other characters, and out of the picture ; but Robert and Hortense in their little parlour and Caroline in the twilight have a grace *d'outre mer*.

Unlike *Jane Eyre, Shirley* is not easy to read. Beautiful as is Caroline's love-story, it is of another order of art altogether from that of the easy masterpiece—possibly of an even rarer order. There is the distinction between what is of great beauty and what is great.

Varying the next few years with visits to London and to friends, Charlotte Brontë found recuperation, and her temperament underwent some steeling. All her loved ones in early graves or separated by 'surge and blast,' she can now bear to look back, not absolutely without repining, but with much of the artist's detached and curious interest at what once was. Another story was owed to the public, and, perhaps, that one, too suddenly told in the unpublished *Professor*, might unroll itself anew. Fresh observations, too, had been added, and, when *Villette* opens, it is the figure of Dr John that catches the eye—the boy John with his tiny companion Paulina—whether or not a personal reminiscence, certainly a charming effort of imagination. But the main theme of *Villette* is the remembrance of Brussels, and we may suppose that the effort to resolve past discords was now largely conscious. In any case, there is no better exercise for the student of art and its processes than to compare the unembarrassed handling of the material of experience in *Villette*, with the treatment of the same material in *The Professor*. For all that, the material still counts for too much, and one feels, as one does not feel in *Jane Eyre* or in the case of Caroline Helstone, that the characters, however changed the circumstances, are, nevertheless, real people, to be actually found somewhere. One does feel, and to a degree which, artistically, is painful, that, after all, all this is observation or record. We have an uneasy fear that we are looking into other people's houses. The result is a novel which is a miracle of characterisation, and most supreme where it seems most literal, as in the wonderful 'patriotic' scene in the schoolroom, or in Lucy's tremors over her letter. Yet, even in such places, our pleasure is alloyed by our consciousness that we are being put off with mere description. At times, too, when we are out of the school and where no great interest is taken by the author in the character observed, it is evident that literalness of transcription has interfered with artistic effort, as in the account of the actress Rachel. As novel-readers, we do not expect to be reading a diary. Nor is this weakness in *Villette*—a weakness due to the absence of imagining and to its author's contentment in merely seeing life's pages turn over—redeemed by the merits of the book. The amazing variety of characters does not remedy it, nor does the fact that this weakness is counted a chief excellence by those whose interest is in the biography rather than in its subject, in her life rather than in her work, in the least degree cure it. *Villette* is a brilliant novel; in it, Charlotte Brontë threw off the incubus of the past, without transforming the past into the ideal; or, in other words, she built on her experience without making her experience our experience of the soul. *Villette* is the work of a great genius; but it does not bring the solace that comes from great art. It makes us sad; but it leaves our eyes dry. We watch beings who suffer, without sharing their suffering; our identity is not merged in the human crisis because, speaking of the book as a whole, it is not poetry. At the end, doubtless, it is, and we put it down, participating in that distant sorrow. But this is only to say that, at the end, it achieves what it has not achieved during its progress.

This *tour de force* was the last of Charlotte Brontë's writings. Two chapters of a novel, strangely called *Emma*—a sort of challenge to fame—remain from her few months of married life. She had said her say as the poets say it, and was dead before she was thirty-nine.

Emily Brontë left only one book and some verses. As to her novel, critical judgment is still in suspense. It is not desirable to read; to take *Wuthering Heights* from the shelf is to prepare for oneself no pleasure. The song of love and of morning that makes *Jane Eyre* an imperishable possession is not sung here. On the contrary, in this strange tale of outland natures on outland moors all is thunder-clad—darkness, and the light more awful that

breaks the storm, passions that, in their tempestuous strength at
once terrify us for human nature and enlarge our conception of its
dignity. It bears the same relation to *Jane Eyre* that Webster
bears to Shakespeare, if one could imagine Webster greater than
Shakespeare. This, indeed, is its defect, and in seeking to estimate
the proportional value of this defect judgment is at a loss. It is
a tale of *diablerie*, not of life. What happened in *Jane Eyre*
might have happened, part of it did actually happen, but all of it,
leaving out of account a little melodrama, here and there, which
is not essential, might have happened. These are beings agitated
by our desires, and we are reading about ourselves. In *Wuthering
Heights*, it is not so ; we see Heathcliff from the outside, and
observe this triumph of imagination. When we have admitted this
—that this is not a tale of our own life—the door is closed upon
detraction. In every other respect and of its kind, the work done
here is absolute. In these chapters, echoing with apprehension,
chapters that

Bring the unreal world too strangely near

and in which the disaster that one would often think has culminated
goes on culminating to the close, everything is found in place, and,
though it is a wild consistency, as Dobell was the first to say,
consonant. Perfectly 'in keeping' with the nature of Heathcliff,
as perfectly as the abduction of Isabella or the forced marriage of
the shivering Linton, are the hanging of the Springer—a demoniac
revelation—and the attack upon the younger Catherine, those
stunning and unceasing slaps on the young girl's face that
madden the reader as if he had been present. Undeviatingly,
almost without thinking, from Lockwood's nightmare at the
beginning to the last scene in Joseph's kitchen, when Heathcliff's
glazing eyes are tense with love's vision, the imagination pursues
its course because the authoress never for a moment dreams of
questioning the imagination.

In reading such a work, we are oppressed by an intensity of
personal feeling. There is no friendly author between us and
what is seen. The fury of the events is by no means harmonised
or softened by human comment explanatory or apologetic. The
hideous drama merely comes before us, and is there; and yet we do
not absolutely hate Heathcliff. The scene in the death-chamber
with Catherine entitles him to speak of his affection as an 'immortal
love,' a feeling which 'shackles accidents and bolts up change,'
and testifies to the infinity of humanity. In those few pages,
where the stormy villain and his dying beloved override time and

snatch a moment from eternity, we learn, as in *Othello*, something of passion's transfiguring power. And this passion is not physical. No doubt, a writer older and with more experience than Emily Brontë must, of necessity, have known that the attraction exercised by such a man, or by any man the least like Heathcliff, could only be of that kind. She did not know, and in her ignorance she gave to the transcendent a new setting, a setting far stranger than that in *Jane Eyre*, but, also, more arresting. It is the main mark of the Brontës' books and the inner reason why they are cherished that, out of the innocence of the heart, the mouth speaketh.

Of Emily Brontë's poems, it may be said that they are on the edge of greatness. So much cannot be pretended for those of her sisters. Charlotte's have a strong autobiographical reference, and, when they are most autobiographical, the truthful tenderness of her emotion sometimes finds expression ; but, in the main, they are not poetry. Charlotte Brontë, though she did not care for three volumes, achieves her results, as a prose authoress, by a series of effects, not by single blows. Such a method is unsuited to short poems, where poetry loses everything if it loses the quint-essential. The verse-writing of the gentle Anne, like all her work, has something winning in its appeal, or, it would be more correct to say, in its absence of appeal. It compasses more only when it is religious ; but the religious poems are distinguished rather by a few rare verses than as complete or satisfying wholes. At their best, they have more sincerity and less sentimentalism than most hymns.

Since the poems of Emily challenge a much graver attention, it should be noted at once that, judged from a higher standpoint, the chief defect of Anne's is, also, very observable here. Except where the poems are very short—such as *The Old Stoic, Remembrance,* or *Stanzas*—they seldom hold attention to the end, and the poetical experience is not coextensive with the poem. It is there often—at the beginnings or episodically—but it is seldom continuous. Besides this, even the best of them are too frequently dependent upon scaffolding. They have a set theme, or they work through to a set pronouncement. They have, generally, something definite to say, as prose has. The poetry does not express itself for its own sake or mould its own setting. Yet, they have been greatly prized by many fine critics. Their independence of the ordinary aids to comfort, their habit of resting on an accepted despondency, predisposes the modern reader in their favour. Especially their pagan feeling for nature, and their deeply melancholy but unrepining sentiment, appeal to minds that have been

already influenced by Meredith. Moreover, Emily's verse has—
what is scarcely to be traced at all in that of her sisters—metrical
music :

> For if your former words were true
> How useless would such sorrow be;
> As wise, to mourn the seed which grew
> Unnoticed on its parent tree,

and, sometimes, a very original feeling in the metre :

> Silent is the house, all are laid asleep,

where the hesitancy of the verse, together with the stumbling treatment of the allegory, expresses perfectly the quiver of the girl as
she withdraws into the world of dream. Occasionally, there is a
tenderness for which one would hardly have looked in the author
of *Wuthering Heights*—the real Emily that lived, one would think,
and to whom that vision came :

> To-day, I will seek not the shadowy region
> Its unsustaining vastness waxes drear.

In one farewell verse only, the great wind blows :

> Though earth and man were gone
> And suns and universes ceased to be
> And Thou wert left alone,
> Every existence would exist in Thee;

for, in poetry, what was elemental in her was not to find expression.
The graves and the moors are in these poems as they are in
Wuthering Heights, and it is the same Emily who is walking by
them, but how differently—without the delirium of strength.
Here, we are in contact with the actual human being, and find
ourselves listening to the low tones natural to the girl who, all
her life, and except when she was writing *Wuthering Heights,*
controlled the utterances of the heart :

> So I knew that he was dying,
> Stooped and raised his languid head,
> Felt no breath and heard no sighing,
> So I knew that he was dead.

The feeling beneath those poems, perhaps just because it is a
controlled feeling, does not always find full expression. One likes
them the better on rereading, one has to come again and taste,
for the atmosphere of the poet's thought is not quite com-
municated : they are not poems that compel one to feel with the
poet. To be complimentary, it might be said that they 'speak in
silences.' They do speak, but to an attentive ear, with something
of soundlessness, something estranged, at least something very

far away from the sounding sureness of the prose. The lyric medium did not supply her with sufficient imaginative material, and this, perhaps, may suffice to explain why there is not more to praise; for, in her verse, though she communes freely with her spirit of imagination, that spirit is not freely exercised. Perhaps it also explains why their constant readers love these poems; for, in them, in the absence of her strange imaginings, what is chiefly disclosed is her individualism, the author of *Wuthering Heights* in her loneliness.

A word may be added as to the novels of Anne Brontë. *Agnes Grey* has interest, a record of her governess experiences, treated, so far as one can judge, not very freely, and, for this reason, affording, in its mild way, something of the pleasure of discovery. The eager interest in everything connected with the biography of the Brontës aroused by Mrs Gaskell's *Life* has given to those faint pages an attraction beyond their own. Yet, what her sister once wrote to Mr Williams, in reply to a letter full of family references, is not without appositeness: 'I think details of character always have a charm, even when they relate to people we have never seen, nor expect to see.' *The Tenant of Wildfell Hall* is as interesting a novel as was ever written without any element of greatness. It is pleasant to read of all sorts of intrigue and bad doings just as if they were a fairy tale and altogether outside the atmosphere of badness. There is one drawback—the tale is told by a man meant by the authoress to be quite 'nice,' but, in fact, less likeable than Crimsworth in *The Professor*. The Brontës had observed men not unclosely; but they were not able to see things through the eyes of men.

APPENDIX

A Chapter in the History of a Tyrone Family being a tenth extract from the Legacy of the Late Francis Purcell P.P. of Drumcoolagh, appeared in *The Dublin University Magazine* for October 1839, pp. 398-415, and was reprinted in *The Purcell Papers*, 1880, and in *The Watcher and other Weird Stories*, 1894, by J. Sheridan Le Fanu.

While nothing could be more probable than that the author of *The Irish Sketch Book* and *Barry Lyndon* had read this story, it is clear that Charlotte Brontë could have had access to it. Her father, when at Cambridge, sent money to his Irish relatives; in his will, he remembered them, and there is an absurd legend that, after the publication of *Jane Eyre*, one of them crossed the Irish sea to deal summary justice to Miss Rigby of *The*

Quarterly, whom he took to be a man. There was, therefore, some 'measure of correspondence.' Charlotte Brontë herself, in requesting Messrs Aylott and Jones to send out review copies of the *Poems*, mentions, alone among Irish papers, *The Dublin University Magazine*. A favourable notice appeared; and, in writing to the editor to thank him for it, 6 October 1846, she signs herself 'your constant and grateful reader.' Later, 9 October 1847, she makes a special request that Messrs Smith and Elder should send *Jane Eyre* to the same review. It is not improbable that a forgotten remembrance of Le Fanu's story, read years before, supplied what was never a fertile inventiveness with the machinery it wanted.

In the story, which is about a twelfth of the length of *Jane Eyre*, lord Glenfallen, who is neither old nor ugly, neither young nor handsome, marries, or pretends to marry, the young Irish girl who is the narrator, Fanny Richardson. The couple then set off for his country house, Cahergillagh court, a large rambling building, where they are welcomed by an old housekeeper who is used as the storyteller's confidante. The day after, lord Glenfallen, beginning in a jocular manner by saying he is to be her Bluebeard, counsels the heroine to ' visit *only* that part of the Castle which can be reached from the front entrance, leaving the back entrance and the part of the building commanded immediately by it to the menials.' He gives no reason for this extraordinary request, further than a mysterious warning of danger; the actual reason being that in that part of the castle there lived his blind wife, who had arrived either from another of his houses or from abroad—one need not understand everything in the story—on the very day of his own arrival. A month later, coming up to her bedroom, the heroine is startled by finding a blind lady seated in a chair. Some sudden talk follows, and, on Fanny's saying that her name is lady Glenfallen, an outbreak of rage on the part of her visitant. 'The violence of her action, and the fury which convulsed her face, effectually terrified me, and disengaging myself from her grasp, I screamed as loud as I could for help. The blind woman continued to pour out a torrent of abuse upon me, foaming at the mouth with rage, and impotently shaking her clenched fist towards me. I heard Lord Glenfallen's step upon the stairs, and I instantly ran out: as I passed him I perceived that he was deadly pale and just caught the words: " I hope that demon has not hurt you." I made some answer, I forget what, and he entered the chamber, the door of which he locked upon the inside. What passed within I know not, but I heard the voices of two speakers raised in loud and angry altercation.' When lord Glenfallen returns after two hours, he is pale and agitated; 'that unfortunate woman,' said he, 'is out of her mind. I daresay she treated you to some of her ravings: but you need not dread any further interruption from her: I have brought her so far to reason.' The heroine can elicit nothing further. Lord Glenfallen becomes silent and distracted, and one morning proposes they should go abroad. That night, however, Fanny is again visited in her bedroom by the blind woman, who tells her that she and not Fanny is the true lady Glenfallen, commands her to leave her pretended husband the next day and threatens her, if she refuses, that she will reap the bitter fruits of her sin. Commenting upon this adventure, Fanny continues—'There was something in her face, though her features had evidently been handsome, and were not, at first sight, unpleasing, which, upon a nearer inspection, seemed to indicate the habitual prevalence and indulgence of evil passions, and a power of expressing mere animal rage with an intenseness that I have seldom seen equalled, and to which an almost unearthly effect was given by the convulsive quivering of the sightless eyes.' She tells her husband, but he meets her with his former defence: 'the person in question, however, has one excuse, her mind is, as I told you before, unsettled. You should have remembered that, and hesitated to receive as unexceptionable evidence against the honour of your husband, the ravings of a lunatic'; and, afterwards, Fanny is told by old Martha that she hears her master had ill-used the poor blind Dutchwoman. 'How do you know that she is a Dutchwoman?' asks Fanny, 'Why, my lady,' answered Martha, 'the master often calls her the Dutch hag, and other names you would not like to hear, and I am sure she is neither English nor Irish; for, whenever they talk together, they speak some queer foreign lingo.' Her maiden name, it appears later, had been Flora van Kemp.

The next incident occurs when Fanny is sitting in the parlour late one evening. 'I heard, or thought I heard, uttered within a few yards of me, in an odd, half-sneering tone, the words—"There is blood upon your ladyship's throat."... I looked around the room for the speaker, but in vain. I went then to the room-door, which I opened, and peered into the passage, nearly faint with horror lest some leering, shapeless thing should greet me upon the threshold.' That same night, in her bedroom, the incident is repeated. 'After lying for about an hour awake, I at length fell into a kind of doze; but my imagination was very busy, for I was startled from this unrefreshing sleep by fancying that I heard a voice close to my face exclaim as before—"There is blood upon your ladyship's throat." The words were instantly followed by a loud burst of laughter.' Sleep forsakes the terrified girl, and, sometime in the small hours, she sees the long wall-mirror fixed opposite the foot of the bed slowly shifting its position. In reality, the mirror was hung on a concealed door now swinging open to admit a figure. 'It stepped cautiously into the chamber, and with so little noise, that had I not actually seen it, I do not think I should have been aware of its presence. It was arrayed in a kind of woollen night-dress, and a white handkerchief or cloth was bound tightly about the head. I had no difficulty, spite of the strangeness of the attire, in recognising the blind woman whom I so much dreaded. She stooped down, bringing her head nearly to the ground, and in that attitude she remained motionless for some moments, no doubt in order to ascertain if any suspicious sounds were stirring.' Then comes the account of the attempted murder, the murderess groping about the room till she finds a razor and then swiftly sliding towards the heroine, who is paralysed by fear. 'A slight inaccuracy saved me from instant death; the blow fell short, the point of the razor grazing my throat. In a moment, I know not how, I found myself at the other side of the bed, uttering shriek after shriek.' Lord Glenfallen rushes in and fells the intruder, and the entrance of a crowd of domestics prevents further danger.

At the trial, Flora van Kemp accuses him of having instigated the attempted murder of the pretended wife and, on its failure, of having turned upon herself. But she does not intend to perish singly, 'all your own handywork, my gentle husband.' This was 'followed by a low, insolent, and sneering laugh, which from one in her situation was sufficiently horrible.' Nevertheless, justice is baulked of its prey and sentence is passed upon her alone. 'Before, however, the mandate was executed, she threw her arms wildly into the air, and uttered one piercing shriek so full of preternatural rage and despair, that it might fitly have ushered a soul into those realms where hope can come no more. The sound still rang in my ears, months after the voice that had uttered it was for ever silent.' The husband becomes a prey to maniacal delusions, hears voices and cuts his throat under circumstances of peculiar horror; while the innocent Fanny seeks the refuge of a convent.

CHAPTER XIII

LESSER NOVELISTS

EDWARD GEORGE EARLE LYTTON BULWER was born on 25 May 1803; on the death of his mother, in 1843, he succeeded to the Knebworth estate and, in the following year, assumed the name of Lytton; he was created baron Lytton of Knebworth in 1866. *Ismael and other Poems* was published in 1820; his first novel, *Falkland*, in 1827; and he continued, in the midst of social, editorial and political concerns and disastrous matrimonial relations, to produce fiction, verse and drama until his death on 18 January 1873. His versatility is not more remarkable than his anticipatory intuition for changes of public taste. In a first phase, he wrote novels dealing with Wertherism, dandyism and crime; in a second, he evolved a variant of the historical romance; in a third, in *The Pilgrims of the Rhine* (1834), he brought together English fairy lore and Teutonic legend; in a fourth, he imported into fiction pseudo-philosophic occultism; in a fifth, he turned to 'varieties of English life,' comparatively staid and quiet; later still, in *The Coming Race* (1871), he outlined a new scientific Utopia; and, finally, in *Kenelm Chillingly* and *The Parisians* (1873), he portrayed character and society transformed by the vulgarisation of wealth.

Lytton's second and best novel *Pelham, or The Adventures of a Gentleman* (1828), is a blend of sentiment, observation and *blague*. Rousseau, Goethe, Byron and some ultra-sentimental experiences of Lytton's own youth are drawn upon for the figure of Sir Reginald Glanville. Pelham, on the other hand, is drawn from life, not from books; he is a more credible character in a more credible world than the almost contemporary Vivian Grey. Pelham is a dandy, coxcomb, wit, scholar and lover, and, in many ways, offensive and exasperating; but he is also a staunch friend and an ambitious and studious politician, in these respects differing from the corresponding figure in the preliminary sketch *Mortimer*.

What distinguishes *Pelham* from its author's later writings is its concentration of creative and expressive effort; Henry Pelham is the most vivid of all Lytton's characters; and the earlier chapters have an incisive humorous cynicism which is all too quickly dissipated into mere discursiveness by an influence everywhere apparent in the book, that of the encyclopaedists. *Pelham* was issued at a time when a publisher's recipe for popular fiction[1] was 'a little elegant chit-chat or so.' The effect was galvanic; Pelhamism superseded Byronism, established a new fashion in dress and made Lytton famous eight years before *Pickwick* began to appear.

In the second quarter of the century, the writings of Pierce Egan, Ainsworth, Whitehead and Moncrieff give evidence of a new lease of interest in criminal biography and low life; Lytton was quick to seize the opportunity. The character Thornton, in *Pelham*, is drawn from the actual murderer Thurtell; in *The Disowned* (1829), Crauford is a representation of the fraudulent banker Fauntleroy; *Lucretia, or The Children of the Night* (1846), is based on the career of the forger Wainewright. The point of view is different in *Paul Clifford* (1830), and *Eugene Aram* (1832), which fall into line with *The Robbers* (1782), *Caleb Williams* (1794), *The Monk* (1795), *The Borderers* written 1795—6, *Melmoth* (1820) and other books[2] concerned with the criminal's justification of himself and demand for sympathy and understanding. *Paul Clifford* won the benediction of Godwin, who thought parts of it 'divinely written,' and of Ebenezer Elliott; in its melodramatic way, it furthered the efforts of Mackintosh, Romilly and others for the reform of prison discipline and penal law; it provided, also, an example, not lost upon Dickens, of the novel of humanitarian purpose. The introduction of picaresque figures, among them the rogue Tomlinson, who stands for 'all the Whigs,' and who becomes a professor of ethics—and, still more, the quips and personal caricatures in the book—rouse suspicions as to the depth of the writer's sincerity. Paul Clifford, the chivalrous highwayman, has his counterpart in the philosophising murderer Eugene Aram; the obscuring of the plain issue of crime by sentimental, or, as in the case of Ainsworth, by romantic sophistry, nauseated Thackeray; in *George de Barnwell*, Thackeray described these heroes as 'virtuous and eloquent beyond belief,' and, in his unvarnished Newgate chronicle *Catherine* (1839—40),

---

[1] Cf. *The Disowned* (1829), chap. xxix.
[2] Cf. Legouis, E., *The Early Life of Wordsworth*, p. 271.

he put the whole matter in its naked and repulsive truth. The melodramatic law-court scenes of *Paul Clifford* and *Eugene Aram* are earlier evidences of the theatrical skill with which Lytton composed his dramas, chief among them *Richelieu* (1838), *The Lady of Lyons* (1838) and the comedy *Money* (1840). In the characterisation of Claude Melnotte, hero of *The Lady of Lyons*, again, the criminal fact is obscured by the veneer of sentiment.

Lytton next turned his attention to the historical novel; his *Devereux* (1829) uses up more of the material (some had already been put into *Pelham*) gathered in his study of the politician Bolingbroke. *The Last Days of Pompeii* (1834) differs from Lytton's chief historical romances in taking for its main interest a natural, instead of a social, convulsion, and in introducing, by the nature of the case, characters entirely invented. It established in public favour the romance of classical days, which Lockhart had attempted in *Valerius* (1821); at the close of his life, Lytton returned to the type in his *Pausanias the Spartan*, published in 1876. In *Rienzi* (1835), *The Last of the Barons* (1843) and *Harold* (1848), he works upon a consistent theory; abandoning the practice of Scott, he elects as his central figure a person of the highest historical importance; his aims are, first, to give a just delineation in action and motive of this character; secondly, to build up, with all the records at hand, a picture of the age in its major and minor concerns; thirdly, to bring to light the deeper-lying causes—personal, social, political—of the events of the period, a period in which the closing stages of an old, and the opening stages of a new, civilisation are in conflict. His skill in divining the forces at work in complex phases of society, and in concocting illustrative scenes, almost nullified by the intolerable diction of *Rienzi* and the facile imaginativeness of *Harold*, is best seen in *The Last of the Barons*; though, even in this last case, the comparison with *Quentin Durward* or *Notre Dame* is fatal. His distinction between Scott's 'picturesque' and his own 'intellectual' procedure has in it a dangerous note of presumption.

Lytton's keen and credulous interest in all forms of the occult first finds expression in the short *Glenallan* and in *Godolphin* (1833). The diabolic aspects of rosicrucianism had been put to use in Godwin's *St Leon*, and in *Melmoth*; spectral figures of more beneficent origin loom in the semi-allegorical *Zanoni* (1842), developed from *Zicci* (1841). The rosicrucian initiate, Zanoni, yields up all he has won of youth and power for the sake of a forbidden human passion; in consequence, he falls a victim to the Terror; the book suddenly ceases to be vague and becomes dramatic when dealing with the fates of Robespierre and Henriot. Lytton's treatment of the Terror falls in date between that of Carlyle and that of Dickens. Two works nearer to the date and manner of Wilkie Collins also make use of the supernatural; in *A Strange Story* (1862), a murder mystery is darkened and complicated by the power which one character possesses of suspending natural law; the short story *The Haunted and the Haunters* (1859) contains Lytton's most impressive use of the occult; the machinery is explained, at the end, in the manner of Mrs Radcliffe— by persistent will-power, a curse is preserved in a magical vessel, generations after a crime has been committed. But the effect of the tale is due less to this than to the half-impalpable loathsomeness which menaces the invader of the haunted house; here, the story may challenge comparison with the Monçada episode in *Melmoth*. For the finer chords of mystery and terror struck by Coleridge and Keats, Lytton had no ear.

Lytton had early premonition of the change in taste which occurred about 1848, and sought to fall in with the new realistic trend in *The Caxtons* (1849), *My Novel* (1853) and *What will he do with it?* (1858). The result is illuminating. The hero of *The Caxtons* is neither 'dandiacal,' overwrought nor perverted; and, while in *Lucretia* the effects of evil home life and upbringing are traced, in *The Caxtons* the conditions are reversed and nearer to common experience. To this degree, Lytton becomes a realist. But he could not bring himself to face life squarely; a great part of *The Caxtons* is devoted to the Byronic youth Vivian; the simple annals of the family are narrated in the manner of Sterne; an elderly impracticable scholar, a lame duck, a street organ-grinder feeding his mice provide some of the occasions for emotional indulgence. If anyone should seek in *My Novel* for varieties of English life, he will be disappointed: only one point of view is possible for the writer, that of 'our territorial aristocracy'; the varieties may be found in Kingsley's *Yeast* (1848).

In the fantastic *Asmodeus at Large* (1836), Lytton had foreshadowed the idea of *The Coming Race*, which antedates by a year Butler's *Erewhon*. Lytton's book gives an original turn to an often-used convention; in this case, the ideal republic is dominated by an irresistible destructive force Vril, and, therefore, is at peace. The inhabitants look down upon civilisations barbarous and unfixed in principle. By its implied criticism of contemporary society, the book is connected with *Kenelm Chillingly* and

The Parisians, which was left unfinished in the same year. These books picture England and the Paris of the second empire, sterile in large ideas and feverishly experimenting with new and untried expedients; vast financial depredations, communism, political shiftiness, muscular religion, realism in art—these are some of the innovations which are contrasted with the older aristocratic pride and conservatism.

Even in an age of voluminousness, Lytton is an outstanding example; to his novels must be added a great mass of epic, satirical and translated verse, much essay-writing, pamphleteering and a number of successful plays. His wide range of accomplishment, his untiring industry, his talent in construction, his practice of dealing with imposing subjects, his popularity with the bulk of readers, give him an air of importance in the Victorian epoch. But he was rooted too deeply in the age of emotionalism and rhetoric. Richardson, Sterne and the weaker part of Byron, on the one hand, and the encyclopaedists on the other, encouraged in him the sentimentalism which, incidentally, ruined *Great Expectations*, and the didactic and abstract habit of thought and expression with which Thackeray made high-spirited play. The novel, in Lytton's view, was a study of the effect of something upon something else; so, after *Pelham*, he rarely ever escaped from the discursive to the idiomatic style, or created character by dramatic sympathy. Finally, his early success confirmed him in the adoption of the pose, hotly resented by Thackeray and Tennyson, of the *grand seigneur*, dispensing the light of reason, knowledge and humanity.

Anthony Trollope, after a wretched boyhood and youth, of which he gives some glimpses in his *Autobiography* and in *The Three Clerks* (1858), entered upon a doubly prosperous career as a civil servant in the post office and as a man of letters. He had behind him, in the work of his mother, Frances Trollope, an incentive to literary fertility; from her, he inherited some prejudices, but little of his art. The two Irish stories *The Macdermots of Ballycloran* (1847) and *The Kellys and the O'Kellys* (1848), and *La Vendée* (1850), were out of accord with his natural aptitudes, which fitted him rather for the treatment of material like that of Jane Austen or Thackeray, for both of whom his admiration was unbounded. The monograph on Thackeray falls below the level of its subject; but the resemblances in essential points between Trollope's best work and Thackeray's show that he understood more as an artist than he could express as a critic. In *The Warden* (1855), a scene from clerical life which precedes by two years those of George Eliot, the individual quality of Trollope's genius first comes to light. Echoes of Titmarsh are heard in the passages satirising Dickens and Carlyle; the characterisation and the creation of a locality show complete originality. In both respects, the novel is the nucleus of the Barsetshire series on which the fame of Trollope most securely rests. Round about Hiram's hospital, the scene of *The Warden*, is built up in *Barchester Towers* (1857), the cathedral city with all its clerical hierarchy. Beyond the city, in successive tales—*Dr Thorne* (1858), *Framley Parsonage* (1861), *The Small House at Allington* (1864) and *The Last Chronicles of Barset* (1867)—come into view the episcopal see with its outlying parishes rich and poor, its houses of middle class folk and gentry, and, looming large and remote, the castle of the duke of Omnium—a country of the imagination which gives the illusion of actual life by the completeness of its visualisation. Clearly as he knows its topography, he has few pages of description, except in his lively hunting scenes. His foremost concern is with people; and the people in his books come to our notice in the natural fashion of acquaintanceship; with the passage of time, characters are hardened or mellowed; Trollope rivals Thackeray and Balzac in the skill with which he suggests changes due to lapsing years. Following the fortunes of Septimus Harding, the one poetic figure Trollope created, we come into contact with the old bishop and his son archdeacon Grantly, the new bishop and Mrs Proudie, Mr Slope, dean Arabin, lord Lufton, the Thornes, the Greshams, the Dales, the Crawleys, the whole multitudinous population of the county. In the main, Trollope delineates quite ordinary types, though, curiously, some of the most famous are drawn larger than life-size— Mrs Proudie, Obadiah Slope, the signora Vesey-Neroni and, in later novels, the famous Chaffanbrass. Trollope was a Palmerstonian, and his predilection was for the middle and upper middle classes, for clerical dignitaries who have more of Johnson's principles than of his piety, for the landed gentry, the county representatives and the hunting set. For intruders in church and state, the evangelical Slopes and Maguires, and for upstart millionaires and speculators, Melmotte and Lopez and others, Trollope has nothing but contempt.

No other writer of fiction has had so keen a perception of the *mœurs* of a distinctive class as Trollope; his triumph is that, like

Chaucer, he preserves the traits of common humanity seen beneath
professional idiosyncrasy. In his ecclesiastical portraits—he knew
little of their prototypes at first hand—inference has the validity
of apparent observation; only less lifelike are his civil servants,
ranging from Charley Tudor to Sir Raffle Buffle, manor house
inhabitants, as in *Orley Farm*, journalists, London clubmen,
electioneering agents and the varied figures of his political
novels from *Phineas Finn* (1869) to *The Duke's Children* (1880).
The rather chilly Plantagenet Palliser and the philandering young
Irishman Phineas Finn link the series together. These novels
suffer by the inevitable comparison with Disraeli's; for, except in
the person and intrigue of Mr Daubeny (a sketch of Disraeli himself), Trollope lacks Disraeli's power of piercing to the core of a
political situation, and his insight into politically minded character.

Trollope went on his way very little distracted by passing
literary fashions; he was just touched by the example of Dickens,
as when he describes the Todgers-like boarding house in *The
Small House at Allington* or the Dickensian bagmen of *Orley
Farm*; forgeries, murders and trials appear after the date at
which Wilkie Collins had made them popular, in *Orley Farm*, for
instance, and in *Phineas Finn*. In *The Vicar of Bullhampton*
(1870), the story of the outcast Carry Brattle, he ventured upon the
problem novel; but, for the most part, he upheld the Victorian
idea of wholesomeness, which included sexual impropriety among
the sweeping omissions which it exacted from the novelist. In
later novels, he unfortunately forsook his earlier practice of holding himself altogether apart from his characters and letting the
story convey his moral (he set as much store by the moral as any
Victorian) without challenge or comment; *The Way We Live
Now* (1875) drifts continually into satire and criticism of no great
pertinence; on the other hand, he scarcely ever used the novel
for the exposure of specific abuses.

These occasional departures from his accustomed practice
affected very little the lifelikeness with which character and occupation are presented, or the unlaboured precision of detail with
which the interiors of households, deaneries, newspaper offices,
lawyers' chambers, clubs and the like are described; the future
social historian will regard Trollope as a godsend—a Trollope
of the Elizabethan age would be invaluable. His best stories
preserve the even texture of average experience; he excels in
imparting interest to commonplace affairs, to hopes and fears of
clerical or political patronage, to minor financial worries, to the

working out in various lives of some initial blunder, or to love affairs in which one of his staid, but attractive and very natural, girls has to decide between two ardent suitors, or one of his youths has two minds in his amatory devotions. In virtue of the verisimilitude of his tales, Trollope has been called by some a photographer, by others a realist; he was neither. He was a day-dreamer who could so order his dreaming that it partook of the very texture and proportion and colour of ordinary life; his genius resides in this. He had but to give some stimulus—the view of Salisbury from the little bridge, for instance—to his dream faculty, and it would improvise for him—effortlessly and without the need of constant reference back to life—places, people and events, having an animation and atmosphere denied to photography, but, at the same time, lacking in the sense of sharpness and solidity which is the first care of the realist. A dreamer has little concern with the profounder causes which underlie action. This view is confirmed in his *Autobiography*, where he speaks of 'constructing stories within himself,' of 'maintaining interest in a fictitious tale,' of 'novel-spinning.' 'I never found myself,' he says, 'thinking much about the work I had to do till I was doing it.' What further supports this idea, is the exception, when he created out of starved flesh and blood, and out of anguish, pride and humility of spirit, the figure of Josiah Crawley, perpetual curate of Hogglestock. In this character, there is a quality different even from such unforgettable strokes in his other manner as bishop Proudie's prayer 'that God might save him from being glad that his wife was dead.'

Trollope's writing is, above all things, easily readable; it is lucid, harmonious, admirable for purposes of even narrative and familiar dialogue; it has a pleasant satiric flavour, but makes no more claim to distinction in rhythm or diction than do his stories to depth or philosophy or intensity. He had command of humour and, much more, of pathos, which rings true even now because the occasions are unforced and the placid and sensible tenor of his narrative enables him to reach emotional climax without pitching the note too high. In *An Autobiography*, written 1875—6 and published 1883, he chose to emphasise the mechanical and commercial aspects of his art. Froude's phrase—'Old Trollope... banging about the world'—has in it a touch of portraiture which corresponds with Trollope's picture of himself. His philistinism was partly innate, partly the outcome of hostility towards affectation; there is legitimate satire in his ironical analogy between the minor novelist waiting for the moment of inspiration and the tallow-chandler waiting for the divine moment of melting. He did, however, make a fetish of mere voluminousness and he became a stand-by of magazines such as *The Cornhill, Blackwood's* and *The Fortnightly,* whose editors valued punctuality in their contributors. He has so vividly described himself ticking off his two hundred and fifty words every fifteen minutes in the morning hours that posterity has been willing to accept his writing at the valuation he seems to put upon it ; his fame has suffered in consequence.

Few writers of the nineteenth century could contend on the score of wide and eager interest in life with Charles Reade, whose physical and mental vigour animate his pages, sometimes to the point of violence. The most characteristic products of the man are those in which he worked, Hugo-like, on a large symbolic scale, for human compassion and justice. These more grandiose compositions have a little obscured from view the novels of manners, in which he exercises a more delicate art. The first of his novels, *Peg Woffington* (1853), was of this lighter kind; it was made, on the advice of his life-long friend Laura Seymour, out of one of his few successful plays, *Masks and Faces* (1852). Reade spent an inordinate amount both of mental energy and of his fortune upon the stage; he wrote in a period of staginess and melodrama and easily succumbed to the taste of the time. He shared the opinion of Wilkie Collins that fiction and drama do not differ in essence, but merely in mechanism of expression. His play *Gold* (1853) could, therefore, be turned into *It is never too late to mend* (1856); *Foul Play* (1869) and other writings could appear either as plays or novels; and his most effective play *Drink* (1879) was made out of Zola's *L'Assommoir*. A scene of crude theatricality which mars the play *Masks and Faces* recurs in the novel *Peg Woffington*; but, apart from that scene, both make skilful use of an old theme, the mingled glamour and pathos in the double life of the stage queen. *Christie Johnstone* (1853) owes much to Maria Edgeworth, not only in its representation of the *ennui* of the leisured lord Ipsden, but, also, in the delineation of the markedly individual Scots fishing village, Newhaven. Christie Johnstone, in her simplicity, devotion and heroism, is the forerunner of other humbly born heroines—Mercy Vint, in *Griffith Gaunt* (1866), and Jael Dence, in *Put Yourself in his Place* (1870). In characters of this type, Reade is evidently breaking with conventional romance and reacting against the satirical tone of Thackeray's realism and the heroic challenge of Carlyle. The other novels of manners have a background more familiar in this kind of fiction, that of English squirearchy. *Love me Little, Love me Long* (1859), which gives the earlier history of characters in *Hard Cash* (1863), has a brilliantly conceived portrait of an elderly egotist, Mrs Bazalgette, going about with premeditated selfishness to have her own way. Her niece, Lucy Fountain, like the Kate Peyton of *Griffith Gaunt* and the Philippa Chester of *The Wandering Heir* (1872), is a girl of graceful person, quick resource, high spirit and incalculable feminine pride, such as Meredith was afterwards to elaborate in Rose Jocelyn. In *Griffith Gaunt*, Reade came nigh to producing a masterpiece; the earlier part, describing the courtship of the young Cumberland girl Kate Peyton, has the brilliance and fineness of style to which Reade could always modulate his strength in his portraits of women. In this part are seen the first phases of jealousy; later comes the masterly diagnosis in dramatic, not analytic, fashion of the moods and devices of that malignant passion. The flaw in the book was indicated by Swinburne; the moving and pathetic development follows from a criminal and incredible act, the bigamous marriage of Gaunt with Mercy Vint, through envy of a rustic rival. The inadmissible plot beneath all the fine workmanship affects us like similar things in the plays of John Ford. The doctrine of the celibate priesthood, a *motif* repeated from *The Cloister and the Hearth* (1861), adds a complicating thread to the web of intrigue; the tractarians had forced the subject to the forefront of controversy, and Kingsley had already raised his protest in *The Saint's Tragedy* in 1848. *A Terrible Temptation* (1871) is altogether coarser in fibre than the novels hitherto named; lurid and sensational elements, a demi-mondaine turned roadside preacher, a kidnapping, asylum horrors and the like, overbear the quieter and more gracious figure of lady Bassett. Nevertheless, it is a book of power, and it anticipates some important developments of the novel; it is a study of a strain of wild blood handing on hereditary qualities of ferocity and brutality. *The Wandering Heir*, which makes use of the murder and peerage trials of the Annesley claimant in 1743, is notable for a passage descriptive of Irish manners in the early eighteenth century. The passage is based largely on Swift's *The Journal of a Modern Lady*, and, on a smaller scale, shows the same power as *The Cloister and the Hearth* of weaving scattered material into a living picture of an unfamiliar period. A charge of plagiarism from Swift, Reade repudiated angrily in a reply appended to a later edition; by what a mass and diversity of reading his pictures are supported may be gathered from that document. This was but one of numerous occasions on which Reade's notions of literary property brought him under suspicion, and his litigious and combative disposition often turned suspicion into active enmity.

Reade was deeply in sympathy with the impulse towards realism which was at work in fiction in the middle of the century. Whereas Trollope thought a kind of 'mental daguerreotype' the ideal manner of presenting truth, Reade put his trust in immense accumulations of reports of actual events, by means of which he supported his boast, that, when he spoke of fact, he was 'upon oath.' In *A Terrible Temptation*, he describes his method of collecting and indexing his material, a task upon which, at one period, he spent five hours a day. The method was, of course, that adopted later by Zola; the differences of temper between the two writers are explained, to some extent, by the fact that Reade comes before, and Zola after, the scientific revolution.

Reade's documentary novels are not all of one kind; there are, first, those in which he makes use of his knowledge, Defoe-like in its intimacy, of out-of-the-way trades and occupations; such are *The Autobiography of a Thief* (1858), *Jack of all Trades* (1858) and *A Hero and a Martyr* (1874). *Jack of all Trades* includes a novel episode of picaresque, describing, with graphic force, the life of a keeper of a murderous performing elephant. Secondly, there are stories of philanthropic purpose; in these, Reade sweeps aside Godwin's theories and Lytton's sentiment, replacing them by fact irrefutably established and by direct denunciation. The ghastly cranks and collars and jackets of *It is never too late to mend* were things he had seen in the gaols of Durham, Oxford and Reading, or knew by report in the trial of lieutenant Austin at Birmingham in 1855. He could cite precedent for every single horror of the asylum scenes in *Hard Cash*; on all the other abuses which he attacked—'ship-knacking' in *Foul Play*, 'rattening' in *Put Yourself in his Place*, insanitary village life in *A Woman Hater* (1877)—he wrote as an authority on scandals flagrant at the moment, not, as sometimes happened in the case of Dickens, about those of a past day. Pitiless, insistent hammering at the social conscience is the method of these novels, which remind us, at times of Victor Hugo, at times of *Uncle Tom's Cabin* and, at times, of Eugène Sue's *Mystères de Paris*. Reade's habit of challenging attention by capitals, dashes, short emphatic paragraphs, changes of type and other Sternean oddities, accentuates the general impression of urgency. This is a small thing in comparison with the gift, exemplified in most of these novels, of sustained and absorbing narrative. The homeward voyage of the 'Agra,' escaping pirates and the tornado to be wrecked amid Hugo-like scenes on the northern coast of France; the rescue of Hardie and Dodd from the burning asylum; the bursting of the reservoir in the Ousely valley : these and other scenes are depicted with a power which makes the reader a participant in the event, sets the pulse throbbing faster and keeps the mind tense with solicitude for the outcome. Hugo's headlong rhetorical outpouring is different in kind; Reade's prose is concentrated, masterful, deliberate and, at the highest pitch of excitement, can bear the closest scrutiny of detail. The humorous English mind does not often produce pure narrative of action ; on Reade's own scale, he has no competitor.

The documentary method has its most triumphant justification, however, in the historical novel *The Cloister and the Hearth*, enlarged from the slight and propitious love-story *A Good Fight*, which appeared in *Once a Week* in 1859. This was Reade's only incursion into the middle ages; the remoteness of the scene relieves his intense humanity from the chafing of its fiery yoke-fellow in the propagandist novels—indignation. His imagination was inspired and steadied by the volume and worth of his documents, the *Colloquies* and *Compendium Vitae* of Erasmus, the satires of Gringoire, the writings of Froissart and Luther, *Liber Vaga-torum* and other beggar books, monkish chronicles, jest books, medieval encyclopaedias of medicine, astrology and the like. He mounts above this mass of learning to view as from a peak the dawn of the renascence over medieval Europe; the survey gives historic significance to the simple closing phrase, *Haec est parva domus natus qua magnus Erasmus.* In two points, in especial, Reade's judgment and prevision are shown: first, in the creation of Gerard the supposed father of Erasmus to fill the *rôle* of pro-tagonist, and, secondly, in seizing upon the rich opportunity afforded by the wandering scholar and soldier of the middle ages. The scenes which are laid in taverns, monasteries, churches, studios, palaces, above all upon the road itself, are not more various than the characters—ruffians, beggars, freebooters, burgomasters, cam-paigners, doctors, penitents, priests of loose or of grave behaviour, artists, printers, bishops and dignitaries higher still in church and state : each is portrayed with appropriate dialect and garb and custom, none more effectively than the master-beggar Cul de Jatte; not one, however insignificant, is feebly imagined or carelessly drawn. What else might have been mere brilliant picaresque gains unity from the large theme of the book, the conflict between ecclesiastical system and human passion, in which the apparent is not the real victor—a theme at once symbolic of the whole age and of dramatic personal concern to Gerard and Margaret. These characters and the Burgundian Denys are drawn with the bold simplicity of outline, the freedom from subtlety, which befit the epic scale; at the same time, their experience never lifts them out of reach of common human sympathy. The endurance of Margaret's passion dominates and ennobles all other impressions; the mind is drawn from every incident to view its effect upon her fortunes in Holland. The plain prose of the philanthropic novels is here coloured and varied and modulated to the expression of every mood of courage, despair, pathos, chagrin, humour, poetic exultation, as the narrative in its course gives occasion. Attempts to classify *The Cloister and the Hearth* fail, because, in spaciousness of design and many-sidedness of interest, in range of knowledge, in fertility of creation, in narrative art and in emotional power, the book is unique; the age must be rich indeed which can afford to consider the author of *The Cloister and the Hearth* a minor novelist.

The habit of minor novelists of inventing a kind of formula or pattern according to which the production of scores or even centuries of novels could go on almost automatically makes it permissible to group the remaining names under some few lines of general development. One of the things which best reveal the practice of the individual writer and the trend of fiction at large is the treatment of setting and scene. The earliest of those to be considered here as making distinctive use of locality is Mary Russell Mitford. She is rather an essayist than a novelist, her one regular novel, *Atherton* (1854), a slight tale of love and a missing legatee, being of small account. Her voluminous gossipy letters (which better deserve the designation *Recollections of a Literary Life* than the anthology of chosen passages and comments to which she gave that title in 1852) reveal some significant preferences; such as those for Cowley, Lamb, Hazlitt, Gilbert White of Selborne, the simpler part of Wordsworth, Steele (whom she thought worth twenty Addisons) and 'Geoffrey Crayon,' whose *Sketch Book* appeared in 1820. Her fame is established by *Our*

Village, begun in *The Lady's Magazine* (1819), published in five volumes between 1824 and 1832. The scene was Three Mile Cross, where she supported her reprobate father for the last twenty years of his life ; the village is near Reading, the county town of her *Belford Regis* (1835). Her inmost desire was to write ambitious tragedies in verse such as her *Rienzi* (1828) ; happily, the art of Jane Austen taught her to work upon a miniature scale. She brushes lightly over her small and rather beggarly world ; she does not falsify it, nevertheless its dullness and insipidity disappear ; places, people, especially children, seasons, sports, atmosphere are touched into bright and graceful animation. *Our Village* evokes the spirit of place through its scene ; *Cranford,* through delicate subtleties of characterisation. An instinctive sense of fitness rules in the apparently spontaneous prose ; its lightness and vivacity and unforced humour are deceptive ; they are, in fact, the outcome of strict discipline, as may be seen from a comparison with the more unstudied letters.

Worthy of notice is a work of very different order, *Chronicles of Dartmoor* (1866), by Mrs Marsh Caldwell, who was a pioneer with Catherine Crowe of the novel of the domestic interior. The scene of *Chronicles* is a village 'deeper in the moor than Chagford.' Though it does not occupy a very large portion of the book, the delineation of the barbaric life of this backwater, untouched by any modern influence, the characters deep-grained by superstition and long-standing irrational custom, is a remarkable anticipation of one aspect of the Wessex novels.

Trollope's Barchester was fruitful in suggestion to other novelists. Mrs Henry Wood's Helstonleigh, a re-creation of Worcester, is on a smaller scale ; the cloisters and the choir-boys, Bywater and the rest of them, help out many of her stories The setting is described with a keener vision in Margaret Oliphant Oliphant's *Chronicles of Carlingford,* one of which, *Miss Marjoribanks* (1866), depicts with engaging humour the campaign of an ambitious young girl for social leadership. Mrs Oliphant gave the surest proof of genius in *Salem Chapel* (1863), the second of the Carlingford series. The sensational part of the story is naught ; the penetrating, not altogether satirical, delineation of the dissenting chapel is masterly ; the tyranny of an antiquated fashion of piety ; the stuffy moral atmosphere ; the intolerance of the congregation for culture and thought ; the singular modes of entertaining ; the revulsion of the young pastor from the sordid and contracted world into which he is thrown—all this is confirmed in the works, at a later date, of 'Mark Rutherford,' closest of all observers of the dissidence of dissent. The butterman Tozer and the pastor's heroic little mother Mrs Vincent might pass unchallenged from the pages of *Salem Chapel* to those of *The Autobiography of Mark Rutherford* (1881).

Another region which Mrs Oliphant's art explored was the unseen world. In *A Beleaguered City* (1880), with eerie imaginative power she depicted the city of Semur in the department of the Haute Bourgogne, 'emptied of its folk' by a visitation of the spirits of the dead, who move about in the streets with a disconcerting purposefulness not to be fathomed by the grosser intellects of men. *A Little Pilgrim in the Unseen* (1882) and other books illustrate, again, this control of the springs of mystery, compared with which Lytton's rosicrucianism seems frigid and mechanical. Setting and place serve Mrs Oliphant well, again, in her stories of her native land, which follow in the established tradition of Mrs Hamilton, Susan Ferrier, Galt and Moir. We pass from the mere facile inventiveness of *Whiteladies* (1876) or *The Cuckoo in the Nest* (1892) (their scenes being laid in England) to people whose dialect, manners and affections derive from roots deep fixed in their native soil, in the Scots stories which begin with *Margaret Maitland* in 1849. One of the best of these stories, *Kirsteen* (1890), which paints the dour pride and passion of a Douglas, the silent affection, quick temper and humorous practicality of the daughter Kirsteen and the fidelity of the old retainer Margaret, gives a living picture of an Argyllshire interior. To the mere volume and miscellaneous nature of her work, undertaken, somewhat apathetically, as the plaintive *Autobiography* (1899) shows, in a heroic effort to provide for a family fated to disaster, must be set down Mrs Oliphant's failure to win a place nearer to George Eliot and Mrs Gaskell.

Other writers, familiar by their birth with various types of Scots character and dialect, are George Macdonald and William Black, early members of the 'kail-yard' school. The county of Macdonald's birth, Aberdeenshire, his fixed belief in human and divine communion, his transition from Calvinism to a less forbidding religious faith and his wide reading in writers such as Crashaw, Boehme, Wordsworth and others of a mystical trend in their interpretation of nature, are the shaping influences upon his work. The farmers, doctors, shepherds and ministers of the Moray country he portrays with most sureness, and especially simple souls such as David and Margaret Elginbrod, deeply taught in scriptural wisdom, and given to an intense practice of piety. Characterisation is freer and more objective than is usual with Macdonald in *Robert Falconer* (1868). The sensational elements with which his stories are eked out are what Swinburne called ' electrified stupidity.' His powers are best revealed in his various fairy tales, in which he shows a fertile invention and a deft poetical handling of the inverted causes and sequences and proportions of that world. *Phantastes* (1858), much influenced by Novalis, presents, in allegory, a mode of escape from the material world, by means of mystical powers in nature ; as, in another way, does a later romance, *Lilith* (1895).

William Black's first popular novel, *A Daughter of Heth* (1871), has its setting in the Ayrshire country ; but his wont is to picture the western islands. He makes full use of the properties, highland pride and feuds, pipers, legends, ballads and super-stitions, the trusted and officious old retainer and dialect; to all this he imparts a personal quality by two rather novel practices. First, he develops the description, in a quasi-poetical style, of the sky and heather and sea of the Hebrides into a separate art, his skill in which won for him a standing among artists; twelve of the most famous illustrators of the day contributed to *Macleod of Dare* (1878). He afterwards employed this gift in the composition of books such as *The Strange Adventures of a Phaeton* (1872), a blend of guide book and novel; an epidemic of word-painting in fiction resulted from his success. A second device which Black elaborated (Susan Ferrier had already hit upon it) was the clash of temperaments of widely differing racial types. The Gaelic Macleod of Dare, moody, passionate, foredoomed, should have shown vividly in contrast with the actress Gertrude White, city-born and bred. More successful, perhaps because it retains some actual memories of youth, is the contrast between the boisterous ' whaup ' and his charming French cousin Catherine Cassilis in *A Daughter of Heth*; but, here and everywhere, Black's vision is impeded by romantic sentiment.

It is only necessary to indicate wider territorial annexations, such as those made in Basil Hall's *Schloss Hainfeld* (1836), a tale of Styria, and colonel Meadows Taylor's *Confessions of a Thug* (1839) ; Lytton, Reade and Trollope send their heroes—fore-runners of imperialism—to the antipodes ; the best use of this opportunity is made by Henry Kingsley in his *Geoffrey Hamlyn* (1859) and other Australian books, in which, in his meandering, anecdotal fashion, he paints the life of the new colony, its vast rolling plains, the industry of the sheep-run, perils from bush-rangers, aborigines, drought, forest fires and other dangers, which he knew by first-hand experience. The strain of adventure appears again in the Crimean scenes of *Ravenshoe* (1862). This latter book and the Australian tales are all deeply scored by the influence of Arnold of Rugby ; but Henry Kingsley was more devoted to an old aristocratic ideal. The intrigue in his stories is rather apt to depend upon mysterious villainies which result in acts of overstrained quixotry, the author too often intervenes to tell how sad a fate menaces his hero. Nevertheless, as in a medieval romance, the fine spirit of courtesy and chivalry shines out. Lord Charles Barty in *Austin Elliot* (1863) and lord Saltire in *Ravenshoe* are 'very parfit gentle knights'; the latter especially illustrates Kingsley's veneration for manners, whether they come of hereditary right, or whether they are the fine flower of character. A pleasing irresponsible humour, a mellow wisdom and an immense fund of affection for men and animals are other elements which blend in the individual quality of Henry Kingsley's books.

The province which George Louis Palmella Busson Du Maurier added in his best known novel *Trilby* (1894) was of a different kind; the book is our English *Scènes de la Vie de Bohème*, appropriate omissions being made; it fails in the attempt to delineate the artist of genius. As in this writer's other novels, *Peter Ibbetson* (1891) and *The Martian* (1896), the story is helped out by fanciful occultism and by melodrama which is stark stagi-ness. The charm of each of the books is found in the *chasse des souvenirs d'enfance*, in the pictures of schools and studios at Passy, Paris and Antwerp, and of early comradeships with Whistler, Poynter, Lamont and the rest; Taffy in *Trilby* is one of the great Victorian sentimental characters. The writing is in the kindlier vein of Thackeray; the colloquial idiom and the confidential atti-tude are other points of resemblance. *The History of the Jack Sprats* is a clever piece of social satire, but, in general, Du Maurier reserved the satire of conventional society for his other art, that of black and white; he does not often escape from the drawing-room; there, however, is to be found the ideal scene for the staging of the mid-century comedy of which the heroine is Mrs Ponsonby de Tomkyns, and the theme, the striving of the plutocrat's women folk to touch the hem of the garment of penniless aristocracy.

Briefly, it may be remarked, in regard to these treatments of place and setting, first, that the novel is seen to be taking possession of its full inheritance, *quidquid agunt homines*; secondly, that a closer presentation of the scene not only helps on the general tendency towards realism, but also conduces to concreteness, and is a safeguard, in some degree, against the intrusion of doctrine and 'viewiness'; and, thirdly, that we may see the process at work by which the individual novel comes to deal with special, almost insulated, areas of life.

In the historical novel, date, as well as setting, is of importance; many variants of Scott's established form make their appearance: the novel of classical times in Lockhart, Lytton, Wilkie Collins (*Antonina* 1850), Whyte-Melville, Kingsley and others; the auto-biographic type, initiated by Hannah Mary Rathbone in her *Diary of Lady Willoughby* (1844), and developed by Anne Manning in *The Maiden and Married Life of Mistress Mary Powell* (1849); the slight pictorial *Lances of Lynwood* (1855) and other such works of Charlotte Mary Yonge. Two novels only are of outstanding rank; the *Lorna Doone* (1869) of Richard Doddridge Blackmore and the *John Inglesant* (1881, privately printed in 1880) of Joseph Henry Shorthouse. In *Lorna Doone*, the proportion of history is exceedingly small, and the episode of Monmouth's rebellion of no great significance ; the form of the historical romance is modified, therefore, in various ways. First, known personages, such as Charles II and the notorious Jeffreys, come only into the remote background of the story ; secondly, the theme treated is that of a medieval romance, the deliverance of a lady in duress from the robber race and stronghold by a chivalrous knight of low degree ; thirdly, there is the more occasion for romance ; and the story is steeped in romance of many kinds—romance of adventure and action, romance of youthful passion, romance of the legendary deeds wrought by the Doones, the herculean John Ridd and the highwayman Tom Faggus, romance of the glorious hills and valleys that lie between Porlock and Lynton. Some of the material existed in manuscript, some in lingering memories of the countryside, some of it is pure happy invention. The scene is thickly peopled with bucolic originals and characters, speaking their own dialect and living their placid lives until the peril of the marauders overtakes them. The style is a little too near the rhythm of verse and overloaded with fantasy and embroidery ; at

the same time, it is redolent of the scents and stained with the
hues which come of the tilling of the soil and the tending of stock;
and it has engaging tricks of humour, often played in the unexpected clause tacked on to the end of a sober sentence.   Of
Blackmore's other novels, *Springhaven* (1887), which gives a
charming picture of a small southern port threatened by Napoleon's fleet and visited, from time to time, by Nelson, is nearest to
Lorna Doone in its blending of chivalry, romance, adventure and
villainy.   *John Inglesant* is a tale of the time of the civil war in
England and of the uprising and suppression of the Molinists in
Rome; and the fortunes of the hero Inglesant become credibly
interwoven in the web of European politics.   In his preface, Shorthouse suggests that the innovation that he is making is the
introduction of a larger measure of philosophy into the historical
framework; more exactly, it is the type of hero which is new to
novels of this kind.   Inglesant is presented in the analytic way,
and he is a figure as complex in inner mental life as are the
personages in purely psychological novels.   He is a mystic, to
whom apparitions and voices are borne through the thin veil of
the material world; he would have spent his life in the pursuit
of the beatific vision, had not his Jesuit tutor distracted his
high-wrought, sensuous, subtle spirit and turned its powers to
the service of intrigue and cabal.   The vision does not desert
him; it withholds him at the verge of temptation by the world,
the flesh and the devil in the three crises of the story; he is
one of those whom 'God saves by love.'   It is a relief to turn
from the tense emotional strain of the mystical story to the
episodes of diplomacy, crime, revenge and passion; to the
historical portraits and to the imaginative scenes—the court at
Oxford, the community of Little Gidding, the papal election at
Rome, Naples under the scourge of the plague: these are firm
in historical and intellectual substance, picturing an age not
only in external detail but in temper and spirit.   The novel
connects itself with the Anglo-catholic movement which preserved
the seventeenth century Anglican alliance with learning and
culture; the mystical fervour of the movement rather than its
symbolic ritual appealed to Shorthouse as being that with which
he could blend most congruously his strongly held Platonic beliefs.

Current moral, religious and domestic ideals, reflected in books
such as *The Heir of Redclyffe* (1853), *John Halifax, Gentleman*
(1857) and *Tom Brown's Schooldays*[1] (1857) illustrate the

---

[1] See, *ante*, chap. XI.

diversity of the exhortations to which the mid-Victorian era submitted; but in the heyday of the preachers and prophets there were mockers and indifferentists as well as enthusiasts. The standard of positive rebellion was raised by two writers chiefly, George Alfred Lawrence and Ouida (Louise de la Ramée), who chose as her audience 'les militaires,' suggesting that they left convention to those who cared to regard it. *Guy Livingstone* 1857, Lawrence's most characteristic book, is laughable in its florid satanism; nevertheless, it has a certain gross power in its portrayal of the social buccaneer, Livingstone, with his vast physical proportions, his untold lawless amours, his insatiable thirst for adventure and blood, and his speech, blended of sporting slang and classical allusion. The historical innovation which Lawrence effects is the endowment of the superhumanly immoral person with heroic qualities and social aplomb. Muscular blackguardism, composed of Byronic and berserker traits (Carlyle and others having brought the sagas into fashion) replaces muscular Christianity. In her early novels of society, Ouida is of the lineage of Lawrence; like him, she extends the world of *Vivian Grey* and *Pelham* on the side of sport; for, total ignorance, except by hearsay, did not prevent her from writing voluminously and with diverting inaccuracy upon every kind of masculine affair. She created artists of the sated Byronic type, and, in especial, superbly insolent guardsmen, exquisite animals, basking in exotic luxury, affecting languor and boredom in the midst of prodigious heroism, equally irresistible in the boudoir, the chase and the battlefield and faithful even in death to their singular code of loyalty. The type is worth notice because it forms the model of the aristocratic hero of novelette literature. For her delineation, in flushed and ornate language, of these military heroes and their world, Ouida has suffered the full measure of ridicule. In truth, her world is operatic rather than romantic, twice removed from reality; nevertheless, within it, she has many gifts, emotional energy, narrative power, the sense of action, a conception of heroism and fidelity, an eye for beauty of scene whether of the warm luxuriance of Italy or of the cooler flower-haunted spaces of Brabant. Her *vivandière* Cigarette, in *Under Two Flags* (1867), comes near to poetry, in her last ride and death; as does the deserted Italian child Musa of *In Maremma* (1882), in her innocence, devotion and suffering. When she curbs her constitutional extravagance, Ouida has command of moving pathos and of a purer style, as in the idyllic *Two Little Wooden Shoes*

(1874), in the best of her animal stories *A Dog of Flanders* (1872) and in some of the children's stories in *Bimbi* (1882). Though her flamboyant style is now out of date, Ouida's outspokenness, rebellious instinct and not altogether specious cosmopolitanism played some part in widening the scope of the novel.

One other considerable development, due to lesser novelists, remains to be chronicled—a new form of the novel of crime, in which the interest turns upon pursuit and detection[1]. Godwin's *Caleb Williams* (1794) is a tentative anticipation. A great fillip was given to the type by the publication in France of Vidocq's *Mémoires* in 1828—9 (Poe's *Murders in the Rue Morgue* is of the year 1841). An early example in England is the *Paul Ferroll* (1855), of Mrs Archer Clive (who is identical with the poetess V.[2] appreciated in *Horae Subsecivae*). *Paul Ferroll* is an admirably restrained story of concealed crime ; the interest, however, is not that of detection, but of the approaching moment at which the murderer must confess in order to save innocent suspects.

The chief master of the devices of the art in England is William Wilkie Collins, the contemporary of Émile Gaboriau in France ; Collins discovered his *métier* in *The Woman in White*, which appeared in *All the Year Round* in 1860. The method is the long pertinacious unravelling of a skein of crime, not by the professional detective, but by a person with a compelling human interest in the elucidation—a more artistic thing than Gaboriau's interpolated biographies. Surprises and false trails keep curiosity on the rack ; the struggle for concealed documents or treasure adds the interest of action ; deeds done in abnormal mental states add the touch of mystery; and the encounter of cunning with cunning, as between Godfrey Ablewhite and the Indians in *The Moonstone* (1868), or between Mrs Lecount and captain Wragge in *No Name* (1862), blends with other sensational elements that of constantly stimulated excitement. Collins brings to bear, also, his accurate knowledge of law, medicine, chemistry, drugs (he was an opium taker), hypnotism and somnambulism. He has the power of generating the atmosphere of foreboding, and of imparting to natural scenes a desolation which befits depression and horror of spirit. Most characteristic of his method is the telling of the story by means of diaries, letters and memoranda supposed to be contributed by the chief actors ; out

---

[1] Cf. Chandler, F. W., *The Literature of Roguery*, vol. II, p. 524.
[2] See, *ante*, chap. VI.

of these materials, he creates a mental labyrinth through the intricate windings of which he conducts the reader, rarely, if ever, losing his bearings, whether as to time, place or person. His tales are saved from being mere literary mathematics by the animation and Dickensian 'humours' of the puppets; we recall Miss Clack by her incontinent evangelism, Betteridge by his admiration for Robinson Crusoe, count Fosco by his corpulence and velvet tread, his magnetic glance and his menagerie of pets; the creation of Fosco is a remarkable effort, composed, as he is, of reflections seen in the mirrors of many different minds. Swinburne has called attention to the author's way of letting stories depend at crucial moments upon characters disordered in mind or body Relying, in the Victorian manner, upon variety rather than upon concentration of interest, Collins's books have a ponderous air (some of his shorter tales excepted) as compared with the economical technique of Poe, or with modern forms of the detective tale which turn upon quick deductions from meticulous detail, discard lumber and aim at a consistent psychology.

The influence of Wilkie Collins was widespread and various; upon Dickens, it was large and reciprocal; the convivial *Letters of Charles Dickens to Wilkie Collins* are full of discussions of intrigues and plots. Collins set a standard of orderly and well knit narrative at a time when both the example of the masters of fiction and the methods of publication, whether in parts or by instalments in magazines, tended to chaotic construction Writers such as James Payn, Miss Braddon and Sir Walter Besant have this skill in composition and combine with it miscellaneous gifts of humour, observation and power to hold attention. But, in the case of these writers, however talented they may be, we are conscious that the impulse which began about 1848 is exhausted. Fiction becomes more and more competent in workmanship, while its themes, characters, scenes and standards become conventionalised. One writer, however, is untouched by these processes—Mark Rutherford (William Hale White). He delineated a noteworthy phase of English life, that of provincial dissent, at the moment when its younger educated ministers became aware of the shaken bases of the beliefs accepted by their congregations. The perplexity and misery of the sincere and thoughtful pastor's situation are revealed with subtle insight and with the poignancy of actual experience in the Mark Rutherford books and in *The Revolution in Tanner's Lane* (1887). The undercurrent of sadness which runs through his pages has,

however, a still deeper cause, namely the constant baffling of the
mind in the pursuit of absolute truth. Rutherford—himself an
authoritative interpreter of Spinoza—commends the avoidance of
metaphysical enquiry to those who value peace of mind. Thought,
deeply pondered, emotional sincerity, vivid descriptive power and
critical restraint distinguish the prose of this singular writer.
Apart from him, the lesser novelists show few signs of originality
until the influence of continental realism comes, belated, to
England through later writers of the first rank.

CHAPTER XIV

GEORGE MEREDITH, SAMUEL BUTLER, GEORGE GISSING

GEORGE MEREDITH was born on 12 February 1828, of parents in both of whom there was a rather remote strain of Celtic blood, Welsh in his father, Irish in his mother. At the age of fourteen, he was sent for two years to the Moravian school at Neuwied. On his return, he came into contact with literary people, among them the son and daughter of Thomas Love Peacock, to whom he dedicated his first published volume, *Poems*, in 1851. In 1849, he married Mary Ellen Nicolls, a widowed daughter of Peacock. Meredith then abandoned the law (he had been articled to a solicitor) and turned to literature and journalism for support. His early contributions to various periodicals[1], together with a first version of *Love in a Valley*, were gathered into the volume named above. He established relations, which continued till about the year 1866, with *The Ipswich Journal*, *Once a Week* and *The Morning Post*. His closest relations, later, were with *The Fortnightly Review*, in which much of his work first appeared; for a brief space, in 1867, he was acting-editor. His first wife, from whom he was separated in 1858, died in 1861. He took a room in Rossetti's house at Chelsea in 1861, but made little use of it, though the friendship established with Swinburne, at that time, bore fruit in the latter's vindication of *Modern Love* in *The Spectator*, 7 June 1862. He became reader to the firm of Chapman and Hall in 1860, and continued in that office for some thirty-five years. In 1864, he married his second wife Marie Vulliamy, to whom, in his poem *A Faith on Trial*, he paid tribute on her death in 1885. He had taken up his residence at Flint cottage, Box Hill, in 1865, and this remained his home until his death on 18 May 1909.

---

[1] Dates of Meredith's known contributions to periodicals are given in *A chronological list of George Meredith's publications*, 1849—1911, by Arundell Esdaile, 1914

A rather loose grouping of the novels may be suggested. The exotic stories *The Shaving of Shagpat* (1856), and *Farina* (1857), have a rich vein of burlesque fantasy and romance which runs on into the earlier novels, especially in characters such as the countess de Saldar and Richmond Roy. To Meredith's maturer taste, when he was revising his novels for later editions in 1878 and 1897, the farcical ebullience of *The Ordeal of Richard Feverel* and *Evan Harrington* seemed excessive, and he pruned them with an austerity which alters the proportions of the tales. *The Ordeal of Richard Feverel* (1859), *Evan Harrington* (1861), *Emilia in England* (1864) (the title was changed to *Sandra Belloni* in 1887) and *The Adventures of Harry Richmond* (1871), all deal with the upbringing of well-born youth to the stage of 'capable manhood.' *Rhoda Fleming* (1865) differs from them in giving prominence to figures of the yeoman class, who, in the earlier novels, are subsidiary. In *Vittoria* (1867), *Beauchamp's Career* (1875) and, to a less degree, in *The Tragic Comedians* (1880) the novelist takes a wider sweep of vision over the world of politics in England and Germany and of high national aspiration in Italy. The short stories, or, rather, the short novels, *The House on the Beach* (1877), *The Case of General Ople and Lady Camper* (1877) and *The Tale of Chloe* (1879), may be grouped together with *The Gentleman of Fifty and the Damsel of Nineteen*, which was not published till 1910. *The Egoist* stands apart, not only in the latter half of the nineteenth century, but even among Meredith's novels, by its complete originality of attitude and technique, the clues to which are disclosed in the essay *On the Idea of Comedy and the Uses of the Comic Spirit* (1877). The four novels *Diana of the Crossways* (1885), *One of Our Conquerors* (1891), *Lord Ormont and his Aminta* (1894) and *The Amazing Marriage* (1895), have in common a chivalrous advocacy of women compromised in honour and in pride by masculine despotism; three of the instances have some historical foundation ; the working out of the situation in *Diana of the Crossways* admittedly departs from historical facts in the climax of the story. The early-written and unfinished *Celt and Saxon*, published in 1910, has resemblances to *Diana of the Crossways*, in particular in its criticism of English temperament. Throughout his career, Meredith continued, without public encouragement, the writing of verse, which, from time to time, was gathered into volumes. In 1862 appeared *Modern Love*, the poet's tragic masterpiece. Some of the poems, printed in the same volume, are in a mood characteristic of Stevenson and of Borrow, with whose Isopel Berners Meredith's portrait of Kiomi may well compare. The volumes *Poems and Lyrics of the Joy of Earth* (1883), *A Reading of Earth* (1888) and *A Reading of Life* (1901), in which, chiefly, Meredith sets forth his cult of 'earth,' stand high in the tradition of metaphysical poetry bequeathed by Wordsworth and Shelley. The work contained in *Ballads and Poems of Tragic Life* (1887) challenges comparison with similar productions of Rossetti, Swinburne and Morris ; *The Empty Purse* was published in 1892 ; the poems in *Odes in Contribution to the Song of French History* (1898) are, in form and thought, allied to the political odes with which Coleridge, Shelley and Swinburne, earlier in the century, had celebrated, the struggle of liberty against tyranny A final collection, *Last Poems*, was published in 1909

Meredith began to write at a time when Dickens, Thackeray, Browning and Tennyson were at the height of their powers and when George Eliot was hardly known ; he is not, in any strict sense, either the disciple or the founder of a school—nevertheless, he receives and hands down many traditions. Deep traces are left upon his thought by the poets of the school of Wordsworth, and by Carlyle, whose influence is tempered by that of Goethe ; indirectly, science taught him accuracy of observation and the elimination of vague optimism. The lingering feudal society he depicts, with its caste-feeling, its medieval view of women, its indifference to thought, its instinct for command, its loyal retinue and its fringe of social aspirants, is the background familiar in the English novel of manners ; the temper in which the portrayal is done is that of keen onlookers, such as Saint-Simon and Molière. Touches of poetic fantasy and caricature (and the praise of old wine) remind us of Peacock. But, when all these links are admitted, the isolation of Meredith (eccentricity, some call it) remains. It is due, in part, to his revulsion from the sentimentality of English, and the realism of French, fiction ; in part, to his rich endowment of the quality which used to be called Celtic ; in part, to the fact that he studies a stratum of experience of an uncommon order ; most of all is it due to the fact that he carried further than any contemporary artist, not excepting Browning, the process of intellectualisation which set in at the middle of the century. This process is manifest in Meredith in various ways ; in his analytical method, in his curbing of emotion, in the prevalence of his wit, above all in his complete re-interpretation of the moral idea. This is what George Eliot essayed, but with too many prepossessions. Meredith had none. He envisaged afresh the whole area of life—natural, human and universal—and aimed at ensuring the truth of his delineations of particular characters and incidents by their consistency with this wide survey. This is his meaning when he stipulates, in *Diana of the Crossways*, that novelists should turn to philosophy rather than to realism (which Meredith was apt to misjudge). The full purport of his novels is not, therefore, to be grasped except in the light of such poems as *The Woods of Westermain, Earth and Man, The Thrush in February* and *The Test of Manhood*. The key is the idea of an evolution carried on into the spheres of mind and spirit. Life is a continuous unfolding of the germinal powers of earth until the spiritual essence in earthly things is liberated. Blood, brain and spirit are the names given to the successive stages of the process. The instincts of the blood govern the primal man ; they breed a progeny of evil and, for this, the ascetic would eradicate them ; but, at the same time, they are, in the poet's view, the means by which man keeps firm hold on life, by which he realises his ancestral kinship with 'earth.' Earth fosters him, allays his fevered blood and prompts him forward. In the strife between the nobler and the baser parts of man, brain is evolved ; men learn that there are unalterable laws, accommodate themselves to a social order, perceive in self-control and fellowship the conditions of welfare and the direction of progress. The brute part of man is ill at ease in this environment, and the shifts of the 'rebel heart' and the 'dragon self' afford material for a great part of Meredithean comedy. Spiritual valiancy, which is tried in passionate ordeals of love, friendship and patriotism, is the final goal ; the 'warriors of the sighting brain' are the ideal type. The sanction of this ethical code is found in the 'good of the race,' the most prevalent idea in Meredith's writing.

The scheme of thought thus baldly abstracted from the poems underlies all Meredith's picturing of the human condition ; as may be seen in many instances. Such an inter-relation of man and nature as is suggested by this doctrine explains how 'earth' can resume her suspended spiritual purpose in men ; it is through the senses that nature works to withhold Susan from tragic error in the poem *Earth and a Wedded Woman* ; and through the senses that the fevered spirit of Richard Feverel is bathed and cleansed in the storm of the Rhine forest ; phrases such as Nataly Radnor's 'Earth makes all sweet' and the equally characteristic 'Carry your fever to the Alps' are steeped in the Meredithean creed.

The identity of human life and nature is so complete that, at supreme moments, passion seeks expression in the language of nature; the surrounding scene prolongs the ecstasy of Richard and Lucy at the weir; the waves are richer in meaning than words for Matey and Aminta. Through this identity of human and natural law comes the perfect fusion of sensuous glory and symbolic truth which characterises the poet's *Meditation under Stars, Dirge in Woods* and *Ode to the Spirit of Earth in Autumn.* The deep veining of Meredith's creative work by his thought may be seen, again, in his studies of the mating of the sexes; rhetorical emotion on the theme of love gave way in France to a pitiless insistence upon physical aspects of passion. Meredith, though equally suspicious of mere sentiment, nevertheless keeps the ideal aspects of love uppermost; to him it is a force 'wrought of the elements of our being.' The unions which win his sanction are those in which passion, mind and spirit each find due response after sharp and long-during trial; from these unions are to come 'certain nobler races now very dimly descried.' His most brilliant diagnosis is practised upon alliances which fail in one or other of those regards, as, for instance, in *A Ballad of Fair Ladies in Revolt*; in *The Sage Enamoured and the Honest Lady*; in darker and intenser mood, in *Modern Love* and in the characters of later novels, Diana, Nesta, Aminta, Carinthia, who add to the qualities of Victorian heroines the greater power of intellect, the 'more brain' which Meredith's ideal of womanhood required and all that follows thence of dignity and largeness of character. From the doctrine embodied in the poems is derived, also, a juster and more delicate scale of judgment for motive and action, a scale called for by the ever-growing consciousness of the complexity of character and morality. Meredith has made it incumbent upon the novelist of the future to take into account remote hidden origins as well as the diverse play of the more immediate forces which shape character. Seen in the perspective of the poet's thought, the egotist Sir Willoughby Patterne proves to be 'the brutish antique' prolonged into the civilised state, and 'become fiercely imaginative in whatsoever concerns himself.' Sentimentalism has its roots, also, in the primitive man; it is a sophisticated form of the instinct of sex; in Diana Warwick's phrase, it is 'fiddling harmonics on the strings of sensualism.' Alvan-Lassalle[1] is brought nearer to comprehension by the same scale; the instance is the more germane because Meredith did not

---

[1] Cf. *The Tragic Comedians*, chap. XIX.

invent either the character or the story. The fine adjustment of the claims of blood, brain and spirit is the ideal illustrated in his grander figures ; Mazzini, 'an orbed mind supplying its own philosophy,' Carinthia, and Vittoria, whose nature, compounded of the elements of woman, patriot and artist, was 'subdued by her own force.' Finally, the conception of retribution in the poems and novels shakes off the scriptural and puritan accretions which cumbered George Eliot ; other orders of human error and punishment come to light, as in the instances of Sir Austin Feverel, Victor Radnor and lord Ormont. On the largest scale, in *Odes in Contribution to the Song of French History*, Meredith's ethic reveals Sedan as the expiation of the errors of seventy years before, when, rejecting her spiritual lover, liberty, France yielded to the glamour of Napoleon.

Meredith summoned the novelist to define not only his philosophy but, also, the temper and intention with which he proposed to depict society. He symbolised the ideal attitude in his creation of the comic spirit, an emanation of 'earth,' and, therefore, endowed with sanity, clear vision, inborn purity and sympathy with the final purpose of 'earth.' Politely but relentlessly, it fulfils its office as guardian spirit of a civilisation of which the members are but quasi-civilised. 'Accord' is its social aim ; it seeks out, therefore, not the obvious sinners, with whom the moralist can deal simply and well, but the Patternes, Poles, Daciers and Fleetwoods, in whom lurking savage instincts are concealed by surface veneer and rectitude. The weapon of the comic spirit is the 'silvery laughter of the mind'; its strokes take the form of satire, humour, wit or irony. It is clear that the comic spirit is a new form of the ideal observer, already known in the Greek chorus, in the spirit of Aristophanes and of Molière and of others reviewed in Meredith's *Essay on Comedy*, in Addison's Mr Spectator, in Goldsmith's Chinaman ; the comic spirit ranges over a wider field in the novel, exercises a more incessant vigilance in its efforts to reconcile the diverse aims of society.

There are two main kinds of structure in Meredith : one, a highly individual form in which an outstanding character appears constantly in the centre of the stage in a succession of loosely connected scenes, for which the focus and angle of vision are determined by the comic spirit. The method is exemplified in miniature in *The Case of General Ople and Lady Camper*, and, at full length, in *The Egoist* ; the model is evidently that of comedy ; *The Egoist* is called a 'comedy in narrative'; if *Le Misanthrope* could be magnified to the proportions of the novel, we should have an exact counterpart. The alternative kind of structure is, however, more common in Meredith. In it is outlined a prolonged situation depending upon delicate adjustments of honour, passion and aspiration in many characters; very often, some kind of problem lies behind the story—educational in *The Ordeal of Richard Feverel*, political in *Beauchamp's Career*, social in *One of Our Conquerors*. The play of influences from nature is, also, unremitting. Action and the older sort of plot can almost be dispensed with; they are exchanged for large organic conception, knowledge of the subterranean processes by which idea and will gather force and externalise themselves, intuition as to the time and places at which the tension and the disturbing vibrations will work towards dramatic conjunctions—such, for instance, as Beauchamp's final encounter with Renée de Croisnel, where we witness the long-impending collision between incompatible French and English customs; or the deep-founded misunderstanding which precedes the apology of lord Romfrey to doctor Shrapnel. The former kind of novel, the comedy in narrative, presents figures, such as Sir Willoughby, who are both individual and typical, after the fashion of Molière's Tartufe or Harpagon; the latter kind, the novel of highly charged situation, presents its characters in more relations and with a more vivid sense of complex personality. In both kinds, we draw our conception of character chiefly from two sources: the first, speech and dialogue, which are idealised and extended so that they offer the largest sensitive surface whereon character may leave its impress; the second, the analysis, sure, delicate and exhaustive, of motive and feeling. In this analysis, Meredith is a realist (though there are occasional failures, such as the central incident of *Diana of the Crossways*), and his figures are distinguished from the pleasing shadows of romance. At times, we feel, as in George Eliot's works, that the novelist is helping us by lucid and dispassionate reasoning to understand a figure viewed as through a glass window; but, in the more notable characters, especially those of women, we feel ourselves continually in the presence of personalities quick with nervous and spiritual vitality and having the power on their own account to engage our concern and memory. Lucy, Rose, Kiomi, Vittoria, Renée, Clara Middleton, Nesta, Carinthia, are as vivid in gesture, speech and movement, in varied mood and in the quality they impart to our own humour, as any figures in nineteenth-century fiction. Meredith's boys are creations of profound insight; his men, even those cast in the mould of Vernon Whitford, do not, in general, lodge so securely in the memory. A rare gift of characterisation, which Meredith possesses in the highest degree, is that of calling into being figures belonging to other nationalities; his Welsh and French and Italian creations are marked both by completeness and by subtlety; this is the basis of the historical power which gives abiding value to the picture of the rising under Mazzini in *Vittoria,* and to that of Napoleon in *Odes in Contribution to the Song of French History.* It is worth notice that, in the main, the analytical method is only practised upon the complex, sophisticated people of the leisured world; the simpler classes are delineated in other ways; for instance, Mrs Berry, who is alive, and Jack Raikes, who is moribund, are in Dickens's manner of humorous exaggeration. Meredith's rustics are apt to savour chiefly of beef and beer. The exception to the avoidance of psychology in the case of humbler folk is in the part of *Rhoda Fleming* which deals with the yeoman's family; the age-long moulding influence of the Kentish soil, the inveigling of the weaker sister, Dahlia, and the savage virginal pride of Rhoda Fleming are set forth in the way of analysis.

The general effect of oracular allusiveness in Meredith's style appears, on examination, to arise mainly from incidental comment, in which the figurative and aphoristic elements, due, in some degree, to the influence of Carlyle and, therefore, indirectly of Jean Paul Richter, abound to such a degree that we often seem to be looking at similes and metaphors instead of at the thing which was to have been said. On the other hand, the narrative prose, and that directly expressive of character, has, in general, a fine precision, an almost ostentatious felicity of phrase and diction. The writings of La Bruyère, Saint-Simon and Stendhal are parallels and, sometimes, models, for the clear exposition of intricate psychological and moral situations, and for the predilection for wit and epigram, which overflow into receptacles such as 'The Pilgrim's Scrip' and 'Maxims for Men.' The pervasive irony, exultancy and poetic distinction of Meredith's writing are native to his own mind. In his middle years, he seems to have retorted upon public indifference by a wilful disregard for the convenience of his readers; he avoids simplicity and indulges in fantastic circumlocution; he sacrifices more and more of the narrative quality, of which, on occasion, as in the duel in the Stelvio pass, he is a master, in favour of effects derived from witty and ironical analogy; there is a wasteful fusillade of phrases which do not carry us forward; imagery, at all times too prodigal, becomes bewildering in its protean transformations. It is unfortunate that these excesses culminate in the early part of *One of Our Conquerors*, and thus bar the way to Meredith's most delicate and poetic study of awakening womanhood, the character of Nesta Victoria Radnor. His poetic style has other features, due, in part, to a revulsion from the manner of *Idylls of the King*, in part to the concentration which was his declared method of craftsmanship. Unessentials are shorn away until words are left to stand side by side, each preserving, sphinx-like, the secret which connects it with other words; it is certain that not all the satisfaction which comes with comprehension arises from poetic sources. At the same time, as in all poets of insubordinate intellect—Donne, Chapman, Browning and others—there are supreme imaginative passages, pellucid in diction, and of radiant beauty and entrancing music.

Meredith is a great metrical experimenter. He devises new forms of stanza in *Modern Love, Hymn to Colour, A Ballad of Fair Ladies in Revolt* (where the rhythm sustains admirably the sense of keen spontaneous debate), *Love in a Valley* (which plays exquisite variations upon a nursery measure), *Earth and Man* and *The Thrush in February* (two variants of the gnomic quatrain). His tragic ballads invite comparison with similar forms in Rossetti, Morris and Swinburne; his sonnets are very various in theme, temper and structure; one of them, *Lucifer in Starlight*, is among the most remarkable technical achievements of Meredith; it evokes the full epic strain of Milton from the restricted keyboard of the brief sonnet form. The travail of creation tortures the form of much of Meredith's poetry; the *Lucifer* sonnet has the repose of perfect achievement. Individual effects are attained, also, in his continuous measures; in the iambic movement of the consummate lyric outburst *The Lark Ascending*; in the anapaestic trimeters of *The Day of the Daughter of Hades* and *A Faith on Trial*, the freedom of equivalence and substitution (and, in the former case, of rime) preserves the emphasis of meaning from the too great insistence of the metrical beat—the pitfall of this metre. *The Woods of Westermain* and *The Nuptials of Attila* are in the trochaic tetrameter catalectic; in the latter poem, the impression of primitive violence in the theme is reinforced by the persistence of four strong stresses within a short line of seven syllables, and by the entire avoidance of weak syllables either at the beginning or the end of the line. *Phaéthôn*, a splendid, if rather free, attempt, in galliambic measure, for which Meredith names the *Attis* of Catullus as his model, and *Phoebus with Admetus*, with its three successive strong stresses at the end of the even lines, and the use of pauses to complete the length of the line, are other instances of the research and the testing of metrical possibilities by the inner ear which impart a fresh and unfamiliar music to his verse. There is evidence that, by its imaginative, intellectual and metrical daring, and by its opening of new springs of poetical inspiration, Meredith's verse has more immediate bearing upon the practice of following writers than his novels ; for, though it is admitted that he has set a high standard to which the novel must attain, if it would be ranked as literature, nevertheless, fiction has quite notably discarded his philosophic way, and is committed to the path entered upon, not with his approval, by the realists.

Samuel Butler was born on 4 December 1835 at Langar rectory, Nottingham ; he was the son of Thomas Butler and grandson of Samuel Butler, headmaster of Shrewsbury school and bishop of Lichfield. Samuel Butler was bracketed twelfth in the first class of the classical tripos at Cambridge in 1858. In the following year, abandoning his intention of taking orders, he went to New Zealand and successfully managed a sheep-run. Some of his leisure was spent in writing for *The Press*, Christchurch, New Zealand, the articles *Darwin on the Origin of Species* (1862) and *Darwin among the Machines* (1863) which were afterwards expanded into *Erewhon* and *Life and Habit*. A volume published in 1863, *A First Year in Canterbury Settlement*, is composed of his letters from the colony. Returning to England in 1864, he settled for the remainder of his life in Clifford's inn. He studied painting and exhibited at the Royal Academy between the years 1868 and 1876. *Erewhon* was published in 1872 ; *The Fair Haven* (1873) provides an ironical setting for the matter of his pamphlet *The Evidence for the Resurrection of Jesus Christ*, written in 1865. Meantime, he had begun, about 1872, *The Way of all Flesh* ; it was laid aside in 1885, and not published till 1903. *A Psalm of Montreal* was written in Canada in 1875. His books of scientific controversy include *Life and Habit* (1877), *Evolution Old and New* and *God the Known and God the Unknown* in 1879, *Unconscious Memory* (1880), *Luck or Cunning* (1887), and the essays *The Deadlock in Darwinism* (1890). His Italian journeys led to the publication, in 1881, of *Alps and Sanctuaries of Piedmont and the Canton Ticino.* His close interest in the art of the Sacro Monte at Varallo-Sesia, especially in that of the artist Tabachetti, is reflected in *Ex Voto* (1888). A number of essays appeared in *The Universal Review*, between the years 1888 and 1890 ; in 1896 was published *The Life and Letters of Dr Samuel Butler.* Butler's admiration for Handel's music, an admiration dating from his boyhood and constantly increasing, led to his attempt to compose in the Handelian manner, collaborating with Henry Festing Jones. One of the subjects chosen as libretto for an oratorio was Ulysses, and, hence, arose an independent study of the Homeric poems, from which resulted Butler's theories of the feminine authorship and Trapanese origin of the *Odyssey.* The substance of many pamphlets and lectures on the subject is contained in *The Authoress of the Odyssey,* published in 1897. He also made prose translations, in a vigorous homely idiom which he called Tottenham Court road English, of the *Iliad* (in 1898) and of the *Odyssey* (in 1900). In 1899 appeared *Shakespeare's Sonnets, reconsidered and in part re-arranged,* in which he combated the view that the poems were academic exercises, and contended that Mr W. H. was a plebeian of low character. These literary controversies illustrate Butler's antipathy to professional critics, and his view that the function of criticism is to disengage the personality of an artist from his medium of expression. *Erewhon Revisited* was published in 1901. Butler died on 18 June 1902. A selection from his manuscript note-books appeared in 1912, under the title *The Note-Books of Samuel Butler.*

Only the briefest reference is possible to Butler's scientific discussions. His interest in them was lifelong, and he imparted to them, at times, an angry temper born of his belief that he was flouted by an oligarchy of men of science, who regarded him as an amateur because he was not a professional collector and experimenter. He accepted all their facts ; but he challenged their interpretations on the ground of what he deemed was their loose reasoning. His contentions turn chiefly upon two points : first, the restoration of the idea of design to the philosophy of evolution—not the old teleological design of Buffon, Lamarck and Erasmus Darwin, but a cunning and will inherent in each separate cell to shape the chances of its environment to ends of comfort and stability. Secondly, he put forward a conception of heredity based on the continuity of each generation with all its predecessors, and the transmission of serviceable habits stored up by unconscious memory. These conclusions are now, in a provisional way, accepted; but the debate has passed away from this region and is concentrated for the present upon the internal economy of the reproductive cell.

Butler's place in literature, however, must be finally determined by his genius as satirist and essayist, as illustrated in *Erewhon*, *Erewhon Revisited*, *A Psalm of Montreal*, *The Way of all Flesh*, *Alps and Sanctuaries* and *The Note-Books*. *Erewhon* was published in 1872 ; Butler's was not a solitary voice ; Carlyle had thundered ; Ruskin and Morris had entered the plea for beauty ; Matthew Arnold, in *Friendship's Garland* (1871), and Meredith had given warning of the shadow looming from the continent upon complacent prosperity in England. But the appeal, in these cases, is to the nation collectively ; some practical reform is in view. Butler's attitude is different; he does not vaticinate ; he has little to say of industry or of democracy. But he is struck by evidences on all sides of the stagnation of thought. In religion, thought, emptied of its propulsive energy, has sunk into the moribund system of the musical banks ; in education, the universities are busied in suppressing originality and cultivating evasion ; youthful mental vigour is dulled by grinding for many years at the hypothetical language ; professors are afflicted with the 'fear-of-giving-themselves-away-disease.' In science, there has been a promising upheaval in the coming of Darwinism ; but the English aversion from mental effort is in process of making Darwinism into a pontifical system for comfortable acceptance. Butler carried on a ceaseless crusade to save science from the fate of the musical banks. In the family, schools and churches, tyrannies have been set up which have vested interests in mental stupor and convention, and which permeate the atmosphere with cant and hypocrisy convenient to themselves. These things are the customary targets for the satirist of the Victorian compromise ; and, when that phase has passed away as completely as the commonwealth phase, *Erewhon* will need a commentary as *Hudibras* does. But there is a profounder criticism in *Erewhon* ; it is embodied in the paradoxical interchange of moral misdemeanour with physical ailment. This is the basis of a classic piece of ironical prose, descriptive of the trial of a youth, who, after being convicted of aggravated bronchitis, is, a year later, condemned on a charge of pulmonary consumption. An obvious interpretation is that the passage is a plea against the puritanic morality which isolates and condemns the individual without consideration of environment, heredity or other uncontrollable factors. This would be the position of a modern humanitarian, who would acknowledge a deep intellectual debt to Butler. Behind this interpretation, however, lies a conception which gives a clue to a large portion of Butler's writing. 'Good-breeding' is the corner-stone of his system, and, in implication, he identifies morality with health; he draws a contrast between puritanism and paganism, if the word may be applied to the ideal of grace, strength and courtesy which gives *Erewhon* its resemblance to *Utopia*. The same idea comes out in his comment on *The Pilgrim's Progress*, which, he says, 'consists mainly of a series of infamous libels upon men and things.' The same opposition, fundamentally that between ἀγάπη and γνῶσις, between spirit and letter, is set forth in sardonic form in his masterpiece *A Psalm of Montreal*; the Discobolus, the emblem of pagan grace, is thrust aside in deference to a person who boasts of his second-hand morality and thrives by a craft which simulates life.

The most illuminating parallel to *Erewhon* is the obvious one, Swift's *Gulliver's Travels*. Both authors adopt the ironical method according to which a commonplace person carries with him his own ingrained prepossessions when he comes upon a race with bodily and mental habits, equally deep-rooted, but long ago given a different direction. Both authors preserve an episcopal gravity while they prolong and enrich the fantasy with witty inventions and oddities of synthesis. Both are wanting in poetic endowment, but rich in the humorous, pictorial gift which has the enduring quality of poetry. Both wield a style keen, serried, precise in an unstudied way, and, at the same time, flexible, calling to mind the image of a Toledo blade. Swift, an eighteenth century politician, has the sharper eye for the hot antagonisms of sects and parties; Butler, for hypocritical mental jugglery; Swift's Laputans enshrine the prejudice of Scriblerus against science; Butler's hostility is for any kind of academicism. Swift, with his acuity of vision for human injustice, portrays it with the passionate self-torturing anger which flames in the later parts of *Gulliver*. Butler sees a perverse indifference to commonsense and, for the most part, paints it with a cool amused irony—the good form of his Ydgrunites—which has become a common trait in later fiction and essay writing.

Erewhon Revisited, published in 1901, is an ironist's way of using the conclusions to which *Essays and Reviews* (1860), and Seeley's *Natural Religion* (1882), had been tending years before.

The book is as much a sequel to *The Fair Haven* as it is to *Erewhon*. In his accustomed way, Butler plants a 'seedling idea,' in this case, the supposed miraculous ascent of Higgs from Erewhon twenty years before. In ironical analogy, he traces from it the origin of religious myth, of sacrosanct scriptures, of legend and sophistry crystallising round public credulity and of the exploiting of the new religion by unscrupulous professional magnates such as Hanky and Panky. *Erewhon Revisited* has less of the free imaginative play of its predecessor; it is apt to seem, in that respect, sterilised and rigid, like the later satires of Swift; but, in sharp brilliance of wit and criticism, in intellectual unity and coherence, it surpasses *Erewhon*. All the skill which Butler had acquired by his controversies in marshalling evidence and in reviewing a whole system of thought in all its bearings is put to the happiest use, especially in the effects of climax made possible by the structural perfection of the work; the furious outburst of Higgs against Hanky, for instance, in the cathedral; and, again, the ecclesiastical round table conference, debating whether Sunchildism shall be supported as a supernatural religion or not—a perfect piece of high intellectual comedy.

There is, apparently, a Voltairean subversiveness about all this which may obscure Butler's real view and intention. Voltaire is the supreme rationalist; Butler puts no excessive faith in reason; he found it, both in its extremes and in its mean, illogical. In *God the Known and God the Unknown,* he offers, seriously, though it is not usual with him to do so, conjectures which transcend reason. He had, moreover, the utmost respect for certain simple religious tenets, which he defined in the concluding chapter of his *Life of Dr Butler*, and in the advice given by Higgs at the ecclesiastical conference, and which he saw, in a measure, exemplified in the religion of the Italian peasantry. He asserted, in jest, his membership 'of the more advanced wing of the Broad Church.'

Butler thought contemptuously of the fiction of his day, in comparison with that of the eighteenth century. *The Way of all Flesh* owes practically nothing to any tradition; its prodigality of idea and suggestion and wit has enabled men to quarry from it books, novels and essays ever since. Butler claimed for it that 'it contains records of things I saw happening rather than imaginary incidents'; it contained, also, things which he had undergone in his own experience. It is like a book of the reign of queen Anne, inspired by a controlled passion of hatred, which surges up with embittered unassuaged memories of youth. As always, Butler breaks down common classifications; he had already obliterated the distinctions between machinery and humanity, and between life and death ; in his novel, he tells the story, not so much of a character as of a family organism, insinuating its nature in the name Pontifex (a more successful effort of nomenclature than the mere inversions of *Erewhon*). The Pontifex cell is transmitted with modifications until it establishes itself in the English country rectory. Theobald Pontifex, at first a victim, and, afterwards, an inquisitor, is the unifying character ; the study of the formalised relationship of parents and children is the central theme. Theobald and Christina take up throughout the pontifical attitude of parents ; this premises, in the father, infallibility, and, in the mother, a recurring state of 'self-laudatory hallucination,' which finds consummate expression in Christina's letter, a brilliant piece of imaginative divination. The native iniquity of the child Ernest is to be trained until it evolves the ' virtues convenient to parents.' Ernest's boyhood, schooling and ordination proceed under this superimposed morality, which, like the system in *Richard Feverel*, bears the strain until adolescence bursts disastrously through it to get at the fresh air of reality. Ernest's misdemeanour and trial are the counterparts of those of the tuberculous youth in *Erewhon*. We learn without surprise that Ernest finally leaves his children in the charge of parents not their own. In these characterisations, there is an incisiveness of satirical effect which leaves a sting upon the memory and feeling ; for the sense of cynical disillusionment with which the first part of Theobald's honeymoon is drawn, we must seek a parallel in de Maupassant. There are more genial elements in the portraits of Alethea (Butler's friend Eliza Mary Ann Savage) and of Mrs Jupps, a pagan of the lower world, free from any shadow of scruple, and mistress of ' the oldë daunce.' Nevertheless, after a time, in spite of its range and fearlessness and truth, the book strikes us as one-sided; we feel as we do sometimes with Meredith's comic spirit that the pursuit is too relentless, the victim is in a hopeless case and the element of sport has gone out of the hunt.

A juster conception of Butler's nature is to be derived from *Alps and Sanctuaries*, in which sensitiveness to the genius of the place and people, humour, enthusiasm and love of beauty blend with the sharp flavour of his wit and clear sense, to produce a travel-book inimitable in its engaging idiosyncrasy. The same genial mind is at play in his brief essays, especially in one entitled *Quis Desiderio...?* in which he laments with airy and irreverent wit the disappearance from the shelves of the British Museum of *Frost's Lives of Eminent Christians*, a book which had served him for many years in the office of a desk.

Butler strove incessantly to irritate thought out of its inertness and convention and credulity, to challenge stifling authority and to undermine hypocrisy. For these purposes, he prepared and stored in his note-books 'little poisonous microbes of thought which the cells of the world would not know what to do with.' He applied them to society in book after book; but, as it seemed to him, in vain; in his own words, 'he was allowed to call his countrymen life-long self-deceivers to their faces, and they said it was quite true, but that it did not matter.' He has not the highest gifts of poetry or emotion, but he is very far from being a mere undiscriminating wit; he has, in the end, a constructive intention, not mockery, but the liberation of the spirit.

George Robert Gissing was born at Wakefield on 22 November 1857; at school, and at Owens college, Manchester, he worked with a furious energy, and seemed destined for a notable career in the academic world. His course was, however, cut short through an ill-starred marriage in 1875; he fled first to London, where he experienced the poverty and wretchedness described in many of his novels; and, afterwards, in 1876, to America, making use of that adventure in the narrative of Whelpdale in *New Grub Street*. After a brief stay in Germany, he returned to London, publishing his first novel *Workers in the Dawn*, at his own expense, in 1880. He made a precarious livelihood by private tuition, going without sufficient food, but steadfastly declining to take up journalism, which offered possible openings. The evidence is a little contradictory; but it seems that by the year 1882 Gissing had emerged from the bitterest of the miseries due to poverty. In 1884 appeared *The Unclassed*, in 1886 *Isabel Clarendon* and *Demos*, and, from that year until 1895, he published one or more books annually; in 1887 *Thyrza*; in 1888 *A Life's Morning*; in 1889 *The Nether World*; in 1890, in which year he entered upon a second unfortunate matrimonial venture, *The Emancipated*; in 1891 *New Grub Street*; in 1892 *Born in Exile* and the short *Denzil Quarrier*; in 1893 *The Odd Women*; in 1894 *In the Year of Jubilee*; and, in 1895, four books, *Eve's Ransom, Sleeping Fires, The Paying Guest* and *The Whirlpool. Human Odds and Ends*, a collection of short sketches, came out in 1898 and in the same year *Charles Dickens: A Critical Study*. Later writings connected with Dickens were the introductions to the (incomplete) Rochester edition beginning in 1900 ; *Dickens in Memory* (1902) ; the abridgment of *Forster's Life of Dickens* in the same year; and a chapter in *Homes and Haunts of Famous Authors*, published in 1906 after his death. Meanwhile, he had written *The Town Traveller* in 1898, *The Crown of Life* in 1899 and *Our Friend the Charlatan* in 1901. The two books that followed were of the essay kind, *By the Ionian Sea* (1901) and *The Private Papers of Henry Ryecroft* in 1903. After his death were published the unfinished *Veranilda* in 1904, *Will Warburton* in 1905 and a second volume of short stories, *The House of Cobwebs*, in 1906. Gissing died at the age of forty-six at St Jean de Luz on 28 December 1903.

The novels of Gissing bear all the marks of a period of transition ; they retain features of the passing Victorian type— sentimental, capacious, benevolently admonitory, plot-ridden ; at the same time, they adumbrate accepted modern forms, which picture a familiar 'slice of life' in a representation saturated with material detail, precise and complete in analysis of the inner world of thought and feeling. The transition was effected at an earlier time, and more consciously, in France, where its principles were formulated by apologists such as Taine, and theorists who were also practitioners, such as the disciples of Flaubert. Gissing was widely read in the fiction of the continent and uses his reading to finely critical purpose in the monograph on Dickens ; it is natural, therefore, to look in him for affinities with these continental writers.

The titles of some of Gissing's books give warrant to a suggestion advanced by one critic[1] that Gissing early burdened himself with a grandiose ambition of emulating Balzac's survey of the whole province of society ; but, in method of representation, there is little that is common to the art of the Frenchman, voracious of reality and teeming with products of his creative genius, and to the fastidious, resentful observation and record of the Englishman. There are points of resemblance, rather than of contact, with the circle of *Soirées de Médan* ; Gissing surveyed his world closely, but he is not 'documented' like the brothers

---

[1] *The Monthly Review*, August 1904 : 'George Gissing,' by H. G Wells.

de Goncourt[1]; he does not attain the controlled objectivity of his contemporary de Maupassant, though it is evident that, by Gissing's time, the question of the intervention of the artist in his work has become, what it was not to Dickens and Thackeray, an artistic problem. Gissing is like Zola in his portrayal of the submerged part of the population of towns and of the squalidness of poverty ; the crowds which gather in districts such as Hoxton, Lambeth and Clerkenwell are more like those of Zola than those of *Barnaby Rudge.* In Gissing's reading of men and women, amorousness, sometimes furtive, sometimes brutal, plays a large part. He is one of the earliest in English fiction to probe deeply into the psychology of sex ; though a certain reserve withholds him from the description of such fervid eroticism as leads to the study of remorse in *Thérèse Raquin.* Gissing was pre-occupied with the environment of poverty, and has little concern with heredity or with the procrustean bed of theory into which the history of the Rougon-Macquart family is forced. He does not deliberately practise the *roman expérimental* ; nevertheless, his treatment of poverty is not altogether unlike the Zolaesque studies of some aspect of commerce or creed or confirmed social habit. A distinction which Zola drew in the manifesto to *Thérèse Raquin* is developed in *Isabel Clarendon,* that between character and temperament. Bernard Kingcote, in that book, is a victim of nervous sensitiveness and exhaustion ; there are no such characterisations in Scott or Thackeray or Dickens. Both Zola and Gissing are apt to evade by some romantic device the full implication of the realistic method. A traceable link with all these writers is found in the thought of Schopenhauer, which leavened the whole mass of realistic fiction. Gissing's sojourn in Germany was given up to the reading of philosophers, chief among them Comte and Schopenhauer. The latter's influence appears constantly in the novels ; Gissing, in his first book, adopted from Schopenhauer his conception of social sympathy, though he quickly rejected it to become a social agnostic ; Schopenhauer's outlook of despair colours some of Gissing's most powerful writing ; it was on this social side that the novelist was influenced most ; Schopenhauer's view of women, applied with ruthless Latin logic by de Maupassant, does not affect Gissing ;

[1] In the privately printed *Letters from George Gissing to Edward Clodd*, the first letter mentions a note-book kept by Gissing containing a long list of barbarisms and superstitions among the lower classes of women in London; a letter printed in Edmund Gosse's *Questions at Issue* (1893) gives Gissing's observations on the reading of the poorer classes.

on the contrary, the delineation of finer feminine characters sets free all the latent idealism of Gissing's nature.

In truth, the term realist implies a homogeneity in his work which does not exist; his most realistic novel has prefixed to it a sentence from Renan which cuts at the root of realism : *La peinture d'un fumier peut être justifiée pourvu qu'il y pousse une belle fleur ; sans cela le fumier n'est que repoussant.* And, however much he may have derived from the practice of the continent, he is, at the same time, in direct continuance from English traditions. He admired and imitated Hogarth—a moralist; Dickens and Meredith left deep impressions on the two main sections of his work. The London of Dickens cast an enduring spell over his youthful imagination ; the *milieu* which he best describes is that of Dickens, the lower middle and the lowest classes. The differences in attitude between Dickens and his disciple are profound; poverty to Dickens was a soil rich in picturesque or sentimental idiosyncrasy; its vulgarity he transformed to magical humour ; its evils, he thought, could be remedied by large-hearted humanity. To Gissing, who was bred in the north of England, poverty was a desolate, mirthless waste on the borders of the evil kingdom of commerce. He does not, as Mrs Gaskell and Charles Reade do, much concern himself with the workshop or conflicts of capital and labour; but, with a profounder knowledge than Ruskin, Carlyle or Morris had when they revolted against its ugliness, he pictured the world of poverty, its streets and purlieus and dens, the whole atmosphere of it, squalid and without a vestige of beauty. Envy, jealousy and revenge are the reigning motives there; the brutal and cunning, such as Clem Peckover, in *The Nether World,* trample upon the impotent and degenerate Pennyloaf Candy and Bob Hewitt, and prey upon those whose instincts are humane, such as Jane Snowden and Sidney Kirkwood. The anatomy of poverty is carried out most fully in the novels *Demos, Thyrza, The Nether World, New Grub Street, Born in Exile, The Odd Women, In the Year of Jubilee, Eve's Ransom,* and in the short sketches contained in *Human Odds and Ends* and *The House of Cobwebs.* In some of these books is described the outcome of attempts at amelioration; Besant's *All Sorts and Conditions of Men* (1882) treats Gissing's material in a mood of resolute optimism ; Gissing is frankly pessimistic. In *Demos,* the suggested remedy of socialism leads to a mob-murder; and wealth, which comes unexpectedly to the lower middle class

family, the Mutimers, only leads to demoralisation. In *Thyrza,*
along with the presentation of the lovely though idealised figure
of Thyrza and her more human sister Lydia, there is a study of
the results of bringing education to the artisan ; the sole outcome
is the bitter tragedy which indirectly befalls the exceptionally
endowed workman Gilbert Grail. The finer characters of the
lower world are those untouched by education ; the wild, frank
Totty Nancarrow, and old Mrs Mutimer, Richard Mutimer's
mother ; the dumb, instinctive honesty of her protest against his
despicable manoeuvre is one of the most masterly, and one of the
few heroic, things in Gissing. In general, his dramatic episodes
are not those depicting resistance.

In all the books named above it is evident that Gissing, a born
hedonist, hated the scene he was portraying ; he could not at
any time sink his own standards, nor could he comprehend the
factors—custom, comradeship, the lowered demand upon life and
characteristic forms of courage and humour—by which their lot
is rendered tolerable to the poor. The picture of poverty is seen
in pleasanter lights (and presented in a less substantial medium)
in the later books, *The Town Traveller* and *Will Warburton.*

Certain of the novels, *New Grub Street, Born in Exile* and
The Odd Women portray a rather higher stratum of society,
whose origins are in the suburbs or the provinces ; but the
malignant effects of poverty or obscure birth invade this region
also. The theme is frequently the endeavour of one born in an
inferior station to grasp at the advantages of culture or ease for
which, by intellect or temperament, he or she is fitted, but
excluded by lack of money or by defect of social aptitude ; it is
the case with Godwin Peak and with Eve Madeley ; they both
seek their prize by dishonourable means ; both, in some shifty
way, have to disavow an earlier hampering alliance ; these de-
teriorations are traced back to poverty. The novels last named
also work out vigorously, and without dogmatism (which Gissing
could not tolerate), problems arising out of distinctly modern
conditions. They exhibit a complete change of temper from the
attacks made on abuses with reforming intent by Dickens and
Reade. In *New Grub Street,* there is the problem of conscience
in the conditions of modern journalism ; in *Born in Exile,*
the conflict between religion and science ; in *The Odd Women,*
the status of women made conscious of their unpreparedness and
superfluousness when the sheltering home collapses. Some of
Gissing's finest work in the more strictly defined business of the

novelist is in these three books; the characterisation in *New Grub Street* of Alfred Yule—pedantic, unimaginatively sincere, ageing, beset by minor ailments, the springs of courtesy and kindliness dried up in him by constant disappointment, swept aside by the tide of progress, but holding sardonically to his place—has a grip and tenacity and a freedom from analytical impediment to which Gissing rarely attained; the characters of Reardon, suffering from 'the malady that falls upon outwearied imagination,' and Biffen, author of the unsuccessful novel *Mr Bailey, Grocer* (an example of the theory of 'absolute realism in the sphere of the ignobly decent') are made the more real by a vein of reminiscence of Gissing's own apprenticeship to want and defeat; his temperament gave him, moreover, a clue to these types, sensitive, self-centred, conceiving themselves the chosen victims of adversity, and lacking in 'social nerve.' In *The Odd Women* is illustrated another way in which Gissing foresaw new directions of technical method and criticism of life in the novel form; it is found in the relentless study, unmoved by any considerations of sentiment or plot, of the beginning, course and ending of Virginia Madden's indulgence in secret drinking.

Gissing wrote novels of another type in which the purpose is the analysis of states of mind. The two kinds of novel cannot be strictly divided; but there is a recognisable boundary between the sociological studies and such stories as *Isabel Clarendon, A Life's Morning, The Emancipated, Eve's Ransom, The Whirlpool, The Crown of Life* and *Our Friend the Charlatan*. Here, Meredith was his master, and the direct influence of *The Ordeal of Richard Feverel* may be traced in *A Life's Morning*, an idyll shadowed, for a while, by tragedy; to Meredith, also, may be due the more frequent occurrence in these novels of concise satirical strokes such as the characterisation of the irresolute artist Mallard in *The Emancipated*, as a 'Janus with anxiety on both faces,' or of Mrs Bradshaw, who 'interested herself greatly in Vesuvius, regarding it as a serio-comic phenomenon which could only exist in a country inhabited by childish triflers.' We miss, however, Meredith's heroic keynote, poetic conception and penumbra of comedy. Gissing's analysis probes deeply, especially in his tracing of the disintegration of ill-starred marriage unions which have no sanction in community of standards, tastes or class-clanship; and in the dissection of modern temperamental types, such as Dyce Lashmar, 'who excelled in intellectual plausibility,' and Alma Fotheringham, whose artistic enthusiasms spring out of too shallow a soil. In these instances, he exhibits the plenitude of interacting motive with practised skill; but, too often, he lacks the magical spell which combines the scattered traits into a breathing personality. One of his analytic studies begins 'Look at this girl and try to know her'; the phrase is indicative of his most serious limitation as a novelist.

Gissing was not without avenues of escape from the dismal world in which for a great part of his career he dwelt and studied; one was his native instinct to idealise womanhood; upon almost all his feminine characters he confers some graceful sensuous charm, and he gives his imagination free rein in bodying forth such visions as Thyrza, Cecily Doran and Sidwell Warricombe. He won a sense of mental liberty, again, in classic poetry and amid the scenes which it calls to mind. The gratification of a long-fostered desire to see Italy gives a momentary richness of colour to the drab expanse of *New Grub Street*; Magna Graecia is the main scene and inspiration of two later books, *By the Ionian Sea* and *Veranilda*. In the former, Gissing proves himself a master of the descriptive essay, as might have been anticipated from many passages in the novels in which the elusive charm of English scenery is sensitively caught and rendered. Impressions of the memorials of antiquity, of the bright or delicate colouring of land and sea-scape, of languorous perfume, of the discomforts of travel, of the sharp, deleterious climate at certain seasons, of strongly marked Italian rustic types, are blended in the exquisite prose narrative, which reveals surpassing beauty in the chapter 'The Mount of Refuge.' A historical novel dealing with the period of Totila—the suggestion dated from his early absorption in Gibbon—had long been a preoccupation with Gissing. He put into *Veranilda* years of patient labour, and wrote with matured power upon a theme which pleased his imagination. The background is skilfully planned, informed by exact knowledge (in great part drawn from Cassiodorus, of whom Gissing wrote charmingly in *By the Ionian Sea*) of habit, custom, religion, law and the daily round of sixth century life. The historical novel of the classical world is a recurrent form in English fiction; but the closest parallel is to be found in *Salammbô*. Gissing's romance, in contrast, fails in intensity of imagination.

A third of these imaginative liberations Gissing found in his lifelong admiration of Dickens. His monograph established a claim for Dickens as a representative of 'national life and sentiment'; it disposed finally of the heresy that Dickens's characters were merely types or caricatures devoid of basis in observation; it brought into relief his skill in the presentation of various types of women; and it accorded due praise to his style, discriminating in it the salutary element which is drawn from the eighteenth century. The book is more than a criticism of Dickens; it is a manual of the art of fiction, which brings to bear upon a mass of problems raised by his work a ripe judgment formed by practice, reading and reflection. One further imaginative solace Gissing found in the solitary retreat outlined in *The Private Papers of Henry Ryecroft*; a retreat freed from the menace of poverty, from the exactions of acquaintanceship, filled with the atmosphere of books and of quiet comfort; even in prosperity, Gissing preferred the *rôle* of social outlaw. In form, *The Private Papers of Henry Ryecroft* lies somewhere between the *journal intime* and the diary, reflection and observation being expanded to the length of brief essays, and 'tuned to the mood of the sky and the procession of the year'; memories of the bitter past, or of vanishing phases of English custom and scenery; thoughts stirred by some phrase of famous authorship, or by the anticipations of mortality, or by things which he resented, such as industrialism, compulsion of the individual, talk of war: all are mingled and unified by the style and tone which echo 'the old melodious weeping of the poets.' The book is not autobiographical, though it seems to be the expression of a personality almost as intimately realised as the autobiographical form presupposes. Gissing wrote of it that it was 'much more an aspiration than a memory.'

In structure, Gissing looks back to the age of the three-volume novel; he uses at times, but impatiently and not well, the old contrived plot, with melodramatic *contretemps* which results from hidden wills, renounced legacies, forced coincidence and the like; his more characteristic work takes the form of studies, rather than tales, of the fates of two or three groups, related by marriage, cousinship or occupation. Each section is dealt with in turn methodically and exhaustively; but, partly through the consequent breaks in the narration and partly through the occasional analytic stagnation, there is some loss of organic continuity; the form is impressed from without, and too little shaped by forces within, the narrative; the characters are hedged about by this absolute exclusion of vagrancy; poles apart from this method stands such a book as Dostöevsky's *Brothers Karamazov*, where the tale affects us like a continuous swirling stream. Gissing's dialogue is apt to be bookish, and, though admirably representative of character, it often fails to create illusion; there is an exception / in his natural unforced pathos. In style, though he is rather consciously literary, he is one of the few novelists who add to the worth of words by the care with which they are used, and his best writing has a rare rhythmical grace and variety. He was an eager student of the rhythm of classical verse as well as of the prose of Landor and the poetry of Tennyson; in the later novels, his prose, always pure and finely chosen, breaks into arresting and felicitous phrase, more often of pungent than of imaginative quality.

CAMBRIDGE: PRINTED BY
W. LEWIS, M.A.
AT THE UNIVERSITY PRESS